ASSESSMENT
in
COUNSELING

A Guide to the Use of
Psychological Assessment Procedures

FOURTH EDITION

Albert B. Hood and Richard W. Johnson

AMERICAN COUNSELING ASSOCIATION
5999 Stevenson Avenue
Alexandria, VA 22304
www.counseling.org

ASSESSMENT
in
COUNSELING

A Guide to the Use of
Psychological Assessment Procedures

FOURTH EDITION

10   9   8   7   6   5   4   3   2

American Counseling Association
5999 Stevenson Avenue
Alexandria, VA 22304

Director of Publications
Carolyn C. Baker

Production Manager
Bonny E. Gaston

Copy Editor
Judith O. Johnson

Editorial Assistant
Catherine A. Brumley

Cover and text design by Bonny E. Gaston

Library of Congress Cataloging-in-Publication Data
Hood, Albert B. (Albert Bullard), 1929–
   Assessment in counseling : a guide to the use of psychological assessment procedures/ Albert B. Hood and Richard W. Johnson.—4th ed.
     p. cm.
   Includes bibliographical references and index.
   ISBN-13: 978-1-55620-261-2 (alk. paper)
   ISBN-10: 1-55620-261-X (alk. paper)
1. Psychological tests. 2. Counseling. I. Johnson, Richard W., 1934– II. Title.
BF176.H66 2006
150.28′7—dc22

                                                                    2006024532

Table of Contents

SECTION

I

Basic Concepts of Psychological Assessment

SECTION

IV

Personality Assessment

Foreword

Written for the First Edition

PSYCHOLOGICAL TESTS first became available in the United States during the early part of the century. Lewis Terman's Stanford–Binet Intelligence Test, a carefully standardized and individually administered intelligence test that initiated the famous MA/CA = IQ, became public in 1916. This remained a basic test for the next 7 decades and beyond. In 1921 Arthur Otis, a former student of Terman's, published the first group intelligence test, a paper-and-pencil test using the extensive research performed on the Army Alpha and the Army Beta tests of World War I. E. K. Strong, Jr., opened another area when the Vocational Interest Blank was published in 1927. This test, with major revisions and additions, has become one of the most widely used tests of the century. Robert Woodworth's Personal Data Sheet appeared early in the 1920s. Around 1930 personality tests began to make their appearance, with pioneering productions by Robert Bernreuter and Hugh Bell. All but one of these early productions originated at Stanford University. They became part of my life because I did my graduate work at Stanford at about that time (1928–1932) with Terman and Strong as my MA and PhD advisors. I did my bit in these early ventures by bringing out the first edition of the Study Habits Inventory in 1935.

Let me add to the personal note of these years by recalling that during my first year at Stanford I was given an appointment as what we would now call a student personnel assistant—Stanford's first. This involved counseling in the registrar's office and giving admissions tests for the university. Stanford had pioneered in those early days by giving what we would now call scholastic aptitude tests as part of the admissions process. I made trips each spring throughout the state giving the Thorndike Intelligence Test to prospective students at Stanford testing centers. Kathleen, my wife, accompanied me and scored the tests as we moved along—at 25¢ an hour!

After 8 years at Stanford, I accepted an appointment at the University of Minnesota (1936–1964) and again moved into another center of intense test activity. Over these past 75 years, I have seen an accelerating development of psychological tests and other types of assessment, tests for many purposes. During World War II, tests were used in selecting millions of war workers, in assigning other millions in the Armed Forces, and in diagnosing the mental and social health problems of men and women under stress. Today also, tests are used to make decisions for or against a client. This is not a counselor's use of tests; a counselor uses tests or other assessment measures to help clients understand themselves. The authors of this book state this very clearly in words that should appear in large black type: "*In the counseling setting . . . psychological tests are used to help clients to understand themselves. . . . [They are used] primarily to assist individuals in developing their potential to the fullest and to their own satisfaction*" [italics mine] from "Final Statement," Chapter 18, p. 242.

This is a significant book in my experience, a book written by two professionals whose scholarship, depth of experience with assessment in counseling, and sheer desire to be helpful to the reader are apparent on every page. It is a pragmatic book, focusing on what has been useful to others and using a simple problem-solving model. The authors clearly indicate how tests are used differently in different counseling settings: schools, university counseling centers, hospitals and mental health centers, banks, business, government, and private practice.

The first four chapters (Chapters 1–4) introduce the reader to basic concepts in psychological assessment and to the statistical understandings necessary in the selection and interpretation of tests, not in their construction. The last three chapters (Chapters 16–18) deal with special populations, communications, and ethics in the use of tests.

Chapters 5–15 treat with care and skill the use of more than 100 tests, inventories, and other assessment measures in each of 11 categories. Numerous tables, figures, appendices, and reference citations provide a great deal of information in compact bundles. The treatment of the literature is admirable—no long quotations in varying styles of writing, but interpretations and applications all in the same simple, consistent wording of the two authors.

By this time, the reader may begin to suspect that I like this book. I do indeed! I commend it to counselors and psychologists without reservation. I wish that it had been available to me during my lifetime of service. I would have been a better counselor.

—C. Gilbert Wrenn
April 2, 1902–December 28, 2001

Preface

The purpose of this book is to provide information about the various psychological assessment procedures that are specifically relevant for practicing counselors. The book deals with the use of these assessment procedures in the counseling process and includes illustrative case studies. It emphasizes the selection, interpretation, and communication of psychological test results and highlights the basic principles of psychological assessment. It emphasizes the importance of integrating test results with other information about the client.

The book is not designed to be a comprehensive textbook or desk manual on the various tests themselves. There are a number of excellent books that describe psychological tests and other assessment procedures in detail (such as Kapes & Whitfield, 2002, and the *Mental Measurements Yearbooks*). We expect that counselors will make use of such publications along with other resources, including the test manuals themselves, that deal with the construction, reliability, and validity of the various assessment instruments. This book assumes that the reader possesses basic knowledge of statistics often required in the evaluation and use of psychological tests. As with the previous editions, we have attempted to include the latest developments regarding those assessment instruments commonly used by counselors and other mental health professionals—and there have been many such recent developments. Some are well known, such as the revision of College Board's SAT, which has become more of an academic achievement test like the ACT and now includes a written essay. Changes in statewide school achievement tests required by the No Child Left Behind Act have resulted in much controversy regarding "high-stakes" testing results for both students and their schools. The concept of intelligence has been broadened as reflected in new and revised intelligence tests, including the Stanford–Binet, Kaufman, and Das Naglieri tests.

We have presented, in particular, new developments in assessment instruments that are widely used by counselors, including those in career counseling, personality assessment, values measurement, and intelligence testing. Major test revisions since the last edition of this book include Stanford–Binet-5th Edition, several of the popular Wechsler intelligence tests, Kaufman assessment tests for adults and children, Strong Interest Inventory, Allport-Vernon-Lindzey Study of Values, and Work Values Inventory. A new set of scales (Restructured Clinical Scales) has been added to the Minnesota Multiphasic Personality Inventory. The California Psychological Inventory (CPI) has been updated (now called CPI-260). New instruments such as the Kuder Skills Assessment, Expanded Skills Confidence Inventory, Career Futures Inventory, and Schwartz Value Survey have been constructed. Some tests have increased significantly in popularity during the past few years, such as the Kuder Career Search with Person Match, U.S. Department of Labor's O*NET Career Exploration Tools, Substance Abuse Subtle Screening Inventory–3, Career Decision-Making Difficulties Questionnaire, and Career Factors Inventory. All of these changes are discussed in some detail in this new edition. Instruments that have become increasingly out-dated and that have declined in popularity, such as the Kuder General Interest Survey, Career Assessment Inventory, and Minnesota Importance Questionnaire, now receive less attention.

We have also provided information concerning new standards and guidelines for the use of psychological assessment procedures, including the new *ACA Code of Ethics* of the American Counseling Association and similar codes established by the American Psychological Association and different specialty counseling groups such as the American School Counselor Association and the American Rehabilitation Counseling Association. Information regarding the revised version of the "Responsibilities of the Users of Standardized Tests" (RUST Statement) and the revised *Code of Fair Testing Practices* is presented. We have added a new section on Outcome Measurement that includes a discussion of client satisfaction forms, client self-report scales, counselor rating scales, client feedback interviews, and tailor-made measures.

There is a trend toward the use of briefer instruments and behavior rating scales, and a number of these measures are described in this edition. We discuss the continuously expanding use of the computer in psychological assessment. Publishers of most widely used assessment instruments now make available programs for test administration, scoring, and interpretation either on an individual computer or over the Internet, or both. New simulations, sophisticated graphics, and resources not feasible by traditional testing are being developed. For example, we describe the Test of English as a Foreign Language that, in addition to reading and writing, assesses listening and speaking skills over the Internet.

New research is reported, including studies of the use of tests to assess different types of client problems, long-term validity studies, and the applicability of particular tests or procedures with different types of populations (racial, ethnic, age, or gender). Also reported are the findings that test results and their interpretation alone, when understood by the client, can be growth producing and/or therapeutic; and that psychological tests have been shown to predict outcomes as well as most medical tests.

As with the previous editions, we have again organized this volume into five sections. Section I presents basic concepts of psychological assessment. It includes an introduction to the nature and use of psychological assessment procedures in counseling, briefly describes certain important measurement concepts, and discusses initial and outcome assessment procedures. This section provides an overview of the commonly used descriptive statistical concepts but is not intended as a substitute for a basic knowledge of psychological statistics. Section II covers cognitive assessment and the various tests that assess intelligence, academic aptitude, and academic achievement. Section III deals with assessment procedures used by counselors to assist clients in making decisions regarding careers and life plans. In Section IV, personality assessment is considered, including the use of personality inventories and other personality measures in counseling. This section also reviews instruments used for assessment of interpersonal relationships, various aspects of mental health, and certain mental disorders. Finally, Section V deals with professional practices and considerations. It includes assessment of ethnic and special populations; guidelines for the communication of test results, both in interviews and in case reports; and a discussion of the significant ethical and social issues that arise with psychological assessment procedures used in counseling.

Appendices A, B, and C provide excerpts from the ethical codes and test standards of professional organizations that are particularly appropriate for counselors. Appendix D lists the names, addresses, and Web sites of publishers of tests commonly used by counselors, along with the names of the instruments that may be ordered from these publishers.

In graduate courses that cover the use of tests and other appraisal procedures in counseling, information about the various instruments is typically covered, but the actual use of psychological assessment procedures in counseling often must be learned through trial and error. This volume should help remedy that situation by providing information to assist the counselor in choosing, administering, and interpreting psychological assessment procedures as part of the counseling process.

Acknowledgments

Albert B. Hood wishes to acknowledge the contributions of many colleagues at various institutions who, at formal presentations as well as informal conversations at lunches and social gatherings, have helped him stay abreast of developments in the psychological testing field. He is grateful for the collections of the Paul Blommers Measurement Resources Library as a valuable resource of test information and particularly for the suggestions and assistance of Anne Marie Guengerich, its librarian.

Richard W. Johnson would like to acknowledge the influence of his mentors at the University of Minnesota, especially Donald G. Paterson, Ralph F. Berdie, Lloyd H. Lofquist, and Wilbur L. Layton, all of whom taught him to appreciate the importance of assessment in counseling. He is thankful to his colleagues, graduate students, and clients at the University of Wisconsin–Madison and elsewhere, who have contributed to his knowledge and understanding of the use of psychological assessment in counseling.

Both authors appreciate the expertise and guidance provided by Carolyn Baker, Director of Publications for the American Counseling Association, in producing the last three editions of this book. Both authors continue to be grateful to their wives—Jean and Adelle—for their patience with curtailed social activities and deferred home maintenance schedules during the time that this volume was being written and revised.

—Albert B. Hood
Iowa City, Iowa

—Richard W. Johnson
Madison, Wisconsin

About the Authors

ALBERT B. HOOD is emeritus professor of education and former chair of the Division of Counselor Education at the University of Iowa. He received his BA degree (1951) from the University of New Hampshire in psychology and his EdD degree (1957) from Cornell University in counseling and student personnel administration.

He has been the assistant director of the Student Counseling Service at Princeton University and a counseling psychologist in the Student Counseling Bureau at the University of Minnesota. In addition to using psychological tests regularly in his counseling practice, he worked with several colleagues at the Educational Testing Service in Princeton and consulted with various test authors as he conducted research studies on academic aptitudes (with Ralph Berdie; the Minnesota Scholastic Aptitude Test), interest inventories (with David Campbell; the Strong Vocational Interest Blank), and personality measures (with Starke Hathaway; the Minnesota Multiphasic Personality Inventory). At the University of Iowa, he coauthored several student development inventories and consulted with staff members of the American College Testing Program. He held a research fellowship in Kyoto, Japan, and a Fulbright lectureship in the Soviet Union, and he has been a visiting faculty member at the University of Utah, at San Francisco State University, and at IKIP Yojyakarta, Indonesia.

Author of more than 100 books, monographs, and professional articles, Dr. Hood received the Contribution to Knowledge Award of the American College Personnel Association (ACPA) in 1985, the American Counseling Association's Extended Research Award in 1994, and the University of Iowa Alumni Association's Distinguished Faculty Award in 2005. He was the editor of ACPA's *Journal of College Student Personnel* from 1970 to 1976 and is a fellow in the American Psychological Association's Division 17 (Counseling) and in the American Psychological Society. Dr. Hood's scholarly work has dealt primarily with research on the psychological, educational, and vocational development of college students, and a large proportion of the over 60 PhD dissertations he has directed have dealt with psychological assessment.

His e-mail address is albert-hood@uiowa.edu.

RICHARD W. JOHNSON is former director of training for Counseling and Consultation Services, a unit of University Health Services at the University of Wisconsin–Madison, where he also served as adjunct professor of counseling psychology until his retirement in 1997. He obtained his PhD degree in counseling psychology at the University of Minnesota in 1961, after graduating with honors in psychology from Princeton University in 1956. Prior to joining the staff at the University of Wisconsin–Madison in 1968, he taught and counseled at the University of Massachusetts–Amherst and at the University of North Dakota.

Dr. Johnson has served on the editorial boards for three journals of the American Counseling Association: *Journal of College Student Development, Measurement and Evaluation in Counseling and Development,* and *The Career Development Quarterly.* He has been a frequent contributor to scholarly journals in the field of counseling psychology. His professional interests include psychological assessment, career development, cognitive–behavioral counseling, and individual differences. He was the recipient of the Exemplary Practices Award from the Association for Assessment in Counseling in 1998.

His e-mail address is rwjohnso@wisc.edu.

SECTION
I

BASIC CONCEPTS
OF PSYCHOLOGICAL ASSESSMENT

1

Use of Assessment Procedures in Counseling

Assessment has always played an important part in counseling. During the early days, counseling and testing were virtually synonymous. Many of the counseling centers established during the 1930s and 1940s were called Counseling and Testing Centers. At that time, counseling typically involved helping students to make educational or vocational plans on the basis of test results.

In recent years, the role of counseling has broadened to include many issues beyond academic and career planning. Counselors help clients address a variety of concerns, such as self-esteem, shyness, personal growth, family and couple relationships, sexual identity, sexual abuse, cross-cultural communication, substance abuse, eating disorders, depression, anxiety, and suicidal ideation. Many counselors now work in community mental health settings, private practices, hospitals, and businesses as well as in educational institutions. During the same time, the nature of psychological assessment has expanded to assist counselors and clients in all of these areas.

Psychological assessment, which includes the use of a wide variety of evaluation methods, enables counselors to identify the nature of a client's concern and to consider possible treatment approaches. Counselors also rely on assessment data for program planning and evaluation. Clients use the results of assessment to understand themselves better and to make plans for the future.

The assessment process can be therapeutic in itself by helping clients to clarify goals and to gain a sense of perspective and support. Research indicates that clients benefit significantly from all forms of assessment, including personality assessment (Finn & Tonsager, 1992), vocational interest assessment (Randahl, Hansen, & Haverkamp, 1993), relationship assessment (Worthington et al., 1995), and alcohol assessment (Kypri et al., 2004), when the assessment is accompanied by a feedback session. As indicated by these studies, the simple act of learning more about oneself and one's situation in a supportive atmosphere can lead to such positive outcomes as increased self-esteem, increased hope for the future, decline in symptomatic distress, and more effective behaviors.

For most purposes, assessment can be conceptualized in terms of problem solving (Brown-Chidsey, 2005; Lovitt, 1998; Nezu & Nezu, 1993). This chapter begins with a discussion of the purpose of assessment within the framework of a problem-solving model. Principles of psychological assessment are then considered, followed by a discussion of attitudes toward psychological assessment. Finally, the usage of psychological tests in different settings is considered.

PURPOSE OF PSYCHOLOGICAL ASSESSMENT

The problem-solving model often used by counselors provides a convenient means for summarizing the purposes of psychological assessment in counseling. Each of the following five steps in the standard problem-solving model entails the need for information that can be gained through psychological assessment (Chang, D'Zurilla, & Sanna, 2004; D'Zurilla & Goldfried, 1971; D'Zurilla & Nezu, 1999).

The first step in the problem-solving model, which assesses how the problem is viewed, differs qualitatively from the remaining four steps, all of which are concerned with how the problem is solved (D'Zurilla & Nezu, 1999). A client's orientation toward problem solving can be either positive or negative. Clients with a positive orientation look upon problems as a challenge (not as a threat), believe that problems can be solved, consider themselves capable of solving problems, and recognize that the solution to problems requires time and effort (Nezu, 2004). Clients who lack these beliefs will need help with their approach to problem solving before they can make much progress in counseling.

The next four steps in the problem-solving model all pertain to the client's manner of solving a problem. Three styles predominate: *rational, impulsive,* and *avoidant.* The rational style, by definition, follows a logical, systematic method of problem solving. In the impulsive style, a person is inclined to solve the problem quickly without much thought by pursuing the first action that comes to mind. Finally, clients who practice an avoidant style resist thinking about the problem or doing anything to solve it.

Clients who use a rational method of problem solving are most likely to enjoy success in resolving their problems (Nezu, D'Zurilla, Zwick, & Nezu, 2004). They will usually follow the steps in the problem-solving model listed here. An individual's problem-solving orientation and style can be assessed by interview or by the Social Problem-Solving Inventory–Revised (SPSI-R; D'Zurilla, Nezu, & Maydeu-Olivares, 2002).

Problem Orientation

The first step requires the client to recognize and accept the problem. If the client denies the problem, it cannot be dealt with adequately. Almost any assessment procedure can be used to increase sensitivity to potential problems. Instruments that promote self-awareness and self-exploration can stimulate clients to cope with developmental issues before they become actual problems.

Surveys of groups or classes can help counselors identify common problems or concerns that can be taken into account in planning programs for clients. A number of needs assessment instruments (e.g., alcohol screening inventories and sexual behavior questionnaires) have been developed for this purpose.

As soon as a problematic situation is identified, the client and counselor can begin to approach it in a systematic fashion as indicated by the problem-solving model. The problem-solving model helps to normalize a client's concerns. It implies an acceptance of problems as a normal part of life. The counselor provides support and perspective for the client as the client begins to address the problem. Recognition of the problem, together with a means of addressing it, helps the counselor to establish rapport with the client.

Problem Identification

In the second step, the counselor and the client attempt to identify the problem in as much detail as possible. Assessment procedures can help clarify the nature of the client's problem. For example, screening inventories or problem checklists can be used to assess the type and the extent of a client's concerns. Personal diaries or logs can be used to identify situations in which the problem occurs. Personality inventories can help counselors and clients understand personality dynamics underlying certain situations. Information gained during the course of identifying client problems can be used to specify counseling goals.

Identification of the problem improves communication with the client. A client is more likely to continue in counseling and to achieve positive outcomes if the counselor and client agree on the nature of the problem (Busseri & Tyler, 2004). Identification of the problem also aids in communication with others, such as referral sources, family, and friends.

Identification of the problem includes *diagnosis,* a term that has been anathema to some counselors because of its medical connotations; however, diagnosis can be broadly defined to pertain to any classification system used in assessment (Hohenshil, 1996). For example, counselors often distinguish between developmental and pathological problems. An increasing number of counselors now work in mental health settings where they need to use the *Diagnostic and Statistical Manual of Mental Disorders* (4th ed., text rev.; American Psychiatric Association, 2000a), the system most often used to classify mental disorders.

Generation of Alternatives

In the third step, the counselor and client generate alternatives to help resolve the problem. Assessment procedures enable counselors and clients to identify alternative solutions for client problems. For example, an interest inventory can suggest alternative career choices for a client. An assessment interview can be used to determine what techniques have worked for the client in the past when faced with a similar problem. Checklists (such as a study skills inventory or work skills survey) yield data that can be used to generate alternatives.

Test results can help clients to view problems from different angles. Instruments that measure personality styles can provide clients with alternative ways of looking at their behavior or the behavior of others. Assessment exercises can be used to identify positive self-statements of clients, which can open up alternatives for clients (Alberti & Emmons, 2001). Counselors use assessment procedures to assist clients in discovering strengths on which they can build to overcome difficulties or enhance development.

Assessment instruments can also be used to stimulate new learning (Krumboltz & Worthington, 1999). For example, the profile report for the Campbell Interest and Skill Survey encourages clients to explore career fields in which their skills are high but their interests are relatively low. Similarly, clients are encouraged to develop skills in those areas in which they have interests but lack skills.

Decision Making

For the fourth step, deciding on a solution to a problem, clients need to anticipate the consequences of the various alternatives. According to classical decision theory, choice is a function of the probability of success and the desirability of the outcome (Horan, 1979). This equation emphasizes the importance of assessing both the likelihood of success of various alternatives and the attractiveness of those alternatives for the client. Clients will usually want to consider those alternatives that maximize the likelihood of a favorable outcome.

Counselors use assessment materials to help clients weigh the attractiveness of each alternative and the likelihood of achieving each alternative. The attractiveness of various alternatives can be assessed by values clarification exercises. The likelihood of achieving different alternatives can be evaluated by expectancy (or experience) tables that show the success rate for people with different types of test scores or characteristics (Anastasi & Urbina, 1997). Balance sheets or decision-making grids enable clients to compare the desirability and feasibility of various alternatives (Howard, 2001).

Counselors can use assessment data to help determine the appropriate treatment for clients. As examples, achievement test scores can be used to guide a student's course selections, scores on the Minnesota Multiphasic Personality Inventory (MMPI) can be used to help decide which type of treatment program to use for a client (Butcher, 1997), and diagnoses of mental disorders based on specified criteria can provide a basis for treatment planning (Spitzer, 2004).

Verification

Counselors need to evaluate the effectiveness of their counseling (Steenbarger & Smith, 1996). They need to verify that the client's problem has been resolved or reduced. The counselor should discuss with the client how the client would know when the problem has been solved. This fifth step requires that goals be clearly specified, that they be translated into specific behavioral objectives, and that the possibility for progress in accomplishing these goals be realistically viewed. Assessment procedures for this purpose include goal attainment scaling (Kiresuk, Smith, & Cardillo, 1994), self-monitoring techniques (Korotitsch & Nelson-Gray, 1999), the readministration of tests that the client completed earlier in counseling, client satisfaction surveys, and the use of outcome questionnaires (Wells, Burlingame, Lambert, & Hoag, 1996).

In addition to serving as a guide for the counseling process, verification efforts also provide a means of accountability for the counseling agency. Positive feedback from clients can be used to gain support for counseling practices, especially in managed-care settings. Negative feedback can be used to help revise programs to make them more effective.

PRINCIPLES OF PSYCHOLOGICAL ASSESSMENT

According to the *Standards for Educational and Psychological Testing* (American Educational Research Association [AERA], American Psychological Association [APA], & National Council on Measurement in Education [NCME], 1999), the term *assessment* refers to "any systematic method of obtaining information from tests and other sources, used to draw inferences about characteristics of people, objects, or programs" (p. 172). The first part of this definition ("any systematic method of obtaining information from tests and other sources") indicates that a broad range of evaluation methods, such as standardized tests, interviews, and rating scales, may be used as a means of obtaining data about clients. Different methods of assessment used by counselors are discussed in chapter 2.

The second part of the definition ("used to draw inferences about characteristics of people, objects, or programs") emphasizes the use of the assessment data to help counselors understand their clients and the situations in which the clients find themselves. Psychological assessment is a more comprehensive activity than testing by itself because it includes the integration and interpretation of the results of the tests and other evaluation methods. The data provide a basis for forming and testing hypotheses regarding the nature of a client's issues and possible treatment approaches.

The process of psychological assessment can be described as both a science and an art. Many of the instruments used in psychological assessment have been developed by means of empirical research; however, the process of interpreting the assessment data often depends on the counselor's best judgment. In addition to learning about different evaluation procedures, counselors need to consider how they can improve the judgments they make in the assessment process.

Basic principles for conducting psychological assessments are listed below. Counselors should be able to improve the validity of their assessments by adhering to these principles.

1. Consider the purpose of the assessment. As noted in the previous section, a problem-solving model can often be used as a means of identifying the purpose of assessment in counseling. Focusing on the purpose of the assessment will aid counselors both in selecting assessment instruments and in interpreting their results. Ultimately, the assessment results should provide the basis for treatment planning and evaluation.

2. Include the client as a collaborator in selecting topics for assessment and in interpreting the results of assessment instruments.

3. Consider the reliability, validity, and utility (see chapter 3) of an assessment method for the purpose for which it will be used. Such "evidence-based assessment" (Hunsley & Mash, 2005, p. 251) should prove to be more consistent, meaningful, and useful than other types of assessments.

4. Use several methods of assessment. A multimodal assessment method provides a broader view of the issue and can also serve as a means of corroborating the results of any one assessment method. For example, impressions from an interview or interviews may be compared with the results from standardized tests and reports from those who know the client.

5. Assess more than a single variable at a time. A multidimensional approach enriches the assessment process by providing additional information that can be helpful in forming assessments. It presents a "big picture" of the client's situation that can be important in viewing a client's concerns from different angles. For example, career counselors may wish to assess such variables as career planning readiness, personal values, interests, and abilities in helping a client with a career planning concern.

6. Use instruments with validity checks, such as "fake good," "fake bad," and "random responding" scales. Make sure that a client's test responses are valid before attempting to interpret the test results.

7. Consider the possibility of multiple problems, such as depression coupled with substance abuse, anxiety, or physical problems. Clients with mental disorders often meet the criteria for more than one disorder at the same time (Kessler, Chiu, Demler, & Walters, 2005).

8. Assess the situation as well as the client. Avoid *attribution bias,* which indicates a predisposition to attribute the cause of problems to the individual rather than to the situation. Environmental factors interact with individual characteristics in affecting a person's behavior in a particular situation (Galassi & Perot, 1992).

9. When possible, combine the different assessment data by means of a systematic approach that has been studied and verified. In general, statistical (objective) means of combining data have proved to be superior to clinical (subjective) means of combining data (Aegisdóttir et al., 2006; Grove, Zald, Lebow, Snitz, & Nelson, 2000).

10. Consider alternative hypotheses. Counselors need to be watchful for *confirmatory bias,* that is, a tendency to look only for evidence that will support a favorite hypothesis. Seek data that may support an alternative hypothesis as well as data that may prove a pre-established hypothesis. For example, a counselor who believes that a student is failing in school because of lack of ability should also consider other factors, such as health, personal or family problems, and study skills, that may be affecting academic performance.

11. Treat all assessments as tentative. As additional data become available, the counselor should be ready to revise the assessment. Information obtained over an extended time period is likely to be more valid and reliable than information obtained at one point in time (Garb, 1998). Clients' viewpoints change, and clients' memories of past events are often inaccurate.

12. Keep in mind the *regression effect* when interpreting very high or very low scores, all of which are influenced to some extent by chance factors. On retesting, a client's scores tend to regress toward the mean of the population that the client represents. "Less likely states tend to be followed by more likely states" (Tracey & Rounds, 1999, p. 126); that is, clients who obtain unusually high or low scores on a test the first time usually will not score as high or low on an equivalent form of that test the next time they take it. For this reason, it is often helpful to test a client more than once.

13. Become familiar with the condition or issue being assessed. Make use of base rates (frequency of occurrence of a particular behavior or diagnosis within a given population) in undertaking and forming an assessment. For example, because of the frequency of problem drinking among college students, counselors should routinely assess college clients for alcohol abuse (Knight et al., 2002).

14. Consider the influence of individual factors, such as age, gender, educational level, and ethnicity, on test results. Use separate norms that take such factors into account when they are available. For example, gender can have a large effect on interest inventory results (Fouad, 2002).

15. Be aware of common cultural or personal biases that may influence assessment decisions. Studies show that race bias, social class bias, and gender bias may affect clinical judgment (Garb, 1997).

16. Identify, interpret, and incorporate cultural data as part of the assessment process (Ridley, Li, & Hill, 1998). Use measures of acculturation, such as number of generations in new culture and language preference, to help determine whether a client fits the population on which a test was developed and normed (Comas-Díaz & Grenier, 1998).

17. Consult with other professionals regarding assessment procedures and outcomes.

18. Use the assessment results to provide feedback to clients as part of the therapy process. Clients can use the information gained in a feedback session to improve self-understanding and to make positive changes in their lives (Finn & Tonsager, 1997). Assessments should include an evaluation of a client's strengths as well as limitations.

ATTITUDES TOWARD PSYCHOLOGICAL ASSESSMENT

Psychological testing, which can trace its modern history to the work of Francis Galton (1883) in England on the measurement of individual differences in various physical and mental characteristics, became very popular during and after World Wars I and II. In the years since that time, people have reported "persistently positive" attitudes toward standardized testing as indicated in numerous public opinion polls (Phelps, 2005a). At the same time, testing has been severely criticized by social and educational reformers ("Controversy Follows Psychological Testing," 1999;

Lehman, 1999; Samuda, 1998b). Tests and other assessment procedures have been criticized from two points of view: (a) shortcomings in the tests themselves and (b) improper use of the tests.

In the first case, critics maintain that the tests lack validity; that is, they believe that tests cannot adequately evaluate one's characteristics or predict future behavior. For example, Kohn (2000) has contended that standardized tests fail to take into account such factors as experiential differences, motivation, and creativity. He has argued that the tests measure superficial knowledge, the exercises are artificial, the questions are ambiguous, the response format is too limited, and too much emphasis is placed on speed of performance.

In reply to criticisms of test validity, Phelps (2005b) has presented evidence from a number of studies to show that standardized tests have led to higher achievement levels and to improved selection of students and personnel for academic and employment situations. Kubiszyn et al. (2000) has provided convincing evidence of the validity and utility of a variety of psychological tests in the assessment and treatment of mental health concerns. G. J. Meyer et al. (2001) found "strong and compelling" (p. 128) evidence for the validity of psychological tests when they were properly used in the situations for which they had been designed. In a comprehensive review of the research literature based on more than 125 meta-analyses, they concluded that the validity of psychological test results, such as those obtained from scholastic aptitude tests and personality inventories, was comparable with that obtained by common medical tests, such as bone density and blood culture tests.

Test authors have responded to criticisms of tests by revising and upgrading them, especially by taking advantage of computer advancements to improve such matters as the nature of item selection, thoroughness of reliability and validity studies, and quality of test reports. The MMPI and the Strong Interest Inventory represent examples of popular instruments that have been thoroughly revised in this way to bring them up to date and to enhance their psychometric characteristics and counseling usefulness (Buchanan, 2002; Donnay, Morris, Schaubhut, & Thompson, 2005).

Regarding the second major criticism noted, people both within and outside the counseling profession are often more upset by the misuse of tests than by their limitations. In particular, they have been concerned about such issues as invasion of privacy, use of tests with minority groups who may differ significantly from the population for whom the test was developed, use of tests to label or stereotype a person based on the test results, and the disproportionate influence of tests in "high-stakes" decisions such as selection for college or employment. In some situations, too much emphasis may be placed on test results, often because of their quantitative or scientific nature; in other situations, pertinent test information may be disregarded, especially if it conflicts with an individual's personal beliefs or desires.

On the basis of a study of improper uses of tests in real-life cases, researchers identified 86 specific elements that represented common problems in test usage (Eyde et al., 1993), such as choosing an incorrect test, helping a favored person receive a good score, and not following scoring directions. Surveys of testing practices by counselors indicate several areas of concern, including inadequate knowledge of test norms, too much reliance on test scores without additional information, and insufficient knowledge of possible test bias and how to use tests fairly (Elmore, Ekstrom, & Diamond, 1993; Elmore, Ekstrom, Diamond, & Whittaker, 1993).

A number of steps have been taken by professional organizations to help prevent the misuse of tests. Professional standards for the construction and usage of tests have been established and refined. Qualifications for the use of tests have been specified and enforced by means of professional associations and state licensing and certification requirements (see chapter 2). Special consideration has been given to the use of tests with ethnic minority groups, clients with disabilities, and other nontraditional populations. (Further information on these matters can be found in chapters 16 and 18.)

To offset criticisms, counselors need to become aware of the strengths and limitations of the assessment procedures used in their counseling. They need to understand both the psychometric properties of tests and the psychological findings regarding the behavior being assessed (Anastasi, 1992). They should understand first the theoretical construct or condition being measured by a test, such as attention deficit disorder, and then whether or not the test adequately measures this construct. They should be well versed in all aspects of test use, including selection, administration and scoring, interpretation, and the communication of results. They should be able to integrate information from a particular test with other relevant information as part of an overall assessment.

Counselors should be aware of those situations in which tests are likely to be most helpful. Tests can be especially beneficial in counseling if they are designed to stimulate self-exploration and self-development, if they are accompanied by extensive interpretive materials, and if counselors are well schooled in their use (Prediger, 1994b). By using tests appropriately, as discussed throughout this book, counselors can surmount many of the criticisms of tests.

TEST USAGE IN DIFFERENT SETTINGS

Although preferences for particular tests have changed somewhat over the years, counselors continue to make extensive use of tests for a variety of purposes. The usage of tests by counselors varies significantly from setting to setting.

In a survey of National Certified Counselors, Loesch and Vacc (1993) found that the majority of counselors in all settings "frequently" or "routinely" assisted clients in understanding test results. Furthermore, this activity was considered to be "very important" or "critically important" by the majority of the counselors. The counselors who responded to the survey considered psychological assessment procedures to be important in both personal and career counseling. In regard to personal counseling, they emphasized the importance of assessing the client's potential for harm to self and others, the client's movement toward counseling goals, and the extent of a client's psychological dysfunction. In regard to career counseling, the counselors stressed the importance of test results for client decision making.

Mental Health Counseling

Counselors often work in mental health agencies with other professionals to assess and treat clients encountering a variety of personal problems. In a survey of licensed mental health counselors, the majority of the respondents reported that they used assessment instruments in their work (Frauenhoffer, Ross, Gfeller, Searight, & Piotrowski, 1998). In addition to an assessment interview, the mental health counselors were most likely to use the MMPI-2, Beck Depression Inventory, Wechsler Intelligence Scale for Children–3rd Edition (WISC-III), Wechsler Adult Intelligence Scale–Revised (WAIS-R), projective tests (House-Tree-Person Projective Technique, Human Figures Drawing Test, and Sentence Completion Test), and Wide Range Achievement Test–3 as assessment procedures. These tests have been designed primarily to measure psychopathology and intellectual status.

In a related study, Camera, Nathan, and Puente (2000) found that clinical psychologists in private practice, with whom community-based counselors often work, were most likely to use measures of personality/psychopathology and intellectual/achievement status. As measures of personality/psychopathology, they most frequently used the MMPI-2, projective tests (Rorschach Inkblot Test, Thematic Apperception Test, and House-Tree-Person Projective Technique), Beck Depression Inventory, and Millon Clinical Multiaxial Inventory (MCMI). To measure intellectual/achievement status, they most often used the WAIS-R, WISC-III, or Wide Range Achievement Test–3. In a similar manner, psychologists who perform assessments with adolescents in clinical and academic settings have reported that they are most likely to use the Wechsler intelligence scales, MMPI, and projective tests, along with an increased use of parent and teacher rating instruments (Archer & Newsom, 2000).

Many of the instruments identified in these surveys require intensive training in their use, particularly the MMPI-2, MCMI, projective techniques, and the Wechsler scales. These surveys show the need for advanced training in the use of assessment procedures for the counselors who work in these settings.

Career Counseling

Career assessment and counseling are pursued by counselors in a broad range of settings, including employment services, Veterans Affairs hospitals and mental health agencies, rehabilitation centers, and school and college counseling offices. Counselors in these settings benefit from a wide variety of career assessment instruments from which to choose for career counseling purposes. Kapes and Whitfield (2002) have described more than 300 instruments used to measure different factors important in career assessment.

Popular instruments designed specifically for career assessment include interest measures such as the Strong Interest Inventory or one of the Kuder interest inventories, aptitude tests such as the

Differential Aptitude Tests or the Armed Services Vocational Aptitude Battery, and values measures such as the Work Values Inventory (Watkins, Campbell, & Nieberding, 1994). Because of their widespread use in career counseling over a number of years, these three types of measures (sometimes called "the Big Three") have been looked on as the most crucial ones to take into account in career assessment (Swanson & D'Achiardi, 2005). Other measures pertinent to career counseling include measures of career choice and development, such as the Career Maturity Inventory and Career Decision Scale. The different career assessment measures have been used (a) to increase client self-knowledge, (b) to help clients make career choices, and (c) to encourage client participation in career counseling (Watkins et al., 1994).

School Counseling

Counselors in elementary, middle, and high school settings frequently are involved with assessment activities in their work with students, parents, and teachers. A survey of members of the American School Counselor Association found that school counselors frequently performed the assessment activities shown in Table 1-1 (Ekstrom, Elmore, Schafer, Trotter, & Webster, 2004). At least 75% of the counselors in the survey indicated that they performed these 12 activities often or occasionally. School administrators and teachers typically consider school counselors to be "test experts," whom they will consult in test matters such as those listed in the Table 1-1 (Impara & Plake, 1995).

Surveys indicate that school counselors are most likely to use tests that measure cognitive abilities, such as the Wechsler Intelligence Scale for Children or the Scholastic Aptitude Tests (Elmore, Ekstrom, Diamond, & Whittaker, 1993; Giordano, Schwiebert, & Brotherton, 1997). In addition to these tests, the surveys indicated that the counselors used a variety of other instruments including achievement, aptitude, interest, personality, and substance abuse measures.

Approximately two thirds of the school counselors in one survey indicated that testing was an "important" or "very important" part of their work (Elmore, Ekstrom, Diamond, & Whittaker, 1993). Nearly all of the respondents in this survey said that they were responsible for interpreting test results to students. In many cases, school counselors do not administer standardized tests, but they are expected to be able to interpret the results from such tests to students, parents, and teachers (Blacher, Murray-Ward, & Uellendahl, 2005; Giordano et al., 1997).

TABLE 1-1
Frequent Assessment Activities of School Counselors

Assessment Activity	Frequency[a] (%)
Referring students to other professionals, when appropriate, for additional assessment/appraisal	98
Interpreting scores from tests/assessments and using the information in counseling	91
Reading about and being aware of ethical issues in assessment	86
Reading about and being aware of current issues involving multicultural assessment, the assessment of students with disabilities and other special needs, and the assessment of language minorities	84
Synthesizing and integrating test and nontest data to make decisions about individuals	84
Reading a variety of professional literature on topics such as use of testing and assessment in school counseling, school counseling research, and career counseling research	84
Communicating and interpreting test/assessment information to parents	81
Communicating and interpreting test/assessment information to teachers, school administrators, and other professionals	80
Helping teachers use assessments and assessment information	80
Make decisions about the types of assessments to use in counseling groups or individual students	78
Use assessment information to evaluate student performance	78
Use assessment information to monitor student performance	78

Note. From "A Survey of Assessment and Evaluation Activities of School Counselors," by R. B. Ekstrom, P. B. Elmore, W. D. Schafer, T. V. Trotter, & B. Webster, 2004, *Professional School Counselor, 8,* pp. 24–30. Copyright 2004 by the American School Counselor Association. Reprinted with permission. No further reproduction authorized without written permission of the American School Counselor Association.

[a]Assessment activities that at least 75% of responding school counselors reported as performing "often" or "occasionally."

School counselors are also likely to be exposed to behavioral assessment procedures, which are often used by school psychologists to evaluate students for developmental disorders. School psychologists frequently use instruments such as the Behavior Assessment System for Children, Achenbach Child Behavior Checklist, or Conners' Behavior Rating Scale for this purpose (Zaske, Hegstrom, & Smith, 1999). Although school counselors may not administer these instruments themselves, they can work more effectively with students if they are familiar with the instruments, both for referral purposes and for understanding and implementing recommendations based on their use.

Most of the specific tests mentioned above that are used in the different types of counseling settings are discussed in this book. It is important for counselors to learn about these tests so that they can use them successfully in their own practices and so that they can interpret scores from tests for clients referred to them by other professionals. Some of these instruments require advanced training beyond that obtained in most master's-degree counseling programs.

SUMMARY

1. Psychological assessment is an integral part of counseling. Assessment provides information that can be used in each step of the problem-solving model. The assessment process can be therapeutic in and of itself.
2. Assessment serves the following functions: (a) to stimulate counselors and clients to consider various issues, (b) to clarify the nature of a problem or issue, (c) to suggest alternative solutions for problems, (d) to provide a method of comparing various alternatives so that a decision can be made or confirmed, and (e) to enable counselors and clients to evaluate the effectiveness of a particular solution.
3. Psychological assessment refers to the process of integrating and interpreting client information from a broad range of evaluation methods. This process can be improved by adhering to the basic principles of psychological assessment outlined in this chapter.
4. Psychological tests have been criticized for both their limitations and their misuse. Counselors need to be aware of test limitations and must obtain appropriate training and supervision in regard to the tests that they plan to use.
5. According to surveys of test usage, counselors often engage in assessment activities in their work. Although there is some overlap in the types of tests used in different settings, mental health counselors are most likely to use measures of psychopathology and intellectual status, career counselors are most likely to use interest inventories and occupational aptitude tests, and school counselors are most likely to use scholastic aptitude and achievement tests.

2

Nature of Psychological Assessment
in Counseling

To make effective use of assessment procedures, counselors need to understand their basic characteristics. In this chapter, the different criteria that have been used to distinguish among psychological assessment procedures are reviewed and then used to describe six common assessment methods. These methods include standardized tests, rating scales, projective techniques, behavioral observations, biographical measures, and physiological measures. The standards that have been established for evaluating tests and test usage are identified, and the chapter concludes with a list of informational sources about psychological tests and assessments.

DISTINCTIONS AMONG PSYCHOLOGICAL ASSESSMENT PROCEDURES

Psychological assessment procedures differ from each other in a variety of ways. As indicated in the following paragraphs, these differences can be categorized by six basic questions regarding the nature of the assessment method itself.

Who Is Making the Assessment?

Is the person making a self-assessment, or is another person making the assessment? Measurement specialists have differentiated between "S-data" based on self-reports and "O-data" based on the reports of others, such as teachers, supervisors, family members, and friends. Both types of data are needed to obtain a full appraisal of the individual. For example, a process known as 360° (full circle) feedback is sometimes used in business settings to evaluate employee performance from multiple points of view, including those of managers, peers, subordinates, customers, and self. Although not readily available, reports from others are particularly helpful in assessing conditions when self-reports may be distorted or limited, such as substance abuse, personality disorders, and childhood disorders (Klein, 2003).

In general, self-reports and other-reports offer different perspectives regarding an individual. Research indicates that the two types of data can complement each other. For example, Fiedler, Oltmanns, and Turkheimer (2004) found that the performance of recruits in the military was more effectively predicted by a combination of S-data (information from a self-report questionnaire) and O-data (ratings made by fellow recruits) than by either type of data by itself.

What Is Being Assessed?

"What" here refers to the subject of the assessment procedure. Is the *individual* or the *environment* the subject of the assessment? Counselors have usually been interested in individual assessment; however, instruments that evaluate the environment (e.g., classroom atmosphere or residence hall settings) can also provide important information for understanding or treating a problem (Chartrand, 1991; S. L. Friedman & Wachs, 1999). The client's behavior depends on both individual and situational characteristics, so counseling can be most effective when psychological assessment includes both the individual and the environment.

If the individual is being appraised, does the content of the assessment deal primarily with *affective* (feeling), *cognitive* (thinking), or *behavioral* (doing) aspects of the individual? These three aspects of the individual may be further subdivided as discussed below.

Affective characteristics may be subdivided into *temperamental* and *motivational* factors (Guilford, 1959). Temperamental factors include the characteristics assessed by most personality inventories, for example, self-sufficiency, stability, and impulsiveness. Motivational factors refer to interests or values. According to Guilford, temperament governs the manner in which an individual performs, whereas motivation determines what activities or goals the individual will choose to pursue.

Cognitive variables may be based on learning that takes place in a specific course *(course-related learning)* or learning that is relatively independent of specific course work *(non-course-related learning)*. This distinction describes a basic difference between achievement and aptitude tests. Achievement tests evaluate past or present performance; aptitude tests predict future performance. Achievement tests measure learning that has taken place in a particular course or series of courses. Aptitude tests assess the capacity to learn on the basis of items that are relatively independent of the classroom or of any type of formal educational experience.

Behavioral measures include responses that are *voluntary* or *involuntary* in nature. Voluntary responses may be assessed either by self-monitoring or by other-monitoring techniques. A systematic record is kept of measurable items such as calories consumed or hours spent watching television. In the case of involuntary responses (e.g., blood pressure or heart rate), various types of physiological measures are used to assess individual reactivity. Biofeedback devices, often used to teach relaxation methods, are a good example of the latter type of assessment measure.

The question of what is being assessed also pertains to the variables chosen for the assessment process. Individuals can be assessed by *common* variables that apply to all people or by *unique* variables that apply only to the individual. In the first case, sometimes referred to as *nomothetic assessment,* emphasis is placed on variables that show lawful or meaningful distinctions among people. The group provides a frame of reference for determining which variables to assess and how to interpret the results. In the second case, sometimes referred to as *idiographic assessment,* emphasis is placed on those variables that can be most helpful in describing the individual. The individual serves as the reference point both to identify relevant variables and to interpret data.

Most psychological tests, such as interest and personality inventories, use the nomothetic approach. These tests use the same scales to describe all clients. Scores are interpreted in regard to a set of norms. In contrast, many of the informal assessment procedures, such as the interview, case study, or card sorts, use an idiographic approach. A different set of variables is used to describe each client. Nomothetic techniques can be more readily interpreted, but they may not be as relevant or as penetrating as idiographic methods, which have been designed to measure variations in individuality (Grice, 2004; Neimeyer, 1989).

Where Is the Assessment Taking Place?

The location in which the assessment takes place is important in the sense that it helps to differentiate between test results obtained in *laboratory* settings and those obtained in *natural settings*. Many psychological tests must be administered under standardized conditions so that the test results can be interpreted properly. For these tests, a testing room or laboratory is usually used. If the circumstances of test administration differ from person to person, differences in the testing conditions can influence test results. Some measures such as employee ratings are obtained in natural settings under conditions that may vary considerably for different individuals. Variations in job circumstances can greatly affect the ratings. Interpretations of the results must take into account the setting in which they were obtained.

When Is the Assessment Occurring?

The question of when an assessment takes place is of value in distinguishing between assessments planned in advance *(prospective)* and those based on recall *(retrospective)*. Self-monitoring techniques are usually planned in advance. For example, students may be asked to keep track of the number of hours that they studied or the number of pages that they read during a study period. In contrast, biographical measures such as life history forms are recorded to the best of the individual's recollection after the event has occurred.

Why Is the Assessment Being Undertaken?

The question of why pertains to the reason for administering the test rather than to the nature of the test itself. The same test can be used for a variety of purposes, such as counseling, selection, placement, description, and evaluation. As noted in chapter 1, tests are often used in counseling as part of the problem-solving process.

When tests are used in counseling, all data obtained must be regarded as confidential. Such *private data* may be contrasted with *public data*—data originally obtained for another purpose, such as selection or placement. Examples of public data include academic grades, educational level, or occupational status. Counselors use public as well as private data in helping clients to address certain issues, because the public data can provide a great deal of information about the client's past performance under various circumstances.

How Is the Assessment Conducted?

"How" here refers to the manner in which the test material is presented, how the data are analyzed, and how the score for the assessment procedure is obtained. First, is the type of behavior that is being assessed *disguised* or *undisguised?* Projective techniques (described in chapter 12) are designed so that the respondent is typically unaware of the true nature of the test or of any "preferred" answer. Because the intent of the test is disguised, it is more difficult for respondents to fake their answers to produce a particular impression.

Second, is the information obtained in the assessment analyzed in a *quantitative* or *qualitative* fashion? Quantitative procedures, which include most psychological tests, yield a specific score on a continuous scale. Qualitative procedures, such as card sorts, work samples, or structured exercises, produce a verbal description of a person's behavior or of a situation that can be placed into one of several categories (e.g., outgoing vs. reserved personality type). By their very nature, quantitative procedures have been more thoroughly studied in terms of reliability and validity. Qualitative procedures, however, are more open-ended and adaptable for use in counseling, especially with a diverse clientele (Goldman, 1992; Okocha, 1998).

Finally, are scores arrived at *objectively,* free of individual judgment, or *subjectively,* based on the scorer's best judgment? Tests that can be scored by means of a scoring stencil are objective. That is, different individuals using the same scoring stencil with an answer sheet should obtain the same score if they are careful in counting the number of correct answers. In contrast, rating scales are subjective—the score assigned will often vary depending on the individual rater.

TYPES OF PSYCHOLOGICAL ASSESSMENT METHODS

The various assessment methods used in counseling may be conveniently classified by using different combinations of the criteria discussed in the previous section. Six popular types of psychological assessment methods are described below.

Standardized Tests

By definition, standardized tests must meet certain standards for test construction, administration, and interpretation (Anastasi & Urbina, 1997). These standards include uniform procedures for test administration, objective scoring, and the use of representative norm groups for test interpretation. Most standardized tests have been studied in terms of their reliability and validity. Many assessment procedures used in counseling fail to meet these standards.

Standardized tests include the following assessment procedures, each of which is discussed in this book: achievement tests, aptitude (or ability) tests, personality inventories, interest inventories, values inventories, and environmental inventories. Strictly speaking, a test refers to a task on which people are asked to try their best, such as an aptitude or achievement test. Tests measure *maximum* performance, in contrast with questionnaires and inventories, which evaluate *typical* performance (Cronbach, 1990). Questionnaires and inventories, such as personality and interest inventories, elicit self-reports of opinions, preferences, and typical reactions to everyday situations. In practice, questionnaires and inventories also are often referred to as tests if they meet the standardization criteria noted above.

Nonstandardized assessment procedures, which are discussed below, include rating scales, projective techniques, behavioral observations, and biographical measures. Nonstandardized techniques produce results that are less dependable (i.e., less reliable and valid) compared with standardized techniques; however, they allow counselors to consider aspects of behavior or the environment not covered by traditional psychological tests. Counselors must be concerned not only about the *dependability* of test results but also about the *exhaustiveness* of the results (Cronbach & Gleser, 1965). Tests that provide highly dependable information often describe only a small part of the information a counselor needs. Assessment procedures such as interviews, projective techniques, or essays, which provide less dependable information, can nonetheless aid counselors in obtaining information on topics that would be missed by formal testing procedures. Exhaustive procedures should be used when counselors need to obtain a large amount of information pertaining to a variety of decisions (e.g., which problems to address or which treatments to consider). Information obtained in this manner can be verified in subsequent assessment with more dependable measures that must be administered and scored according to specified procedures.

Rating Scales

Rating scales, which provide estimates of various behaviors or characteristics based on the rater's observations, are a common method of assessment. In contrast with standardized tests, rating scales are derived from subjective rather than objective data. Rating scales include self-ratings, ratings of others, and ratings of the environment. Interview data are often summarized by means of rating scales.

Because of their subjectivity, rating scales have a number of disadvantages. Three common errors associated with rating scales are (a) halo effect, (b) error of central tendency, and (c) leniency error. In the case of the halo effect, raters show a tendency to generalize from one aspect of the client to all other aspects. For example, if a person is friendly, that person may also be rated highly in unrelated areas such as intelligence, creativity, leadership, and motivation. The error of central tendency describes the tendency to rate all people as "average" or near the middle of the rating scale. The leniency error refers to the tendency to rate the characteristics of people more favorably than they should be rated.

To control for such errors, raters are sometimes asked to rank people one against the other on each rating scale. As an alternative, raters may be forced to distribute their ratings across the entire rating scale according to the normal curve or a similar system. When these techniques are applied to a large number of people, they prevent ratings from bunching up in the middle of the distribution or at the top end of the distribution. Kenrick and Funder (1988) offered the following suggestions for improving the validity of ratings: (a) Use raters who are thoroughly familiar with the person being rated, (b) require multiple behavioral observations, (c) obtain ratings from more than one observer, (d) use dimensions that are publicly observable, and (e) identify behaviors for observation that are relevant to the dimension in question. These suggestions can help counteract limitations posed by the various sources of invalidity.

Examples of rating techniques include the semantic differential and situational tests. The semantic differential technique requires raters to rate concepts (e.g., "my job") by means of a series of seven-step bipolar scales (e.g., competitive vs. cooperative). This technique can be readily adapted to a variety of situations, including cross-cultural assessment (Osgood & Tzeng, 1990).

Situational tests require the person to perform a task in a situation that is similar to the situation for which the person is being evaluated. For example, the in-basket technique requires candidates for an administrative position to respond to the daily tasks of an administrator by means of an in-basket (work assignment basket) that simulates the actual work assignments of administrators. Situational tests can often meet the conditions suggested by Kenrick and Funder (1988) noted above. For this reason, they often prove to be beneficial in predicting performance in a situation similar to that of the test. Situational tests are frequently used to assess leadership or management skills.

Projective Techniques

Projective tests use vague or ambiguous stimuli to which people must respond. Because the stimuli (e.g., inkblots, ambiguous pictures, and incomplete sentences) are vague, people tend to make interpretations of the stimuli that reveal more about themselves than they do about the stimuli. They "project" their own personality onto the stimuli. Responses are usually scored subjectively. Common projective techniques include the Rorschach Ink Blot Test, Thematic Apperception Test, and Rotter Incomplete Sentences Blank. For many years, projective tests dominated the field of personality testing, but during the past few decades objective (standardized) tests have become more popular. The use of projective techniques in counseling is discussed further in chapter 12.

Behavioral Observations

Behavioral observations refer to behaviors that can be observed and counted. The observations are planned in advance or based on recent events. The behaviors, which usually occur in a natural setting, are monitored by the client, by an observer such as a spouse or parent, or both. The observer usually records the frequency of a discrete behavior, for example, the number of "I" statements made in an interview or the number of conversations initiated. Frequently, the duration of the response and the intensity of the behavior (as rated by the observer) are also recorded.

Behavioral observations have the advantage of pertaining directly to a behavior that a client is concerned about. The behavior can usually be included as part of a goal. The measure is directly related to the client's treatment.

Biographical Measures

Biographical measures refer to accomplishments or experiences as reported by the client or as reflected in historical records. For example, an employment résumé or college application form usually provides an extensive amount of biographical information. Biographical measures differ from behavioral measures in that the observations are not planned in advance. They differ from rating scales in that the information is usually a matter of fact rather than a matter of judgment. Biographical data (biodata) include information maintained in cumulative records by schools or in personnel records by businesses, such as academic grades, extracurricular achievements, job promotions, hobbies, and volunteer work experiences.

The value of biographical measures in assessment is expressed in the well-established psychological maxim: "The best predictor of future performance is past performance." As a rule, the best single predictor of college grades for an individual is usually that person's high school grades. A person who has functioned well in a particular job in the past will probably perform well in related types of activities in the future.

Biographical data are usually collected by means of a written form or during the course of an initial interview with a client. Although this information is most often used in a qualitative manner, it can also be quantified for assessment purposes (Dean, 2004; Oswald, Schmitt, Kim, Ramsay, & Gillespie, 2004).

On the one hand, biographical measures are both economical and efficient. They can provide information on topics such as leadership experiences or creative accomplishments that may be difficult to assess by other means. On the other hand, they may be inappropriate or difficult to interpret if the person's experiences have been unusual or severely limited. Biographical measures yield a broad range of information, but the meaning of the information requires additional interaction with the client or others familiar with the situation.

Work résumés and curricula vitae represent examples of biographical measures. These biographical summaries can be used to review one's accomplishments in terms of transferable work skills (Bolles, 2005). They provide a systematic means of analyzing one's history in regard to career opportunities. Other examples of biographical measures include career assessment portfolios (Satterthwaite & D'Orsi, 2003) and psychosocial inventories such as the Quickview Social History (Giannetti, 1992).

Physiological Measures

Physiological assessment can be particularly helpful in understanding and monitoring client behavior because of the unique information that it provides. It enables a client's condition, such as anxiety, to be assessed at a more basic level than that made possible by traditional assessments such as standardized tests and behavioral observations (Berntson & Cacioppo, 2006). Measures such as heart rate, breathing rate, muscle contractions, and blood pressure, which are primarily involuntary in nature, can reveal information regarding a client's condition that might otherwise be missed (Lawyer & Smitherman, 2004). Advances in instrumentation and procedures (e.g., biofeedback devices, cardiac monitoring systems, and alcohol biomarkers) and collaboration with other professionals in a team approach make it feasible to include such variables in the assessment process.

STANDARDS AND GUIDELINES FOR EVALUATING TESTS AND TEST USAGE

Several sets of standards have been published by professional organizations concerning the development and use of psychological assessment procedures. Counselors should be familiar with each set of standards or guidelines for test usage presented in this section.

ACA Code of Ethics

The American Counseling Association (ACA; 2005) *ACA Code of Ethics* specifies principles of ethical conduct and standards of professional behavior for counselors. Sections of this document devoted to psychological assessment are reproduced in Appendix A. Other professional organizations have also published ethical codes that address the use of psychological assessment procedures in a similar fashion (American Mental Health Counselors Association, 2001; American Psychological Association, 2002; American Rehabilitation Counseling Association, Commission on Rehabilitation Counselor Certification, & National Rehabilitation Counseling Association, 2002; American School Counselor Association, 2004; National Board of Certified Counselors, 2005).

"Responsibilities of Users of Standardized Tests" (RUST Statement–3rd Edition)

The Association for Assessment in Counseling and Education (AACE; 2003b), one of the subdivisions of ACA, has developed a policy statement titled "Responsibilities of Users of Standardized Tests." This statement, referred to as "the RUST statement," lists responsibilities of test users in seven categories: qualifications of test users, technical knowledge, test selection, test administration, test scoring, interpreting test results, and communicating test results. Counselors should be familiar with this policy statement and each of its recommendations. This document is reproduced in Appendix B.

Guidelines similar to the RUST statement have also been prepared by ACA (2003), the American School Counselor Association and Association for Assessment in Counseling (1998), and the American Psychological Association (Turner, DeMers, Fox, & Reed, 2001). These guidelines delineate the basic knowledge and skills required for the competent and responsible use of tests by members of the helping professions. Such guidelines can serve as a means for counselors to evaluate their individual professional development and to consider their need for continuing education. They can also be used in developing and evaluating training programs in psychological assessment for counselors.

Standards for Educational and Psychological Testing

The *Standards for Educational and Psychological Testing* (AERA, APA, & NCME, 1999) provide criteria for evaluating both the tests themselves and use of the tests. The criteria were prepared by a joint committee of the American Educational Research Association, American Psychological Association, and National Council on Measurement in Education. The most recent version of the *Standards* represents the sixth in a series of documents on this issue beginning in 1954. Originally, this publication emphasized technical standards for test construction and evaluation. As the editions evolved, the joint committee placed increased emphasis on the responsibilities of the test user and the need for fairness in testing. Adherence to the *Standards* by counselors should help to improve testing practices and reduce criticism of tests and test usage (Association for Assessment in Counseling, 2002). Excerpts from the *Standards* that pertain to the responsibilities of test users (Standards 11.1–11.24) are presented in Appendix C in this book.

Statements of Joint Committee on Testing Practices (JCTP)

The JCTP, which includes members from ACA, the American Educational Research Association, American Psychological Association, American Speech-Language-Hearing Association, National Association of School Psychologists, National Association of Test Directors, and National Council on Measurement in Education, represents an interdisciplinary effort to improve the use of tests (JCTP, 2006). This committee has stressed educational efforts, not restriction of access, as a means of ensuring qualified test users.

The JCTP has issued several publications designed to improve test usage. Its publications include *Responsible Test Use* (Eyde et al., 1993), *Rights and Responsibilities of Test Takers* (JCTP, 1999), and *Code of Fair Testing Practices in Education* (JCTP, 2004), each of which is discussed below.

Responsible Test Use

Research conducted under the auspices of JCTP has identified a total of 86 competencies required for the proper use of different instruments (Eyde et al., 1993; Moreland, Eyde, Robertson, Primoff, & Most, 1995). Of the 86 competencies, 12 embody minimum proficiencies for all test users, such as avoiding errors in scoring and recording, using settings for testing that allow for optimum performance (e.g., adequate room), and establishing rapport with examinees to obtain accurate answers (see Table 2-1).

Factor-analytic research indicates that the 86 competencies can be reduced to seven broad factors: comprehensive assessment, proper test use, psychometric knowledge, integrity of test results, scoring accuracy, appropriate use of norms, and interpretive feedback. On the basis of research regarding test misuse, the relative significance of the seven factors varies with the particular type of test. For example, competencies in comprehensive assessment are more important in using clinical tests, whereas skills in the appropriate use of norms are more important in vocational tests

TABLE 2-1
Twelve Minimum Competencies for Proper Use of Tests

Item No.	Competency
1.	Avoiding errors in scoring and recording
2.	Refraining from labeling people with personally derogatory terms like *dishonest* on the basis of a test score that lacks perfect validity
3.	Keeping scoring keys and test materials secure
4.	Seeing that every examinee follows directions so that test scores are accurate
5.	Using settings for testing that allow for optimum performance by test takers (e.g., adequate room)
6.	Refraining from coaching or training individuals or groups on test items, which results in misrepresentation of the person's abilities and competencies
7.	Being willing to give interpretation and guidance to test takers in counseling situations
8.	Not making photocopies of copyrighted materials
9.	Refraining from using homemade answer sheets that do not align properly with scoring keys
10.	Establishing rapport with examinees to obtain accurate scores
11.	Refraining from answering questions from test takers in greater detail than the test manual permits
12.	Not assuming that a norm for one job applies to a different job (and not assuming that norms for one group automatically apply to other groups)

Note. From "Assessment of Test User Qualifications: A Research-Based Measurement Procedure," by K. L. Moreland, L. D. Eyde, G. J. Robertson, E. S. Primoff, and R. B. Most, 1995, *American Psychologist, 50,* p. 16. Copyright 1995 by the American Psychological Association. Reprinted with permission of the author.

(Moreland et al., 1995). Examples of appropriate and inappropriate test usage based on the 86 competencies and seven broad factors are provided in the casebook, *Responsible Test Use: Case Studies for Assessing Human Behavior* (Eyde et al., 1993).

Rights and Responsibilities of Test Takers

In one of its efforts to improve testing practices, the JCTP has developed a statement that lists the rights and responsibilities of individual test takers (JCTP, 1999). For example, test takers have a right to know the purpose of testing, who will have access to their scores, how the tests will be used, and possible consequences of taking or not taking the test. They also have personal responsibilities, such as reading or listening to descriptive test information, informing test administrators of special needs, and asking questions about specific concerns they might have.

This document also provides detailed guidelines for test administrators to ensure that test takers receive their rights and understand their responsibilities. As test administrators, counselors should clarify the rights and responsibilities of test takers and obtain informed consent before proceeding with testing. They should be able to offer reasonable accommodations for test takers with disabilities. Counselors should provide appropriate information to clients concerning the testing process, such as suggestions for test preparation, scoring procedures, opportunities to re-take the test, provisions for feedback, availability of interpretive materials, and confidentiality safeguards. The full statement is available online on the Internet (JCTP, 1999).

Code of Fair Testing Practices in Education

This code, first issued by the JCTP in 1988, has been updated and expanded (JCTP, 2004). The code focuses on the development and use of educational tests from the standpoint of fairness to all test takers regardless of age, gender, disability, race, ethnicity, or other personal characteristics. The revised version of the code lists a total of 31 standards for test developers and test users in four areas: developing and selecting appropriate tests, administering and scoring tests, reporting and interpreting test results, and informing test takers.

These standards, which complement the *Standards for Educational and Psychological Testing,* are not mandatory as such, but they are intended to inspire test developers and test users to consider the importance of fairness in all aspects of testing. For example, test users are encouraged to evaluate test materials for offensive language, to select tests that have been modified appropriately for clients with disabilities, and to consider to what extent test performance for individuals from diverse subgroups may have been affected by factors unrelated to the skill being assessed.

Test Publisher Requirements

Requirements for test usage depend on the complexity of the test. Test publishers often distinguish between Level A tests (no restrictions), Level B tests (purchaser must have a 4-year college degree and must have completed a college course in tests and measurements), and Level C tests (purchaser must have completed an advanced degree in an appropriate profession, belong to an appropriate professional organization, or be licensed or certified in an appropriate profession). Specific levels and qualifications vary according to the test publisher. Because some efforts have been made to restrict access to psychological tests to members of a certain profession such as psychologists or psychiatrists, the Association of Test Publishers (ATP, 2006) has issued a policy statement emphasizing that the qualifications to use different tests should be based on an individual's education, training, and experience in using an assessment instrument, not solely upon his or her membership in a particular profession.

Most test publishers require potential customers to complete qualification forms in which they must indicate the purpose for which they will use the test, their level of training, their professional credentials, their educational background, the specific training they have received in the use of tests, and their testing competencies. Counselors need to be aware of the necessary qualifications for the specific tests they wish to use. *Counselors should not attempt to use tests for which they lack adequate preparation.*

Multicultural Assessment Standards

The *Standards for Multicultural Assessment,* a publication of the Association for Assessment in Counseling (2003), a division of ACA, lists 68 standards of test practices that are relevant for clients from multicultural populations. The booklet lists standards compiled from different sources mentioned above, especially the *Standards for Educational and Psychological Testing,* that should be followed in selecting, administering, scoring, and interpreting instruments for clients from minority cultures. These standards also stress the importance of multicultural counseling competencies, such as the need to understand how race, culture, and ethnicity may affect such matters as personality formation, vocational choice, and the manifestation of psychological disorders (Association for Multicultural Counseling and Development, 1992). *Standards for Multicultural Assessment* is available on the Internet at http://aac.ncat.edu/resources.html.

SOURCES OF INFORMATION ABOUT ASSESSMENT PROCEDURES

Although there are a vast number of tests available in the United States and there is a constant stream of new tests and revisions of old tests on the market, most of the tests are published by a few large publishers, such as Psychological Assessment Resources, Consulting Psychologists Press, and Pearson Assessments (formerly NCS Assessments). These publishers distribute test catalogs from which manuals, scoring keys, and the tests themselves may be ordered. Appendix D gives the names, addresses, Internet Web sites, and related information for the publishers of tests most likely to be used by counselors.

The best general source of information about commercial tests is the *Mental Measurements Yearbook* series. First published in 1938 by Oscar K. Buros at Rutgers University, the series is now published at the Buros Institute of Mental Measurements at the University of Nebraska–Lincoln. The yearbooks provide descriptive information about each test, including the publisher, prices, and persons for whom the test is appropriate, along with critical reviews by test experts and a list of recent publications pertaining to the test. *The Sixteenth Mental Measurements Yearbook* (Spies & Plake, 2005) contains information for nearly 300 new or revised instruments. Critical reviews are not published for each test in each yearbook because each new volume is designed to add to, rather than replace, information found in prior volumes.

A comprehensive listing of all tests currently available for purchase in English-speaking countries is provided in another publication, titled *Tests in Print,* also initiated by Buros. *Tests in Print VII* (Buros Institute of Mental Measurements, 2006) provides information, such as purpose, target population, and types of scores, for more than 4,000 tests. The tests listed in *Tests in Print* are cross-referenced to the test reviews found in all previous editions of the yearbooks.

The publisher plans to issue a new edition of *Tests in Print* every 3 years. The yearbooks are now published every 18 to 24 months. Recent test reviews awaiting publication, as well as already published test reviews, can be accessed for a fee on the Internet at Test Reviews Online (Buros Institute of Mental Measurements, 2005).

In addition to the publications of the Buros Institute, counselors can consult *Tests* and *Test Critiques,* a series of reference books published by PRO-ED test publishing company. *Tests* (5th edition) provides updated information on approximately 3,000 tests available from a total of 219 test publishers (Maddox, 2003). The information includes a description of each test, its cost, scoring procedures, and publisher information. *Test Critiques* (Keyser, 2005) offers in-depth reviews of popular psychological assessment instruments. The reviews, which average eight pages in length, provide a discussion of the practical applications of each test as well as its technical aspects.

Information regarding many standardized tests and research instruments can also be obtained by searching TestLink (Educational Testing Service [ETS], 2005b) on the Internet. This resource, described as the "World's Largest Test Collection Database," provides access to the ETS Test Collection, which contains information regarding more than 25,000 tests and other measurement devices dating from the early 1900s to the present.

Most of the information required for evaluating any particular test should be available in documents provided by the test publisher. In addition to the test manual, these documents may include a technical manual, user's guide, and supplementary materials. The test manual should contain information regarding the construction of the test together with directions for administering, scoring, and interpreting the test. Norms should be reported, including a comprehensive description of the norm group and the sampling techniques used to obtain the norms. Information regarding the reliabilities of the test scores and the validity evidence for proposed interpretations should be presented in the manual. Examples of comprehensive, well-documented manuals include the *Manual for the Campbell Interest and Skill Survey* (D. P. Campbell, Hyne, & Nilsen, 1992) and the *Strong Interest Inventory Manual* (Donnay et al., 2005). For a fee, most test publishers will provide qualified test users with a specimen set of a test that includes the test itself, answer sheets, scoring keys, and a test manual.

Professional books and journals also provide extensive information about tests. *A Counselor's Guide to Career Assessment Instruments* (Kapes & Whitfield, 2002) reviews popular assessment procedures used in career counseling along with a list of sources of information about assessment procedures in general. Copies of selected tests together with brief test reviews can be found in a number of sourcebooks (Allen & Wilson, 2003; Corcoran & Fischer, 2000; Fischer & Corcoran, 2000; Nezu, Ronan, Meadows, & McClure, 2000).

Counselors are most likely to find information about assessment procedures pertinent to their work in the following journals: *Measurement and Evaluation in Counseling and Development, Journal of Counseling & Development, The Career Development Quarterly, Journal of Counseling Psychology, Psychological Assessment, Journal of Personality Assessment, Journal of Career Assessment,* and *Assessment.* Information may be difficult to obtain for some proprietary tests that are exclusively owned and used within an organization such as a psychological consulting firm. Counselors should be cautious in relying on the results of a test that has not been submitted for professional review.

SUMMARY

1. Psychological assessment procedures can be distinguished from each other in terms of who is making the assessment, what is being assessed, where the assessment takes place, when the assessment occurs, why the assessment is undertaken, and how the assessment is conducted. These distinctions can be used to classify tests into six broad categories: standardized tests, rating scales, projective tests, behavioral observations, biographical measures, and physiological measures.

2. Standardized tests have been the most thoroughly studied of all psychological assessment procedures in terms of reliability and validity; however, they cover a limited domain of behavior or situations. Counselors need to use a broad range of assessment procedures to obtain information on relevant matters not included in standardized tests.

3. Counselors should be familiar with professional recommendations for evaluating tests and test usage. Important sets of guidelines include the *ACA Code of Ethics,* "Responsibilities of Users of Standardized Tests" (The RUST statement), and *Standards for Educational and Psychological Testing.*

4. The most important sources of information about psychological tests are the *Mental Measurements Yearbooks, Test Critiques,* test manuals, and professional journals.

3

Measurement Concepts and
Test Interpretation

To make effective use of tests, counselors must understand certain elementary statistical concepts that are used in conjunction with the development and interpretation of tests and test scores. In this chapter, only a few descriptive statistical concepts involved in understanding and interpreting tests are presented. Neither the underlying concepts of statistics nor their calculations, elements commonly found in a basic statistics course, are included. This chapter describes (a) some of the measures used to organize and describe test information, (b) the concepts of test reliability and test validity, and (c) the interpretation of reliability and validity information.

A simple raw score on a psychological test, without any type of comparative information, is a meaningless number. If a graduate student obtains a raw score of 58 on a midsemester examination in a course called "Theories of Counseling," the student's next question will be about the meaning of that score. A student whose score falls in the top 5% of the class will obviously react very differently from one whose score falls in the bottom 5%.

Some type of interpretive or comparative information is necessary before any information is conveyed by a score. To say that a client obtained a raw score of 37 out of 60 on an anxiety measure conveys no useful information, nor does the fact that this score of 37 meant that the client answered 62% of the anxiety items. To know that the same client obtained a raw score of 48 on a 60-item measure of tolerance does not indicate that he or she is more tolerant than anxious, nor does it yield any other useful information. Some frame of reference is necessary to give a test result meaning (Anastasi & Urbina, 1997).

Scores on tests can be interpreted from three points of view: (a) comparison with scores obtained by other individuals, (b) comparison with an absolute score established by an authority, and (c) comparison with other scores obtained by the same individual. The first type of comparison is usually referred to as a *norm-referenced* interpretation. This type of comparison is used most often in interpreting scores on standardized tests. The second type of comparison is often described as a *criterion-referenced* interpretation. For example, a program administrator may require students to understand 90% of the material in a course before they receive credit for that course. Scores for tests based on this course would then be compared with this 90% passing score, not with the scores of other students.

Both of the first two types of comparisons use an external frame of reference. The third type of comparison, which uses an internal frame of reference, can be best thought of as a *self-referenced* (or ipsative) measure (e.g., "At age 35, he weighs substantially more than he did in his late 20s"). An article in the local newspaper carried the following headline: "Smith's Is Best for Breakfast." This headline could imply that Smith's restaurant was the best restaurant in the city for breakfast. In the article, however, it was pointed out that Smith's was not a particularly good place to eat, but if one had to choose, it was better for breakfast than it was for lunch or dinner. The restaurant was being compared with itself at different times of the day (an internal comparison) rather than with other restaurants or with an absolute standard (both external comparisons).

In a norm-referenced interpretation, individuals' scores are compared with others' scores so various statistics are used for these interpretations. A frequency distribution is constructed with the scores on the test indicated on a horizontal axis and the number of individuals receiving a particular score shown on the vertical axis. This produces a frequency polygon, which when smoothed for the typical distribution results in the familiar normal or bell-shaped curve shown in Figure 3-1.

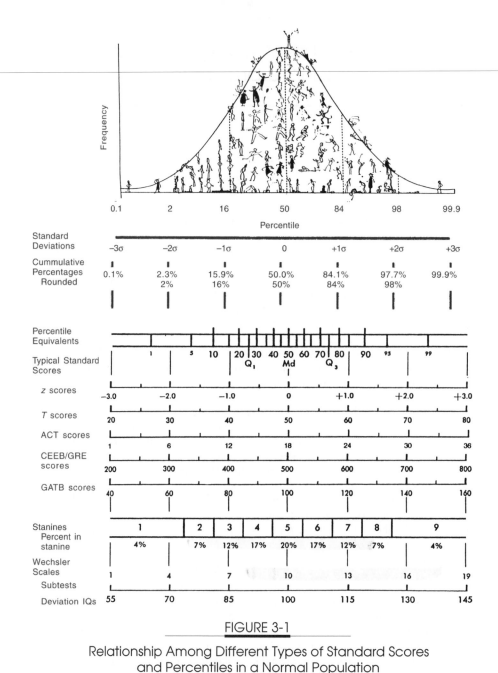

FIGURE 3-1

Relationship Among Different Types of Standard Scores
and Percentiles in a Normal Population

Note. CEEB/GRE = College Entrance Examination Board/Graduate Record Examination; GATB = General Aptitude Test Battery.

MEASURES OF CENTRAL TENDENCY AND VARIABILITY

When examining an individual's score, it is often useful to have some indication of the typical or average score and how scores are distributed. Different measures for these purposes, usually referred to as measures of central tendency and variability, are discussed below.

Measures of Central Tendency

There are three measures of central tendency that are often computed. The mean, or arithmetic average, has algebraic properties that make it the most frequently used measure of central tendency. It is equal to the sum of the scores divided by the number of individuals in the group. The median is the middle score below which one half, or 50%, of the scores will fall and above which the other half will fall. The mode is the score that appears the most frequently in a set of scores.

In a perfectly normal frequency distribution, such as that shown in Figure 3-1, all three measures have the same value. When larger numbers of individuals score at one of the ends of the distribution, the distribution is not symmetrical and becomes skewed (pulled) in one direction or the other (Figure 3-2). Differences that result between these measures of central tendency indicate the magnitude and direction of this skewness. If the mean is higher than the median, the distribution is positively skewed; if the mean is lower than the median, the distribution is negatively skewed. In a skewed distribution, the median becomes the better measure because it is not affected by extreme scores.

Measures of Variability

A number of measures of variability have been developed over the years to indicate to what extent scores on a test differ from each other. Of the various measures, the range and the standard deviation are the best known and most frequently used. The easiest measure of the variability to understand is the range, which simply indicates the distance between the lowest and the highest scores. Although knowing the range can be informative, it does not help very much in interpreting an individual score. The standard deviation is a much more meaningful and useful measure, as seen in the following description.

If a frequency distribution is constructed of a sufficiently large number of measurements of many naturally occurring phenomena, a bell-shaped curve is likely to be produced. Results of most measurements occur close to the average, and relatively few are found at either extreme. For this type of distribution, the most dependable measure of variability is the standard deviation. The larger the standard deviation, the wider the spread or scatter of scores is from the mean. The standard deviation is the most widely accepted measure of variability for test users because (a) it is the basis for standard scores, (b) it yields a method of presenting the reliability of an individual test score as described in a later section, and (c) it is used in research studies for statistical tests of significance.

In a normal curve, the numerical value of the standard deviation divides the raw score range into approximately six parts, with three above the mean and three below. Scores occurring above

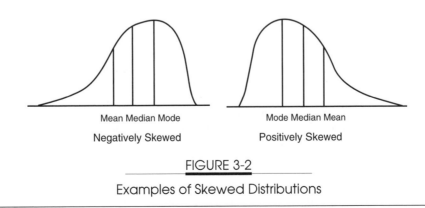

Mean Median Mode	Mode Median Mean
Negatively Skewed	Positively Skewed

FIGURE 3-2

Examples of Skewed Distributions

or below the distance of 3 standard deviations occur only very rarely. In a normal distribution, shown in Figure 3-1, approximately 34% of the sample lies between the median and 1 standard deviation above it and another 34% within the standard deviation below it. Thus, the distance of 1 standard deviation in each direction encompasses approximately 68% of the sample. An additional 14% or so of the sample is found within the second standard deviation above the mean and 14% below the mean, and approximately 2% is found in each of the measurements occurring in the third standard deviation above the mean and below the mean.

A person scoring 2 standard deviations below the mean, therefore, falls at the second percentile; at 1 standard deviation below, he or she falls at the 16th percentile. A person scoring at the median or mean is at the 50th percentile, a person scoring 1 standard deviation above the mean is at the 84th percentile, and a person scoring 2 standard deviations above the mean is at the 98th percentile. These percentages and points along the normal curve are shown in Figure 3-1. Because the standard deviation is the basis of standard scores, which are used in reporting the results of most psychological tests used by counselors, these percentages and points along the normal curve should be thoroughly understood and *memorized* by anyone who makes substantial use of psychological test results.

NORMS AND TYPES OF SCORES

Standardized tests by nature are norm referenced. Norms are established by administering the instrument to a standardization group and then referencing an individual's score to the distribution of scores obtained in the standardization sample. The individual's raw score is converted into some type of derived score, which indicates the individual's relative standing to the normative sample. This, then, provides a comparative measure of the individual's performance on whatever characteristic that instrument is assumed to measure.

It is important to note that the standardization sample should be representative of the population with which the student or client is being compared. For example, if a student is being compared with 10th-grade students, the sample should include a cross-section of students in the 10th grade from his or her city, state, region, or country, depending on the type of comparison one wishes to make. Norm groups should be systematically assembled, and fully described, in regard to significant variables such as grade, age, sex, type of school, and location. Separate norms should be developed if certain characteristics, such as ethnicity or socioeconomic background, are to be taken into account in interpreting test results.

Rank

A person's rank or standing within a group is the simplest norm-referenced statistic, with its interpretation based on the size and composition of the group. It is used extensively for grades—for example, a high school student who ranks 12th in grade point average (GPA) in a graduating class of 140—but it is seldom used in describing psychological test results.

Percentile Rank

Percentile rank is much more often used because it is not dependent on the size of the comparison group. Percentile scores are expressed in terms of the percentage of people in the comparison group who fall below them when the scores are placed in rank order. A percentile rank of 65 indicates a score or rank that is as high as or higher than those made by 65% of those in the comparison group. A percentile can be interpreted as a rank out of 100 persons in the comparison group (see Figure 3-1). Higher scores yield higher percentile ranks, and the lower the percentile, the lower the person's standing. The 50th percentile corresponds to the middle-most score, or the median. The 25th percentile is the first quartile point, marking the bottom quarter of the distribution, and the 75th percentile is the third quartile point, above which is found the top one quarter of the scores. The advantage of using percentiles is that they are easily calculated and easily understood by most people (provided it is made clear that a percentile indicates ranking in the comparison group rather than the percentage of correct responses).

The principal disadvantage of percentile ranking is that the distribution of most scores resembles the familiar bell-shaped curve (as in Figure 3-1), whereas the distribution of percentiles is always rectangular in shape. Ten percent of the cases fall between the 40th and 50th percentiles, in the same way that 10% fall between the 80th and 90th percentiles. Because of the pile-up of scores near the center of a distribution, a small difference in middle raw scores can yield a large difference in percentile ranks, as can be seen in Figure 3-1. At the extreme high and low ends of the distribution, however, large raw score differences may yield only small differences in percentile ranks. Percentile ranks are generally intended as a means of conveying information concerning a person's relative rank in a group, but because of the nature of percentiles, they are generally not used in additional statistical computations.

Grade Equivalents

Grade equivalents are often used on educational achievement tests to interpret how a student is progressing in terms of grade level. Grade equivalent scores consist of a number representing a grade followed by a decimal representing the 10 months of the school year from September through June. The grades range from K (kindergarten) to 12. Grades above 12 are occasionally used but are not particularly meaningful. The mean raw score obtained by students in each grade is computed, with fractions of a grade determined either by interpolation or by testing students at different times during the school year.

The principal advantage of grade equivalents is the seeming ease of interpretation to those without any understanding of measurement concepts. Actually, grade equivalents are subject to considerable misinterpretation. A sixth grader obtaining a grade equivalent score of 9.3 in arithmetic could easily be assumed by parents and teachers to have a knowledge of mathematics equivalent to the average student in the ninth grade at that time. A more correct interpretation would be that the student obtained a score on the arithmetic test equivalent to the score the average ninth grader would have obtained on that test in the unlikely event that ninth graders might have a sixth-grade arithmetic test administered to them. It would not mean that the sixth grader would have obtained a score equal to the average ninth-grade student on the ninth-grade test, which would undoubtedly have included algebraic and other mathematical concepts unfamiliar to sixth graders. Such a score would certainly indicate superior performance by a sixth grader but could not be regarded as equivalent to a ninth-grade performance (Urbina, 2004). In addition, because grade equivalents are computed from mean raw scores, students will vary in a bell-shaped curve above or below the mean. Thus, a teacher might attempt to bring each student up to grade level—all students scoring at or above the mean. If national grade equivalents are used, this could perhaps be accomplished in a particular classroom, but if local norms are used, such a feat would obviously be impossible.

Standard Scores

Because there are several problems related to using percentiles and other types of scores, many tests make use of standard scores as the most satisfactory method of reporting test results. Standard scores are based on standard deviations and means. A standard score is defined as a score expressed as a distance, in standard deviation units, between a raw score and the mean. The basic standard score is the z score. A z score of -1.5 on this scale indicates that the raw score falls $1\frac{1}{2}$ standard deviations below the mean of the reference group. A z score of 0 means the raw score falls exactly at the mean, and a raw score falling 2 standard deviations above the mean would yield a z score of $+2.0$. Because z scores produce both decimals and negative values, they cause difficulties in computations and interpretation, so other types of standard scores have been developed based on a linear transformation of the z score.

The most common standard score is the T score, which is used on a number of the most widely used educational and psychological tests. By definition, the T score has an arbitrary mean of 50 and an arbitrary standard deviation of 10. The T score is rounded to the nearest whole number, and because most raw scores do not exceed plus or minus 3 standard deviations from the mean, T score distributions usually range from 20 to 80. The results of many aptitude, interest, and personality measures are profiled in terms of T scores. To aid in the interpretation of T scores, half standard deviation units along with their comparable percentiles are shown in Table 3-1. The interpretations commonly given to the different ranges of T scores (along with percentile equivalents) are also given in that table (assuming of course that the norms are appropriate to the individual or group being assessed). It can be seen in Table 3-1 that T scores of 45 to 55, the middle 38% of the

TABLE 3-1

Interpretation (Assuming Appropriate Norms) for Given
T Scores and Percentile Ranks

T Score	Percentile Rank	Interpretation
70	98	Very high
66	94	
65	93	
60	84	High
56	70	
55	69	
50	50	Average
45	31	
44	30	
40	16	Low
35	7	
34	6	Very low
30	2	

distribution, are commonly interpreted as *average,* those above 55 as *high,* and those above 65 as *very high*. *T* scores below 45 can be interpreted to clients as *low,* and those below 35 as *very low*.

Other test publishers have selected different scales using different means and standard deviations, which can be interpreted the same way as *z* scores or *T* scores. The College Entrance Examination Board and the Graduate Record Examination (GRE) scores are reported in standard scores that use a mean of 500 and a standard deviation of 100. Thus, a raw score falling 1 standard deviation above the mean, which would yield a *z* score of 1.0 produces a standard score of 600. All scores are reported in increments of 10. This produces a scale that is recognizable for these instruments, although the scores may be thought of simply as *T* scores with an additional zero added. This type of scale can cause a minor problem in that small differences in raw scores may seem to be much larger because of the large-scaled score differences that range through 600 points (200 to 800).

For many years, there was considerable confusion concerning the Scholastic Aptitude Test (SAT) portions of the College Entrance Examination Board (which is discussed further in chapter 6). A mean of 500 was established years ago, when a smaller proportion of college-bound students took those tests. The typical college-bound student in more recent years scored well below the supposed mean of 500. In 1995, the scores were "re-centered," and 500 again became the college-bound student mean (College Board, 1994). The total scores of the three parts of the SAT now range from 600 to 2,400.

ACT, Inc., uses standard scores similar to those developed for the Iowa Tests of Educational Development ($M = 15$, $SD = 5$). The ACT tests have been standardized with a mean of 18 and a standard deviation of 6, yielding a range of standard scores from 1 to 36. Standard scores developed for the General Aptitude Test Battery (GATB) used for many years by the U.S. Employment Service yielded a mean of 100 and a standard deviation of 20.

When the first intelligence tests were developed, a ratio of mental age to chronological age was developed, and this ratio multiplied by 100. This ratio was later called the Intelligence Quotient, or IQ. The ratio IQ had a number of problems, including the fact that the ratio became invalid beginning in the adolescent years. Deviation IQ standard scores have since been developed to replace ratio IQs. Current results still report the mean at 100, as was the case with ratio IQs, but they report a standard score based on standard deviation units. Therefore, tests such as the Wechsler scales and the Stanford–Binet established a mean of 100 and a standard deviation of 15 or 16, depending on the test. The positions at which these standard scores fall along the normal curve are shown in Figure 3-1. Again it is important in interpreting test results with any of these types of standard scores to have firmly in mind the points along the normal curve where these scores fall and the proportions of the population on which the standard scores are based that fall at various points on the normal curve.

Another type of standard score is the *stanine*, based on the term *standard nine*. Stanines have a range of 1 to 9 and a mean of 5. The stanines of 1 and 9 at the ends of the distribution contain

4% of the cases, and these increase as in the normal curve so that the center stanine of 5 includes 20% of the cases. Test scores can be converted to stanines by referring to the normal curve percentages in Figure 3-1. Stanines are infrequently used because of the difficulty in explaining their meaning. Their chief advantage lies in the single-digit numbers, which do not imply greater accuracy than most tests can deliver. However, single digits can sometimes suggest a significant difference between two individuals when none exists.

CORRELATION

The correlation statistic assesses the degree to which two sets of measures are related—for example, how a tested trait or ability is related to a behavior. If a counselor had a score on a mathematics achievement test and the grades in arithmetic achieved by each student in a class, the counselor might wonder to what extent those students who scored well on the mathematics test also get good grades in arithmetic. To the extent that the rank orders of the students on each of these indices were similar—that is, those who scored high on the test obtained good grades and those with lower scores obtained poorer grades—the counselor would conclude that a relationship existed between the two indices. Such a relationship is expressed through a statistic known as a correlation coefficient. Each correlation coefficient contains two bits of information: The sign of the correlation tells whether the two variables tend to rank individuals in the same order or in their reverse order, and the magnitude of the correlation indicates the strength of this relationship. The smaller the number of individuals on whom a correlation is based, the larger the correlation must be to indicate a relationship that is statistically significant.

Among the several different types of correlation coefficients that can be computed, the Pearson product–moment coefficient (r) is the most common and can range in value from +1.00, a perfect positive relationship; through .00, no relationship or a chance relationship; to –1.00, indicating a perfect negative, or inverse, relationship. For example, the correlation between scores on a college entrance test and the freshman-year GPA of college students might yield a correlation coefficient of .40. The distance of students' homes from the college might yield a random or complete lack of a relationship, .00, with grades, and number of hours that students spent watching television might yield a low negative relationship with grades of –.20.

It must be remembered that a substantial correlation between two variables does not imply that either variable causes the other. They both can be under the influence of a third variable. Heights of children could show a significant correlation with their scores on a vocabulary test, but both of these variables could be related to the children's ages and maturational growth.

RELIABILITY

Reliability and validity are two technical subjects that may not be of great interest to most people-oriented counselors, but they are extremely important for those who use psychological tests. They are concepts that need to be well understood when selecting, administering, and interpreting psychological tests. Also, in many school districts, counselors are the most knowledgeable persons regarding the technical aspects of educational and psychological measurement. Their training and experience with standardized tests usually exceeds that of classroom teachers and most administrators. This role of school counselors has been magnified by the measurement demands of the No Child Left Behind Act (2002) legislation, and reliability issues will be among those they will be expected to address (Feldt, 2004).

Inherent in the concept of reliability of psychological tests is the recognition that none of these instruments measure perfectly. Educators and behavioral scientists are interested in measuring much more complicated human characteristics than people's physical aspects. Anxiety, intelligence, depression, and potential to become a substance abuser are complex qualities that are difficult both to define precisely and to measure.

Reliability refers to how consistently a test measures and the extent to which it eliminates chance and other extraneous factors in its results. Synonyms for reliability include dependability, reproducibility, stability, and consistency. A score that a person receives on a test is made up of two elements: the person's true score and an error score that may add to or subtract from the true score. A test with perfect reliability would be one on which everyone's scores remained in the same relative position on each administration (although they would not necessarily receive the exact same scores each time). Although people refer to the reliability of a test, reliability is actually the property of the test scores for the particular group on which it was administered—not of the test itself. In computing a correlation coefficient for a group of people on two sets of scores on different forms of the same instrument, the perfect relationship would yield a correlation of 1.00. If the test scores were completely unreliable, the relationship between the two would be a chance relationship, and the correlation would be approximately 0.

Reliability is concerned both with the natural variation in human performance and with the technical aspects of psychological measurement. The stability of the trait or variable being measured obviously influences the amount of variation expected or considered normal when measured at different times. On the one hand, it would be expected that ability variables would have less variation than psychological states, but changes in ability measures can still occur as a result of growth and development. On the other hand, measures of personality variables, such as a state of depression, a state of anxiety, or a state of stress, could be expected to vary considerably at different times and under different circumstances.

Factors that are irrelevant to the purpose for which the test is designed represent error variance. Attempts to maintain uniform test conditions by controlling the instructions, time limits, and the testing environment are undertaken to reduce error variance and make test scores more reliable. No test produces scores that are perfectly reliable, and because psychological measurement is often imprecise, it is important to check the accuracy and consistency of the instrument constantly to ensure that the unreliability is kept within reasonable limits. The current *Standards for Educational and Psychological Testing* (AERA, APA, & NCME, 1999) emphasizes that test developers should provide test users with substantial amounts of information on test reliability and standard errors of measurement. This includes reporting in test manuals specific details about populations on which reliability data were obtained, standard errors of measurement for all types of scores reported, and intervals between retests and interrater consistency where appropriate.

Reliability coefficients usually run within the range of .80 to .95, but what is considered to be acceptable reliability varies substantially depending on both the testing circumstances and the type of reliability. For national testing programs such as the GRE or the Iowa Tests of Educational Development, reliability coefficients are expected to be above .90. For certain other types of psychological tests, this type of reliability is substantially lower. A score on the Depression scale of the Minnesota Multiphasic Personality Inventory (MMPI), for example, is an indication of the person's mood at the time the inventory was administered. Because people's moods change, a very high test–retest reliability would be neither expected nor desired. Thus, for personality measures, interest measures, and attitudinal measures, test–retest reliability coefficients often fall below .90, although if they fall below .70, the consistency of the instrument becomes suspect (Cicchetti, 1994).

Types of Reliability

Reliability can be measured in several different ways, so there is not a single measure of reliability for a set of test scores but different coefficients depending on how the coefficients are determined. Test scores can vary in their consistency in terms of time, test forms, or test items. Traditionally, there are three basic methods of estimating the reliability of an instrument based on these variables: test–retest, alternate forms, and internal consistency. The proportion of test error attributable to each of these sources of unreliability can be calculated by analysis of variance procedures with an approach to reliability measurement known as generalizability theory (AERA, APA, & NCME, 1999).

Test–Retest Reliability

Test–retest reliability, which is a common method of estimating traits, measures consistency over time. The correlation coefficient in this case indicates the relationship between scores obtained by individuals within the same group on two administrations of the test. Test–retest correlations tend to decrease as the interval between the test administrations lengthens. If the interval is brief, there are potential problems of practice and memory, which tend to make the reliability estimation spuriously high. If the time interval is too long, variation can be influenced by events that occur to participants between the two test administrations, and spuriously low estimates of reliability may be obtained.

Alternate-Form Reliability

Alternate-form, or parallel-form reliability, is computed by comparing the consistency of scores of individuals within the same group on two alternate but equivalent forms of the same test. Because the test items are different, the effect of memory and other carryover effects are eliminated. The crucial question remains whether in fact the two alternate forms of the test are actually equivalent.

Two tests that measure the same content or variables and that are equivalent in difficulty level can be administered on the same day or very close to each other without concern about the practice effect. They can be alternated so that Test A is given to one group first and Test B to the other group first, and the practice effect can thus be controlled.

The problem with this type of test reliability is that it is often difficult enough to come up with one good form of a test, much less two good forms. Therefore, unless there is a national testing program with a staff working on developing test forms, as is the case with some of the national testing programs such as the Medical College Admissions Test or the ACT tests, hope for this form of reliability is unrealistic.

In national testing programs, the problem of developing equivalent forms is met by administering experimental items with each test administration. The people taking the test respond both to items that count and to those that are being tried out. The latter do not count in scoring for that administration but provide data for the construction of future forms of the test. The experimental items do not need to be the same for all those taking the test on a particular date because item information can be collected from random subsamples. This is how national testing programs are able to produce equivalent forms year after year.

Internal Consistency

Measures of internal consistency provide an estimate of test score reliability that indicates the consistency of responses to the different items or parts of a test during a single test and administration (AERA, APA, & NCME, 1999). Two common measures of internal consistency are split-half and interitem consistency.

Split-half reliability is a popular form of establishing reliability because it can be obtained from a single administration by dividing the test into comparable halves and comparing the resulting two scores for each individual. It is administered all at once, so no time-to-time fluctuation occurs. From this point of view, it can be thought of as a special case of alternate-form reliability. In most tests, the first half and the second half would not be comparable because of differences in the difficulty of the items, as well as effects of practice and fatigue that are likely to vary from the beginning to the end of the test. Therefore, most tests are split into odd and even items, except when several items deal with a specific problem, in which case the entire group of items is assigned to one or the other half. An important weakness in the split-half approach lies in the general principle of sampling—that is, usually the greater the number of items, the more stable will be the concept being measured. All things being equal, the longer the test, the more reliable its scores will be. The split-half procedure cuts the test length in half, thus decreasing the reliability estimate. To correct the computed reliability based on the shorter length, the Spearman–Brown Prophecy Formula can be used to yield an estimate of what the reliability would be if it were obtained on the test's full length.

Interitem Consistency

Interitem consistency is a measure of internal consistency that assesses the extent to which the items on a test are related to each other and to the total score. This measure of test score reliability provides an estimate of the average intercorrelations among all of the items on a test. Depending on the type of response called for on the instrument, formulas known as the Kuder–Richardson Formula 20 for two-response answers (e.g., true or false, yes or no) or Cronbach's alpha reliability coefficient for more than two alternatives are computed. All individual item responses for each person in the entire sample are placed in a computer, and the resulting reliability coefficients indicate the consistency with which the items sample the trait being measured.

Profile Reliability

For tests that yield a profile of scores on a number of different scales, the concept of profile reliability may be more appropriate than a mean reliability coefficient from a number of different scales of varying reliability. Profile reliability is obtained by computing the overall similarity of two profiles obtained for the same person at two different times. If the profile reliability is greater than .75, there is little difference in the interpretation given to the profile by counselors (Hoyt, 1960).

Considerations in Reliability

The appropriateness of a particular method depends on the nature of the trait being measured, particularly in terms of the stability of the trait. If one is interested in a measure that indicates the degree to which the items in a scale are interrelated, then the interitem consistency technique would be recommended; if the concern is with dependability for predictive purposes, then the test–retest or parallel forms with an increased time interval would be more appropriate.

The interpretation of a reliability coefficient also depends on the nature of the trait being measured. A paper-and-pencil IQ test with a reliability coefficient of .75 would not be acceptable, whereas the same coefficient for a measure of anxiety would be fairly acceptable for use. Reliabilities of test scores can be compared with the reliabilities of similar instruments, remembering that the lower the reliability, the less confidence can be placed in the use and interpretation of the resulting test data.

Reliability estimates are influenced by the nature of the group on which the reliability measure was computed. In a group that is heterogeneous on the characteristic being measured, there will be a greater range and greater variability and hence a higher reliability coefficient. An introductory course at the undergraduate level is likely to have a relatively heterogeneous group of students, with the result that a relatively poorly constructed final examination may yield a considerably higher reliability coefficient than a carefully constructed final examination in a graduate-level course, which will likely contain a much more homogeneous group of students. Thus, in examining the reliability of test scores for a particular instrument, it is necessary to look at the type of sample on which the reliability coefficient was obtained as well as the type of reliability that was obtained. Information on reliability in a test manual should include the means and standard deviations, as well as the demographic characteristics of the sample on which the reliability coefficients were computed (AERA, APA, & NCME, 1999).

An important point to remember regarding reliability is that longer tests are usually more reliable than shorter tests (although brief computer-administered adaptive tests with specifically selected items often yield high reliabilities). It is also true that speed tests such as those assessing clerical aptitude or manual dexterity can yield reliability coefficients that are spuriously high. On speed tests, individuals are likely to complete approximately the same number of odd and even items and do not receive credit for items at the end of the test because they did not get that far. This results in a similarity of performance between the two halves and yields a high split-half reliability coefficient. The split-half method takes into account accuracy of performance on the odd versus even items but not the number of items completed, which is usually the most important consideration on the speed test. Another form of test reliability should be used to determine the consistency of speed at which a person works.

When subjective judgments are involved in scoring test items, the problem of interrater or interscorer reliability results. Reliabilities of scored essay tests have always been quite poor, a problem faced by national testing organizations as they have developed writing samples as criteria for college admissions. By giving clear instructions to the examinees regarding length, format, and content and extensive training to the raters, they have attempted to meet this problem. Even so, well-trained raters often vary substantially in the ratings they give to writing samples.

Standard Error of Measurement (SEM)

The *SEM* yields the same type of information as does the reliability coefficient but is specifically applicable to the interpretation of individual scores. Its most common use is to construct bands of confidence around an individual's obtained score. It represents the theoretical distribution that would be obtained if an individual were repeatedly tested with a large number of exactly equivalent forms of the same test. Such a cluster of repeated scores would form a curve, with a mean and standard deviation of the distribution, and that standard deviation is called the *SEM*. An individual's single score on a test is assumed to be the mean of repeated scores, and the *SEM* can be interpreted in terms of normal curve frequencies. Thus, if a student's true raw score was 40 on a particular test and the *SEM* was 3, then if the test were repeated many times, 68% of the individual's scores would fall between 37 and 43, and we could be 95% confident that the individual's true score would be between 34 and 46—2 *SEM* units above or below the obtained score.

The *SEM* is easily computed when the standard deviation and the reliability coefficient of the test are known by using the following formula: The *SEM* equals the standard deviation *(SD)* of the test times the square root of the quantity 1 minus the reliability of the test:

$$SEM = SD \times \sqrt{1 - \text{reliability}}.$$

As an example, the SAT scores of the College Entrance Examination Board have a standard score mean of 500, a standard deviation of 100, and test–retest reliability of approximately .91 for college applicants. The *SEM* is 30 ($100 \times \sqrt{1 - .91} = 100 \times \sqrt{.09} = 100 \times .3 = 30$). If Susan, a college applicant, scores 490 on the test, the odds are high (68% of the time) that her true score falls between 460 and 520 (i.e., plus and minus 1 *SEM* of the obtained score) and 95% between 430 and 550—2 *SEM*s. Similar estimates can be made of the true scores for individuals on the ACT test, which, with a mean of 18, a standard deviation of approximately 6, and reliability coefficients of about .90, has an *SEM* in the vicinity of 2. In the case of the Wechsler intelligence scales with full-scale score standard deviations of 15 (*M* = 100) and reliability coefficients in the vicinity of .96, the *SEM* equals 3.

Although most test manuals interpret *SEM* according to classical test theory in the manner discussed above, item response theory recognizes that the interpretation of SEM varies depending on the degree to which the individual scored above or below the mean. In general, test error is higher for extreme scores because there are fewer items of appropriate difficulty at these levels to measure the variable in question (Embertson, 1996). In addition, extremely high or low scores can be expected to change more on retesting than scores in the average range due to regression toward the mean (Charter & Feldt, 2002).

VALIDITY

Whereas reliability is concerned with whether the instrument is a consistent measure, validity deals with the extent to which meaningful and appropriate inferences can be made from the instrument. Is there evidence to support the interpretation of test scores for the purpose for which they will be used? It is possible for test scores to have high reliability with little or no validity for a particular purpose (but in order to have good validity, high reliability is necessary).

According to the *Standards* (AERA, APA, & NCME, 1999), test validity should be assessed in terms of the use to which the test is put, such as counseling, selection, or classification. Once the use of the test is clear, the test user should study the evidence of the validity of the test for that particular purpose. It is therefore important that test manuals contain detailed information regarding both theoretical and empirical evidence of validity for the interpretation and use of test scores.

The question "validity for what?" must always be asked, because the validity of a test varies depending on the purpose and the target population. For example, scores on the Strong Interest Inventory (the Strong) have considerable test–retest reliability even when the second test is taken many years later. Validity, however, is much more complicated. Because of the large number of scales and the different types of scales, specific definitions must be developed before they can be applied to a criterion to obtain validity. As will be seen later (in chapter 9), scores on the Strong can be used effectively to predict the occupation that a person is likely to enter in the future. However, it is not particularly valid for predicting success in an occupation. People who enter an occupation for which they get a low score on the Strong may very well not stay in that occupation. People who score high are much more likely to stay in the occupation, but the few low scorers who stay in that field are just as likely to be successful as those who score high. Therefore, a score on a scale of the Strong may have some validity for predicting whether people will enter an occupation and, if so, how long they will stay in it, but it will have little validity when it comes to predicting success in that occupation.

Validity also asks the question of whether the test scores measure what they purport to measure. Does a test that is supposed to measure arithmetic skills really measure arithmetic skills, or is it composed of word problems of such reading difficulty that it is actually measuring reading ability instead?

The range of validity coefficients runs much lower than that of reliability. Whereas coefficients of .80 to .95 are common for reliability, validity coefficients seldom run above .60 and are more typically in the range of .20 to .40 (Hemphill, 2003). Validity coefficients as low as .10 and .20 can still be useful in predicting future behavior (Rosenthal, 1990; Rosnow & Rosenthal, 1988). In predicting grades in college from test scores, coefficients are almost never obtained above .60. Even when other measures of high school achievement, personality, and some type of achievement motivation are all combined, validity coefficients above .60 are seldom achieved for college grades.

We emphasize here that psychological test data provide unique information beyond that obtained from relying only on the interview. As indicated in chapter 1, large-scale studies of psychological tests have found that they yield validity coefficients as high as medical tests and that the evidence for using them in clinical and counseling practice can be "strong and compelling" (G. J. Meyer et al., 2001, p. 128).

Evidence of a test's validity for a particular purpose can be assessed in different ways, as noted in the *Standards* (AERA, APA, & NCME, 1999; Urbina, 2004). Emphasis is placed on the nature and strength of the evidence for a particular interpretation. Different types of validity evidence are discussed below.

Evidence Based on Test Content and Response Processes

In the case of *content validity* evidence, the items on a test are examined carefully to determine whether the items measure what the test is intended to measure. For educational assessment in schools, test items are selected by examining curricula, textbooks, and other materials as well as performance objectives. If the test is designed to measure achievement in high school physics, a number of high school physics teachers, and perhaps some college physics teachers, examine the items on the test to determine whether these items are in fact measuring knowledge of what is typically taught in high school physics. Content validity involves judgment by competent experts in that discipline. The rationale and criteria that examinees use in choosing their responses can be investigated through observation and interviews to determine whether they are responding as intended (Goodwin & Leech, 2003).

Content validity should not be confused with face validity, which is not really validity at all but merely deals with the question of whether the items seem to be relevant to the person taking the test. Validity from the perspective of the test taker can nevertheless be important for acceptance of the testing process and of the test results.

Evidence Based on Relations to Relevant Criteria and Other Variables

Test-Criteria Relationships

Criterion-related validity pertains to validity evidence that is obtained by comparing test scores with performance on a criterion measure such as grades or job satisfaction. All criterion-related measures can be described as empirical (as contrasted with theoretical or logical) in that they involve the collection of data.

In the case of *concurrent validity,* the test scores and the criterion performance scores are collected at the same time. Correlation coefficients are calculated between the test score and the scores on the criterion variable. For example, a test of mechanical aptitude might be given to a group of working machinists, and then the ratings that they receive by their supervisors might be examined to determine whether the mechanical aptitude scores are related to their current work. Often measures of concurrent validity are obtained because the test is going to be used in the future to predict some type of behavior—such as the ability to do the work of a machinist.

A second type of criterion-related validity is *predictive validity.* In this case, the person's performance or criterion measure is obtained some time after the test score. For a scholastic aptitude test designed to predict college grades, the grades that the students earn in college are examined to determine whether the scholastic aptitude test given in high school has predictive validity. Does it predict what it is supposed to be predicting—in this case, college grades?

One of the problems in measuring either concurrent or predictive validity is that the size of the correlation coefficients will be reduced if the range of scores on either the test or the criterion variable is restricted in any way. Because scholastic aptitude test scores are often used to select students for a particular institution, and many students with low scores are eliminated, the group being studied to measure the test's predictive validity will have a narrower range, with a resulting lower validity coefficient. One way of avoiding this is to administer the instrument before any selection has taken place and to have the selection take place without regard to the criterion being assessed. For example, in one of the validation studies for the GATB of the U.S. Employment Service, the entire battery was given to all applicants for jobs in an industrial plant that was being built in a particular town. Workers were then selected without regard to their GATB results. Performance ratings for the workers were obtained at a later date, and these were then related to the previously obtained GATB results showing substantial predictive validity.

Spuriously high validity coefficients can be obtained from a form of criterion contamination if, for example, the people doing the rating know the test results. University professors' knowledge of graduate students' GRE test results might (but obviously should not) influence the grades they assign, which could result in a higher relationship between test results and graduate GPAs.

An important concept related to the validity of a test concerns the base rates of the characteristic that is being measured in the population. *Base rates* refer to the proportion of people in a population who represent the particular characteristic or behavior that is being predicted. Base rates are important because they have a marked influence on how useful or valid tests are in making predictions. If the base rates are either very low or very high, the predictions made from the tests are not likely to be useful. If almost every student admitted to medical school graduates, then scores on the Medical College Admission Test (MCAT) are unlikely to differentiate between those who will graduate and those who will not. The best prediction to be obtained would be not to use the test scores but merely to predict that every student admitted will graduate. Suicide rates are examples of low base rates. Although people who obtain high scores on a scale that measures depression are more likely to commit suicide than those with lower scores, most people who obtain high scores on a measure of depression do not commit suicide. Because suicide is relatively rare, the base rate is so low that even with a high score on a depression scale, the most accurate prediction to be made would still be that any individual is not likely to commit suicide.

For many widely used instruments, large numbers of individual predictive studies have been conducted, often with conflicting results. Meta-analyses techniques now allow researchers to collect and synthesize results of many studies. They statistically correct for different sampling and measurement problems and are able to clarify issues and provide considerable evidence for the predictive validity of these instruments (Urbina, 2004).

The purpose of tests is, of course, to provide more information than could be obtained by chance or other unreliable means. Validity of tests is evaluated in terms of how much they contribute beyond what could be predicted without them. The concept of incremental validity refers to the extent to which a particular assessment instrument adds to the accuracy of predictions obtained from other tests or other less-extensive methods of assessment. This improvement can result in increased accuracy of prediction, better specificity or sensitivity, or increased efficacy of decision-making judgments beyond that generated on the basis of other data (Hunsley & Meyer, 2003). The real value of the MCAT would be if the correct prediction rate could be increased beyond that available without the use of the test. Incremental validity should be taken into account in deciding whether to use an additional assessment instrument, and, of course, the financial cost of acquiring more data should be weighed against the importance and the clinical utility of the new information.

The amount of variability in a criterion that a correlation coefficient is considered to account for is determined by the square of the correlation. Thus, a correlation coefficient of .30 means that 9% of the variance is explained. In using a correlation coefficient for prediction, however, Rosnow and Rosenthal (1988) showed that the correlation coefficient can be taken to indicate the improvement in success of prediction over chance alone by the percentage indicated by that correlation. Thus, a correlation of .30 means that using that variable in prediction improves the prediction by approximately 30%. When considered in this way, a moderate correlation can be seen to have considerable usefulness in counseling over that which would have been obtained had that test not been taken into consideration.

When a test is used to make a dichotomous, either/or decision (e.g., acceptable or unacceptable, successful or unsuccessful, positive diagnosis or negative diagnosis), cutoff scores are usually used. The point at which the cutoff score is established is often a matter of relative cost. In some cases, a miss can be very costly, for example, concluding that someone is not suicidal because he or she is below a cutoff score on a suicide potential scale when in fact the person is suicidal. The cost of this type of miss could be that a suicide takes place that might have been preventable. This type of case is called a *false negative*. The person fell below the cutoff score and was therefore predicted not to be suicidal when in fact he or she was suicidal. A false positive occurs when a person obtains a score above the cutoff score and, for example, is predicted to be successful on the job but in fact fails and is discharged. Again, the time and money invested in training the person are likely to influence where the cutoff score is placed and, therefore, to influence the proportion of false positives.

The accuracy of classification of individuals into different diagnostic categories or related groups based on a particular cutoff score can be expressed in terms of *sensitivity* and *specificity*. Sensitivity refers to the accuracy of a cutoff score in detecting those people who belong in a particular category. By definition, testing procedures that are sensitive produce few false negatives. Specificity indicates the accuracy of a cutoff score in excluding those without that condition. Testing procedures that possess specificity yield few false positives. Sensitivity and specificity will vary depending on the particular cutoff score used to select individuals considered to be meeting the condition. Generally, if sensitivity is increased, specificity will be reduced and vice versa.

For example, most clients who commit suicide or have seriously considered suicide obtain an elevated score (T score > 65) on the Depression scale of the MMPI. However, a large number of individuals who are not suicidal also obtain elevated scores on this scale. When the MMPI Depression scale is used in this manner, it can be said to possess sensitivity in identifying potentially suicidal individuals but to lack specificity in ruling out individuals who are not suicidal (Cicchetti, 1994). If a higher cutoff were used (e.g., T score > 75), specificity would be increased, but sensitivity would be lessened (there would be more false negatives because although most people who commit suicide are depressed, their depression scores may not exceed 75).

Where a test has been shown to possess considerable validity for predictive purposes, counselors are encouraged to produce materials adapted for local needs (American School Counselor Association & Association for Assessment in Counseling, 1998). An example is the expectancy table shown in Table 3-2, in which ACT Math scores are related to success in a university mathematics course typically taken by freshmen. Such a table would be useful not only for determining a cutoff score for placement into this particular mathematics course but also as a valuable counseling tool. We could say to a student who scored a 20 on the ACT Math, "Of those who achieved your ACT score, 9 students out of 100 got a *B* or higher, 43 got a *C* or higher, and therefore 57 did not get a passing *C* grade. Now we don't know whether you will be 1 of the 9 who gets at least a *B*, 1 of the 43 with a *C*, or 1 of the 57 falling below—but this gives you a chance to see what the odds are if you decide to take it."

Convergent and Discriminant Evidence
Another type of validity evidence asks the question: Are the test results related to variables that they ought to be related to and not related to variables that they ought not to be? For example, do

TABLE 3-2
A Locally Produced Expectancy Table

ACT Mathematics Score	Percentage Obtaining a *B* or Better	Percentage Obtaining a *C* or Better
33+	88	98
31–32	81	96
28–30	67	93
25–27	44	85
21–23	18	64
18–20	9	43
15–17	3	23
12–13	1	9
11–	1	6

Note. From *Using the ACT in Advising and Course Placement 1999–2000,* by the American College Testing Program, 1999. Copyright by ACT, Inc. Adapted with permission.

results on the test change according to what is known about developmental changes? Do older students do better on the test than younger students; for example, do sixth graders do better on arithmetic tests than third graders?

Patterns of relationships to other variables yield validity evidence known as *convergent validity* and *discriminant validity.* On the one hand, tests scores should be expected to show a substantial correlation with other tests and assessments that measure similar characteristics. Measures of mathematical aptitude ought to be related to grades in mathematics studies. On the other hand, test scores should not be substantially correlated with other tests from which they are supposed to differ; that is, they should show discriminant validity. A test of mathematical ability probably should not show a strong correlation with a test of clerical speed and accuracy. A measure of sociability should be negatively related to the score on a schizophrenic scale and positively related to the score on a scale of extraversion. Most validation studies report convergent validity.

Evidence that pertains to the theoretical basis of a test, such as that emphasized in this section and the next, is sometimes referred to as construct validity—a type of validity that has been used as a means of explaining the psychological meaning of the variable ("construct") measured by the test. In essence, construct validity is synonymous with the term *validity* itself, which focuses on the extent and the nature of the evidence used to support all test interpretations (AERA, APA, & NCME, 1999).

Evidence Based on Internal Structures

A component of internal validity is *internal consistency*. Measures of internal consistency, which are used primarily to indicate reliability, show the extent to which the items in the test are related to each other and to the total score on the test. High internal consistency is therefore one indication of construct validity. When test scales are internally consistent, they are easier for the counselor to interpret because all of the items are measuring the same construct.

The statistical procedure known as factor analysis is used to extract the various dimensions or factors assessed by the different items on the test. This type of analysis can answer such questions as, Do the test results make psychological sense? and What are the underlying constructs (or factors or characteristics)?

If an instrument is related to a particular psychological theory, then the results should fit that theory. Factor analysis can determine whether the test items fall together in different factors the way that the theory suggests they should. If a test is constructed along the lines of Jungian theory, such as the Myers–Briggs Type Indicator, the resulting factors from a factor analysis should be related to such Jungian concepts as introversion versus extraversion, sensing versus intuition, and thinking versus feeling.

Evidence Based on Consequences of Testing

A relatively new type of validity evidence proposed by Messick (1995), sometimes called *consequential validity,* examines both the expected and unexpected consequences of testing. Cost–benefit ratios for each situation, the risks involved in making false positive and false negative decisions, and the efficiency of tests compared with other alternatives must be taken into account. In particular, attempts need to be made to determine the long-term consequences to society of large-scale testing programs. Obvious examples would include the testing required by the No Child Left Behind Act or the addition of the SAT essay.

Treatment Validity

Another type of validity important for counselors and clinicians has been termed *treatment validity:* Do the results obtained from the test make a difference in the treatment? (Barrios, 1988; Holland, 1997). If the test results are useful, if they make a difference in the counseling process, then the test could be said to have treatment validity. For example, Finn and Tonsager (1992) found that clients who had their MMPI scores interpreted to them showed significant improvement on several treatment variables. In a similar fashion, Randahl et al. (1993) found that clients who had their Strong profile interpreted to them made significant progress on their career planning.

The question, then, is not simply, Is the test valid? but, What is the validity evidence to support the planned use of the test? Criterion-related validity is important, for example, if the test is to be used for selection, whereas content validity is important if it is to be used as a measure of achievement. In the overall construction and development of a test, various validation procedures are applied throughout the developmental stages. All the types of validity can be conceived as contributing to the validity of a test score, which may also include the social value consequences of its use. Measures of internal consistency are built into the early stages of development; criterion-related validation typically occurs in some of the latter stages. Validation continues long after the test has been published and distributed for use.

TEST DEVELOPMENT

To produce a well-designed standardized psychological test or inventory, the test developer generates a large amount of data. First, test items are written, usually by specialists or experts in the field according to the objectives and purpose of the test (Drummond & Jones, 2006). They are then checked for cultural, sexual, or regional bias, and items that might be unfair or offensive to any group are eliminated. They are then tried out on sample populations similar to the targeted group, and the results are analyzed to determine those items that are of appropriate difficulty and discriminating power. The items must differentiate between people who represent more and less of the behaviors or the domain that is being measured using item response theory models. After the resulting items have been assembled into a test and scored, the scores must be converted into a continuous scale, norms must be developed that are applicable to the groups for which the test is designed, and reliability estimates must be calculated. Correlations of the test with other similar variables, with background variables, and with predicted criteria must then be determined. The effectiveness of the test or inventory in accomplishing the objectives for which it was created should continue to be studied on a regular basis after it has been published and put to use.

SUMMARY

1. Test scores may be interpreted in terms of a comparison group (norm-referenced), a preestablished standard (criterion-referenced), or one's earlier performance on the same measure (self-referenced).
2. The proportion of individuals who fall within each of the 6 standard deviation units on the normal curve must be thoroughly understood to accurately interpret most test scores.
3. Correlation coefficients indicate the degree and direction of a relationship between two measures or variables.
4. Reliability refers to the consistency or generalizability of test scores over time (test–retest reliability), forms (alternate-form reliability), and items (internal consistency).
5. The *SEM* indicates the amount of variation that can be expected in an individual's score on retesting because of test unreliability.
6. Validity refers to the degree to which accumulated evidence supports the proposed interpretation of test scores for the purpose for which they will be used.
7. Different types of validity evidence that may be used to support a test interpretation include information pertaining to the test (Is the content appropriate for the intended use?), criterion-related relationships (Are the test scores significantly correlated with relevant criteria, such as school or work performance?), convergent and discriminant relationships (Do the test scores correlate with other variables in the expected direction?), internal consistency of test items (Are the test items related to each other and to the total score?), factor structure of the test (Do the factors measured by the test fit its planned usage and help to explain the meaning of the test scores?), and the consequences of testing (Are people helped or hurt by participating in the testing process?).

4

Initial and Outcome Assessments in Counseling

W hat assessment procedures should counselors pursue at the beginning of counseling? What outcome assessments can best be used at the end of counseling to evaluate the effectiveness of the counseling? What steps should be taken to ensure that assessment procedures are appropriately selected, administered, and scored? This chapter addresses these questions.

Both initial and outcome assessments are discussed in this chapter because the same instruments are often used in both cases to evaluate the nature and severity of an individual's concerns. By using the same or similar instruments, counselors can easily evaluate a client's progress. In this chapter, we also discuss the principles of test selection, administration, and scoring as issues that often need to be considered at the beginning of counseling.

CLIENT ORIENTATION TOWARD PROBLEM SOLVING

Clients differ in their readiness for counseling, their expectations of counseling, and their problem-solving styles. Counselors can be more effective with clients if they take these differences into account.

Readiness for Counseling

In their work with individuals with addictive behaviors, Prochaska, DiClemente, and Norcross (1992) noted five stages of change experienced by their clients: *precontemplation, contemplation, preparation, action,* and *maintenance.* These same stages of change pertain to clients with a wide variety of problems (Petrocelli, 2002).

In the precontemplative stage, individuals are not especially aware of their problem and have no plans to change their behavior in the foreseeable future. Individuals who seek counseling while in the precontemplative stage usually do so at the insistence of someone else who is concerned about their problems. Research indicates that such individuals benefit less from counseling and perceive their counseling relationship less favorably than do those in more advanced stages of change (Rochlen, Rude, & Baron, 2005).

Clients in the contemplative stage are aware of their problem but have not yet made a serious commitment to do anything about it. Individuals in this stage are considering making changes in their behavior sometime within the next 6 months; however, it may be much longer before they actually do make changes.

In the preparation stage, clients have begun to make small changes in their problematic behaviors, with the intention of making more complete changes within 1 month. The action stage is reached when clients successfully change their behavior for short periods of time. If the changes persist for longer than 6 months, the client enters the maintenance stage, in which the goal is to maintain the behavioral and attitudinal changes that have occurred.

Assessment of the client's stage of change is crucial for determining the most effective treatment technique. As noted by Prochaska et al. (1992), different approaches should be used for clients in different stages. For example, individuals in the precontemplative and contemplative stages can be helped most by early intervention techniques such as consciousness raising and dramatic relief, whereas individuals in the action and maintenance stages can benefit most from later intervention techniques such as reinforcement management and support groups.

It is important to note that most clients recycle through some or all of the stages several times before successfully achieving long-term changes. Although recycling is the norm, most clients learn from their previous attempts so that they make faster progress through the cycle in subsequent attempts to resolve their problems. The University of Rhode Island Change Assessment (URICA), a 32-item questionnaire that assesses attitudes and behaviors associated with different stages of change, can be used to help determine a client's readiness for change (P. J. Cohen, Glaser, & Calhoun, 2005).

Expectations of Counseling: Models of Helping and Coping

Clients' expectations for counseling will vary depending on their view of the problematic situation. Clients differ in the extent to which they accept responsibility for the problem or its solution. This distinction is important because it makes it possible to separate blame for the problem from control of its solution. Brickman et al. (1982) identified four different orientations toward counseling based on the client's views. As indicated below, clients may subscribe to any one of these four models.

- *Moral Model.* People are responsible for their problems and solutions. Clients who fit this model look on counselors as consultants who can help direct them to resources, such as self-help books and personal growth groups, that they can implement on their own. They perceive themselves as lazy people who must work harder. Clients seek stimulation from counselors to do what they know they must do.
- *Compensatory Model.* People are not responsible for their problems but are responsible for solutions. Clients with this point of view perceive counselors as advocates who can help them to overcome a problem that they did not cause (e.g., poor education, which can be helped by tutorial programs). They think of themselves as deprived individuals who must assert themselves. Clients look to counselors for empowerment to help them correct situations that cause problems.
- *Enlightenment Model.* People are responsible for their problems but not for solutions to the problems. Clients who endorse this model look on counselors as saviors who can provide long-term care for them by means of ongoing support groups or other methods. They see themselves as guilty individuals who must submit to a higher authority. Clients expect counselors to help provide them with discipline they lack themselves.
- *Medical Model.* People are not responsible for problems or solutions. Clients who fit this model view counselors as experts who will be able to remedy their problems by external means (e.g., by prescribing a treatment program). They regard themselves as ill people who must accept advice or treatment from the proper authority. Clients expect counselors to prescribe the solution, which they will then follow.

The problem-solving process can be aided by taking into account the orientation of the client and that of the counselor. Clients report more satisfaction and work more effectively with counselors who agree with them regarding responsibility for the problem and its solution (Hayes, Wall, & Shea, 1998). Clients who accept responsibility for causing or solving their problem respond better to insight-focused counseling; those who attribute their problem or its solution to outside forces show greater improvement with symptom-focused interventions (Beutler, 2000).

Counselors can usually determine the client's orientation by means of an interview. They can ask clients who (or what) is to blame for their problem and who (or what) is in control of solving the problem. They can use the distinctions among the models indicated in the preceding paragraphs to help frame questions for clients. Internal versus external locus of control scales may also be helpful in this regard (Corcoran & Fischer, 2000). Clients who believe that they are in control of their destiny (internal locus of control) fit the moral or compensatory models; clients who believe that they are the victims of chance or their environment (external locus of control) conform to the enlightenment or medical models.

The compensatory model produces the best results for counselors in many situations (Brickman et al., 1982). It has the advantage of absolving clients of blame for the problem, thus justifying their request for assistance. At the same time, it places them in control of removing or reducing the problem. As indicated in a number of studies reviewed by Brickman et al., changes that occur as a result of counseling are most likely to persist when clients feel that they are responsible for the change. If change is attributed to the counselor's efforts, the change in client behavior is less likely to endure. Counselors can help clients to reattribute solutions for their problems to factors that they can control (Dorn, 1988).

Problem-Solving Style

Individuals differ in how they define the problem, how they solve the problem, and which part of the problem-solving process they tend to emphasize (defining the problem or solving the problem). The Myers–Briggs Type Indicator (MBTI) can be used as a means of analyzing an individual's problem-solving style. As indicated in chapter 11, the MBTI includes four bipolar dimensions. Each of these dimensions can be used to describe an important aspect of the client's problem-solving style.

First, the Extroverted versus Introverted dimension indicates the extent to which the person chooses to solve problems as part of a group or individually. Second, the Sensing versus Intuition dimension offers insight into the manner in which the client defines a problem. Does the client give predominant consideration to facts (Sensing type) or possibilities (Intuitive type)? Third, the Thinking versus Feeling dimension indicates the extent to which the person solves the problem by logic (Thinking type) or values (Feeling type). Finally, the Judging versus Perceiving dimension shows which function (problem definition or problem solving) the client will emphasize. Judging types place greater importance on solving the problem, whereas Perceiving types give primary consideration to defining the problem.

These same personality variables are also included as part of the Millon Index of Personality Styles–Revised (MIPS Revised; Millon, 2003). Counselors can use the MBTI or the MIPS Revised to help clients identify their problem-solving style. They can help clients to recognize both strengths and weaknesses in their preferred styles. Counselors can teach clients to "stretch" their styles when necessary to include some of the advantages of the other personality styles.

Problem-solving style can also be assessed by means of several instruments specifically designed to measure the manner in which individuals cope with difficult situations. The Social Problem-Solving Inventory–Revised (SPSI-R) assesses both problem orientation and problem-solving style (D'Zurilla et al., 2002). The Problem-Focused Style of Coping inventory measures reflective (rational), suppressive (denial), and reactive (impulsive) styles of coping (P. P. Heppner, Cook, Wright, & Johnson, 1995). Other instruments of this sort include the Ways of Coping Questionnaire (Folkman & Lazarus, 1988), the Problem-Solving Inventory (P. P. Heppner, 1988), and the Coping Inventory for Stressful Situations (Endler & Parker, 1994).

DEFINING THE PROBLEM

What is the nature of the client's problem? How severe is it? How does it affect the client's life? Answers to these questions can help counselors to plan and to evaluate treatment for their clients. In this section, a number of systematic procedures for addressing these questions are considered.

Counselors can gather significant information from clients in a short period of time by means of an intake (initial contact) questionnaire, a screening inventory, and an interview. The intake counselor uses this information in arranging counseling for the client or in making a referral.

Intake Form

An intake form contains questions about client status and presenting issues that can help guide the first counseling session. Common questions include name, address, sex, age, ethnicity, educational and work history, presenting problem (or problems), previous counseling, and urgency of request for counseling. Intake forms vary somewhat from agency to agency, depending on the particular type of services offered by the agency.

In general, the intake form should be kept relatively short so that it does not become an imposition in counseling. The form can be supplemented with additional questionnaires designed for particular issues, such as career planning, study skills, or relationships, as counseling progresses.

If desired, an agency's intake questionnaire can be supplemented with a standardized questionnaire to obtain more complete information regarding a client's background. As an example, the Quickview Social History contains 130 questions pertaining to the client's developmental history, family of origin, educational history, marital history, occupational history/financial status, and legal history, together with 105 additional questions that address psychological and medical issues (Giannetti, 1992). The client's answers are processed by computer to provide a four- to five-page narrative report plus a follow-up section that highlights the client's problems and areas that the counselor may wish to explore further with the client.

Information obtained from the intake form orients the counselor toward the client's problem, serves as a checklist to make sure that important points are covered, and provides a record for future counseling contacts. This information can also be compiled and used to describe the nature of the clientele served by a counseling center during a given time period. These data can be helpful in budget and program planning.

Screening Inventories

Counselors often use brief, self-report screening instruments to obtain a preliminary, overall view of a client's concerns. Clients are asked to indicate which of a wide range of symptoms or concerns may have been troubling them during the recent past. The screening inventory can provide an initial measure of both the nature and the intensity of a client's concerns. Because of its scope, it can detect issues of possible importance that might otherwise be overlooked. Once detected, such issues can then be further assessed in the interview and by other means as necessary.

Several inventories that have proved to be particularly valuable for use in counseling are described below. In addition to these instruments, other popular or promising screening inventories include the College Adjustment Scales (Anton & Reed, 1991), Holden Psychological Screening Inventory (Holden, 1996), Multidimensional Health Profile, Part I: Psychosocial Functioning (Ruelhman, Lanyon, & Karoly, 1999), Psychological Distress Inventory (Lustman, Sowa, & O'Hara, 1984), and Psychological Screening Inventory (Lanyon, 1978).

Inventory of Common Problems (ICP)
The ICP was developed by Jeffrey Hoffman and Bahr Weiss (1986) for use as a screening instrument in college counseling centers. It lists 24 specific problems that college students may confront (see Figure 4-1). These items represent six major types of problems as follows:

- Depression: Items 1–4
- Anxiety: Items 5–8
- Academic problems: Items 9–12
- Interpersonal problems: Items 13–16
- Physical health problems: Items 17–20
- Substance-use problems: Items 21–24

Clients must indicate to what extent each of the 24 problems has distressed, worried, or bothered them in the past few weeks. Answers range from 1 *(not at all)* to 5 *(very much)*. Scores for each scale can range from 4 to 20; total scores can range from 24 to 120.

Normative data for a sample of college students collected by Hoffman and Weiss (1986) showed no significant sex differences. Thus, the same set of norms may be used with both male and female clients. The highest mean score (11 points) was obtained on the Academic Problems scale, whereas the lowest mean score (5 points) was recorded for the Substance Use scale. The mean total score for college students was approximately 45 points, with a standard deviation of about 10 (Hoffman & Weiss, 1986).

The ICP possesses sufficient reliability and validity evidence for its use as a screening instrument with most college students, but it should not be regarded as a diagnostic instrument (Hoffman

Instructions: The following items represent common problems of college students. How much has each problem distressed, worried, or bothered you in the past few weeks? Please circle the answer that is most nearly correct for you.

Not at all	A little bit	Moderately	Quite a bit	Very much
1	2	3	4	5

1. Feeling depressed, sad, dejected?	1 2 3 4 5
2. Blaming, criticizing, or condemning myself?	1 2 3 4 5
3. Feeling discouraged or like a failure?	1 2 3 4 5
4. Suicidal thoughts or concerns?	1 2 3 4 5
5. Feeling irritable, tense, or nervous?	1 2 3 4 5
6. Feeling fearful?	1 2 3 4 5
7. Spells of terror or panic?	1 2 3 4 5
8. Feeling like I'm "going to pieces"?	1 2 3 4 5
9. Academic problems?	1 2 3 4 5
10. Difficulty caring about or concentrating on studies?	1 2 3 4 5
11. Indecision or concern about choice of career or major?	1 2 3 4 5
12. Feeling like I'm not doing as well in school as I should?	1 2 3 4 5
13. Problems with romantic or sexual relationships?	1 2 3 4 5
14. Family problems?	1 2 3 4 5
15. Difficulty getting along with others?	1 2 3 4 5
16. Feeling lonely or isolated?	1 2 3 4 5
17. Physical health problems?	1 2 3 4 5
18. Headaches, faintness, or dizziness?	1 2 3 4 5
19. Trouble sleeping?	1 2 3 4 5
20. Eating, appetite, or weight problems?	1 2 3 4 5
21. My use of alcohol?	1 2 3 4 5
22. My use of marijuana?	1 2 3 4 5
23. How many psychoactive drugs I use?	1 2 3 4 5
24. How many prescribed drugs I use?	1 2 3 4 5

If so, what? _____

FIGURE 4-1

Inventory of Common Problems

Note. From "A New System for Conceptualizing College Students' Problems: Types of Crises and the Inventory of Common Problems," by J. A. Hoffman and B. Weiss, 1986, *Journal of American College Health, 34,* p. 262. Copyright 1986 by the Helen Dwight Reid Educational Foundation. Published by Heldref Publications, 4000 Albermarle Street, NW, Washington, DC 20016. Reprinted with permission.

& Weiss, 1986). The results should be used primarily to suggest topics for further exploration in counseling. Counselors can easily readminister the ICP to clients to obtain a rough measure of progress during the course of counseling. If administered to all clients as part of the intake process, it can also be used to provide a comprehensive picture of the types of psychological problems presented at the agency (Keutzer et al., 1998).

From a practical point of view, the ICP offers several advantages for counselors. It can be completed by most clients within 5 to 10 minutes, it represents most of the problems that clients are likely to encounter, and it can be reproduced economically.

The ICP has been designed so that it can be used together with the Therapist Rating Form, which asks therapists to classify the type of crisis encountered by the client as psychopathological, developmental, or situational (Hoffman & Weiss, 1986). A case example based on the use of the ICP with a college student is presented below.

Case Example

Linda came to the university counseling center as a senior because of dissatisfaction with her major. She felt particularly uneasy because most of her peers were participating in job interviews for the next year. She was majoring in finance but was not happy with it. She did not like the competitiveness of the students in her field. According to the intake form that she completed at the same time as the ICP, she wanted help in "choosing a major" and "career planning." She marked all of the items except one in the first three categories (Depression, Anxiety, and Academic Problems) of the ICP as 4 or 5. She was feeling very distressed by her career indecision.

On the Therapist Rating Form, the intake counselor attributed Linda's problems primarily to developmental issues, not psychopathological or situational factors. Short-term counseling was arranged, based on the counselor's judgment. Linda needed help in dealing with developmental tasks, especially in resolving her career choice, not in making fundamental changes in other aspects of her life.

Linda met with a counselor for six sessions for help in acquiring decision-making and assertiveness skills and for assistance in working through conflicted feelings about her career choice. She decided to add human resources management as a second major to that of finance. This combination was supported by the tests (including the Strong Interest Inventory) that she had taken and by the information that she had gained in career exploration.

The ICP was readministered at the conclusion of counseling. Linda marked no 4 or 5 responses the second time she completed the inventory. Her total score, which dropped from 66 to 34, and all of her subscores fell well within the normal range compared with other college students. For Linda, the ICP was helpful both in determining the nature and the severity of her initial complaints and in evaluating the progress that she showed in counseling. Linda's rapid progress in counseling supported the perception of the intake counselor that her problems were developmental, not psychopathological, in nature.

Symptom Check List–90–Revised (SCL-90-R)

The SCL-90-R has been widely used for research and clinical purposes in a variety of medical and mental health settings (Derogatis, 1994). As indicated by its name, the SCL-90-R contains a list of 90 symptoms such as "headaches," "feeling critical of others," and "feeling tense or keyed up." Clients respond to items in terms of how much they were distressed by that symptom during the past week. Each item is answered on a five-step scale ranging from 0 *(not at all)* through 4 *(extremely)*. Most clients complete the SCL-90-R within 15 minutes. With practice, it can be easily hand scored.

The SCL-90-R provides scores for the following nine scales: Somatization, Obsessive–Compulsive, Interpersonal Sensitivity, Depression, Anxiety, Hostility, Phobic Anxiety, Paranoid Ideation, and Psychoticism. Scores for each scale show the mean response for the items in that scale. It also yields three total scores: Global Severity Index (GSI), Positive Symptom Total (PST), and Positive Symptom Distress Index (PSDI). The GSI, the best single index of psychological disturbance, shows the mean response to all 90 items. The PST indicates the number of symptoms reported (all items marked 1 or higher). The PSDI, which shows the mean response to all items included in the PST, reflects the severity of the client's symptoms.

Scores on the SCL-90-R vary depending on age and sex. Adolescent nonpatients report more symptomatology than do adult nonpatients. Women acknowledge more symptoms than do men. The SCL-90-R manual provides separate norms for adolescent nonpatients, adult nonpatients, adult psychiatric inpatients, and adult psychiatric outpatients. Each norm is "gender keyed" (Derogatis & Fitzpatrick, 2004, p. 5) to take into account sex differences.

Scores on the different scales show adequate internal consistency and test–retest reliability over short time periods for psychiatric patients. Overall, the SCL-90-R appears to be most valid as a broad measure of psychological disturbance. The test scores have demonstrated sensitivity to many forms of treatment, which indicates that they can be used effectively to monitor the improvement of clients during the course of counseling (Vonk & Thyer, 1999).

The SCL-90-R is particularly valuable as a screening instrument to detect cases that need additional assessment. As a general rule, Derogatis (1994, p. 58) suggested that counselors should refer clients for psychiatric evaluation if their scores on the GSI or any two of the individual scales equal or exceed the 90th percentile (*T* score = 63) compared with adult nonpatients.

Several abbreviated versions of the SCL-90-R have been developed. The Brief Symptom Inventory (BSI) contains 53 of the 90 items on the SCL-90-R (Derogatis, 1993). Administration time for the BSI is approximately 10 minutes, compared with 15 minutes for the SCL-90-R. Intercorrelations between the two sets of scales range from .92 to .99. According to Derogatis and Fitzpatrick (2004), the BSI is often preferred over the SCL-90-R by clinicians and researchers, even in situations lacking time constraints. The BSI can also be administered as an 18-item form (BSI-18); however, this version of the instrument includes only Somatization, Depression, and Anxiety scales (the three scales most commonly associated with psychological distress and disorder; Derogatis, 2000).

In addition to the self-report forms described above, Derogatis has constructed matching rating scales for use by clinicians familiar with the client. The Derogatis Psychiatric Rating Scale and the SCL-90-Analogue can be used to obtain clinician ratings on the same symptom constructs included in the SCL-90-R and BSI. Counselors can obtain a more thorough and accurate assessment of a client's status by using both self-rating scales and clinician rating scales.

The SCL-90-R and BSI have been used extensively in different cultures throughout the world. The instruments have been translated into more than two dozen languages (Derogatis & Fitzpatrick, 2004).

Inventories for Assessing Mental Disorders
Some screening inventories have been designed specifically for use in making psychiatric diagnoses. These include the Psychiatric Diagnostic Screen Questionnaire (PDSQ) and the Patient Health Questionnaire (PHQ). The PDSQ contains 13 scales, each of which is related to a mental disorder as defined by the *Diagnostic and Statistical Manual of Mental Disorders* (4th ed., text rev.; *DSM-IV-TR;* American Psychiatric Association, 2000a; Zimmerman & Mattia, 1999). The PHQ includes scales for eight common mental disorders, such as major depressive disorder and panic disorder (Spitzer, Kroenke, Williams, & the Patient Health Questionnaire Primary Care Study Group, 1999). Both of these inventories have proved to be helpful in medical settings in identifying individuals with diagnosable psychiatric disorders unknown to their primary physician.

Suggestions for Using Screening Inventories in Counseling

1. Identify critical items on the screening inventory (e.g., items that refer to thoughts of suicide or violent behavior) that can be used to help determine whether the client is in a state of crisis. Be sure to make a suicide risk assessment (see chapter 14) if the client shows signs of suicidal thinking.
2. Examine general level of responses. If a client marks a large number of extreme responses, consider the need for immediate counseling and possible psychiatric referral. Ask clients to discuss each of these responses, especially ones that they perceive to be most crucial.
3. Note the client's responses for substance abuse and health items. These problems may be overlooked in the counseling interview if the counselor does not bring them up with the client.
4. Readminister the inventory at the conclusion of counseling or after a significant time period has elapsed to evaluate changes that have taken place during the course of counseling. Clients who have shown little improvement may need to be referred.
5. Use screening inventory scores to consult with supervisors or colleagues regarding the treatment of a case. Screening inventory scores can be used to communicate the nature and severity of the client's issues within a few minutes.
6. Add items to screening inventory to assess matters of importance to your agency. For example, one agency added the following items to the ICP to identify potentially dangerous situations: "Urge to harm myself," "Plan to harm myself," "Urge to harm someone else," "Plan to harm someone else," and "Concern that someone else may harm me."
7. Administer screening inventories for specific topics (e.g., Michigan Alcoholism Screening Test, My Vocational Situation, or Eating Attitudes Tests) when these seem to be appropriate. Ask clients to identify any issues that they might be experiencing that are not represented on the screening inventory.
8. Consider the possibility that clients could be minimizing or exaggerating their problems. Use both number and intensity of symptoms to help gauge possible distortion. If clients mark most items at a low level of intensity, they could be minimizing their problems. Similarly, if they mark a large number of problems at a high level of intensity, they could be exaggerating their concerns.

9. Screening inventories should be used in conjunction with other assessment methods. Use individual scales and items primarily as a means of identifying significant subject matter for discussion and further assessment.

10. Use screening inventories to monitor the caseload in your agency. What types of clients are receiving treatment at the agency? How many of the clients express suicidal ideation? How many of the clients indicate problems with substance abuse? Use these data to develop local norms to help interpret screening inventory responses. The data may also be used to help decide which types of services to emphasize in the agency.

Intake Interview

The purpose of the intake (or assessment) interview is to assess the nature and severity of the client's problems and to determine possible treatment programs (Nelson, 2002). The interview, which provides more flexibility than most other assessment procedures, enables the counselor to clarify the client's responses on the intake forms and to explore the client's concerns in some depth.

Most intake interviews cover the following topics: (a) general appearance and behavior; (b) presenting problem; (c) history of current problem and related problems; (d) present level of functioning in work, relationships, and leisure activities; (e) use of alcohol or other drugs, including medications; (f) family history of mental illness; (g) history of physical, sexual, or emotional abuse; (h) risk factors, including urge to harm self or others; (i) previous counseling; and (j) attitude of client toward the counseling process. The interviewer should explain the policies of the agency, such as session limits, rules of confidentiality, and referral options. The intake interview should help the counselor to decide the immediacy of the need for counseling, the type of expertise required, and the type of service (e.g., individual counseling, couples counseling, group counseling, or consultation and referral).

Interview Guidelines

Initial interviews usually progress on a continuum from minimal structure to more structure. As the interview proceeds, the client may need help or direction in continuing to respond. Questions that probe or clarify can be used to obtain a clearer understanding of what the client feels or means. Statements like "Can you tell me more about . . ." or "Tell me more about how you felt when . . ." or "I don't think I understand what you mean by . . ." provide relevant information from the client's point of view and help to maintain rapport. Rephrasing of questions can sometimes help to clarify a client's responses if other techniques have not been effective. In general, it is best not to ask "why" questions because they may cause the client to become defensive.

It is important to determine what factors led the client to seek help at this particular time. Has the problem recently become worse? Have other people become concerned about the person? Has the problem begun to interfere with the client's functioning at work or home? Answers to such questions can help clarify the nature of the client's problem and assess the client's motivation for participating in counseling.

As part of the intake interview, counselors should also seek information about behaviors or events that have been helpful in the past or that the client expects might be helpful in the future. For example, when has the problem been least likely to occur in the past? What has kept the problem from getting worse? What is one small step the client could take to improve the situation? Answers to such questions can be useful in considering possible solutions for the client's problem (Dejong & Berg, 1998).

The counselor should pay attention to the client's nonverbal behavior, such as eye contact, facial expression, and activity level. Observations of the client's nonverbal behavior can be particularly important for clients who may have difficulty in communicating with the counselor.

The information obtained in the initial interview needs to be organized systematically to help identify significant patterns of behavior. Fong (1993) suggested that counselors sort observations of client functioning into four broad areas: (a) cognition, (b) affect, (c) behavior, and (d) physiological functioning. Figure 4-2 shows an example of a worksheet based on this system for a client named "Charles." Each of the items represents an observation that can be helpful in diagnosing Charles's mental condition.

In preparing such a worksheet, the counselor's observations should be described in an objective manner, for example, "moved slowly" or "didn't smile," instead of in the form of an inter-

Cognitions
    Oriented to person, place, and time
    Goal directed, precise speech
    Worried about "experiences" of intense anxiety and impact on him
    Thinks job is stressful, but proud of success at sales

Affect
    Controlled, somewhat limited range of affect

Behaviors
    Well groomed, expensive suit and watch
    Insomnia several nights per week
    Divorced, now engaged to be married
    Good working relationships, but prefers not to socialize outside
    Intense anxiety attacks without warning
    Has started to drive only in right hand lane, avoids crowds
    Separation anxiety and shyness as child
    Denies drug use, infrequent drink with client

Physiological Functioning
    Heart palpitations, sweating hands, difficulty breathing, and weakness
     during intense anxiety attacks
    Diagnosed irritable bowel syndrome
    Frequent headaches, "tight band around my head"

FIGURE 4-2

Observation of Client Functioning Worksheet: Charles

Note. From "Teaching Assessment and Diagnosis Within a *DSM-III-R* Framework," by M. L. Fong, 1993, *Counselor Education and Supervision, 32,* p. 286. Copyright 1993 by the American Counseling Association. Adapted with permission. No further reproduction authorized without written permission of the American Counseling Association.

pretation such as "seemed sad." Interpretations of behavior, which may vary greatly from counselor to counselor for the same behavior, should be reserved until sufficient data have been collected to formulate hypotheses regarding the client's problem and possible interventions. In the case of Charles, the worksheet reveals a pattern of anxiety symptoms that merits further examination, especially in regard to a possible anxiety disorder (see Fong & Silien, 1999).

The intake counselor should also be aware of the possibility that the client's psychological symptoms may be caused by physical illness, particularly if (a) the client has not responded well to counseling or psychotherapy; (b) the symptoms have not occurred previously, especially for older clients; (c) the onset of symptoms has been relatively abrupt; (c) the client has suffered from recent or multiple medical disorders; (d) the client is disoriented or confused; or (e) psychosocial stressors are absent or minor (Pollak, Levy, & Breitholtz, 1999). If the client is on medications, possible side effects of these medications should be checked in the current edition of the *Physicians' Desk Reference* (published annually by Thomson Healthcare).

Although interviews can serve as a rich source of information, observations based on interviews are frequently biased or subject to misinterpretation. Common errors of judgment based on interview assessments include the following (Spengler, Strohmer, Dixon, & Shivy, 1995):

- *Anchoring:* placing too much emphasis on information obtained early in the interview;
- *Availability:* relying too much on one's favorite theory or on popular diagnoses such as borderline personality disorder or adult child of dysfunctional family;
- *Diagnostic overshadowing:* ignoring or minimizing problems because they are less noticeable or are of less interest to the counselor;
- *Attribution:* attributing the problem primarily to the client without giving sufficient consideration to the environment.

Counselors may combat these errors by adhering to the principles of assessment listed in chapter 1. In particular, it is important to keep an open mind and to use a multimethod, multifactor approach to assessment. Multimethod assessments include a variety of assessment methods such as interview schedules, objective instruments, and observations of the client and others. Multifactor assessments provide data concerning a range of individual and environmental factors. A multimethod, multifactor approach enables counselors to see issues from different viewpoints and to consider alternative explanations of client problems.

Mental Status Exam (MSE)

In some mental health settings, counselors routinely administer an MSE during the intake interview. In other settings, counselors may perform an MSE if they perceive the client to be disoriented, confused, or out of touch with reality. Information obtained by means of an MSE can be especially important when the counselor does not have access to psychological test data (Groth-Marnat, 2003).

The MSE consists of a series of questions and observations designed to evaluate the client's current level of functioning (Polanski & Hinkle, 2000; Waldinger, 1986). It provides a format for organizing information provided by clients (referred to as subjective data) and information based on observations of clients (referred to as objective data) that have been collected in a scattered fashion throughout the interview. It usually includes a consideration of the client's general appearance and behavior, speech, emotions, thoughts, perception, and cognition. The cognitive section of the MSE is the only part that involves the use of specific tests (e.g., counting backward by sevens or threes from 100 to test concentration).

The MSE is usually administered informally. Interviewers ask questions only in those areas in which they have concerns. Information is picked up naturally during the course of interviewing the client. Anything that seems unusual should be explored in depth. Vague or puzzling matters should always be clarified.

The results of the MSE can usually be reported in one or two paragraphs. Attention is drawn to any usual features of the client that may demand further attention. The MSE should not be used by itself to make a diagnosis, but it can be helpful in suggesting areas in which further assessments should be made.

Structured Interviews

At times, counselors may wish to use a structured interview to improve the reliability and validity of their assessments (Garb, 1998). Structured interviews have a standardized format for content, presentation, recording, and scoring of questions. As such, they can enhance rapport with clients, reduce errors of clinical judgment, ensure comprehensive coverage of symptoms, and increase commitment to counseling (Vacc & Juhnke, 1997).

In a review of structured and semistructured interviews most likely to be used by counselors, Vacc and Juhnke (1997) cited the Composite International Diagnostic Interview, the Diagnostic Interview Schedule, the Psychiatric Research Interview for Substance and Mental Disorders, and the Structured Clinical Interview for *DSM-IV* Disorders for adults. For children, they found the Diagnostic Interview for Children and Adolescents and the Diagnostic Interview Schedule for Children to be most noteworthy. All of these interview schedules can be used to assess the broad spectrum of mental disorders as defined in the *DSM-IV-TR*. Most counselors, who usually use open-ended questions and nondirective leads in the initial interview, probably would not use one of these instruments in an initial interview; however, they may find such an approach beneficial as part of an extended intake process.

In contrast with the lengthy structured interviews mentioned above, the Primary Care Evaluation of Mental Disorders (PRIME-MD) involves a brief, guided interview (usually less than 8 or 9 minutes) designed to detect and diagnose mental disorders among patients in primary care settings (S. R. Hahn, Sydney, Kroenke, Williams, & Spitzer, 2004). When used together with a brief patient questionnaire, this process has been found to be reliable and valid in detecting and diagnosing the most common types of psychopathology found among individuals in a general population. Although not often used in counseling settings, the PRIME-MD approach can be easily adapted to aid counselors in screening clients for mental disorders that otherwise might be overlooked. The PRIME-MD questions can also be asked in a self-report form (PHQ; Spitzer et al., 1999) with equivalent results, thereby reducing the time required to consider this information with the patient to about 3 minutes.

In addition to the general interview schedules listed above, specialty interview schedules have been constructed to evaluate specific disorders or concerns. Specialty interview schedules can be useful for counselors who wish to focus on a particular issue, such as substance abuse or suicide risk (Vacc & Juhnke, 1997). Intake interview schedules that emphasize multicultural factors include the Person-in-Culture Interview and the Career-in-Culture Interview (Ponterotto, Rivera, & Sueyoshi, 2000).

EVALUATING COUNSELING OUTCOMES

At the conclusion of counseling, as well as at intervals throughout counseling, it is important to evaluate its effectiveness. Has counseling achieved the purposes for which it was sought? As the last step in the problem-solving model, the counselor needs to determine whether the client's problem has been resolved or reduced (see chapter 1).

Outcome assessments should be related to the purpose of counseling, appropriate for the client's development level, valid and reliable for the purpose for which they are used, and sensitive enough to show change at the level expected (Granello & Granello, 2001; Whiston, 2001). They should employ well-established instruments with adequate normative data to aid in the interpretation of a client's scores (Leibert, 2006). When feasible, outcome assessments should use more than one source of feedback (e.g., client, counselor, and observer) and consider more than one outcome variable (e.g., changes in knowledge, understanding, and behavior). Counseling outcomes should take into account immediate, intermediate, and ultimate goals, such as a more positive attitude toward school, improved grades, and school graduation, and should include evaluations taken at different points in time. As a practical matter, outcome assessments should be brief, be easy to administer and score, and be cost effective.

Typical outcome assessment instruments include client satisfaction forms, client self-report scales, client interviews, and rating scales. Outcome instruments vary in their degree of specificity. Global measures focus on such matters as general well-being or career maturity. Specific measures assess particular factors such as level of depression or career planning difficulties. Some examples of the different types of outcome measures are provided below.

Client Satisfaction Forms

These measures assess the degree to which counseling fulfilled the client's expectations. A number of client satisfaction scales or rating forms have been developed for local use, especially in medical or mental health settings. These forms provide valuable feedback for administrators and professionals; however, they pose difficulties in interpretation because they lack standardization.

Two standardized measures of client satisfaction—one global and the other specific—have been developed at the University of California, San Francisco (UCSF). The UCSF Client Satisfaction Questionnaire–8 (CSQ-8) provides a global measure of a client's satisfaction with mental health services received (Attkisson & Greenfield, 2004). The UCSF Service Satisfaction Scale–30 (SSS-30), which uses 30 items compared with 8 items used by the CSQ-8, provides a more detailed measure of client satisfaction. The SSS-30 yields scores on several subscales, such as counselor manner and skill, office procedures, and access, as well as an overall satisfaction score (Greenfield & Attkisson, 2004). These instruments have extensive norms that can be used to interpret the results. They can be supplemented with open-ended questions regarding the client's reaction to treatment.

Client satisfaction can also be inferred by means of therapeutic relationship scales, such as the Working Alliance Inventory, that measure the degree to which the client and the counselor agree on counseling goals and tasks and the extent to which they have bonded together for counseling purposes (Horvath & Greenberg, 1989). As a rule, the strength of the therapeutic alliance, as rated by the client, counselor, or observer, correlates significantly with progress in counseling (Martin, Garske, & Davis, 2000).

Client Self-Report Scales

These instruments evaluate changes in the client's status or functioning as perceived by the client. Many of the self-report inventories used in the initial stages of counseling to identify a client's problems, such as the ICP, SCL-90-R, and BSI discussed earlier in this chapter, can also be used later in counseling to evaluate progress in resolving these problems. In many ways, these instruments are ideal for outcome assessment because they provide comparable information at different points in time that can be used to show changes that occur during the course of counseling. Because of their brevity and broad focus, results from these instruments should not be relied on exclusively, but they can be used informally to judge progress and to guide the counseling process.

Several self-report measures have been designed specifically to assess the outcomes of counseling or therapy. These include the Outcome Questionnaire–45 (Lambert, Gregersen, & Burlingame, 2004), revised Behavior and Symptom Identification Scale (Eisen, Normand, Belanger, Spiro, & Esch, 2004), and Treatment Outcome Package (mental health symptoms and functional modules; Kraus, Seligman, & Jordan, 2005). All of these measures are short self-report questionnaires with several subscales that are sensitive to changes in a client's symptoms or behaviors. They all provide reliable and valid measures of a client's functioning and normative data to aid in interpretation of scores.

Depending on the issues involved, other brief measures such as the Beck Depression Inventory, Beck Anxiety Inventory, and Holland's My Vocational Situation can be used to assess progress in specific areas. These instruments are each discussed in chapters dealing with these particular topics. Self-monitoring of one's behavior, such as alcohol drinking, can also be helpful in assessing counseling outcomes (W. R. Miller & Muñoz, 2005).

Client Feedback Interviews

Interviews can also be used to obtain feedback regarding a client's progress. Talmon (1990) described a brief telephone interview that he used routinely with clients who had been seen for brief counseling. Clients were asked in the intake process for permission to contact them by telephone sometime about 3 months after the end of counseling. At that point, they were asked 12 questions regarding such matters as their satisfaction with counseling (5-point scale), change in the problem they presented at counseling (5-point scale), what they found to be most helpful or harmful, and what recommendations they wished to make to the counselor for improvement of counseling. This procedure lets clients know that the counselor cares about them and their situation and provides counselors with helpful information (both quantitative and qualitative in nature) regarding their counseling procedures.

Ratings by Counselors and Other Observers

In addition to feedback from the client, evaluation of a client's functioning can also be sought from the counselor or others in a position to judge the client's behavior, such as parents, spouses, teachers, supervisors, coworkers, or trained observers. Counselors can provide a more detailed, specific description of client outcome by the use of instruments such as the Brief Psychiatric Rating Scale for major psychopathology (Lachar, Espadas, & Bailley, 2004) or the Hamilton Depression Rating Scale, a measure of depression based on interview data (Hamilton, 1967). Teachers, parents, or others can use observer rating forms such as the Conners' Rating Scales–Revised for Teachers and Parents to evaluate problem behavior in children (Conners, 1997). Observation of a client's behavior by someone close to the client is important in obtaining information regarding the progress of clients who cannot accurately or consistently report this information themselves.

In some situations, counselors are required to complete the Global Assessment of Functioning (GAF) Scale (Axis V on the *DSM-IV-TR*) for every client they see, often at both the beginning and end of counseling. This measure provides a single score, ranging from 1 to 100, regarding the client's psychological, social, and occupational functioning (American Psychiatric Association, 2000a). The GAF scale is anchored with behavioral descriptions at each 10-point interval; for example, ratings in the "71 to 80" range indicate transient symptoms (such as difficulty concentrating after a family conflict) or slight impairment in functioning (such as falling behind in one's work on a temporary basis).

Tailor-Made Measure

Some outcome measures, such as Goal Attainment Scaling (GAS) or the Target Complaints (TC) procedure, are designed specifically for individual clients to assess their progress in therapy. With GAS, the counselor or other expert judges establish specific goals for a client based on his or her concerns (Kiresuk et al., 1994). The judges then rate the client's success in attaining these goals at the end of counseling on a 5-point scale. This measure has proved to be a reliable and valid measure of progress for clients receiving time-limited psychotherapy (Shefler, Canetti, & Wiseman, 2001).

The TC measure requires clients (with the help of a counselor) to identify three specific complaints that they wish to address in counseling and then to rate these complaints according to their severity (Battle et al., 1966). Counseling outcomes are assessed in terms of reductions in the severity of a client's complaints. This method has been used effectively to evaluate the success of clients in resolving problems during counseling (Kivlighan, Multon, & Patton, 2000).

Use of Outcome Measures

Outcome measures can be helpful at three levels: (a) individual, (b) agency, and (c) profession. At the individual level, both the client and counselor can benefit. Clients can profit by seeing progress in resolving issues and improvement in well-being. Counselors can use feedback from clients to learn what counseling approaches are most effective with different types of clients. At the agency level, information obtained from clients can help in establishing and modifying counseling programs and in gaining support from those who fund the programs. Finally, for the profession as a whole, outcome studies can lead to more successful, evidence-based treatments and strengthen its viability and credibility overall (Leibert, 2006).

When outcome studies are undertaken by the combined resources of a professional organization or a counseling agency, it is possible to conduct a much more thorough and comprehensive evaluation of counseling effectiveness than would otherwise be possible. The American Counseling Association Practice Research Network (ACA-PRN) enables practitioners to work together to evaluate the effectiveness of their counseling activities (Bradley, Sexton, & Smith, 2005). In research designed by this organization, individual counselors practicing in a variety of settings are asked to rate the outcomes of their counseling with specific clients. Clients are administered the Outcome Questionnaire–45 both before and after counseling. Data are entered by both the counselor and client at the ACA-PRN Web site to help ensure timely, comprehensive, and confidential reporting.

Although it may not be feasible for all counselors to be involved in a comprehensive outcome study, some effort should be undertaken to evaluate the effectiveness of all counseling interventions (Granello & Granello, 2001). If only one outcome measure can be obtained, it is probably best to obtain it directly from the client, possibly at the conclusion of counseling or shortly thereafter. As an informal procedure, counselors can readminister a client self-report form such as the ICP or the Beck Depression Inventory–II to note changes. They can also ask clients at that point what was most helpful, what was least helpful, and what recommendations they would make for future counseling. The use of a brief, semistructured interview such as that proposed by Talmon (1990; see above) can be especially productive for counselors evaluating the effectiveness of their counseling on an individual basis.

TEST SELECTION, ADMINISTRATION, AND SCORING

Test Selection

Assessment should be seen as a part of the counseling process and not as an interruption of it. People often approach psychological tests with some anxiety, particularly aptitude and achievement tests where they may fear failure. Anxiety regarding testing can influence the entire counseling process. Even interest and personality inventories can reveal aspects of a person's character that may indicate weaknesses or undesirable features. To reduce the threatening aspects of tests, the counselor should make clear to clients that the purpose of testing is to provide self-understanding, not evaluation of the client by the counselor. The counselor needs to convey to clients the feeling that they will be accepted whatever the test results happen to be.

If at all possible, clients should actively participate in the selection of tests that will be used in counseling. From a therapeutic point of view, clients should collaborate with counselors in deciding what questions they wish to answer by the use of tests or other assessment procedures (Finn & Tonsager, 1997). If convinced of the usefulness of the tests, clients will be more motivated to do their best on ability tests and to be accurate and truthful in responding to items on interest and personality inventories. By having participated in the decisions to use the tests, clients are also more likely to accept the results and their interpretations with less defensiveness. They can be more objective in their perception of the results of the tests.

In the case of academic or career counseling, clients often feel dependent on tests. They perceive the counselor as an expert who will select tests that will tell them what to do. Active participation by clients in test selection helps to counteract overreliance on the counselor.

Generally, the client does not select specific tests. That is a technical matter that counselors must decide on the basis of their knowledge of tests. Instead, the client helps to decide the types of tests that can provide the information most useful for whatever actions or decisions are going to be made. Clients are not nearly as interested in specific characteristics of tests as they are in the implications the results will have for them. The types of tests are therefore described in a general fashion. For example, a counselor should describe the Strong Interest Inventory to a client simply as "an interest inventory that enables you to compare your likes and dislikes with those of people in different occupations." The counselor should not overwhelm the client with a detailed description of the instrument itself.

After the client and counselor have agreed on the type of test, the counselor must decide which specific test would be best to use. In particular, the counselor needs to consider the test's reliability, validity, normative data, and practicality for its intended purpose. Does the test possess sufficient reliability and validity to answer the questions posed by the client and his or her situation? Does the test provide appropriate normative data for the client? Is the test easy to administer and score? How expensive is it? Is the reading level appropriate? Is this assessment procedure culturally appropriate for the client? The counselor can best answer these questions, which require specialized knowledge regarding the technical quality of different assessments.

A client's statement of need for tests should not necessarily be taken at face value. An initial request for a personality inventory should result in an effort to explore the meaning of the request, not simply acceptance of it. The client may be experiencing a significant problem such as anxiety or depression that should be explored before tests are assigned. The client may be asking for help regarding a particular problem but having difficulty revealing the problem or asking for help directly. The request for tests serves as an avenue to get at the major problem.

Tests should not be used unnecessarily. Other sources of data in addition to tests should also be explored. In a college counseling center, little is gained by selecting scholastic aptitude tests when records of college entrance tests, high school grades, and college grades are readily available. Other counseling agencies, of course, often start with no previous information. Nevertheless, counselors can first attempt to explore with the client previous experiences that may provide relevant information and self-descriptions. Recall of previous experiences can provide a great deal of information either to supplement test results or to eliminate the need for particular tests.

Test Administration

Standardized tests must be administered in a specified manner under controlled conditions with uniform instructions and materials. The person who administers the test must be familiar with the instructions and other aspects of the administration. The knowledge necessary for administering the test differs greatly depending on the test. On the one hand, standardized scholastic aptitude tests can be administered with relatively little training. On the other hand, the knowledge and skill needed to administer individual intelligence tests require extensive course work and practicum experience.

Inexperienced test administrators often do not fully appreciate the importance of the test administrator's role. Irregularities identified in test administrations in school settings include inaccurate timing, altering answer sheets, coaching, teaching the test, scoring errors, recording errors, and student cheating (Gay, 1990). Most test manuals provide detailed instructions for the administration of a particular test, which should be followed exactly. It is the standardization of instructions that makes it possible to compare one person's scores with those of another or with different groups.

In administering tests, the examiner must elicit the interest and cooperation of the test taker. In obtaining rapport, the examiner should attempt to convince test takers that the results will be useful and that they are not wasting their time in a task that will be of little consequence or value to them. Usually clients are cooperative if they have voluntarily sought counseling. If they are being tested against their will, perhaps because of a court order or because they feel that the test information is not important, good rapport may be difficult to establish.

Individuals should be informed prior to testing about conditions that may improve their performance on aptitude or achievement tests, such as taking a practice test or reviewing certain material (American Counseling Association, 2005). During the test administration itself, the test administrator must encourage examinees to follow instructions carefully and to perform as well as they can. With small children, tests may be presented as a game. For interest or personality inventories, examinees should be encouraged to answer honestly and frankly to preclude invalid results.

The administrator should be familiar with the test being administered so that clients do not doubt the administrator's competence. Self-confidence, together with a warm and friendly manner, should be exhibited.

The testing environment should be suitable for test administration, with adequate seating, lighting, ventilation, and temperature. It should be free from noise, interruptions, and other distractions. Time limits should be followed exactly, and measures taken to prevent cheating. Factors, even minor ones, that can alter test performance should be recognized and minimized. These factors contribute to the error variance in test scores. Any problems in administering the test should be noted and taken into account when interpreting the test results.

At times, the test administration procedures may need to be altered to take into account such matters as a client's disability or language problems (AERA, APA, & NCME, 1999). Accommodations in test administration, such as additional time or the use of an interpreter, should be made if they can improve the opportunity for the client to demonstrate his or her abilities but not if they provide that client with an advantage over other test takers. Sometimes it is difficult to make this distinction, but the test administrator must make the best decision possible. Any alterations in administration procedures should be noted and included in the report of test results.

Individual Versus Group Tests

Some tests are designed to be administered to one individual at a time by a trained examiner; other tests can be administered to a group of people. Group tests allow information to be obtained from many people within a short period of time at relatively little cost, whereas individual tests allow the examiner to adapt the test administration to the needs of the client. Individual tests must be used with certain populations, such as very small children and those with particular handicaps. Individual tests permit observational data, such as the client's language proficiency and level of cooperation, to be obtained in addition to the test scores.

Speed Versus Power Tests

Some ability tests place a heavy emphasis on speed of response. These tests often consist of a large number of easy items that a person must complete quickly. Examples of speed tests with relatively short time limits include finger and manual dexterity tests and clerical speed and accuracy tests.

In contrast, power tests contain items of varying difficulty, most of which the person is expected to complete within the time limits. If 90% of the people for whom the test is designed can complete the test within the time limits, the test can be described as a power test. Although speed can still be a factor for some students on power tests, speed would not have much influence on the total score for most students. Most intelligence tests, scholastic aptitude tests, and achievement tests are basically power tests.

Computer-Based Test Administration

In recent years, testing by means of computer has become widespread as computers have become much more readily available. The computer offers a number of advantages compared with paper-and-pencil testing (Naglieri et al., 2004; S. Wang, 2004). Computer-based testing is usually faster, less expensive, and more convenient. It enables immediate feedback, greater test security, more flexibility in test administration, briefer test administration time, a greater degree of test standardization, and increased possibilities for data analysis. In some cases, test reliabilities have been improved (Kapes & Vansickle, 1992; Vansickle & Kapes, 1993).

The computer can be used to administer tests with new types of items, including items that use movement or sequential arrangements, dynamic graphics, split or multiple screens, voice-activated responses, and multimedia presentations. For example, the Test of Variables of Attention is a game-like test that uses continuous movement in the form of a target stimulus to assess individuals for attention deficit disorder. It yields scores for several variables, including reaction time, errors of omission (inattention), errors of commission (impulsivity), and anticipatory and multiple responses, that would be difficult to obtain with paper-and-pencil testing (Greenberg, 1994). In a similar manner, the Educational Testing Service (2006b) has created an Internet version of the Test of English as a Second Language that uses multimedia items for the first time to test different aspects, including reading, writing, listening, and speaking, of learning a language.

The length of the test administered to an individual on the computer can often be reduced by one half or more by means of computerized adaptive testing (D. J. Weiss, 2004). Based on item response theory, an examinee's item responses are analyzed as he or she progresses through a test so that items that are likely to be too difficult or too easy can be identified and eliminated from the test for that individual. Adaptive versions of the Graduate Management Admission Test, Armed Services Vocational Aptitude Test Battery, and the Minnesota Multiphasic Personality Inventory (MMPI) represent examples of the use of the computer to administer individualized tests based on the examinee's pattern of test responses (Handel, Ben-Porath, & Watt, 1999). Scores obtained in this manner are just as reliable and valid as scores based on the complete test.

Both counselors and clients report positive attitudes toward computer-based test administration and interpretation. Counselors prefer the computer because it can free them from rather elementary and repetitive tasks involved in test administration and because it can help prepare clients for counseling sessions by providing them with preliminary test interpretations. Clients have reported a preference for computer-based testing, especially when it provides individualized interpretive information not available in paper-based testing (J. C. Hansen, Neuman, Haverkamp, & Lubinski, 1997; Lumsden, Sampson, Reardon, Lenz, & Peterson, 2004). Clients are generally more open and often prefer computer-administered tests instead of clinician-administered tests when responding to sensitive matters such as psychological symptoms, suicide, alcohol or drug abuse, sexual behavior, and HIV-related symptoms (Chinman, Young, Schell, Hassell, & Mintz, 2004; Kobak, Greist, Jefferson, & Katzelnick, 1996).

Computer-based testing also presents some problems, especially for tests that are administered via the Internet. Many of the new instruments developed for use on the Internet have not been sufficiently studied in regard to reliability and validity (Naglieri et al., 2004). The traditional standards regarding test quality and test usage that have been applied to paper-based tests must also be applied to computer-based tests.

Tests administered via the computer may produce results that differ from the same tests administered by paper and pencil. Although several studies have reported equivalent results for the two modes of administration (Finger & Ones, 1999; Lumsden et al., 2004; S. Wang, 2004), other studies have noted differences, especially for tests that are speeded, involve writing, or use more than one screen to present an item (Wall, 2004a). If more than one mode of administration is possible, counselors should inspect the results reported in the test manual or elsewhere to determine whether the modes provide equivalent results.

Some individuals may have trouble using the computer. Students have reported difficulty in responding to items presented on the computer where they cannot easily go back to check previous answers or leave an item blank for later consideration. Computer anxiety may interfere with the performance of some people on tests administered by the computer, especially older people, women, and individuals from a lower socioeconomic background (Bozionelos, 2004; Meloun, 2005). A study of eighth-grade students found that familiarity with the computer was significantly correlated with performance on computer-based mathematics and writing tests after controlling for paper-based performance in these subjects (Sandene et al., 2005). Counselors should make certain that examinees are familiar and comfortable with using the computer. Examinees should be given the opportunity to practice responding to computer-based items prior to testing.

Test Scoring

Tests can be scored by hand or by computer. Tests that are scored by hand often involve the use of a scoring template that can be placed over the answer sheet to identify incorrect responses. In some cases, clients score their own tests by the use of "self-scorable" answer sheets that reveal the correct answers behind a seal on the reverse side of the answer sheet. Examples of measures for which clients score their own answer sheets include the MBTI and the Self-Directed Search. If more than a few tests or scales are involved, hand scoring can become time consuming, tedious, and subject to error. If at all possible, another person should also score tests that are scored by hand to ensure accuracy of results.

Compared with hand scoring, computer scoring is more rapid, accurate, and thorough. The computer makes it possible to undertake elaborate test scoring programs such as those required for the Strong Interest Inventory and the Campbell Interest and Skill Survey that would be virtually impossible to do by hand. For the most part, the computer is an exceedingly efficient scoring machine, and at times may appear to be infallible; however, it is important to remember that scoring errors can and do occur, especially at the programming level. In one large statewide testing operation, a number of schools received inaccurate test reports, which led to "demoralization" of teachers and students until the errors were detected and corrected (Tareen, 2005). In a national testing program, thousands of SAT exams were found to have been scored incorrectly (after two students asked to have their tests rescored) during one examination period, possibly because of wet weather conditions that affected the accuracy of the computer scoring program (Setoodeh, 2006). If test results appear questionable, they should be rechecked.

In addition to specific scores, computers can also generate test interpretations by means of scoring rules, or algorithms, stored in the computer's memory. Computer-based test interpretations (CBTIs), such as those that have been developed for the MMPI, provide a "second opinion" that counselors can use both to create and to test hypotheses about clients. Compared with counselor interpretations, CBTIs that have been derived from extensive databases by test experts can be more comprehensive, objective, consistent, and reliable (Sampson, Purgar, & Shy, 2003).

Despite their apparent advantages, CBTIs can also pose a number of problems. In some cases, the developers of CBTIs lack appropriate qualifications. In other cases, the interpretations can be too general (e.g., they may be statements that are true for just about everybody) or they may contradict one another. Frequently, they are accorded "unrealistic credibility" because of their computer origin (Sampson et al., 2003). To prevent misuse of CBTIs, counselors should not rely on them unless they possess sufficient knowledge about the assessment instrument itself to be able to evaluate independently the accuracy of the interpretations. In addition, clients should not be expected to be able to use CBTI reports without the aid of a counselor unless the reports have been specifically validated as "self-interpreting" (National Career Development Association, 1997).

A test can have well-established validity for various uses, but that does not necessarily ensure the validity of a CBTI derived for that test. The scoring rules on which the CBTIs are based are often a "trade secret" so that it is difficult to evaluate how adequately they have been developed. In fact, the publishers of the *Mental Measurements Yearbooks* abandoned an effort to provide a separate volume of reviews of CBTIs because of the difficulty they encountered in obtaining information from the test publishers regarding the computer programs and their algorithms (Kramer & Conoley, 1992). Counselors must examine CBTIs in light of other information that they have been able to collect about the client. They should use their best professional judgment to take into account any individual or situational factors that could alter the CBTI for a particular client. As with any test data, the results should be viewed as hypotheses that need to be confirmed or revised on the basis of other information that is collected regarding the particular client.

SUMMARY

1. A client's readiness for counseling can be assessed in terms of five stages of change: precontemplative, contemplative, preparation, action, and maintenance.
2. Counselors can use Brickman's (Brickman et al., 1982) "models of helping and coping" to clarify a client's expectations of counseling. Clients differ in their expectations of counseling based on the degree to which they see themselves as responsible for causing or solving their problems.
3. The MBTI can be used to help clients identify their orientation toward problem solving. Clients should be helped to recognize the advantages and disadvantages of their particular problem-solving style.
4. The nature and severity of a client's problems can best be determined by means of an intake form, a problem checklist or screening inventory, and an intake interview used in com-

bination. Both the ICP and the SCL-90-R contain comprehensive lists of client problems or symptoms that can be used systematically to clarify a client's concerns.

5. The intake interview provides a flexible format for assessing a broad range of topics as needed. The client's psychological well-being can be assessed systematically by means of a mental status examination or a structured interview.

6. Ideally, counseling outcomes should be assessed by the means of multiple methods (e.g., client satisfaction scales; self-report scales such as the ICP, SCL-90, and Outcome Questionnaire–45; and counselor rating scales) used with multiple sources (clients, counselors, and significant others) in regard to multiple outcomes (e.g., general level of functioning, level of depression, and marital satisfaction) over different time periods to gain a complete picture of the effectiveness of counseling. Such comprehensive studies are important to advance the counseling profession as a whole.

7. From a practical point of view, some type of outcome assessment, possibly obtained by means of a client satisfaction scale or a brief interview, should be conducted for each client at the end of counseling with that client.

8. The client should be integrally involved in all aspects of test selection. A variety of assessment procedures should be considered for this purpose.

9. The counselor should be careful to establish rapport with the client and to follow the prescribed procedures for test administration.

10. Tests administered via the computer must meet the same professional standards for test quality and test usage as traditional paper-and-pencil tests.

11. Computer-based test interpretations (CBTIs), which have become increasingly popular, require thorough knowledge and understanding of the test itself, the testing circumstances, and characteristics of the client to ensure proper use. CBTIs do not replace the need for counselor training and experience in psychological assessment.

SECTION
II
COGNITIVE ASSESSMENT

5

Assessment of Intelligence

Counselors who work in certain settings, such as schools, or who are involved in employment or vocational counseling make considerable use of the results of intelligence tests. Others, working in colleges and secondary schools, constantly make use of a particular type of intelligence measure (a scholastic aptitude test), whereas marriage counselors and those working with substance abusers, for example, may only occasionally use such instruments. Some general knowledge of intelligence assessment is important, and test results influence many decisions clients make. All counselors are expected to have some knowledge of intelligence assessment and the ability to make use of test results in assisting clients to make decisions. In this chapter, some of the most often used instruments are described, along with considerations regarding their use. Scholastic aptitude measures are discussed in the next chapter. Assessment instruments designed for special populations are described in chapter 16.

Intelligence has been one of the most thoroughly studied fields throughout the history of psychology. It was Alfred Binet in France who, in the early 1900s, conceptualized intelligence as a general ability to judge, to comprehend, and to reason well. With this definition, he then developed a series of measures by which he could identify children for whom it was necessary to provide special educational programs. The measures he used showed that mental processes increase as a child grows older. Three-year-olds could be expected to be able to point to their nose, eyes, and mouth and repeat two digits. The typical 7-year-old could distinguish right from left and name various colors, and the typical 12-year-old could define various abstract words and make sense of a disarranged sentence.

In 1916, Lewis Terman, at Stanford University, revised and standardized Binet's test for use in the United States. It became known as the Stanford–Binet Intelligence Scale. Making use of the concept of mental age developed by Binet, Terman devised the concept of the now-outdated intelligence quotient (IQ). This IQ score is a ratio calculated between an individual's mental age and chronological age. A child's mental age is divided by the child's chronological age and multiplied by 100. A child exactly 10 years of age with a mental age of 12 will obtain an IQ score of 120. A mental age substantially below a child's chronological age was considered evidence of mental retardation. This type of an IQ score has a number of problems connected with it. In the first place, answering all of the items correctly on the original Stanford–Binet yielded a maximum mental age of less than 20. Thus, anyone 20 or older automatically received an IQ score of less than 100. The usefulness of the ratio score therefore disappears during the teen years. In addition, the concept of a person's IQ has been erroneously viewed by the public as a fixed measure, similar to the color of a person's eyes, rather than as a particular score on a particular test at a particular time. The ratio IQ has therefore been replaced by a derived IQ standard score (known as the deviation IQ) to circumvent some of these problems.

The question of what it is that actually makes up intelligence and what it is that intelligence tests actually measure has long been the subject of much controversy. One conceptualization divides intelligence into two types: *crystallized* and *fluid*. Crystallized intelligence deals with an individual's ability to solve problems and make decisions on the basis of acquired knowledge, experiences, and verbal conceptualizations. Fluid intelligence is an individual's ability to be adaptable and flexible in solving new problems (Carroll, 1993a). Most of the tests in the content areas of verbal reasoning and quantitative reasoning would be considered crystallized intelligence and those in the abstract/visual reasoning area fluid intelligence. The Cattell-Horn-Carroll three-stratum theory of cognitive abilities has had a significant impact on many of the tests that have been constructed or revised since 1990 (Alfonso, Flanagan, & Radwan, 2005). In this theory, the general mental ability factor (known as *g*) is made up of a second stratum of eight subfactors (of which fluid and crystallized are two of the most prominent), and these subfactors are each made up of a number of narrower abilities, which constitute the third stratum.

More recently various authorities have argued that it is time to move on beyond the general intelligence model that has dominated psychology over the past many decades and recognize a much broader view of what makes up intelligence and include such factors as creativity and practical intelligence (Sternberg, 2002, 2005) or planning and simultaneous processing mental activities (Naglieri & Das, 2005). However defined, *g* has nevertheless been shown to affect a very large number of life tasks—literacy and educational attainment, job performance, ability to handle job complexity, and ability to meet life's risks (L. S. Gottfredson, 2002).

POPULAR INDIVIDUAL INTELLIGENCE TESTS

Stanford–Binet

The Stanford–Binet became the best-known intelligence test in the world and was used as the "gold standard" against which all other intelligence tests being developed were validated. The 1916 Stanford–Binet Intelligence Scale had a number of weaknesses and was therefore revised to produce the 1937 scale in two parallel forms (L and M). The ratio IQ score was eliminated, and standard scores were calculated to provide each age with a mean of 100 and a standard deviation of 16. A 1960 revision was developed and was restandardized in 1972 to provide more adequate norms intended to be representative of the entire U.S. population. A fourth edition was constructed in 1986, in which the authors attempted to provide a continuity with the previous editions by retaining the advantages of the early editions as an individually administered intelligence test and still take advantage of the more recent theoretical developments in cognitive psychology.

In 2003, the Stanford–Binet Intelligence Scales, Fifth Edition (SB5) was published as an update of the fourth edition (Roid, 2003). This revision follows the Cattell-Horn-Carroll hierarchical model of cognitive abilities.

It consists of five verbal and five nonverbal individually administered subtests; the full scale battery takes from 45 to 75 minutes to administer. It can be administered to examinees from 2 years to over 85 years of age. As in the case of the previous editions, individuals are administered a range of tasks suited to their abilities. Testing is begun with two routing subtests (Object Series-Matrices and Vocabulary) to determine the starting point for the remaining subtests. Depending on the performance on these subtests, the examiner begins at one of five developmental levels on each of the other eight tests. Testing then proceeds on each test until at least three out of four items are missed, which determines a ceiling level on that test at which further items can be expected to be answered incorrectly. The routing subtests can be used by themselves as an abbreviated IQ test taking only 15 to 20 minutes to administer.

The battery yields a Full Scale IQ score, Nonverbal and Verbal IQs, and five Factor Indexes—Fluid Reasoning, Knowledge, Quantitative Reasoning, Visual-Spatial Processing, and Working Memory. Standard scores have a mean of 100 but, unlike previous editions, have a standard deviation of 15, as in other major intelligence tests. Individual subtest scores have a mean of 10 and a standard deviation of 3. A standardization sample of 4,800 individuals was stratified by age, gender, race/ethnicity, geographic region, and educational attainment to match U.S. census data.

High reliability of SB5 scores has been reported for all three of the methods used—internal consistency, test–retest, and interscorer agreement. Internal consistency coefficients ranged from .95 to .98 for the IQ scores and from .90 to .92 for each of the Factor Index scores. The 10 subtest reliabilities ranged from .76 to .91. Test–retest reliability coefficients of .89 to .95 for the IQ scores and .83 to .95 for the Factor Index scores were reported. Interscorer agreement was also high (median correlation .90). Standard errors of measurement are 2.30 for Full Scale, 3.26 for Nonverbal, and 3.05 for Verbal IQs. High correlations with other cognitive tests, including the Wechsler scales and previous editions of the Stanford-Binet, give evidence of convergent validity (Bain & Allin, 2005). A confirmatory factor analysis of the subtests yielded evidence for the five-factor solution. Construction of the SB5 was based on a five-factor hierarchical model of intelligence from overall (Full Scale IQ or g), to a second level of domains (Five Factors), to a third level of subtests (Kush, 2005).

The SB5 may be hand scored, but it is easier to score with the Windows-based Scoring Pro, in which the examiner enters information and raw scores and receives an extended score report and a brief narrative summary (Roid & Barram, 2004). The factor Working Memory had been added to the SB5. This factor, which was not in the previous edition, is related to children's learning problems and includes an increased number of nonverbal measures that are useful in working with clients from diverse backgrounds. There are more high-end items to assess gifted performance and more low-end items to better measure children and adults who are functioning at a low level. The colorful toys and materials are especially appealing to children (J. A. Johnson, D'Amato, & Harrison, 2005).

Wechsler Scales

The Stanford–Binet was originally developed for children, with some more difficult items added for adults. David Wechsler, working at Bellevue Hospital in New York, believed that there was a need for an intelligence test more suitable for adults, and he therefore developed the Wechsler Bellevue Intelligence Scale in 1939. In addition, believing that the Stanford–Binet placed too much emphasis on language and verbal skills, he developed a totally different performance scale measuring nonverbal intelligence. The Wechsler scales are reported to be the most frequently used instruments by school counselors (Wechsler Intelligence Scale for Children) and among the four instruments used most often by mental health counselors (Wechsler Intelligence Scale for Children and Wechsler Adult Intelligence Scale; Elmore et al., 1993; Frauenhoffer et al., 1998; Giordano et al., 1997).

Wechsler Adult Intelligence Scale–Third Edition (WAIS-III)

The 1939 scale was revised in 1955 to correct a number of deficiencies that had been found in the earlier form and became the WAIS. The WAIS was revised in 1981 to produce the WAIS-R and standardized on a sample selected to match the proportions of the U.S. population in regard to race, occupational level, education, and residence (Wechsler, 1981). During the 1990s, it was expanded as the WAIS-III by adding three new optional subtest scores on four factor-analysis-based indexes. It was also was restandardized to yield more comprehensive and updated norms (Kaufman & Lichtenberger, 1999; Wechsler, 1997a). A Spanish version is also available.

There is a core of nine subtests, with two added to obtain IQ scores and a different two added to obtain factor-based index scores. Thirteen are administered to obtain both, and there is an optional Object Assembly subtest that may be substituted for a "spoiled" performance subtest. IQ scores are derived from norms on 13 age bands (ages 16–89 years) and can range from 45 to 155 (Hess, 2001).

The Wechsler tests yield a profile of scores (such as that of the case example for the WAIS-III, some of which are displayed in Figure 5-1) showing the scale score for each of the 13 subtests along with verbal IQ, performance IQ, and the full-scale IQ scores. The mean and standard deviation for each of the subtests are 10 and 3, respectively. For the performance, verbal, and full-scale IQ scores, the mean is 100 with a standard deviation of 15 (compared with 16 for the earlier Stanford–Binets). Standard error of measurement for the three IQ scores is reported to be approximately 2.5 for the full-scale IQ, 2.7 for the verbal IQ, and 4.1 for the performance IQ. A client's true full-scale score could thus be assumed at a 95% level of confidence to fall within 5 points in one direction or the other from the client's obtained full-scale IQ score.

The manual (Psychological Corporation, 1997) contains information regarding the comparison of index and subtest scores; however, such pairwise comparisons remain problematic. Comparisons of these index and subtest scores with the overall verbal and performance scores yield more accurate interpretations (Longman, 2004). Following is a case example of a WAIS-III administered at the time of admission to a residential alcoholism treatment facility.

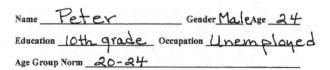

Name **Peter**   Gender **Male** Age **24**

Education **10th grade**   Occupation **Unemployed**

Age Group Norm **20-24**

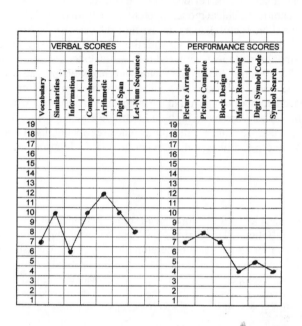
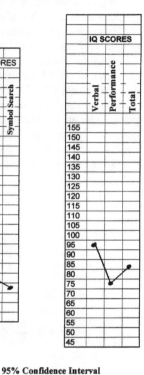

	IQ	Percentile	95% Confidence Interval
Verbal	95	37	90 – 100
Performance	76	5	71 – 84
Total	85	16	81 – 89

FIGURE 5-1

Wechsler Adult Intelligence Scale–III Summary

Case Example

Peter, 24 years old and single, completed the WAIS-III while undergoing treatment for alcoholism in a residential alcohol detoxification center. He had been treated twice before for alcoholism, but being single and without family or other support systems, he found it easy to drift back into alcoholism upon discharge. He had mild depression and antisocial tendencies and had been in trouble with the law in addition to his problems with alcohol. In the center, however, he was a model client and cooperated fully with the treatment and testing he received. His verbal score on the WAIS-III fell in the normal range although he scored substantially lower on the performance subtests, giving him a total score that would place him in the dull-normal range. The large difference between the verbal and performance portions of the WAIS-III may very likely have been caused by the effects of continued alcohol abuse.

Wechsler Intelligence Scale for Children (WISC-IV)
The WISC was originally developed as a downward extension of the Wechsler Bellevue Intelligence Scale for use with children ages 6 to 16 years. It was revised in 1974 (WISC-R) to contain more

child-oriented items, to include more African American and female figures, and to provide a normative sample more representative of children in the U.S. population (Wechsler, 1974). A revised, updated, and restandardized edition was published in 1991 as the WISC-III and a fourth in 2003 as the WISC-IV. The WISC-IV standardization sample consisted of 2,200 children, ages 6 to 16, with 200 in each of the 11 age groups and stratified by age, sex, parent education level, geographic region, and race/ethnicity.

The WISC-IV contains 15 subtests, 5 of which are supplementary, to be used if the examiner meets with difficulty in administering one of the regular subtests to a particular child. The subtests generally parallel those in the WAIS-III and are administered by alternating the verbal and performance subtests. The WISC-IV provides four Index scores: Verbal Comprehension, Perceptual Reasoning, Working Memory, and Processing Speed, important indicators of a child's cognitive strengths and weaknesses (L. G. Weiss, Saklofske, & Prifitera, 2005). Each Index score is derived from two or three of the subtest scores (Maller, 2005).

The Index scores and the full-scale IQ score have means (100) and standard deviations (15) similar to those of the WAIS-III. Norms are provided for each 4-month age group between 6 and 16 years. The WISC has been found to be a useful instrument for the diagnosis of learning disabilities and mental retardation. An expanded version, titled the WISC-IV Integrated, provides 16 Process Subtests related to the four Index scores to provide measures of how a child's problem-solving strengths and weaknesses may be affecting his or her results. There is also a Spanish edition of the WISC-IV.

Index score split-half reliabilities exceeding .90 (full scale IQ, .96) and test–retest reliabilities at or above .84 (full scale IQ, .91) are reported for all age groups. The standard error of measurement for the full-scale IQ test is approximately 3 points. Thus, a child's true WISC-IV IQ score would be estimated to be no more than 6 points above or below the obtained score at a 95% level of confidence (Wechsler, 2003).

Wechsler Preschool and Primary Scale of Intelligence (WPPSI-III)
In 1967, a downward extension of the WISC was developed for use with children 4 to $6\frac{1}{2}$ years of age, called the Wechsler Preschool and Primary Scale of Intelligence (WPPSI), which was revised in 1989 to become the WPPSI-R (Wechsler, 1989). In 2002, the WPPSI was revised and divided into two age bands, allowing for a lower age range down to $2\frac{1}{2}$ years. Four subtests are administered to $2\frac{1}{2}$- to 4-year-olds and seven subtests to those between 4 and 7 years, yielding verbal IQ, performance IQ, and full scale IQ scores. There are supplemental and optional subtests that can be substituted for certain of the core subtests. Normalized standard scores for subtests and IQs are similar to those on the other Wechsler tests (Lichtenberger & Kaufman, 2004; Madle, 2005).

Wechsler Abbreviated Scale of Intelligence
There is also a short-form Wechsler instrument, the Wechsler Abbreviated Scale of Intelligence (WASI; Wechsler, 1999). Taking only 15 to 30 minutes to administer and appropriate for individuals ages 6 to 89, the WASI is a brief measure tied to both the WISC-III and the WAIS-III. Because its results are less stable, it should not be used when a more accurate estimate from a full version is needed (Alexrod, 2002).

Kaufman Batteries

More recently, several tests have been developed that make use of Luria's (1980) neuropsychological theory of intelligence. These include the Kaufman tests and the Das Naglieri system. Known as the PASS model, it consists of Planning (selecting a strategy to efficiently solve a problem), Attention (selectively attending to a stimulus and inhibiting competing stimuli), Simultaneous (integrating several stimuli into a single whole), and Successive (working with things in a specific serial order). The Kaufmans have developed several intelligence test batteries, including the Kaufman Assessment Battery for Children (KABC-II) and the Kaufman Adolescent and Adult Intelligence Test (KAIT). The KABC-II is composed of 18 subtests of which up to 10 are administered depending upon the age of the child (American Guidance Service, 2005; Kaufman, Lichtenberger, Fletcher-Janzen, & Kaufman, 2005). It is designed for children 3 to 18 years old and yields scores on six different ability indices. It was standardized with the Kaufman Test of Educational Achievement. The KABC-II is considered to be more cross-culturally fair than most comparable tests of intelligence, in part because it separates processing scores from crystallized scores (Samuda, 1998a).

The KAIT consists of six core subtests and four additional subtests in an expanded battery and is normed for ages 11 to 85 years (Kaufman & Kaufman, 1993). It yields scores on both crystallized and fluid intelligence and a composite IQ score, each with reliability coefficients above .90. A short form, the Kaufman Brief Intelligence Test (Kaufman & Kaufman, 2002), which can be administered in 15–30 minutes, consists of a vocabulary (through pictures) portion and a matrices portion using pictures and abstract designs. It is useful when time constraints preclude the use of a longer measure.

Cognitive Assessment System

Another instrument developed to provide a broader measure of children's cognitive abilities is the Das Naglieri Cognitive Assessment System (CAS; Naglieri, 2005). Based on Luria's (1980, Naglieri & Das, 2005) cognitive-processing theory of intelligence, it contains 13 subtests (only 12 are used in any administration), yielding four scales labeled Planning, Attention, Simultaneous Processing, and Successive Processing (PASS) and a full-scale score ($M = 100$, $SD = 15$). Internal consistency and test–retest reliabilities are in the vicinity of .90, and the planning and attention scales assess concepts not found on traditional intelligence tests.

Woodcock–Johnson

The Woodcock–Johnson III (WJ III) consists of two separate instruments, the Test of Cognitive Abilities (WJ III COG) and the Tests of Achievement (WJ III ACH). The WJ III COG contains 10 tests in its Standard Battery, 10 in its Extended Battery, and 11 in the Diagnostic Supplement. There are 12 tests in the WJ III ACH Battery (Schrank, 2005). The two instruments were normed together on a sample that ranged from 2 to 90 years of age, and there are two parallel forms of each battery. The WJ III is often used in the diagnosis of learning disabilities and in determining the need for special education resources (Gregg, Coleman, & Knight, 2003). WJ III score reliabilities are mostly in the .90s and yield cluster scores that are consistent with current factor theories of ability (Sandoval, 2003).

Other Individual Intelligence Tests

There are several individually administered intelligence tests designed to provide brief assessments of cognitive abilities for individuals of widely varying ages. The Peabody Picture Vocabulary Test–Third Edition (PPVT-III; L. M. Dunn & Dunn, 1997) is a brief (10–15 minutes) screening test of listening comprehension and verbal ability. A word is given, and the examinee is told to point to the appropriate one picture out of four on a card. There are two parallel forms.

The Slosson Intelligence Test–Revised (SIT-R3) is an individual screening test of verbal intelligence made up of items similar to those found on the verbal subtests of the Wechsler scales (C. A. Campbell & Ashmore, 1995; Nicholson & Hibpshman, 1998). It requires 10–25 minutes to administer and was renormed in 1998. There is a Primary form (SIT-P) for ages 2 through 7 that includes a nonverbal scale (Erford & Pauletta, 2005).

Both the PPVT-III and the SIT-3 can be administered to individuals of widely varying ages (from 3 or 4 years to 65 and older), both report reliability coefficients of above .9, and both show substantial concurrent validities with the verbal portions of other instruments such as the Wechsler and Kaufman batteries. They yield deviation IQs with a mean of 100 and standard deviations of 15 for the PPVT-III and 16 for the SIT-R3.

The Wide Range Intelligence test (WRIT) is a brief, individually administered test of intellectual ability for ages 4–85. It contains four subtests that yield a verbal (crystallized) IQ and a visual (fluid) IQ, with both alpha and test–retest reliabilities of above .90 (Widaman, 2003b).

Advantages and Disadvantages of Individual Intelligence Tests

Each of these intelligence tests is individually administered and requires a highly trained examiner. Considerable training and practice in administering each test are necessary for a competent administration that produces reliable results without the scoring errors that are an inherent aspect of individual assessment. An experienced examiner has the opportunity to observe and judge a variety of behaviors and aspects of the individual's personality. Thus, for the competent examiner, these tests provide aspects of a clinical interview as well as a standardized test.

Because these individual intelligence tests provide several different types of IQ scores, the counselor has the opportunity to pay particular attention to those clients for whom the difference between the scores is substantial. In such cases, an exploration is warranted to attempt to discern factors that might account for the differences. The different subtest scores also provide an opportunity to examine the pattern of scores that appear as a profile on the report form, such as that shown for the WAIS-III case example of Peter in Figure 5-1.

There have been a number of hypotheses advanced regarding emotional, neurological, and pathological problems that yield differential subtest scores. Considerable research has shown differential diagnoses resulting from patterns on such profiles to be questionable. Because the different subtests vary in reliability, difference scores obtained among the subtests can be particularly unreliable. Nevertheless, most sophisticated users of the Stanford–Binet and the Wechsler tests regard differential patterns as suggesting certain types of dysfunction. For example, higher scores on various verbal scales and lower scores on certain of the performance scales are suggestive of such problems as brain damage; drug abuse (as in the case example); or, in an older person, Alzheimer's dementia. Verbal subtest scores falling well below performance scores may suggest poor reading ability or lack of motivation for academic achievement.

The primary disadvantages of individual intelligence tests are their costs, both in terms of time and money, and the extensive training required for them to be properly administered and interpreted. Counselors often lack both the resources and the training to use these instruments themselves. Instead, they refer clients in need of individual testing to competent examiners and receive the results from them. Counselors should encourage such examiners to report their observations and any other information that can assist counselors in interpreting the results, particularly regarding information that can help to explain any discrepancies. In place of individual intelligence tests, counselors are more likely to use group intelligence tests to assess the cognitive abilities of their clients.

GROUP INTELLIGENCE TESTS

Group intelligence tests are considerably more cost efficient than individual tests in the time and expense required for administration and scoring. They require simpler materials; typically only a printed booklet, a multiple-choice answer sheet, a pencil, and a scoring key are needed. They also usually offer more normative information because this type of data is easier to collect for group tests.

The development of group tests was stimulated by the need to classify almost 2 million U.S. Army recruits during World War I. The Army Alpha and the nonreading companion test, the Army Beta (now in its 1999 nonverbal civilian form the Beta III), were developed for military use. Group intelligence tests designed for educational and personnel uses were developed shortly thereafter, with these two tests as models. Such group-administered tests are now used at every educational level from kindergarten through graduate school. They are also used extensively by industry, by the military, and in research studies. The Beta III is widely used when hiring non-English-speaking or illiterate unskilled laborers for whom a verbal test would not be appropriate (Bellah, 2005). To avoid the term *intelligence test,* because the term *intelligence* is so often misunderstood and misinterpreted, counselors are encouraged to describe these tests, particularly those designed for school use, in terms of mental maturity, cognitive ability, school ability, or academic ability.

Group Intelligence Tests for School Use

Because these tests are administered across a number of grades throughout entire school systems, they are administered in the hundreds of thousands each year. The market for these tests is therefore a profitable one, and a large number are available for use. Four of the most popular and most psychometrically sound instruments are briefly described here. Results are typically reported in a variety of forms: national and local age and grade percentiles, stanines, and normal curve equivalents.

Cognitive Abilities Test (CogAT)
The Cognitive Abilities Test, Form 6 (CogAT-6) is the modern version of the Lorge–Thorndike Intelligence Tests (Riverside Publishing Co., 2001). The test has two editions: the Primary Edition

with three levels for kindergarten through Grade 2 and a Multilevel Edition with levels for use in Grades 3 through 12. The CogAT-6 is composed of three batteries assessing verbal, quantitative, and nonverbal abilities with each battery consisting of three separate tests with a composite score (B. G. Rodgers, 2005). The nonverbal section uses neither language nor numbers but rather uses geometric figures for tasks that require classification, analogies, or figure synthesis. In this portion, the effects of formal schooling, poor reading ability, or non-native-English speaking are minimized. Raw scores on each section can be converted into stanine and percentile scores for both age and grade levels so that the three scores can be compared both with norm groups and within each individual. In addition, the scores can be converted to standard scores that have a mean of 100 and a standard deviation of 16 to produce a deviation standard age score (SAS) or IQ score. The Cognitive Abilities Tests were standardized along with the Iowa Tests of Basic Skills for kindergarten through Grade 9 and with the Iowa Tests of Educational Development for Grades 9 through 12. They were standardized on a sample of 180,000 students representative of the U.S. census population, with high and stable predictions found at all grade levels between CogAT-6 scores and future scores on the Iowa achievement tests (DiPerna, 2005).

Kuhlmann–Anderson Test

The Kuhlmann–Anderson Test is made up of seven separate levels for kindergarten through 12th grade, with each level containing eight tests (Scholastic Testing Service, 1997). It is the contemporary version (restandardized and renormed in 1997) of one of the earliest and most popular intelligence tests used in the schools. It is less dependent on language than most similar tests and yields verbal, nonverbal, and total scores. Scores are presented as age- and grade-related percentile bands (confidence intervals) as well as deviation IQ (cognitive skills quotient) scores.

Test of Cognitive Skills (TCS/2)

The TCS/2 is the contemporary version of the long-used California Test of Mental Maturity–Short Form (CTB/Macmillan/McGraw-Hill, 1993). In its original form, the instrument was designed to be the group-test equivalent of the Stanford–Binet and to yield scores similar to those that would be obtained by individually administering the Stanford–Binet. In addition to verbal and nonverbal ability subtests, it also contains a section designed to assess short-term memory. There are six levels, each designed for two grade levels ranging from Grade 2 through Grade 12. The Primary Test of Cognitive Skills is available for grades K–1. Age and grade stanines, percentiles, and standard score norms are available for each subtest. A Combined Cognitive Skills Index provides a deviation IQ score. It was standardized with the Terra Nova and the California Achievement Tests–5.

Otis–Lennon School Ability Test

The Otis–Lennon School Ability Test, 8th Edition (OLSAT8) has seven levels ranging from kindergarten to Grade 12 (Harcourt Assessment, 2003). The test is published in two forms and yields verbal and nonverbal scores based on 36-item subtests and a total IQ score. The test represents a contemporary version of a series of former Otis tests. The OLSAT8 was jointly normed with the Metropolitan Achievement Tests 8 and the Stanford Achievement Tests 10.

Other Group Intelligence Tests

Shipley Institute of Living Scale

The Shipley Institute of Living Scale–Revised (SILS-R) is a 60-item (40 vocabulary, 20 abstract reasoning) intelligence test that takes approximately 20 minutes to administer. IQ and standard scores are obtained based on age-adjusted norms (Zachary, 1986). Correlations in the vicinity of .8 with Wechsler tests are reported in the manual, along with reliabilities of .8 to .9 for internal consistency and .6 to .7 for test–retest. Originally constructed to assess cognitive impairment, this test is now used as a brief screening device for overall intellectual ability.

Wonderlic Personnel Test

The Wonderlic Personnel Test is a brief 12-minute, 50-item, speeded test of mental ability for adults (Wonderlic, 1999). Sixteen forms of this paper-and-pencil intelligence test are available, along with Braille and audiotape editions for persons with disabilities. There are extensive norms.

It is administered in business and industry to 2.5 million job applicants each year for the selection and placement of employees. It is available in 14 languages and can be administered on a personal computer. Validity data in regard to job success are undoubtedly available locally in many companies but typically are not found in the research literature. The test's validity has been questioned in regard to selection for certain positions when minorities obtaining lower scores on the instrument are screened out of various entry-level positions. This has resulted in the Wonderlic Personnel Test becoming the subject of various court cases in which its use was declared not legitimate when testing procedures resulted in denying fair opportunities to prospective minority employees but acceptable when test results could be shown to be substantially related to the performance on specific jobs.

Multidimensional Aptitude Battery

The Multidimensional Aptitude Battery–II (MAB-II) was developed by the late Douglas Jackson as a group-administered paper-and-pencil test to yield the same types of results and scores as the WAIS (D. N. Jackson, 1998). This test battery contains five tests on the verbal scale and five tests on the performance scale that involve very similar tasks to the subtests on the WAIS but in a paper-and-pencil format. Scores on the various subtests have a mean of 50 and a standard deviation of 10, and total scores on the verbal, performance, and full scale have a mean of 100 and a standard deviation of 15. It is available in English, French, and Spanish versions.

In the design of the MAB, Jackson made use of the capabilities of modern computers in developing items and scales through item analysis and factor-analysis techniques. The battery can be taken directly on most computers with software that presents instructions and practice items, times the subtests, scores them, and produces four different types of interpretive reports. The advantage of the battery is its ease of administration and scoring; the highly trained examiner necessary to administer the WAIS or the Stanford–Binet is not required. As a group-administered battery, however, it does not provide the examiner with the observational data obtained in using individual instruments. Therefore it is generally not administered in high-stakes testing situations such as the determination of mental retardation (Widaman, 2003a).

INTERPRETING INTELLIGENCE TEST RESULTS

The typical intelligence test administered in the United States assumes a relatively common cultural background found in contemporary society and English as the native language. For tests above the lower elementary levels, reading ability in English is also necessary to obtain valid results on most of the group-administered tests. To provide valid assessment devices useful in other cultures or for use with subcultures or minority cultures in the United States, test developers have made attempts to develop culture-fair tests that function independently of a specific culture, primarily by eliminating, or at least greatly reducing, language and cultural content. These are discussed in chapter 16.

Robert Sternberg has refocused attention on some of the fundamental questions regarding intelligence (Sternberg, 1985; Sternberg, Wagner, Williams, & Horvath, 1995). He has proposed a triarchic theory of intelligence with each of the three factors made up of several different elements that interact with one another. The componential (cognitive) factor deals with information processing and is made up of crystallized abilities measured by such subtests as vocabulary and reading comprehension and fluid abilities measured by subtests such as abstract analogies and series completions. His experiential (creative) factor embodies the ability to deal with novel activities and situations and the ability to automatize high levels of information processing. His conceptual (practical) factor contains the components of practical intelligence and social intelligence. His triarchic intelligence test (not yet published) consists of 12 subtests, 4 for each of the three factors. He believes that a single index of IQ does more to obscure than describe a person's abilities, and his measures vary widely from the tasks typically involved in the more traditional attempts to assess intelligence (Sternberg, 1988, 1998a).

Howard Gardner has also proposed a theory of multiple intelligences (called the MI theory) with seven different and relatively independent intelligences: logical-mathematical, linguistic, musical, special, bodily-kinesthetic, interpersonal, and intrapersonal (Gardner, 1999). He and his colleagues are attempting to develop instruments to assess these various intelligences, but at present his theory lacks a strong empirical base (Groth-Marnat, 2003).

Meanwhile, John Carroll in England has reanalyzed 461 data sets of various cognitive abilities (Carroll, 1993b). He has described a more traditional theory of intelligence of three strata in a hierarchical model, similar to that of Vernon (1961). It contains a single general ability g at the apex, a second stratum of eight broad abilities, and a third with many narrow abilities. Numerous studies have continued to show that cognitive ability as measured by the traditional intelligence test is a valid predictor of educational achievement, occupational success, and work performance (Barrett & Depinet, 1991; Schmidt & Hunter, 1998).

For many reasons, controversy continues regarding the concept of intelligence, the specific abilities that constitute intelligent behavior, and the magnitude of the roles played by heredity and environment. There has been a curious trend in which mean IQ scores have increased about 3 points per decade over the last 50 years. This trend, known as the "Flynn effect" after James Flynn, who noted it early, is not easily explained—this effect has been variably reasoned to be caused by education, nutrition, media, and even hybrid vigor (Neisser, 1998; Whiston, 2000). Using a sophisticated mathematical model, Dickens and Flynn (2001) suggested that industrialization's rising cognitive demands of work and leisure have created a steadily increasing environmental "social multiplier" effect that could account for the higher IQ scores across many nations. At the same time, academic achievement and scholastic aptitude test scores have not shown similar increases and occasionally have shown actual decreases.

Perhaps the most important point to remember in the interpretation of intelligence test results is that the IQ score obtained does not represent a fixed characteristic of the individual. Instead, it should be interpreted as a particular score obtained on a particular test at a particular time. As has been mentioned, this is especially important for younger clients, for whom test–retest reliabilities are lower, indicating that considerable change and development take place over time. In interpreting the result to a client, rather than say that he or she has an IQ of 112, the counselor would provide a better interpretation by saying that the client scored in the top quarter of his or her peers on a test that measures an ability useful in learning academic subjects.

GIFTEDNESS AND CREATIVITY

There is no single method for identifying children who are gifted; however, the best available for identifying children with superior cognitive abilities is the standardized, individually administered, multidimensional test of intelligence such a Wechsler test or the Stanford–Binet. In some schools, group tests must be substituted for screening purposes when the administration of large numbers of individual tests is not feasible. Other areas of giftedness, such as creativity or talent, are more difficult to assess and must include a combination of procedures including achievements, achievement tests, portfolios, auditions, and teacher and parent nominations (McIntosh & Dixon, 2005; Sattler, 2005).

The Torrance Tests of Creativity (Torrance, 1974) are the most widely used tests to assess creativity. They consist of both nonverbal and verbal forms assessing four creative abilities—fluency, flexibility, originality, and elaboration. The nonverbal form uses drawing activities, and the verbal form involves activities such as generating questions or suggesting alternative uses for an object. Each activity is timed and scored on the first three of the creative abilities. The nonverbal activities are also scored for elaboration. Research has shown adequate score reliability. An interesting 22-year longitudinal validity study showed student scores to be related to accomplishments in adulthood (Kerr & Gagliardi, 2003).

SUMMARY

This chapter dealt with the assessment of intelligence through the use of both individual and group assessment instruments.

1. The concept of intelligence is widely studied in psychology, but IQ scores are widely misunderstood by the general public.
2. Binet designed the first intelligence test in France in the early 1900s; it was revised in 1916 at Stanford for use in the United States. The 2002 revision of the Stanford–Binet intelligence tests contains 10 subtests, only parts of which are administered to any individual, depending on chronological age and answers on two of the routing subtests.

3. Four different Wechsler scales represent individually administered intelligence tests designed specifically for different age ranges.
4. Large numbers of group intelligence tests are administered each year in U.S. schools, and seven of these tests were briefly described in this chapter.
5. Fundamental questions regarding the range of abilities that constitute intelligent behavior are still being explored along with instruments to assess these abilities.
6. Giftedness, creativity, and talent must be assessed with a variety of procedures.

6

Academic Aptitude and Achievement

The assessment of various aptitudes has played an important role in the field of psychological testing. An aptitude is generally thought of as an ability to acquire a specific type of skill or knowledge. In the field of aptitude testing, the assessment of scholastic aptitude is particularly important, because academic or scholastic aptitude is significantly related to achievement in various educational programs in high schools, colleges, and professional schools. Because of the importance of higher education as a prerequisite for entering the majority of higher status occupations and professions in today's society, achieving acceptable scores on scholastic aptitude measures is becoming increasingly crucial for those aspiring to such occupations.

Even counselors in elementary schools or mental health agencies who seldom see scholastic aptitude test scores in their work are expected to be knowledgeable about these tests. They will probably at least be consulted by their relatives, friends, and colleagues whose children are beginning to apply to undergraduate or professional colleges and universities.

In this chapter, information about the two major national college testing programs is presented, along with considerations and data useful in the interpretation of test scores. Academic aptitude tests used for admission to several of the different types of professional colleges are briefly described, followed by a few points regarding the administration and interpretation of academic aptitude tests. Examples of academic achievement test batteries commonly used in the schools are briefly described, along with a discussion of the use and misuse of such test batteries. Finally, the relatively new cognitive development theories and assessment instruments are mentioned because of the expectation that they will be of increasing interest to counselors.

TESTS FOR HIGHER EDUCATION

Scholastic aptitude tests are used as sources of information for the selection and admission of students to institutions of higher education at the undergraduate and graduate or professional levels. They are also used for awarding academic scholarships, in determining athletic eligibility, for awarding financial aid, for placing students in courses, as well as for academic and vocational counseling and advising. The two national college-level aptitude tests are the College Entrance Examination Board's (CEEB) SAT and ACT, Inc.'s, ACT Assessment.

SAT

The SAT has been given since 1926 and is now taken by over a million college-bound high school students each year. Its design, administration, and reporting are carried out by the Educational

Testing Service (ETS) in Princeton, New Jersey. Originally called the Scholastic Aptitude Test, it was revised in 1994 and given the redundant name—the Scholastic Assessment Test–I (SAT-I). The 2005 version is known simply as the New SAT or the SAT Reasoning Test. It is a 4-hour, primarily multiple-choice test with three major sections: (a) Critical Reading (formally Verbal), containing 67 multiple-choice items dealing with critical reading and sentence completion (70 minutes); (b) Mathematical (M), with 54 both multiple-choice items dealing with regular mathematics and quantitative comparisons and 10 completion items that require student-produced responses (70 minutes; College Board, 2005b); and (c) Writing (W). The Writing section consists of 49 multiple-choice items—improving sentences, improving paragraphs, identifying sentence errors (35 minutes)—and writing an essay (25 minutes). There is an additional 25-minute unscored section of experimental items being tried out for future tests. Scores on the three multiple-choice portions and the essay are then combined and placed on the same type of 200–800 standard scale as the Critical Reading and Mathematical sections. The total of an individual's standard score from each of the three sections of the SAT can thus range from 600 to 2,400 (College Board, 2006a).

Traditionally, the SAT attempted to measure developed abilities or intellectual skills and was not meant to be an achievement test tied to particular high school courses or curricula. Criticisms of that approach have led to revisions that are more closely related to secondary school subjects (and in that way has grown more similar to its competition, the ACT). Reliabilities of the SAT Verbal and Mathematical portions have generally been found to be in the vicinity of .90 for college-bound students, yielding standard errors of measurement of approximately 30 points.

In 1941, the mean on each section for students taking the test was set at 500 with a standard deviation of 100, and scores therefore ranged on a standard scale from 200 to 800. Since 1941, the college-bound cohort completing the test each year had changed drastically, and 500 no longer approximated the college-bound mean. In the spring of 1995, scores on the SAT-I were "recentered" with the mean on each of the two portions reset at 500 (College Board, 1994). By the year 2004, mean scores had edged up slightly to 508 on the SAT-I Verbal and 518 on the SAT-I Mathematical sections.

The Mathematical section of the SAT is more dependent on curriculum-based learning than is the Critical Reading section; the further the student progresses in mathematics courses in high school, the better the student will be prepared for the SAT Mathematics test. Students should plan to take math courses at least through Algebra II and be encouraged to review some of their basic algebra and geometry before sitting for the SAT.

The essay on the Writing section is scanned into a computer and sent to two readers (usually English teachers) who read it on their terminals. They score it on a 1–6 scale, and if they disagree by more than 1 point, it is sent to a third reader. The two scores are then added for a 2–12 total and combined with the multiple-choice results. In one study, the estimated true score reliability for the essay was .76 and on alternate forms .67. This yields a standard error of measurement *(SEM)* of approximately 1.0 (Kobrin & Kimmel, 2006). Thus an essay score of 7 (on the 2–12 range) would mean that 68% of the time the student's true score would fall between 6 and 8. The essay score contributes about 25% of the Writing section score.

The CEEB also administers the 1-hour SAT-II subject tests in 18 specific subjects (e.g., biology, Spanish), one or more of which are required by some colleges.

Preliminary Scholastic Aptitude Test/ National Merit Scholarship Qualifying Test (PSAT/NMSQT)

The PSAT/NMSQT is typically taken in the 11th grade (College Board, 2000). It is considered by some students to be a practice or trial run for the SAT to be taken the following year. It is also used to help students choose which colleges to consider in their college decision-making plans. It plays an important role as the initial step in qualifying for National Merit Scholarships.

Scores on the PSAT/NMSQT, which range from 20 to 80, are designed to be comparable—with an additional 0 added—to the SAT scores that students would be expected to obtain when they take that test in their senior year. Like the SAT, it yields Critical Reading and Math scores (from two 50-minute sections) and includes a 30-minute Writing Skills section but without writing an essay. The Math portion cannot include junior and senior year mathematics concepts because a large number of sophomores also take it (perhaps as a pre-PSAT) and are included in its norms (College Board, 2005c).

The PSAT/NMSQT was also recentered in the fall of 1994 in order that those juniors could predict the scores they would receive when they took the recentered SAT-I in 1995 (College Board, 1992). Thus, a student who receives a 50 on the PSAT Critical Reading, a 55 on the PSAT Math, and a 45 on the PSAT Writing would be expected to receive scores somewhere in the vicinity of 500 on the SAT Critical Reading, 550 on the SAT Mathematical, and 450 on the SAT Writing. Such a student who had been planning to apply to a very highly selective institution at which the majority of those students admitted score above 650 on all portions of the SAT-I might wish to reconsider his or her chances of admission to that institution. An additional score, known as the "Selection Index," is computed for scholarship consideration by summing the Verbal, Math, and Writing Skills scores on the PSAT/NMSQT. The approximately 16,000 highest scoring students become National Merit Scholarship semifinalists, with actual selection index cut-off scores varying among the different states to obtain the top 1% of the scholarship qualifiers from each state.

ACT

The other national college testing admissions program is that of ACT, Inc., established in 1959 and based in Iowa City, Iowa. The ACT tests tend to be used more often by colleges in the Midwest and less often by those on the East Coast, although the majority of institutions in the United States will accept either SAT or ACT scores. The current revision, termed the ACT Assessment, consists of four academic achievement tests, an interest inventory, and a questionnaire regarding student backgrounds and plans. It is administered on six national testing dates. The academic tests take 2 hours and 55 minutes to complete and are designed to assess academic ability in four areas: English, mathematics, reading, and science reasoning. There is also an optional 30-minute ACT Writing Test, an essay that is required by a number of institutions (ACT, Inc., 2005a).

The item content of the ACT Assessment is similar to that of the Iowa Tests of Educational Development, on which the ACT tests were originally based. For example, the ACT-Math consists of 60 items from pre-algebra, intermediate algebra, geometry, and trigonometry. The Science Reasoning test contains 40 items dealing with concepts from biology, physics, and chemistry. Results are reported on a standard score scale that ranges from 1 to 36 for each of the four academic tests and their seven subscales, along with a total composite score. The mean for college-bound students who take the ACT Assessment is approximately 21 on each of the four academic tests and the composite score. Standard deviations vary from 4.5 to 6.0. The *SEM* is approximately 2 for the academic tests and 1 for the composite score.

Essays are scored by two readers on a 1 to 6 scale and added to give a 2 to 12 score that is reported to the student along with readers' comments. A combined English and writing score is also reported using the 1 to 36 standard scale.

The 90-item UNIACT Interest Inventory is taken along with the ACT Assessment, and provides scores on six interest areas similar to Holland's (1997) hexagon and a method of plotting interests on the accompanying World-of-Work Map (ACT, Inc., 2000b). In addition to information sent to the college, ACT reports that are sent to both the high school and the student contain much information useful in academic and career planning. The reports include student plans, perceived educational needs, interest inventory scores, and rankings of the students' scores at the colleges to which the scores are being sent.

There are two preliminary ACT batteries useful for occupational and, especially, educational planning. The EXPLORE program taken by eighth and ninth graders consists of four academic achievement tests along with an interest inventory, educational plans, and background information. The PLAN Program for 10th-grade students consists of (a) four academic tests of 20 to 45 minutes each, yielding standard scores of 1 to 32 that are linked to junior/senior year ACT Assessment scores; (b) the UNIACT Interest Inventory; (c) a student Needs Assessment; (d) a high school grade/course information section; and (e) an educational/occupational plans section (ACT, Inc., 2005a).

ACT's ASSET Student Success System is administered in nearly 400 community and technical colleges to assess student skills with three 25 minute tests—Writing Skills, Numerical Skills, and Reading Skills. The program also collects information about students' educational backgrounds, their plans, and their needs. Additional tests have been constructed to assess skills in certain other academic areas (e.g. chemistry, geometry, college algebra; ACT, Inc., 2006a).

Validity of Scholastic Aptitude Tests

The ACT and the SAT are approximately equal in their ability to predict college grades. Thousands of studies have been conducted assessing the ability of these tests to predict grades, with the typical correlation ranging in the vicinity of .30 to .50 for freshman grade point averages (GPAs). Correlations tend to be higher at institutions with more heterogeneous freshman classes and lower among homogeneous student bodies, particularly at the very highly selective institutions with restricted ranges of student scores.

Most studies have found that high school grades are the best predictors of college GPAs but that scholastic aptitude tests are able to improve the prediction over high school GPAs or high school ranks alone (College Board, 2000). That scholastic aptitude test scores would add to the prediction of college success is not surprising. The particular high school GPA that a student obtains depends on a number of factors: the general competitiveness of the high school attended, the grading curve used in that high school, and the types of courses taken, as well as other personal factors. Thus, a high school GPA of 3.2 achieved by a particular student who has taken all college preparatory subjects in a school with a low grading curve and where the majority of classmates are college-bound represents a very different level of achievement than that obtained by a student from a less competitive high school who has taken a number of vocational or commercial courses. A national college admissions test represents a common task for all students and therefore can operate as a correction factor for the high school GPA. In addition, for the student with low grades but with substantially higher scholastic aptitude test scores than would be expected from those grades, the scores may suggest hitherto unrecognized academic potential. These scores may represent a "second chance" for such a student.

These tests are generally equally predictive for different racial groups. In those instances in which differences have been found, the group with the lower scores tends to obtain lower than predicted college GPAs rather than higher, as might be expected (Cleary, Kendrick, & Wesman, 1975).

Test scores tend to be greatly overemphasized by many parents and their college-bound students. Only at the most highly selective institutions are very high scores generally required, and even there, much other information goes into admissions decisions. Students with good high school grades can obtain admission to most colleges unless their test scores are extremely low.

When scholastic aptitude test scores are interpreted to students and their parents, the standard error should be taken into account. On the SAT-Critical Reading and SAT-Mathematical, the standard error is in the vicinity of 30, suggesting that two thirds of the time the student's true score will fall within 30 points in one direction or the other from the obtained score. For the ACT, with a standard error of approximately 2 points, two thirds of the time students' true scores could be expected to fall within 2 points on either side of their obtained ACT standard scores.

Academic Aptitude Test Scores and College Admission

Although the number of U.S. colleges and universities that require very high ACT or SAT scores is not large, almost all 4-year institutions claim to maintain some type of a selective admissions policy. This selectivity varies greatly. Some public institutions will take any student in the top half of his or her high school class or one who obtains a test score at least equivalent to that level. Others take only those in the top quarter, or in the top three quarters, or have other means of selection using formulas with high school rank or high school grades and SAT scores. A few private institutions admit perhaps only one in five applicants from an already very selective applicant pool. There are many other private colleges that, although maintaining that they are selective in their admissions, in fact will admit almost every high school graduate who applies, as will most public community colleges. The result is a great variation in the abilities of the average or typical student on various campuses.

It is definitely not true in the United States that a particular GPA earned at one institution is equivalent to that earned at another institution or that college degrees are equivalent from wherever they are obtained (Hood, 1968). Although some differences in levels of competition among colleges are recognized to at least a limited extent by the general public, and perhaps to a greater degree by those in higher education, the actual differences are far greater than all but the most sophisticated observers of American higher education imagine. Levels of competition vary so greatly among institutions that a student obtaining an honors GPA of 3.4 at one institution could easily fail out of a much more competitive institution.

These differences can be understood by examining the scholastic aptitude test scores in various institutions. Scholastic aptitude test scores of entering freshmen at particular institutions of several different types are shown in Table 6-1. This table includes ACT-English and College Board SAT Critical Reading scores as rough equivalents. It should be recognized that the equivalence between these two tests shown in this table was based on a large and relatively heterogeneous population but at a single institution. Populations at particular institutions of varying ability levels and with differing proportions of the two sexes may result in concordance tables that differ substantially from this table. The equivalent scores given in this table should be read as only rough equivalents and not as exact mathematical equivalents. The scores given for the different types of institutions represent a specific institution and are provided here as general examples and do not represent the typical or median institution of that type.

By comparing scores in Table 6-1, one can see, for example, that the median student at the Ivy League institution falls above the 90th percentile for students at the midwestern state university. At the same time, the median student at the midwestern university falls in the lower 5% for students at the Ivy League institution. Students at the midwestern university actually tend to score well above college-bound students nationally: The median student at the midwestern university falls at about the 75th percentile of the national college-bound population. The median student at the private liberal arts college included in Table 6-1 is practically never found in an Ivy League school and falls in the bottom quarter among students at the midwestern state university. The median student at the southern state college (an accredited institution) is found only in the lower 1%–2% of students at the midwestern state university, and very few students at this private liberal arts college score that low. The highest scoring student at the southern state college does not reach the mean at the midwestern state university, and only a handful of students at the Ivy League university obtain scores as low as the highest student at the southern state college. Thus, between the southern state college and the Ivy League institution there is virtually no overlap among the scores of their students.

In assisting college-bound students in their decision making about the institutions they might choose, counselors should consider these types of differences. Information regarding the levels of academic competition at particular institutions can be found in certain college guides, such as *Profiles of American Colleges* (Barrons Educational Series, 2004) or *The College Handbook* (College Board, 2005a). Anyone involved in college counseling should obtain a guide that contains information regarding high school ranks and test scores of students at different institutions. Armed with the knowledge that the standard deviation on an academic aptitude test at a given institution is likely to be in the vicinity of two thirds or three quarters that of the normative standard deviation of the instrument (4 or 5 points on the ACT Assessment or 60 to 75 points on the SAT) and with the mean score or the range of the middle 50% given in one of the college guides, a counselor can easily calculate a rough estimate of the point at which the student is likely to fall in regard to academic aptitude at that institution.

Combining this with knowledge of the student's achievement level in high school, it is possible to estimate the general level of competition that a student will find at a given institution. Combined with other information about the student, his or her chances of obtaining admission at that institution can also be estimated. A student might therefore be encouraged to apply to several different institutions, including one or two in which chances for admission and satisfactory performance are favorable. The following illustrates how counselors can use academic aptitude test information in their discussions of college choices.

Case Example

Jason is just beginning his senior year in high school, and he and his parents are having a conference with his guidance counselor. He has a 2.9 GPA in the academic program in his high school and received scores ranging from 18 to 22 for a composite score of 20 on the ACT battery that he took the previous spring. His parents want to talk about colleges and universities that he should investigate and his chances of being admitted to them. Included in their consideration is an Ivy League institution that their nephew attends.

TABLE 6-1

Percentiles of Students With Certain Academic Aptitude Test Scores (Verbal) in Different Types of Institutions

ACT English Standard Score	SAT-CR	ACT National Norms English 1999–2000	Ivy League University (SAT-CR)	A Midwest State University (ACT-E)	A Small Liberal Arts College (ACT-E)	A Southern State College (SAT-CR)
33	730	99	95	—	—	—
32	700	98	80	99	—	—
30	660	97	60	94	98	—
29	640	94	45	90	95	—
27	600	88	23	74	89	—
24	540	76	3	44	71	99
20	460	52	1	14	34	91
18	420	37	—	8	19	76
12	290	8	—	1	2	44
6	270	1	—	—	—	11
1	230	—	—	—	—	2

Note. Institutions shown were selected to show the great variation among them and are not meant to be representative of those types. SAT-CR = SAT Reasoning Test, Critical Reading Section; ACT-E = ACT–English.

The counselor reports to them that Jason's score on the ACT is about an average score for college-bound students in the United States. When he takes the SAT a few weeks hence, if he obtains comparable scores, they are likely to be in the 400s. She suggests that unless he were class valedictorian or a star athlete (which he is not), he has little chance of being admitted to a highly competitive institution. She tells them that because the state university admits any high school graduate who is in the top two fifths of his or her graduating class, and because Jason is at the 65th percentile, he would be admitted to the state university. He would, however, rank toward the bottom at that institution, both in terms of high school record and test scores, and could find it difficult to achieve more than barely passing grades.

Because Jason is undecided as to a career or a major, he is planning to enter a general liberal arts program and therefore has a wide range of institutions from which to choose. At some 4-year institutions, he would fall well above the mean and at others well below the mean. At the particular small college he is considering, he would be below the middle but still above the bottom third. His chances of success there would be better than at a number of other institutions that he and his parents have considered.

The level of competition a student is likely to meet if admitted should also be discussed. Although there are many, including parents, who feel that a student should attend the highest status institution to which he or she can be admitted, some evidence suggests that for many students this is not the wisest move. A 1969 study conducted by Werts and Watley indicated that, holding ability constant, those students who attended an institution at which they fell in the bottom portion of the students at that institution were less likely to go on and attend graduate or professional school than those students who had attended an institution at which they were closer to or above the middle of the distribution. This finding is supported by recent research on the "big-fish–little-pond effect," which indicates that gifted children who participate in regular classes report higher academic self-concepts than do those who are placed in gifted programs (Zeidner, 1999). This effect, in which students in highly competitive settings tend to report lower academic self-concepts, has been tested in a cross-cultural study of samples of 4,000 students in each of 26 countries (Marsh & Hau, 2003). Results consistent with this effect were found in all of the 26 samples. In essence, it may not always be desirable for students to pursue the most competitive programs for which they can gain admission.

When students transfer from college to college, much of the difference in the GPAs obtained at the new institutions can be accounted for by differing levels of competition. Students transferring from community colleges to more competitive 4-year institutions often experience a drop in grades known as "transfer shock." Students transferring from more competitive institutions to less competitive ones will, on the average, see their GPAs increase.

GRADUATE AND PROFESSIONAL SCHOOL ADMISSIONS TESTS

Graduate Record Examination (GRE)

The GREs are administered by ETS of Princeton, New Jersey. They consist of two separate types. The first is the GRE General Test, which consists of three portions: Verbal Reasoning (GRE-V), Quantitative Reasoning (GRE-Q), and Analytical Writing (GRE-W; Educational Testing Service, 2005a). The Verbal portion, two 40-minute sections, includes reading comprehension, analyzing written materials, and recognizing relationships between words and concepts. The Quantitative portion, two 40-minute sections, requires mathematical reasoning and interpreting graphs and diagrams and includes items dealing with arithmetic, algebra, and geometry. The Analytical Writing portion requires writing two 30-minute essays, one dealing with an issue and the other with an argument. The second type is the GRE Subject Tests, which are available in eight academic areas, such as physics, psychology, and literature in English.

Scores on the Verbal and Quantitative portions of the General test were formerly reported in standard scores, 200–800 with a mean of 500 and a standard deviation of 100. The scores were standardized on a group of college seniors who took the test in 1952, and scores were equated to this reference group in order that scores remain constant over time. They are now reported on a scale that runs from 110 to 150 (ETS, 2006a). The GRE General Test scores show high internal consistency reliabilities (.90 or above).

The Writing portion is similar to the writing tests now found on both the undergraduate admissions testing programs and those for most of the graduate and professional schools such as the Medical College Admission Test (MCAT) and the Graduate Management Admission Test (GMAT). In each testing program, the writing samples are sent over the Internet to two raters who score them on a 1–6 scale. If there is a discrepancy between the readers of more than 1 point, the samples are sent to a supervisory reader who determines the score. The two scores are added to yield a score in the 2–12 range that may be reported directly or converted to a standard score, or in the case of the GRE, the two scores on the Analytical Writing portion are averaged and reported on a 0– 6 scale in half-point increments. Administrations of the GRE General Test are scheduled on an individual basis at a large number of ETS-approved testing sites throughout the world, eliminating the requirement that the test be taken on national testing dates.

For a time, the GRE General Test used an adaptive format in which the examinee was presented with questions of average difficulty, after which the computer selected questions based on the difficulty level of the questions answered correctly and incorrectly. Each correct answer leads to a more difficult question, whereas a wrong answer leads to an easier one. Scores on the test are based both on the number of questions correctly answered and on the difficulty level of these questions (Sireci, 2004). This resulted in an efficient individualized test; however, item security became a problem because examinees, particularly in certain Asian countries, were memorizing questions and answers from previous test takers. Therefore ETS lengthened the test and returned it to its current format, with the paper-and-pencil version continued only in a few countries where computers are not available.

The GRE Subject Tests are still in paper-based format and are administered on three national testing dates. They are required less often by graduate institutions or by graduate departments than is the General Test. They last 2 hours and 50 minutes and have been developed by committees of faculty members in the appropriate academic departments working with the ETS staff. The results are also reported on a standard scale resembling that of the Aptitude Test with a mean of 500; however, the actual mean, range, and standard deviation of scores are different for each of the advanced tests. Certain of the advanced tests provide subscores for specific subject matter areas within the larger test, for example, a subscore on Experimental Psychology and one on Social Psychology within the Psychology Examination.

The GRE is used in selecting students for admission into graduate school and into specific graduate departments. Norms on the tests vary greatly among institutions and among specific departments. A physics department could require substantially higher scores on the Quantitative section than on the Verbal section, whereas requirements by an English department would be the opposite. An art department might require a portfolio and pay little attention to either. Because of these differences, use of GRE test scores to assist students in selecting institutions and departments in which they are likely to be admitted and are likely to be successful is difficult without knowledge of the norms in specific graduate institutions and departments.

Using the GRE scores to predict success in graduate school is particularly difficult for a number of reasons. There is likely to be the problem of restriction in range within particular departments, because GREs and undergraduate GPAs are the major criteria on which students are selected for graduate programs, thus eliminating low scores. In addition, graduate school GPAs may be highly restricted in range because grades of *A* and *B* are often the only grades given. For a typical department, however, GRE scores plus undergraduate GPAs still provide a better prediction of academic success than any other readily available variables (ETS, 1990; Jaeger, 1985; Kuncel & Hezlett, 2001).

Miller Analogies Test (MAT)

The MAT, published by the Psychological Corporation (1991, 1994), is a second test used for the selection of graduate students. The test consists of 120 complex analogy items drawn from the subject matter across a number of academic fields (100 items count and 20 are experimental). It is available in both paper-and-pencil and computer formats and can be taken in various Harcourt-approved centers around the country (Harcourt Educational Measurement, 2006). Although the test is administered with a 60-minute time limit, it is largely a power test, not a speed test. It includes items of considerable difficulty so that resulting scores are purported to differentiate reliably among people of superior intellect. It is available in a number of parallel forms, with reliabilities in the general magnitude of .90. In a meta-analysis study of the MAT (Kuncel, Hezlett, & Ones, 2004), the instrument was shown to be not only a valid predictor of academic variables such as graduate school grades and time taken to finish a graduate degree but also of vocational and career criteria. Familiarity with the kinds of items on this type of test can significantly affect scores, with substantial improvement resulting from studying practice items or from previous experience with an alternate form. As with the GRE, norms among graduate students in different institutions and different departments vary widely, and knowledge of normative data in relevant comparison groups (provided in the MAT manual) is a necessity if predictive information based on the scores is to have any value. The problems of predictive validity of graduate school success discussed for the GRE are also present for the MAT.

Professional School Tests

A number of aptitude tests have been developed by different professions for selection into their professional schools. In many cases, these tests are universally required for admission to such schools. Such tests include the MCAT (Association of American Medical Colleges, 2000), the Dental Admission Test (DAT; Division of Educational Measurements, Council on Dental Education, 1994), the Law School Admission Test (LSAT; Law School Admission Council, 2005), and the GMAT; ETS, 2004). These admission tests are typically developed and administered by one of the national testing programs such as ACT or ETS, and the cost to applicants can be quite expensive.

These tests usually include items similar to those found on scholastic aptitude tests, including measures of verbal and numerical ability. In addition, they usually contain subtests with items relevant to the particular profession. The LSAT includes sections that attempt to assess competence in analytical and logical reasoning. The GMAT, which is administered on demand in a computer-adaptive format only at test centers throughout the world, includes a quantitative and an analytical writing section. The DAT has a perceptual ability portion, and the MCAT includes scores in such areas as the physical and biological sciences as well as a writing sample. Scores on each of the tests are reported in very different types of standard scores with different means and standard deviations. For example, the MCAT yields standard scores ranging from 1 to15 with a mean of approximately 8 and a standard deviation of approximately 2.5. The LSAT now reports scores ranging from 120 to 180 with a mean of approximately 150 and a standard deviation of approximately 10. For the DAT, scores range from 1 to 30 with a mean of 15 and a standard deviation of 5. The GMAT, used by most graduate schools of business, reports subtest scores ranging from 0 to 60 with a mean of 30 and total scores similar to those of the GRE with a range of 200 to 800 and a mean of 500. The writing portion receives a score of 1 to 6.

ADMINISTERING AND INTERPRETING ACADEMIC APTITUDE TESTS

Test Anxiety

During aptitude and achievement tests administration, it is generally considered a good procedure to attempt, while building rapport, to reduce test anxiety (Zeidner, 1998). Small but significant negative relationships have been found between test anxiety and scores on these types of tests. This relationship, of course, does not necessarily mean that high levels of anxiety cause lower test scores. Often those who have done poorly on these types of tests in the past are likely to experience more anxiety. Some studies suggest that a moderate amount of test anxiety can actually benefit test scores, whereas a high level of anxiety may be detrimental. Individuals differ in the amount of anxiety that can be considered to be optimal for best test performance.

These results have been obtained when tests have been given under experimental conditions of high tension and of relaxed situations. For example, in an early study (French, 1962) on this topic, students took the test under normal conditions when the scores were to be reported to the institutions to which they applied and a second time on an equivalent form under instructions that the test results were to be used only for research purposes and not otherwise reported. The results showed essentially equal performance under both the anxious and relaxed conditions. The only difference was that certain students under the anxiety conditions attempted more of the mathematical items and therefore achieved slightly higher scores on that subtest than they did under the relaxed conditions. Apparently, under the relaxed conditions, they gave up a little earlier and therefore achieved slightly lower scores.

When test anxiety involves an excessive amount of worry and fear, clients may have difficulty thinking clearly or organizing their thoughts or experience mental blanking. Interventions that counselors can use include (a) emphasizing adequate preparation; (b) teaching cognitive-behavioral techniques such as challenging irrational beliefs, thought stopping; (c) using desensitization techniques; and (d) encouraging relaxation exercises (Goonan, 2004). In general, testing procedures that are well organized, that are smoothly run, and that reassure and encourage should help to reduce the anxiety felt by highly anxious test takers.

Coaching

The effect of coaching or practice on test scores is a controversial one that has received much attention and has been the subject of a number of studies. Obviously, practice or coaching that provides the answers to, for example, an individual IQ test such as the Stanford–Binet or Wechsler Intelligence Scale for Children would invalidate the results as an accurate assessment. However, completion of a high school course in mathematics that results in a higher score on a mathematics achievement test probably accurately reflects the student's knowledge of mathematics outside the testing situation. The distinction therefore must be made between broad training and specific training or coaching focused on specific test items.

Coaching has been particularly controversial because of the existence of commercial coaching programs designed to raise scores on admissions tests such as the CEEB's SAT, the GRE, or the MCAT. These coaching programs advertise and almost promise substantially better test performance for those who enroll in their programs. Many of the studies reported have substantial weaknesses that usually include the absence of a noncoached but equally highly motivated control group that is comparable with the coached group in all important ways, including performance on initial tests.

The CEEB has been particularly concerned for two reasons. First, if coaching could help students to improve their scores substantially, then the test results for all students would lose some validity. Second, the commercial coaching programs charge substantial fees and can represent a waste of money if coaching yields little improvement. A number of CEEB's studies investigating different types of coaching methods among different types of students indicate that coaching is unlikely to produce substantial gains on the SAT (Aiken, 2000; Powers & Rock, 1998). An ACT study showed that students' scores tend to increase on a second testing, most of which can be accounted for by the general development that has occurred as students take additional high school courses (Lanier, 1994).

A small amount of increase is perhaps due to a practice effect, that is, familiarity with the types of problems and the problem-solving skills required. As a result, most of the testing programs— the College Board, the ACT, and the various professional school testing programs—now provide considerable information about the tests, including booklets with a number of practice test items. Thus, all applicants have the opportunity to take practice tests and to become familiar with the types of items that appear. In addition to those provided by the testing programs, a number of test-familiarization books have been published, with practice examinations in all of these areas. Usually titled *How to Take the . . . Examination,* these books can be found in many bookstores. For certain tests such as the SAT, these materials are not limited to printed booklets but also include a variety of audiovisual and computer software materials as well as programs available on the Internet. A free, full-length SAT practice test is available at www.collegeboard.com. ACT sells a CD-ROM personalized test preparation program using real ACT tests (ACTivePrep), and the ETS sells GRE and GMAT CD-ROMs that contain two complete computer-administered practice tests and hundreds of practice test items (POWERPREP).

It should be remembered that although specific coaching provides little improvement in test performance over that achieved by a little familiarization and practice (and this is particularly true on the verbal portions of these tests), additional training in the form of course work is likely to result in improvement. In addition, a general review of the subject matter covered can substantially increase scores. For example, a student who has not taken any mathematics during the last 2 years in high school can improve scores on the Mathematics portion of the SAT by review of the courses in algebra and geometry that were taken earlier. A college senior who has not taken any mathematics in college since the freshman year can also improve his or her scores on the Quantitative portion of the GRE by a review of the mathematical and algebraic concepts learned in high school and as a college freshman. In addition to a review of basic skills in the area being tested, taking as many as four or five full-length practice tests with standard time limits, paying attention to item format, pacing and priority setting, can lead to a moderate score increase (Rubinstein, 2004).

Coaching for achievement tests has been generally shown to produce positive results but with increases averaging less than one fourth of a standard deviation. The best results are when the coaching occurs not just before a major assessment but over longer periods and when incorporated into regular classroom instruction (Crocker, 2005).

Counselors often receive questions from students, parents, and those involved in the selection and interpretation of such scores regarding the efficacy of coaching programs and other review procedures. They need to be cognizant of the effects of different types of training and other activities on test performance.

ACADEMIC ACHIEVEMENT TESTS

Hundreds of thousands of achievement tests are administered each year, primarily in educational institutions ranging from kindergarten through graduate and professional schools. Others are administered for licensing and certification in trades and professions, in medical specialties, or for the selection and promotion of postal workers.

Achievement tests differ from aptitude tests in that they attempt to assess learning that takes place under relatively standardized conditions or as a result of a controlled set of experiences. Aptitude tests are more typically used for prediction purposes and do not assume previous standardized learning experiences. Achievement tests are designed to measure what has already been learned or knowledge or skills that have been attained, whereas academic aptitude tests attempt to measure learning ability, although such ability is usually related to that which has been developed up to the time of testing. Achievement tests are usually evaluated on the basis of content validity, that is, the extent to which the test includes content similar to that which those tested are expected to have experienced. Aptitude tests are usually evaluated in terms of predictive validity, that is, the extent to which success in whatever it is the aptitude test attempts to measure can be predicted from the test results. The distinction between achievement and aptitude tests is not absolute, however. Some aptitude tests are based on some generally standardized prior experience, whereas some achievement tests are designed to measure some generalized educational experiences that are not especially uniform in nature (Anastasi & Urbina, 1997). For example, the ACT test serves as a scholastic aptitude test to predict success in college; however, its items represent subject matter areas taught in all high school curricula. The new SAT is now similar in this regard, a departure from the previous SAT that was designed to assess aptitude rather than achievement.

Achievement tests vary from the brief achievement test administered by a teacher to evaluate the learning that has taken place during a single lesson to the nationally available achievement test programs produced by the major commercial test publishers. These achievement test batteries are generally designed across a number of grade levels from kindergarten through the 12th grade. The test batteries provide profiles of scores in various academic skill areas. They tend to be based on the "three *Rs*" in the early grades and to measure information and knowledge in specific academic areas at the secondary school levels. The tests are generally carefully prepared in regard to content, with items written by teachers and consultants and examined by expert reviewers. The items are then subjected to analyses of item difficulty and item discrimination, with attempts made to eliminate gender and ethnic bias.

School Achievement Tests

The most commonly used national achievement test batteries include (a) the Iowa Tests of Basic Skills/Iowa Tests of Educational Development, (b) the Stanford Achievement Tests, (c) the Metropolitan Achievement Tests, and (d) the TerraNova Tests. Results are usually reported in a full range of derived scores, including scale scores, national and local percentile ranks, normal curve equivalents such as stanines, and grade equivalents. These four test series are briefly described as examples of such batteries.

Iowa Tests of Basic Skills/Iowa Tests of Educational Development

The Iowa Tests of Basic Skills (ITBS) form a battery of achievement tests covering kindergarten through Grade 8 (Hoover, Dunbar, & Frisbie, 2003a). They are considered to be some of the oldest and best of their type (Brookhart, 1998). The tests are designed to measure basic educational skills, including vocabulary, reading, language, and mathematics for the early grades, with the addition of social studies, science, and information utilization tests for the upper grades. Complete, Core, and Survey Batteries are available. The Complete Battery consists of 5 to 15 subtests depending upon the level, the Core consists of 3 to 12. The Survey Battery contains three 30-minute tests in reading, language, and math. They were normed on large and well-documented samples and were jointly standardized with the IQ-type Cognitive Abilities Test (Hoover, Dunbar, & Frisbie, 2003b).

The Iowa Tests of Educational Development (ITED) are designed for use at the high school level (Forsyth, Ansley, Feldt, & Alnot, 2001). There are six tests in the Core Battery (Vocabulary, Reading Comprehension, Revising Written Materials, Spelling, Math Concepts and Problem Solving, and Computation) and three additional tests in the Complete Battery (Analysis of Social Science Materials, Analysis of Science Materials, and Sources of Information). The ITED was standardized on a national sample stratified by geographic region; district enrollment; socioeconomic status; and public, private, and Catholic schools.

Results are reported in a variety of derived scores, including standard scores ($M = 15$, $SD = 5$). Studies have shown the ITED to be good predictors of the ACT (.85–.89), the SAT (.71–.83), and even college GPA (.24–.50). Predicted ranges are reported for both the ACT composite (within a 5-point range) and SAT (within a 100-point range). Results can therefore be used in counseling for making decisions about high school programs and college planning. Both of the Iowa test batteries have been produced in two equivalent forms—Form A and a secure Form B that is only available by special arrangement. There are also Braille and large-type editions. Different sets of ITBS and ITED interpretive materials are published for counselors and school personnel to use, and messages and interpretative guides for parents and students are provided (Bugbee, 2005).

Iowa Early Learning Inventory (IELI)

The IELI is an observational instrument to be completed by kindergarten or early first-grade teachers to measure six behavioral areas related to school learning. It is intended to be administered in conjunction with an achievement measure such as the ITBS (Lukin, 2005).

Stanford Achievement Test

The Stanford Achievement Test Series, 10th Edition (Stanford 10) is a series of achievement tests from kindergarten through Grade 12, with separate tests for each of the 13 levels that do not repeat item content except for Grades 11 and 12 (Harcourt Educational Measurement, 2003). Each test battery contains a number of different subtests, with the Stanford Early School Achievement Tests (SESAT) for kindergarten and the first grade and the Tests of Academic Skills (TASK) for Grades 9–12. The typical battery is composed of 8–10 untimed subtests yielding total scores in six or seven subject areas. They contain multiple-choice, open-ended, and writing-prompts items. Easy and difficult items are mixed to prevent students from feeling frustrated and giving up as they reach increasingly difficult items (Carney, 2005). It was standardized in combination with the Otis–Lennon School Ability Test, 7th Edition. The Stanford 10 is available in four equivalent forms, two of which are secure, along with Spanish (Aprenda 3), Braille, and large-type editions.

Metropolitan Achievement Tests

The Metropolitan test was first published in the 1930s and has undergone a number of revisions since then. Examination of subject matter textbooks, curricula, and educational objectives and trends has gone into the item development for each revision. The METROPOLITAN8 (MAT8) is the 8th edition of the Metropolitan Achievement Tests, which provides 13 overlapping batteries from kindergarten through Grade 12 (Harwell, 2005). The battery consists of a varying number of subtests in basic skills areas beginning with reading, mathematics, and language to which science and social studies are added in the early primary grades and research skills and thinking skills are added in the remaining grades, yielding a total of seven achievement areas. Open-ended versions are available for Reading and Math, and there is a separate test for Writing. It too was standardized along with the Otis-Lennon, 7th Edition. Predicted scores for both the PLAN Program and the PSAT in Grades 9 and 10 and ACT and SAT scores for Grades 11 and 12 are available using MAT8 results.

TerraNova Tests

TerraNova is the name of a family of assessments based on versions of what would have been the sixth edition of the California Achievement Test. There are three different batteries available, the Basic, the Complete, and the Survey that vary according to length, subjects tested, and item-task format (Cizek, 2005). They assess academic achievement from kindergarten through Grade 12 (K–12) with two forms and a Spanish edition (referred to as SUPERA). The test series include assessments of reading/language arts, mathematics, science, and social studies for all school grades using both multiple-choice and student-constructed response items. They are designed to be customized to meet different states' No Child Left Behind (NCLB) requirements. Items have been designed to represent diverse cultures, with topics and content to represent national standards. There are 13 levels (K–12), and the battery was standardized along with the Test of Cognitive Skills (CTB/McGraw-Hill, 2001).

All of these national batteries of achievement tests are highly reliable, with internal consistency reliabilities for individual tests ranging from .80 to .90 or above for appropriate populations. Composite scores based on the complete batteries produce internal consistency reliabilities well above .90. The item pools have been administered to large samples, and sophisticated item analyses to detect gender and cultural biases are used. They have been standardized on very large samples carefully stratified to mirror the total U.S. student population. In order to establish local validity, of course, the test content must be examined to determine whether it mirrors the curricula and goals of the particular school or district.

The procedures that the authors and publishers of each of the sets of tests have established for ensuring content validity are thorough and detailed. An example of the extent of test development procedures is illustrated in Figure 6-1 for the ITED (Forsyth, Ansley, Feldt, & Alnot, 2003). After reviewing local, state, and national guidelines for curriculum (an ongoing activity), test items were written, examined, and edited. The resulting 5,000 items were then tried out on samples of 100,000 Iowa students in 350 school systems. After being analyzed for difficulty, discrimination, readability, and fairness, the items were again tried out on a national sample of 10,000 students. After a further review two forms (A and B) were standardized and published for administration to students in Grades 9 to 12.

Although the results of these test batteries are often grossly misinterpreted by different publics, considerable pains have been taken to provide the results in understandable language and formats. The test publishers market a wide variety of support and interpretative materials for use with teachers, counselors, parents, and students.

Most students take standardized achievement tests, which are used for a variety of purposes, at regular intervals during their first 12 years of schooling. They are used in a diagnostic way to identify the strengths and weaknesses of specific skills and achievements in individual students. As a result of such diagnoses, students can be selected for specific types of instruction, either remedial or advanced in nature. For this reason, the tests are often used as a part of the regular guidance and counseling program in an institution. Counselors thus become involved in interpreting the results to the students themselves, to their parents, and to teachers and other professionals (Ekstrom et al., 2004; Thorn & Mulvenon, 2002).

High-Stakes Testing

Achievement tests are also used (and often misused) in attempts to evaluate the quality of the curricula and instruction within courses, programs, schools, or school systems. Large-scale assessments are designed to serve a variety of purposes, including acting as a barometer of the effects of efforts to improve education as a part of the educational reform movement (Plake, 2002). The tests can provide information regarding what has been actually taught in a course or curriculum, especially in regard to educational goals. They can also be used to assess change in performance over time within a school or school district or to compare the achievement of schools in a district or with national norms.

In 1969, the National Assessment of Educational Progress (NAEP) was established to report student performance in various subjects in Grades 4, 8, and 12. Nationally representative samples

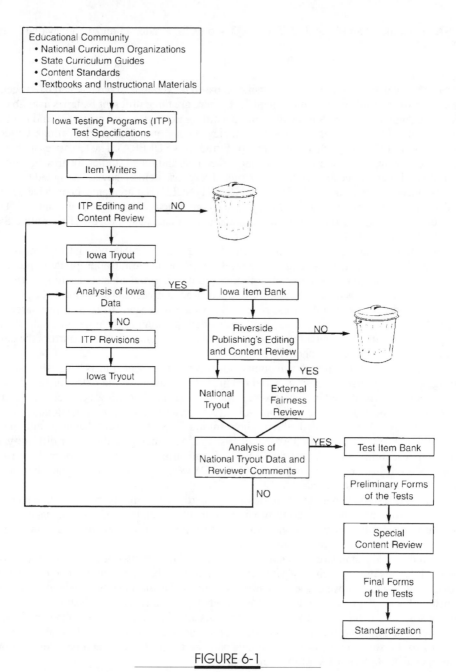

FIGURE 6-1

Steps in Development of the Iowa Tests of Educational Development (PDFC)

of students are tested to yield reports that became known as the "Nation's Report Cards," summarizing what students know and can do in different subjects and different grades. In 1990, NAEP initiated a process of defining student achievement levels as Below-Basic, Basic, Proficient, or Advanced (Wise, 2004). Percentages of students who fall in different achievement levels on a state's assessments can be compared with national and other states' data. Particular attention is placed on the percentages of students who reach the Proficient level.

Although the public is asking for accountability in education, which usually involves achievement test results, there are many important factors and complex issues, such as the academic backgrounds of the students and the goals of the educational programs, that make such comparisons difficult and frequently invalid. The complexity of such accountability is often not well understood, but counselors who better understand the effects of ability, socioeconomic status, and ethnic backgrounds should strive to prevent the misuse of achievement testing.

In high-stakes testing, it is necessary to be especially wary if there is a suspicion that cultural characteristics affect the validity of the scores and to understand the possible limitations of typical test norms for such students (Frisby, 1998; Scheuneman & Oakland, 1998). As a resource, the U.S. Department of Education, Office of Civil Rights (2000) has issued a document of principles and warnings regarding the high-stakes testing of students with disabilities or limited English proficiency.

These test batteries have traditionally been used to assess the academic strengths and weaknesses of individual students for use by teachers, parents, and counselors. Now, however, they are also found in mandatory statewide programs of "high-stakes" testing required by Federal legislation in the NCLB. States are required to implement reading/language arts and mathematics assessments annually and science at least once in Grades 3–8 and at least once during Grades 10–12, with serious consequences for schools whose students do poorly (Bourque, 2005). They are used to assess student achievement to determine whether a student is promoted or graduates and to reward or penalize teachers, schools, or school systems. Some states make use of tests specifically developed for particular grades in those states, whereas others adapt one of these batteries for this purpose. California and Tennessee add a few items to the Stanford 10 to fit their specific curriculum standards. New York City customizes the TerraNova for certain grades, whereas Philadelphia makes use of the unmodified ITBS. All juniors in Illinois and Colorado take an exam that includes the ACT Assessment along with several state-designed tests. In Maine, the SAT is administered to all juniors and the PSAT to all sophomores, components of the statewide assessment program that were opposed by most of the state's school counselors.

Two national organizations, the American Educational Research Association (AERA; 2000) and the American Psychological Association (2005a) have issued documents dealing with this subject: "AERA Position Statement Concerning High-Stakes Testing in Pre K–12 Education" and the American Psychological Association's "Appropriate Use of High Stakes Testing in Our Nation's Schools." These documents emphasize the need for test content to be aligned with the curriculum, for test results to be validated for their intended use, and for accommodations made for students with disabilities or from non-English-speaking backgrounds (Plake, 2002).

High-stakes testing programs have been widely criticized for possessing arbitrary standards, penalizing schools with students from diverse backgrounds or having diverse learning skills, and turning schools into test-preparation courses (Sternberg, 2004b). Also schools under pressure may be encouraged to cheat by teaching to the test or excluding certain students from testing. Nevertheless, in addition to improving the diagnosis of individual students' strengths and weaknesses and improving selection and placement for future educational and employment opportunities, the preponderance of research evidence indicates that standardized testing also significantly improves student achievement (Phelps, 2005b).

School counselors, who typically have the responsibility of coordinating the administration of these test batteries, need to be aware of the anxiety and stress levels of many of the students as they approach the tests. With the increased importance of high-stakes testing felt by teachers, school administrators, and parents, increased stress is transmitted to the students, which has led to difficulty sleeping, to becoming sick, to vomiting before or during the test, and even to such extremes as attempting to break bones in the hand or fingers to get out of taking the tests (Myers, Villalba, & Sweeney, 2005). Counselors can make use of various stress reduction and relaxation techniques to help reduce such detrimental anxieties as well as help students appropriately prepare for the tests, as mentioned earlier.

College-Level Achievement Tests

Several college-level testing programs have been created as a basis for awarding college credit other than by enrolling in college courses. These programs include the College-Level Examination Program (CLEP; College Board, 2004) and the Advanced Placement (AP) program (College Board, 2006b) administered by the CEEB.

The CLEP contains (a) general examinations that assess college-level achievement in five basic liberal arts areas usually covered during the first 2 undergraduate years and (b) 35 multiple-choice subject examinations, each taking 90 minutes to complete, covering a wide range of popular introductory college-level courses. By achieving a satisfactory score (typically 50 on a 20- to 80-point scale) students can, subject to college policy, receive 3 to 12 credits toward their degree (College Board, 2004). The examinations are administered on a computer, and results are immediately available. There is usually a test center charge in addition to the cost of the examination.

The AP program provides materials and examinations for college-level courses to be offered in secondary schools for which high school students may gain college credit or obtain advanced placement in college courses (College Board, 2002, 2006b). Once a program for a few select high school students, it now reaches over a million students, and a majority of American high schools now participate. Passing a number of AP examinations can save substantial tuition fees once in college, although it appears that for many, a more important reason for participation in the AP program is to impress college admissions offices (T. Lewin, 2006). The examinations, for which there is a fee, are 3 hours in length and contain both multiple-choice and either essay or problem items. The AP provides 35 different examinations in 19 different academic fields. AP examinations are scored on a 1–5 basis, with colleges typically giving credit for a 3 or better but with some of the choosier ones now requiring a 4 or 5.

Both ACT and ETS have developed instruments to assess the proficiency in English of individuals who are not native English speakers. ACT has constructed a computer-adaptive, multiple-choice testing program called COMPASS/ESL (ACT, Inc., 2006b) that offers diagnostic and placement testing in mathematics, reading, and writing and placement testing for English as a second language (ESL). The ESL portion consists of three modules—Reading, Listening, and Grammar/Usage—each of which yields a score that classifies students into one of four proficiency levels for course placement.

The ETS's Test of English as a Foreign Language (TOEFL) has been administered in its paper-and-pencil version since the mid-1960s to international students around the world who have applied for admission to North American colleges and universities. The current TOEFL iBT (Internet-based testing) represents the latest advance in computer-administered testing. All the four English skills necessary for success in American institutions—reading, writing, listening, and speaking—are assessed over the Internet. The test consists of four sections: Listening, Speaking, Reading, and a Written Essay. For the Listening and Speaking sections, examinees read some text, listen to a brief lecture, and then respond to questions. They wear a headphone and speak into a microphone, and their speech is digitally recorded and transmitted to a scoring network where humans score the responses. The scores on each section are converted to a 0–30 scale, yielding a Total Score of 0–120 (ETS, 2005b). It is administered at technology and university centers throughout the world. Tutorials and practice exercises are available on a CD-ROM or can be downloaded from the TOEFL Web site. Students applying to professional and graduate schools from foreign countries are usually required to obtain certain minimum scores on the TOEFL.

Adult Achievement Tests

Several test batteries have been created to assess the general achievement of adults. These test batteries include the Tests of Adult Basic Education 9/10 (TABE 9/10), the Adult Basic Learning Examination (ABLE), and the Basic Achievement Skills Inventory (BASI). The TABE are designed to assess the basic skills that adults need to live and work (CTB/McGraw-Hill, 2003). There are five levels, with two parallel forms and a Spanish edition, representing difficulty levels ranging from less than a first-grade level to college level. Reading, mathematics, and language skills are assessed. A locator test of 25 vocabulary words and 25 mathematical items yields scores that indicate the appropriate level to use. Although scores are based on adult norms, grade equivalents to California Achievement Test grade levels are reported along with estimated scores on the Tests of General Education Development, or GED (pre-2002 battery), which are taken by candidates for high school equivalency diplomas.

The ABLE, 2nd Edition (Karlsen & Gardner, 1986) provides assessment of adult learning in vocabulary, reading comprehension, spelling, language, number operations, and problem solving. All tests are untimed and may be self-scored. A Spanish edition is available. This battery is often used in adult education programs.

The BASI is designed for use with students and adults. It includes six subtests assessing language, reading, and mathematics skills. It is published in two equivalent forms for four age levels (Bardos, 2004).

Individual Achievement Tests

There are several academic achievement tests administered on an individual basis to obtain diagnostic information about such skills as reading, mathematics, and spelling. These tests include the Wide Range Achievement Test, Fourth Edition (WRAT4; Wilkinson & Robertson, 2005), the Kaufman Test of Educational Achievement–Normative Update (K-TEA-II; Kaufman & Kaufman, 2003), and the Wechsler Individual Achievement Test–2nd Edition (WIAT-II; Wechsler, 2001). All provide norms based on national samples ages 6 through adult. The WRAT4 has two equivalent forms and a large-print form. The K-TEA-II has a brief screening form and provides an error analysis form for identifying remediation needs for writing Individual Educational Programs. The WIAT-II contains nine achievement subtests (e.g., listening comprehension, reading comprehension, mathematics reasoning) and is linked to the Wechsler Adult Intelligence Scale–III, the Wechsler Intelligence Scale for Children–III, and the Wechsler Preschool and Primary Scale of Intelligence–Revised (Doll, 2003).

STUDY HABITS INVENTORIES

Counselors in high schools and colleges often work with students who are having difficulties with their course work or are not achieving academically up to their potential. In working with such students, counselors find that a study habits inventory is often useful for several reasons: first, to allow students to understand how adequate their study habits are as compared with those of other students; second, as a teaching tool, because the items on such inventories have useful instructional value; and third, to point out particular weaknesses, which is useful in discussing specific activities for improvement. In addition to their diagnostic purposes, these inventories also act as structured exercises that can help teach good study techniques and point out ineffective attitudes and behaviors. Several of the achievement test batteries used at the high school level, such as the California or Metropolitan achievement batteries, contain subtests that assess study skills.

The Study Attitudes and Methods Survey (SAMS) was developed to assess noncognitive factors associated with success in schools (Michael, Michael, & Zimmerman, 1988). The 148-item inventory provides scores for six factor dimensions: Academic Interest, Academic Drive, Study Methods, Study Anxiety, Manipulation, and Alienation Toward Authority. The survey, which takes approximately 30 minutes to complete, has available both high school and college norms.

The College Student Inventory of the Noel-Levitz Retention Management System is designed to identify academic and affective factors related to student attrition (Noel-Levitz, 2006). It contains 17 scales such as Study Habits, Intellectual Interests, Attitude Toward Educators, and Math and Science Confidence. Form A has 194 items, and Form B has 100 items. It is typically administered to entering college students at orientation and yields scores that can alert advisers, instructors, and student service providers to potential problems that a student might face.

The Learning and Study Strategies Inventory (LASSI) is the most widely used learning inventory on college campuses (B. Murray, 1998). The 77-item inventory contains 10 seven- or eight-item scales, 5 of them assessing personal factors related to academic achievement (Attitudes, Motivation, Time Management, Anxiety, and Concentration) and 5 cognitive factors (Information Processing, Selecting Main Ideas, Study Aids, Self Testing, and Test Strategies; Weinstein, Palmer, & Schulte, 1987, 1997). The inventory is available in both secondary school and college forms, and alpha reliabilities are reported in the .7 to .8 range (Weinstein, 1987). The LASSI is also available in a computer-administered and computer-scored format.

Knowledge that individuals prefer different types of learning styles and, in fact, often learn more effectively when the instructional technique matches their preferred learning style has led to the development of inventories designed to assess such individual learning styles. There are four such inventories, all titled Learning Style Inventory (Canfield & Canfield, 1988; R. Dunn, Dunn, & Price, 1987; Kolb, 1985; Renzulli & Smith, 1978). They are designed to help individuals assess their preferred methods of learning and to identify differences among individual learning styles and corresponding learning environments. This information can then be used to provide more individualized instructional methods. These inventories typically yield scores on three or four dimensions of learning styles or modes, such as need for structure, active experimenting, or abstract conceptualizing. Robert Sternberg proposed a theory of 13 thinking styles that he termed *mental self-government*. He constructed the Thinking Styles Inventory to assess them (Zhang & Sternberg,

2001). Because there are significant differences in the types of learning styles assessed by these instruments, the particular purpose for which the inventory is to be administered should be evaluated so that the inventory that best meets that purpose can be selected.

COGNITIVE DEVELOPMENTAL THEORIES

In addition to the learning of substantive knowledge that takes place in school, college, work, and daily life, other types of cognitive development, such as rationality, intellectual tolerance, and intellectual integrity, are now beginning to be assessed as well. One of these areas is ethical development as conceptualized by Kohlberg (1969, 1971), building on the structuralist view articulated by Piaget (1965). Kohlberg's theory holds that moral values are first external, then conventional in upholding and maintaining the social order, and at the highest levels maintained through individually held principles. Rest (1979; Rest, Narvaez, Thoma, & Bebeau, 1999) developed a paper-and-pencil instrument, called the Defining Issues Test, using Kohlberg's hypothetical moral dilemmas to assess this type of cognitive development.

Based in part on the work of both Piaget and Kohlberg, Perry (1970) developed a cognitive developmental scheme of positions of intellectual development that take place during adolescent and adult years. Perry's theory is composed of nine positions representing a continuum of development that can be clustered into four general categories: dualism, multiplicity, relativism, and commitment in relativism. Assessing cognitive development on Perry's scheme has been difficult, although five different measures have been constructed that attempt to place individuals along these positions. Three of these (Baxter-Magolda, 1992; King & Kitchener, 1994; Moore, 1988) require free responses that must be classified using trained raters—thus making for high costs in terms of money and convenience. Two inventories that make use of objective-style responses to assess cognitive development are the Scale of Intellectual Development (Erwin, 1983) and the Parker Cognitive Development Inventory (J. Parker & Hood, 1997). Although these inventories are in a form that could be used by counselors, more validity studies and probable revisions need to be undertaken before they will be ready for use by counselors with individual clients.

Stages of cognitive development represent important concepts for counselors to explore, because these stages influence many of the decisions that clients make and the processes by which they arrive at these decisions. These concepts can provide an understanding of why one client seeks only one "right" answer to a problem whereas another is willing to explore a number of alternatives.

SUMMARY

1. Almost all counselors can expect to be consulted about scholastic aptitude tests, even if they work in settings where they seldom make use of them.
2. Test results on the College Board, National Merit, and ACT college admissions tests have often been misinterpreted, even by those with some understanding of their standard score distributions.
3. Scholastic aptitude tests contribute to academic selection and placement by identifying unrecognized academic potential and by acting as a correction factor for high school grades resulting from differing levels of competition.
4. There are great differences in the distribution of students in regard to academic aptitude among the different institutions of higher education in the United States. These differences can greatly affect both the chances for admission and the chances for success at specific institutions.
5. Academic aptitude tests required for admission to graduate and professional programs typically have similar verbal and quantitative sections but otherwise vary considerably in subjects that are assessed and in the types of standard scores with which they report results.
6. Although some practice and familiarity with the types of problems and skills required on academic aptitude tests may make slight improvements in scores, extensive coaching has not been shown to produce substantial gains.
7. Academic achievement batteries are administered in virtually all primary and secondary schools to provide useful diagnostic information regarding the strengths and weaknesses of specific skills and achievements of students. The results are increasingly used and mis-

used in high-stakes testing and to evaluate the quality of instruction within classes, schools, and school systems.

8. Cognitive developmental theories can provide useful concepts in working with adolescent and postadolescent clients, but instruments to assess these stages need considerable additional refinement to be useful to most counselors.

SECTION
III

CAREER AND LIFE PLANNING ASSESSMENT

7

Measures of Career Choice and Development

Careers play a predominant role in the lives of most people. Counselors help clients with the process of making educational and career choices and adapting to the challenges inherent in career development. To help clients with this process, counselors must assess the clients' readiness for these activities as a first step in a comprehensive career counseling program. Fostering a client's readiness for career decision making has been described as "the cornerstone of effective career counseling" (Levinson, Ohler, Caswell, & Kiewra, 1998, p. 476).

Measures that focus on the *process* of career choice and development are discussed in this chapter. These measures, which evaluate a client's readiness to choose and pursue a successful and satisfying career path, encompass both attitudinal and cognitive factors (Lent, Brown, & Hackett, 1994; Super & Thompson, 1979; Thompson, Lindeman, Super, Jordaan, & Myers, 1981). Factors that pertain to the *content* of career choice and development, such as work values, career interests, special abilities, and occupational characteristics, are considered in subsequent chapters.

The measures of career choice and development discussed in this chapter are important in determining appropriate counseling interventions for clients (Sampson, Peterson, Reardon, & Lenz, 2000). Clients with low levels of readiness for career planning profit from interventions designed to improve the process of career planning, which include issues such as increasing self-confidence, clarifying outcome expectations, reducing perceived barriers, and enhancing social support (Lent et al., 1994). Such clients are more likely to need individual or long-term group counseling. Clients with high levels of readiness benefit more from interventions focused on the content of career planning, such as helping clients to identify occupations that match their interests (Toman & Savickas, 1997). These clients can often be helped by means of brief staff-assisted and self-help services such as workshops, computer-based career planning programs, and occupational information.

ATTITUDES TOWARD CAREER PLANNING

Attitudinal factors involved in career planning include both career beliefs and career concerns. Career beliefs refer to the client's assumptions regarding career choice and development, for example, the belief that there is one "right" career choice for each individual or that people will not be able to change their careers as they progress through life. Career concerns include difficulties in decision making and in resolving developmental tasks, such as choosing a major or career or making satisfactory progress in one's work. Career concerns involve both personal and environmental factors.

Measures of Career Beliefs

The instruments described in this section have been influenced by theory and research in the field of cognitive psychology, which maintains that an individual's actions are based on how he or she thinks about an issue or situation. By examining their thinking in regard to career choice and development, clients should be in a better position to understand and modify their behaviors.

Career Beliefs Inventory (CBI)
The CBI identifies beliefs that may block career goals (Krumboltz, 1991). It contains 96 items answered on a Likert scale (*strongly agree* to *strongly disagree*) that provide the basis for scores on 25 scales, such as Openness, Control, and Taking Risks. The beliefs are not considered to be "good" or "bad" by themselves; however, individuals frequently possess assumptions about themselves and their careers that may interfere with their career planning. Low scores indicate career beliefs that may be problematic depending on the individual's situation.

The CBI should be used early in the counseling process to expose questionable attitudes and assumptions related to career planning that might not otherwise be addressed. The counselor can then help the client to test the accuracy of these beliefs in his or her particular situation. Mitchell and Krumboltz (1987) found that focusing on the career beliefs of undecided clients proved to be more effective than teaching decision-making skills for stimulating career exploration and reducing anxiety.

The CBI provides unique information for career counseling not available by means of traditional interest and aptitude measures (Naylor & Krumboltz, 1994). As such, it can provide valuable information for discussion purposes, but it should not be used as a basis for decision making because of its limited psychometric properties. The CBI scales, most of which contain four items or fewer, yield relatively low internal consistency coefficients and test–retest reliabilities. In regard to validity, Krumboltz (1991) found that the CBI scores correlated with career satisfaction; however, the correlations were relatively low. Despite its limitations as a measurement tool, M. E. Hall and Rayman (2002) concluded that the CBI has "great promise as a career-counseling tool" (p. 321) when used as an interview or discussion aid. They point out that it can be used effectively with groups as well as individuals, that it can be used to discuss a client's strengths as well as problems, and that the instrument is accompanied by a large amount of "user-friendly" materials that can be helpful in understanding the impact of career beliefs on career decision making.

The following case is discussed in the CBI manual (Krumboltz, 1991, p. 10).

Case Example

Ted, a college student, disliked his college major (premed) but did not believe that he had any other options. Ted obtained a low score on Scale 12, Approval of Others, which indicated that approval of his career plans from someone else was very important to him. When the counselor asked Ted about the possible meaning of this score, he said that he wanted to please his father, who wanted him to become a physician. The counselor asked him to discuss this matter with his father, which Ted did despite fears that it was a hopeless matter. In so doing, he learned that his father's actual goal was to be supportive, not demanding, at which point Ted felt free to change his major from premed to art. Ted's desire to enter art had been blocked by his belief that his father would "simply die" if he did not fulfill the ambitions he had for him, a belief that was at the root of his difficulties. Use of the CBI helped to expose his thinking on this matter, which was then addressed in counseling by encouraging him to gather further evidence to test the accuracy of his thinking.

Career Thoughts Inventory (CTI)
The CTI, which is based on cognitive information processing (CIP) theory, assesses dysfunctional thinking in career problem solving and decision making for adults, college students, and high school students (Sampson, Peterson, Lenz, Reardon, & Saunders, 1996). It includes 48 items designed to measure misperceptions in eight content areas related to career choice and development, such as self-knowledge, occupational knowledge, and communication. It provides a total score and scores on three scales: Decision-Making Confusion, Commitment Anxiety, and External Conflict. It can be easily administered and scored in a relatively short period of time. Local norms are recommended in addition to those provided in the manual.

Counselors are urged to discuss high scores on any of the scales or individual items with clients. Counselors help clients to reframe negative thoughts regarding the career process into positive thoughts that are true for them. For example, clients who mark *agree* or *strongly agree* to the item "no field of study or occupation interests me" could be encouraged by their counselors to examine extracurricular or leisure-time activities to help identify interests. They could also be encouraged to broaden their life experiences as a means of clarifying and developing their interests.

According to Pickering (1998), the CTI is "a well designed, theoretically based, reliable and valid measure of dysfunctional career thoughts" (p. 6) that can be used effectively with career planning clients. Counselors should become well acquainted with both CIP theory and the CTI materials (especially the *Workbook* and *Professional Manual*) to gain the greatest benefit from this combined assessment and treatment approach to career planning (Feller & Daly, 2002).

Measures of Career Concerns for Students

As suggested by career development theory, the career concerns of students differ from those of adults. The inventories of career concerns discussed below focus on the decision-making process of high school and traditional-age college students.

All of the measures discussed in this section contain scales that assess the degree to which clients may be encountering difficulty in choosing a career. Clients who score high on scales of indecision may be in the precontemplation or contemplation stage of change (Prochaska et al., 1992); that is, they may not be prepared or ready to make a career choice. They may lack the self-confidence, the autonomy, or the maturity to make a decision. Instead of administering interest inventories or ability tests to these individuals to help them make a decision, the counselor should explore further with them factors that underlie their indecision or, in some cases, indecisiveness (Osipow, 1999).

Four measures of career decision-making difficulties are discussed below. Two of these measures—My Vocational Situation (MVS) and the Career Decision Scale (CDS)—were among the first instruments to formally assess career decision problems. The MVS is frequently used as a screening inventory to detect career planning concerns that need to be addressed in counseling. The CDS has been widely used as an outcome instrument, often as a pre–post measure in evaluating counseling interventions. The Career Factors Inventory (CFI) and the Career Decision-Making Difficulties Questionnaire (CDDQ) are newer "second or third generation" (Osipow, 1999, p. 150) measures of career decision that are multidimensional in nature. Research supports the utility of both of these two new instruments for clarifying factors associated with a student's indecision (Dickinson & Tokar, 2004; Kleiman et al., 2004).

My Vocational Situation (MVS)

The authors of this inventory attributed difficulties in decision making to three main factors: (a) problems of vocational identity, (b) lack of information about careers, and (c) environmental or personal obstacles (Holland, Daiger, & Power, 1980). The MVS includes scales to measure clients' concerns in each of these areas

The first scale on the MVS, the Vocational Identity scale, contains 18 items related to career choice uncertainty that must be answered *true* or *false*. *True* responses suggest problems with one's vocational identity. Normative data indicate that high school students mark about seven *true* answers on the average, whereas college students usually mark about two or three *true* responses. Individuals with a large number of *true* responses compared with those of their age group may profit from career workshops, personal counseling, or additional work experiences.

Each of the two remaining scales, Occupational Information (OI) and Barriers (B), consists of one question with four parts. The OI scale provides data concerning the client's need for occupational information (e.g., how to obtain training or employment in an occupation), whereas the B scale points out barriers (e.g., lack of needed abilities or family support) that may be impeding career development. These scales can be used as checklists to suggest specific steps that counselors can take to assist their clients in the career planning process.

Because of its brevity, clients can easily complete the MVS before the first counseling interview, in the same manner as other screening inventories described in chapter 4. Research indicates that the meaning of the scores on the MVS may differ somewhat based on gender and race (Toporek & Pope-Davis, 2001). For this reason, MVS results can best be used at the item level as a stimulus for further discussion to determine their significance for the client, rather than as a means of identifying or diagnosing the nature of an individual's vocational problems.

Career Decision Scale (CDS)

The CDS was developed by Samuel Osipow and his colleagues to identify the antecedents of career indecision (Osipow, 1987). It includes two scales: a 2-item Certainty scale and a 16-item Indecision scale. The 16 items on the Indecision scale represent 16 reasons for career indecision based on interview experiences with clients. For each item, clients indicate on a 4-point scale to what extent the item accurately describes their situation.

The target population for the CDS includes high school and college students in the process of deciding on a career. Because of its brevity, the CDS can be quickly administered (about 10 minutes) and scored (2 minutes). The manual provides normative data for high school students, college students, and continuing education students.

For counseling purposes, the items from the CDS can be used to explore possible causes of a client's indecision. Despite relatively low test–retest reliabilities, results from individual items can be helpful in suggesting hypotheses that can be explored in counseling. It has been used effectively in a wide variety of cultural settings (Osipow & Winer, 1996). Although it has some shortcomings, principally in clarifying the meaning of its scores, it has been praised for its ease of use, its applicability in counseling and research, and its extensive research support (Levinson et al., 1998; Savickas, 2000). Kelly (2002a) found that its coverage of different types of career planning problems was somewhat limited compared with other instruments. He concluded that it probably functioned better as a research or outcome instrument to assess the effectiveness of counseling than as a counseling or diagnostic tool.

Career Factors Inventory (CFI)

The CFI is a 21-item, self-scorable inventory that provides scores on four scales: Need for Career Information, Need for Self-Knowledge, Career Choice Anxiety, and Generalized Indecisiveness (Chartrand, Robbins, & Morrill, 1997). The scales were designed to measure need for information (first two scales) and difficulty in decision making (last two scales). It provides a relatively broad coverage of the factors underlying career indecision (Kelly, 2002a).

Research supports the structural and discriminate validity of the CFI results when used with college students (Dickinson & Tokar, 2004). D'Costa (2001) noted that the CFI is somewhat limited both in terms of score reliabilities and available normative data, but that it is a "reasonable counseling tool" (p. 221). He described it as a "quick and simple tool designed to do a simple job" (p. 220), that is, discern the client's readiness for deciding upon a career. It is a valuable instrument for this purpose.

Career Decision-Making Difficulties Questionnaire (CDDQ)

The CDDQ is a 44-item questionnaire that assesses a student's ability to cope with different types of difficulties in deciding on a career (Gati, Kraus, & Osipow, 1996). The items are derived from a taxonomy of career-decision difficulties that distinguishes between difficulties that occur prior to the decision-making process (lack of readiness) and those that occur during the process (lack of information and inconsistent information). It is scored on three broad categories that are divided into 10 subcategories as indicated below.

- Lack of Readiness (Motivation, Indecisiveness, and Dysfunctional Beliefs)
- Lack of Information (About Process, About Self, About Alternatives, and About Sources of Information)
- Inconsistent Information (Unreliable Information, Internal Conflicts, External Conflicts)

The validity of the taxonomic structure underlying the CDDQ has been supported in studies based on high school students, college students, military recruits, and adults (Albion & Fogarty, 2002; Gati & Saka, 2001). Kelly (2002a) found a somewhat similar structure in a factor analytic study based on a large sample of undecided college students. The nature of the taxonomic structure may vary some for different cultures (Mau, 2001).

Studies indicate that the CDDQ yields reliable and valid results when used to identify the difficulties experienced by students and young adults in making career decisions (Camp, 2000; Gati et al., 1996). Some cultural, gender, and age differences have been noted. Mau (2001, 2004) found that Asian American students reported more difficulties in career decision making than did students from other cultures. Boys have reported greater difficulties than girls in external conflicts and dysfunctional beliefs (Gati & Saka, 2001). High school students have reported more difficulties than older career deciders (Albion & Fogarty, 2002).

The CDDQ results can be interpreted at three levels—the 3 major scales (Lack of Readiness, Lack of Information, and Inconsistent Information), the 10 subscales, and the 44 items, each of which represents a specific difficulty. Such information can be used as a basis for deciding what type of intervention is needed, for example, personal counseling for internal or external conflicts, testing for lack of information regarding an individual's interests or abilities, or referral to an occupational library for lack of information about occupations (Gati et al., 1996).

Measures of Career Concerns for Adults

Several measures have been developed to assess career issues of adults in the working world. In addition to the Adult Career Concerns Inventory (ACCI) and the Career Attitudes and Strategies Inventory (CASI), both of which are discussed below, the Career Transitions Inventory can provide helpful information for the counselor and client. The Career Transitions Inventory analyzes the psychological resources—including readiness, confidence, perceived support, control, and decision independence—of clients undergoing a career transition (M. J. Heppner, Multon, & Johnston, 1994). Low scores on any of the five factors represent barriers to career change that may need to be addressed in counseling.

Adult Career Concerns Inventory (ACCI)
The ACCI measures the career concerns of adults at different stages in their development (Super, Thompson, & Lindeman, 1988). It contains 61 items, which are scored in terms of four developmental stages (Exploration, Establishment, Maintenance, and Disengagement) and 12 substages. Sample items from each of the 12 substages are listed in Table 7-1. Clients rate each item on a five-step scale ranging from *no concern* to *great concern* on the basis of their present situation. Most clients complete the ACCI, which requires an eighth-grade reading ability, within 15 to 30 minutes.

The manual reports preliminary norms for each gender and for different age groups (Super et al., 1988). In addition to making normative (interindividual) comparisons, Super et al. also stressed the importance of ipsative (intraindividual) comparisons. Ipsative comparisons enable the counselor and the client to identify the predominant developmental tasks facing the person. Although most people obtain their highest score (indicating greatest concern) in the stage that is most common for their age, adults who are in the process of career change can be expected to recycle through some of the early developmental stages.

The test scores show a high degree of internal consistency for samples of employed adults. Factor-analytic studies support the construct validity of the ACCI. Such studies have identified factors similar to the four developmental stages that provide the framework for the ACCI (R. M. Smart & Peterson, 1994).

The ACCI clarifies the nature of the developmental tasks of greatest concern to the client at the present time. It can also be used as a teaching device to alert clients to future career challenges. As noted by Cairo, Kritis, and Myers (1996), "the ACCI remains one of the few measures capable of illuminating our understanding of the career issues facing adults" (p. 200). Professional counselors can gain access to the ACCI on the Internet, where their clients may complete it online free of charge (Glavin, 2005).

For situations in which time may be of concern, counselors can use a short, 12-item form of the ACCI consisting of 1 item from each of the 12 substages (Perrone, Gordon, Fitch, & Civiletto, 2003). These items, each of which possessed the highest factor loading for its substage, are the ones listed in Table 7-1. The ACCI short form proved to be a reliable and valid measure of adult career concerns in the research conducted by Perrone et al.

Career Attitudes and Strategies Inventory (CASI)
Like the ACCI, the CASI was developed to identify and clarify the career problems confronted by adults (Holland & Gottfredson, 1994b). In contrast to the ACCI, the construction of the CASI was

TABLE 7-1

Representative Items From the Adult Career Concerns Inventory

Scale	Item
	Exploration Stage (typically ages 15 to 25)
Crystallization	"Finding the line of work that I am best suited for"
Specification	"Finding a line of work that interests me"
Implementation	"Getting started in my chosen career field"
	Establishment Stage (typically ages 25 to 45)
Stabilizing	"Settling down in a job I can stay with"
Consolidating	"Becoming especially knowledgeable or skillful at work"
Advancing	"Planning how to get ahead in my established field of work"
	Maintenance Stage (typically ages 45 to 60)
Holding	"Keeping the respect of people in my field"
Updating	"Attending meetings and seminars on new methods"
Innovating	"Identifying new problems to work on"
	Disengagement Stage (typically ages 60 and over)
Deceleration	"Developing easier ways of doing my work"
Retirement Planning	"Planning well for retirement"
Retirement Living	"Having a good place to live in retirement"

Note. From *Adult Career Concerns Inventory* by D. E. Super, A. S. Thompson, R. H. Lindeman, R. A. Myers, & J. P. Jordaan (1985). Palo Alto, CA: Consulting Psychologists Press. Reproduced by permission.

influenced primarily by practical rather than theoretical considerations. It includes a broad range of personal and situational factors known to affect a person's career status.

The CASI consists of 130 items that survey nine aspects of career or work adaptation, such as Work Involvement, Risk-Taking Style, and Geographical Barriers. The instrument is designed to be self-administering and self-scoring; however, counselors are usually needed to help interpret the results.

The items for each scale are grouped together in the CASI booklet to facilitate scale interpretation. For example, clients who mark *true* or *mostly true* to items such as "family responsibilities limit my career responsibilities," "I short-change my family or partner by working too much," and "I have changed my work schedule to better meet my family responsibilities" will obtain high scores on the Family Commitment scale. As indicated by the item content, high scores on this scale indicate the realities and some of the difficulties of dual-role responsibilities.

Two large samples of adults who completed the CASI obtained scores with moderately high coefficients of internal consistency (mostly in the .80s). Scores on the scales are correlated with other measures of career concerns according to expectations (Holland & Gottfredson, 1994a). M. B. Brown (1998) recommended that the CASI be used primarily as a checklist to generate discussions with clients and to identify potentially problematic areas for further assessment.

CAREER PLANNING COMPETENCIES

Measures of career planning competencies focus on the cognitive aspects of career development, including occupational knowledge, decision-making skills, and employment-seeking skills. An individual's competencies can be assessed by both self-ratings and different types of tests. Different testing methods include objective paper-and-pencil tests, performance tests, and various exercises in which a person demonstrates his or her understanding or knowledge of career matters (G. W. Peterson, 1998; Walls, 2000; Westbrook, 1995). Examples of both a self-rating instrument and an informal testing procedure based on a vocational card sort are discussed below.

Career Decision-Making Self-Efficacy Scale (CDMSE)

The CDMSE assesses a client's perceptions of his or her ability to make effective career decisions (Betz & Taylor, 1994). This instrument has been developed as a means of testing and implementing self-efficacy theory and, by extension, social cognitive career theory (Bandura, 1986, 1997; Lent et al., 1994). According to these theories, individuals who express confidence in their ability to perform a task (independent of their actual abilities) show greater decisiveness, higher levels of accomplishment, and greater persistence in that activity than do individuals who lack such confidence.

The CDMSE consists of 50 items that represent the critical skills in career decision making suggested by Crites's (1978) model of career maturity. It can be scored on five scales (Self-Appraisal, Occupational Information, Goal Selection, Planning, and Problem-Solving); however, factor-analytic studies indicate that it is best interpreted in terms of the total score as a global measure of career decision-making self-efficacy (Luzzo, 1996). As predicted by self-efficacy theory, individuals who score low on the CDMSE (indicating lack of confidence in career decision-making ability) are likely to have trouble in deciding on an occupation. CDMSE total scores significantly differentiate among college students with declared majors, tentative majors, and no majors in the expected manner (Betz & Luzzo, 1996).

Self-efficacy theory maintains that individuals can learn how to increase their self-confidence in an area, a feat that should increase their willingness and their ability to undertake activities in that area. Strategies for increasing self-confidence in career decision making include (a) successful experiences, (b) vicarious learning or modeling, (c) encouragement or support from others, and (d) emotional arousal (Bandura, 1986). Research indicates that a variety of counseling interventions, including exposure to the DISCOVER computer-based career planning program, verbal persuasion, career exploration workshops, and interest assessment, have successfully increased students' scores on the CDMSE (Betz & Luzzo, 1996; Uffelman, Subich, Diegelman, Wagner, & Bardash, 2004). The CDMSE can be helpful both in detecting students in need of counseling assistance and in assessing their responsiveness to counselor interventions (R. W. Johnson, 2001a).

The test authors have developed a shortened, 25-item version of the CDMSE that has produced validity coefficients comparable with or higher than those obtained with the full-scale form (Betz, Klein, & Taylor, 1996). The short version can be easily used as an intake form and in program evaluation research.

In addition to the CDMSE, instruments that measure an individual's belief in his or her ability to cope with other career-related tasks, such as search for a job, manage multiple roles, and perform certain occupational tasks, have been developed (Lent & Brown, 2006). As a rule, counselors should inquire about an individual's self-confidence in performing a specific type of activity, not just self-confidence in general, and then consider strategies for enhancing the individual's self confidence in that activity as needed (Betz & Hackett, 2006).

Vocational Card Sort

As an alternative means of assessing an individual's occupational competencies, counselors may use a vocational card sort, which can provide an informal assessment of occupational knowledge. According to a procedure developed by G. W. Peterson (1998), clients sort occupational titles into separate piles on the basis of the titles' similarity to each other. The clients then label and make comparisons among the piles. They are asked to name the attributes of the occupations in the occupational pile that they believe they most resemble.

As they engage in this process, clients verbalize the reasons for their decisions. This process provides helpful insights regarding the maturity of the client's knowledge and understanding of careers. This procedure can serve as a simple means of evaluating a client's career development and as a stimulus for career exploration.

COMBINED MEASURES OF CAREER PLANNING ATTITUDES AND COMPETENCIES

Inventories that include scales for both career planning attitudes and competencies provide a comprehensive measure of a client's readiness to engage in career planning. High scores on such measures are associated with *career maturity* or *career adaptability*.

Career maturity, which served as the ultimate goal of career development in Super's early work, indicates a client's readiness to accomplish the career developmental tasks appropriate for his or her age. In later work, Super and others shifted the goal of career development from career maturity to career adaptability (Savickas, 1997; Super et al., 1988).

Career adaptability, which emphasizes situational factors as well as developmental tasks, refers to a client's readiness to cope with both the predictable and unpredictable aspects of career selection and participation. It broadens the criteria for evaluating career development by acknowledging the client's need to respond to new or novel circumstances. The concept of career adaptability is more appropriate for nontraditional clients, for adults, and for individuals from different cultures (Vondracek & Reitzle, 1998).

In general, counselors should interpret the results from the measures in this section in terms of career adaptability; that is, what do the measures indicate about the client's readiness to cope with the challenges faced in his or her career development? Such an interpretation should take into account cultural context, situational pressures, and personal goals, as well as normal developmental expectations.

Four broad measures of career planning readiness are discussed below. The first two are designed for use with secondary and postsecondary school students in the exploratory stage of career development (Super, 1990). The third instrument is constructed for use with adults who are in the establishment or maintenance stages of career development. The fourth is a short instrument that can be used with college students or other adults to assess their overall readiness for career planning. In addition to these four instruments, the Childhood Career Development Scale is a new measure of career progress based on Super's theory for children (Grades 4 through 6) that shows "excellent promise" (Dagley & Salter, 2004, p. 108; Schultheiss & Stead, 2004).

Career Development Inventory (CDI)

Donald Super and his associates designed the CDI "to assess students' readiness to make sound educational and vocational choices" (Thompson et al., 1981, p. 7). The present version of the CDI includes the School Form (Grades 8 through 12) and the College and University Form. Although the CDI was constructed some time ago, it "remains the pre-eminent operational definition of career development during adolescence and young adulthood" (Savickas, Briddick, & Watkins, 2002, p. 32).

Part I of the CDI, which includes 80 items, provides two scales each for career planning attitudes and career planning competencies. Scores on the two scales that measure attitudes—Career Planning (CP) and Career Exploration (CE)—are added together to provide a total score for Career Development Attitudes (CDA). Similarly, scores on the two scales that measure competencies—Decision Making (DM) and World-of-Work Information (WW)—are summed to obtain a total score for Career Development Knowledge and Skills (CDK). A Career Orientation Total (COT) score, which serves as a comprehensive measure of career maturity, combines the scores for all four scales.

Part II of the CDI evaluates the client's knowledge of the occupational field to which he or she is most attracted. The Knowledge of Preferred Occupational Group (PO) scale uses the same 40 multiple-choice items for each occupational group. The correct response for each item (e.g., employment opportunities or educational requirements) varies depending on the occupational field. Part II differs from Part I because of its emphasis on occupational knowledge that pertains to a particular occupational field instead of occupations in general. Under ordinary circumstances, this part of the CDI should not be administered to students below the 11th grade.

The composite scores (CDA, CDK, and COT) show sufficient internal consistency and test–retest reliability (2- to 3-week intervals) when used with high school and college students (Savickas & Hartung, 1996). Scores on the individual scales, particularly PO, WW, and DM, should be interpreted with caution because of relatively low alpha coefficients and test–retest reliabilities found in studies conducted with high school and college students.

In terms of validity, the items for each scale were selected by expert judges to be representative of the different dimensions of Super's model of career development. The scores for most of the scales increase for each age group in the manner suggested by Super's model (Thompson et al., 1981). Savickas and Hartung (1996) noted that the CDI has been used successfully to predict both career choice perseverance and academic success. Higher levels of career maturity on the CDI are associated with higher levels of personal and social adjustment as measured by the California Psychological Inventory (Savickas et al., 2002).

As proposed by its authors, the CDI should be helpful in counseling individuals, in planning guidance programs, and in evaluating programs and conducting research. In a review of the career literature, Savickas and Hartung (1996) concluded that research based on the CDI "strongly supports the sensitivity and specificity of the inventory as a measure of readiness to make educational choices, vocational choices, or both" (p. 185). The CDI can be administered online to clients without cost under the direction of a qualified counselor through Vocopher, an "online career collaboratory" of career counselors and researchers that provides access to a number of counseling instruments (Glavin, 2005).

Career Maturity Inventory–Revised (CMI-R)

The CMI is based on John Crites's (1978) model of career development. According to his model, career maturity encompasses a hierarchy of factors. He hypothesized a general factor of career maturity similar to the g factor in intelligence testing, several group factors, and a large number of specific factors. The group factors pertain to both the process of career planning (attitudes and competencies) and the content of career planning (consistency and realism of career choice).

Crites developed the CMI to measure the career planning attitudes and competencies of secondary school students (Grades 6 through 12). In 1995, he revised the CMI to pertain to college students and young adults as well as adolescents (Crites & Savickas, 1996). He made a conscious effort to shorten the CMI by reducing the number of items and by eliminating subscales. He also added self-help material (the *Career Developer* supplement) to the test package to aid in the interpretation of the instrument and to help nurture the client's career development. According to McDivitt (2002), the revised version of the CMI "has greatly enhanced" (p. 341) its usefulness for teaching students the process of career decision making and for helping them to gain career maturity.

The CMI-R resembles the CDI in its focus on the career planning process variables. It yields a career planning attitude score, a career planning competency score, and an overall career maturity score in a manner similar to the CDI. It differs from the CDI in its brevity (50 items altogether) and its lack of subscales.

Crites selected items for the CMI-R in terms of theoretical specifications and age and grade differentiations. Validity studies with the original CMI showed that students in higher grades scored higher (albeit modestly) on the scales than did students in lower grades. Scores on the Attitude Total scale correlated significantly with performance and satisfaction in both academic and work settings.

In a study of high school students, Busacca and Taber (2002) found "modest but limited support" (p. 450) for the reliability and validity of the CMI-R scores. They noted that "supplemental and supporting evidence" (p. 454) should be obtained to confirm the CMI-R results for clients. Although the current version of the CMI resembles the original version in many respects, its reliability and validity need to be examined with new studies, especially in view of its brevity.

Career Mastery Inventory (CMAS)

The Career Mastery Inventory (abbreviated CMAS to differentiate it from the CMI described above) was constructed by Crites (1993) to assess the career development of adults in the same manner that the CMI assessed the career development of adolescents. Part 1 of the CMAS consists of 90 items on a 7-point Likert scale that assess work attitudes and behavior. Part 2 contains 20 multiple-choice items that measure skill in handling problems in one's work situation.

For Part 1, clients receive a Career Development total score plus scores on six career developmental tasks: Organizational Adaptability, Position Performance, Work Habits and Attitudes, Coworker Relationships, Advancement, and Career Choice and Plans. For Part 2, they receive a Career Adjustment total score together with scores on three adjustment scales: Integrative (reduces anxiety and solves work problems), Adjustive (reduces anxiety only), and Nonadjustive (neither of the above). The test booklet, which has been uniquely designed so that duplicate copies are provided by means of carbon paper, can be both self-scored to provide immediate feedback and machine scored for aggregate data analysis and program evaluation.

The CMAS has been used primarily in business and industrial settings to help design career development programs, to identify common problems among workers within the organizational culture, and to diagnose individual career development task and job adjustment problems. High total scores on the CMAS are correlated with worker satisfaction and job success as measured by performance appraisals and standardized measures (Crites, 1993). Scores on the career development subscales are associated with an individual's age in the manner predicted by Crites's career development model.

Both of the career development instruments by John Crites described here (the CMI-R and the CMAS) will soon be available for use by counselors on the Internet by means of Vocopher, "A Web-Library of Free Career Inventories" (Glavin, 2005).

Career Futures Inventory (CFI)

The CFI is a new, brief inventory that provides the same type of information as that obtained from the combined measures of career planning attitudes and competencies described above, but in a much more circumscribed manner (Rottinghaus, Day, & Borgen, 2005). It includes scales that measure attitudes (Career Optimism, 11 items), competencies (Perceived Knowledge, 3 items), and overall career maturity or adaptability (Career Adaptability, 11 items). College students with high scores on these scales explore career options more actively and report greater certainty in regard to their career plans than do those with low scores.

USE OF CAREER DEVELOPMENT MEASURES IN COUNSELING

Several guidelines concerning the use of career development measures in counseling are listed below:

1. Determine type of counseling intervention based on the client's level of career planning readiness. Clients with low levels need individual counseling or long-term group counseling; clients with high levels can be benefit from short-term group counseling, workshops, or self-directed activities.
2. Use items from the career development measures as a checklist to identify problematic issues for further consideration. Counselors can use the items themselves, especially together with supplementary materials such as the *Career Developer,* to "teach the test" to clients as a means of fostering career maturity (McDivitt, 2002).
3. Use career development measures to survey the needs of student groups for particular services or resources, such as computer-based career planning programs, career exploration workshops, or career courses (Folsom & Reardon, 2003).
4. Help clients to identify and challenge career myths or distorted beliefs about careers that may be interfering with their career development.
5. Distinguish between indecision and indecisiveness. Clients who are indecisive will probably need personal counseling in addition to assistance for career planning.
6. Consider a client's decision-making style when deciding upon a counseling intervention. For example, structured workshops have proved to be more effective with individuals who prefer a rational decision-making style than with those who favor an intuitive or dependent style (Tinsley, Tinsley, & Rushing, 2002).
7. When working with multicultural clients, keep in mind the need to evaluate and to address the institutional and personal challenges they may face, both in entering an occupation and in progressing in it. Such challenges include limited educational experiences, low self-confidence, less access to mentors, and lack of political skills and savvy (Eby, Johnson, & Russell, 1998). Consider using local norms for cultures with different approaches to career planning (Mau, 2001, 2004).
8. In addition to quantitative assessment procedures, counselors should use qualitative techniques, including interviews, observations, and structured career assessment activities, to help evaluate and foster a client's readiness to engage in career planning (Levinson et al., 1998; McMahon, Watson, & Patton, 2005).
9. In planning interventions, take into account the complexity of a client's situation (family, social, economic, or organizational factors) as well as the client's capability to make ap-

propriate career choices (Sampson et al., 2000). External factors include both barriers and supports that can detract from or contribute to a client's readiness to engage in career planning (Swanson, Daniels, & Tokar, 1996; Wettersten et al., 2005)

10. Ask students or clients to retake career development measures as counseling or education progresses to assess changes in dealing with developmental tasks. Use career development measures as criteria for evaluating the effectiveness of career counseling programs.

SUMMARY

1. Instruments that assess readiness to engage in the career planning process include both attitudinal (career beliefs and concerns) and cognitive (career planning competencies) scales. The results from such instruments can be used to choose counseling and educational interventions that may be most appropriate and effective for a particular client.

2. It is important for counselors to identify assumptions of clients that may be blocking their progress in career planning. Inventories that counselors can use for this purpose include the Career Beliefs Inventory and the Career Thoughts Inventory.

3. Several instruments have been designed to evaluate the concerns of high school and college students that affect career planning. My Vocational Situation can be used effectively as a screening instrument to pinpoint career concerns that need to be addressed in counseling. The Career Decision Scale has proved to be particularly helpful in evaluating the outcomes of interventions selected to improve career planning readiness.

4. The Career Factors Inventory and Career Decision-Making Difficulties Questionnaire are two newer instruments that assess the concerns of young people. Both of these measures are multidimensional inventories that provide a systematic assessment of career concerns.

5. The Adult Career Concerns Inventory and the Career Attitudes and Strategies Inventory focus on the career difficulties of adults. These instruments can serve as a springboard for discussing critical issues in counseling sessions.

6. Career planning competencies can be assessed by self-rating methods or by different types of tests. The Career Decision-Making Self-Efficacy Scale indicates the degree to which individuals consider themselves competent to decide upon a career. Peterson's vocational card sort can be used as an informal means of assessing one's occupational knowledge.

7. Several instruments have been designed to assess both career planning attitudes and career planning competencies. The Career Development Inventory and the Career Maturity Inventory-Revised provide comprehensive measures of career planning readiness for high school and traditional-age college students. The Career Mastery Inventory provides a comprehensive measure of career adaptability for adults. The Career Futures Inventory is a new, brief measure of career planning attitudes and competencies that has been used effectively with college students.

8

Measures of Work and Personal Values

Counselors often need to help clients evaluate their motivations in regard to work or other aspects of living. Measures of both values and interests can be helpful for this purpose. Values define what a person thinks is *important;* interests refer to what an individual *likes* to do. According to Nevill and Super (1986b), "values are the objectives sought in behavior, whereas interests are the activities in which the values are sought" (p. 3). In essence, values pertain to *why* a person works or undertakes an activity, whereas interests refer to *what* the person chooses to do. Values are more highly correlated with work satisfaction than are interests (Rounds, 1990). In contrast, interests are more closely related to academic and career choices (Pryor & Taylor, 1986). Measures of values are considered in the following paragraphs; measures of interests are discussed in the next chapter.

Assessment procedures for both work and personal values are discussed. Work values are a subset of personal values that describe different motivations for working. Personal values include a broader range of motivations that pertain to school, family, community, and leisure, as well as work (Super, 1990). Research indicates that the structures of both work values and personal values are similar across different cultures (Schwartz & Boehnke, 2004; Sverko, 1995).

VALUES INVENTORIES

Values can be assessed either by a values inventory or by values clarification exercises. Inventories of both work and personal values are considered in this section. Values clarification exercises are discussed in the next section.

Inventories of Work Values

Work values inventories assess values that pertain primarily to work situations. They measure objectives that can be satisfied in the work itself (intrinsic values) or through work as a means to an end (extrinsic values). Intrinsic values include creativity, mental challenge, and achievement. Extrinsic values include prestige, income, and working conditions. Both types of values need to be taken into consideration in career planning.

Four standardized measures of work values are discussed below in some detail. All of these measures have been designed so that they can be used as stand-alone instruments or as part of a larger, more comprehensive career planning program that also assesses such factors as interests, abilities, and career development. The values inventories are most likely to be used independently when the counselor wants to help a client focus on what is most important to that client in his or her work situation. All of the values inventories discussed here assess primary needs or values related to worker satisfaction.

O*NET Work Importance Profiler (WIP)

The WIP is one of the career exploration tools used in the O*NET (Occupational Information Network) career exploration system established by the U.S. Department of Labor (see chapter 10). This instrument is derived from the Minnesota Importance Questionnaire (MIQ), an established measure of values based on the Theory of Work Adjustment (Dawis & Lofquist, 1984; U.S. Department of Labor, Employment and Training Administration [ETA], 2002b). Because of its ready availability and ease of scoring, the WIP replaces the MIQ for many purposes; however, the MIQ can still be purchased and scored at Vocational Psychology Research at the University of Minnesota (P. M. Hanson, personal communication, April 20, 2006; Web site: www.psych.umn.edu/psylabs/vpr).

The WIP is a computer-based instrument that may be administered and scored on the Internet. An equivalent paper-and-pencil version, known as the Work Importance Locator (WIL-P&P), has also been created for use where a computer may not be available (U.S. Department of Labor, ETA, 2000). Compared with the WIP, the WIL-P&P uses a simpler item format that requires one fewer item and many fewer comparisons among the items. The WIL-P&P is an easier instrument for clients to complete; however, the results are somewhat less reliable.

Both instruments provide rankings on six "core values"—Achievement, Independence, Recognition, Relationships, Support, and Working Conditions—that are similar to the values assessed on the MIQ. The rankings are based on responses to 21 (20 for the WIL-P&P) "work need statements" similar to those originally used on the MIQ. Individuals rank these items in comparison with each other as a means of determining which values are most important for them. The number of statements (items) per category ranges from 2 to 6 as can be seen in Table 8-1. The computer analyzes the individual's responses and presents the results by first listing the top two values in red and then the remaining four values in black. No scores are given, but the values are listed in order of importance for each individual.

Preliminary research has shown that test–retest profiles are moderately stable for college students over short time periods (U.S. Department of Labor, ETA, 2002b). The top one or two values probably will not change substantially over short time periods, although the stability of other values is less certain, especially for the WIL-P&P. Administration of the WIP and WIL-P&P to the same students yields profiles that show relatively high agreement with each other. Both instruments produce results that are moderately correlated with results on the MIQ, their parent instrument. The correlations are somewhat suppressed by the ipsative nature of the questionnaire, the use of fewer items in a simplified response format (for the WIL-P&P), and changes in the wording of some of the items. Additional research is needed to establish the validities of the WIP and WIL-P&P in their own right.

The WIP or the WIL-P&P can be helpful in counseling when used together with the other O*NET instruments for career exploration under the guidance of a skilled counselor (Michael, 2005). The work value ratings for all of the occupations included in the O*NET database can be found on the Internet (U.S. Department of Labor, ETA, 2006). Counselors or clients can check occupations directly, or they can enter particular values one at a time to find occupations in which those values rank highest. For example, occupations in which Achievement values are highest include Interior Designers (Job Zone 3), Airplane Pilots (Job Zone 4), and Architects (Job Zone 5). ("Job Zones" indicate amount of education, training, and experience required in order to perform a job, ranging from 1—*little or no preparation* to 5—*extensive preparation*.)

The User's Manual (U.S. Department of Labor, ETA, 2002b, p. 41) provides an example of the use of the WIP for "Mary Q." who obtained her highest scores on the Achievement and Relationships values scales. She wished to consider occupations in the Job Zone 3 category (medium preparation). She obtained a list of 12 occupations in this category that matched her values. The three occupations that most closely matched her values were employment interviewers, private or public employment service; personal financial advisors; and hosts and hostesses, restaurant, lounge, and coffee shop. Other matching occupations included gaming managers and supervisors, orthotists and prosthetists, and interpreters and translators. The computer screen provides a link to the O*NET database, which makes available extensive information for each of these occupations. The instructions indicate that if she is dissatisfied with these choices, she could consider occupations in another Job Zone, consider occupations for just her highest value, retake

TABLE 8-1

Scales and Item Content of O*NET Work Importance Profiler

Work Values	Work Need Statements *On my ideal job, it is important that. . .*
Achievement	
Ability Utilization	. . .I make use of my abilities.
Achievement	. . .the work could give me a feeling of accomplishment.
Independence	
Creativity	. . .I could try out my own ideas.
Responsibility	. . .I could make decisions on my own.
Autonomy	. . .I could plan my work with little supervision.
Recognition	
Advancement	. . .the job would provide an opportunity for advancement.
Authority	. . .I could give directions and instructions to others.
Recognition	. . .I could receive recognition for the work I do.
Social Status	. . .I would be looked up to by others in my company and community.
Relationships	
Co-workers	. . .my co-workers would be easy to get along with.
Ethics	. . .I would never be pressured to do things that go against my sense of right and wrong.
Social Service	. . .I could do things for other people.
Support	
Company Policies & Practices	. . .I would be treated fairly by the company.
Supervision—Human Relations	. . .I have supervisors who would back up their workers with management.
Supervision—Technical	. . .I would have supervisors who train their workers well.
Working Conditions	
Activity	. . .I could be busy all the time.
Compensation	. . .my pay would compare well with that of other workers.
Independence	. . .I could work alone.
Security	. . .the job would provide for steady employment.
Variety	. . .I could do something different every day.
Working conditions	. . .the job would have good working conditions.

Note. From the O*NET™ *Work Importance Profiler User's Guide,* U.S. Department of Labor, 2002b. Retrieved February 17, 2006, from http://onetcenter.org/dl_files/WIP.pdf. O*NET™ is a trademark of the U.S. Department of Labor, Employment and Training Administration.

the WIP, or place greater emphasis on occupations suggested by the other O*NET Career Exploration Tools (see chapter 10).

The WIP, which can be downloaded from the O*NET Web site, has the advantage of being free of charge (Lewis & Rivkin, 2004). The WIL paper-and-pencil form can be purchased from the Department of Labor. There is a commercial version of the WIL-P&P, known as the O*NET Career Values Inventory (CVI), available through JIST Publishing (2006). The CVI provides the same information as the WIL-P&P, but it uses a compact, fold-out paper format that costs significantly less for customers to purchase.

Work Values Inventory–Revised (WVI-R)

The WVI, which was originally developed by Donald Super (1970) for career development research and counseling, has recently been revised (National Career Assessment Services, Inc., 2004; Rottinghaus & Zytowski, 2006). It is often used together with the Kuder Career Search interest inventory as part of the Kuder Career Planning System (see chapter 9).

In its revised form, clients rate the relative importance in their work situation of 12 values or goals, on the following scales: Creativity, Mental Challenge, Achievement, Independence, Prestige, Income, Security, Work Environment, Supervision, Co-workers, Lifestyle, and Variety. Three (Altruism, Esthetics, and Management) of the original 15 scales, all of which overlapped with interest measures, have been dropped. The 12 remaining scales (some of which have been renamed) were increased in length from three to six items each with five response options ranging from *not important at all* to *crucial*. The revised version uses a combined norm group of 7th- through 12th-grade boys and girls for converting raw scores to percentile scores.

The emphasis in interpretation is placed on the rank of an individual's scores, that is, what is relatively most important for that individual compared with his or her other values. Clients are reminded that some values are associated with an occupation (e.g., business management occupations often have a higher income), whereas other values may be satisfied by a particular position within an occupation (e.g., a salesperson who works independently).

Career Orientation Placement and Evaluation Survey (COPES)

The COPES is one of three instruments used in the Career Occupational Preference System. It measures work values on eight bipolar scales as indicated below (Knapp, Knapp-Lee, & Knapp, 1995; Knapp-Lee, 1996):

- Investigative versus Accepting
- Practical versus Carefree
- Independence versus Conformity
- Leadership versus Supportive
- Orderliness versus Flexibility
- Recognition versus Privacy
- Aesthetic versus Realistic
- Social versus Reserved

Each bipolar scale consists of 16 pairs of items that represent the opposite ends of the scale. For each item pair, clients must choose which activity or type of work they value more. For example, "work on my own without direction" versus "work under careful supervision" is an item pair scored on the Independence versus Conformity scale.

The COPES has been designed so that it may be used with the COPSystem Interest Inventory and Career Ability Placement Survey (see chapter 10). Based on a review of the career literature, the scale authors have identified the three most relevant values for each of the 14 occupational clusters used within this system. For example, outdoor careers are matched with Practical, Independence, and Privacy values.

Studies indicate that the eight COPES scales measure values that are relatively homogeneous and independent of each other. Students in different occupational groups obtain COPES scores according to expectations. Longitudinal data indicate that the COPES scores successfully predict future job or college program placement (Knapp-Lee, 1996).

Values Scale (VS)

Donald Super and Dorothy Nevill collaborated with vocational psychologists from a number of different countries as part of the Work Importance Study to construct both the VS and the Salience Inventory (Nevill & Super, 1986a, 1986b). The VS builds on the research conducted by Super on the Work Values Inventory (WVI). It contains 21 scales, which represent the 15 work values originally measured by the WVI, plus 6 additional values measured on the following scales: Physical Activity, Physical Prowess, Risk, Advancement, Personal Development, and Cultural Identity.

Each VS scale contains five items with four response options ranging from 1 *(of little or no importance)* to 4 *(very important)*. For each scale (except Working Conditions), at least two of the five items pertain to nonwork situations, whereas two others pertain to work. Most people complete the inventory in 30 to 45 minutes. The VS, which is intended for people age 13 and older, requires an eighth-grade reading level. It can be easily scored by hand in a few minutes.

Studies of the VS with cross-national samples indicate that five factors (or orientations) account for most of the variance in test scores (Sverko, 1995). The five factors together with the scales that best represent them are listed below:

- Utilitarian Orientation (Economics, Advancement, Prestige, Authority, Achievement)
- Orientation Toward Self-Actualization (Ability, Personal Development, Altruism)
- Individualist Orientation (Lifestyle, Autonomy)

- Social Orientation (Social Interaction, Social Relations)
- Adventurous Orientation (Risk)

These five factors can be used to help organize and explain the information obtained from the 21 scales. The Utilitarian and Individualist orientations primarily assess extrinsic values that can be satisfied by the outcomes of work, whereas Orientation Toward Self-Actualization, Social Orientation, and Adventurous Orientation measure intrinsic values that can be satisfied by participation in the work itself.

From a psychometric point of view, questions have been raised regarding the reliabilities of the scale scores, the representativeness of the norms, and the lack of predictive validity studies (Green, 1998). Despite its limitations, the VS can be helpful in counseling for focusing on the importance of values in life and career planning (Nevill & Kruse, 1996). At this point, the VS can be best used for intraindividual comparisons, that is, to help clients determine the relative strength of their values when compared with each other. Schoenrade (2002), who noted that the VS might be better named the Work-Related Values Scale, concluded that it is a "sound instrument for career counseling purposes" (p. 301) that helps individuals take an in-depth look at what they seek from a job. The VS has been designed for use with other measures of career development, including the Adult Career Concerns Inventory and the Career Development Inventory (see chapter 7), as well as the Strong Interest Inventory, as described in the C-DAC model (Career-Development Assessment and Counseling; Super, Osborne, Walsh, Brown, & Niles, 1992).

Additional Inventories
Other inventories of work values include the Inventory of Work-Relevant Values (IWRV), Hall Occupational Orientation Inventory (4th ed.; HOOI), and the Physician Values in Practice Scale (PVIPS). The IWRV has been developed by ACT, Inc., for use in the DISCOVER computer-based, career-planning program (Bobek & Gore, 2004). The HOOI (L. G. Hall, 2000) assesses a broad range of career factors, including values, from a nonnormative, "humanistic perspective" (Law, 2005, p. 428). The PVIPS is an example of a scale designed to measure "context-specific values" within a limited occupational category, such as medical specializations (Hartung, Taber, & Richard, 2005).

Inventories of Personal Values

Inventories of personal values can be used to evaluate what goals or objectives an individual considers to be important in a variety of situations beyond work itself. Some of these instruments, such as the Rokeach Value Survey (RVS) and the Schwartz Value Survey (SVS), are broad measures of values that have been used primarily for research purposes; however, counselors may find their comprehensive coverage of different types of values to be helpful in some counseling situations. Other instruments, including the Study of Values (SOV), Salience Inventory (SI), and Quality of Life Questionnaire (QOLI), have been specifically validated for use in counseling situations to predict criteria such as educational and occupational membership or life satisfaction. All five of these inventories are discussed below, together with outcome expectation questionnaires, which consider the degree to which particular values may be realized in different situations.

Rokeach Value Survey (RVS)
The RVS is a short inventory that consists of two sets of 18 words or phrases that measure instrumental and terminal values (Rokeach, 1973). Instrumental values, such as obedience, forgiveness, and imagination, represent "modes of conduct." Terminal values, such as beauty, adventure, and friendship, represent the "end-states of existence." Respondents must rank each of the two sets of 18 items in order of their preferences for the different values.

Although designed for individuals age 11 and over, the results tend to be unreliable for younger individuals, especially those who lack the ability to handle verbal abstractions. Brookhart (1995) recommended that the use of the RVS be limited to "literate adults who are used to dealing with abstractions" (p. 879). Although the RVS has been used primarily for research purposes, Sanford (1995) noted that it can be "useful for examining an individual's value system and for determining if change has occurred within [it]" (p. 880). Because of limited norms, the results should be interpreted simply by comparing the ranks of the different values for an individual with each other (i.e., in an ipsative fashion), not by comparison with a norm group.

Schwartz Value Survey (SVS)

The SVS is a newer, 57-item instrument that is based in part on Rokeach's original work. Schwartz (1994) has attempted to develop a broad measure of "basic values" that would be applicable in most human cultures. He has identified a total of 10 basic values that can be arranged in a circular fashion (a circumplex) with two bipolar dimensions running through it at right angles: *Self-Transcendence vs. Self Enhancement* and *Openness to Change vs. Conservation* (see Figure 8-1). The SVS structure of values has been tested and confirmed in more than 60 countries (Schwartz & Boehnke, 2004).

The values are arranged on the circumplex so that those close together have the most in common and those across from each other have the least in common. The two values, Tradition and Conformity, are both diametrically opposed to Stimulation (excitement, novelty); however, Tradition, which indicates an adherence to cultural and religious customs and ideas, is even further removed from Stimulation than is Conformity, which shows a tendency to agree with family and friends more than with the culture as a whole. Values that tend to be more popular in general, such as Benevolence (concern for the welfare of others) and Universalism (understanding, appreciation), are shown by larger sizes in the circumplex.

Men and women show moderate differences in values across most cultures. Men score higher on the Power, Stimulation, Hedonism, Achievement, and Self-Direction values scales; women score higher on the Benevolence and Universalism values scales. Sex differences are not as great as age and cultural differences in most studies. Cultural differences are especially large in regard to Tradition, Conformity, Security, and Hedonism values scales (Schwartz & Rubel, 2005). Scores on the values scales have effectively predicted behavior in many situations, including sexual behavior, delinquency, and cooperation (Schwartz & Bardi, 2001). Psychological well-being has been predicted by congruence between an individual's value system and that of the prevailing culture (e.g., academic department; Sagiv & Schwartz, 2000).

Research indicates that values as measured by the SVS overlap somewhat with interests; however, most of the relationships are modest. Studies involving the SVS and the Self-Directed Search show the following positive relationships, which conform to expectations (Sagiv, 2002):

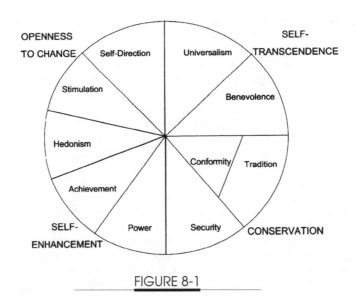

FIGURE 8-1

Structure of Personal Values

Note. From "Sex Differences in Value Priorities: Cross-Cultural and Multimethod Studies," by S. H. Schwartz and T. Rubel, 2005, *Journal of Personality and Social Psychology, 89,* p. 1011. Copyright 2006 by the American Psychological Association. Reprinted with permission.

- Conventional interests—Conformity, Security, and Tradition values
- Enterprising interests—Power and Achievement values
- Social interests—Benevolence values
- Artistic interests—Self-Direction and Universalism values
- Investigative interests—Self-Direction and Universalism values
- Realistic interests—No significant relationships

These relationships were stronger for individuals who had made a career decision in counseling than for those who were undecided, suggesting that decided individuals may have been experiencing less conflict in their decision making.

Instead of the SVS, counselors may use the Portrait Values Questionnaire (PVQ) or the Short SVS, both instruments that contain the same 10 scales as the SVS (Lindeman & Verkasalo, 2005; Schwartz et al., 2001). The PVQ asks responders to indicate to what degree values portrayed by different individuals compare with their own. Both instruments produce results similar to those found with the SVS.

Study of Values (SOV), 4th Edition

The SOV is a venerable measure of personal values that enjoyed wide usage for many years until it gradually became out of date in the 1980s (Allport & Vernon, 1931; Allport, Vernon, & Lindzey, 1960). This instrument has been updated by rewriting 15 of the original 45 items (Kopelman, Rovenpor, & Guan, 2003). Items that used sexist language (all male pronouns), dated examples (e.g., Amundsen, Byrd), and limited religious references (all Christian) were revised to make them more relevant and acceptable. The items ask people to choose among different values in terms of their preferences in particular situations, such as which individual (Aristotle or Abraham Lincoln) they feel has made the greatest contribution to society. Studies indicate that the updated version (SOV-U) compares favorably with the original version in terms of its psychometric properties.

The SOV-U measures the relative strength of an individual's values in six areas: theoretical, economic, aesthetic, social, political, and religious. Because of its ipsative nature, emphasis should be placed on intraindividual comparisons in interpreting the test results. Research indicates that the SOV-U predicts external criteria, such as graduate field of study, more accurately than the RVS (Instrumental and Terminal versions) and the SVS (Kopelman, Prottas, & Tatum, 2004), presumably because of its use of behavioral items instead of items that ask about abstract values. Individuals may not be aware of their values until they are forced to choose among them in life-like situations. The SOV-U is reprinted in Kopelman et al.'s (2003) article and may be used with permission of its authors.

Salience Inventory (SI)

The SI measures the importance of different life roles for individuals in the context of Super's "life-space, life-span" model of career development (Nevill & Super, 1986a; Super, 1990). Five life roles, Studying, Working, Community Service, Home, and Leisure Activities, are assessed from three perspectives: Participation, Commitment, and Value Expectations. The five Participation scales measure the extent of a person's actual behavior in each of the five roles. The five Commitment scales assess the client's emotional attachment to each role. Finally, the five Value Expectations scales measure the degree to which a client expects that his or her values will be fulfilled in each of the five roles.

The instrument, which includes 170 items rated on a 4-point scale, requires about 30 to 45 minutes to complete. It can be hand scored easily without the use of templates.

The SI scales have yielded high coefficients of internal consistency for student and adult samples; however, test–retest coefficients for college students have been somewhat low. A client's test scores can be expected to change somewhat over short time periods. Validity studies indicate that the SI differentiates among different occupational and cultural groups in expected directions. Individuals vary in the relative importance they place on the different roles on the basis of such factors as age, gender, and culture.

The SI provides information for counseling purposes that is not readily available from other instruments. It can help clarify the client's readiness to engage in career planning by indicating the relative significance of career in the client's life. It can be used to identify and explore role conflicts within clients or between clients and their environment. For example, discrepancies between Commitment or Value Expectations and Participation scores may suggest important topics for consideration.

When used in combination with the VS (or other measure of work values), the SI can help identify outlets for values not realized in one's career. Because the SI has been developed for use in multicultural settings, it can be particularly valuable in counseling students from different cultural backgrounds (Nevill & Calvert, 1996). The SI will be available via the Vocopher Web site in the near future (K. Glavin, personal communication, April 27, 2006; Internet Web site: www.vocopher.com). In the meantime, SI materials can be obtained from the test author (D. D. Nevill, personal communication, January 25, 2006; e-mail address: nevill@ufl.edu).

QOLI

The QOLI is a short, 32-item instrument that can be used to rate the importance of 16 different aspects of life, such as learning, helping, and health (Frisch, 1994). Individuals also rate the degree to which they are satisfied with each of these aspects of their lives. Total Quality of Life scores can be obtained by multiplying the Importance ratings by the Satisfaction ratings for each of the 16 areas, and then adding these figures together. National norms have been supplemented by clinical norms drawn from various mental health settings (Frisch et al., 2005).

Longitudinal research shows that the QOLI predicts academic retention 1 to 3 years in advance and that it is a sensitive indicator of treatment-related changes (Frisch et al., 2005). In general, it can serve as a vehicle for the discussion of values with clients. It has the advantages of being brief, comprehensive, easy to administer and score, and based on a quality of life model that can be used to interpret scores and suggest possible interventions (R. W. Johnson, 2001b).

Outcome Expectations Questionnaires

In some cases, the relationship of values to decision making or behavioral change has been studied in terms of outcome expectations. Cognitive theories of behavioral change, such as the social cognitive career theory of Lent et al. (1994), suggest that an individual's behavior is dependent, at least in part, on the expected outcomes of that behavior. A number of outcome expectation questionnaires have been developed to assess an individual's expectations based on that person's behavior in specific situations, such as taking math courses, majoring in engineering, or entering a weight loss program (Finch et al., 2005; Fouad & Guillen, 2006; Lent & Brown, 2006). Because of the specificity of the situations, the particular values involved vary from questionnaire to questionnaire. For example, weight loss programs may inquire about expectations in regard to physical fitness, avoidance of disease, and physical attractiveness as a result of participating in the program. In general, positive expectations are associated with increased participation in a particular activity, such as academic or career planning. In the course of considering values, counselors should explore with clients the extent to which they believe their values could be fulfilled by various options. In some cases, these beliefs may need to be challenged or strengthened if they are not well supported.

Use of Values Inventories in Counseling

The following points pertain to the use of all values inventories in counseling:

1. Use a measure of values when a client wishes to clarify work or life goals and objectives. Integrate measures of values with measures of interests in attempting to understand client motivation for work or other activities.
2. Use the scales or factors from a values inventory to provide a meaningful structure by which clients can consider their values. A structure of this sort enables the client to consider the nature of values expressed in various activities.
3. Ask clients to estimate their own profile. Ask them to separate those needs that are most important for them from those that are least important. This approach will teach clients to apply a values structure to their own situation.
4. Try to estimate the client's profile. This type of exercise helps the counselor to become more familiar with both the values inventory and the client. The counselor is forced to organize his or her thinking about the client's values in a systematic fashion.

5. Compare the client's and the counselor's estimates with the actual profile from the values inventory. If they do not match, try to determine the reasons for the discrepancies. Clarify the meaning of both estimated and measured values.
6. To what extent do the values scores agree with the client's experiences? Clients should report satisfaction with previous occupations and activities that provide rewards that agree with their needs and values.
7. Ask clients to interpret individual items in regard to their situation. What do the items mean to them, particularly those items that they may be most concerned about?
8. Look at the relationship between values scores and values that rank highest for different occupations as listed in the O*NET database to obtain a list of occupations that provide rewards appropriate to clients' values (U.S. Department of Labor, ETA, 2006).
9. Consider work values within a larger context of life values and life planning (L. S. S. Hansen, 1999). Help clients to consider a range of values that may be expressed within a variety of roles and situations.
10. Take into account the possible influence of cultural values, such as collectivism versus individualism, linear versus circular time orientation, and person–nature relationship, on career choice and development (D. Brown, 2002).
11. Use the results from values inventories to stimulate self-exploration. The results should be used in conjunction with other data that take into account interests, abilities, previous experiences, and opportunities.
12. Keep in mind that values can change. As basic needs (such as survival, safety, and belonging) are satisfied, higher order needs (such as esteem and self-actualization) become more important (Maslow, 1987). Counselors may need to help clients review their values as their situation changes.

VALUES CLARIFICATION EXERCISES

Values clarification exercises are strategies that enable clients to identify and to make comparisons among their values. Compared with values inventories, values clarification exercises require clients to engage in self-assessment at a deeper level that takes into account actual behavior as well as preferences. The exercises ask clients to review their beliefs and behaviors in response to different situations. They encourage clients to assume a more active role in exploring and expressing their values. They possess all of the advantages of qualitative assessment procedures, including more active participation on the part of the client and a more holistic approach (Goldman, 1992).

For example, a typical values clarification exercise invites clients to list 15 to 20 things they love to do. For each activity, they are then asked to consider such matters as how long it has been since they participated in the activity, if it is something that they do with others or alone, how much the activity costs, how important that activity is compared with other activities, how much planning the activity requires, and whether or not this is a new activity for them. The exercise requires clients to analyze their activities in terms of the values expressed. A value is considered to be fully developed when it meets the following six criteria: It has been (a) chosen freely (b) from among alternatives (c) after careful consideration of the consequences, (d) prized and (e) publicly affirmed, and (f) acted on repeatedly (Raths, Harmin, & Simon, 1978).

Values clarification exercises have been used in regard to a wide variety of issues, including substance abuse, career transitions, grieving, and sex education. Singelis (1998) provided a number of value clarification exercises that can be used to increase understanding of and communication with different ethnic and racial groups.

Most career planning workbooks (e.g., Bolles, 2005; Figler, 1993) contain several values clarification exercises. The workbooks help clients to integrate information derived from the values clarification exercises with other information about themselves and with occupational information. Different types of exercises include the values auction, values card sort, and guided fantasy. Other values clarification assessments include the use of stories in which work values are embedded (Krumboltz, Blando, Kim, & Reikowski, 1994) and the use of the Repertory Grid to help clients create their own values categories for making comparisons among occupations (Zytowski, 1994). Brott (2005) described several activities, including the life line, the life-space genogram, and life-roles analysis, that counselors can use with clients to help clarify life roles and construct meaningful life stories. Knowdell (1998) has constructed a Career Values Card Sort (CVCS) that requires clients to sort a total of 41 value-label cards into five categories ranging from "most valued" to "never valued." The CVCS has been described as a "useful device" that should provide clients with "an enjoyable and a helpful experience" (Kinnier & Kernes, 2002, p. 221).

The Life Values Inventory combines qualitative and quantitative assessment of an individual's values (D. Brown, 1995; Crace & Brown, 1992). It is particularly helpful for identifying and addressing both intrarole conflicts (when values held by the individual conflict with values espoused in the workplace) and interrole conflicts (when values held by the individual conflict with his or her values expressed in another role outside of work). The scales from the inventory provide a structure for analyzing the types of values demonstrated in an individual's life experiences or career choice. Clients repeat the quantitative section of the inventory after performing the qualitative exercises as a means of reviewing the priority of their values. This same technique can be used with other combinations of values inventories and values clarification exercises.

Kinnier (1995) noted that values clarification exercises have come under attack for the superficial and irrelevant manner in which they have been applied at times. He argued that values clarification can be most meaningful when it is applied to specific values conflicts, such as the relative importance that an individual places on family versus career commitment. He described a number of strategies (both rational and intuitive), such as problem solving, cognitive restructuring, life review, incubation ("sleeping on it"), and the "two-chair technique," that can be used for this purpose. He has designed an assessment instrument—the Values Conflict Resolution Assessment (VCRA)—that can be used to identify a values conflict, guide its resolution, and evaluate the desirability of the resolution (Kinnier, 1987). VCRA scores correlated positively with self-reports of conflict resolution and self-esteem for a sample of graduate students.

SUMMARY

1. Values refer to a person's objectives or goals in work or other settings. Counselors usually assess client values by means of values inventories or values clarification exercises.

2. The O*NET Work Importance Profiler (WIP), a computer-based instrument, provides a measure of work values based on the Theory of Work Adjustment. Counselors can compare client values identified by WIP (or the Work Importance Locator, a paper-and-pencil version of the WIP) with values expressed in different occupations by means of the O*NET database on the Internet.

3. The revised version of the Work Values Inventory provides a relatively pure measure of work values with 12 six-item scales.

4. The Career Orientation Placement and Evaluation Survey assesses work values by means of eight bipolar scales.

5. The Values Scales provides a broad measure of work and personal values based on research conducted in cross-national settings.

6. The Rokeach Values Survey and Schwartz Values Survey both measure personal values that can be used to assess motivational priorities in a variety of situations. The Schwartz Values Survey assesses values by means of a two-dimensional circumplex that has applicability in most cultures.

7. The Study of Values, one of the first psychological instruments to be used in career counseling, has been updated and shown to be effective in discriminating among students in different occupational fields.

8. Both the Salience Inventory and the Quality of Life Inventory can be used to assess personal values that affect life satisfaction. These inventories enable individuals to compare the relative importance of different life roles or aspects of their life and to determine to what degree their values are being met in their activities.

9. Outcome expectations questionnaires can be used to assess the degree to which clients believe that certain behaviors will help them to attain their goals. High expectations will influence their choices.

10. Values clarification exercises require clients to identify and compare their values with their behaviors. As such, they can be particularly valuable in stimulating exploration and development of client values.

9

Assessment of Interests

Since at least 1909, when Frank Parsons published his classic book, *Choosing a Vocation,* counselors have tried to devise ways to assess people's career interests. Interest inventories, which ask clients to report their likes and dislikes for various activities, have proved to be particularly useful for this purpose. Several interest inventories that counselors use frequently are discussed in this chapter, together with guidelines for their selection and interpretation.

TYPES OF INTEREST INVENTORIES

Interest inventories can be classified in a variety of ways, for example, by age level, occupational level, or type of item. In many ways, the most useful distinction pertains to type of scale. Two types of interest scales predominate. The first type measures the strength of an individual's interests in broad fields of activity, such as art, mechanical activities, or sports. These scales are frequently described as *general* or *basic* interests. They are *homogeneous* in nature because they refer to one type of activity. For this reason they are relatively easy to interpret.

In contrast, the second type of scale assesses the similarity of an individual's interest patterns with those of people in specific occupations. These scales, usually called *occupational* scales, are *heterogeneous* in terms of item content. The scales include a variety of items that distinguish between the interests of people in an occupation and those of people in general. Because of the mixed item content, scores on these scales are more difficult to interpret.

The first type of scale is usually constructed by a rational process. The scales are designed to include items that logically fit together. Examples are the Occupational Theme scales and Basic Interest scales on the Strong Interest Inventory™ (Strong). Internal validation procedures such as factor analysis are usually undertaken to ensure that the item content of the scales is relatively pure. Scales of this type belong to a "closed system" of scales; that is, the system includes all the scales that are necessary to represent all the different types of interests.

Scales of the second type are based on those items that differentiate between the interests of people in an occupation and people in general. Item selection depends on an empirical process (observed differences between groups), not on theoretical or logical considerations. Examples are the Occupational scales on the Strong and the Campbell Interest and Skill Survey (CISS). External validation procedures such as discriminant analysis are frequently used to determine the effectiveness of the scales in differentiating among the interests of people employed in different occupations. Empirical scales are usually part of an "open system"; that is, no one set of scales is established to represent the universe of occupational interests. New scales must be constructed as new occupations emerge or as old occupations change.

Both types of scales contribute to the career or life planning process. Because they are easy to interpret, the basic interest scales can be used in a variety of situations in which counseling contact may be limited. The basic interest scales can also be helpful in interpreting the scores on the occupational scales when both types of scores are available. The occupational scales, on the other hand, provide a means of comparing an individual's interest pattern as a whole with those of people in different occupations. These scales include in a single score the information that is distributed over a number of basic interest scales.

In most cases, counselors should use interest inventories that provide broad measures of interest with high school age or younger students. Such scales are not only easier to interpret but they also preclude young students from focusing too early on specific occupations before they have had sufficient opportunity to explore different occupations. Inventories that show scores for specific occupations are more appropriate for college students or other adults.

SELECTION OF INTEREST INVENTORIES FOR COUNSELING

Counselors most often use interest inventories to aid clients with academic or career planning. Interest scores can be used to help clients to explore or discover new academic or career possibilities, to decide among various alternatives, or to confirm a previous choice. Interest scores can also be used for considering ways in which a job might be modified to produce greater job satisfaction or for planning leisure-time activities. In addition, interest scores can serve as a starting point for discussing future plans with parents or other significant people in a person's life.

The following guidelines should help counselors to decide when to use an interest inventory with a client. First, counselors should keep in mind that interest inventories measure likes and dislikes, not abilities. Most studies show a negligible relationship between inventoried interests and tested abilities. Interest inventories identify careers or work situations that clients should find satisfying, but they do not indicate how successful the person would be in those settings. For this reason, interest inventories are often administered together with a measure of abilities (self-rated or tested) so that both interests and abilities can be taken into account in considering career options (Betz & Rottinghaus, 2006).

Second, clients should be positively motivated to participate in the assessment process. Clients are more likely to benefit from taking an interest inventory if they express an interest in the results beforehand. They are also more likely to present an honest picture of their interests or intentions if they clearly understand and accept the purpose of testing. Large changes in interest scores can occur when clients change the manner in which they approach the test. Sometimes clients answer items in terms of what they think other people (especially parents) would like them to say, or they may respond to the items in regard to their abilities or opportunities instead of their interests. Clients may answer the questions hastily or insincerely, especially if they take the inventory as part of a classroom administration. Test scores will be less valid and reliable under such circumstances.

Third, general interest inventories are of limited value for people who must make rather fine distinctions, such as choosing between civil and electrical engineering. Special purpose inventories such as the Purdue Interest Questionnaire for engineering and technical students (Shell, LeBold, & Ward, 1991), the Business Career Interest Inventory for business students (Butler & Waldroop, 2004), or the Medical Specialty Preference Inventory for medical students (Borges, Gibson, & Karnani, 2005; Zimny, 2002) can provide some assistance in these cases. Under any circumstance, interest inventories must be supplemented with other information about the person and his or her situation, including abilities, values, previous work experiences, and job availability, before a decision is made.

Fourth, interest inventories may be inappropriate for people with emotional problems. Disturbed people make more negative responses and endorse more passive interests than do people who are not disturbed. Personal issues can interfere with decision making. Counselors usually must address the emotional difficulties before career planning can take place.

Fifth, scores on interest inventories can show significant changes for clients who are young or after long time periods. As a rule of thumb, counselors should consider readministering an interest inventory if it has been longer than 6 months since the client last completed one. Interests are most likely to change for people under age 20 who have experienced large changes in their situation (e.g., new work or school experiences).

Finally, counselors may wish to use an interest card sort instead of an interest inventory if they are interested in the underlying reasons for the client's choices (Slaney & MacKinnon-Slaney, 2000). The card sort functions as a structured interview. As originally designed by Leona Tyler, clients sort cards with occupational titles on them into piles of "would choose," "would not choose," and "no opinion." They then subdivide the three piles into smaller piles based on their reasons for placing the cards into those piles. This technique helps counselors to understand the reasons for a client's choice. The counselor and the client together look for themes in the client's preferences that can guide the career exploration process. Examples of such card sorts include the Missouri Occupational Card Sort, Missouri Occupational Preference Inventory, Nonsexist Vocational Card Sort, Occ-U-Sort, and Slaney's Vocational Card Sort (Slaney & MacKinnon-Slaney, 2000). The Vocational Exploration and Insight Kit, which includes an 84-item card sort together with other career exploration activities, is especially appropriate for highly motivated clients who wish to consider their career choices in some depth (Holland, 1992).

POPULAR INTEREST INVENTORIES

Several of the most popular interest inventories used for career or life planning are discussed in this chapter. These measures include the Strong Interest Inventory, Campbell Interest and Skill Survey, Kuder Career Search with Person Match, Self-Directed Search, Career Decision-Making System–Revised, and Jackson Vocational Interest Survey.

All of these interest inventories, except for the Jackson Vocational Interest Survey, also include a parallel measure of self-rated competencies, either as part of the inventory itself or as a paired instrument (Betz & Rottinghaus, 2006). The two types of measures together can often predict occupational criteria more effectively than either measure by itself. In essence, they fit together well for this purpose in that they both emphasize typical (as opposed to maximal) modes of behavior (Darcy & Tracey, 2003),

Strong Interest Inventory™ (Strong)

The 2004 Strong is the most recent version of a series of interest inventories that began with the publication of the Strong Vocational Interest Blank (SVIB) by E. K. Strong Jr. in 1927 (Donnay et al., 2005). The SVIB included two forms, one for men and one for women, that were merged when the SVIB was replaced by the Strong-Campbell Interest Inventory (SCII) in 1974. The SCII was ultimately revised and renamed to become the Strong Interest Inventory (Strong or SII) in 1994. This version of the Strong was extensively revised in 2004.

The Strong is particularly noteworthy because of its wide usage, its extensive research base, and its innovative role in the field of career assessment. The Strong has been the subject of extensive research studies in regard to occupational norms, long-term test–retest reliability, concurrent and predictive validity, cross-cultural differences, and counseling applications (Donnay et al., 2005; J. C. Hansen, 2000; Harmon, Hansen, Borgen, & Hammer, 1994; Lattimore & Borgen, 1999). This "landmark" inventory has led the way for other inventories in the use of criterion-related scale development and in the application of Holland's theory to interest measurement (D. P. Campbell & Borgen, 1999; Donnay, 1997).

The 2004 version of the Strong differs from 1994 version in the following ways:

- The number of items has been reduced from 317 to 291 (98 of these are new or revised items). All items now have a 5-point response format for each item, and all forced-choice items, previously found on two sections of the Strong, have been eliminated.
- The Basic Interest Scales have been revised and expanded in number from 25 to 30.
- The number of Occupational Scales has been increased from 211 to 244 (122 for each sex). Forty-eight of these scales (24 for each sex) have been added or updated for this edition. The new scales emphasize business and technology occupations, such as financial analyst and technical support specialist.
- A new Personal Style Scale, titled Team Orientation, has been added to the profile (Donnay et al., 2005).

The 291 items on the present version of the Strong are divided into six sections (occupations, subject areas, activities, leisure activities, people, and your characteristics). For the first five sections, clients indicate whether they *strongly like, like,* are *indifferent to, dislike,* or *strongly dislike* the activity represented by that particular item. For the last section, they indicate to what degree a characteristic is like them on a 5-point scale. Most people complete the Strong in 25 to 35 minutes.

The new Strong is based on a new norm group, called the General Representative Sample (GRS), which is more representative of the general population in terms of race, ethnicity, and occupational diversity than previous norm groups. The GRS consists of 1,125 men and 1,125 women culled from a large number of individuals who volunteered to take the Strong on the Internet in return for a free career assessment and report (Donnay et al., 2005). This combined group of men and women is used to provide the norms for both the General Occupational Themes and Basic Interest Scales. The separate groups of men and women that make up the GRS are used to represent the interests of men or women in general in constructing the Occupational Scales for each sex.

The answers must be scored by means of a computer program by the publisher or one of its agents. The scores are reported to the client on a multipage profile or as a computerized narrative interpretation. Standard, High School, and College Edition profiles are available, all of which present the same scores, but with different interpretive information. Besides several Administrative indexes, the Strong produces scores on four sets of scales—the General Occupational Themes (GOTs), Basic Interest Scales (BISs), Occupational Scales (OSs), and Personal Style Scales (PSSs)—each of which is described below.

The different parts of the Strong profile are discussed in regard to Michael, a 20-year-old college junior, who completed the Strong to help him in career planning. He felt that he had the ability to succeed in "almost anything" but could not decide which career he would find most satisfying. He marked a large number of concerns on the My Vocational Situation checklist (see chapter 7) that he completed at the same time as the Strong. In particular, he expressed a need to reduce his career uncertainty, to learn more about his career options, and to gain reassurance that he was moving in the right direction. He was considering the possibilities of majoring in chemistry, kinesiology, or some other scientific or technical field at that time. The most pertinent results from his Strong profile are shown in Table 9-1. (Sample reports of complete Strong profiles can be viewed on the Internet at http://cpp.com.)

Administrative Indexes

The Strong contains three administrative indexes that provide valuable information for interpreting the rest of the profile. These indexes are (a) Item response percentages, which show the percentages of *strongly like, like, indifferent to, dislike,* and *strongly dislike* responses for the different sections of the inventory; (b) Total responses index, which indicates number of items completed (if this number falls to less than 276, the answer sheet is not scored); and (c) Typicality index, a new measure on the Strong that reveals the consistency with which a person has responded to the items.

The Typicality index tallies the number of inconsistent responses to 24 pairs of items that possess similar content (Donnay et al., 2005). For example, if a person marks *like* for accountant as an occupation, but *dislike* for accounting as a subject, the responses would be scored as inconsistent for that pair of items. If the number of consistent responses falls to fewer than 17 (out of 24), the counselor should try to determine the reason for the inconsistency. The client may have a reading problem; misunderstood the directions; answered the items hurriedly or carelessly; or, in fact, may have an unusual pattern of interests.

Michael's scores on the Administrative indexes (not shown in Table 9-1) are all within normal response ranges. His total response percentages for the different parts of the inventory were *strongly like* = 10%, *like* = 19%, *indifferent to* = 23%, *dislike* = 27%, and *strongly dislike* = 20%, which is a fairly typical response pattern (Donnay et al., 2005, pp. 154–155). He answered all of the items on the Strong with no omissions as indicated by his response total of 291. Finally, he obtained a score of 22 (out of 24) on the Typicality index, which suggests a high level of consistency. Overall, the Administrative indexes indicate that he was discriminating, conscientious, and consistent in his approach to the inventory and that the results can be viewed as trustworthy. The Administrative indexes, which appear at the end of the profile under "Response Summary," should be inspected first before interpreting the rest of the profile to make sure that the results are reliable and to note any unusual pattern of responses.

TABLE 9-1
Strong Interest Inventory Scores for Michael, a College Student

Scale	Score	Scale	Score
General Occupational Themes		Military (R)	36
Investigative (I)	64	Taxes & Accounting (C)	36
Artistic (A)	56	Office Management (C)	35
Realistic (R)	51		
Social (S)	46	Occupational Scales[a]	
Enterprising (E)	42	Biologist (IA)	57
Conventional (C)	34	Artist (A)	56
		Graphic Designer (A)	54
Basic Interest Scales		Musician (A)	54
Science (I)	70	Geologist (IRA)	53
Athletics (R)	57	Photographer (ARE)	53
Nature & Agriculture (R)	56	Technical Writer (AI)	51
Performing Arts (A)	56	Elementary School Teacher (S)	50
Research (I)	56	Psychologist (IA)	48
Visual Arts & Design (A)	56	University Professor (IAS)	48
Religion & Spirituality (S)	53	Librarian (A)	47
Mechanics & Construction (R)	52	Medical Illustrator (AIR)	47
Medical Science (I)	52	Forester (RI)	43
Social Sciences (S)	52	Reporter (A)	43
Teaching & Education (S)	52	Social Worker (SA)	43
Culinary Arts (A)	51	Speech Pathologist (SA)	43
Writing & Mass Communication (A)	50	Translator (AI)	43
Entrepreneurship (E)	48	Urban & Regional Planner (AI)	43
Marketing & Advertising (E)	46	Broadcast Journalist (AE)	42
Politics & Public Speaking (E)	45	College Instructor (S)	42
Computer Hardware & Electronics (R)	44	Editor (AI)	42
Counseling & Helping (S)	44	Science Teacher (IRS)	41
Healthcare Services (S)	44	Chiropractor (ISA)	40
Law (E)	44	Medical Technologist (IRC)	40
Protective Services (R)	40	Parks & Recreation Manager (SE)	40
Finance & Investing (C)	39		
Human Resources & Training (S)	38	Personal Style Scales	
Management (E)	38	Learning Environment	61
Mathematics (I)	38	Risk Taking	54
Sales (E)	38	Leadership Style	45
Programming & Information Systems (C)	37	Team Orientation	41
		Work Style	36

Note. Scales in each category are ranked from highest to lowest score. Holland codes for each scale are shown in parentheses. A = Artistic; C = Conventional; E = Enterprising; I = Investigative; R = Realistic; S = Social.
[a]Only the Occupational Scales for which Michael obtained a score of 40 or above (indicating similarity of interests with men employed in the occupation) are listed.

General Occupational Themes (GOTs) and Basic Interest Scales (BISs)
The Strong contains two sets of general or homogeneous scales: the GOTs and the BISs. These scales have been developed by a combination of logical and statistical means to ensure that all of the items for each scale represent a single type of interest.

The GOTs provide a summary or overview of the Strong profile as well as a framework for interpreting the other scales. Each of the six GOTs contains items selected to fit Holland's (1997) descriptions of six types of occupational personalities. Holland found that people (as well as environments) could be broadly classified according to the six types of interests or skills shown in the hexagon in Figure 9-1. This figure shows the nature of the relationship among the six categories, which holds true across both sexes and all major ethnic and racial groups (Day & Rounds, 1998; Fouad, Harmon, & Borgen, 1997). The closer the categories are to each other on the figure, the more they have in common with each other. For example, people with Social interests are more likely also to possess Artistic or Enterprising interests (interests represented by adjacent categories) than they are the other types of interests. The two dimensions underlying this figure can be described as *people versus things* (Enterprising–Social vs. Realistic–Investigative) and *data versus ideas* (Conventional vs. Artistic).

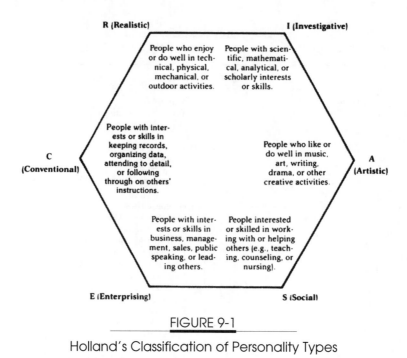

FIGURE 9-1

Holland's Classification of Personality Types

Note. Adapted from *Making Vocational Choices: A Theory of Vocational Personalities and Work Environment* (3rd ed., p. 35) by John. L. Holland, ©1997. Reproduced by permission of Psychological Assessment Resources, Inc., Lutz, Florida.

The 30 BISs function as subscales for the six GOTs. They are grouped into the six GOT categories on the basis of correlations between the two sets of scales. Each of the GOTs subsumes four or more of the BISs. As with the GOTs, the BISs are helpful in understanding the interest patterns associated with different occupations. Compared with the GOTs, the BISs are relatively short, with lengths ranging from 6 to 12 items (Donnay et al., 2005). Scores on these scales can be significantly affected by responses to a few items.

The GOTs and BISs have been standardized so that the combined group of men and women in the GRS will obtain a mean *T* score of 50 and a standard deviation of 10 on each scale. In general, scores above 57 indicate high interest (top 25% of norm group) in that activity, whereas scores below 43 indicate little interest (bottom 25% of norm group); however, interpretation of scores varies somewhat based upon the client's gender. The following interpretive comments are used in the Strong reports to indicate the level of one's interest in an activity compared with others of the same sex: "Very High" (91st to 100th percentile), "High" (76th to 90th percentile), "Moderate" (26th to 75th percentile), "Little" (11th to 25th percentile), and "Very Little" (0 to 10th percentile; Donnay et al., 2005). For example, a *T* score of 60 on the Mechanics and Construction BIS is interpreted as Moderate for men, but Very High for women

Gender differences are most notable on scales in the Realistic category. Men in the GRS averaged between 5 to 10 points ($\frac{1}{2}$ to 1 standard deviation) higher than women on the Realistic GOT and the Mechanics & Construction, Military, Computer Hardware & Electronics, Athletics, and Protective Services BISs (Donnay et al., 2005). Such differences pertain not only to men and women in general, but also to men and women employed in the same occupations, such as engineering (Harmon et al., 1994). Counselors should take such differences into account when interpreting scores on these scales, particularly for individuals who may be considering nontraditional occupations.

High scores on both the GOTs and BISs are based on *like* responses, whereas low scores are based on *dislike* responses. A large number of *likes* indicate broad interests; a large number of *dislikes* indicate fairly focused interests. In either case, the interest scores should be interpreted in relationship to one another. That is, clients should give careful consideration to their highest scores regardless of their absolute level.

The GOTs and BISs yield results that are highly reliable both in terms of internal consistency and test–retest consistency over extended time periods. Empirical validity studies indicate that both sets of scales effectively discriminate among people employed in different types of occupations (Donnay et al., 2005: Donnay & Borgen, 1996). Cross-cultural research with the Strong indicates that the results are equally valid for members of different racial and ethnic groups (Fouad & Mohler, 2004; Lattimore & Borgen, 1999).

The GOT scores can be used to arrive at a Holland code to summarize a person's interest. To determine Michael's Holland code, his highest scores on the GOT scales must be identified. As shown in Table 9-1, his highest scores were Investigative (I) and Artistic (A), in that order, which remain the same when gender norms are taken into consideration. Therefore, his Holland code is IA. With this information, a large number of occupations with similar codes can be identified for the client's consideration by checking resources such as the *Dictionary of Holland Occupational Codes* (G. D. Gottfredson & Holland, 1996) or the O*NET database on the Internet (U.S. Department of Labor, Employment and Training Administration [ETA], 2006).

As a counseling technique, it is usually helpful to ask clients to look at their four or five highest and lowest scores on the BISs. Do they agree with this description of their interests? Can they think of ways in which they could combine the activities represented by their highest scores in a career or life plan? Michael received his highest scores on the Science, Athletics, Nature & Agriculture, Performing Arts, Research, and Visual Arts & Design scales. These scores show a pronounced interest in investigative activities in addition to relatively high interests in athletic, outdoor, and creative endeavors.

Occupational Scales (OSs)

The Strong profile provides scores for 122 pairs of OSs for men and women. The OSs were developed by selecting items that significantly differentiated between the interests of men or women in the occupation and men or women in general. The typical scale contains 25 to 30 items selected in this manner.

Members of occupational criterion groups used to develop the OSs were screened on the following characteristics:

- Employed in occupation for 3 years or more
- Satisfied with their work
- Perform typical duties of members of the occupation

Information regarding the specific characteristics of each occupational criterion group, such as number of participants, year tested, mean age, mean years of experience, education, and typical duties, can be obtained from the Strong manual (Donnay et al., 2005, pp. 183–263).

Each of the OSs is coded in terms of the predominant interest pattern of people employed in that occupation based on Holland's classification system (see Figure 9-1). For example, the Biologist scale for men is coded IA (as noted in Table 9-1) because men who are biologists more frequently express Investigative and Artistic interests than do other men. The Holland codes are helpful in organizing the OS scores and in understanding the nature of the interests underlying the scores.

The OSs have been normed so that men or women in the occupation (depending on which sex was used for constructing the scale) obtain a mean T score of 50 with a standard deviation of 10. Men and women in general obtain mean T scores of approximately 20 to 35 for most scales. A score of 40 or above (referred to as "similar interests" on the Strong profile) indicates that a client endorses many of the same likes and dislikes as those that differentiate men or women in a particular occupation from men or women in general. A score of 29 or below ("dissimilar interests") indicates a rejection of this interest pattern.

Some clients receive few or no high scores on the OSs. In such cases, scores can still be interpreted in relation to each other. Students with "flat" (undifferentiated) profiles may need additional time and experience to clarify their interests. A 12-year follow-up study indicated that students with flat profiles took longer to get established in their careers; however, at the end of 12 years, they were just as satisfied and successful in their careers as those with differentiated profiles (S. A. Sackett & Hansen, 1995). In fact, the male students with flat profiles in this study showed a higher level of satisfaction with their jobs after 12 years than did those with differentiated profiles, possibly because they may have been more flexible and easier to please.

Separate-gender scales have been established to take into account differences in social conditioning. Contrary to previous editions of the Strong, which reported scores on both the male and female OSs for all respondents, the new form of the Strong provides scores for only the same-sex scales. Because the same occupations are now represented on both the male and female scales and because most of the mean differences between scores on the male and female scales are relatively small, it is not as important to know the scores of clients on the opposite-sex scales as it once was (Donnay et al., 2005).

In contrast with the GOTs and BISs, high scores on the OSs are based on both *like* and *dislike* responses. People obtain high scores when they share the same likes and dislikes as people in the occupation. In essence, high scores on the OSs point to occupations in which individuals can pursue those activities they enjoy and avoid those they dislike.

A few scales, such as Farmer/Rancher and Radiologic Technologist, include a relatively large number of items with positive weights for *dislike* responses. People in these occupations possess rather narrow or focused interests. If clients mark a large number of *dislikes,* they will probably obtain elevated scores on these scales. High scores that are based primarily on dislikes can be misleading. It is important to look at the specific likes and dislikes (as revealed by the BISs) that underlie an OS score.

OS scores are highly reliable, particularly for people 20 years of age and older and over short time periods (less than 1 year). Even over very long time periods (10 to 20 years), the OSs produce similar results for most people based on research conducted with earlier versions of the Strong.

Concurrent validation studies show that the OSs significantly differentiate between people in the occupation and people in general (Donnay et al., 2005). A number of longitudinal research studies (ranging in length from 3 to 18 years) have been conducted to examine the predictive validity of earlier versions of the Strong. These studies found that from one third to two thirds of the people who took the Strong were later employed in occupations related to their high scores (Donnay, 1997). J. C. Hansen and Dik (2005) found that 57% of college students tested as freshmen were employed in an occupation related to their Strong results 12 years later. This figure increased to 73% for a subset of the sample when their scores from the Strongs completed in the senior year were compared with their occupation 8 years later. The Strong scores were equally predictive for men and women.

Scores on the OSs show greater validity when they are supported by scores on the BISs that are most relevant; for example, high scores on the Life Insurance Agent OS possess greater predictive validity when they are paired with high scores on the Sales BIS. OS scores are also more valid when clients report that they have had work or volunteer experiences in those fields.

Research indicates that the OSs predict occupational membership just as accurately for college students who are undecided as they do for those who are decided (Bartling & Hood, 1981). This finding is important because the Strong is frequently used with students who are having difficulty in making a career decision.

When OS scores agree with expressed interests (career choice stated at the time that the Strong was completed), the predictive accuracy of Occupational scores significantly increases (Bartling & Hood, 1981). When OS scores disagree with expressed interests, the latter are more accurate. Expressed interests take into account factors that are not measured by the Strong, such as values, abilities, and opportunities. For example, students may follow family traditions in choosing occupations instead of basing their choices on measured interests. Counselors should recognize the limitations of an instrument such as the Strong. It provides helpful information about an individual's interests, but it needs to be incorporated with other relevant information.

In general, people report greater job satisfaction when their occupation matches the type of occupation suggested by their Strong scores than when it does not; however, the relationship tends to be modest. Presumably, factors other than interests, such as salary, opportunities for advancement, and relationships with supervisors or coworkers, account for much of an individual's satisfaction or dissatisfaction. In addition, some individuals appear to be more flexible in the expression of their interests so that they can learn to adapt to a wide variety of situations (Darcy & Tracey, 2003).

As indicated in Table 9-1, Michael obtained high scores (*T* score of 40 or above) on a relatively large number of the OS scales. His interests resembled those of men in 26 of the 122 Occupational scales for men.

Scores on the OSs can be interpreted by referring to both the GOTs and the BISs. Most of the OSs for which Michael obtained a high score have Investigative or Artistic primary codes in keeping with his highest scores on the GOTs and BISs. His high score on the Biologist OS can be directly related to his high scores on the Investigative GOT and on the Science, Nature & Agriculture, and Research BISs. His Biologist score is also elevated because of his preference for cultural-esthetic activities (indicated by high scores on Artistic GOT and Performing Arts and Visual Arts & Design BISs) and his rejection of business activities (as shown by low scores on Conventional and Enterprising scales), both common features of the interest patterns of scientists and others in similar occupations (Donnay et al., 2005; Harmon et al., 1994). The scores on the GOTs and BISs can be used in a similar manner to clarify the nature of the interest patterns underlying his other OS scores.

Personal Style Scales (PSSs)
The 2004 version of the Strong includes five PSSs that measure personality factors related to educational and career planning. These five scales, each of which is bipolar in nature, are briefly described below (Donnay et al., 2005).

- Work Style: High scorers prefer to work with people; low scorers prefer to work with ideas, data, or things.
- Learning Environment: High scorers possess academic interests associated with advanced degrees; low scorers possess practical interests associated with technical or trade school attendance.
- Leadership Style: High scorers prefer to direct others; low scorers prefer to lead by example.
- Risk Taking/Adventure: High scorers prefer to take chances; low scorers prefer to play it safe.
- Team Orientation: High scorers prefer to accomplish tasks as a team; low scorers prefer to accomplish tasks independently.

Although these scales have been constructed by different techniques, they are all intended to provide information concerning personality factors associated with career development. Research indicates that the PSSs significantly add to the validity of both the GOTs and BISs in differentiating among occupational groups (Donnay & Borgen, 1996). The PSSs can be used as a means of introducing personality factors into career planning that might otherwise be overlooked.

Low and high *T* scores (scores below 46 or above 54) are said to be "clear" scores that can be interpreted as indicating a preference for one end or the other of the bipolar scales. As indicated in Table 9-1, Michael obtained clear scores on four of the five PSSs. Three of the clear scores fall below 46, namely, Work Style, Team Orientation, and Leadership Style. These scores show a preference to work independently with things or ideas instead of people in situations where he is not expected to lead others. He also obtained a clear score above 55 on the Learning Environment scale, which supports his pursuit of a college degree, especially if he can find a compatible major and career field.

Interpretation of Client Profile
Much of Michael's profile has been discussed in preceding paragraphs. In addition to the profile, he received a copy of an interpretive booklet that provided helpful information for understanding and applying the Strong results in career exploration (Borgen & Grutter, 2005).

As a means of obtaining some focus, his counselor asked him to select several occupations on the Strong profile that had the most appeal to him. He was asked to look particularly at the scales for which he received scores indicating similarity of interests but not to exclude any occupations. He chose the following occupations: photographer, university professor, librarian, science teacher, and parks and recreation manager. He had obtained scores showing similarity between his interests and those of men employed in each of these occupations. He also expressed an interest in several other occupations with Investigative and Artistic Holland codes as listed in the interpretive booklet that he was provided, including laboratory technician, biochemist, astronomer, chemical engineer, medical research, scientific researcher, and anthropologist.

In addition to the occupations mentioned above, Michael expressed an interest in chemist (IR code) and pharmacist (ICE), occupations in which his OS scores were in the midrange (Chemist = 33; Pharmacist = 36). His Chemist score was lowered because of his very low score ($T = 38$)

on the Mathematics BIS. His Pharmacist score is affected by both low math interests and low business interests. If he were to enter pharmacy as a career, he said it probably would be as a hospital or clinical pharmacist, not as a community (business-oriented) pharmacist. He believed that his Mathematics interest score may have increased from what it was when he completed the Strong 2 months earlier. He was failing his calculus course (a course for which he was not well prepared compared with other students) at the time. Since that time, he had re-enrolled in calculus for a second semester, signed up for tutoring, and improved his performance considerably, which helped to increase his liking for the subject. Aside from math, his other grades were very good (primarily *A*s and *B*s).

At this point, he thought he would decide to major in chemistry, which would allow him to pursue his interests in science and research. He would like to work for a while as a lab technician after graduating from college and then consider the possibility of returning to graduate school. His counselor discussed with him ways in which he could obtain more information about all of the career possibilities mentioned above, including visiting departmental representatives on campus for each of the academic majors in these fields, interviewing people employed in these fields, using the career research features of O*NET OnLine (the occupational information network sponsored by the U.S. Department of Labor, ETA, 2005b) , and possibly taking a course in these areas or doing volunteer work in a related field.

He was pleased to obtain information from his Strong profile that supported his interests in science and research. He recognized the potential conflict caused by his low interest in math, which he was attempting to address. He appreciated the information that he received regarding other career possibilities suggested by his interest profile. The Strong enabled him to evaluate systematically his interests in regard to different career fields, which was the type of information that he needed at the time.

Strong Interest Explorer (SIE)

The SIE is a simplified, self-scorable version of the Strong for use with young people beginning in the eighth grade (Morris, Chartrand, & Donnay, 2002). It contains 130 items that can be completed in 10 to 15 minutes. This instrument, which provides scores for 14 basic interest areas, can be used in either individual or group settings with students or others in the early stages of career exploration.

Skills Confidence Scales

The Strong, which focuses on interests, may be supplemented with instruments that ask clients to evaluate their abilities to succeed in different types of activities. Two instruments—the Skills Confidence Inventory (SCI) and the Expanded Skills Confidence Inventory (E-SCI)—have been developed specifically for this purpose (Betz, Borgen, & Harmon, 1996; Betz et al., 2003). The SCI contains six scales that match the six Holland interest scales used on the Strong. The E-SCI contains 17 scales that parallel many of the Basic Interest scales found on the Strong. Research shows scores from either the SCI or E-SCI significantly enhance the validity of Strong scores in predicting occupational criteria (Donnay & Borgen, 1999; Rottinghaus, Betz, & Borgen, 2003). Both types of measures (interests and self-rated skills) should be taken into account in considering career options.

Campbell Interest and Skill Survey (CISS®)

David Campbell, who is known for his work in updating and revising early forms of the Strong (previously titled the Strong-Campbell Interest Inventory), created the CISS subsequent to his work on the Strong (D. P. Campbell, 2002). The CISS is one of several inventories in an integrated battery of psychological surveys called the Campbell Development Surveys (D. P. Campbell, 1993). The CISS is similar to the Strong in that it includes both general and occupational interest scales; it differs from the Strong by its inclusion of a set of self-report skill scales to match each of the interest scales (D. P. Campbell et al., 1992).

The CISS provides interest and skill scores for 7 Orientation scales, 29 Basic scales, 60 Occupational scales, and 3 Special scales (Academic Focus, Extroversion, and Variety). The 7 Orientation scales are similar to the 6 Holland scales on the Strong. The Strong Realistic scale has been subdivided into Producing and Adventuring scales to create the seventh Orientation scale. The Basic scales on the CISS have much in common with the Basic scales on the Strong.

In contrast with the Strong, the CISS uses unisex Occupational scales instead of separate scales for men and women. These scales were formed by comparing the interests and skills of a combined sample of men and women in the occupation with a general reference sample of men and women. The proportions of men and women in the general reference sample were adjusted for each occupation to match the proportions of men and women in the occupational sample as a means of controlling for gender differences. On the basis of a study on eight occupations, D. P. Campbell et al. (1992) found that combined-sex scales worked about as well as single-sex scales in representing the interests of people within and outside the occupation.

Reliability studies conducted with employed adults indicate that the CISS results are internally consistent (general scales) and stable over a 3-month time period (all scales). In regard to validity, people in the occupation score substantially higher on the interest and skill scales for that occupation than do people in general. On the average, people in the occupational criterion group used in creating an occupational scale scored about 2 standard deviations higher (18 to 20 points) on the Occupational scale than did people in the general reference sample (D. P. Campbell et al., 1992). These results compare favorably with those reported for the Strong.

Validity studies indicate that the CISS interest scales effectively differentiate among students in different academic majors (J. C. Hansen & Neuman, 1999; Pendergrass, Hansen, Neuman, & Nutter, 2003). About 65% to 75% of the students in these studies were engaged in college majors compatible with their interest scores.

Scores on the skill and interest scales for the same activities or occupations are interpreted in terms of the following four categories:

- *Pursue:* high interest, high skill
- *Explore:* high skill, lower interest
- *Develop:* high interest, lower skill
- *Avoid:* low interest, low skill

For example, individuals with a high score on the Attorney skill scale but a relatively low score on the Attorney interest scale are encouraged to explore this occupation with the thought that their interests in it might be enhanced or that they might find a niche in the occupational field that they would enjoy.

The test publishers provide a *Career Planner* booklet that may be used as an aid in interpreting and acting on the CISS results. According to Boggs (2002), the CISS is "a useful instrument for career assessment" that is "well constructed and technically tested" (p. 199).

In addition to the CISS, other instruments in the Campbell Development Surveys include the Campbell Organizational Survey, Campbell Leadership Index, Campbell–Hallam Team Development Survey, and Campbell Community Survey (D. P. Campbell, 1993). These instruments, which possess many characteristics in common to aid interpretation, can help counselors in their work with teams, organizations, and communities in addition to individuals.

An example of the use of the CISS in counseling is presented below.

Case Example

When Tess first came to the Counseling Center as a 31-year-old returning adult student, she had just graduated from college with a degree in business administration. At that time, she was actively involved in a job search. She wanted to learn more about herself and how her interests and skills related to a variety of occupations and leisure activities. The counselor assigned the CISS to help her in this process.

Her scores on the CISS report summary are shown in Figure 9-2. She produced a valid profile as shown by the Procedural Checks on the bottom of the second page of the report summary. Her response percentages for the interest and skill items were normally distributed, her responses to pairs of similar items were consistent in all but one case, and she omitted no items.

She obtained high scores (*T* score of 55 or higher) on all seven Orientation skill scales but on only two (Organizing and Analyzing) of the Orientation interest scales. As indicated

TESS — **Orientations and Basic Scales**

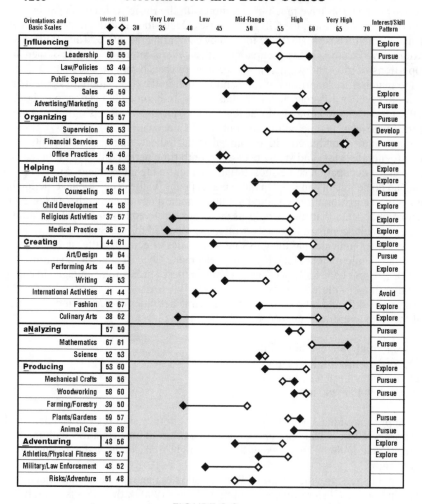

Orientations and Basic Scales	Interest ◆	Skill ◇	Interest/Skill Pattern
Influencing	53	55	Explore
Leadership	60	55	Pursue
Law/Policies	53	49	
Public Speaking	50	39	
Sales	46	59	Explore
Advertising/Marketing	58	63	Pursue
Organizing	65	57	Pursue
Supervision	68	53	Develop
Financial Services	66	66	Pursue
Office Practices	45	46	
Helping	45	63	Explore
Adult Development	51	64	Explore
Counseling	58	61	Pursue
Child Development	44	58	Explore
Religious Activities	37	57	Explore
Medical Practice	36	57	Explore
Creating	44	61	Explore
Art/Design	59	64	Pursue
Performing Arts	44	55	Explore
Writing	46	53	
International Activities	41	44	Avoid
Fashion	52	67	Explore
Culinary Arts	38	62	Explore
aNalyzing	57	59	Pursue
Mathematics	67	61	Pursue
Science	52	53	
Producing	53	60	Explore
Mechanical Crafts	58	56	Pursue
Woodworking	58	60	Pursue
Farming/Forestry	39	50	
Plants/Gardens	59	57	Pursue
Animal Care	58	68	Pursue
Adventuring	48	56	Explore
Athletics/Physical Fitness	52	57	Explore
Military/Law Enforcement	43	52	
Risks/Adventure	51	48	

FIGURE 9-2

Campbell™ Interest and Skill Survey (CISS®) Report Summary
for Tess, a 31-Year-Old Recent College Graduate *(Continued next page)*

on the profile, she was encouraged to pursue Organizing and Analyzing occupations and to explore occupations in the other fields.

Tess showed high interests and self-rated skills on the Leadership, Advertising/Marketing, Financial Services, Counseling, and Mathematics Basic scales, all areas that can be related to her major in business administration. She also obtained high interest and skill scores on the Art/Design, Mechanical Crafts, Woodworking, Plants/Gardens, and Animal Care scales, which can be looked on as possible leisure-time pursuits as well as career alternatives.

Tess obtained a large number of high scores on both the Occupational interest and skill scales (see second page of report summary), especially in the Organizing and Analyzing areas. She felt encouraged by the test results. She planned to investigate the following occupations in greater detail, all of which she was advised to pursue on the CISS report: financial planner, corporate trainer, bank manager, CEO/president, and restaurant manager. All of these occupations were consistent with her major in business administration.

In a follow-up interview conducted 4 years later, Tess reported that shortly after completing counseling, she obtained a job as a program manager that involved both organizing and influencing skills and interests. She disliked the influencing (public speaking) aspect of that job and left it after 6 months. She then obtained a job as a bookkeeper for a public

TESS
Female
Age 31

Occupational Scales

DATE SCORED: 2/06/97
White
College Graduate

Report Summary

Influencing

	Orientation Code	Standard Scores	Interest/Skill Pattern
Attorney	I	I 43 / S 49	
Financial Planner	IO	I 65 / S 66	Pursue
Hotel Manager	IO	I 53 / S 64	Explore
Manufacturer's Representative	IO	I 54 / S 75	Explore
Marketing Director	IO	I 61 / S 59	Pursue
Realtor	IO	I 58 / S 73	Pursue
CEO/President	IOA	I 65 / S 66	Pursue
Human Resources Director	IOH	I 71 / S 61	Pursue
School Superintendent	IOH	I 71 / S 61	Pursue
Advertising Account Executive	IC	I 45 / S 68	Explore
Media Executive	IC	I 41 / S 57	Explore
Public Relations Director	IC	I 52 / S 55	Explore
Corporate Trainer	ICH	I 76 / S 57	Pursue

Organizing

	Orientation Code	Standard Scores	Interest/Skill Pattern
Secretary	O	I 44 / S 43	Avoid
Bank Manager	OI	I 56 / S 68	Pursue
Insurance Agent	OI	I 56 / S 69	Pursue
Retail Store Manager	OI	I 63 / S 64	Pursue
Hospital Administrator	OIH	I 61 / S 58	Pursue
Accountant (CPA)	ON	I 74 / S 69	Pursue
Bookkeeper	ON	I 63 / S 59	Pursue

Helping

	Orientation Code	Standard Scores	Interest/Skill Pattern
Child Care Worker	H	I 36 / S 65	Explore
Guidance Counselor	H	I 47 / S 68	Explore
Religious Leader	H	I 16 / S 53	
Teacher K-12	H	I 43 / S 65	Explore
Social Worker	HC	I 49 / S 72	Explore
Psychologist	HNC	I 47 / S 72	Explore
Nurse (RN)	HN	I 35 / S 68	Explore
Nursing Administrator	HIO	I 42 / S 65	Explore

Creating

	Orientation Code	Standard Scores	Interest/Skill Pattern
Commercial Artist	C	I 40 / S 67	Explore
Fashion Designer	C	I 57 / S 71	Pursue
Liberal Arts Professor	C	I 40 / S 52	
Librarian	C	I 52 / S 43	
Musician	C	I 34 / S 53	
Translator/Interpreter	C	I 47 / S 46	
Writer/Editor	C	I 34 / S 56	Explore
Restaurant Manager	CO	I 55 / S 57	Pursue
Chef	CP	I 43 / S 63	Explore

aNalyzing

	Orientation Code	Standard Scores	Interest/Skill Pattern
Physician	N	I 42 / S 62	Explore
Chemist	NP	I 53 / S 61	Explore
Medical Researcher	NP	I 61 / S 63	Pursue
Engineer	NP	I 63 / S 63	Pursue
Math/Science Teacher	NPH	I 62 / S 61	Pursue
Computer Programmer	NQ	I 62 / S 60	Pursue
Statistician	NO	I 72 / S 68	Pursue
Systems Analyst	NOP	I 69 / S 63	Pursue

Producing

	Orientation Code	Standard Scores	Interest/Skill Pattern
Carpenter	P	I 51 / S 63	Explore
Electrician	PN	I 53 / S 64	Explore
Veterinarian	PN	I 29 / S 62	Explore
Airline Mechanic	PNA	I 62 / S 59	Pursue
Agribusiness Manager	PO	I 57 / S 61	Pursue
Landscape Architect	PNC	I 69 / S 73	Pursue
Architect	PC	I 57 / S 66	Pursue

Adventuring

	Orientation Code	Standard Scores	Interest/Skill Pattern
Police Officer	AI	I 38 / S 56	Explore
Military Officer	AIO	I 61 / S 55	Pursue
Ski Instructor	AP	I 55 / S 56	Pursue
Test Pilot	APN	I 48 / S 58	Explore
Athletic Coach	AH	I 55 / S 64	Pursue
Athletic Trainer	AH	I 44 / S 61	Explore
Emergency Medical Technician	AH	I 44 / S 61	Explore
Fitness Instructor	AH	I 55 / S 60	Pursue

Special Scales

	Standard Scores
Academic Focus	I 50 / S 56
Extraversion	I 56 / S 54

Procedural Checks

Response Percentage Check

Interest Items	19	18	15	11	22	16	Valid
Skill Items	4	38	28	23	8	0	Valid

	Inconsistency Check		Omitted Items Check	
Interest Items	1	Valid	0	Valid
Skill Items	0	Valid	0	Valid

* Standard Scores: I = Interests; S = Skills   ** Interest/Skill Pattern (Pursue, Develop, Explore, Avoid)
*** Orientation Code: I = Influencing. O = Organizing. H = Helping. C = Creating. N = aNalyzing. P = Producing. A = Adventuring

FIGURE 9-2

Campbell™ Interest and Skill Survey (CISS®) Report Summary for Tess, a 31-Year-Old Recent College Graduate (*Continued*)

agency, from which she was soon promoted to chief financial officer and assistant director. She thrived in this work, which matched her interests and skills on the Financial Services, Mathematics, and Leadership scales. The CISS helped Tess to identify a career field that proved to be satisfying and fulfilling for her.

Kuder® Career Search (KCS) With Person Match

G. Frederic Kuder (1903–2000) contributed greatly to the field of interest measurement by developing three different types of interest inventories over a lifetime of work. First, he created the Kuder Preference Record–Vocational (KPR-V) in 1939, an instrument that was widely used in counseling settings for many years (Zytowski, 1992; Zytowski & Austin, 2001). The KPR-V, which measured interests in broad domains such as art and science, was revised several times and eventually replaced in 1963 by the Kuder General Interest Survey (KGIS), a simplified version of the KPR-V with a sixth-grade reading level.

Second, he constructed the Kuder Occupational Interest Survey (KOIS), Form D, in 1956 to measure interests with occupational scales in a manner similar to the Strong. This instrument evolved into the KOIS, Form DD, which used improved test construction procedures and added college major scales. Finally, as a third type of inventory, he developed the KCS with Person Match, a "truly innovative" inventory that compares an individual's interests with those of specific people in various occupations (Kelly, 2002b; Zytowski, 1992).

Kuder's first two interest inventories, the KGIS (former KPR-V) and the KOIS, have both become somewhat dated and less useful for counselors (Kelly, 2002b; Pope, 2002). The broad interest scales used on the KGIS can also be found on the KCS, so that the latter instrument can essentially serve as a replacement for the KGIS as well as provide the Person Match information when desired. The KOIS has not been revised for some time. Most of the criterion groups upon which its scales are based are now more than 30 years old and need to be updated (Kelly, 2002b). Similar information based upon more recent research can be obtained from other interest inventories, such as the Strong or CISS. For these reasons, only the KCS with Person Match will be discussed in detail here.

The KCS contains 60 forced-choice triads (48 triads adapted from the KOIS and 12 new triads) written at a sixth-grade reading level (Zytowski, 2006). Each triad includes three activities, such as "Build birdhouses," "Write articles about birds," and "Draw sketches of birds," which clients rank in order according to their preferences. The use of forced-choice items makes it possible to control for response styles such as acquiescence (marking "like" to most items) and deviation (making extreme responses to most items). The forced-choice item format affects the interpretation of the results. The scores must be interpreted in regard to each other. A high score indicates that the person likes that type of activity more than other activities compared with members of the norm group, but it does not indicate the absolute magnitude of the interest.

The KCS can be taken and scored on the Internet or by paper and pencil. Clients receive scores on 6 Career Cluster scales similar to the six Holland categories used on other interest inventories and on 10 Activity Preference (AP) scales similar to the 10 broad interest scales that appeared on the KGIS. The relationships among the Holland categories, Career Cluster scales, and the AP scales are indicated below:

Holland Category	Career Cluster Scale	Activity Preference Scale
Realistic	Outdoor/Mechanical	Nature, Mechanical
Investigative	Science/Technical	Science/Technical
Artistic	Arts/Communication	Performing Arts, Communications
Social	Social/Personal Service	Human Services
Enterprising	Sales/Management	Sales, Management
Conventional	Business Operations	Computations, Office Detail

The six Career Cluster scales show the degree of similarity between an individual's interests and those of people classified in six different career areas. These scales are "criterion scales" similar to the occupational scales on the KOIS that clients can use to identify career fields that attract people with their same types of interests. With special arrangements, the KCS can also be programmed to provide scores for other career clusters, such as those used in some career information systems or school curriculums (Zytowski, 2006).

A "single grand norm group" consisting of both males and females from sixth grade through adults is used to obtain percentile scores for the Career Cluster scales and the AP scales. Some sex differences have been found on the scales, however, Zytowski (2006) noted that such differences do not significantly affect the score interpretations because of the emphasis on rank order of scores within the individual.

In terms of reliability, scores on the AP scales showed satisfactory internal consistency and test–retest consistency for a sample of college students who completed the KCS online (Ihle-Helledy, Zytowski, & Fouad, 2004). Whole profiles for individuals tested twice over a 3-week period also proved to be reasonably stable (Zytowski, 2006).

Longitudinal research studies conducted with earlier versions of the Kuder indicate that most of the students tested in their teenage years are employed in occupations consistent with their basic interests in later years (Kuder, 1988). People employed in occupations related to their interests also reported greater job satisfaction compared with individuals in jobs unrelated to their interests. These studies support the validity of the general interest scores such as those found on the KCS; however, these same studies also show that a surprisingly large number of students become happily employed in occupations that would not have been predicted by their scores. This latter finding supports the use of the Person Match of the KCS, which underlines the fact that people with the same basic interests can find satisfaction with employment in a broad array of occupations.

The Person Match part of the KCS has been designed to help clients identify and explore various career possibilities. Clients are provided with detailed descriptions of the type of work pursued by individuals with their same interests. This process helps clients to realize their multipotentiality, as shown by the wide range of occupations typically represented by the individual descriptions that they receive. This technique uses "stories instead of scores" to suggest a variety of career paths to a client (Savickas, 1993).

To obtain "person matches," a client's scores on the 10 AP scales are ranked in order and correlated with the rank orders of activity preferences for nearly 2,000 individuals in the KCS occupational database. Nearly all of the occupations included in the *Occupational Outlook Handbook* (U.S. Department of Labor, Bureau of Labor Statistics, 2006) are represented within the KCS occupational database. Occupations with a large number of members are represented by at least several individuals; for example, the database includes descriptive information for more than 30 registered nurses. All members of the database must be satisfied in their work and must have at least 3 years of work experience.

Clients receive detailed descriptions of the individual careers and lifestyles of the 14 people (7 from each of their two highest career clusters) who most closely resemble them in terms of interests. The descriptions include information about how their career was chosen, specific job duties, likes and dislikes, and future career plans. In essence, this approach provides a client with the equivalent of 14 informational interviews with employed adults who are similar to the client and who have found satisfying occupations. The client report form includes a number of suggestions to help individuals interpret their inventory results and investigate career options.

Because the Person Match part of the KCS is intended to motivate clients to engage in career exploration, it needs to be validated according to its success in accomplishing this purpose. One recent study along this line found that individuals who completed the KCS reported more confidence in their career exploration and planning activities than did individuals who did not complete the KCS (Ihle-Helledy et al., 2004).

The KCS can be used effectively with two audiences. First, the homogeneous scales on the KCS can be used to provide general information regarding interest patterns for young people in middle school or high school who are just beginning to think about careers. Second, the Person Match part of the KCS can be helpful in expanding the career exploration of college students and older people who can benefit from consideration of multiple options. Some individuals who wish to focus their career search may be frustrated by the multiple options provided by Person Match. These individuals may prefer an interest inventory such as the Strong or CISS that provides scores for specific occupations.

The KCS is part of the Kuder Career Planning System, which also includes the Kuder Skills Assessment (KSA) and the revised Super's Work Values Inventory (see chapter 8). The KSA is a 90-item inventory that asks clients to rate their skills in six types of activities (Zytowski & Luzzo, 2002). These six activities match the six interest areas measured on the Kuder Career Search. Each item includes four response options ranging from "I don't think I could ever learn to do this task" to "I can already do this task." As with the KCS, this instrument may be used with individuals from middle school age through adult. By using the KSA, counselors are able to take into account a client's perception of his or her abilities as well as interests in different type of activities.

Information derived from the Kuder Career Planning System is designed for self-interpretation with the aid of ancillary materials including the book *Take Hold of Your Future* (Harris-Bowlsbey, 2005). Clients may use the KCS and other instruments in the Kuder Career Planning System in conjunction with the Kuder Online Career Portfolio, a career planning tool and resume builder (National Career Assessment Services, Inc., 2006).

Self-Directed Search (SDS)

The SDS (4th edition), which can be self-administered, self-scored, and self-interpreted, is based on Holland's (1997) theory of vocational choice. Holland's theory can be summarized as a "person–environment congruence" theory (Spokane & Catalano, 2000, p. 137) that assumes that people will be most satisfied and successful if they live and work in an environment that is compatible with their interests and skills. The same six categories used to describe an individual's personality type are also used to describe occupational environments, so that comparisons between an individual's characteristics and occupation's attributes can easily be made by means of the SDS.

Although it is often classified as an interest inventory, the SDS is actually an inventory of both interests and abilities. Holland referred to it as a career counseling simulation. It consists of four sections: two that ask about liking for activities (66 items) or occupations (84 items) and two that that inquire about competencies (66 items) and abilities (12 self-rating scales).

Four versions of this instrument have been created for different populations (Holland, Powell, & Fritzsche, 1994). These versions include the Regular Form (Form R) for high school students, college students, and adults; the Easy Form (Form E) for adults or high school students who possess limited education or reading ability; the Career Planning Form (Form CP) for adults in career transition and those seeking occupations at upper levels of educational requirements; and the SDS Career Explorer for middle school and junior high school students.

In addition to the traditional paper-and-pencil format, the SDS Form R may be completed by means of software installed on a personal computer (SDS: Computer Version) or by accessing it on the Internet at the Psychological Assessment Resources Web site (http://www3.parinc.com/). All three versions of the inventory produce equivalent SDS scores (Lumsden et al., 2004). Students prefer the computer versions, both of which include an interpretive report, over the paper-and-pencil version. For individuals engaged in counseling, the personal computer version of the SDS is desirable because it includes a professional summary for the counselor. The Internet version, which does not include such a summary, is basically a self-help or "stand-alone" instrument

Each part of the SDS includes an equal number of items from each of the six Holland categories (Realistic, Investigative, Artistic, Social, Enterprising, and Conventional) as described earlier in this chapter. Based on the test taker's responses, a three-letter Holland code is derived that can then be compared with the Holland code for various occupations or college majors. The *Occupations Finder,* a booklet that accompanies the SDS, lists over 1,300 occupations according to their Holland code and the amount of education required. Holland codes for nearly all occupations can be obtained via the O*NET occupational database on the Internet (U.S. Department of Labor, ETA, 2006) or by consulting the *Dictionary of Holland Occupational Codes* (G. D. Gottfredson & Holland, 1996). Codes for more than 750 postsecondary fields of study are given in *The Educational Opportunities Finder* (Rosen, Holmberg, & Holland, 1994). Finally, two-letter codes for more than 750 leisure activities have been published for use in life planning outside of careers (Holmberg, Rosen, & Holland, 1990).

Many of the codes that Holland and his colleagues have assigned to different occupations are based primarily on judgments of job analysts. These codes may differ from the codes assigned by authors of interest inventories based on actual test scores. For example, food service manager is coded as an ESR (Enterprising-Social-Realistic) occupation in the *Occupations Finder,* whereas it is coded as a CES (Conventional-Enterprising-Social) occupation for both men and women on the Strong. In most cases, the codes based on the two types of systems agree. When they disagree, codes derived by means of actual data should be given greater weight.

The SDS uses the client's raw scores in determining Holland codes. Holland has been criticized for this approach in that it reinforces sexual stereotypes. With the use of raw scores, men are more likely to obtain high scores on the Realistic, Investigative, and Enterprising scales, and women are more likely to score high on the Social, Artistic, and Conventional scales than they would if scores based on separate-sex norms were used. Holland defended his approach as reflecting the real world, namely, that men and women are in fact attracted to different types of activities (Holland, Fritzsche, & Powell, 1994).

Holland has recommended that the SDS be supplemented with the My Vocational Situation (MVS) inventory, which measures aspects of vocational identity not measured by the SDS (see chapter 7). Clients with a clear vocational identity probably need relatively little assistance from counselors. The SDS by itself may be sufficient for such clients. Clients who score low on the Vocational Identity scale (indicating difficulties in self-perception) are more likely to need individual counseling or other interventions, such as career seminars or volunteer experiences, in addition to the SDS. Similarly, clients who show a need for occupational information or who face external barriers to their career development, such as lack of financial support, parental disapproval of career choice, or lack of ability to complete a training program, probably could profit from individual counseling. The SDS may also be supplemented with the Vocational Exploration Insight Kit for clients who desire a more intensified assessment (Holland, 1992).

A large number of research studies have found that taking, scoring, and interpreting the SDS can be therapeutic in itself even without the aid of a counselor. People who participate in this process report an increased number of career options, increased satisfaction with career choice, and increased self-understanding (Holland et al., 1994). Results have been equally positive for clients from different cultures.

Because it is easy to use and self-interpreting, has multiple formats, and has been in existence for some time, the SDS is, as proclaimed by its publisher (Psychological Assessment Resources, 2006), probably "the most widely used career interest inventory in the world" (p. 99). Ciechalski (2002) described it as an "outstanding instrument" that has "numerous studies to support its use" (p. 286).

A case example illustrating the use of the SDS in counseling is presented below.

Case Example

Lisa, a college sophomore, completed both the SDS and the MVS to help her in career exploration after she was dropped from her academic program for poor grades. She had been majoring in biology, with plans to become a dentist, but had lost interest in this career goal some time ago. She planned to reconsider her career plans during the next 3 to 4 months, and then reapply to the university the following semester. According to the SDS, her Holland code was ESI (Enterprising–Social–Investigative). In discussing these results, she indicated that she wished to consider the possibility of pursuing a career in business with an emphasis on the environment, a career choice suggested by her SDS scores. The MVS indicated that she lacked occupational information. She planned to take advantage of the time that she would not be in college to explore this type of career direction by talking with people in the field, reading relevant materials, and obtaining volunteer or paid employment in a related field.

Career Decision-Making System–Revised (CDM-R)

The CDM-R, by Harrington and O'Shea (2000), offers a broad, simplified approach to career planning based on self-assessments that requires relatively little testing time (20 to 40 minutes altogether). Students rate themselves in terms of interests, career choices, school subjects, work values, abilities, and educational plans. Most emphasis is placed on an individual's interests, which are scored in terms of the six Holland interest categories.

The CDM-R is available in two versions: Level 1 (Grades 7 through 10) and Level 2 (high school students and adults). For both versions, students score their own answer sheets by simply counting the number of responses in each of the six interest categories. Raw scores (instead of standardized scores) are used in the same manner as with the SDS. (The authors have published a set of norms for the interest scales in the manual for those who wish to use them.) In a long-term follow-up study of high school students who completed the original CDM in the 10th grade, Harrington (2006) found that most of them (61% of the boys and 52% of the girls) were employed in an occupation compatible with their Holland code (two highest scores) 20 years later.

Results from the CDM-R are used to suggest career clusters to students that they may wish to investigate. The CDM-R is accompanied by an extensive manual and helpful interpretive materials. This comprehensive, low-cost assessment package has received favorable reviews from guidance experts, especially as a means of stimulating career exploration (V. L. Campbell & Raiff, 2002).

Jackson Vocational Interest Survey (JVIS)

The JVIS, originally published in 1977, has been designed for counselors to use in educational and career planning with high school students, college students, and other adults. A new set of norms, based on a sample of 3,500 adults and secondary school students, and new reliability analyses and interpretive materials were provided in 1999 (D. N. Jackson & Verhoeve, 2000).

Respondents must choose between 289 pairs of items that measure interests in different types of job-related activities. The items have been paired to control for response bias. Most people can complete the JVIS in 40 minutes to 1 hour.

Similar to the Strong, the JVIS includes administrative indices, general occupational theme scales, basic interest scales, occupational scores, and a nonoccupational scale (Academic Satisfaction). It differs from the Strong by including measures of academic interests and by its emphasis on occupational clusters instead of specific occupations. Scores are provided for a total of 17 academic major clusters, such as Performing Arts and Environmental Resource Management, and for 32 occupational clusters, such as Agriculturalists and Health Service Workers.

The JVIS differs from most other interest inventories by including items that measure interests in different types of work environments (work style items) as well as different types of work activities (work role items). Of the 34 Basic Interest scales, 8 reflect work style preferences. The work style scales, such as Independence and Job Security, are similar to the types of scales often included on values inventories.

The measures of occupational and academic major interests are unique in that these measures are derived from the scores on the Basic Interest scales. Scores for each of the 17 academic major and 32 occupational clusters are reported as correlation coefficients that show the degree of similarity between an individual's basic interest profile and the average basic interest profiles of people in different majors and occupations. In this manner, Jackson was able to make use of vast amounts of archival data accumulated for the Strong.

Sanford (2003) described the JVIS as "a well-developed test for examining occupational interests for career planning" with "adequate validity and reliability evidence for this use" (p. 487). A sample copy of an 18-page JVIS Extended Report for a 30-year-old man can be accessed on the Internet (Sigma Assessment Systems, 2005). The report is noteworthy for its detailed information including lists of suggested reading materials and activities based upon the individual's scores.

Other Interest Inventories

Two other interest inventories worth noting are the Interest Determination, Exploration and Assessment System (IDEAS) by Charles Johansson (1996) and the Vocational Interest Inventory–Revised (VII-R) by Patricia Lunneborg (1993). The IDEAS, which has both a School Version and an Adult Version, can be used with students beginning in the seventh grade. The VII-R is designed primarily for use with college-bound high school students and college students.

Several interest inventories that were discussed in this section of the book in previous editions have become dated and are now dropped from consideration here. In addition to the two Kuder instruments (KGIS and KOIS-DD), the Career Assessment Inventory–Vocational Version and Career Assessment Inventory–Enhanced Version need to be updated to take into account changes within career fields during recent years (Kelly, 2002b; Miner & Sellers, 2002; Pope, 2002).

INTERPRETATION OF INTEREST INVENTORIES IN COUNSELING

The following guidelines should be considered in interpreting interest inventories to clients.

1. Check to make certain that the client has answered all or nearly all of the items and to ensure that the client understood and followed the directions. Total response and infrequent response indices should be helpful for this purpose. Check all validity indices, such as the Typicality index on the Strong.
2. Keep the purpose for assigning the inventory in mind. Review this purpose with the client before interpreting the results.
3. Ask clients about their reactions to the inventory before interpreting the results. If possible, allow clients time to inspect their profile and to formulate questions before discussing the results with them.
4. Note the percentage distribution of *like, indifferent,* and *dislike* responses for interest inventories with this type of response format. Remember that high scores on general or basic interest scales are based on likes, whereas low scores on these scales are based on dislikes. If a client marks an unusually high or low percentage of either *likes* or *dislikes,* be sure to

interpret scores relatively; that is, give greatest consideration to the highest scores, regardless of their absolute level.

5. Interpret the general (homogeneous) scales first. Help the client to determine his or her Holland code. Use the basic interest scales when available to clarify the meaning of the Holland codes, which can vary significantly for an individual from one interest inventory to another (Savickas & Taber, 2006). Use the Holland code together with the basic interest scales as a framework for interpreting the occupational scales.

6. If feasible, adapt the interpretation interview to the client's personality style as indicated by the Holland code (Prince, 1998). For example, Artistic types may prefer an interpretation process that is relatively unstructured and that encourages the client to be creative in reflecting on test scores. Investigative types may wish to know more about how the inventory was constructed and validated as part of the interpretation process.

7. When available, use separate-sex norms in interpreting scores on the interest scales. The separate-sex norms take into account the differences in the socialization process for men and women, which can affect the validity of the scales.

8. Interpret the occupational scores as measuring similarity of interest patterns compared with those of people in the occupation. Emphasize that the scores reflect interests rather than abilities. The scores can be used to help predict job satisfaction but not job success.

9. Do not overinterpret small differences in scores between scales. If T scores fall within 8 to 10 points of each other, do not consider them to be significantly different from each other for most scales.

10. Refer to *dislike* as well as *like* responses in interpreting high scores on occupational scales. A client can obtain high scores for some occupational scales simply by sharing the same dislikes that people in the occupation possess.

11. Use information from self-rated ability tests to take into account the client's confidence in pursuing different types of activities. Special attention may need to be devoted to those situations in which the client's interests and self-rated abilities disagree with one another.

12. Use information from personality scales, such as the Personal Style Scales on the Strong or the Special Scales on the CISS, to introduce personality factors into career planning that can help to enhance the predictive validity of the occupational scales.

13. Relate the scores to other information concerning the client, such as stated interests, work experience, academic background, and career plans. Help the client in integrating the assessment data and in generating hypotheses that may be helpful in interpreting the data and in suggesting directions for further career exploration.

14. Bring into consideration occupations that are not on the profile by using Holland's occupational classification system (G. D. Gottfredson & Holland, 1996). Use the O*NET database on the Internet to identify occupations related to the client's interest pattern (U.S. Department of Labor, ETA, 2006)

15. When feasible, use the interest inventory together with other assessment procedures to obtain a more complete picture of the client's situation. For example, the Strong may be used productively with the Myers–Briggs Type Indicator in career planning (Katz, Joyner, & Seaman, 1999) or with the Adult Career Concerns Inventory, Career Development Inventory, Values Scale, and Salience Inventory as part of a career development assessment package (Osborne, Brown, Niles, & Miner, 1997).

16. Ask clients to identify four or five occupations or two or three career-related questions suggested by the interest inventory that they would like to investigate. Suggest sources of occupational and educational information, including the *Occupational Outlook Handbook,* O*NET Online, career pamphlets, informational interviews, and volunteer work.

17. Schedule a follow-up interview with clients to help them review their progress and address issues that they may have identified during the career exploration process.

SUMMARY

1. Interest inventories differ in the types of scales they use. General (homogeneous content) scales, which measure interests in different types of activities, provide scores that are relatively pure and that can be easily interpreted. Occupational (heterogeneous content)

scales measure combinations of interests that show in a single score the extent to which an individual's likes and dislikes match those of people employed in a particular occupation.

2. Counselors should carefully consider the circumstances for assigning an interest inventory to a client. These circumstances include the purpose for testing, the client's motivation for taking the inventory, the client's emotional adjustment, and the availability of other interest measures, among other matters. Card sorts can be used to explore underlying reasons for career preferences.

3. The Strong Interest Inventory, the oldest and most thoroughly researched measure of career interests still in use, has been extensively revised and updated in recent years. It now contains a total of 6 Occupational Theme scales, 30 Basic Interest Scales, and 122 pairs of Occupational scales for men and women, all based on Holland's theory of vocational choice.

4. The Campbell Interest and Skill Survey uses self-rated abilities as well as self-rated interests to assess one's similarity to people in 60 different occupations. This instrument has been designed so that it is compatible with other instruments included in the Campbell Development Surveys.

5. The Kuder Career Search (KCS), which contains 10 general interest scales, can be used with younger clients beginning in Grade 6 as an introductory step in career exploration. The KCS with Person Match, which provides career sketches of 14 satisfied and successful individual workers with interests similar to those of the client, can be used with older clients to illustrate the broad range of career paths open for them to consider.

6. Holland's Self-Directed Search provides a self-administering, self-scoring, and self-interpreting measure of occupational preferences that helps clients to organize their thinking about careers and guide their career exploration. This instrument appears to be used more often than any other instrument for career planning purposes.

7. The Harrington–O'Shea Career Decision-Making System–Revised offers a simplified assessment of individual factors important in career planning that can be especially helpful in stimulating career exploration.

8. The Jackson Vocational Interest Survey provides a comprehensive view of an individual's preferences for work environments as well as work activities.

9. Counselors should use all of the scales on an interest inventory in combination to understand a client's profile. The administrative scales, especially response patterns, should be reviewed. Scores on the general scales should be used to help interpret scores on the occupational scales. Scores on special (personality) scales and on parallel measures of self-rated abilities should be used to further clarify the interpretation of the interest scores and to enhance their predictive validity.

10

Comprehensive Assessment Programs for Career and Life Planning

---

Comprehensive assessment programs measure a combination of a person's values, interests, and aptitudes. All of these programs include a means for identifying academic, career, or social environments that would be compatible with a person's preferences and abilities. Some of the programs are informal, nonstandardized programs. Others adhere to test standardization procedures that include systematic item selection, establishment of representative norms, and ongoing studies of reliability and validity. Both types of comprehensive assessment programs are discussed in this chapter. Only those standardized programs with objective tests of ability are reviewed in this chapter.

NONSTANDARDIZED ASSESSMENT PROGRAMS

Career and life planning programs based on nonstandardized assessments include computer-based programs and career education workbooks. These programs use self-ratings to help clients organize their thinking about themselves and various opportunities. They have been validated primarily in terms of their success in encouraging people to explore various occupations and in enabling individuals to make progress in their career decision making.

Research shows that *informed* self-ratings can predict performance at least as accurately as standardized tests in many situations (ACT, Inc., 2000a; Prediger, 2004; Shrauger & Osberg, 1981). In addition, self-ratings can be used to assess abilities in many areas (e.g., creativity, leadership skills) not easily assessable by standardized tests. Self-ratings will be most accurate when clients know specifically what aspects of their behavior are being assessed, when questions are phrased as directly as possible, when the counselor helps the client to recall previous behavior in similar situations, and when clients are motivated to cooperate (Shrauger & Osberg, 1981).

Computer-Based Programs

A number of computer-based career and life planning programs have been developed in recent years. These programs assist clients in self-assessment, environmental assessment (i.e., educational and occupational information), and decision making. The self-assessment modules usually ask clients to evaluate their interests, values, and skills. On the basis of the self-evaluations, the computer generates a list of appropriate occupations.

Two popular programs are SIGI PLUS (System of Interactive Guidance and Information), a product originally developed by Educational Testing Service, and DISCOVER, a creation of ACT.

Both programs are comprehensive, interactive, and simple to use, and both are updated each year. Both programs are now available on the Internet as well as by means of software programs installed on local computers. SIGI PLUS can be accessed on the Internet through many schools, libraries, and community centers as SIGI-3, a new Web version of SIGI that is easier to navigate and updated more frequently than SIGI PLUS (Valpar International Corporation, 2005). An Internet version of DISCOVER for Grade 9 through Adult is also available for students at schools and colleges who subscribe to this service (ACT, Inc., 2005b).

Research indicates that use of computer-based programs leads to increased retention of career information and to greater certainty of occupational choice (Eveland, Conyne, & Blakney, 1998; Pyle, 1984). In a comprehensive review of research on the effectiveness of DISCOVER, Taber and Luzzo (1999) found that it increased users' vocational identity, level of career development, and self-confidence in career decision making. The programs are most effective when they are used in conjunction with counseling (Eveland et al., 1998; Taber & Luzzo, 1999; Whiston, Brecheisen, & Stephens, 2003). The effectiveness of computer-based programs does not appear to be influenced by a client's age, gender, or race (Eveland et al., 1998).

Career and Life Planning Workbooks

Career and life planning workbooks play an important part in comprehensive self-rating programs used by counselors. These workbooks usually include a number of exercises that can be used by clients to assess their interests, values, personality style, and skills. Additional exercises aid clients in exploring the work environment by means of informational interviews and reviews of career literature. The workbooks are well suited to career education classes or career exploration groups. They often use a decision-making or problem-solving model as a framework for presentation of the exercises.

Examples of effective career and life planning workbooks include *What Color Is Your Parachute?* (Bolles, 2005), *Career Development and Planning: A Comprehensive Approach* (textbook, student manual, and instructor's manual; Reardon, Lenz, Sampson, & Peterson, 2005), and *Making Career Decisions That Count: A Practical Guide* (Luzzo, 2002). Exercises provided in the workbooks are informal or qualitative in nature. They are meant to stimulate interest in career exploration by offering a variety of assessment procedures in a systematic fashion.

STANDARDIZED ASSESSMENT PROGRAMS

Although most standardized assessment programs use self-report inventories to evaluate motivational factors such as interests and values, they vary in their approach to measuring abilities. Assessment programs are likely to use self-reports to evaluate abilities when the results are used for counseling. Many of these programs are best known for their interest inventory, which often serves as the centerpiece of the assessment program, such as the Strong Interest Inventory, Campbell Interest and Skill Survey, and Self-Directed Search. All of these programs have been discussed in chapter 9.

In contrast with the assessment programs that use self-ratings to measure abilities, a number of programs use objective tests to assess abilities. Objective tests help ensure the validity of test results in those situations in which clients' responses may be biased or distorted, such as may occur when tests are used as a basis for selection. Objective tests can also be used in assessing the abilities of clients who may not have an adequate basis for judging their own abilities.

Each of the assessment batteries discussed in this section includes objective tests of abilities in addition to inventories of interests, values, or experiences. In contrast with self-report ability measures, objective tests assess the client's abilities on the basis of actual performance in a test situation. Six frequently used programs—ACT Career Planning Survey, DAT Career Planning Program, WorkKeys, Armed Services Vocational Aptitude Battery, O*NET Career Exploration Tools, and Career Occupational Preference System—are discussed in this section. Some of these programs supplement the objective aptitude testing with subjective (self-ratings) assessments to expand the number of abilities taken into consideration for career planning. These batteries have been validated most often in terms of their effectiveness in predicting educational or occupational membership and performance.

ACT Career Planning Survey (CPS)

The CPS is a comprehensive career guidance program designed to aid students in Grades 8–10 in educational and career planning (ACT, Inc., 2000a). It includes two self-report inventories and a pair of objective tests of ability as indicated below.

- *Inventory of Work-Relevant Abilities (IWRA)*. This inventory asks students to rate their skills in 15 areas. Many of the areas, such as Sales, Helping Others, and Leadership, entail abilities that cannot be measured adequately by objective tests. The results are reported in six categories that correspond to the six Holland types.
- *Unisex Edition of the ACT Interest Inventory (UNIACT)*. The UNIACT assesses a student's interests in the same six fields as the IWRA. It consists of 90 items that yield equivalent responses for men and women. All items that produced significant sex differences have been eliminated so that combined-sex norms could be used.
- *Reading and Numerical Skills Ability Tests*. These two tests measure basic concepts and skills essential in reading and mathematics. The tests are intended to identify students in need of remedial or refresher training in either of these areas. High school teachers and representatives from different cultural groups have reviewßed the test items for content and fairness. These two tests (which together require 30 minutes of testing time) may be excluded from the assessment battery if desired.

The CPS differs from the EXPLORE and PLAN assessment programs also offered by ACT for high school students in that it places more emphasis on career development and less emphasis on academic evaluation and planning. The latter two programs, developed for use with 8th and 10th graders, respectively, measure academic abilities and career interests (ACT, Inc., 2005a). They assess a student's proficiency in the same subject matter areas as those included in the ACT college admissions testing program. The CPS provides information on a much wider variety of abilities (most of which are self-rated) along with career interests so that it can be used effectively in considering a broad range of occupational opportunities.

ACT provides a *Career Planning Guide* to help students apply their survey results in career exploration. The *Guide* includes a Work-Relevant Experiences Checklist and a Job Characteristics Checklist as additional assessment tools. Students use these instruments to review their work experiences and to consider what characteristics (e.g., recognition, physical activity, or variety) they prefer in their work.

Clients can compare their self-rated abilities and interests with those typically expressed by people in different career areas by means of the World-of-Work Map (shown in Figure 10-1). The map shows the relationships among 26 career areas grouped into 12 interest and ability regions (Prediger, 2002). The arrangement of these regions on the map closely resembles that of the Holland hexagon (see Figure 9-1 in chapter 9). As indicated on the map, the career areas differ from each other in regard to two basic dimensions: *data versus ideas* and *people versus things.* For example, career areas in Region 2 (Management, Marketing & Sales, Employment-Related Services) represent occupations that are people and data oriented.

The CPS Report shows the regions on the World-of-Work Map in which a student obtains his or her highest interest and ability scores by means of a color code (abilities = gray; interests = red; both abilities and interests = red–gray mixture). By inspecting this report, students can easily make comparisons among their abilities, their interests, and relevant career areas.

Self-estimates of interests and abilities are reported as stanine scores (standardized scores ranging from 1 to 9) in the counselor report. Interest self-estimates are simply listed in rank order, and ability self-estimates are reported as bands (instead of single points) on the student profile. Academic Ability test scores are reported in terms of five broad categories (upper 10%, upper 25%, middle 50%, lower 25%, and lower 10%) based on the student's performance in comparison with a national norm group. All these reporting methods have been designed to prevent the overinterpretation of small differences in scores.

Validity studies indicate that both the interest and self-estimated ability measures predict occupational choice for large samples of students with greater than chance accuracy. The prediction accuracy is significantly increased when the results of the two measures are in agreement (ACT, Inc., 2000a).

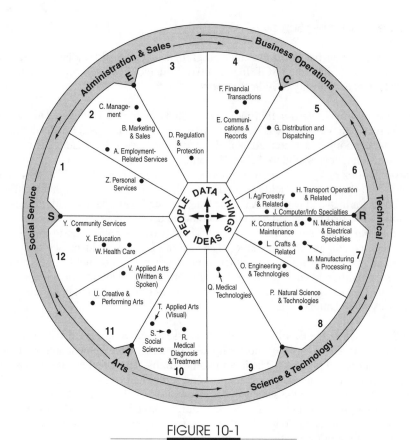

FIGURE 10-1

ACT World-of-Work Map (3rd edition—Counselor Version)

Note. The World-of-Work Map arranges 26 career areas (groups of similar jobs) into 12 regions. Together, the career areas cover all U.S. jobs. Most jobs in a career area are located near the point shown. However, some may be in adjacent map regions. A career area's location is based on its primary work tasks. The four primary work tasks are working with DATA (facts, numbers, files, accounts, business procedures), IDEAS (insights, theories, new ways of saying or doing something; e.g., with words, equations, or music), PEOPLE (people you help, serve, inform, care for, and sell things to), and THINGS (machines, tools, living things, and materials such as food, wood, or metal). Copyright 2000 by ACT, Inc. All rights reserved. Reprinted with permission.

The CPS is well designed for use with individuals or groups of students. It is comprehensive, thoroughly researched, relatively brief, clearly reported, and well integrated with career exploration activities. As noted by Loew (2003), the CPS is "a very useful tool for school counselors" (p. 165).

Differential Aptitude Tests (DAT)

The DAT can be used together with the Career Interest Inventory (CII) to generate educational and career planning reports for counselors and students. The DAT, originally published in 1947, was last revised in 1990 as the fifth edition, Forms C and D (G. K. Bennett, Seashore, & Wesman, 1990). The CII measures work and school interests.

Both the DAT and CII include two levels of assessment: Level 1 for Grades 7 through 9 and Level 2 for Grades 10 through 12. Both levels of the DAT and Level 2 of the CII may also be used with adults. When the DAT and the CII are administered together, the results can be integrated by means of a computerized educational and career planning report.

The DAT contains eight subtests: Verbal Reasoning, Numerical Reasoning, Abstract Reasoning, Perceptual Speed and Accuracy, Mechanical Reasoning, Space Relations, Spelling, and Language

Usage. The eight tests require $2\frac{1}{2}$ to 3 hours to complete. The CII provides scores for 15 occupational groups plus additional information regarding interests in school subjects. The DAT and the CII have been normed jointly with students drawn from different parts of the country, different socioeconomic classes, and different ethnic groups.

Scores on the DAT subtests show high internal consistency and acceptable alternate-form reliabilities across samples. Test scores are reported as percentile bands (test score ± 1 standard error of measurement) that take test error into consideration.

The DAT has been validated primarily in terms of educational criteria. Typically, DAT scores have been correlated with course grades from a variety of subjects. In most cases, combined scores on Verbal Reasoning plus Numerical Reasoning (VR + NR) produce the highest correlations with course performance. Except for Perceptual Speed and Accuracy, test scores are highly intercorrelated, so that differential prediction (the goal of the DAT) is questionable. Despite some problems, L. Wang (2002) noted the "lasting popularity" of the DAT, which he attributed to "the quality, credibility, and utility" (p. 127) of the instrument. Its most significant shortcoming at the present time is its age (1990 publication date); it needs to be updated to stay abreast of developments in the field and changes in the population for which it was designed.

Armed Services Vocational Aptitude Battery (ASVAB)

The ASVAB Career Exploration Program consists of a multiple aptitude test battery, a career interest inventory, and career planning materials and exercises that aid students in identifying and investigating career possibilities, The ASVAB (Forms 23 and 24) is administered and interpreted without charge by representatives of the Armed Services (U.S. Department of Defense, 2005). Test results are used by the military for recruitment, for assessing qualifications of students for different military occupations, and for research. School counselors use the results to help high school students (Grades 10 through 12) and community college students in educational and vocational planning. Testing time, including instructions, is approximately 3 hours. More than one fourth of U.S. high school seniors participate in the ASVAB Career Exploration Program sometime during their high school years (Baker, 2002).

The ASVAB includes the following eight individual ability scales: General Science (GS), Arithmetic Reasoning (AR), Word Knowledge (WK), Paragraph Comprehension (PC), Mathematics Knowledge (MK), Electronics Information (EI), Auto & Shop Information (AS), and Mechanical Comprehension (MC). (The two scales that emphasized speed of performance—Numerical Operations and Coding Speed—have been dropped in the revised version.) Scores on these scales are added together to form three composite scores, known as Career Exploration Scores, that are used for general counseling purposes, and a fourth composite score, known as the Military Entrance Score (also identified as the Armed Forces Qualification Test or AFQT), that is used to determine eligibility for military service. These composite scores, which have been derived from factor analyses of the individual scales, are calculated as follows:

Verbal Skills = WK + PC,
Math Skills = MK + AR,
Science and Technical Skills = GS + EI + MC, and
Military Entrance Score = Verbal Skills + Math Skills.

The Military Entrance Score can be considered a measure of general academic ability similar to the combined Verbal Reasoning plus Numerical Reasoning (VR + NR) score on the DAT. Only the composite scores are used for counseling and selection purposes.

In addition to the ASVAB test scores, the Career Exploration Program includes a new 90-item interest inventory. This inventory, called Find Your Interests (FYI), consists of six scales to assess career interests in the same six Holland categories used on many other interest inventories (U.S. Department of Defense, 2005). Work values are assessed informally by means of exercises in the *Exploring Careers: The ASVAB Career Exploration Guide.* This guidebook is given to all students who complete the ASVAB, or it can also be accessed on the Internet (U.S. Department of Defense, 2006).

The guidebook also includes OCCU-Find, a chart used to identify occupations that match an individual's abilities and interests. The student's three Career Exploration (composite) Scores and two-letter Holland code (obtained from FYI) are compared with the interest codes and skill importance ratings for different occupations in the booklet. Research indicates that participants in the ASVAB Career Exploration Program show reduced career indecision and increased career exploration knowledge compared with nonparticipants (Baker, 2002).

According to numerous studies conducted with earlier versions of the ASVAB and the General Aptitude Test Battery (upon which the ASVAB is modeled), the test scores are valid in predicting training and job performance in a wide variety of military and civilian occupations (U.S. Department of Defense, 2005). This research also indicates that the test scores predict equally well for men and women and for different racial and ethnic groups.

In general, the ASVAB, together with its accompanying materials, has shown great improvement since its inception in 1968, especially in selecting candidates for military careers (J. E. Rogers, 2002). It is limited in its measurement of specific abilities because of its heavy loading on g (general intelligence). Research indicates that informed self-estimates across a broad range of abilities (e.g., meeting people, leadership/management, and creative/artistic) can significantly enhance the effectiveness of the ASVAB in differentiating among students in various career fields (Prediger, 2004; Prediger & Swaney, 1992).

WorkKeys

The WorkKeys system is a comprehensive work skills assessment program developed by the publishers of the ACT tests (ACT, Inc., 2005e). The program is built around a common scale that measures both the skills of an individual and the skills required for successful job performance. Counselors and educators can use WorkKeys to help students understand their preparedness for specific jobs and careers; employers can use it to establish selection and training programs. WorkKeys may be used with either high school students or adults.

WorkKeys measures foundational skills ("skills needed to learn other skills") in 10 areas related to work on the following scales: Applied Mathematics, Applied Technology, Business Writing, Listening, Locating Information, Observation, Reading for Information, Readiness, Teamwork, and Writing (ACT, Inc., 2005e). The Readiness test, which assesses basic skills in reading and mathematics, can be used as a screening tool to determine if a person is sufficiently prepared to take the other tests in the WorkKeys system. In addition to the foundation skills, the WorkKeys system has recently been expanded to include two measures (called Performance and Talent) to evaluate attitudes and a third measure (called Fit) to assess how well an individual's interests and values match those of a specific job (ACT, Inc., 2006c).

The skill tests were defined and developed by panels of employers, educators, and ACT staff. All of the test items are based on work situations. They are designed to measure generic work skills that pertain to a variety of work situations, not skills that are specific to a particular job. The tests typically are scored in terms of skill levels ranging from Level 1 (lowest) to Level 7 (highest); however, "finer-grained" scale scores with 40- to 65-point ranges have also been established for use when it is important to detect smaller differences (ACT, Inc., 2005d). Depending on the nature of the test, items are presented in a paper-and-pencil, computer, video, or audio mode with a multiple-choice or constructed-response format. The 10 skill tests vary in testing time from 30 to 64 minutes. Individuals, educational institutions, and employers select the tests most relevant for their particular situation. The tests are usually administered and scored on a selected basis, not as a battery, by service centers certified by ACT, such as a community college.

WorkKeys enables students to assess their qualifications for different occupations by means of eight skill areas (all but Business Writing and Readiness). Job analysts have collaborated with subject matter experts (usually workers in the job under study) to judge the appropriate skill levels for different occupations. With these data, ACT has prepared a table of occupational profiles, which shows the median skill level in each of the eight skill areas for nearly 1,400 occupations (ACT, Inc., 2005c). An individual's skill levels are compared with the skill-level requirements for a particular job or occupation by means of this table to determine whether he or she is prepared to enter that job or occupation. For example, the occupational profile for accountants shows that they obtain their highest scores in Applied Mathematics (Level 6), Locating Information (Level 5), and Reading for Information (Level 5). Individuals who obtain similar or higher scores would appear to be good candidates for further training in this field.

WorkKeys differs from traditional ability tests in that it is criterion referenced, not norm referenced. A test taker must correctly answer 80% of the items representing any skill level to be qualified at that level. For those cases in which a person does not attain the skill level required for a particular occupation, the test report includes suggestions for improving his or her skills. In addition, organizations endorsed by ACT, such as KeyTrain and WIN Career Solutions, provide interactive instructional materials designed to improve the generic work skills assessed by WorkKeys (ACT, Inc., 2005e).

The WorkKeys system has been extensively validated by ACT, especially in regard to content validity (ACT, Inc, 2005e). Outside consultants reviewed the test items for content accuracy and fairness to minority groups. Statistical analyses were used to identify and eliminate items that functioned differently for various groups of people, such as men versus women or African Americans versus Whites. Subject matter experts confirmed that the eight skill areas adequately represented the type and the range of skills required in the majority of jobs. Ongoing research studies show that scores on the WorkKeys scales correlate significantly with scores on comparable instruments and with job performance ratings in related fields (ACT, Inc., 2005f).

Counselors will find the WorkKeys system to be most valuable in helping clients to appraise their basic work skills compared with those required in various occupations. Case examples illustrating the use of the WorkKeys system in counseling and employment situations can be found on the ACT Web site (ACT, Inc., 2005e).

O*NET System and Career Exploration Tools™

The U.S. Department of Labor created the Occupational Information Network (O*NET™), a comprehensive career information system, in the 1990s to replace the *Dictionary of Occupational Titles (DOT),* which had become dated and cumbersome (Mariani, 1999; N. G. Peterson et al., 2001). The O*NET system includes (a) the O*NET database, (b) O*NET Career Exploration Tools, and (c) O*NET OnLine.

The O*NET database provides extensive information about the primary occupations found in the United States. By combining occupations and eliminating obsolete and obscure occupations, the number of occupations included in O*NET was reduced from the 12,741 occupations defined in the *DOT* to 974. Compared with the *DOT,* the O*NET system places greater emphasis on transferable skills than on job duties (Mariani, 1999).

Each occupation is described in terms of six content areas: (a) worker characteristics (abilities, interests, and work styles), (b) worker requirements (education, knowledge, and skills), (c) experience requirements (training, work experience, and licensing), (d) occupational-specific information (job duties and tasks), (e) occupational requirements (work activities and work context), and (f) occupational characteristics (labor market information). The first three content areas describe individual attributes. Worker characteristics refer to worker traits that are relatively stable over time. In contrast, worker requirements and experience requirements refer to worker qualities that are likely to change with the passage of time.

The O*NET database indicates the relevance and the importance of each of the variables for the different occupations based on the ratings of experts, employers, and employees (U.S. Department of Labor, Employment and Training Administration [ETA], 2006). Occupations are coded according to the 2000 Standard Occupational Classification (SOC) System used by the federal government for collecting, calculating, and disseminating information about occupations. The database is partially updated twice a year, with plans for it to be completely updated in 5-year cycles.

The Career Exploration Tools have been constructed to measure an individual's abilities, interests, and values, that is, those variables that have been most valid in predicting occupational criteria. The following three instruments have been developed for this purpose: Ability Profiler, Interest Profiler, and Work Importance Profiler. Although these instruments may be used separately, the Department of Labor (2005a) recommended using them together as part of a "whole person" approach to counseling. The three assessment tools are described below.

Ability Profiler

This instrument, which replaces the General Aptitude Test Battery (GATB) for counseling purposes, includes nine scales that are similar to the nine scales that appeared on the GATB. The nine scales make up three cognitive factors (Verbal Ability, Arithmetic Reasoning, and Computation), three perceptual factors (Spatial Ability, Form Perception, and Clerical Perception), and three psychomotor factors (Motor Coordination, Manual Dexterity, and Finger Dexterity). The GATB

General Learning Ability scale has been dropped, and the GATB Numerical Aptitude scale has been divided into Arithmetic Reasoning and Computation scales.

The Ability Profiler differs from the GATB in that it provides new items, revised instructions and scoring procedures, new portions, fewer subtests, and more flexible administration. Additionally, time limits were modified to ensure that examinees had sufficient time to complete subtests in which speed of answering questions was not important to test performance.

The Ability Profiler includes both paper-and-pencil (first seven scales) and apparatus (last two scales) tests. If preferred, the paper-and-pencil tests can be administered without the apparatus tests. Total testing time for the paper-and-pencil part of the testing process is 1.5 to 2 hours. When apparatus tests are included, total testing time is 2 to 3 hours. The Ability Profiler has been designed specifically for use in counseling and should *not* be used for selection or placement.

The examinee's scores on the Ability Profiler are compared with the ability profiles for the different O*NET occupations. Ability profiles for the different O*NET occupations have been estimated by means of GATB validity data and occupational data from the *DOT*. The O*NET system includes five job zones that represent five different levels of experience, education, and training. Within each job zone (which the examinee selects), the computer uses a correlational procedure to determine which occupations have ability patterns that most closely match those of the examinee (U.S. Department of Labor, ETA, 2002a).

Interest Profiler

This inventory measures occupational interests in the same six categories used by most interest inventories: Realistic, Investigative, Artistic, Social, Enterprising, and Conventional (see Holland, 1997). Both paper-and-pencil and computerized versions are available. It is designed to be self-administered and self-interpreted. It requires about 30 minutes to complete.

An individual's highest scores on the Interest Profiler are compared with the interests that are most characteristic for different occupations as means of identifying compatible occupations. Occupational experts designated the predominant interest fields for different occupations. Although the expert raters used the same Holland categories to classify interests as those used by the Strong Interest Inventory and the *Dictionary of Holland Occupational Types,* the agreement among the Holland codes assigned to the same occupations by these three sources is only moderate (Eggerth, Bowles, Tunick, & Andrew, 2005). Counselors should keep in mind that the interpretation of a particular Holland code may vary somewhat from one source to another.

Work Importance Profiler

The third O*NET assessment tool measures six types of work values: Achievement, Independence, Recognition, Relationships, Support, and Working Conditions. Similar to the Interest Profiler, the Work Importance Profiler may be completed in paper-and-pencil form (titled Work Importance Locator) or computer form in about 30 minutes. It is also self-administered and self-interpreted. The relative significance of the different values in various occupations has been determined by job supervisors. This instrument is described in greater detail in chapter 8.

All three of the O*NET instruments are based on extensive research by leading vocational psychologists. The instruments were developed and tested with populations that varied in terms of race, age, gender, ethnic background, geographic location, and educational and economic background. The tools' psychometric properties (e.g., validity, reliability, and fairness analyses) are reported in research reports, which are published along with user's guides on the O*NET Center Web site (http://www.onetcenter.org/tools.html) as they become available. These reports support the technical quality of the instruments and allow confidence in their use (Lewis & Rivkin, 2004).

O*NET OnLine enables users to gain easy access to the O*NET database on the Internet (U.S. Department of Labor, ETA, 2005b). Individuals can readily compare information gained from the Career Exploration Tools and from self-estimates with pertinent information reported in the database for the various occupations.

For example, according to the O*NET database, the work of a mental health counselor best fits with Social, Investigative, and Artistic interests and Achievement, Independence, and Relationship work values (U.S. Department of Labor, ETA, 2004). The database indicates that the following abilities (as defined by the O*NET system) are most important for mental health counselors: Oral Expression, Oral Comprehension, and Problem Sensitivity. This occupation falls in Job Zone 5 ("extensive preparation needed"). Individuals can compare this information with their scores on the

O*NET Career Exploration Tools and with self-rated abilities to help determine to what degree this occupation matches their interests, values, and abilities.

In addition to the individual attributes measured by the Career Planning Tools, the detailed report for any occupation listed in the O*NET database also provides ratings for the importance of other worker requirements (Knowledge, Skills, Work Styles, and an expanded list of Abilities) and occupational requirements (Tasks, Work Activities, and Work Context). Many variables or elements are rated in each category. For example, the relevance and importance of 52 abilities for each occupation are rated by a panel of experts (Byrum & Tsacoumis, 2005). A complete printout of the occupational profile for mental health counselors requires 17 pages. The O*NET system provides a rich source of information that enables users to gain a thorough analysis of the occupation.

An individual's standing on many of the variables used in the O*NET system to describe workers and occupations must be measured by self-estimates. Prediger (2004) has pointed out the advantages of broadening the number of variables taken into consideration in career exploration and the surprising validity of self-estimates for career planning under the proper circumstances. The validity of self-estimates can be improved by paying close attention to definitions of the self-estimates, which are clearly indicated in the O*NET system. The O*NET system should be used in its entirety to be most effective.

Career Occupational Preference System (COPSystem)

The COPSystem provides a comprehensive assessment of interests, values, and abilities designed for use in a wide variety of settings. According to one statewide survey (Giordano et al., 1997), the COPSystem was used more frequently by the school counselors in that state than any other standardized test except for the Wechsler Intelligence Scale for Children–Revised or the SAT (with which it was tied).

The COPSystem includes the following measures (Knapp-Lee, 2000): (a) The Career Occupational Preference System (COPS) Interest Inventory, which assesses interests in 14 occupational clusters at different educational levels; (b) the Career Orientation Placement and Evaluation Survey (COPES), which measures eight bipolar personal values related to the work one does (see chapter 8); and (c) the Career Ability Placement Survey (CAPS), which measures eight abilities that are important for different types of work. The complete battery can be administered in less than 2 hours. Answer sheets may be self-scored or machine scored.

Several versions of the COPS Interest Inventory have been developed to take into account different grade levels and reading abilities of clients. The COPS Interest Inventory itself may be used with seventh-grade students through adults. The COPS-II (Intermediate Inventory), a highly visual, simplified version of the COPS Interest Inventory based on knowledge of school subjects and activities familiar to younger students, may be used with elementary school children or with adults who have a limited reading ability (fourth-grade level). The COPS-R (Form R) differs from the COPS Interest Inventory in that it contains sex-balanced items, combined-sex norms, and simplified language (sixth-grade reading level). The COPS-R more closely parallels the COPS Interest Inventory than does the COPS-II. The COPS-P (Professional level) provides an advanced version for college students and adults who may be considering professional occupations. Finally, the COPS-PIC (Picture Inventory) uses pictures only to assess the interests of nonreaders or those with reading difficulties.

The CAPS consists of the following brief, 5-minute tests: Mechanical Reasoning, Spatial Relations, Verbal Reasoning, Numerical Ability, Language Usage, Word Knowledge, Perceptual Speed and Accuracy, and Manual Speed and Dexterity. Validation studies indicate that scores on these tests correlate highly with scores for similar tests from other batteries, such as the Differential Aptitude Tests (Knapp, Knapp, & Knapp-Lee, 1992).

Both the COPS Interest Inventory and the COPES were revised in 1995 (EdITS, 1995). Since that time, extensive norms for the COPSystem instruments have been established based on large samples of intermediate, high school, and college students (EdITS, 2004). Separate norms have been prepared as needed for boys and girls and for high school students and college students. Research with earlier versions of the COPSystem indicates that it can be used effectively to predict educational and occupational status.

The COPSystem contributes significantly to the counseling process by stimulating clients to explore career fields from different viewpoints (Wickwire, 2002). Eby et al. (1998) noted that "the COPSystem may be particularly useful as a career exploration tool for diverse individuals" (p. 293) who have had fewer opportunities to engage in career planning. The publisher has prepared a *Comprehensive Career Guidebook* and *Self-Interpretation Profile and Guides* to aid in the interpretation of the COPSystem assessments (EdITS, 2004).

Other Standardized Assessment Programs

In addition to the six comprehensive assessment programs discussed above, the Occupational Aptitude Survey and Interest Schedule–Third Edition (OASIS-3) and the Ball Career System are worthy of note. Both of these programs have recently been revised. Both use the 12 interest factors from the *Guide for Occupational Exploration (GOT;* Farr, Ludden, & Shatkin, 2001) to help in the interpretation and application of aptitude test results.

The OASIS-3 Aptitude Survey, which can be used with students beginning in the eighth grade, measures six broad aptitude factors: General Ability, Verbal Aptitude, Numerical Aptitude, Spatial Aptitude, Perceptual Aptitude, and Manual Dexterity (R. Parker, 2002). The Interest Schedule that accompanies the Aptitude Survey measures the 12 *GOT* interest factors (e.g., Artistic, Scientific, and Plants & Animals). Bunch (2005) described OASIS-3 as "an exceptional tool to help junior high, high school, or postsecondary students explore vocational options" (p. 715).

The Ball Career System is based on the Ball Aptitude Battery (BAB), Form M (Ball Foundation, 2002). The BAB, which consists of 12 aptitude subtests, builds on the work of Johnson O'Conner, a pioneer in the development of work-sample aptitude tests. The tests are presented at two levels: Level 1 for 8th through 10th grades and Level 2 for 11th and 12th grades and beyond. The tests results are interpreted in terms of the interest categories used in the *GOT* as a means of including interests in career counseling based on the BAB results. Kelley (2005) recommended the Ball Career System for students as "a good foundation to begin exploring their career options" (p. 79). Rein (2005) has expressed some concerns about the BAB, Form M, especially Level 2, because of the lack of criterion-related validity and need for updated norms.

USE OF COMPREHENSIVE ASSESSMENT PROGRAMS IN COUNSELING

Several recommendations for the use of comprehensive assessment programs discussed in this chapter are listed below:

1. Use self-rating career and life planning programs such as DISCOVER or SIGI PLUS to promote self-examination and career exploration, especially for people who are unwilling or unable to see a counselor.
2. Use standardized career and life planning programs to identify educational or career fields that match a client's interests, values, and abilities.
3. Use objective tests of abilities with clients who may lack an adequate basis for assessing their own abilities or who may be motivated to distort self-assessments.
4. Supplement objective tests of abilities with informed self-ratings to enlarge the number of abilities considered in career planning. Self-ratings can be helpful in assessing abilities such as interpersonal skills, leadership, organizational skills, and creativity that are difficult to assess with objective tests.
5. Disregard small differences between test scores on multiple aptitude tests. When feasible, report test results as a band or range of scores (usually spanning 2 standard errors of measurement) instead of reporting them as a precise point on a scale.
6. Use combined verbal and numerical ability measures to predict school or job success. Not only is this measure more valid than the other test scores in most cases, but it also yields results with smaller differences between males and females.
7. Develop local norms for interpreting results, especially if the results are used to estimate performance in local courses.
8. Help students with low ability scores consider how they may improve their scores through appropriate course work or related experiences.
9. Interpret aptitude scores as measures of developed abilities. Exposure to the subject matter represented within the test is necessary for the student to perform well on the test.

10. Use nonlanguage tests, such as the Abstract Reasoning and Spatial Relations tests from the DAT, for students with limited English language skills to determine general ability to learn new material or to perform tasks for which knowledge of English is not required.
11. Consult supplementary materials provided by most publishers of comprehensive career planning programs. Use student workbooks to encourage active participation on the part of clients.

SUMMARY

1. Comprehensive self-assessments based on computer programs or career and life planning workbooks can be used to stimulate career exploration and to improve capacity for career planning.
2. Standardized assessment programs for career and life planning provide measures of an individual's values, interests, and abilities that can be compared with the requirements of different educational and occupational environments.
3. Programs with objective tests of abilities help ensure validity of results, especially in situations in which the results may be used for selection or placement.
4. Career planning programs that add the use of self-ratings for abilities not assessed with objective tests are more successful in predicting occupational criteria than those that rely on objective tests alone.
5. The ACT Career Planning Survey and the DAT Career Planning Program can be used in educational settings to help students choose an academic field or training course based on their interests and abilities.
6. The Armed Services Vocational Aptitude Battery can be used to predict success in both military and civilian occupations for students from a variety of backgrounds.
7. The WorkKeys system enables individuals to compare their basic work skills in eight areas with those required in a broad range of occupations.
8. The O*NET (Occupational Information Network) database provides a means of directly comparing individual characteristics (as measured by the Career Exploration Tools and by self-estimates) with requirements for more than 900 occupations. This system may be easily accessed on the Internet at the O*NET OnLine Web site.
9. The COPSystem provides a systematic assessment of interest, values, and ability measures that can be used in a variety of settings to assist individuals or groups in career exploration and planning.

SECTION
IV

PERSONALITY ASSESSMENT

11

Personality Inventories

The term *personality* is often used to cover a very broad concept. When applied to psychological assessment instruments, however, it is used more narrowly to describe those instruments designed to assess personal, emotional, and social traits and behaviors, as distinguished from instruments that measure aptitudes, achievements, and interests. The instruments discussed in this chapter are generally referred to as self-report personality inventories in which respondents check or rate items that they believe are most descriptive of themselves.

This chapter first discusses the different approaches used to construct these inventories, followed by a description of 11 inventories often used by counselors. Personality inventories primarily designed to assess psychopathology are presented in chapter 15.

INVENTORY DEVELOPMENT

Four methods have been used to construct personality inventories (Anastasi & Urbina, 1997): (a) logical content, (b) theoretical, (c) criterion group, and (d) factor analysis. These four methods are described below. In the logical content method, the inventory author uses a rational approach to choosing items. Statements related to the characteristic being assessed are logically deduced to be related to the content of the characteristic being assessed. The Basic Interest Scales of the Strong Interest Inventory (the Strong) and the content scales of the Minnesota Multiphasic Personality Inventory (MMPI-2; discussed in chapter 15) use this method. The principal limitation of this approach is that it assumes the validity of each item—that individuals are capable of evaluating their own characteristics and that their answers can be taken at face value. If a client checks an item related to "not getting along with parents," this approach assumes that the client is having parental difficulties.

In the theoretical method, items are developed to measure constructs represented by a particular theory of personality. After the items have been grouped into scales, a construct validity approach is taken to determine whether the inventory results are consistent with the theory. Two examples of this approach are Jackson's Personality Research Form (PRF), based on H. A. Murray's (1938) theory of needs, and the Myers–Briggs Type Indicator (MBTI), based on Jung's (1960) theory of personality types.

Two methods make use of empirical (data-based) strategies to develop personality inventories. The criterion group method begins with a sample with known characteristics, such as a group of individuals diagnosed with schizophrenia. An item pool is then administered to individuals in the known sample and to a control group (usually a "normal" population). The items that distinguish the known sample from the control group are then placed in a scale in a manner similar to the method used to construct the Occupational scales on the Strong. Typically, these items are then used on another similar sample (a process called cross-validation) to determine whether the scale continues to distinguish between the two groups. This method can also be used with groups that present contrasts on a particular trait. For example, members of fraternities and sororities are asked to judge the five most and the five least sociable individuals in their group, and then items that distinguish between these two groups are used in the development of a sociability scale. The MMPI-2 clinical scales and the majority of the scales on the California Psychological Inventory (CPI) are based on the criterion group method of inventory construction.

The factor-analytic method is the second method using an empirical strategy in test development. In this method, a statistical procedure is used to examine the intercorrelations among all of the items on the inventory. This technique, which can effectively be completed only on a computer, groups items into factors until a substantial proportion of the variability among the items has been accounted for by the dimensions that have resulted. An example of this approach is Cattell's Sixteen Personality Factor Questionnaire (16 PF), which resulted from a factor analysis of 171 terms that describe human traits and that, in turn, had been developed from a list of thousands of adjectives that in one way or another describe humans. Items that appear on particular dimensions resulting from a factor analysis are combined to form homogeneous scales.

Researchers using factor-analytic techniques across a number of personality inventories have synthesized personality traits into five major dimensions nicknamed the "Big Five." These five factors are

1. Neuroticism—insecure versus self-confident,
2. Extraversion—outgoing versus shy,
3. Openness—imaginative versus concrete,
4. Agreeableness—empathic versus hostile, and
5. Conscientiousness—well-organized versus impulsive.

The NEO Personality Inventory–Revised (NEO PI-R) has been developed specifically to assess these Big Five factors (Costa & McCrae, 1992; Costa & Widiger, 2002; Goldberg, 1993; McCrae & Costa, 1986). The four dimensions of the MBTI are related to each of the last four of these factors but not to neuroticism. The MMPI, on the other hand, contains numerous items related to neuroticism and fewer relating to the remaining four factors. These same personality dimensions are also found across diverse cultures as similar factor structures have appeared in Portuguese, German, Chinese, and Japanese samples (McCrae & Allik, 2002; McCrae & Costa, 1997). Although there has been considerable agreement regarding the existences of these general dimensions, several authorities, including two of the most famous, disagree. Eysenck said that there were only three, and Cattell was convinced there were far more (Goldberg, 1993). There is also disagreement regarding some of the labels that have been given to these dimensions as well as disagreement regarding some of the specific personality characteristics and behaviors deemed associated with certain of these dimensions (Whiston, 2000).

Because most personality inventories are self-report instruments, they can typically be distorted in a negative direction if individuals are motivated to present a poor image or in a positive direction if, for example, they are applying for a desired job or perhaps just wish to make a good impression in general. Several inventories contain validity or social desirability scales to detect such distortion. For counselors, this is less often an important problem because the purpose for taking the inventories is self-understanding and counselor understanding. Nevertheless, it is often helpful to point out such purposes and instruct clients to answer openly and honestly to obtain the most valid results.

SELF-REPORT PERSONALITY INVENTORIES

Myers–Briggs Type Indicator (MBTI)

Work on the MBTI was begun in the 1920s by Katherine Briggs when she developed a system of psychological types by conceptualizing her observations and readings (I. B. Myers, McCaulley, Quenk, & Hammer, 1998). Upon finding much similarity between her conclusions and those of Carl Jung, who was working at the same time, she began using his theory. Together with her daughter, Isabel Myers, she developed an inventory now known as the Myers–Briggs Type Indicator.

The inventory, in its several forms, was slow in gaining acceptance but is now reported to be the most widely used personality inventory in the world. More than 2 million are administered each year, and the majority of the Fortune 100 companies use it for hiring or training.

The MBTI is based on Jung's concepts of differences in perception and judgment that are used by different types of people. Each of the several forms of the MBTI (in both self-scored and computer-scored formats) is scored on eight scales (four pairs) that yield four bipolar dimensions. More sophisticated item response theory methods were used for the item development and scoring weights in the latest versions, the 93-item Form M and the more recent 144-item MBTI Step II (Form Q). Jung's theory proposes that apparently random variations in human behavior can be systematically accounted for by the manner in which individuals prefer to use their capacities for perception and judgment. The MBTI is a self-reporting instrument designed to identify these preferences.

The first of the four dimensions involves the preference for extraversion versus introversion (E-I). Extraverts prefer to direct their energy to the outer world of people and things, whereas introverts tend to focus energy on the inner world of ideas.

The second dimension measures personal preference for mode of perceiving and is labeled the sensing–intuition (S-N) dimension. Sensing individuals prefer to rely on one or more of the five senses as their primary mode of perceiving. Intuitive people, in contrast, rely primarily on indirect perception by the way of the mind, incorporating ideas or associations that are related to perceptions coming from the outside.

The third MBTI dimension is designed to measure an individual's preference for judging data obtained through sensing or intuition by means of either thinking or feeling (T-F). A thinking orientation signifies a preference for drawing conclusions using an objective, impersonal, logical approach. A feeling-oriented individual is much more likely to base decisions on personal or social rationales that take into account the subjective feelings of others.

The fourth dimension measures a person's preference for either a judging or perceiving (J-P) orientation for dealing with the external world. Although individuals must use both perception and judgment in their daily lives, most find one of these orientations to be more comfortable than the other and use it more often, in the same way that a right-handed person favors the use of the right hand. People with a judgment orientation are anxious to use either the thinking or feeling mode to arrive at a decision or conclusion as quickly as possible, whereas those with a perceptive orientation are more comfortable continuing to collect information through either a sensing or intuitive process and delaying judgment as long as possible. This fourth dimension was not defined by Jung but represents an additional concept of Briggs and Myers.

Although the four dimensions of the MBTI are theoretically independent, significant correlations in the vicinity of .30 have been found between the S-N and J-P scales. This finding tends to support Jung's theory, which included only the first three dimensions. Other than the relationship between these two sets of scales, the remaining scales are statistically independent of each other.

A person's MBTI personality type is summarized in four letters that indicate the direction of the person's preference on each of the four dimensions. All possible combinations of the four paired scales result in 16 different personality types. Thus, an ENTJ is an extravert with a preference for intuition and thinking who generally has a judging attitude in his or her orientation toward the outer world. An ISFP type indicates an introvert with a preference toward sensing and feeling who has a perceptive orientation toward the outer world. The manual (I. B. Myers, McCaulley, et al., 1998) provides a summary of the processes, characteristics, and traits of each of the 16 types.

In computing personality type, scores resulting from forced-choice items are obtained for each of the opposite preferences and then subtracted to obtain the particular type. A large difference between the two scores indicates a clear preference and yields a higher score on that type, whereas a smaller difference yields a low score, indicating a preference on that type that is considered less strong and less clear. Even though the difference is small (the scoring formula eliminates ties), one or the other letter is included in the four-letter code type. These preferences are presumed to interact in complex, nonlinear ways to produce the 16 types. There is, however, little support for these 16 personality types as separate entities or clusters. Another major criticism of the MBTI is that the variables assessed are assumed to result in dichotomies, although there is little psychological or empirical evidence of such dichotomies or bimodal distributions. Instead, the variables can best be represented as continuous bipolar distributions that fall along the normal curve (Pittenger,

1993, 2005). An additional component of MBTI theory involves dominant and auxiliary functions that are controversial and lack substantial research.

Although an individual's type is supposed to remain relatively constant over a lifetime, norms on several MBTI dimensions change substantially between adolescence and adulthood as well as during the adult years (Cummings, 1995). Internal consistency studies of the MBTI Form M have generally yielded correlation coefficients exceeding .90. In terms of the four letter types, test–retest reliability data tend to be somewhat discouraging in that an individual's four-letter MBTI type has only about a 50–50 chance of being identical on retesting. On the average, 75% of the people completing the instrument will retain three of the four dichotomous type preferences on retesting.

The most recent form of the MBTI, known as the MBTI Step II, yields an additional 20 facet scores—five 5- to 9-item subscale or facet scores for each of the four dichotomies. Developed using item response theory, the facet scores allow a more complete, although less simple, description of an individual's personality. For example, among thinking types, one person may be more logical and reasoning whereas the other may be more questioning and critical, and the facet scores can reveal this difference (Lanning, 2003). Scores on the 20 facets require mail-in or online scoring.

One of the reasons the MBTI is attractive to many individuals is that there are no good or bad scores or good or bad combinations of types. Because both polarities can be viewed as strengths, this nonjudgmental quality facilitates interpreting results to clients. A score indicates a preference to use certain functions or behavioral preferences, although most individuals have the capacity to make use of the opposite preference as well. Each preference includes some strengths, joys, and positive characteristics, and each has its problems and blind spots. In the interpretive materials in the manual, as well as in a number of other publications, the strengths, weaknesses, abilities, needs, values, interests, and other characteristics are provided for scores on each of the scales as well as for the 16 types. Resources include *Essentials of Myers-Briggs Type Indicator Assessment* (Quenk, 2000); *Gifts Differing* (I. B. Myers & Myers, 1995); *Critical Reflections on MBTI: Theory and Practice* (Bayne, 2005); *Introduction to Type* (I. B. Myers, Kirby, & Myers, 1998); *MBTI Applications: A Decade of Research on the Myers–Briggs Type Indicator* (Hammer, 1996); *I'm Not Crazy, I'm Just Not You* (Pearman & Albritton, 1997); *Applications of the MBTI in Higher Education* (Provost & Anchors, 1987), and *Do What You Are: Discover the Perfect Career for You Through the Secrets of Personality Type* (Tieger & Barron-Tieger, 2001).

The MBTI is used in a number of counseling situations. It is often used to explore relationships between couples and among family members (chapter 13). It is used to develop teamwork and an understanding of relationships in work situations and in vocational counseling by examining the effects of each of the four preferences in work situations. For example, introverts like a work situation that provides quiet or concentration and may have problems communicating, whereas extraverts like variety in action and are usually able to communicate freely. People with strong thinking preferences are interested in fairness and logic and may not be sensitive to other people's feelings. Feeling types tend to be very aware of other people's feelings and find it difficult to tell people unpleasant things. Thus, preferences and strengths on the MBTI can be discussed in terms of occupational functions and work environments, although solid validity data for such use still need to be obtained.

In addition, the manual lists the types of people found in various occupations from a vast data pool of people in different occupations who have completed the MBTI. People with certain MBTI types are found in substantially higher proportions in certain occupations. All types may enter all types of occupations, but certain types choose particular occupations far more often than they do others. For example, although all types are represented among psychologists, 85% of psychologists are intuitive types and only 15% are sensing types, but, like the general population, they are evenly split on the introvert–extravert dimension. The MBTI is seldom used by itself in career counseling but is often used along with interest inventories and other psychological test results to add an additional dimension in vocational counseling (Tieger & Barron-Tieger, 2001).

Individuals who are intuitive, feeling, and perceptive seem to be more likely to seek counseling than individuals with other MBTI types (Mendelsohn & Kirk, 1962; Vilas, 1988). Counselors often share these preferences. A few counselors administer the MBTI before counseling has begun so that they can use the results, along with the knowledge of their own type, in structuring the counseling process for a particular client.

Because of the wide variety of settings in which counselors use the MBTI, no specific list of guidelines for its use or interpretation is included here. Because of its popularity and seemingly simplistic interpretation of results, however, it is often administered and interpreted by those who are overly enthusiastic about its use or who have little background in psychological assessment. Counselors who make use of this personality inventory should be aware not only of its strengths and usefulness in various settings but also of its various weaknesses, including ipsative scoring and lack of criterion-related validity studies in certain settings.

The MBTI should not be used to label or narrowly categorize people. Also, people should not feel limited by their personality type. Although most people have a preferred personality style that they can learn to use to their advantage, they can also learn to express the less dominant aspects of their personality when appropriate. Counselors can teach clients to become more flexible in the manner in which they respond to different situations.

An alternative to the MBTI is the Keirsey Temperament Sorter II (KTS-II; Keirsey, 2006) designed for personnel, consulting, and training settings (Zachar, 2005). It contains 70 questions similar to MBTI items and classifies individuals into four temperaments similar to MBTI personality types (Quinn, Lewis, & Fischer, 1992; Tucker & Gillespie, 1993). These temperaments, each of which consists of four MBTI letter codes, are titled Guardians, Artisans, Idealists, and Rationalists. The KTS-II yields an individual's four-letter MBTI type in addition to the Keirsey temperaments. The KTS-II may be taken without cost on the Internet to obtain a four-letter code but with a fee if a person wishes to have it completely scored.

California Psychological Inventory (CPI)

The CPI was developed for use with relatively well-adjusted individuals (Gough & Bradley, 1996). It is a popular inventory because it assesses an individual's strengths and positive personality attributes. Although the MMPI was used as a basis for development of this inventory (over one third of the CPI items), the CPI is designed to measure everyday traits that its author, Harrison Gough, called "folk concepts"— traits such as sociability, tolerance, and responsibility, terms that people use every day and across cultures to classify and predict each other's behavior (Donnay & Elliott, 2003). The 1995 version of the CPI (3rd Edition), containing 434 items and 30 scales, was normed on standardization samples of 3,000 men and 3,000 women. The CPI 3rd Edition was restandardized in such a way that the scales on the earlier and 1995 forms can be considered interchangeable. It takes 45–60 minutes to complete and can be administered as a paper-and-pencil instrument for hand or mail-in scoring or taken on a computer on a local or Internet system. The CPI has been used in organizational training and evaluation, and a briefer form, the CPI 260, has been specifically developed for managerial assessment and leadership training.

The CPI items deal with typical behavior patterns and attitudes with less objectionable content than the MMPI. The scales are designed to assess positive personality characteristics and to aid in the understanding of the interpersonal behavior of normal individuals. Thus, the CPI is sometimes termed "the sane person's MMPI."

The CPI contains 20 folk scales that are organized into four separate clusters or classes (see Figure 11-1):

1. Class I is designed to assess interpersonal adequacy of poise, self-assurance, and ascendancy and contains seven scales titled Dominance, Capacity for Status, Sociability, Social Presence, Self-Acceptance, Independence, and Empathy.
2. Class II contains measures of socialization, responsibility, and character with seven scales titled Responsibility, Socialization, Self-Control, Good Impression, Communality, Well-Being, and Tolerance.
3. Class III contains scales measuring intellectual and academic themes useful in educational counseling. The three scales in this cluster are titled Achievement via Conformance, Achievement via Independence, and Intellectual Efficiency.
4. Class IV contains a mixed group of three scales that do not fit well together or are not highly related to scales in the other three clusters. They include Psychological-Mindedness, Flexibility, and Femininity–Masculinity.

Of the 20 CPI scales, 13 were developed by the criterion group method, 4 (Social Presence, Self-Acceptance, Self-Control, and Flexibility) by internal consistency analysis, and 3 (Good Impression, Communality, and Well-Being) by a combination of these two methods (Gough & Bradley, 1996).

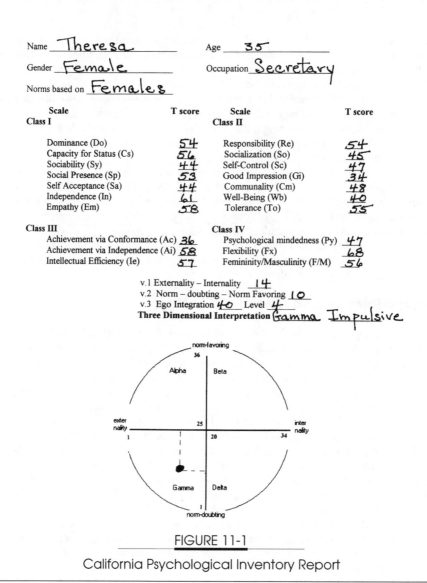

Name __Theresa__   Age __35__

Gender __Female__   Occupation __Secretary__

Norms based on __Females__

Scale	T score	Scale	T score
Class I		**Class II**	
Dominance (Do)	54	Responsibility (Re)	54
Capacity for Status (Cs)	56	Socialization (So)	45
Sociability (Sy)	44	Self-Control (Sc)	47
Social Presence (Sp)	53	Good Impression (Gi)	34
Self Acceptance (Sa)	44	Communality (Cm)	48
Independence (In)	61	Well-Being (Wb)	40
Empathy (Em)	58	Tolerance (To)	55
Class III		**Class IV**	
Achievement via Conformance (Ac)	36	Psychological mindedness (Py)	47
Achievement via Independence (Ai)	58	Flexibility (Fx)	68
Intellectual Efficiency (Ie)	57	Femininity/Masculinity (F/M)	56

v.1 Externality – Internality __14__
v.2 Norm – doubting – Norm Favoring __10__
v.3 Ego Integration __40__ Level __4__
Three Dimensional Interpretation Gamma Impulsive

FIGURE 11-1

California Psychological Inventory Report

Three of the scales are validity scales developed to detect faking or other test-taking attitudes. "Faking bad" is detected by T scores of 35 or less on the Well-Being, Communality, or Good Impression scales. Low scores on the Well-Being scale reflect endorsement of items representing various physical and psychological complaints. Scores on the Communality scale are based on a frequency count of popular responses, with low scores ($T = 29$ or less for men, 24 or less for women) suggesting that the inventory has been taken in a random or idiosyncratic fashion (Groth-Marnat, 2003). When a "fake bad" profile is obtained, the counselor should ask why the individual feels a need to create an impression of serious problems. The person might in fact have very serious problems or might be malingering for some reason, or the low score might represent a cry for help. The Good Impression scale is based on responses by normal individuals asked to "fake good" to identify persons who are overly concerned about making a good impression. "Faking good" is suggested by a Good Impression T score of 65 or more, with this score as the highest on the profile. Generally, most other scales will also show scores in the positive direction, which makes it difficult to differentiate between an individual with an excellent level of adjustment and one who is faking good. Here an individual's history can usually help the counselor to differentiate between faking good and superior adjustment.

Standard scores (*T* scores) are reported with a mean of 50 and a standard deviation of 10 (see Figure 11-1; Donnay & Elliott, 2003; Gough, 1999, 2000). High scores (*T* scores of 60 or above) tend to indicate psychological health and lower scores (40 or below) psychological inadequacy or distress (except for the Femininity–Masculinity scale). Different profiles reflecting different gender norms are used to plot scores for men and women. Results can be obtained on a profile report, a narrative report, or a configural analysis report.

Norms in the current version are based on the 6,000 men and women who represent heterogeneous samples from high school and college students, teachers, business executives, prison executives, psychiatric patients, and prison inmates. Fifty percent are high school students, and 17% are college undergraduates. The manual (Gough & Bradley, 1996) contains many specialized norm groups—a total of 52 for males and 42 for females—that counselors should consider using with clients who match the characteristics of the norm group (Hattrup, 2003). Reliability coefficients for some scales show substantial reliability, whereas for others, coefficients are more moderate. Median alpha coefficients for the 20 folk concept scales were .72 for men and .73 for women. Test–retest reliabilities ran relatively high, from .51 to .84 after a 1-year period. The many validity studies conducted with the CPI, usually exploring either predictive or concurrent validity, have yielded validity indices that have varied widely among the scales and among different types of validity criteria, typically predicted behavior.

On the basis of factor-analytic work, Gough developed three "vector" scales to measure broad aspects of personality structure. Because a number of the 20 scales on the CPI show considerable overlap, the three dimensions (vectors) can be used to facilitate understanding and interpretation of the 20-scale profile. The three vectors are described generally as (a) internality versus externality, (b) norm favoring versus norm questioning, and (c) self-doubting vulnerability versus self-actualization. These factors have been placed in an interpretive three-dimensional model (see Figure 11-1). The first two vectors measure personality type, whereas the third vector measures levels of personality adjustment.

- *Vector 1:* High scorers tend to be viewed as reticent, modest, shy, reserved, moderate, and reluctant to initiate or take decisive social action. Low scorers are talkative, outgoing, confident, and poised.
- *Vector 2:* High scorers are viewed as well organized, conscientious, conventional, dependable, and controlled. Low scorers are seen as rebellious, restless, self-indulgent, and pleasure seeking.
- *Vector 3:* High scorers are described as optimistic, mature, insightful, and free of neurotic trends and conflicts and as having a wide range of interests. Low scorers are seen as dissatisfied, unsure of themselves, and uncomfortable with uncertainty and complexity and as having constricted interests.

The intersection of Vectors 1 and 2 form four quadrants or lifestyles. Personality characteristics can be inferred from membership in one of these four quadrants: Alphas are ambitious, productive, and socially competent; Betas are responsible, reserved, and conforming; Gammas are restless, rebellious, and pleasure seeking; and Deltas are withdrawn, reflective, and detached. These four lifestyles are related both to going to college and college majors (Gough, 2000). Among almost 3,500 high school graduates in 16 cities, the college-going rate for Alphas, who were most likely to major in engineering or business, was 61%; for Gammas, who were most likely to major in the social sciences, it was 40%; for Betas, who were most likely to major in teaching or nursing, it was 39%; and for Deltas, who were most likely to seek out the humanities or music, it was only 27%.

In addition to the 20 folk scales, there are 13 special purpose or research scales: Management Potential, Work Orientation, Creative Temperament, Baucom's Unipolar Masculinity scale, Baucom's Unipolar Femininity scale, Leventhal's Anxiety scale, Dicken's scale for Social Desirability, Dicken's scale for Acquiescence, Leadership, Amicability, Law Enforcement Orientation, Tough-Mindedness, and Narcissism (Gough, 1999, 2000). A 33-item Depression scale has recently been constructed to identify depressive symptomatology (Jay & John, 2004).

The CPI has been shown to be useful in predicting success in a number of educational and vocational areas. Achievers in both high school and college have been shown to obtain relatively high scores on the Achievement via Conformance, Achievement via Independence, Responsibility, and Socialization scales. Studies making use of CPI scale scores have been shown to predict school and college performance beyond that using IQ scores or Scholastic Assessment Test scores alone. Other scores (Achievement via Conformance, Capacity for Status, Sociability, Good Impression, and Intellectual Efficiency) have been shown to be related to achievement in different types of vocational and professional training programs. The Dominance scale has proved to be effective in differentiating leaders from nonleaders. The CPI has not been shown to be effective for clinical assessment because it was not designed for that purpose, although extreme scores can provide useful information about an individual's maladjustment. An individual's general level of adjustment or maladjustment is indicated by the overall level of the profile, but the scales do not yield much information related to a specific diagnosis. Juvenile delinquents and criminals tend to have low scores on the Responsibility and Socialization scales. Solitary delinquents tend to obtain low scores on the Intellectual Efficiency and Flexibility scales, whereas social delinquents tend to obtain high scores on the Sociability, Social Presence, and Self-Acceptance scales.

When interpreting the CPI results, the three validity scales (Good Impression, Communality, and Well-Being) should be inspected first. If the CPI results are valid, the three vector scales should then be reviewed to provide a broad overview of the results—including classification into one of the four lifestyles and the level of self-realization. After that, the profile for the 20 individual scales should be examined.

In analyzing the CPI profile, the counselor should begin by paying attention to the overall height of the profile. Higher scores represent psychologically healthy responses, and these should be compared not only with the standard scores on the profile but also, where possible, with an appropriate norm group. The mean on most of the scales, for example, is higher for college students than for high school students. Next, the counselor should pay attention to the highest scores (T score of 60 or above) and the lowest scores (40 or below) on the profile. The next step in examining the profile is to attend to the height of the scores within each of the four classes. The class in which the scores tend to run the highest and those in which they tend to run the lowest are examined and interpreted. Continuing to examine the profile, the counselor should interpret and discuss the highest scales within each class and the lowest scales within each class. Finally, the counselor should pay attention to the remaining scales on the profile to be described and interpreted. With this method, the most important aspects of the profile are discussed first and receive the most emphasis and are less likely to become lost by the client in the detailed interpretation that follows. Finally, all of the data, including scale interactions where appropriate, are integrated with other client information in the overall interpretation (P. Meyer & Davis, 1992).

The manner in which the elevation of the scales can be interpreted is seen in Table 11-1 for the Dominance scale of the CPI (Craig, 1999; Gough, 2000; Groth-Marnat, 2003; McAllister, 1996). Similar information for all the CPI scales can be found in these sources.

Because of the care with which the CPI was originally constructed and has since been revised, along with the many hundreds of studies using this instrument, the CPI has become one of the best and most popular personality inventories available. Because the majority of the scales were empirically constructed and scale scores can be compared with different norm groups, the counselor

---

TABLE 11-1

Sample Interpretive Descriptions for the California Psychological Inventory Dominance Scale

Very High (T = above 65): Highly assertive, frequently seeks power and leadership positions in a direct manner, is confident, ambitious, and dominant, may be overbearing.

High (T = 60–65): Reasonably dominant and assertive, likely to take charge of situations, confident, optimistic, task oriented.

Moderately High (T = 55–60): Generally self-confident, can assume leadership roles when called upon.

Average (T = 45–55): Neither strongly dominant nor inhibited, not characterized by strongly assertive or unusually nonassertive behavior.

Moderately Low (T = 40–55): Likely to be hesitant to take the initiative, generally uncomfortable in leadership positions, may have difficulty making direct requests.

Low (T = 35–40): Likely to appear dependent, generally prefers a nonassertive participant role, may resist change and be seen as lacking in self-confidence.

Very Low (T = below 35): Likely to be socially withdrawn, appears shy and insecure, tends to avoid tension and pressure situations, usually seen as submissive and inhibited.

can make use of the instrument in assessing and comparing the strength of various personality characteristics of clients, and clients can use the interpretation to assess their own strengths and weaknesses in comparison with normative samples.

Computer-based profile interpretation is also available. A limitation of the CPI is that few studies have examined the meaning of elevations on more than one scale, in contrast to the considerable research that has been conducted on two and three high-point codes of the MMPI.

An example of an interpretation of a CPI profile is provided below:

Case Example

The CPI profile of scores for Theresa, a 35-year-old divorced secretary, is shown in Figure 11-1. She sought counseling because of a general dissatisfaction with her current situation. She is not happy with her job; she has had three serious relationships with men since her divorce, none of which have developed into marriage; and she is often in conflict with her 15-year-old daughter. After graduation from high school, she attended college sporadically for 2 years, earning fewer than 40 credits and a grade point average of 1.6. She attributes her poor record to a lack of goals and interest in liberal arts subjects and to "too much partying."

The validity scales from Theresa's CPI profile show a tendency to present herself in a negative fashion (Good Impression = 35). Her personality type, Gamma, suggests self-confidence and social competence together with restlessness, pleasure seeking, and non-conforming beliefs and behaviors. At Level 4 (out of seven levels) on Vector 3 (Realization), she shows average integration and realization of potential. As a Gamma at this level, she may feel somewhat alienated from society. At a higher level, she might be seen as creative or progressive; at a lower level, she might be viewed as antisocial.

In general, the scores on Theresa's profile fall near the midpoint, which corresponds with her Level 4 score on Vector 3. Her two high scores (T score of 60 or above) indicate that she is "self-sufficient, resourceful, detached" (Independence) and that she "likes change and variety"; that she is "easily bored by routine life and everyday experience"; and that she "may be impatient, and even erratic" (Flexibility; Gough, 1987, pp. 6–7). Her three low scores (T score of 40 or below) indicate that she "insists on being herself, even if this causes friction or problems" (Good Impression); that she is "concerned about health and personal problems; worried about the future" (Well-Being); and that she "has difficulty in doing best work in situations with strict rules and expectations" (Achievement via Conformance; Gough, 1987, pp. 6–7). Theresa used the information from the CPI together with other information to gain a better understanding of herself and her situation.

Sixteen Personality Factor Questionnaire (16 PF)

The 16 PF (5th Edition) is a personality inventory developed through the factor-analytic technique by Raymond B. Cattell and others (H. E. P. Cattell & Schuerger, 2003; Karson, Karson, & O'Dell, 1997; Russell & Karol, 1993). On the basis of the commonsense theory that if a human trait exists, a word in the language would have been developed to describe it, Cattell began from a list of all adjectives that could be applied to humans from an unabridged dictionary and produced a list of 4,500 trait names. These were combined to reduce the list to 171 terms that seemed to cover all of the human characteristics on the longer list. He then asked college students to rate their acquaintances on these terms and, through factor analysis, arrived at 16 primary factors that were developed into the 16 scales. Additional scores are now also obtained on five global factors—extraversion, anxiety, tough-mindedness, independence, and self-control (note resemblance to the Big Five)—as well as on a number of additional derived scales.

The adult edition now contains 185 items. High and low scores on each of the scales represent opposite characteristics. Thus, the scales are labeled Practical versus Imaginative, Trusting versus Suspicious, Concrete versus Abstract, Shy versus Socially Bold, and Relaxed versus Tense. Separate-sex and combined-sex norms are available for adults, college students, and high school juniors and seniors. Scores are given in terms of "stens"—standard scores with a mean of 5.5 and a standard deviation of 2.0. Scores below 4 (10th percentile) are considered low, and scores above 7 (90th percentile) are considered high. Because the scales are bipolar, both high and low scores can be interpreted as representing a particular characteristic (H. E. P. Cattell & Schuerger, 2003).

Several sets of equivalent forms of the inventory have been developed. In addition, the adult level has been extended downward to develop a form for high school students ages 12 to 18 (the High School Personality Questionnaire) and another one for use with children ages 8 to 12 (the Children's Personality Questionnaire).

Three different validity scales have been developed, one to detect random responding, one to detect faking-good responses (called the Motivational Distortion scale), and a third to predict attempts to give a bad impression (called the Faking Bad scale). Additional adaptations and computer-generated interpretations of the 16 PF have been published and promoted for use in marriage counseling, career counseling, job proficiency, and the assessment of managers.

The following steps constitute a suggested strategy for interpreting the 16 PF. After considering client information and the context of the assessment, the counselor should first inspect the three validity scales to determine whether the results are trustworthy. Second, the counselor should interpret global scores and their patterns and evaluate overall adjustment level (Craig, 1999). Third, the counselor should interpret very high or very low primary factor scores, and fourth, the counselor should interpret patterns (interrelationships) of primary factor scores. The counselor should pay attention to any inconsistencies among the primary scores within the global factors that may affect the interpretation of the global scores (Karson et al., 1997; Schuerger, 2000). Another approach in using the 16 PF is to compare the client's overall profile with typical profiles of certain groups. This approach is aided by the use of computer programs available for such interpretation.

The 16 PF is based on a large amount of research both in the construction of the instrument and in the examination of its reliability and validity. Test–retest reliability coefficients over short periods tend to range from .60 to .85. The reliability coefficients are somewhat low because the scales are made up of relatively few items (10 to 13 items per scale). A wide variety of validity data is available, including the prediction of academic grades and mean profiles for many groups such as delinquents, neurotics, and workers in a variety of different occupations.

NEO Personality Inventory–Revised (NEO PI-R)

The NEO PI-R was developed to assess the Big Five personality factors previously mentioned (Costa & McCrae, 1992). It consists of five 48-item scales answered on a 5-point *agree–disagree* continuum. Scores are obtained on each of the five domains of Neuroticism (high scores: poor adjustment and emotional distress; low scores: self-confident, free of neurotic conflicts), Extraversion (high scores: sociable, energetic; low scores: reserved, even-paced), Openness (high scores: imaginative, curious; low scores: practical, traditional), Agreeableness (high scores: sympathetic, dependent; low scores: egocentric, antagonistic), and Conscientiousness (high scores: organized, self-controlled; low scores: easygoing, disorganized) as well as on 30 facet subscales. Each of the five global dimensions is composed of six subscales of eight items each designed to measure facets of the global dimension. The Neuroticism domain includes facets such as anxiety, hostility, and depression, whereas the Conscientiousness domain includes facets such as competence, order, and self-discipline. Except for the Neuroticism scale, higher scores are indicative of positive characteristics, but on two of the scales (Agreeableness and Conscientiousness), very high scores can indicate a lack of balance in the individual's personality structure.

Reliability coefficients ranging from .8 to .9 are reported for the global dimensions with the facet scales ranging from .6 to .8. Separate profile sheets are provided with differing norms for males, females, and college students. The inventory is easy to administer and hand score, although computer administration, scoring, and interpretation are available. Concurrent validity studies (primarily with other personality measures) have yielded moderate to strong correlations in expected directions.

The NEO PI was originally developed on populations available from two large studies of aging adults, indicating that the inventory can be used throughout the full range of adult ages. Because it was developed primarily with adults, different norms must be used with adolescents and college-age adults, because they tend to achieve particularly high scores on certain of the inventory's five dimensions. In addition to the individual form (Form S), an additional form (Form R) is available with the same items but designed to be completed on an individual by another rater—someone who knows the individual well, such as a spouse or peer. The scores representing an individual's self-perception and another's perception can then be compared. Correlations that range from .5 to .7, which are typically obtained between individual and spouse or peer ratings, can be interpreted as evidence of the validity of the instrument.

A form for use in employment and career counseling settings where the Neuroticism factor is not relevant is the NEO-4. It can provide feedback in nonthreatening terms appropriate for both group and individual sessions. Again, two forms are provided: self-reports (Form S) and ratings by another individual (Form R). A shortened version, the NEO Five Factor Inventory, which yields scores only on the five domains, is also available.

A rapidly increasing number of research studies using the NEO PI-R have been conducted, and it has emerged as one of the better inventories available for the assessment of normal adult personality. In addition, when administered to clinical samples, NEO-PI-R scores have been shown to add incremental predictive validity to MMPI-2 results (Costa & Widiger, 2002). It increased diagnostic classification an additional 7% to 23% beyond that obtained with 28 MMPI-2 scores. The NEO-PI-R may have the potential to bridge the gap between general personality and psychopathological instruments (J. D. Miller, Reynolds, & Pilkonis, 2004; Quirk, Christiansen, Wagner, & McNulty, 2003).

Eysenck Personality Questionnaire–Revised (EPQ-R)

The EPQ-R offers a brief, broad, and well-researched measure of personality characteristics (Eysenck & Eysenck, 1993). It yields scores for three personality scales, an addiction scale, and a validity scale. The three personality scales—Extraversion, Neuroticism, and Psychoticism— measure independent factors that account for most of the variance among different personality measures. The scales were designed to be used primarily with a nonpathological population; however, extreme scores on the Neuroticism or Psychoticism scales usually indicate psychopathology. The Lie scale measures the extent to which a client may have distorted his or her answers to give a good impression. The 100 items on the EPQ-R describe behaviors that fall primarily within the normal range, not psychiatric symptoms.

For normal clients, the Neuroticism scale can be relabeled as a measure of "emotionality" and the Psychoticism scale as a measure of "tough-mindedness." The Lie scale, although primarily a measure of dissimulation, also may reflect social naïveté. A scoring algorithm has been developed to provide an addiction scale.

The EPQ-R has been validated primarily in terms of factor analysis and related procedures. The statistical analyses show that the scales do represent independent dimensions of personality that are important in describing variations in human behavior. The scales significantly discriminate among different groups (e.g., mental patients, criminals, business leaders) in the expected manner. The scales exhibit satisfactory test–retest reliabilities for short time periods and moderately high alpha reliabilities.

Separate age and sex norms are needed. Men score higher on the Psychoticism scale; women score higher on the Neuroticism and Lie scales. Men score higher than women on the Extraversion scale when they are young (less than age 50) but lower than women as they become older. Both sexes obtain lower scores on the Psychoticism and Neuroticism scales as they become older. Scores on the Lie scale are positively correlated with age. A separate form of the EPQ-R, the EPQ Junior, should be used for younger age groups.

Personality Research Form (PRF)

The PRF is one of two personality inventories authored by the late Douglas Jackson that represent a method of test construction using the availability of high-speed computers (D. N. Jackson, 1997b). It is based on H. A. Murray's (1938) personality theory and yields scores on 20 scales that assess personality traits, such as Affiliation (friendly and accepting of others), Endurance (patient and persevering), Nurturance (sympathetic and comforting), and Play (easygoing and participates in many fun activities). In addition to the 20 personality scales, there are two validity indices: a Social Desirability scale and an Infrequency scale. High scores on the Social Desirability scale indicate that the clients may be distorting their answers by primarily saying socially desirable things about themselves. Low scores suggest faking bad or malingering by saying undesirable things about themselves. High scores on the Infrequency scale, which is based on items with highly unlikely responses, suggest careless or random responses. The manual (D. N. Jackson, 1997b) contains norms for sixth grade through college.

Jackson Personality Inventory–Revised (JPI-R)

The JPI-R was also developed by D. N. Jackson (1997a) to assess normal personality characteristics but is designed to provide a more practical orientation than the PRF. It consists of 300 true–false items yielding 15 scales organized into five higher order clusters measuring traits such as anxiety, tolerance, energy level, responsibility, risk taking, and social astuteness. The norms are based on samples of college students and white-collar and blue-collar workers. Each of the 15 scales yields a standard score with a mean of 50 and a standard deviation of 10. The instrument is designed to be easily and quickly scored (10 minutes). High scores represent the traits mentioned by the scales. For example, a high scorer on the Cooperativeness scale is described as susceptible to group influence and pressure and tends to modify behavior consistent with standards set by others. High scorers are described as compliant, agreeable, and cooperative. Low scorers are described as individualistic, self-reliant, and contradicting. Low scorers tend not to go along with the crowd and are independent in thought and action.

Alpha reliabilities, which are somewhat low, range from .65 to .90, with a median of approximately .80. Validity studies, primarily correlations with appropriate scales on other personality inventories, indicate reasonable concurrent validity.

Both of the Jackson instruments represent contemporary methods of constructing psychometrically sound personality instruments, but they are not well known and have not yet received much use in counseling and other applied settings. Jackson accomplished the construction of psychometrically sound inventories but did not produce the validity data and the interpretive materials that make them useful in applied settings.

Millon Index of Personality Styles–Revised (MIPS-R)

The MIPS is an inventory, first developed in 1994 and revised in 2003, that is designed to assess personality styles for adults within the normal range (Millon, 2003). It is intended for various counseling situations involving relationships, career placement, or problems in daily living. It consists of 180 true–false items yielding 24 scales and 4 validity indices. The scales are grouped into three dimensions of normal personality: (a) motivating styles, which assess a person's emotional style in dealing with his or her environment; (b) thinking styles, which examine a person's mode of cognitive processing; and (c) behaving styles which assess a person's way of interrelating with others. The inventory is useful for counseling and helping professionals, including those in family and career settings. As a relatively recently developed instrument, it does not possess an extensive research base (Choca, 1998). Millon has also authored the Millon Adolescent Personality Inventory, which can be used to assess the personality of adolescents who have at least a sixth-grade reading level (Millon & Davis, 1993).

Hogan Development Survey (HDS)

The HDS is one of several instruments from Hogan Assessment Systems developed for use in particular contexts (Hogan, 1997). Although designed for normal clients, this 168-item instrument measures 11 dysfunctional dispositions that disrupt relations with others and hamper occupational, career, or marital success. It can be used for selection for high-stress jobs, for working clients with interpersonal or situational adjustment problems, or in career development programs.

Coopersmith Self-Esteem Inventories (SEI)

Stanley Coopersmith, who devoted a large part of his career to the study of factors related to self-esteem, defined self-esteem as "the evaluation a person makes and customarily maintains with regard to him- or herself" (Coopersmith, 1993, p. 5). He reasoned that people who have confidence in their abilities will be more persistent and more successful in their activities than will those who perceive themselves negatively. He looked on self-esteem as a global construct that affects a person's evaluation of his or her abilities in many areas. Because of its importance to the individual, in terms both of school or work performance and of personal satisfaction, he believed that counselors and teachers in particular should be aware of deficits in children's self-esteem and that they should be aware of methods for helping to improve self-esteem.

He developed three forms of the Coopersmith Inventory (so named to avoid influencing responses) to measure self-esteem. The longest and most thoroughly developed form is the School Form (Form A). This form, which contains 58 items and six scales, was designed for students ages 8 to 15. An abbreviated version of this form, the School Short Form (B), was constructed from the first 25 items in the School Form for use when time is limited. (The School Form requires about 10 to 15 minutes for most students, whereas the School Short Form can usually be answered in about 5 minutes.) The Adult Form (C), which also contains 25 items, was adapted from the School Short Form. All items, such as "I'm a lot of fun to be with," are answered "like me" or "unlike me."

The School Form provides six scores: a total self-esteem score; four scores derived from subscales that measure self-esteem in regard to peers, parents, school, and personal interests; and a score based on a Lie scale that checks for defensiveness. The School Short From and the Adult Form yield only one score: the total self-esteem score. Measures of internal consistency show acceptable reliabilities for both the subscores and the total scores (Lane, White, & Henson, 2002). Studies based on the School Form show significant relationships between self-esteem and school performance (C. Peterson & Austin, 1985; Sewell, 1985).

As a check on the individual's self-report on the SEI, Coopersmith and Gilberts (1982) developed the Behavioral Academic Self-Esteem (BASE) rating scale for teachers to use in evaluating a student's performance in 16 situations. The scale contains items similar to "this child likes to work on new tasks" and "this child readily states his/her opinion." Teachers rate students on a 5-point scale based on the frequency with which they perform the behavior indicated. The BASE provides outside information to check the accuracy of a student's self-perception; however, it should be remembered that teacher ratings only infer student self-esteem and should only be used along with student responses (Marsh, 1985). Counselors can profit from both types of information in helping clients to enhance their self-esteem.

Tennessee Self-Concept Scale (2nd Edition)

This revision of a famous measure of self-concept is a 90-item instrument that yields a total of 14 scales for counseling purposes. The scales assess self-concept in terms of identity, feelings, and behavior (Fitts, 1996). Items are answered on a 5-point scale ranging from completely false to completely true. Nine different measures of self-concept have been derived for areas such as identity, physical self, moral/ethical self, self-satisfaction, and social self. In addition, there are two summary scores and four validity scales. The second edition was standardized on a nationwide sample of 3,000 individuals ages 7 to 90. There is a child form for ages 7 to 14 and a young person–adult form for ages 13 and older. The first 20 items on either version can be administered as a short form when only a quick summary is needed. A similar instrument designed especially for younger children is the Piers–Harris Children's Self-Concept Scale, an 80-item instrument designed for children in Grades 3 through 12 and written at a third-grade level (Piers & Harris, 1996).

Computer Administration and Interpretation

Computers are playing an increasing role in the administration, scoring, and interpretation of personality instruments. Almost all publishers offer mail-in computer-scoring services that provide results with colorful and easy-to-interpret profiles. For additional fees, computer-generated narrative reports can be obtained for specific purposes such as selection for sales or police positions, staff or leadership development, or career counseling. Counseling agencies can often purchase software for their own computers that can provide immediate scoring and interpretation as well as actual administration of the inventory itself on computer screens. Because these features have substantial costs associated with them, counselors, in addition to determining the most appropriate inventory to use, must decide which type of scoring and interpretation report to purchase on the basis of usefulness, value, and cost.

SUMMARY

1. To interpret results of a personality inventory competently, the counselor must understand both the personality characteristics being assessed and the approach used to develop the various inventory scales.

2. The Myers–Briggs Type Indicator has gained great popularity and is used in many settings in addition to its use by counselors and clinicians.
3. The California Psychological Inventory, the Sixteen Personality Factor Questionnaire, and the Eysenck Personality Questionnaire–Revised are carefully developed inventories, with much research backing, that assess everyday personality traits.
4. The NEO Personality Inventory–Revised provides measures of the Big Five personality factors that account for most of the variance among personality measures.
5. The Personality Research Form and the Jackson Personality Inventory–Revised are two personality inventories that have capitalized on the capabilities of modern computers in their construction. The Millon Index of Personality Styles–Revised and the Hogan Development Survey are other personality inventories that have potential usefulness for counselors.
6. Two inventories useful in assessing self-concept are the Coopersmith Self-Esteem Inventory and the Tennessee Self-Concept Scale (2nd Edition).

12

Projective Techniques and Other Personality Measures

Techniques used to assess personality include the interview, behavioral observations, and personality inventories, as discussed in the previous chapter. In this chapter, four of the most commonly used projective personality measures are briefly discussed. Projective techniques are less often used by counselors than other personality assessment procedures for both practical and psychometric reasons.

Influences on personality include both environmental and developmental factors. Several instruments are described that have been constructed to assess different environments in which individuals find themselves and several others dealing with health and lifestyle influences. The chapter concludes with a summary of the assessment of adolescent and postadolescent psychosocial development.

PROJECTIVE TECHNIQUES

In using projective techniques as a method of assessment, counselors present unstructured tasks to the examinee, whose responses to these tasks are expected to reflect needs, experiences, inner states, and thought processes. This concept is known as the *projective hypothesis*—that responses to ambiguous stimuli reflect a person's basic personality. People often reveal more about themselves in their interpretation of a situation than they do about the situation itself, especially if the situation is ambiguous. A variety of ambiguous stimuli have been used for assessment purposes, such as inkblots, pictures, and incomplete sentences. Examinees usually respond in the form of stories, descriptions, completed sentences, or associations. Interpretations have generally drawn on psychoanalytic theory.

Because there is an infinite variety of possible responses to ambiguous stimuli, no particular conclusion can be drawn from any single response. Responses may be classified, however, and from a number of responses, general impressions and inferences regarding a person's personality may be derived. The administration and scoring of most projective instruments require considerable training and experience on the part of the examiner. The scoring process may be quite complex or subjective. In addition, even highly experienced examiners frequently disagree on the interpretations and inferences drawn from projective data. In addition, there is growing controversy regarding "the shortcomings of projective techniques . . . that can lead to poor assessment decisions and harm to clients" (Garb, Wood, Lilienfeld, & Nezworski, 2002, p. 454).

Rorschach Ink Blot Test

The most widely used projective test has been the Rorschach Ink Blot Test (Goldfried, Stricker, & Weiner, 1971; Ulett, 1994), developed in 1921 by Hermann Rorschach, a Swiss psychiatrist. Placing ink on a piece of paper and folding the paper to form ink blots, he asked people to say what images the ink blots suggested to them and used the responses to assess personality.

A series of 10 ink blots have become the standardized stimuli, some of them in gray and several with combinations of colors. Several different methods of administration, along with various systems to score the responses, have been developed. Responses are classified and scored according to set criteria, such as the location of the response on the ink blot, the feature that determined the response, and the content of the response.

Exner's (1993, 2001) Comprehensive System (CS) has emerged as the most popular scoring scheme and has been shown to have considerable interscorer reliability. Each response given to each ink blot is scored for (a) location (which part or whole of blot), (b) determinant (which feature or color), (c) content (clouds, geography, anatomy), and (d) popularity (common or original). Numbers and ratios of responses in different categories are related to the interpretation given to the test protocol. The Exner system has been shown to have considerable validity in identifying certain personality characteristics. It has been criticized, however, for problems with CS norms and its tendency to make normal individuals appear as if they suffer from severe psychopathology (Garb, Wood, Lilienfeld, & Nezworski, 2005).

Although the Rorschach is difficult to evaluate because of its complexity, a meta-analysis of validity studies conducted with the Rorschach indicated that it showed more success than the Minnesota Multiphasic Personality Inventory (MMPI) in predicting objective criterion variables. The MMPI proved to be more effective in predicting psychiatric diagnoses and self-report criteria (Hiller, Rosenthal, Bornstein, Barry, & Brunell-Neuleib, 1999). An extensive amount of training, usually more than one graduate course plus experience, is required to adequately understand and interpret the Rorschach, and the instrument continues to elicit variable reliabilities and validities and mixed reviews (Krishnamurthy & Archer, 2003). Nevertheless, the Rorschach continues its popularity in many clinical settings (Groth-Marnat, 2003).

Thematic Apperception Test (TAT)

The TAT was developed by Christina Morgan and Henry Murray based on Murray's theory of needs (*apperception* means to perceive in terms of past perceptions; H. A. Murray, 1943). It consists of 30 black-and-white picture cards, most containing one or more human figures, and 1 completely blank card. Twenty of the 30 cards are presented in a test administration, the selection of the 20 depending on the age and sex of the examinee. The examinee is asked to make up a story about each picture and to include what is currently happening in the picture, what led up to that situation, how the people in the story feel, and how the story ends. If examinees fail to include any of these elements, they are asked to fill in the information after the initial story has been completed. They are expected to identify with the hero in their story and project their needs, attitudes, and feelings on this character (Groth-Marnat, 2003).

When the entire test is administered, it is usually broken down into two sessions on 2 different days, with 10 cards administered at each session. The cards that illustrate more threatening material are usually included in the second session. Many of those who use the TAT do not use all 20 cards but select 8 to 12 of them and administer them (in the sequences noted by numbers on the back) in a single session. The TAT is usually not scored in any objective fashion, but the frequency of various themes, the intensity and duration of the stories, and the outcomes are taken into account. It is assumed that the hero in the story is the person with whom the examinee identifies. The assumption in interpreting the results is that examinees reveal their conflicts, experiences, needs, and strivings in their storytelling responses. A number of more objective scoring systems have been developed for the TAT to assess such concepts as achievement, ego development, or gender identity (Teglasi, 2001), but most are complex and do not provide the overall qualitative view of the individual usually sought by those using this instrument. To extend the range to broader groups, the Children's Apperception Test (CAT), the Senior Apperception Technique (SAT), and a modified 10-card version for African Americans have been developed.

The TAT is widely used and has many supporters, but it has been attacked primarily on psychometric grounds. Subjective interpretations of TAT results often result in different or opposite conclusions even by experienced users.

Instead of administering the entire TAT, counselors often select a few cards for use in an early interview. The cards can be used as a method of initially gaining rapport and as a method of encouraging the client to open up and talk during the counseling session. At the same time, the storytelling responses can yield considerable insight into the needs and personality of the client.

House–Tree–Person (HTP)

The HTP Projective Drawing Technique evolved from the earlier "draw-a-person" method of attempting to assess a child's level of cognitive maturity. It is one of the more widely used projective techniques because it often yields considerable clinical information and is easy to use (Buck, 1992). The individual simply draws a house, a tree, and a person, usually on three separate sheets of paper. Then the individual is asked to describe, define, and interpret each of the drawings. Characteristics of the drawings are scored, and interpretive concepts are applied to the characteristics and the responses. Interpretive guidelines are available, but they lack independent validation and any extensive research base (Groth-Marnat, 2003).

Rotter Incomplete Sentences Blank

In the sentence completion technique, a person is asked to complete a number of sentence fragments that are related to possible conflicts or emotions. The most popular sentence completion test is the Rotter Incomplete Sentences Blank, Second Edition (Rotter, Lah, & Rafferty, 1992), which consists of 40 sentence fragments. It has been updated with new norms and more reliability information. Most of the sentence fragments are written in the first person, such as "my mother . . ." or "what bothers me most is. . . ." There are three forms: one for high school, one for college, and one for adults. It is expected that attitudes, traits, and emotions will be expressed in the responses. Responses are compared with sample answers in the manual (Rotter et al., 1992) and scored on a continuum of 6 to 0, from unhealthy or maladjusted through neutral to healthy or positive responses (higher scores suggest greater maladjustment). Thus, a single overall adjustment score is produced that makes this particular form useful as a gross screening instrument.

Because sentence fragments are easy to construct, counselors often develop their own incomplete sentence instruments to deal with various types of conflicts and problems presented by clients. Thus, one counselor-constructed incomplete sentence instrument will deal with problems and conflicts revolving around educational/vocational decision making, another might deal with family conflicts, another with interpersonal conflicts, and yet another with school difficulties.

Early Recollections

Alfred Adler's use of early recollections has been described as the first truly projective test (Aiken, 1999). Counselors sometimes use it as a brief projective device. Emphasizing the importance of early experiences in the formation of personality, the technique involves asking the client to "think back to when you were very little and try to remember one of your first memories—one of the earliest things you remember." As a relatively nonthreatening procedure, it tends to involve clients in an interesting and participatory task with no right or wrong answers. The memories, which should be specific rather than general, can be analyzed for cognitive and behavioral patterns. The themes, outlooks, and attitudes revealed by the recollected behavior are examined and interpreted rather than the behavior itself. Standardized questions and a scoring system have been developed to assess and to interpret these early memories (Clark, 2002).

PERSON–ENVIRONMENT INTERACTION

Almost all of the developments of applied psychology on which the field of counseling is based have concentrated on the individual and the individual's specific traits, states, aptitudes, and attitudes. Except for the fields of academic and career planning, relatively little attention has been paid to the environments in which individuals function, although some theorists such as Williamson (1939) have emphasized environmental manipulation as a counseling tool. Certain behavioral settings have a very strong and often coercive influence on individuals, and it is necessary to pay particular attention to the perceived situations and environments that influence human behavior. The emphasis thus far has been an attempt to assess the environment and thereby help people to understand and organize their behavior in the social environments in which they find themselves in order to behave more effectively. Several theories have been developed that emphasize the importance of the environment to the way that individuals think and behave. They emphasize the value that can often result from changes in the environment, as opposed to the more typical counseling approach of assisting the individual to adapt to the situation.

Person–environment interaction theories are usually based on the work of Kurt Lewin (1935) and his famous formula $B = f(P \times E)$, in which behavior (B) is a function (f) of the interaction of the person (P) and the environment (E). These theories give particular attention to the environment portion of this formula, emphasizing the important role that environments play in shaping behavior. Another theorist (Barker, 1968) maintained that individuals tend to behave in similar ways in similar environments (e.g., in church vs. at a football game) even though, as individuals, they differ from each other in many important ways. He pointed out that human environments often have a powerful effect on behavior, for example, the amount of alcohol consumed. Environmental or situational variables are seen as the primary influences on behavior, with individuals behaving in a variety of ways depending on the social environments in which they find themselves.

According to Holland's theory (introduced in chapter 9), human behavior is a function of the interaction between personality and environment, and the choice of a vocation is in part an expression of personality. The ways people think about occupations and vocational stereotypes influence vocational preferences. People with particular personality types create the environments within these occupations, and thus the process is a circular one. People in each of Holland's six personality and environmental types create an atmosphere that reflects that type, and people search out and choose environments in which their interests, attitudes, and personalities fit. Their behavior is thus determined by an interaction between their personality and their environment. Individuals choose environments because of their personalities and remain in these environments because of the reinforcements and satisfactions they obtain in these environments.

Holland developed the Position Classification Inventory (G. D. Gottfredson & Holland, 1991), an 84-item inventory that enables an employee or a supervisor to assess and classify work environments in terms of their demands, rewards, and opportunities. Occupational positions are thus assessed on Holland's six-category classification system and can be used to examine person–job fit and for understanding satisfaction and dissatisfaction with a position or occupation.

Several researchers have developed instruments to use in the assessment of different environments. Rudolph Moos (1974; Moos & Moos, 1994b, 1994c) studied social climates in such widely varying institutions as hospitals, military companies, nursing homes, school classrooms, and university student living units. He developed a series of Social Climate Scales to assess the psychosocial dimensions of environment in these settings. His scales provide information about how those in a particular psychosocial environment perceive that environment. The inventories can be used to compare perceptions of different environments over time or to evaluate how individuals or groups of people differ in their perceptions of an environment.

One of Moos's findings was that the social environments in a variety of settings can be described by common sets of dimensions. These dimensions generally fall under three categories. The relationship dimension refers to the extent to which individuals are involved in the setting, the extent to which they generally support and help each other, and the extent to which they feel able to express themselves. The personal growth dimension includes the extent to which personal growth and self-enhancement occur within the basic functions of the setting. The third dimension is that of system maintenance or change and includes the extent to which the environment is structured and expectations are clear, the extent to which control is maintained in the setting, and how changes can occur.

Individuals are usually more satisfied and successful in those environments in which positive social climates exist. Under these circumstances, workers report greater satisfaction with their jobs, psychiatric patients become less depressed, and students show more interest and become more engaged in their course materials (S. L. Friedman & Wachs, 1999).

Pace (1987) developed the College Student Experiences Questionnaire to assess the quality of students' college experiences. Now in its fourth edition, the questionnaire assesses 10 dimensions of college environments in addition to 13 dimensions of college activities and 25 estimates of outcomes of undergraduate education (Pace & Kuh, 1998). The College Environment scales are composed of 10 one-item rating scales, of which 7 reflect the purposes of the environment: scholarship, aesthetic awareness, critical analysis, understanding diversity, vocational emphasis, information skills, and personal relevance emphasis. The other 3 dimensions focus on the supportiveness of interpersonal relationships at the college among students, with faculty, and with the administration.

HEALTH AND LIFESTYLE INVENTORIES

Recognition of the importance that psychosocial factors play in the efforts of individuals in recovering from injury or illness as well as in their overall lifestyle satisfaction has led to the development of several, what might be termed, *biopsychosocial* inventories. Such inventories assess the psychosocial issues that encourage or inhibit the recovery of individuals from injury or illness. They can be particularly useful to rehabilitation counselors and other mental health professionals. Other inventories assess the overall physical and psychological wellness of clients.

The Battery for Health Improvement 2 (BHI-2; Bruns & Disorbio, 2003) is designed to identify relevant factors that may interfere with health improvement or injury recovery. Its 217 items yield 16 scales plus 2 validity scales. There are 3 Affective Scales (e.g., Depression, Anxiety), 4 Physical Symptom Scales (e.g., Somatic Complaints, Pain Complaints), 5 Character Scales (e.g., Substance Abuse), and 4 Psychosocial Scales (e.g., Family Dysfunction). The instrument was normed on a sample of 527 patients in actual treatment for physical rehabilitation and chronic pain as well as an additional 725 community individuals. Scale score reliabilities ranged from .74 to .92 for internal consistency and for test–retest from .88 to .98 (Fernandez, 2001). There is a shorter 63-item form, the Brief Battery for Health Improvement 2 (BBHI-2), developed to help practitioners quickly evaluate psychosocial factors commonly seen in medical patients. It was derived from the longer form using the same norm groups.

The Coping With Health Injuries and Problems (CHIP; Endler, Parker, & Summerfeldt, 1998) inventory can be used to examine a client's psychological strategies that he or she is using to cope with physical health problems and suggest more effective ones. It was normed on more than 2,500 adult and university students, including almost 400 who were seeking medical treatment.

The Wellness Evaluation of Lifestyle (WEL) is a 131-item inventory that deals with lifestyle behaviors, perceptions, and attitudes (J. E. Myers, Luecht, & Sweeney, 2004). It is designed to assess five lifestyle tasks (examples: Self-Regulation, Work and Leisure, Love) and 14 dimensions of wellness (examples: sense of control, exercise, intellectual stimulation; Cox, 2003). Two briefer forms have been developed using factor analysis techniques—a 73-item five-factor WEL (5F-Wel) and a 56-item four-factor WEL (4-Wel; Abrahams & Balkin, 2006).

The Lifestyle Assessment Questionnaire is published by the National Wellness Institute of Stevens Point, Wisconsin. It contains 227 questions dealing with the assessment of lifestyles in six areas. The instrument is not well developed in terms of reliability and validity studies but can be useful in reviewing current behavior and planning future lifestyle activities.

PSYCHOSOCIAL DEVELOPMENT

Several theories have been advanced regarding the developmental changes that occur as an individual moves through various life stages. Instruments designed to assess the effect of these influences and to substantiate the relevant theories have been constructed, but at this point they are not yet ready for use in individual counseling. Nevertheless, these concepts are important for counselors to take into consideration in their work with individuals and groups, and several examples of theories related to these concepts are presented.

These theories have generally built on the work of Erik Erikson (1968), who believed that an individual develops through a sequence of stages that define the life cycle. Each phase or stage is created by the convergence of a particular growth phase and certain developmental tasks. These tasks include learning certain attitudes, forming particular facets of the self, and learning specific skills that must be mastered if a person is to successfully manage that particular life phase. In these theories, the development follows a chronological sequence: At certain times of life, a particular facet of the personality emerges as a central concern that must be addressed. The particular timing and methods by which the concerns are addressed are influenced by the individual's society and culture. Psychosocial theorists examine these particular concerns or personal preoccupations that occur at various points in the life cycle. The adolescent is likely to be preoccupied with the concerns of "Who am I?" or "What am I to believe?" The young mother wonders, "What type of parent shall I try to be?" and the older worker, "What type of identity will I have when I retire from my professional position?"

Analogous to the moral and cognitive theories in chapter 6 advanced by Kohlberg and Perry, Arthur Chickering (Chickering & Reisser, 1993) developed a theory of college student development that is an elaboration of Erikson's stages of identity and intimacy. Chickering focused on the particular developmental concerns of students that are relevant to the social situation in which they find themselves during their years at the university. He attempted to construct a framework of the developmental changes occurring in young adulthood in a more detailed way than did the psychosocial theorists such as Erikson. This framework has been presented in a form that draws on and gives coherence to the wealth of empirical data on college student change reported by a variety of researchers who have studied college students.

Chickering postulated seven vectors or dimensions of development, rather than the developmental tasks or developmental stages used by other theorists. The seven vectors along which development occurs in young adulthood are as follows: Achieving Competency, Managing Emotions, Developing Autonomy, Establishing Identity, Freeing of Interpersonal Relationships, Developing Purpose, and Developing Integrity.

Two sets of inventories have been developed to assess status on these developmental vectors. They include the Student Developmental Task and Lifestyle Assessment (Winston, Miller, & Cooper, 1999) and the Iowa Student Development Inventories (Hood, 1997). These inventories are designed to assess status on these vectors and the changes on them that occur during the college years. Recommendations regarding activities students might undertake to help them develop on those vectors on which they feel they would like to grow might be made from an individual's scores on these instruments. At this point, however, they do not represent instruments on which reliance can be placed in regard to differential diagnoses or selection.

SUMMARY

1. For both practical and psychometric reasons, projective instruments such as the Rorschach Ink Blot Test and the TAT are seldom used by counselors.

2. Condensed or adapted versions of projective tests such as the Thematic Apperception Test and Rotter Incomplete Sentences Blank are sometimes used by counselors as rapport-building techniques that may also yield insight into the client's personality.

3. Person–environment theories and inventories emphasize situational variables that often have been overlooked by counselors who have traditionally placed more emphasis on the assessment and treatment of individuals. Environmental assessment inventories include the Position Classification Inventory and the Social Climate Scales.

4. Biopsychosocial factors affecting health and lifestyles can be assessed using several recently developed inventories.

5. Psychosocial developmental theories offer useful concepts (e.g., life stages and developmental vectors) for assessing individuals with particular concerns that occur at various points in the life cycle.

13

Assessment of Interpersonal Relationships

Counselors who deal with educational and vocational issues often make extensive use of interest and aptitude tests, and those who deal with personal adjustment problems often make use of personality tests. Snyder, Heyman, and Haynes (2005) pointed out that the assessment of couples differs from individual assessment in a number or ways: (a) It focuses on the relationships and interactions between two or more persons, (b) it can provide the opportunity to directly observe interpersonal communication, and (c) it may involve attempting to maintain a supportive alliance while assessing antagonistic partners. They also believed that when counseling individuals, assessment of couple functioning should be a standard practice and that, similarly, partners should be assessed for serious emotional or behavioral problems when counseling couples.

Although a number of instruments have been designed specifically for marriage and relationship counseling, relatively few of these instruments are used as a part of the counseling process. When tests are used in relationship counseling, they are often those commonly used in other types of counseling, such as the Minnesota Multiphasic Personality Inventory (MMPI), the California Psychological Inventory (CPI), or the Myers–Briggs Type Indicator (MBTI). The relationship inventories most likely to be used in counseling are briefly discussed in this chapter. Most of the other instruments lack substantial amounts of normative and validity data. They have also almost always been developed with White, middle-class couples. Many of these instruments, which can be considered experimental at this point, are primarily used in research studies in this field.

INVENTORIES FOR MARRIAGE, COUPLES, AND FAMILY COUNSELING

Myers–Briggs Type Indicator (MBTI)

The MBTI (see chapter 11) is the standardized assessment instrument most often used by marital and family therapists in counseling with couples and families (Boughner, Hayes, Bubenzer, & West, 1994). Here its use is to help couples understand their differences in the four dimensions measured by the MBTI and therefore to help them use these differences constructively rather than destructively. Data accumulated by the Center for Applications of Psychological Type indicate that people are only slightly more likely to marry individuals of similar than of opposite types (I. B. Myers et al., 1998). The proportion of couples alike in three or all four dimensions is only slightly higher than would be expected from a random assortment of types. The MBTI thus can be used to assist couples in understanding their differences and similarities.

When couples differ on the thinking–feeling dimension, feeling spouses may find their partner cold, unemotional, and insensitive, whereas the thinking spouse can become irritated with the seeming lack of logic of feeling types. Counselors can help thinking types to improve relationships by openly showing appreciation and by refraining from comments that sound like personal criticism. They can encourage feeling types to state wishes clearly, so the thinking partner does not have to guess their wishes. One spouse may be an extrovert who needs considerable external stimulation, whereas the other may be an introvert who needs sufficient time alone. This becomes a problem when the introverted partner expends a good deal of energy in extroverted work all day and has little energy left for sociability in the evening. The extroverted partner, on the other hand, may work in a more solitary setting and look forward to an evening of social stimulation and activity. Problems arising from judging–perceiving differences can be found when planning, order, and organization are important to the judging partner whereas freedom and spontaneity are important to the perceptive partner, who also has a great deal more tolerance for ambiguity.

In using the MBTI with couples, counselors sometimes ask couples to guess the types of their partners after describing the types briefly. It is also possible to have partners answer the MBTI twice, once for themselves and once as they believe their partner will respond. In either case, the accuracy of type descriptions of partners can be discussed, and these differences can be useful to them as they see how they affect their relationship.

The MBTI can also be useful in family counseling in discussing issues such as difficulties in communication, differences in child-rearing styles, and in attitudes toward other family members. For example, a counselor can help an orderly, practical, sensing–judging parent to see that it is easier for him or her to raise a sensing–judging child, who desires structure and organization, than it is for that parent to raise an independent, intuitive–perceptive child, who rebels against structure and order.

Taylor–Johnson Temperament Analysis (TJTA)

The TJTA is second only to the MBTI in popularity for use in premarital and marital counseling (Boughner et al., 1994). It consists of 180 items equally divided among nine scales measuring traits (e.g., Nervous–Composed, Depressive–Lighthearted, Responsive–Inhibited, Dominant–Submissive, and Self-Disciplined–Impulsive; Taylor & Morrison, 1996). Norms are based on large but not necessarily representative samples, including a separate set of norms based on high school students. An additional edition is available for use with populations whose vocabulary and reading comprehension are below the eighth-grade level.

A unique feature of this instrument is the "crisscross" procedure in which one person records his or her impressions of another person. This use can be valuable in family counseling involving parent–adolescent interaction, in situations involving sibling conflict, or in premarital or marital counseling.

Marital Satisfaction Inventory, Revised (MSI-R)

The MSI-R is a self-report inventory designed to assess marital interaction and the extent of marital distress (Snyder, 1997). Scores are obtained on 13 different subscales with titles such as Affective Communication, Problem-Solving Communication, Disagreement About Finances, Sexual Dissatisfaction, Conflict Over Child-Rearing, and a Global Distress scale, which measures general unhappiness and uncertain commitment in the marriage or partnership. A Social Desirability scale (conventionalization) and an Inconsistency scale are included as a check on the response set of the test taker, and an Aggression scale has been added. The scales contain 9 to 19 true–false items per scale. In the revised version, items were changed to be appropriate for both traditional and nontraditional couples, and the inventory was restandardized on a larger and more representative sample of couples.

The MSI-R is intended to be used in couples counseling, with both partners taking the scale and the results displayed on a single profile that indicates areas of agreement and disagreement. It is typically administered during the initial contact with the counselor or agency so that results are available for the ensuing counseling sessions. The MSI-R provides useful information for counselors by providing a picture of the couple's overall marital distress, the general quality of their communication, and the differences between their perceptions of aspects of their relationship. In addition to the paper-and-pencil instrument, there is a computerized version that generates a test report and an interpretation (Brent, 2001). Validity studies of the MSI-R scales generally show reasonable correlations with other measures of marital satisfaction. The MSI-R significantly differentiates between various criterion groups experiencing marital dissatisfaction. The manual (Snyder, 1997) for the MSI-R reports internal consistency coefficients and test–retest reliability coefficients in the .80 to .95 range.

Derogatis Sexual Functioning Inventory (DSFI)

The DSFI yields 12 scores and consists of 10 scales with titles such as Information, Experience, Psychological Symptoms, Gender Role Definition, and Sexual Satisfaction (Derogatis, 1979). A total score and the client's evaluation of current functioning are also included. The Information subscale consists of 26 true–false items measuring the amount of a client's accurate sexual information. The Experience subscale lists 24 sexual behaviors ranging from kissing on the lips to oral–genital sex. The Sexual Drive subscale measures the frequency of various sexual behaviors, and the Attitude subscale measures the diversity of liberal and conservative attitudes.

The entire inventory can be expected to take 45 minutes to 1 hour to complete and was designed to assess individual rather than couple sexual functioning. The DSFI primarily measures current functioning, although the Sexual Experience and the Sexual Fantasy subscales ask the client to report lifetime experiences. Because the DSFI is one of the most studied instruments in sexual research, several different types of norms are available for the instrument (Weis, 1985). Certain of the subscales, such as Sexual Information, Sexual Desire, and Gender Roles, have produced relatively low internal consistency coefficients (below .70). Others tend to be more adequate, falling in the .80 to .92 range (Berman, Berman, Zicak, & Marley, 2002). The instrument can provide counselors with considerable information regarding sexual functioning. A computer-administered version is also available that yields extensive interpretive information.

Couple's Precounseling Inventory (CPCI)

The CPCI is a revision of the Stuart Couple's Precounseling Inventory (Stuart & Jacobson, 1987). Norms are based on a small representative sample (60 couples) that includes nonmarried heterosexual and homosexual couples. The purpose of the instrument is for use in planning and evaluating relationship therapy based on a social learning model. From a 16-page form, scores are obtained in 12 areas of relationships on scales such as Communication Assessment, Conflict Management, Sexual Interaction, Child Management, Relationship Change Goals, General Happiness With the Relationship, and Goals of Counseling. The authors reported high levels of internal consistency reliabilities (from .85 to .91). In taking the instrument, couples describe current interaction patterns rather than personality characteristics. Items tend to emphasize positive characteristics, and, if taken with some seriousness by the couple, the instrument can be educational and therapeutic. The CPCI is based on social learning theory and is designed to examine relationship characteristics and motivations that can be useful in suggesting avenues of treatment if the relationship is to survive (Touliatos, Perlmutter, & Holdon, 2001).

Family Environment Scale (FES)

The FES (3rd Edition) is one of a number of social climate scales developed by Moos and his associates (Moos & Moos, 1994a). It consists of three forms that assess the client's perception of the family as it is (the Real Form), as he or she would prefer it to be (the Ideal Form), and as he or she would expect it to react to new situations (the Expectation Form). The three 90-item inventories yield standard scores for 10 scales with titles such as Cohesion, Intellectual–Cultural Orientation, Active Recreational Orientation, Moral–Religious Emphasis, Expressiveness, and Control. Any of the three forms can be used alone or in combination with various family members to allow the counselor to explore differences between spouses' perceptions and between parent and child perceptions as a means of identifying family treatment issues. There is also a children's pictorial version (CVFES).

The 10 scales are grouped into three underlying domains: the relationship domain, the personal growth domain, and the system maintenance domain. The assumption behind all of the social climate scales is that environments, and in this case families, have unique personalities that can be measured in the same way as individual personalities can. Norms are based on a group of 1,432 nondistressed and 788 distressed families. The items on the FES are statements about family environments originally obtained through structured interviews with family members. The items have been criticized for possessing a middle-class bias and for not taking into consideration today's varying family patterns (Mancini, 2001). Validity evidence is based primarily on the difference in mean scores between nondistressed and distressed families.

Family Assessment Measure–III (FAM-III)

The FAM-III is a diagnostic tool for therapy that assesses family structure and strengths and weaknesses. It consists of three interrelated forms: a 50-item General Scale that examines general family functioning, a 42-item Dyadic Relationship Scale that examines how a family member perceives his or her relationship with another family member, and a 42-item Self-Rating Scale on which each individual rates his or her own functioning within the family (Skinner, Steinhauer, & Santa-Barbara, 1995). The FAM-III yields scores on seven scales, such as Role Performance, Affective Expression, and Communication, and two validity scales. It is available in paper-and-pencil and computer formats, in several languages, and in a brief screening version (Brief FAM). Administration, scoring, and interpretation of three forms for multiple family members can be very time-consuming although computer administration can shorten the process (Manages, 2001).

Sternberg's Love Scales

Sternberg's Triangular Love Scale (STLS) is a 45-item scale that measures the three components of romantic relationships identified by Sternberg (1998b): intimacy, passion, and commitment. Devising scales to measure these separate components, however, has been difficult (J. E. Myers & Shurts, 2002). According to Sternberg, all three components must be assessed in evaluating the quality of a romantic relationship. A copy of the STLS can be found in Sternberg's (1998b) book, *Cupid's Arrow: The Course of Love Through Time.*

He is also developing a technique of analyzing individual's and couple's love stories, which helps clients identify stories of what they perceive love to be (Sternberg, 1998c). This assessment can be helpful in exploring couple relationships with clients because those with similar profiles of stories tend to be more satisfied with their relationships than those with dissimilar profiles.

NEO Couples Compatibility Report

A software program for the NEO Personality Inventory–Revised (NEO PI-R; see chapter 11) has been developed to identify aspects of each partner's personality that may be affecting a couple's compatibility. Each partner takes the NEO PI-R, and his or her NEO facet scores are entered into the computer program. A report is generated that indicates how the partners' personalities fit together and how each partner's personality characteristics are likely to influence the couple's compatibility.

INTERPERSONAL ASSESSMENT INVENTORIES

Contemporary theories of interpersonal functioning assert that an individual's behavior can be understood only in relation to transactions with others and not for the individual in isolation. In the generally accepted model of interpersonal theory, each interaction represents a combination of two basic dimensions of interpersonal behavior: control (dominance vs. submission) and affiliation (friendliness vs. hostility; VanDenberg, Schmidt, & Kiesler, 1992). In any interaction (including client and counselor), individuals continually negotiate these two relationship issues: how friendly or hostile they will be and how much in control they will be in their relationship. This approach uses a circular rather than a linear model; behavior is viewed not solely by situational factors or psychic motivation but instead within a group of two or more people exerting mutual influence. These two dimensions are incorporated into a model called the interpersonal circle, or circumplex. It is organized around the horizontal and vertical axes representing affiliation and control (Tracey & Schneider, 1995).

Among the inventories designed to assess interpersonal interactions are the Checklist of Interpersonal Transactions (CLOIT), a 96-item interpersonal behavior inventory, and the Checklist of Psychotherapy Transactions, a parallel version of the CLOIT for rating clients and counselors, both developed by Kiesler (1987). Other promising measures of interpersonal functioning include the Interpersonal Compass (Fico & Hogan, 2000) and the Impact Message Inventory (Kiesler, Schmidt, & Wagner, 1997).

The Interpersonal Adjective Scales (IAS), a self-report instrument that assesses the two primary interpersonal dimensions of dominance and nurturance, builds on experience gained with previously developed interpersonal assessment inventories (Wiggins, 1993). The IAS yields scores on eight interpersonal variables that are ordered along the two primary axes of the interpersonal circumplex. It is designed to provide information about how an individual typically behaves in different interpersonal situations. The instrument consists of 64 adjectives that are descriptive of interpersonal interactions and are responded to in an 8-point Likert format, with respondents rating how accurately each word describes them as individuals. Responses yield octant scores, which are then plotted on the circumplex. The rational for the circumplex is that personality structure is not made up of independent dimensions but a blending of dimensions (Adams & Tracey, 2004). The titles of the eight interpersonal octants are shown on the circumplex profile in Figure 13-1. Based on scores shown in this example, this individual would be described as coldhearted, aloof, introverted, unassured, and submissive.

In interpreting the results of the circumplex profile, counselors should use all of the information provided on the profile and not focus solely on the highest segment score or scores. By paying attention to only one or two octants, the counselor may miss considerable information regarding

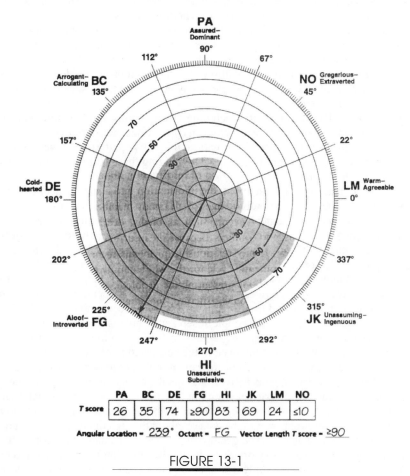

FIGURE 13-1

Interpersonal Adjective Scales Profile of
Extreme Depression in a Former Bank Manager

the client's interpersonal behavior, and the advantage of the circumplex model is lost (Pincus & Gurtman, 2003). Because interpersonal transactions include those between the client and counselor, the counselor's perception of client interactions should be compared with those of the client's self-report represented by the circumplex profile. Counselors can examine the components of a client's interpersonal functioning and identify topics that will be more or less anxiety provoking to a client. Many client difficulties can be viewed as maladaptive transactional patterns. Clients can be helped to understand the predominantly automatic and unaware manner in which they communicate to others through their verbal and nonverbal behavior. Individuals often use a narrow range of interpersonal responses that may not be appropriate to the situation.

The Thomas–Kilman Conflict Mode Instrument is the inventory most often used in situations calling for conflict resolution (Thomas & Kilman, 1974). Individuals respond to 30 pairs of forced-choice statements to determine their preferred style or mode of handling conflict: competing, avoiding, compromising, collaborating, or accommodating. The inventory is quick and easy to take, score, and graph. Reliability indices, both internal consistency and test–retest, only range from .4 to .7 (R. Johnson, 1989). According to a study that compared MBTI types with conflict resolution styles, thinking types preferred collaboration, and introverts preferred conflict avoidance (A. K. Johnson, 1997). Results can lead to a discussion about how conflict affects personal and group relations and suggest a practical approach to conflict resolution.

GENOGRAMS

A genogram is a map that provides a graphic representation of a family structure and is usually associated with Bowen's family system theory (Marchetti-Mercer & Cleaver, 2000). It involves the collection of information for approximately three generations of a family and organizes the information into a kind of family tree. It contains the names and ages of all family members, along with information about major events such as births, deaths, marriages, divorces, adoptions, and conflicts. As the information is collected, it allows family relationship problems to be seen in the context of the developmental cycle for the whole family in addition to the situation of the individual who is presenting the problem.

By examining the relational structure, including family composition, sibling constellations, and unusual family configurations, the counselor can hypothesize certain roles or relationships that can then be checked by eliciting further information. Repetitive patterns of functioning and relationships often occur across generations, and by recognizing these patterns, counselors can help family members to alter them.

In drawing a genogram, some counselors obtain the basic information to structure the genogram and then go back and question each individual about it and their relationships with other family members, both within and across generations. Others obtain this information as each individual is placed on the genogram. Some counselors obtain only a basic genogram illustrating the general family structure; others, through the use of figures, abbreviations, and symbols, develop a genogram that contains a great deal of organized data, including educational and occupational patterns, about the generations of a family system (McGoldrick, Gerson, & Shellenberger, 1999). In the case of a multihome stepfamily, the genogram can show (on a very large sheet of paper) all the members who are genetically, emotionally, and legally connected within three or more generations (Gerlach, 2003). A sample basic genogram for the couple Joseph and Paula is shown in Figure 13-2.

The construction of a genogram is a cooperative task between the counselor and the client. Clients readily become interested and involved in the construction of a genogram; they enjoy the process and usually reveal much significant information about various relatives and their relationships with them. While seeming deceptively simple, the construction of a genogram provides much insight into both the family constellation and the individual's interpersonal relationships within the family system. Even from reticent clients, both the quantity and the emotional depth of the data produced are often superior to the data obtained through the typical interview process and are more easily obtained as well. The genogram can easily be adapted for counseling clients from diverse backgrounds on a variety of issues. Particular attention is usually paid to two opposite types of interactions linked to family dysfunction: enmeshed (too emotionally close) or disengaged (too emotionally distant; Penick, 2000).

The construction of genograms in marriage and relationship counseling, as well as in other types of counseling, has thus been enthusiastically embraced by many counselors and has become an

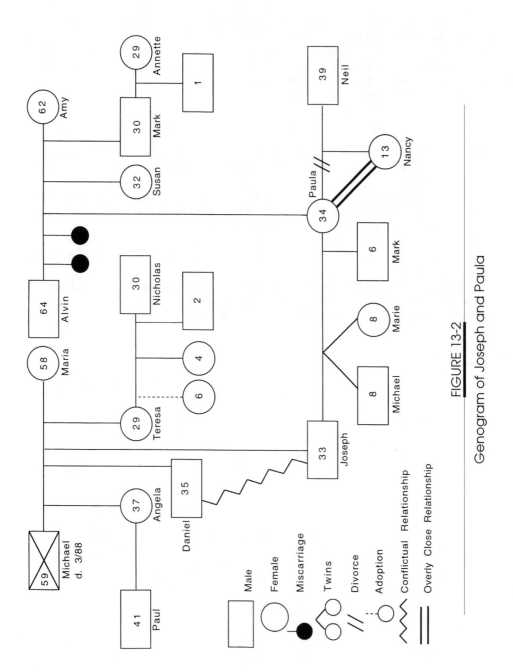

FIGURE 13-2

Genogram of Joseph and Paula

increasingly commonly used assessment technique. Although popular, the technique has been subjected to only a few studies of reliability, and there is little validity evidence. Counselors should therefore consider such interpretations as only hypotheses and use caution in drawing conclusions from genograms without other confirming evidence.

Career genograms have also been found useful in developmental guidance programs in elementary and secondary schools (Gibson, 2005). An ordinary genogram is drawn that includes parents and grandparents, with the occupations of each included in the genogram. Children can be encouraged to determine what their parents and grandparents do for a living, what they do in that type of work, and why they chose that occupation— thus enhancing the children's career awareness. At the secondary level, career genograms can be used to examine themes, patterns, and educational and life decisions.

SUMMARY

1. Personality inventories such as the MMPI, the CPI, and especially the MBTI, commonly used in other types of counseling, are most likely to be used by counselors with clients concerned with marriage or relationship issues.
2. There are instruments specifically developed to assess marital satisfaction, sexual functioning, communication issues, and family environments that counselors can use to assist clients to understand and deal with relationship problems.
3. Interpersonal assessment instruments usually evaluate an individual's interaction with others in terms of two dimensions: control (dominance vs. submission) and affiliation (friendliness vs. hostility).
4. Through the cooperative construction of a multigeneration graphic family structure—the genogram—insight into family constellations and interpersonal relationships within the family can be revealed to both the counselor and the client.

14

Mental Health Assessment:
Interview Procedures

In the course of helping people solve problems, counselors will work with a number of clients who could be diagnosed as mentally ill. On the basis of an interview survey of a large, representative sample of the U.S. population, it has been reported that more than 25% of Americans experience a mental disorder within a 12-month period (Kessler, Chiu, et al., 2005). Anxiety disorders (about 18%) are most common, followed by mood (10%) and impulse-control (9%) disorders. Estimates from the survey indicate that approximately one half of all Americans will meet the diagnostic criteria for a mental disorder sometime in their lifetime (Kessler, Berglund, Demler, Jin, & Walters, 2005). About one half of all lifetime mental illnesses begin by age 14.

Mental disorders are not only widespread but, for the most part, they remain untreated. Although the rate of treatment for those with mental disorders has increased during the past decade, the majority (67%) of those with diagnosable mental disorders have not sought treatment from any sector of the mental health services (Kessler, Demler, et al., 2005). Among those who have received treatment, approximately one half meet the criteria for a mental illness. The typical delay between onset and treatment of a mental illness is nearly a decade.

These statistics indicate the need for counselors to be familiar with procedures for assessing mental illness. Many of their clients will exhibit symptoms of mental illness, especially depression and anxiety. Many of the people in the population the counselors serve will also show signs of mental illness even though they do not seek treatment. Counselors must be able to recognize the symptoms of mental illness and to provide at least a preliminary assessment of the client's mental state. They must be able to determine when services such as crisis intervention, psychiatric consultation, long-term treatment, and outreach programs may be necessary. Interview procedures to aid counselors in this endeavor are presented in this chapter. The use of standardized inventories for this purpose is discussed in the next chapter.

DIAGNOSTIC AND STATISTICAL MANUAL OF MENTAL DISORDERS, FOURTH EDITION, TEXT REVISION (DSM-IV-TR)

The *DSM-IV-TR* (American Psychiatric Association, 2000a) provides a means of classifying psychiatric and psychological disorders for treatment and research purposes. This diagnostic manual, which assumes an atheoretical position, classifies mental disorders based on descriptive, not etiological, factors. The diagnostic categories used by the *DSM-IV-TR* serve as the official means of classifying mental disorders in most medical and psychological settings in the United States. The text revision of the *DSM-IV* provides updated information regarding many of the mental disorders;

however, the specific criteria used in making the different psychiatric diagnoses remain unchanged from the 1994 *DSM-IV.*

The *DSM-IV-TR* uses a multiaxial classification system as indicated below.

- Axis I: Clinical disorders and other conditions that may be a focus of clinical attention
- Axis II: Personality disorders and mental retardation
- Axis III: General medical conditions
- Axis IV: Psychosocial and environmental problems
- Axis V: Global assessment of functioning

The clinical disorders included on Axis I encompass all mental disorders except personality disorders and mental retardation. The Axis I disorders are classified into 15 broad categories, such as mood, anxiety, and adjustment disorders. The broad categories are further subdivided into subcategories, such as major depressive, dysthymic, bipolar I or II, or cyclothymic disorders for the mood disorder category. Developmental disorders such as learning, motor skills, and communication disorders, which used to be classified on Axis II, are now classified on Axis I. In addition to the clinical disorders, nonpsychiatric conditions that may be a focus of clinical attention are noted on Axis I. These conditions include the V-codes, which pertain to relational problems, bereavement, identity problems, phase-of-life problems, academic problems, occupational problems, and other issues often addressed in counseling.

Each disorder is defined in terms of specific criteria. For example, the diagnostic criteria for dysthymic disorder (*DSM-IV-TR* code number 300.4), a chronic state of low-grade depression, are summarized below (American Psychiatric Association, 2000a).

- Depressed mood for most of the day during the majority of the days over a 2-year period (1-year period for children and adolescents)
- Presence of at least two of the following six symptoms while depressed: poor appetite or overeating, insomnia or hypersomnia, low energy, low self-esteem, poor concentration or difficulty making decisions, and feelings of hopelessness
- Symptoms must cause significant distress or impairment in social, occupational, or other areas of functioning

In addition, the person must never have been without these symptoms for more than 2 months during the 2-year period (1 year for children and adolescents) and must not meet the criteria for a major depressive episode during this time period. It is also important to differentiate this disorder from other disorders, such as cyclothymic disorder, chronic psychotic disorders, and substance-related disorders, and from general medical conditions, such as hypothyroidism. Note that the criteria describe the frequency, duration, and severity of the symptomatic behaviors. A person must meet all of these criteria to be classified as an individual suffering from dysthymic disorder.

The diagnosis of mental disorder has become much more reliable since the advent of the *DSM* system, which lists specific, well-defined criteria as the basis for the diagnosis. Axis I disorders can be assessed by means of a structured or semistructured interview (1–2 hours in length) or by brief screening instruments (10 to 20 minutes) that inquire about matters identified in the *DSM* criteria (see chapter 4). Counselors can use the *Quick Reference to the Diagnostic Criteria from DSM-IV-TR* (American Psychiatric Association, 2000c) to guide their interviewing of a client when forming a diagnosis.

Axis II differs from Axis I in focusing on personality disorders or mental retardation conditions that may underlie the presenting problem. These conditions, which are often longstanding in nature, may be overlooked if not recorded on a separate axis (American Psychiatric Association, 2000a). Personality disorders refer to lifelong maladaptive behavior patterns that are often triggered by specific events in the person's life. *DSM-IV-TR* identifies a total of 10 personality disorders grouped in three clusters as indicated below.

- Cluster A: *Emotional withdrawal and odd behavior* includes paranoid, schizoid, and schizotypal personality disorders.
- Cluster B: *Exaggerated, dramatic emotionality* includes antisocial, borderline, histrionic, and narcissistic disorders.

- Cluster C: *Anxious, restive submissiveness* includes avoidant, dependent, and obsessive–compulsive disorders.

In addition, "personality disorder not otherwise specified" also serves as a diagnostic category for individuals who meet the general definition for personality disorder but who do not fit neatly into any of the 10 categories.

Personality disorders represent extreme forms of personality traits (i.e., enduring and pervasive patterns of behavior) that have become dysfunctional for the person. The trait is expressed in such a rigid or inappropriate manner that it interferes with that person's adjustment. People with personality disorders usually lack insight regarding the source of their difficulties. Clients usually do not seek counseling because of a personality disorder itself but because of difficulties associated with the disorder. For example, a person with a dependent personality disorder might seek counseling because of loneliness or indecisiveness but not for dependency. The counselor needs to look beyond the symptoms to find the personality disorder.

According to Fong (1995), any of the following signs may suggest a client with a personality disorder.

- Counseling seems to come to a sudden stop in progress after initial success.
- The client seems entirely unaware of the effect of his or her behavior on others.
- The problems seem acceptable to the client.
- The client is underresponsive or noncompliant with therapeutic regime.
- The client enters into intense conflictual relationships with institutional systems. (p. 636)

Fong recommended the use of a semistructured interview such as the Personality Disorder Interview–IV (Widiger, Mangine, Corbitt, Ellis, & Thomas, 1995) to ascertain the presence of a personality disorder. In addition to interviewing the client, it may be advisable (with the client's permission) to seek information from a spouse, close friend, or colleague regarding the client's behavior because of the distortions in self-perceptions common to individuals with a personality disorder (Widiger, 2002).

The third axis of the *DSM-IV-TR* lists any current physical illness or condition of the individual. In some cases, a physical illness may mask itself as a psychiatric ailment. The counselor needs to be aware of physical disorders that might be influencing a client's mental state, as noted in chapter 4 (Pollak et al., 1999).

The first three axes provide the official classification of psychiatric patients for most purposes; however, information provided by the last two axes allows the counselor to gain a more complete picture of the person. The fourth axis identifies psychosocial stressors faced by the client, such as problems with primary support group or occupational problems. The fifth axis rates the client's general level of functioning on a 100-point scale at the time of evaluation. The five axes together offer an integrated view of a client's problems from the standpoint of a biopsychosocial model of human functioning.

Revisions of the *DSM* have included a number of changes designed to enhance its use with clients from different cultures. D. W. Smart and Smart (1997) noted the following five improvements: (a) Specific culture, age, and gender features are described for many of the disorders; (b) a glossary of culture-bound syndromes limited to certain societies or cultural areas has been added; (c) an "Outline for Cultural Formulation" is provided in the Appendix as a means of systematically taking into account cultural context; (d) Axis IV has been broadened to include psychosocial and environmental problems such as difficulty with discrimination, inadequate housing, and inadequate health care services; and (e) the V-codes now include "acculturation problem" as a nonpsychiatric condition that may be the object of clinical attention.

As a diagnostic system, the *DSM* has continued to evolve since its first edition in 1952. Widiger and Clark (2000) suggested that future versions of the *DSM* be based on a dimensional model of classification that makes systematic use of laboratory or psychological tests in determining diagnoses. A dimensional model recognizes a "continuum of functioning" in various psychological domains (such as personality or cognitive ability factors) that can be used to differentiate between psychopathology and normality and among different types of mental disorders. Such a model (based on cognitive ability factors) is now used in diagnosing learning disorders and mental retardation but not for any of the other *DSM* disorders. They also argued that the *DSM* should place more emphasis on assessments made over a period of time, in contrast with those made at just one point in time.

The following points should be considered in using the *DSM-IV-TR* in counseling:

1. Use the *DSM-IV-TR* with clients who appear to have a psychiatric disorder. Use of the *DSM-IV-TR* classification system improves the reliability and validity of the assessment process. Diagnoses of mental disorders made by means of specific criteria such as those listed in the *DSM-IV-TR* are as reliable as diagnoses of general medical disorders (Satcher, 2000).

2. Become familiar with case study materials and interviewing techniques for determining *DSM-IV-TR* classifications (Frances & Ross, 2002; Othmer & Othmer, 2001a, 2001b; Spitzer, Skodol, Williams, & First, 2001). Appropriate use of the *DSM-IV-TR* requires systematic training and experience in its use.

3. Consider using a guided interview such as the Primary Care Evaluation of Mental Disorders or a questionnaire such as the Patient Health Questionnaire, both developed for use with primary care patients, to assist in the screening and diagnostic process (S. R. Hahn et al., 2004). Use the decision-tree approach described in the *DSM-IV-TR* to help make differential diagnoses (American Psychiatric Association, 2000a, Appendix A).

4. Take into account both inclusion and exclusion criteria. A person who meets the inclusion criteria for a mental disorder actually may have a related disorder, a physical illness, or substance abuse, which may not be clear until exclusion criteria are considered. Recent versions of the *DSM* place greater emphasis on exclusion criteria than did earlier versions of this manual.

5. Assess for the possibility of more than one disorder occurring at the same time. Dual and triple diagnoses of mental disorders for the same person are relatively common (Kessler, Chiu, et al., 2005).

6. Keep in mind the distinction between symptom-oriented interviewing and insight-oriented interviewing (Othmer & Othmer, 2001a). The first yields descriptions of the client's behavior, which is necessary for *DSM-IV-TR* classifications. The second provides possible explanations for the client's behavior. Both types of interviewing need to be pursued in counseling.

7. Be careful to use the *DSM-IV-TR* categories to classify a client's condition, not to label the client. For example, a client should be viewed as a person with schizophrenia, not as a schizophrenic. Labeling can lead to stereotyping and self-fulfilling prophecies.

8. In making *DSM-IV-TR* diagnoses, consider a person's strengths as well as weaknesses, especially as an aid in treatment planning (Ivey & Ivey, 1998; S. J. Lopez et al., 2006). C. Peterson and Seligman (2004) described six character strengths—wisdom, courage, humanity, justice, temperance, and transcendence—that can be particularly helpful for this purpose.

9. Use the *DSM* classification system to enhance communication with medical and mental health referral sources (Geroski, Rodgers, & Breen, 1997; Hinkle, 1999). Most agencies require that clients or patients be assigned a *DSM-IV-TR* code for diagnostic and treatment purposes as well as for third-party payments.

10. Consult guidebooks such as the *Treatment Companion to the DSM-IV-TR Casebook* (Spitzer, 2004) and *DSM-IV-TR Mental Disorders: Diagnosis, Etiology and Treatment* (First & Tasman, 2004) for treatment suggestions for the different types of mental disorders listed in the *DSM-IV-TR*.

11. In planning treatments, take into account the client's environment and developmental history as well as the *DSM-IV-TR* diagnosis (Axis IV can be helpful for this purpose). *DSM-IV-TR* diagnoses primarily focus on the individual without giving sufficient attention to the context in which the problem developed (Ivey & Ivey, 1999; S. J. Lopez et al., 2006). Psychopathology can often be reframed as a logical response to developmental history (Ivey & Ivey, 1998).

12. Be careful not to equate cultural differences with psychological deficits (Kress, Eriksen, Rayle, & Ford, 2005; Rollock & Terrell, 1996). The *DSM-IV-TR* is biased toward the North American culture in which it was developed. Counselors need to develop a broad aware-

ness of social and cultural issues to be able to apply the *DSM-IV-TR* effectively with multicultural clients.

13. Keep in mind the limitations of the *DSM-IV-TR* classification system. Because of its categorical nature, it does not adequately indicate the severity of a particular condition, nor does it sufficiently differentiate among individuals classified within the same broad categories. Furthermore, the categories themselves suffer from artificial boundaries and extensive overlapping.

14. Consider the *DSM-IV-TR* diagnosis as a hypothesis that is subject to review as circumstances change or as additional data are collected. Determining a *DSM* diagnosis should be looked on as a process, not a static event (Hinkle, 1999).

SUICIDE RISK ASSESSMENT

Counselors must always be ready to evaluate the risk of suicide among the clients they see. As indicated in chapter 4, it is a good practice to routinely ask clients about any recent thoughts of suicide. The National College Health Risk Behavior Survey found that 10% of college students had seriously considered attempting suicide during the 12 months preceding the survey (Brener, Hassan, & Barrios, 2000). Chiles and Strosahl (2005) found in surveys of the general population that 40% of those asked had periods of suicidal thinking at some time in their lives, including the formation of a suicide plan by one half of this number. The counselor should be careful to establish rapport with each client so that the assessment can be as complete and as accurate as possible.

Clients should be asked directly about their suicidal thoughts if there is any hint of suicidal thinking. The counselor can usually approach this with a series of graded questions. For example, the counselor might ask, "How have you been feeling lately?" "How bad does it get?" "Has it ever been so bad that you wished you were dead?" and "Have you had thoughts of suicide?" If the client has had thoughts of suicide, the counselor needs to inquire about the extent of these thoughts.

Some counselors are apprehensive about bringing up the topic of suicide with a client for fear that this will encourage the client to think about suicide as an option. In reality, clients who have had suicidal thoughts need the opportunity to talk about these thoughts. The great majority of clients are receptive to the routine assessment of suicide risk, including past suicide attempts. Only 3% of the clients in one study did not think that it was a good idea to assess past suicide attempts routinely (W. K. Hahn & Marks, 1996).

In essence, suicide risk assessment becomes part of the treatment. Talking about suicidal thoughts helps to validate the client's experience. It provides a sense of relief and communicates hope to the client that the problem can be addressed. In contrast, clients who have not had suicidal thoughts will usually reassure the counselor that this is not a concern. In fact, it is sometimes a relief for such clients to see their problems from this perspective: Even though they are struggling with a problem, things are not so bad that they think of suicide.

In making a suicide risk assessment, counselors should be both calm and direct. Calmness indicates that it is acceptable for clients to talk about the things they find to be most troubling. Counselors help clients to look at problems in depth and from different points of view. They should make a point of using the words *suicide* or *kill yourself* while conducting the suicide risk assessment. The enormity of the act should be faced directly. It should not be romanticized.

Significant Factors in Suicide Risk Assessment

The assessment of suicide risk is basic to the formulation of a treatment or intervention plan. The assessment should involve a consideration of the factors discussed below (American Psychiatric Association, 2003; Cesnik & Nixon, 1977; Stelmachers, 1995).

Self-Reported Risk
After clients have acknowledged suicidal ideation, they will usually tell the counselor of their perception of their risk level when asked. Questions such as "How likely do you think it is that you will act on your thoughts of suicide?" or "How long can you continue to tolerate the situation as it is?" will often generate responses that will be helpful in the assessment process. A self-report of high risk must always be taken seriously.

Suicide Plan

For those clients with thoughts of suicide, the counselor should ask if they have considered a plan. If they have a plan, do they intend to act on it? Information about the plan is critical in helping to assess a client's suicide potential.

A suicide plan should be evaluated in terms of the three factors listed below.

- *Lethality.* Some plans are much more lethal, or likely to succeed, than others. Firearms, jumping from great heights, and hanging are highly lethal. More people kill themselves with firearms than by any other method (National Institute of Mental Health, 2004).
- *Availability of means.* Does the client have access to the means of killing himself or herself? Is a gun available? Has ammunition been purchased? The counselor needs to obtain clear answers to these specific questions. At times, it may be necessary to interview friends or family members to obtain this information.
- *Specificity.* Finally, how detailed are the client's plans? The risk of suicide increases as plans become more detailed and specific. For example, has the client made plans to give away possessions? Has the client considered what he or she might write in a note? Where would the suicide take place? When would it take place? Even more alarming are clients who have started to act on their plans, for example, those who have written a suicide note or given a pet animal to a friend.

According to Haley (2004), the best indicators of suicidal risk are ideation, plan, intent, and means. If the client is thinking about suicide, has made a plan, intends to carry it out, and has the means, he or she is at extreme risk and immediate intervention is needed. Chiles and Strosahl (2005) described a number of steps that should be taken with clients at this point, including validating the emotional pain, exploring the ambivalence felt by the client and connecting to that part of the client that wants to live, developing a crisis management plan, and referring the client for psychiatric consultation and treatment, while maintaining a calm and supportive atmosphere.

Suicide History

A history of suicide attempts, the medical seriousness of previous attempts, and a family history of suicide are all critical factors in assessing suicide risk (Peruzzi & Bongar, 1999). If a person has attempted or seriously thought about suicide at some earlier time, particularly by lethal means, the risk of suicide for that person is significantly increased. Individuals who have made more than one attempt are especially at risk (Joiner, Walker, Rudd, & Jobes, 1999).

The counselor should check on the history of suicide in the family and among friends. Have family members or friends committed suicide or made suicide threats or attempts? If so, what was the nature of the relationship between that person and the client? Did that person represent a model for the client? How does the client feel about these situations? When did the suicide or suicide attempt take place? Anniversary dates can sometimes provide the impetus for suicide attempts.

Psychological Symptoms

Clients who have mental disorders or psychological distress are much more likely than others to commit suicide (American Psychiatric Association, 2003). All client symptoms should be reviewed. Critical symptoms include acute suicidal ideation, severe hopelessness, attraction to death, and acute overuse of alcohol (Peruzzi & Bongar, 1999).

Suicidal ideation can be predicted by asking clients if they had relatively long periods of time (2 weeks or more) during the past year in which they (a) experienced sleeping problems, (b) felt depressed or lost interest in things they usually enjoyed, (c) felt guilty or worthless, or (d) felt that life was hopeless (Cooper-Patrick, Crum, & Ford, 1994). Clients who respond positively to any of these items should be asked if they have thoughts of suicide. According to experts on the topic, hopelessness stands out as "the most powerful antecedent" (Stelmachers, 1995, p. 374) of suicide. Restlessness or agitation associated with any of the above symptoms increases the risk for suicide.

Alcohol or other drug abuse significantly increases the risk of suicide for a client. The risk of suicide in alcoholics is 50% to 70% higher than in the general population (American Association of Suicidology, 2004). Counseling programs designed to prevent suicide must also address the related problem of alcohol or other drug abuse (Brener et al., 2000).

Medications can also be associated with suicide. The side effects of many medications include depression. The counselor should note if the client is taking any medications, including any recent change in medications. Medications are also frequently used as a means of suicide. As a safety precaution, someone else should control antidepressant medications prescribed for highly suicidal clients.

Symptoms that suggest severe mental illness such as schizophrenia, bipolar disorder, or other psychotic disorders demand prompt attention. Has the client lost contact with reality? Does the client hear voice commands (auditory hallucinations) telling him or her what to do? All psychotic individuals with thoughts of suicide should be hospitalized immediately to provide protection and relief from their psychosis. Many people who kill themselves are people with severe and persistent mental illness (Harris & Barraclough, 1997). Psychological autopsy studies indicate that more than 90% of those who commit suicide have a mental disorder (American Association of Suicidology, 2004).

Sometimes signs of improvement can increase the risk of suicide. Clients may become more actively suicidal as they begin to come out of a deep depression, that is, when they acquire enough energy to act on their suicidal thoughts. In a similar fashion, clients sometimes will give an appearance of improvement when they have resolved their ambivalence by deciding to commit suicide.

Environmental Stress

Stressful situations are often the precipitating cause of suicidal ideation. What is the nature of the client's environment? Why is the client feeling suicidal at this particular time? What are the precipitating factors? How would the client benefit from suicide? Clients who wish to commit suicide to escape from stressful situations represent a greater risk than clients who see suicide as a means of manipulating the environment.

Has the client encountered significant changes in his or her life, such as divorce, death of a family member, sickness, loss of job, academic failure, or an overwhelming work assignment? Any change, even one that is positive, such as a job promotion or the end of an unhappy relationship, can be perceived as stressful. Change involves loss. Losses that pose the greatest threat include loss of a relationship, loss of a significant role, loss of a dream, or a large financial loss. Sometimes anticipating a loss can be more stressful than the actual loss. Loss can be particularly stressful if the client accepts most of the blame. Client stress can be systematically assessed by means of the Life Experiences Survey (Sarason, Johnson, & Siegel, 1978) or the Life Stressors and Social Resources Inventory–Adult or Youth Form (Moos & Moos, 1994b, 1994c).

Sometimes stress can be associated with an event that happened years earlier if this event has not been addressed. Such events include sexual abuse, physical abuse, the suicide of a parent or sibling, and other traumatic events. Ask clients if there are things from their past that they find very difficult to talk about. If so, help them to begin to look at these issues in a supportive atmosphere. Recognize the need for long-term treatment for many of these issues.

Available Resources

Counselors need to determine what resources are available for the client. Three levels of resources should be considered: (a) internal; (b) family, close friends, neighbors, coworkers, and others who may have contact with the client; and (c) professionals.

First of all, what are the client's internal resources? In trying to assess these resources, the counselor should ask what has helped the client in the past in similar situations. What is keeping the client from committing suicide? Does the client have plans for the future?

To what degree can the client cope with the stress that he or she may be encountering? For example, can the client identify a solvable problem? Can the client distinguish between wanting to die and wanting to be rid of a problem? Can the client see more than one solution to a problem? Some clients experience "tunnel vision" so that they cannot conceive of options other than suicide for dealing with their stress. Does the client benefit from the counselor's attempts to provide assistance? Positive answers to these questions help to reduce the risk of suicide for the client.

Second, find out what type of support system the client has. If nobody seems to be involved with the client at the present time, ask who used to care. Does the client have regular contact with anyone else? Does the client have any confidants? Would the client be willing to share his or her concerns with family members or close friends? In some respects, suicide can be looked on more as a social than as a psychiatric phenomenon. Evaluation of the client's social support system is critical from this point of view. A client's social support system can be evaluated by means of the Multidimensional Scale of Perceived Social Support (Zimet, Dahlem, Zimet, & Farley, 1988) or the Life Stressors and Social Resources Inventory–Adult or Youth Form (Moos & Moos, 1994b, 1994c).

Finally, what community resources are available for the client? Possibilities include a 24-hour crisis phone line, emergency treatment center, or mental health specialist with whom the client has good rapport. Would the client make use of these resources in case of a crisis? Will the client sign a contract that he or she would contact the counselor or another mental health professional before attempting to commit suicide?

In addition to the risk factors discussed above, suicide risk is affected by both personality and demographic characteristics. Individuals with impulsive personality styles are more likely to attempt suicide than are other individuals (Joiner et al., 1999). Women make three times as many suicide attempts as men; however, four times as many men as women succeed in actually killing themselves (National Institute of Mental Health, 2004). The suicide rate is significantly higher for both adolescents and older adults than it is for the general population (Westefeld et al., 2000). Married people or people with dependent children at home are less likely to attempt suicide (J. R. Rogers, Alexander, & Subich, 1994). Personality factors, such as impulsivity, perfectionism, and negativity, and demographic factors, such as sex, age, and marital status, should be considered together with the other risk factors in making a suicide risk assessment.

Suicide Risk Assessment Aids

As indicated above, a large number of factors are associated with suicidal thinking and behavior. An assessment aid can help ensure that the counselor does not overlook crucial factors in making a risk assessment.

Three aids for assessing suicide risk are described below. These aids are designed for use as part of the interview process. All of these aids emphasize the importance of assessing current suicidal symptoms and suicide history. They can provide a guide both for the assessment interview and for documenting the comprehensiveness of the assessment.

SAD PERSONS Scale

This scale provides a convenient acronym for 10 factors to keep in mind when assessing a client for suicidal risk (Patterson, Dohn, Bird, & Patterson, 1983). These 10 factors (arranged in order of the first letter for each factor to spell SAD PERSONS) include *Sex*, *Age*, *Depression*, *Previous* attempt, *Ethanol* abuse, *Rational* thinking loss, *Social* support loss, *Organized* plan, *No* spouse, and *Sickness*. All of these risk factors have been discussed above.

Clients receive 1 point for each of these factors that pertain to them based on the counselor's judgment. All clients who receive more than 2 points should be considered for psychiatric referral or hospitalization. The counselor needs to weigh all aspects of the situation in making a decision. Some factors may deserve greater consideration than others, depending on the particular situation. An organized plan is always cause for serious concern. When working with children, counselors may use the Adapted–SAD PERSONS Scale, which takes into account such factors as negligent parenting and school problems (Juhnke, 1996).

Students who have been taught how to use the SAD PERSONS Scale make judgments similar to those of experienced psychiatrists (Juhnke & Hovestadt, 1995; Patterson et al., 1983). Those who do not know how to use the SAD PERSONS Scale tend to overestimate the suicide risk of the people they evaluate.

Suicide Assessment Checklist (SAC)

J. R. Rogers et al. (1994) developed the SAC, which is based on a review of the literature. It includes 12 items based on the client's suicide planning, suicide history, psychiatric history, drug use, and demographic characteristics and 9 items based on the counselor's ratings of significant factors (hopelessness, worthlessness, social isolation, depression, impulsivity, hostility, intent to die, environmental stress, and future time perspective).

The items are weighted in terms of their criticalness. The authors of this checklist assigned the highest weights to the following factors: having a definite suicide plan, planning to use a highly lethal method (firearm, hanging, car exhaust, drugs/poison, or suffocating), making final plans (such as giving away possessions), writing a suicide note, and being a suicide survivor (having a close friend or relative who has committed suicide). In general, higher scores indicate greater risk; however, counselors also need to take into account other pertinent information such as third-party reports and their own clinical judgment in making a final assessment of suicide risk.

Research evidence indicates that the instrument can be used effectively by counselors with a broad range of education and experience (J. R. Rogers et al., 1994). High interrater and test–retest reliabilities were obtained for SAC ratings by counselors (both experts and crisis-line volunteers) who judged the suicide risk of individuals role-playing suicidal clients. A large-scale study by J. R. Rogers, Lewis, and Subich (2002) found support for the reliability and validity of SAC ratings when used with clients in an emergency crisis center to assess suicide risk.

Decision-Tree Assessment Strategy

This approach uses three risk factors—(a) past suicide attempts, (b) suicide plans and preparation, and (c) suicidal desire and ideation—as a basis for assessing suicidality (Joiner et al., 1999). All clients with these risk factors are assessed further. Clients who have made more than one previous suicide attempt (multiple attempters) or who have made suicide plans and preparation are classified as at least moderate suicide risks if they possess one other significant risk factor, such as depression, alcohol abuse, or impulsivity. Clients who express suicidal ideas and desires (but who have not made multiple attempts or who have not developed plans and preparations) are regarded as at least moderate risks if they possess two other significant risk factors. Clients with none of the three risk factors listed above are considered to be at low risk.

The decision-tree approach helps the counselor to readily identify clients who need further assessment. It provides a systematic means for determining which clients are at greatest risk for attempting suicide.

The authors of this assessment strategy suggest a range of possible interventions for clients judged to be at least moderate risks for committing suicide. These interventions include increase of frequency and duration of counseling sessions or telephone contacts, a detailed emergency plan (presented in writing to the client), 24-hour availability of emergency or crisis services for the client, professional consultation or referral for psychiatric treatment or hospitalization, active involvement of family and supportive others, and frequent reevaluation of suicide risk and treatment goals.

In summary, counselors should use some form of comprehensive and systematic assessment to determine a client's suicide risk. Each of the interview aids described above focuses attention on significant factors that should be included in a suicide risk assessment. By using a systematic approach, the counselor can be sure to assess critical factors relevant to most situations in addition to other factors that may be pertinent in particular situations. Counselors should ask for more detail in those areas in which a problem is detected.

Suicide risk factors should be reviewed during each counseling session for clients who may be suicidal. Such a review can serve both as a risk management strategy by assessing and documenting changes in suicidal thinking and behavior over time and as a basis for ongoing treatment planning.

When the counselor makes a suicide risk assessment, it is often important to consult with another mental health professional. Clients who are at risk for suicide may need to be referred for psychiatric evaluation. Psychiatrists can evaluate the client's need for medication, hospitalization, or long-term treatment. The assessment and treatment of suicidal clients frequently requires a team approach.

ASSESSMENT OF ALCOHOL USE

A section on the assessment of alcohol use is included in this chapter because of the prevalence of abusive drinking and alcohol-related problems in American culture. Almost one third (31%) of students in a survey of 119 four-year colleges met the *DSM-IV-TR* criteria for alcohol abuse; that is, they continued to use alcohol despite significant problems they encountered (Knight et al., 2002). According to a national study of psychiatric disorders, approximately 15% of the U.S. population will meet the diagnostic criteria for substance abuse or dependence some time in their lifetime (Kessler, Berglund, et al., 2005). Most of the substance use disorders involve the use of alcohol. Because denial is a central issue in the abuse of alcohol or other drugs, counselors may not learn of the problem if they do not systematically review this matter with clients.

A variety of assessment procedures may be used to evaluate alcohol use. In most cases, the interview will probably be used to determine the nature and the gravity of drinking problems. Self-monitoring methods and physiological indices such as blood alcohol concentration levels can be used to supplement the interview. Standardized measures (discussed in the next chapter) may also be used as part of the assessment process. In addition to individual assessment, the counselor will often need to assess the environment in which the drinking takes place.

Diagnostic Criteria for Alcohol Dependence or Abuse

Although this chapter focuses on assessment of alcohol disorders, similar diagnostic criteria are used to determine dependence or abuse for all psychoactive substances. Psychoactive drugs include all drugs that alter an individual's mood or thought processes by their effect on the central nervous system. *DSM-IV-TR* recognizes 10 classes of psychoactive drugs (alcohol, amphetamines, cannabis, nicotine, cocaine, PCP or phencyclidine, inhalants, hallucinogens, opioids, and sedatives) that can lead to dependence. The drugs show some differences in respect to tolerance and withdrawal symptoms as indicated in the *DSM-IV-TR*.

The specific criteria used to determine alcohol (or other substance) dependence are summarized below (American Psychiatric Association, 2000a).

- Tolerance to the effects of the substance, so that markedly increased amounts of the substance are needed over time to attain intoxication or desired effect, or markedly diminished effect occurs with continued use of same amount of the substance
- Withdrawal symptoms that significantly interfere with everyday functioning when the substance is no longer available
- Compulsive use of the substance as indicated by consuming the substance in larger amounts or over a longer time period than intended
- Unsuccessful efforts to cut down on use of the substance
- Expenditure of a great deal of time in obtaining the substance, using it, or recovering from its effects
- Reduction or cessation of important social, occupational, or recreational activities because of substance use
- Continued use of the substance despite the physical or psychological problems that it is known to produce

Of the seven criteria listed, three or more must be manifested over a 12-month period for a person to be diagnosed as alcohol dependent. The diagnostic classification includes the specifier "with physiological dependence" (American Psychiatric Association, 2000a, p. 198) if the person shows evidence of either tolerance or withdrawal. Alcohol withdrawal symptoms include "the shakes," transient hallucinations or illusions, anxiety, depressed mood, headache, insomnia, rapid heart rate, or sweating.

Alcohol abuse refers to problematic drinking that does not fulfill the criteria listed above for alcohol dependence. People who suffer from this condition continue to drink within a 12-month period despite significant problems. These problems include failure to fulfill major role obligations at work or home, repeated use in dangerous situations (e.g., driving while intoxicated), recurrent legal problems, or recurrent social and interpersonal problems.

Counselors will often see clients because of the problems produced by drinking, such as deterioration in work performance, conflicts with others, depression, or poor health. The counselor will need to be careful to assess for drinking (or other substance) abuse that may have caused the problem. In general, counselors should assess clients' ability to control their use of alcohol and the degree to which alcohol usage causes problems in their lives.

Interview Schedules for Assessment of Alcohol Use

A number of interview schedules have been developed to aid in the assessment of alcohol use. The schedules vary in length from a few questions designed to be used for screening purposes to extensive forms used for diagnostic purposes that may require as much as 3 hours to complete (Evans, 1998).

Brief Assessments

The CAGE questionnaire (named for the key words in each of four questions) can be readily used to screen clients for problems related to alcohol use (Ewing, 1984; Kitchens, 1994). The interviewer asks clients if they have ever (a) felt the need to *cut* down their drinking, (b) become *annoyed* when others ask them about their drinking, (c) felt *guilty* about their drinking, or (d) needed to take an *eyeopener* to start the day. If clients acknowledge any of these feelings or behaviors, they are likely to have experienced problems with alcohol, and additional inquiry should be undertaken.

Heck (1991) found that the effectiveness of the CAGE questionnaire in identifying problem drinkers could be significantly improved by asking clients about their social drinking habits, driving habits, and the age at which they began to drink. Problem drinkers rarely or never choose non-alcoholic beverages at social events, frequently drive while under the influence of alcohol, and started drinking on a regular basis while they were still in high school.

Researchers in Copenhagen modified the CAGE by changing the wording in each question from "ever" to "anytime with the past year" (Zierau et al., 2005). They also added two questions that ask about number of days a week that a person drinks and if drinking occurs outside of mealtime on weekdays. This modified version, known as the CAGE-C (for Copenhagen), proved to be particularly effective when used for screening purposes in a population with a large number of "at risk" drinkers

In several studies, Cherpitel (2000, 2002) found that a shortened version of the Rapid Alcohol Problems Screen (RAPS) was more effective than the CAGE and other standard screening instruments in detecting alcohol dependence across gender and ethnic groups. The RAPS4 contains four items, each of which has shown high sensitivity and specificity in identifying individuals with alcohol dependence. These four items relate to guilt about drinking (*R*emorse), blackouts (*A*mnesia), failing to do what was normally expected (*P*erform), and need for an eyeopener or morning drink (*S*tarter). Individuals who respond positively to any one of these items should be referred for a more thorough assessment of alcohol problems.

To ensure that primary care practitioners take the time to screen patients for alcoholism, the National Institute on Alcohol Abuse and Alcoholism (2005) has recommended using just one basic question for all patients to determine whether further assessment is necessary. Men who drink are asked "How many times in the past year have you had 5 or more drinks in a day?" (A drink is defined as 12 ounces of beer, 5 ounces of wine, or 1.5 ounces of 80 proof spirits.) For women, the number of drinks is reduced to four. People who answer one time or more are then asked about heavy weekly drinking (more than 14 drinks for men or 7 drinks for women within a 1-week time period). Those who have drunk heavily within 1 week during the past year are then assessed more thoroughly in terms of the *DSM-IV-TR* criteria listed above.

Comprehensive Assessments

Several structured interviews have been developed to assess a client's current and past alcohol or other drug use in considerable detail. These measures include the Addiction Severity Index (ASI), Comprehensive Drinking Profile (CDP), and Time-Line Follow-Back (TLFB).

The ASI assesses the impact of the client's use of alcohol or other drugs on the client's medical status, employment or school status, legal status, family and social relationships, and psychiatric status (McLellan et al., 1992). According to Budman (2000), this instrument has become the standard measure of substance abuse in many agencies, with more than 1 million administrations a year in the United States. Research indicates that it yields internally consistent and valid information regarding a client's functioning even when administered in less-than-ideal circumstances, such as inner-city alcohol and drug abuse clinics (Leonhard, Mulvey, Gastfriend, & Schwartz, 2000). The ASI may also be administered in a multimedia version (called the ASI-MV) by virtual interviewers. The ASI-MV provides computer-generated ratings of addiction severity that match (or surpass) those of trained interviewers in terms of reliability and validity (Budman, 2000).

The CDP is a structured intake interview procedure requiring 1 to 2 hours for completion (Marlatt & Miller, 1984). It provides detailed information regarding the history and current status of an individual's drinking problems and related matters. It assesses both consumption and problematic behaviors. A short form of the CDP, the Brief Drinker Profile, is also available, as well as the Follow-Up Drinker Profile (a measure of client progress) and the Collateral Interview Form (an instrument for obtaining information from other people who are close to the client).

The TLFB enables the client and the counselor to reconstruct the client's drinking or other drug-using behavior for the past year (Sobell et al., 1980). It analyzes the patterns (e.g., daily, weekly, sporadically) and the intensity (light, heavy) of such behavior. Connections between drinking or other drug-use episodes and significant events ("anchor points") in the person's life are studied. Research indicates that the TLFB is reliable and valid when used with adult substance abusers from different countries and cultures (Fals-Stewart, O'Farrell, Feitas, McFarlin, & Rutigliano, 2000; Sobell et al., 2001). TLFB reports obtained from clients agree reasonably well with those that are obtained from clients' spouses or partners or from urine assays. This procedure yields information that is enlightening to clients as well as to counselors.

Self-Monitoring Methods

Self-monitoring can enhance assessments made by means of interview procedures in a number of ways. Because self-monitoring is based on planned observations, data obtained in this manner should be more accurate and more complete than data based on recall. Self-monitoring has the added advantage of helping clients to see more clearly the relationship between certain events and their drinking behavior. Finally, self-monitoring provides a means of plotting the client's progress in controlling drinking behavior.

Self-monitoring charts typically include the amount of alcohol consumed in a given period of time, the situation in which the alcohol was consumed, and the presence of other people (Vuchinich, Tucker, & Harllee, 1988). The thoughts or feelings of the person at the time may also be recorded. Temptations to drink, as well as actual drinking behavior, may be tracked.

Self-monitoring assumes that individuals will comply with the instructions to keep a regular record of their drinking. Such recording can be facilitated by use of a log book, handheld computer, or telephone answering service. For example, the use of an interactive voice response system allows clients to record their drinking by telephone. This type of system has proved to increase accuracy of reporting and lead to reduction in drinking by itself without additional interventions (Helzer, Badger, Rose, Mangeon, & Searles, 2002; Searles, Helzer, Rose, & Badger, 2002).

Motivational Interviewing

Motivational Interviewing, as described by W. R. Miller & Rollnick (2002), can be looked on as a type of guided self-assessment. The counselor, in an empathic, nonjudgmental manner, explores with clients a particular behavior in which change is desired (e.g., excessive drinking or unsafe sex). The counselor aids the client in identifying and clarifying ambivalent feelings regarding the problematic behavior.

In one study of Motivational Interviewing, the interviewer asked college students (all of whom had engaged in excessive drinking) to prepare a written list of "pros" and "cons" for drinking alcohol (LaBrie, Pederson, Earleywine, & Olsen, 2006). The interviewer, while maintaining a neutral position, helped students to make sure that they had evaluated all aspects of their drinking behavior, often by the use of reflections, open-ended questions, and prompts as part of the assessment process. Follow-up research indicated that the students significantly reduced their drinking. The success of this approach was attributed to the careful assessment of pros and cons (called the "decisional balance" method) within the context of a supportive, nonconfrontational interview. In essence, the assessment also became the treatment.

Use of Alcohol Assessment Procedures in Counseling

Guidelines concerning the assessment of problems related to alcohol or other substance use are listed below.

1. Be alert to possible substance abuse problems of individuals with other *DSM-IV-TR* diagnoses. Dual diagnoses involving substance abuse with other mental disorders are relatively common (Grant et al., 2004; Kessler, Chiu, et al., 2005).

2. Be sure to ask about the use of alcohol or other drugs as part of the intake procedure. Evans (1998) pointed out that it is important to diagnose and treat substance use disorder early in counseling when the client is under duress and less guarded.

3. Be aware of crucial signs ("red flags") that indicate possible substance abuse. In the case of adolescents, these red flags include such matters as physical or sexual abuse, parental substance abuse, peer involvement in substance abuse or serious delinquency, sudden downturns in school performance or attendance, marked change in physical health, HIV high-risk activities, and severe depression (Winters, 1999).

4. Inquire about problems related to drinking. Abusive drinking may be most evident in the problems it produces. Checklists can be helpful for this purpose. For example, "An Inventory of Alcohol-Related Problems" lists 45 drinking-associated problems that can be used by clients to review the outcomes of their drinking behavior (W. R. Miller & Muñoz, 2005, pp. 193–194).

5. Ask if other people have been concerned about the client's drinking behavior. Use the CAGE or RAPS4 questions as part of the screening process.

6. Keep the *DSM-IV-TR* criteria in mind in assessing for alcohol dependence or abuse. Determine frequency, duration, and severity of pertinent symptoms. Remember that these same criteria can be used in assessing other types of psychoactive substance dependence or abuse.

7. If alcohol or other drug problems are detected, use a more thorough assessment procedure to gain a better understanding of the problem or refer the client to specialists for this purpose. Interview schedules such as the CDP or TLFB or the Alcohol Use Inventory (briefly discussed in the next chapter) could be used for a more extended assessment.

8. Engage the client in self-assessment. Self-monitoring of drinking behavior can be helpful both in defining the problem and in gauging the success of treatment efforts. Motivational Interviewing can help clients assess and resolve ambivalent attitudes toward drinking.

9. Help clients to become aware of those situations that may trigger drinking for them, such as being with a friend who drinks heavily or drinking late at night.

10. Teach the use of blood alcohol concentration (BAC) tables to clients with drinking problems so that they can assess the influence of alcohol consumption on their judgment and reaction time (W. R. Miller & Muñoz, 2005). Help them to use these tables to set alcohol consumption limits.

11. When clients do not accept the fact that they have a problem of control of their drinking behavior (an essential feature of dependency), ask them to try to limit their drinking to a certain amount (e.g., no more than three drinks) on any one occasion for a period of 3 months. This has sometimes been referred to as the "acid test" of an individual's ability to control drinking behavior.

12. If denial appears to be a problem, obtain permission from the client to speak with family members or friends as a means of gaining information about his or her drinking behaviors. Interview these people with the client present in the room.

13. Use information from all available sources, including work, school, and community records or personnel. Assessment will be more accurate if it is based on multiple sources of information.

14. Seek supervision to avoid frustration and to improve skills for gathering information from clients who may be in a state of denial (Evans, 1998).

15. Refer clients with persistent drinking problems to specialists for assessment and treatment. Assessment should include a physical exam by qualified medical personnel. Inpatient or intensive outpatient treatment in a multidisciplinary setting may be necessary.

SUMMARY

1. Mental illnesses, particularly anxiety and mood disorders, occur frequently in the United States. Counselors need to be able to detect psychopathology among clients in their caseload.

2. The *DSM-IV-TR* offers a clear and comprehensive means of diagnosing possible mental disorders among clients.

3. All counselors should be able to undertake suicide risk assessments and substance abuse assessments within the counseling session.

4. If counselors are concerned about a client's suicide risk, they should ask about suicide intentions, specific suicide plans, previous suicide attempts, psychological symptoms, environmental stress, and available resources.
5. Alcohol assessment should focus on (a) the client's ability to control his or her drinking and (b) the problems in the client's life associated with drinking. The *DSM-IV-TR* criteria can be used to diagnose alcohol dependence or abuse.

15

Mental Health Assessment: Standardized Inventories

S tandardized measures of mental health are presented in this chapter. General-purpose measures contain a variety of scales that assess different aspects of psychopathology, whereas specific-purpose measures focus on a particular type of mental health problem, such as depression, anxiety, alcohol abuse, or eating disorders. The use of both types of measures in counseling is discussed below.

GENERAL-PURPOSE MEASURES

Five of the most popular inventories used to assess psychopathology are reviewed. The Minnesota Multiphasic Personality Inventory–2 (MMPI-2), the oldest of these measures, stands out as "the most widely used and widely researched test of adult psychopathology" (Pearson Assessments, 2006, MMPI-2, ¶ 1). The adolescent form of the MMPI (MMPI-A), first published in 1992, is one of the most frequently used inventories for young people (Archer & Newsom, 2000). The characteristics and uses of both of these instruments are considered below. In addition, three other broad measures of psychopathology—Millon Clinical Multiaxial Inventory–III (MCMI-III), Personality Assessment Inventory (PAI), and Basic Personality Inventory (BPI)—that can serve as alternatives to the MMPI-2 are also reviewed.

Minnesota Multiphasic Personality Inventory–2 (MMPI-2)

The MMPI-2 replaces the MMPI, which was first published in 1943 (Graham, 2005). This instrument, which requires a sixth-grade reading level, may be used with clients beginning at age 18.

The original MMPI, as developed by Starke Hathaway and J. Charnley McKinley, contained a total of 4 validity scales and 10 clinical scales that formed the standard MMPI profile (see Table 15-1). The validity scales enable the counselor to assess the client's attitude toward the testing process. Most of the clinical scales consist of items that significantly differentiated between people in a particular psychiatric diagnostic category (e.g., depression) and people in the general reference group (often referred to as "the Minnesota normals"). For example, the Depression scale (Scale 2) contained 60 items that people with depression endorsed significantly more (or less) often than did the Minnesota normals.

Subsequent research has indicated that the MMPI scales cannot be used to classify individuals into psychiatric categories with a high degree of accuracy. Instead, the scales are most useful in providing descriptions of personality and as a source of inference regarding a person's behavior. Because of the large amount of research that has been conducted with the MMPI, the scales

TABLE 15-1

Description of Standard Scales on the Minnesota Multiphasic Personality Inventory–2

Scale	Behaviors Associated With Elevated Scores
Validity scales	
? Cannot say (?)	Indecisiveness, rebelliousness, defensiveness
L Lie (L)	Faking good, naivete, scrupulosity
F Frequency (F)	Faking bad, unusual behavior, confusion while taking test, self-critical
K Correction (K)	Faking good, defensiveness, self-reliance
Clinical scales	
1 Hypochondriasis (Hs)	Bodily complaints, fatigue, weakness
2 Depression (D)	Dejection, dissatisfaction, tendency to give up
3 Hysteria (Hy)	Denial of problems, desire for social acceptance, psychosomatic symptoms
4 Psychopathic deviate (Pd)	Impulsivity, acting out, not bound by rules
5 Masculinity–femininity (Mf)	Men: Cultural-aesthetic interests, passivity, academic achievement
	Women: Outdoor-mechanical interests, dominating, competitive
6 Paranoia (Pa)	Sensitive, suspicious, preoccupied with rights and privileges
7 Psychasthenia (Pt)	Anxious, obsessive, compulsive
8 Schizophrenia (Sc)	Unusual thoughts or behavior, detached, introspective
9 Hypomania (Ma)	High energy level, restless, distractible
0 Social introversion–extroversion (Si)	Introverted, reserved, reticent

convey a wealth of information about an individual's personality that transcends the original purpose of the scales. For this reason, the original names for the MMPI scales have been replaced by the scale numbers for most purposes (e.g., Scale 7 instead of Pt or Psychasthenia).

The authors of the MMPI-2 corrected problems with the original normative sample and brought the instrument up to date in 1989 (Butcher, Graham, Ben-Porath, Tellegen, & Dahlstrom, 2001). The total number of items (567) remains about the same. Ineffective, offensive, and repeated items have been eliminated. Sexist or dated items have been reworded. New items tap areas not well represented in the original MMPI item pool, including family relationships, eating disorders, and drug abuse.

In contrast to the original standardization procedures, members of the new normative sample (1,462 women and 1,138 men) were selected so that they would be representative of the adult U.S. population in terms of age, marital status, ethnicity, and geography. The percentage of college graduates in the new normative sample is much higher than that found in the original sample or reported by the U.S. Census Bureau. According to Butcher, Ben-Porath, et al. (2000), the change in the educational level of the normative sample has a minimal impact on the interpretation of the MMPI-2 scores.

With the new norms, the cutoff score used to detect psychological problems dropped from 70 on the MMPI to 65 on the MMPI-2. Research indicates that a T score of 65 provides optimal separation between clinical groups and the standardization sample (Butcher et al., 2001). The scores on the MMPI-2 have also been adjusted so that the distribution of the profile scores will be the same for the eight clinical scales (Scales 1, 2, 3, 4, 6, 7, 8, and 9) used to assess psychopathology. For example, a T score of 65 equals the 92nd percentile (based on the restandardization sample) for each of these scales.

Several new validity scales were developed for the MMPI-2. In addition to the number of item omissions (? score), the original MMPI validity scales measured "fake good" (L and K scales) and "fake bad" (F scale) response tendencies. The new validity scales include TRIN (True Response Inconsistency, which measures acquiescence or negativity), VRIN (Variable Response Inconsistency, which measures random responding), and Back F (a fake bad measure for the back, or new, part of the inventory). Counselors should check the validity scores first to make certain that the client has been honest and cooperative in responding to the inventory before they attempt to interpret the other scores.

The MMPI-2 scales should be interpreted in conjunction with the other scales on the profile, not in isolation. A number of MMPI-2 reference books provide personality descriptions and possible psychiatric diagnoses associated with different profile configurations (e.g., Butcher, 1997, 2005; Butcher, Williams, & Fowler, 2000; A. F. Friedman, Lewak, Nichols, & Webb, 2001; Graham, 2005; Greene, 1999). Counselors should be acquainted with the vast literature pertaining to the MMPI-2 if they work with clients who are mentally disturbed; however, they cannot expect to become proficient in its use without specialized training and extensive clinical experience.

Counselors should note critical items that the client has checked as well as scale scores. For example, if the client marked true to Item 506, "I have recently considered killing myself," or Item 524, "No one knows it but I have tried to kill myself," the counselor should review these items with the client. Clients might not bring these topics up on their own initiative. They may assume that the counselor already knows this information from their responses to these items on the MMPI-2.

Several critical item lists have been developed. For example, the Koss–Butcher critical item set contains 78 items related to six crisis areas. These items typically differentiate normal from psychiatric samples. Most computer-based MMPI-2 scoring programs will flag critical items checked by the clients. This information can also be obtained by means of hand scoring. The critical item lists provide a simple and straightforward means for counselors to discuss MMPI-2 results with clients and to identify topics that may need additional inquiry.

A number of additional scales have been created for the MMPI-2 that can be used to help interpret the clinical scales. Most of the clinical scales have been divided into subscales that can help clarify the meaning of scores on the scales (Graham, 2005). The Depression scale, for example, has been divided into the following subscales: Subjective Depression, Psychomotor Retardation, Physical Malfunctioning, Mental Dullness, and Brooding.

In addition to the subscales, 15 content scales devised by Butcher, Graham, Williams, and Ben-Porath (1990) can also be used to clarify the meaning of the MMPI-2 clinical scales. In contrast with the clinical scales, which were developed by empirical means, the content scales were constructed by logical analysis of the item content on the MMPI-2. The scales were refined by statistical procedures to ensure homogeneity of item content. Scales developed in this fashion are easier to interpret than empirical scales. The content scales also assess aspects of personality not measured by the standard scales, including Type A ("hard-driving") behavior, work interference, family problems, and negative treatment indicators. The content scales significantly add to the validity of the clinical scales in predicting symptomatic and personality characteristics of clients (Barthlow, Graham, Ben-Porath, & McNulty, 1999).

The Restructured Clinical (RC) scales (nine in all) were added to the MMPI-2 to provide relatively pure measures of the psychopathological factors measured by the clinical scales (Tellegen et al., 2003). The first RC scale, Demoralization, measures a broad factor of general complaint or malaise that runs throughout the eight clinical scales that assess psychopathology (Scales 5 and 0 were excluded because they are not measures of psychopathology). Each of the remaining eight RC scales was designed to assess the primary dimension of the clinical scale with which it was matched. For example, the RC scale Somatic Complaints is matched with Scale 1 (Hypochondrias). Because of their purity of content, the RC scales can be easily interpreted by themselves and can be used to help interpret the original scales. Although based on fewer items, the RC scales produce results that are as reliable and valid as the original scales (Simms, Casillas, Clark, Watson, & Doebbeling, 2005). The authors plan to develop a short form of the MMPI based on the RC scales.

In addition to the scales discussed thus far, many other scales have been constructed from the MMPI item pool for various purposes. Popular supplementary scales include A (Anxiety), R (Repression), and Es (Ego Strength). The A and R scales represent the two main factors derived from factor analyses of the clinical scales. As such, they offer a quick summary, or overview, of the MMPI-2 results. Scale A provides a measure of anxiety or general maladjustment; Scale R shows the client's tendency to repress or deny psychological difficulties. The Es scale is based on items that distinguished between clients with psychological problems who responded to therapy and those who did not. In contrast with most of the scores on the MMPI-2, high scores on the Es scale should be interpreted favorably.

Research on the MMPI-2 indicates that it can be used effectively with clients from minority groups if moderator variables such as socioeconomic status, education, and acculturation are taken into account (Anderson, 1995; Greene, 1999; Tsai & Pike, 2000). These variables have a greater influence than ethnic status on MMPI-2 scores. Timbrook and Graham (1994) found that the MMPI-2 predicted criterion variables (based on partner ratings) as accurately for African Americans as it did for White men and women. Similarly, McNulty, Graham, Ben-Porath, and Stein (1997) found no evidence of test bias in a study of African American and White mental health center clients. A review of 25 MMPI and MMPI-2 comparative studies found no substantive differences in test scores among European Americans, African Americans, and Latino Americans (Nagayama Hall, Bansal, & Lopez, 1999).

Although the MMPI-2 has many advantages, it is not without faults. In a comprehensive critique of the MMPI-2, Helmes and Reddon (1993) noted the following shortcomings: (a) lack of a consistent measurement model, (b) heterogeneous item content within clinical scales, (c) suspect diagnostic criteria, (d) overlapping of item content among scales, (e) lack of cross-validation of scoring keys, (f) inadequate measures of response styles, and (g) suspect norms. They urged clinicians to consider alternative measures such as the MCMI, PAI, and BPI, because these measures are "more likely to incorporate modern developments and have fewer serious conceptual problems" (Helmes & Reddon, 1993, p. 467).

The use of the MMPI-2 in a counseling situation is illustrated in the following case example.

Case Example

Janet, a 19-year-old college sophomore, requested counseling because of low self-esteem, relationship difficulties, family conflict, and eating concerns. She marked 5 *(very much)* to the following items on the Inventory of Common Problems:

- Feeling irritable, tense, or nervous
- Feeling fearful
- Feeling lonely or isolated
- Eating, appetite, or weight problems

She also completed the Beck Depression Inventory as part of the initial contact session, for which she received a raw score of 32, indicating "severe depression." The counselor asked Janet to complete the MMPI-2 during her next visit to the counseling center to assess more thoroughly the nature and the level of her psychological problems. She obtained the profile shown in Figure 15-1.

The scores on the three validity scales (L, F, and K) indicate self-criticism and a possible plea for help. Her low L and K scores indicate that she is describing herself in a negative fashion. The elevated F score suggests self-criticism together with moderately severe psychopathology. Among the clinical scales, she obtained elevated scores on Scales 2, 6, 7, and 0. Her highest two scores are on Scales 7 and 2. According to Graham (2000), individuals with this code type (27 or 72) "tend to be anxious, nervous, tense, high-strung, and jumpy. They worry excessively, and they are vulnerable to real and imagined threat. They tend to anticipate problems before they occur and to overreact to minor stress. Somatic symptoms are common" (p. 96). Because of their acute discomfort, they are likely to respond well to psychotherapy. They are most likely to receive a psychiatric diagnosis of anxiety disorder, depressive disorder, or obsessive–compulsive disorder.

Janet's elevated scores on Scales 6 and 0 indicate possible difficulties in interpersonal relationships. Scores between 66 and 75 on Scale 6 can possibly be interpreted as follows: angry and resentful, displaces blame and criticisms, hostile and suspicious, rigid and stubborn, and misinterprets social situations (Butcher et al., 2001). Similarly, scores between 66 and 75 on Scale 0 suggest behavior that is introverted, shy, lacking self-confidence, moody, submissive, and rigid (Butcher et al., 2001).

The counselor provided counseling to Janet to help her deal with her immediate situation. At the same time, she made arrangements to refer Janet to a psychiatrist for a more complete assessment of some of the psychological problems suggested by the MMPI-2 and other assessment procedures.

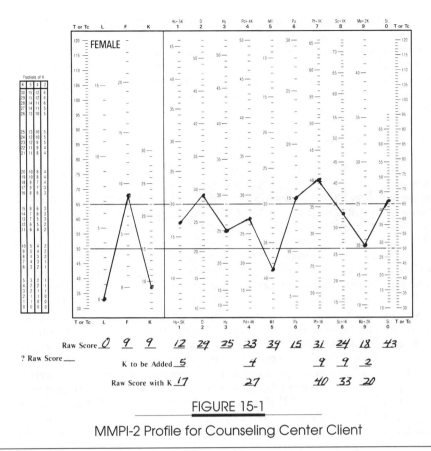

Raw Score _0_ _9_ _9_ _12_ _29_ _25_ _23_ _39_ _15_ _31_ _24_ _18_ _43_

? Raw Score ____

K to be Added _5_   _4_   _9_ _9_ _2_

Raw Score with K _17_   _27_   _40_ _33_ _20_

FIGURE 15-1

MMPI-2 Profile for Counseling Center Client

Note. From Minnesota Multiphasic Personality Inventory–2 (MMPI-2). Copyright 1942, 1943 (renewed 1970), 1989 by the Regents of the University of Minnesota. This profile form 1989. Reprinted with permission.

Minnesota Multiphasic Personality Inventory–Adolescent (MMPI-A)

Prior to the construction of the MMPI-A in 1992, adolescents were frequently administered the adult version of the MMPI despite the difficulties in adapting this version for adolescents. The adolescent version of the MMPI is similar to the new adult version in that it retains the same clinical scales as the old MMPI and also includes a new set of content scales (Archer, 2005; Butcher, Williams, et al., 2000). As with the MMPI-2, the MMPI-A clinical scales and content scales both contain a number of subscales that can be used to help explain the meaning of the scale scores.

The MMPI-A differs from the MMPI-2 in regard to its norms, its item content, and the nature of some of its scales. The MMPI-A provides separate-sex norms for adolescents ages 14 through 18 years. (The test authors recommend that the MMPI-2 be used with 18-year-olds who have moved away from their parental home.) The MMPI-A contains 89 fewer items than the MMPI-2 to help encourage cooperation by clients. Most of the omitted items are items that were not scored on any of the clinical scales, items found on Scales 5 and 0 (both exceptionally long scales on the MMPI-2), or items on the Fears content scale (which has been dropped from the MMPI-A). The MMPI-A includes a number of items from the original MMPI that have been rewritten to pertain to adolescents, as well as a number of new items that deal specifically with adolescent circumstances (such as school, peers, teachers, and parents).

Whereas 11 of the 15 content scales on the MMPI-A are similar to those found on the MMPI-2, 4 of the scales—School Problems, Low Aspirations, Alienation, and Conduct Disorder—have been designed specifically to address issues common to adolescents. The F validity scale, which often produced high scores for adolescents on the MMPI, has been redesigned for the MMPI-A by including only those items answered infrequently (20% of the time or less) by adolescents. The MMPI-A also includes a new supplementary scale, the Immaturity scale, not found on the MMPI-2.

Scores on the clinical and content scales yield adequate test–retest reliability and internal consistency coefficients when used with adolescents. Both sets of scales have proved to be effective in predicting adolescent behavior and personality characteristics, especially when used in combination (Forbey & Ben-Porath, 2003). Much of the validity for the MMPI-A can be inferred from validity established for the MMPI because of the comparability of the instruments. As with the MMPI-2, *T* scores of 65 or greater suggest possible psychopathology. Scores between 60 and 65 should be viewed as indicating possible psychological problems.

Millon Clinical Multiaxial Inventory–III (MCMI-III)

The MCMI-III provides an attractive alternative to the MMPI-2 for diagnosing psychopathology (Millon, Davis, & Millon, 1997). First, it is considerably shorter than the MMPI-2, containing 175 items compared with 567 items on the MMPI-2. Most people can complete the MCMI-III in 20 to 30 minutes. Second, it is more closely tied to the *Diagnostic and Statistical Manual of Mental Disorders (*4th ed., text rev.; *DSM-IV-TR;* American Psychiatric Association, 2000a) so that psychiatric classifications can be made more easily. Finally, it is more closely related to psychological theory, which can serve as a basis for interpreting test results (Millon, 1990, 2003).

The MCMI-III provides two broad sets of scores that correspond with Axis I (clinical syndromes) and Axis II (personality disorders) on the *DSM-IV-TR*. It includes a total of 4 validity scales, 10 clinical syndrome scales, and 14 personality disorder scales. It also includes 42 facet scales (3 content scales for each of the 14 personality disorder scales) that have been added to help interpret the meaning of the personality disorder scales (Millon, Millon, Davis, & Grossman, 2006).

The Axis I and II scales are scored in terms of base rates so that the percentages of people classified by means of the MCMI-III as undergoing particular psychological problems correspond with the actual percentages found in society. Because of the scoring procedure, it is important that the MCMI-III be used only with people who fit the normative population, that is, people suspected to have a mental disorder. The MCMI-III will overpathologize for people who do not belong to this population. Clients should be screened by other criteria such as an interview, the Beck Depression Inventory–II, or the Inventory of Common Problems before they are assigned the MCMI-III.

The MCMI-III has been validated in terms of its effectiveness in differentiating individuals with particular psychiatric diagnoses from other psychiatric patients. This is a more rigorous criterion than differentiating these same types of individuals from a "normal" population, such as that originally used with the MMPI. The technique used with the MCMI-III has proved to be more accurate in identifying the psychiatric diagnoses of patients in subsequent studies than has the technique used with the MMPI.

Although hand scoring is possible, MCMI-III answer sheets can be much more efficiently scored by means of computer-based scoring programs available from the publisher. The scoring programs provide comprehensive narrative interpretations of the scores, together with suggested psychiatric diagnoses and treatment possibilities.

Counselors should consider the use of the MCMI-III with adult clients whom they believe may have psychiatric disorders. For adolescents, counselors should use the Millon Adolescent Clinical Inventory (MACI), the "junior version" of the MCMI-III (Millon & Davis, 1993).

Psychiatric diagnoses suggested by the MCMI-III or MACI need to be verified by further assessment (Widiger, 2001).The counselor can use information gained from these instruments in the referral of clients for psychiatric assessment and treatment. Considerable training and experience are required for the use of either instrument. Several MCMI-III and MACI reference books are available, including those by Jankowski (2002) and Strack (2002) for beginners and Choca (2004) and Millon and Craig (2005) for advanced users.

Personality Assessment Inventory (PAI)

The PAI was designed to provide information on "relevant clinical variables" for individuals 18 years of age and older (Morey, 1991, 2003). Content areas for the PAI were selected on the basis of current diagnostic schemes and treatment planning. It consists of 344 items (selected from an original item pool of 2,200 items) that are scored on 22 scales. Final items for the PAI were selected on the basis of expert ratings, statistical analysis, and related criteria in a 10-stage process.

The 22 full scales on the PAI include four different types of scales, as follows:

- *Validity Scales:* Inconsistency (ICN), Infrequency (INF), Negative Impression (NIM), Positive Impression (PIM)
- *Clinical Scales:* Somatic Complaints (SOM), Anxiety (ANX), Anxiety-Related Disorders (ARD), Depression (DEP), Mania (MAN), Paranoia (PAR), Schizophrenia (SCZ), Borderline Features (BOR), Antisocial Features (ANT), Alcohol Problems (ALC), Drug Problems (DRG)
- *Treatment Scales:* Aggression (AGG), Suicidal Ideation (SUI), Stress (STR), Nonsupport (NON), Treatment Rejection (RXR)
- *Interpersonal Scales:* Dominance (DOM), Warmth (WRM)

The clinical scales, which resemble many of the MMPI clinical scales, can be subdivided into three broad categories of disorders: (a) neurotic spectrum scales (SOM, ANX, ARD, DEP), (b) psychotic spectrum scales (MAN, PAR, SCZ), and (c) behavior disorder scales (BOR, ANT, ALC, DRG). The treatment scales focus on issues important in treatment not necessarily apparent from the clinical scales. The interpersonal scales measure two critical bipolar dimensions in interpersonal relations: *domination versus submission* (DOM) and *friendliness versus hostility* (WRM). Information is also provided on the client's answers to 27 critical items, which were selected because of their potential seriousness and low endorsement rates.

Because of the heterogeneous nature of the clinical scales, nine have been divided into subscales. For example, the ANX scale includes Cognitive, Affective, and Physiological subscales, and the ARD scale includes Obsessive–Compulsive, Phobias, and Traumatic Stress subscales. The treatment scale for aggression has also been divided into three subscales: Aggressive Attitude, Verbal Aggression, and Physical Aggression.

The PAI has a fourth-grade reading level and requires about 50 minutes to complete. The item response format provides four alternatives: *false–not at all true, slightly true, mainly true,* or *very true.* All of the scales can be easily hand scored without the use of a template in 10 minutes or less. In contrast with the MMPI-2, none of the full scales contain overlapping items.

The PAI has been normed on a sample of 1,000 community-dwelling adults selected to match the characteristics of the U.S. population in terms of sex, race, and age. In addition to adult norms, comprehensive norms have also been established for college students and clinical populations.

The full scales exhibit adequate test–retest reliabilities over short time periods and relatively high internal consistency coefficients for samples of college students and community-dwelling adults. The PAI shows substantial convergent and discriminant validity based on its correlations with scales from other psychological measures.

The PAI is an appealing instrument because of its ease of scoring and interpretation. It has been carefully constructed and appears to be psychometrically sound. In a short period of time, it has become one of the most frequently used personality tests in practice and clinical training (Piotrowski, 2000).

The author of the PAI has also developed a brief, 22-item version of the PAI, the Personality Assessment Screener (PAS), that can be used as a screening device to distinguish between those clients free from psychopathology and those in need of follow-up evaluation with the full PAI (Morey, 1998). Burns (2001) described the PAS as "a well developed screening instrument based on an impressive parent scale" (p. 933).

Basic Personality Inventory (BPI)

The BPI is intended for use with both adolescents and adults in clinical and normal populations (D. N. Jackson, 1989). It consists of 240 true–false items scored on 11 clinical scales and 1 critical-item scale (20 items per scale). The categories for the clinical scales were derived from factor analysis of other personality inventories, including the MMPI. As a result, the clinical scales on the BPI have much in common with the clinical scales on the MMPI.

The 11 clinical scales assess neurotic tendencies (Hypochondriasis, Depression, Anxiety, Social Introversion, and Self-Depreciation), psychotic tendencies (Persecutory Ideas, Thinking Disorder), and antisocial tendencies (Denial, Interpersonal Problems, Alienation, and Impulse Expression). Items for each scale were selected to maximize item–scale correlations and minimize interscale correlations.

The BPI, which requires approximately 35 minutes to complete, can be hand scored in less than 10 minutes. The manual (D. N. Jackson, 1989) provides separate-sex norms for both adults and adolescents and reports respectable reliability and validity data. Validation procedures primarily involved correlating the scores on the BPI scales with clinical ratings and other measures of psychopathology.

In comparison with the MMPI-2, the BPI has been praised for its brevity, ease of administration and scoring, and "purity" (homogeneity) of its clinical scales (Urbina, 1995; Yelland, 1995); however, it lacks the diagnostic utility and extensive normative data of the MMPI-2, especially for ethnic populations.

SPECIFIC-PURPOSE MEASURES

A number of standardized inventories have been developed to assess mental health problems in specific areas of interest to counselors. These areas include emotional states such as depression, anxiety, and anger, as well as behavioral problems such as alcohol and other drug abuse, eating disorders, and attention deficit disorders. Measures of emotional states serve as "emotional vital signs" that can be used to assess the individual's psychological well-being in the same sense that physical vital signs such as heart rate and blood pressure are used to evaluate an individual's physical health (Spielberger, Reheiser, Owen, & Sydeman, 2004). Measures of specific behavioral or psychological disorders can be used to determine to what extent an individual may be suffering from a particular problem.

Most of the specific-purpose instruments (sometimes referred to as focus measures, rapid assessment instruments, or "narrow-band" scales) discussed in this section are relatively brief and easy to administer and score. For this reason, they can be readily readministered to monitor a client's progress in dealing with a specific issue.

Depression

One of the most common psychiatric disorders experienced by people in the United States is depression. In the National Comorbidity Survey Replication conducted by Kessler, Berglund, et al. (2005), the lifetime prevalence of major depressive disorder was estimated to be 17% in the general population. On the basis of the survey results, it was estimated that 7% of the population would meet the diagnostic criteria for major depressive disorder in any one year (Kessler, Chiu, et al., 2005).

A large number of self-rating scales have been devised to assess depression. Several of the most popular instruments of this sort are discussed below.

Beck Depression Inventory–II (BDI-II)
The BDI-II replaces the BDI, which was first published in 1961 (Beck, Steer, & Brown, 1996). The current version reflects *DSM-IV-TR* criteria for depression more closely than did earlier versions. The instructions have been changed to pertain to a 2-week period instead of a 1-week period, four items have been replaced with new items, and two items have been reworded. Item responses have been simplified so that the BDI-II can be used with clients as young as 13 years of age.

The BDI-II includes 21 items that describe symptoms of depression of an affective, cognitive, behavioral, or physiological nature (Beck, 1996). Each item uses a 4-point scale of severity ranging from 0 to 3. Clients mark the level of severity for each symptom that best describes how they have been feeling over "the past 2 weeks, including today."

Most clients complete the BDI-II within 5 to 10 minutes. Scoring, which involves tallying answers for 21 items, takes just a minute. For this reason, it can easily be administered, scored, and interpreted as part of a regularly scheduled counseling interview.

Scores on the BDI-II are internally consistent for college students and psychiatric outpatients but are subject to change over time (Beck et al., 1996). The BDI-II was designed to be highly sensitive to changes in mood over short time periods. If people experience significant changes in their lives or if they are responding positively to a counseling program, their BDI-II scores should reflect these events. Validity studies indicate that the BDI-II total score effectively differentiates between depressed and nondepressed individuals (Beck et al., 1996). Scores on the BDI-II correlate highly with clinical ratings of depression.

The BDI-II manual (Beck et al., 1996) recommends that scores be interpreted as follows:

0–13 = minimal depression
14–19 = mild depression
20–28 = moderate depression
29–63 = severe depression

The cutoff scores shown above should be looked on as general guidelines. The counselor will need to obtain more information to judge the severity of a client's depression. The duration of the symptoms and the possible cause of the symptoms (e.g., loss of a loved one) need to be considered. If the symptoms are of short duration (less than 2 weeks) or if they can be attributed to a grief reaction, they are less likely to indicate psychopathology.

As a general rule, if the score exceeds 28, especially for two administrations of the BDI-II separated by 2 weeks, the counselor should consider referring the client for psychiatric evaluation and possible medication. The item content of the BDI-II can be easily reviewed with clients to obtain more information about a symptom. It usually helps to ask clients which items they are most concerned about. Counselors should pay particular attention to symptoms of hopelessness (Item 2) and suicidal thinking (Item 9). The counselor should be sure to evaluate the risk of suicide for such clients.

BDI-II scores for young people often drop upon retesting, even without treatment. Depression for these individuals may be caused by situational factors, such as impending exams or relationship conflicts, which can change rather quickly. Such factors must be taken into account. For this reason, it is a good idea to readminister the BDI-II periodically during the course of counseling to help monitor changes that may occur. Information obtained from readministrations of the BDI-II can often be helpful in trying to decide if the client should be referred for additional assessment or treatment or if the client has made sufficient progress so that regular sessions are no longer needed.

In summary, the BDI-II can be looked upon as the "test of choice" for initially identifying individuals who may be experiencing depression (Stehouwer & Stehouwer, 2005). Additional assessment, especially a clinical interview, must be undertaken to ascertain a diagnosis of depression.

Children's Depression Inventory (CDI)

The CDI is a self-report measure of depression for children and adolescents ages 8 to 17 years (Kovacs, 1992). This instrument, which is a downward extension of the BDI, consists of 27 self-report items written at a third-grade reading level. For each item, the child or adolescent chooses the one statement from among three listed that most closely describes his or her thoughts, feelings, or behaviors for the past 2 weeks. The CDI yields a total score together with scores on five factors: Negative Mood, Interpersonal Problems, Ineffectiveness, Anhedonia (inability to find enjoyment in any activities), and Negative Self-Esteem. The manual (Kovacs, 1992) provides separate-sex norms for children (ages 7 through 12) and adolescents (ages 13 through 17). Kovacs has also created a 10-item version of the CDI for group administration when time is limited. Parent (CDI-P) and teacher (CDI-T) versions have also been developed, each with two scales—Emotional Problems and Functional Problems (Kovacs, 2003).

The CDI is one of the most thoroughly researched of all instruments designed to measure depression in children. Although it was developed primarily for research purposes, it has been used increasingly for clinical purposes because of the lack of effective instruments in the field. Kovacs recommended that a T score of 65 be used to indicate possible depression in screening situations. If a client obtains a T score of 65 or greater on two administrations, he or she should then be evaluated by means of a diagnostic interview.

Although some studies support the validity of the CDI in differentiating between adolescent inpatients diagnosed with major depression and those diagnosed with other psychiatric disorders, studies reported in the manual indicate mixed results (Craighead, Curry, & Ilardi, 1995; Kovacs, 1992). At this point, the CDI can best be used as an adjunct to other diagnostic tools, including the clinical interview.

Geriatric Depression Scale (GDS)

The GDS is a short, self-administered inventory that effectively differentiates between depressed and nondepressed older clients (Yesavage et al., 1983). It consists of 30 yes–no items that focus on affective and cognitive symptoms of depression. Items that assess somatic symptoms have been largely excluded because these items do not detect depression as well in older people as they do in younger populations. Holroyd and Clayton (2000) concluded that the GDS is "the best validated instrument" (p. 6) for measuring depression in geriatric clients who are not cognitively impaired.

Hamilton Depression Inventory (HDI)

The HDI is a paper-and-pencil version of the Hamilton Depression Rating Scale, a well-established measure of depression for adults based on a clinical interview (W. M. Reynolds & Kobak, 1995). In contrast to the BDI-II, the HDI measures the frequency as well as the intensity of symptoms. Some of its 23 questions contain subquestions so that a total of 38 items are included. In addition to the total score, the HDI also provides a relatively pure measure of melancholia (HDI-Mel Scale), that is, endogenous (originating within the organism) depression, which can be helpful in identifying individuals who may benefit from antidepressant medications (Kobak & Reynolds, 2004). Scores on the HDI have proved to be highly effective in differentiating individuals diagnosed with clinical depression from nondepressed individuals.

Anxiety and Fear

More than one fourth of the population in the United States can be expected to experience an anxiety disorder sometime during their lifetime (Kessler, Berglund, et al., 2005). Anxiety disorders, which tend to be chronic, include social phobias, panic disorder, agoraphobia, simple phobia, generalized anxiety disorder, and related ailments. Approximately 18% of the population is likely to have experienced an anxiety disorder during any given year (Kessler, Chiu, et al., 2005).

Popular measures of the symptoms of anxiety and fear are discussed below. *Anxiety* can be defined as "a pervasive feeling of dread, apprehension, and impending disaster" (Goldenson, 1984, p. 53). The cause of the anxiety is usually unknown or unclear. In contrast, *fear* is an intense emotional response to a known danger, such as snakes or crowded places.

State–Trait Anxiety Inventory (STAI)

The STAI, the most popular and well researched of all anxiety measures, was first published by Charles Spielberger and his associates in 1970; the current version (Form Y) was published in 1983 (Spielberger, Gorsuch, Lushene, Vagg, & Jacobs, 1983). The STAI consists of two scales: a State–Anxiety scale (S-Anxiety) that measures transitory anxiety and a Trait–Anxiety scale (T-Anxiety) that measures persistent anxiety. Both scales contain 20 items marked on a 4-point scale.

Instructions for the S-Anxiety scale ask clients to indicate how they feel "at this moment"; they indicate to what degree (*not at all, somewhat, moderately so,* or *very much so*) they may be experiencing different feelings, such as tension or calmness. Instructions for the T-Anxiety scale ask clients to rate how they "generally feel"; they indicate how often (*almost never, sometimes, often,* or *almost always*) they experience different feelings, such as restlessness or self-satisfaction. Responses to the S-Anxiety scale show the intensity of an individual's anxious response at the time of measurement; responses to the T-Anxiety scale show the frequency of such responses.

The STAI is untimed but can usually be completed within 10 minutes. The instrument can be easily hand scored; however, the scorer must take into account that approximately one half of the items measure the absence of anxiety, whereas the other half measure the presence of anxiety. For those items that measure the absence of anxiety, the scoring must be reversed.

Reliability studies indicate that scores on the S-Anxiety scale are internally consistent but can change substantially over time depending on the individual's circumstances. For example, scores on this scale can be expected to rise markedly when a person is confronted with a threatening situation, such as an exam or surgery. Individuals who score high on the S-Anxiety scale are usually experiencing a number of symptoms associated with activation of the autonomic nervous system, such as rapid heart rate, perspiration, shortness of breath, shakiness, and hot or cold flashes.

Scores on the T-Anxiety scale are both internally consistent and relatively stable over time for most populations. Individuals who score high on the T-Anxiety scale will usually show a larger increase in their S-Anxiety scores in a threatening circumstance, especially in situations that involve social evaluations, than will individuals who score low on this scale. In addition to measuring anxiety proneness, the T-Anxiety scale also taps other psychological problems, especially depression (Bieling, Antony, & Swinson, 1998).

A children's version of the STAI, The State–Trait Anxiety Inventory for Children (STAIC), has also been established for counselor use. The STAIC provides extensive norms for fourth, fifth, and sixth graders. Because the reading level for the STAIC is relatively high, the STAIC should be used only with elementary school students who possess above-average reading ability. Research indicates that the STAIC effectively differentiates between children with and without an anxiety disorder (Seligman, Ollendick, Langley, & Baldacci, 2004).

Beck Anxiety Inventory (BAI)

The BAI was designed to measure symptoms of anxiety that are relatively independent of depression (Beck & Steer, 1993). The BAI parallels the BDI-II in its manner of construction and interpretation. Similar to the BDI-II, the BAI contains 21 items, each of which is answered on a 4-point scale. Each item measures a separate symptom of anxiety. Raw scores on the BAI are interpreted in terms of four categories (minimal, mild, moderate, or severe anxiety). As with the BDI-II, the BAI can easily be administered as part of the counseling interview to monitor a client's progress over time. The BAI results can be analyzed in terms of four clusters of scores—neurophysiological, subjective, panic, and autonomic—that can be helpful in differentiating among different types of anxiety disorders.

Other Measures of Anxiety or Fear

Other standardized inventories of anxiety or fear that are of interest to counselors include the Test Anxiety Scale (Sarason, 1980), Mathematics Anxiety Rating Scale–Revised (Plake & Parker, 1982), Maudsley Obsessional–Compulsive Inventory (Hodgson & Rachman, 1977), Posttraumatic Stress Disorder Symptom Scale (Foa, Riggs, Dancu, & Rothbaum, 1993), and Fear Questionnaire (Marks & Mathews, 1978). These instruments assess specific types of anxieties or fears often encountered by clients.

The Multidimensional Anxiety Questionnaire (MAQ) provides scores for overall anxiety plus different types of anxiety or fears (physiological-panic, social phobia, worry-fears, and negative affectivity; W. M. Reynolds, 1999). According to Stein (2003), the MAQ is "an excellent choice of a current anxiety assessment tool for clinicians" (p. 601).

Several anxiety scales have been developed for special populations (C. R. Reynolds, Richmond, & Lowe, 2003). These include the Adult Manifest Anxiety Scale for College Students and the Adult Manifest Anxiety Scale for the Elderly, which have been described as "especially welcome instruments" (Kagee, 2005, p. 31) that counselors may find useful in their work with younger and older populations.

Anger

Anger is a universal emotion that underlies hostile attitudes and aggressive behaviors. Assessment of anger can aid in crisis intervention and increase understanding of factors related to an individual's anger.

An individual's anger can be assessed by means of the State–Trait Anger Expression Inventory–2 (STAXI-2; Spielberger, 1999). This instrument is designed to measure the experience, expression, and control of anger in individuals who are 16 years of age or older. It consists of 57 items that can be completed in 10 to 15 minutes and scored in about 5 minutes. Norms are available for both adolescents and adults.

The STAXI-2 is analogous to the STAI in that it provides measures of anger both as a state (actual anger at any point in time) and as a trait (potential anger). The Trait–Anger (T-Anger) scale consists of two subscales: Angry Temperament and Angry Reaction. The State–Anger (S-Anger) scale has been subdivided into three subscales: Feeling Angry, Feel Like Expressing Anger Verbally, and Feel Like Expressing Anger Physically. In addition to the T- and S-Anger scales, the STAXI-2 contains several measures of anger expression and anger control. An Anger Expression Index provides an overall measure of total anger expression. Factor-analytic research supports the creation of the separate scales (Forgays, Forgays, & Spielberger, 1997).

Although initially developed for research purposes, the STAXI-2 can also be helpful in counseling situations by providing a format for considering the different dimensions of anger. The STAXI-2 provides a broad assessment of an individual's anger that can be useful in counseling clients with issues related to anger, hostility, and aggression. It provides an "excellent conceptual foundation" (Freeman, 2003, p. 876) for understanding and assessing anger; however, its scores may be somewhat difficult to interpret because of the unknown composition of the normative sample.

Alcohol or Other Drug Problems

As indicated in chapter 14, alcohol or other drug problems are relatively common in the United States. A number of instruments have been designed to identify and evaluate individuals with alcohol or other problems. Two screening inventories (Michigan Alcoholism Screening Test and Substance Abuse Subtle Screening Inventory) and a comprehensive assessment instrument (Alcohol Use Inventory) are described below.

Michigan Alcoholism Screening Test (MAST)

The MAST, which has received wide usage over the years, is a brief instrument that can be answered by the client in less than 15 minutes (Evans, 1998; Selzer, 1971). The items describe (a) symptoms of excessive drinking, (b) various problems (e.g., social, family, work, legal, and health) that an individual may have encountered as a result of drinking, (c) concerns expressed by others about an individual's drinking, and (d) efforts that an individual may have made to control drinking or to obtain treatment for excessive drinking. The instrument and the scoring weights for each item are shown in Figure 15-2. Scores of 5 or more indicate alcoholism, scores of 4 suggest the possibility of alcoholism, and scores of 3 or less indicate the absence of alcoholism. Some authorities have suggested using a higher cutoff score (as high as 13) to reduce the number of false positives (Ross, Gavin, & Skinner, 1990).

Research indicates that the MAST can effectively identify individuals with alcohol-related diagnoses (Teitelbaum & Mullen, 2000). MAST results should be confirmed by means of other assessment procedures. The MAST is limited in that its entire item content is obvious and it does not address substance abuse problems other than alcohol. For clients who may be defensive or who may have problems with drugs other than alcohol, other measures should be considered such as the Substance Abuse Subtle Screening Inventory (see below).

The MAST, or abbreviated versions of it (Evans, 1998), can be used routinely with all clients in a counseling service to detect possible alcohol problems that otherwise might be missed. It has been adapted for use with both younger and older people (Luttrell et al., 1997; Snow, Thurber, & Hodgson, 2002).

A case example showing the use of the MAST in counseling is presented below.

Case Example

Sally, a client at a community counseling service, received a score of 16 on the MAST. She answered Items 1, 2, 5, 6, 8, 10, 11, 12, and 23 in the scored direction. Friends had brought Sally to the counseling agency because of problems related to her drinking. Her score of 16 far surpassed the cutoff score of 5 used on the MAST to signal alcoholism.

The MAST contributed to counseling by emphasizing the importance of Sally's drinking problem. Information obtained from the MAST was confirmed by other information related to Sally's drinking habits. Her weekly consumption of alcohol (13 drinks) exceeded that of 97% of American women (W. R. Miller & Muñoz, 2005, p. 32). Counseling with Sally revealed that she came from a troubled family and she frequently fought with her mother while she lived at home. Sally suffered from low self-esteem and a perfectionistic nature. She was demanding and dependent in her relationships. Testing with the California Psychological Inventory revealed that she was highly critical of herself (low Good Impression score; $T = 34$), undercontrolled (low Self-Control score; $T = 39$), and lacking confidence (low Capacity for Status score; $T = 39$). Her personality type was Gamma (externally oriented and norm-questioning) at the midpoint (Level 4 of seven levels) of self-realization.

The counselor worked with her on family issues and relationship matters. Sally became more self-sufficient during the course of counseling and more confident in her relationships with others. She began to deal with some of the personal issues represented by her drinking problem. By addressing unresolved problems and by the use of self-monitoring techniques, Sally was able to reduce the amount of her drinking during the course of counseling.

MICHIGAN ALCOHOLISM SCREENING TEST (MAST)

Instructions: Please answer each question "Yes" or "No" as it pertains to you.

(2) *1. Do you feel you are a normal drinker?

(2) 2. Have you ever awakened the morning after some drinking the night before and found that you could not remember a part of the evening before?

(1) 3. Does your spouse (or do your parents) ever worry or complain about your drinking?

(2) *4. Can you stop drinking without a struggle after one or two drinks?

(1) 5. Do you ever feel bad about your drinking?

(2) *6. Do friends or relatives think you are a normal drinker?

(0) 7. Do you ever try to limit your drinking to certain times of the day or to certain places?

(2) *8. Are you always able to stop drinking when you want to?

(5) 9. Have you ever attended a meeting of Alcoholics Anonymous (AA)?

(1) 10. Have you gotten into fights when drinking?

(2) 11. Has drinking ever created problems with you and your spouse?

(2) 12. Has your spouse (or other family member) ever gone to anyone for help about your drinking?

(2) 13. Have you ever lost friends or girlfriends/boyfriends because of drinking?

(2) 14. Have you ever gotten into trouble at work because of drinking?

(2) 15. Have you ever lost a job because of drinking?

(2) 16. Have you ever neglected your obligations, your family, or your work for two or more days in a row because you were drinking?

(1) 17. Do you ever drink before noon?

(2) 18. Have you ever been told you have liver trouble? Cirrhosis?

(5) 19. Have you ever had delirium tremens (DTs), severe shaking, heard voices, or seen things that weren't there after heavy drinking?

(5) 20. Have you ever gone to anyone for help about your drinking?

(5) 21. Have you ever been in a hospital because of drinking?

(2) 22. Have you ever been a patient in a psychiatric hospital or on a psychiatric ward of a general hospital where drinking was part of the problem?

(2) 23. Have you ever been seen at a psychiatric or mental health clinic, or gone to a doctor, social worker, or clergyperson for help with an emotional problem in which drinking had played a part?

(2) 24. Have you ever been arrested, even for a few hours, because of drunk behavior?

(2) 25. Have you ever been arrested for drunk driving after drinking?

*Negative responses to these items indicate alcoholism; for all other items, positive responses indicate alcoholism.

FIGURE 15-2

Items and Scoring Weights (Shown in Parentheses) for the Michigan Alcoholism Screening Test

---

Note. Adapted from "The Michigan Alcoholism Screening Test: The Quest for a New Diagnostic Instrument" by M. L. Selzer, 1971, *American Journal of Psychiatry, 127*, p. 1655. This instrument is in the public domain.

Substance Abuse Subtle Screening Inventory–3rd Edition (SASSI-3)

The SASSI-3 has been designed as a screening instrument for detecting adults who may be suffering from substance abuse, especially those who may be defensive or who may deny problems (G. A. Miller, 1999). It is a brief paper-and-pencil instrument that can be completed in 15 minutes and hand scored within a few minutes. It can also be administered by computer or audiotape. According to a survey of 350 addiction counselors, the SASSI is used more often and considered to be more important than any other substance abuse screening instrument (Juhnke, Vacc, & Curtis, 2003).

The SASSI-3 provides scores on 10 scales including face valid and subtle scales. The face valid scales ask about the frequency of alcohol and other drug usage and problems. The subtle scales contain a number of true–false items about matters that may be indirectly associated with substance abuse. Research studies indicate that this instrument effectively identifies individuals with substance abuse problems (Lazowski, Miller, Boye, & Miller, 1998). One validation study concluded that "the SASSI-3 appears to the strongest screening instrument of its kind" (Emanuelson, Perosa, & Perosa, 2005, p. 2). Additional research is needed to verify these findings (Fernandez, 2003; Pittenger, 2003).

Another form of this instrument, known as the SASSI-A2 (Adolescent version, 2nd edition), can be used with young people (ages 12–18; F. G. Miller & Lazowski, 2001). The SASSI instruments can serve as "quick and ready triage" (Pittenger, 2003, p. 918) tools for assessing substance abuse; however, their findings need to be supplemented with additional, more in-depth evaluations (Bauman, 2002).

In addition to the MAST and SASSI-3, the following measures of alcohol or other drug problems may be used for screening purposes: the Personal Experience Screening Questionnaire (Winters, 1991), Alcohol Use Disorders Identification Test (Saunders, Aasland, Amundsen, & Grant, 1993), Health Screening Survey–Revised (M. F. Fleming & Barry, 1991), and Adolescent Drinking Index (Harrell & Wirtz, 1989).

Alcohol Use Inventory (AUI)

The AUI is a comprehensive self-report inventory that assesses patterns of behavior, attitudes, and symptoms pertaining to the use of alcohol for individuals 16 years and older (Horn, Wanberg, & Foster, 1986). Most people complete the AUI, which requires a sixth-grade reading level, within 35 to 60 minutes. It contains 24 scales based on 228 items organized at three levels: 17 primary scales, 6 second-order scales, and 1 general alcohol use scale. The scales evaluate alcohol usage in terms of benefits, styles, consequences, and concerns. It is most appropriate for individuals who enter a treatment program as a result of alcohol dependence or abuse. It can be used to establish a treatment plan for a person with alcohol-related issues.

Other comprehensive measures of substance abuse include the Personal Experience Inventory for adolescents ages 12 to 18 years (Winters & Henley, 1989) and the Personal Experience Inventory for Adults (Winters, 1996). Both inventories include a problem severity section and a psychosocial section. The Inventory of Drinking Situations can be used to identify personal or social situations in which a person may drink excessively based on that person's previous experiences in those situations (Annis, Graham, & Davis, 1987). These situations can be summarized as (a) negative situations (e.g., "feeling fed up with life"), (b) social situations (e.g., "wanting to celebrate"), and (c) temptation situations (e.g., "passing a bar"; Parra, Martin, & Clark, 2005).

Eating Disorders

The major eating disorders include anorexia nervosa (restricting type), anorexia nervosa (binge-eating/purging type), bulimia nervosa, and eating disorders not otherwise specified (American Psychiatric Association, 2000a). The *DSM-IV-TR* does not list obesity as an eating disorder because it is not usually associated with a specific psychological or behavioral syndrome.

Women are 6 to 10 times as likely as men to experience an eating disorder. The lifetime prevalence of anorexia nervosa among women ranges from 0.5% to 3.7%, depending on the breadth of the definition. The lifetime prevalence of bulimia nervosa among women ranges from 1.1% to 4.2% (American Psychiatric Association, 2000b). A number of women also have eating disorders not otherwise specified. In addition, studies indicate that many women express some of the symptoms of eating disorders, such as binge eating and purging, without meeting the diagnostic criteria for an eating disorder (Mulholland & Mintz, 2001).

According to the *DSM-IV-TR,* the essential features of anorexia nervosa include refusal to maintain normal body weight (e.g., the person weighs less than 85% of expected body weight), intense fear of gaining weight, a disturbed body image, and loss of menstrual cycle for females. Anorexia nervosa, which means nervous loss of appetite, is a misnomer; the person resists eating, but actual loss of appetite is rare. Bulimia nervosa, in contrast, is characterized by binge eating (rapid consumption of food in a short period of time), a feeling of lack of control of one's eating behavior while binge eating, drastic attempts to prevent weight gain (e.g., self-induced vomiting, use of laxatives or diuretics, strict dieting or fasting, or vigorous exercise), and persistent overconcern with body shape and weight (American Psychiatric Association, 2000a). Some individuals share the symptoms of both disorders and may be diagnosed as having anorexia nervosa, binge-eating/purging type.

Individuals suspected of meeting the *DSM-IV-TR* criteria for an eating disorder should be referred to an eating disorders clinic or health service with a multidisciplinary team that includes a physician, nurse, dietitian, and mental health professional. The person may require a complete medical examination, nutritional assessment, and psychological assessment. Treatment also entails cooperation among the different disciplines to help clients address medical complications, alter eating habits, and alleviate psychological problems by such means as improving social skills and self-image.

Individuals with eating disorders typically wait several years from the onset of the disorder before entering treatment. Early assessment of a person's eating problems can reduce the length of this time period. Counselors can use standardized tests to assess the severity of an individual's eating problems and to help structure a discussion on this topic in counseling. To ensure full and honest reporting, the counselor must establish a trusting relationship with the client before undertaking the assessment.

The Eating Attitudes Test and the Eating Disorders Inventory–3, both discussed below, are two widely used standardized measures available for evaluating eating problems. A third instrument, the Eating Disorder Diagnostic Scale (EDDS) is a relatively new, 22-item inventory that has proved to be effective in diagnosing anorexia nervosa, bulimia nervosa, and binge eating disorder in adolescent girls and young women (Stice, Fisher, & Martinez, 2004). In addition to these measures, the Questionnaire for Eating Disorder Diagnoses, which is based on *DSM-IV-TR* criteria, shows promise for use in counseling (Mintz, O'Halloran, Mulholland, & Schneider, 1997).

Eating Attitudes Test (EAT)

The EAT is a 40-item screening inventory that measures the symptoms and behaviors associated with anorexia nervosa and other eating problems (Garner & Garfinkel, 1979). Total scores on the EAT have clearly differentiated between individuals with and without eating disorders in research investigations (Mintz & O'Halloran, 2000). The scores are sensitive to treatment so that recovered anorectics obtain scores similar to individuals without eating disorders.

The EAT can be scored in terms of three subscales—Dieting, Bulimia, and Oral Control—to help determine the nature of the eating problems. The EAT and EAT-26 (an abbreviated version of the EAT) have been used effectively in a number of different cultural settings (Alvarez-Rayón et al., 2004; Canals, Carbajo, & Fernández-Ballart, 2002). The following case illustrates the use of the EAT with a client in an intake interview.

Case Example

Jodie's intake counselor asked her to take the EAT as a means of reviewing her eating habits and assessing the need for a referral to an eating disorders clinic. Jodie had come to the community mental health service for assistance with relationship issues, family conflicts, and eating problems. She ate large quantities of bakery goods and sweets about once a week and then used laxatives to purge the extra food.

Jodie obtained a score of 36 on the EAT, which placed her almost 2 standard deviations above the mean (98th percentile) of adult women. Scores above 30 suggest serious eating concerns. She marked *always* or *very often* to items such as "am terrified about being overweight," "am preoccupied with a desire to be thinner," and "feel that food controls my life." Her EAT score and other intake data indicated that she could probably benefit from a referral to an eating disorders clinic with a multidisciplinary staff for a more thorough assessment of her eating and nutritional habits as well as her physiological and psychological well-being. After discussing the matter with her, the counselor made arrangements for such a referral.

Eating Disorders Inventory–3 (EDI-3)

The EDI-3 consists of 91 items that assess the psychological and behavioral characteristics that underlie eating disorders (Garner, 2005). It differs from the EAT by the inclusion of personality items as well as behavioral and symptomatic items. The EDI-3 provides scores on 12 scales—3 that measure attitudes and behaviors specific to eating disorders and 9 that measure personality characteristics related to eating disorders. In addition, it yields scores on six composite scales: Eating Disorder Risk, Ineffectiveness, Interpersonal Problems, Affective Problems, Overcontrol, and General Psychological Adjustment.

In addition to the EDI-3 itself, the total EDI-3 assessment package includes two auxiliary forms: the EDI-3 Symptom Checklist and the EDI-3 Referral Form. The EDI-3 Symptom Checklist is used by clients to report frequency of symptoms related to eating disorders (e.g., dieting; exercising; binge eating; purging; use of laxatives, diet pills, and diuretics; menstrual history). This information is useful in forming a *DSM-IV-TR* diagnosis. The EDI-3 Referral Form is based on a short form of the EDI-3, and is used for screening and referral purposes in nonclinical settings, such as high schools, colleges, and athletic programs..

The EDI-3 manual provides normative tables for patients with (a) anorexia nervosa (restricting type), (b) anorexia nervosa (binge-eating/purging type), (c) bulimia nervosa, and (d) eating disorders not otherwise specified (Garner, 2005). Both adolescent and adult clinical norms are provided.

The EDI-3 scales produce reliable (internally consistent) results for people with eating disorders. The results are somewhat less reliable for nonpatient samples, presumably because of the restricted range of scores for these samples. Validity studies with earlier forms of the EDI show that it differentiates patients with eating disorders from various control groups (general psychiatric patients, recovered patients, and nonpatients) in a variety of settings (Niv, Kaplan, Mitrani, & Shiang, 1998; Podar, Hannus, & Allik, 1999; Schoemaker, Verbraak, Breteler, & vanderStaak, 1997).

Attention-Deficit/Hyperactivity Disorder (ADHD)

In recent years, ADHD has become a popular, but somewhat controversial, diagnosis for children and adolescents with behavioral problems (Panksepp, 1998; Zwi, Ramchandani, & Joughin, 2000). Professionals have been accused of both overdiagnosing and underdiagnosing ADHD in the populations they serve (Higgins, 1997). According to the Practice Guidelines of the American Academy of Pediatrics (2000), ADHD is the most common neurobehavioral disorder of childhood, with prevalence rates varying from 4% to 12% for school-age samples. Between 30% and 70% of children diagnosed with ADHD continue to meet the criteria for ADHD as adolescents and adults (Heiligenstein, Guenther, Levy, Savino, & Fulwiler, 1999; B. Jackson & Farrugia, 1997).

The *DSM-IV-TR* provides diagnostic criteria for three subtypes of ADHD: predominantly inattentive, predominantly hyperactive, and combined (American Psychiatric Association, 2000a). An individual must exhibit (a) six of nine symptoms for inattention (such as makes careless mistakes, easily distracted, disorganized, and forgetful) to meet the criteria for ADHD Predominantly Inattentive Type or (b) six of nine symptoms for hyperactivity–impulsivity (such as fidgets, runs about, talks excessively, and interrupts others) to satisfy the criteria for ADHD Predominantly Hyperactive Type. Individuals who exhibit six or more of the nine symptoms in both categories fulfill the criteria for ADHD Combined Type.

Symptoms must be pervasive, maladaptive, and inconsistent with normal developmental expectations. They must have occurred for at least 6 months, must occur in more than one setting (such as school and home), and must interfere with an individual's functioning. Some of the symptoms must have been present before age 7. Symptoms must not be attributable to some other disorder, such as a learning disability, anxiety, or depression.

Because of potential problems with misdiagnosis, a multimodal approach should be used in assessing a client for possible ADHD (M. B. Brown, 2000). Such an approach should include reports from parents and teachers (or other school professionals) as well as the client. Historical information and observational data may be obtained by interviews, questionnaires, and rating scales (see Barkley & Murphy, 2006). Evidence should be obtained regarding the core symptoms of ADHD, age of onset, duration of symptoms, extent of functional impairment, and associated conditions (American Academy of Pediatrics, 2000).

"Broadband" behavior rating scales, such as the Behavior Assessment System for Children–Second Edition (C. R. Reynolds & Kamphaus, 2005) and the Achenbach System of Empirically Based Assessment (Achenbach et al., 2003), can be used as screening devices to identify possible ADHD problems among a number of other behavioral problems. Broadband instruments can be helpful in identifying children in need of further evaluation; however, they should not be relied on as a basis for diagnosing ADHD (American Academy of Pediatrics, 2000).

"Narrowband" scales, such as the Conners' Rating Scales (Revised)–ADHD Index and *DSM-IV* Symptoms Scales (Conners, 1997), ADHD Rating Scale-IV (DuPaul, Power, Anastopoulos, & Reid, 1998), and Barkley Screening Checklist for ADHD (Barkley & Murphy, 2006), focus specifically on ADHD symptoms. These instruments are relatively short, able to discriminate between children with and without ADHD, and sensitive to treatment effects (M. B. Brown, 2000). Studies indicate that ADHD-specific checklists are much more accurate than broadband scales in distinguishing between children with and without ADHD (American Academy of Pediatrics, 2000). The Adult Attention Deficit Disorders Evaluation Scale (McCarney & Anderson, 1996), Conners' Adult ADHD Rating Scales (Conners, Erhardt, & Sparrow, 1998), and Brown Adult ADHD Rating Scales (T. E. Brown, 1996) are narrowband instruments that may be used to assess symptoms among adults.

SUMMARY

1. The MMPI-2 provides a more comprehensive assessment of a client's mental health than any other personality inventory. The MMPI-A provides comparable information for adolescents.
2. The MCMI-III represents a viable alternative to the MMPI-2 for assessment of client psychopathology. It is shorter and more closely related to theory and to the *DSM-IV-TR* categories than is the MMPI-2.
3. Two relatively new measures of psychopathology are the Personality Assessment Inventory and the Basic Personality Inventory. Both of these instruments can be self-scored, contain scales that are relatively easy to interpret, and circumvent some of the difficulties inherent in the MMPI-2.
4. The Beck Depression Inventory–II serves as a quick, yet reasonably thorough, measure of a client's state of depression. It is particularly helpful for monitoring changes in depression over time.
5. The State–Trait Anxiety Inventory yields valid and reliable scores for anxiety that can be distinguished as either transitory (state anxiety) or enduring (trait anxiety). In a similar fashion, the State–Trait Anger Expression Inventory–2 measures an individual's actual and potential anger and provides information on how anger is likely to be expressed.
6. Problems related to alcohol use can be detected by the Michigan Alcoholism Screening Test, Substance Abuse Subtle Screening Inventory–3, or comparable screening inventory. Individuals with problems can be further evaluated by means of the Alcohol Use Inventory and an assessment interview.
7. The Eating Attitudes Test can be used to screen clients for possible eating disorders. The Eating Disorders Inventory–3 provides information regarding the psychological traits and symptom clusters of clients with eating disorders.
8. A multimodal approach based on the use of interviews, questionnaires, and rating scales with clients, parents, and teachers should be used in the assessment of attention-deficit/ hyperactivity disorder.

SECTION

V

PROFESSIONAL PRACTICES
AND CONSIDERATIONS

16

Assessment of Minority and Special Populations

Controversy has surrounded psychological tests almost from their beginnings. The development of the Army Alpha for testing World War I recruits caused much debate (Haney, 1981), particularly when differences between socioeconomic and ethnic groups became known. Since then, controversy has continued, especially regarding the fairness of aptitude tests used for selection procedures for people of different ethnic or racial groups (Gross, 1962; Neisser et al., 1996; Sandoval, 1998). Assessment of individuals with disabilities is a complex problem often requiring modifications of standardized instruments and caution in interpreting the results. This chapter examines the issues of psychological and aptitude assessments for different racial/ethnic groups, people with mental and physical disabilities, and older populations.

CULTURAL BIAS IN TESTING

There are three commonly considered ways in which tests may be biased against a person or group of persons. First, they may contain items that favor one group over another (lack of content equivalence). For example, an item on a verbal analogies test that includes the word *toboggan* might tend to favor people from northern states over those from southern states. Similarly, a test may be biased because it includes language or values that are typical to White middle-class people but not to Blacks, Latinos/Latinas, or other distinct racial/cultural groups (Lonner & Sundberg, 1987). Many sociocultural factors—ethnicity, socioeconomic class, region, and situation—contribute to mismatches between the language of test takers and that of test makers (lack of conceptual equivalence). Most test authors now include carefully chosen normative samples to include members of diverse groups. Counselors should consult the test manuals for specific information about translations and different gender and minority norm groups (Association for Assessment in Counseling and Education, 2003b; Fouad & Chan, 1999).

The second source of bias comes from test-related factors such as the motivation, anxiety, or test sophistication of those taking the test—sources of bias that are external to the test itself. Extreme forms of test anxiety, self-esteem, and achievement motivation have been found to be related to test performance, but there has been little evidence that there are substantial differences in these areas among races, sexes, or social classes. However, clients from minority groups who are not motivated to perform well on a test or who are not sophisticated in regard to the nature of the test items cannot be expected to perform as well on tests as those from the dominant culture, in which these factors have been emphasized.

A third possible source of bias comes from the use of test results in selection for employment or college admissions—if the model used for selection and prediction produces results that vary greatly among different groups. When the use of a test or other selection procedure results in a substantially higher rejection rate for minority candidates than for nonminority candidates, the use of the test must be justified by proving it is valid for the job in question (Anastasi, 1988). In general, a test used in selection can be defined as fair if it does not lead to differential prediction for any minority group (Geisinger, 1998).

In discussing the problem of test bias or group differences, one must distinguish between test results and innate aptitude. The statement that men as a group achieve higher levels of competence in mathematics than women do is a statement regarding past achievement on a given test. This does not imply that men possess a greater aptitude for mathematics than women—a statement that suggests innateness or biological or genetic determinism. Almost no one these days believes that intellectual functioning, no matter how it is measured, by tests or academic achievement, is exclusively a function of either an individual's heredity or his or her environment; it is a complex function of both.

Recognizing that increasing diversity in clients' backgrounds presents special challenges in testing, committees of the Association for Assessment in Counseling established a set of multicultural counseling standards first in 1993 (Prediger, 1994a) and revised in 2003 (Association for Assessment in Counseling, 2003). These standards have particularly addressed the selection of assessment instruments appropriate to multicultural populations and the validity of the resulting interpretations. Both the American Psychological Association (2002) and the American Counseling Association (2005) have stated in their ethical codes that professionals should consider socioeconomic, ethnic, and cultural backgrounds; beliefs; and values when administering and interpreting psychological tests. The American Psychological Association (2005b) has established further specific guidelines on this topic. School counselors, who often coordinate school testing and assessment activities, should be aware of the cultural appropriateness of their tests and of the options for students whose first language is not English (Holcomb-McCoy, 2003). They must also be careful to follow the testing procedures of the Individuals With Disabilities Act (IDEA) that provides safeguards and guidelines to protect the rights of linguistically and culturally diverse students (Gopaul & Armour-Thomas, 2002).

It is important in the assessment and treatment of multicultural clients for the counselor to display both the sensitivity to be aware of the cultural variables that affect assessment and the competence to translate this awareness into effective assessment (Arbona, 1998). An understanding of the client's worldview is important, because the initial step in the counseling process is to understand the client and his or her issues and problems. Worldview includes the individual's perceptions of human nature (good or evil) and the individual's focus on the past, present, or future; it also includes the emphasis given to individual or group goals and locus of responsibility (internal or external), including causes of behavior. On the basis of knowledge of the client's worldview and the client's cultural group, counselors are better able to determine the approaches, techniques, and goals needed for a specific client (Lonner & Ibrahim, 1996; Sue, 1978). If the counselor's and client's worldviews clash, the client may find the services not understandable or unacceptable (Dana, 1998). Counselors, regardless of their ethnic or racial backgrounds, should become aware of how their own cultural background, experiences, attitudes, and values can influence the assessment process (American Psychological Association, 2005b). Vernon and Clemente (2005) have developed a 16-item questionnaire, the Counselor's Self-Assessment of Cultural Awareness Scale, that can be used for this purpose.

Acculturation is defined as the degree of integration of new cultural patterns into a person's original cultural patterns. To competently assess and counsel members of multicultural groups, counselors must consider the level of the client's acculturation and determine the potential impact of this variable (Dana, 1993). In assessing the level of a client's acculturation, the counselor should take into account the age of the client, the number of generations in the new culture (e.g., first, second, third), the language generally preferred, and the extent of activities and relationships within and beyond the client's own cultural group (Paniagua, 2005). Additional factors to be attended to include clients' racial or ethnic identity and their dominant language. Even though multicultural competence has become a significant force in the counseling field, with numerous research studies and position papers, there is still little consensus as to what actually constitutes multicultural competence (A. L. Reynolds & Pope, 2003).

In using standardized tests in counseling with a person from another culture, a general rule is that the less the counselor knows of the client's culture, the more errors the counselor is likely to make. It is important for the counselor to be knowledgeable about the culture of the person being assessed and to develop skills for dealing with culture-related behavior patterns. Conversely, it is important not to "overculturalize." Culture is important in understanding an individual, but it is not the only variable influencing human behavior. Attempting to remove all cultural differences from a test is likely to compromise its validity as a measure of the behavior it was designed to assess. There are many factors that all people experience that lead them to seek counseling, and these are all important in assessing a person (Lonner & Sundberg, 1987).

Culture has an influence on psychopathological expression, and differences on personality tests across cultures should be taken into account. Psychological tests are measures of behavior, and to the extent that culture affects behavior, its influence is going to be detected by tests. Resulting psychological and educational diagnoses made as a result of such testing data should be made with caution (Sue, 1990).

APTITUDE AND COGNITIVE ASSESSMENT

A basic assumption of standardized testing is that it is perfectly appropriate for the test taker to be willing to provide obvious information and to give a performance for a total stranger—the examiner. These basic social assumptions may be in conflict with the interactional rules for individuals in some cultures. For example, it might be hypothesized that Black working-class children or American Indian working-class children are less oriented to public performance for unfamiliar adults than are White middle-class children. It might even be argued that child-rearing practices of many White middle-class parents, which encourage public verbal performance for strangers, program their children for eventual success on standardized tests.

The combination of constriction imposed in most American schools and the competition encouraged there can conflict directly with aspects of African American and Native American cultures. Such conflict may lead to alienation of these students from both the experiences and products of education, of which assessment instruments are a part (Neisser et al., 1996).

African Americans

Counselors must remember that there are large within-group differences among the millions of African Americans in regard to social class, rural/urban, and racial/bicultural identities. For example, the middle-class African Americans who make up 25% of their minority group tend to be similar to their Anglo American middle-class counterparts in regard to personal resources and expectations (Dana, 1998).

Although tests could be biased against any minority group, the most serious controversy exists over the fact that, as a group, African Americans score approximately 1 standard deviation below White Americans on most standardized tests of cognitive ability (Hacker, 1992; Lichtenberger & Kaufman, 1998). Even more aggravating is the fact that the magnitude of this difference persists from preschool children through college applicants (ACT, Inc., 2004). There is, however, some evidence that this differential is decreasing among children and adolescents (Neisser et al., 1996). Of course, there is a great deal of overlap between the two distributions, with almost 20% of Blacks scoring above the mean for Whites and 20% of Whites scoring below the mean for Blacks. Because counselors usually deal with individuals rather than total populations, group differences are of less importance. The counselor is concerned only with the particular ability of a particular individual, whether Black or White. The counselor is not concerned with overall mean differences among populations but with the question of whether a particular aptitude test score has equal validity, that is, whether it predicts equally well for Black as for White Americans.

Because African Americans as a group have experienced great racial discrimination in the past and this discrimination has had an impact on their socioeconomic status, their opportunities, and their home environments, it is not surprising that this would have an effect on test results. Much of the controversy centers on the cause of the differences. Some attribute the differences to the disadvantages that African Americans experience in their economic status and their educational and occupational opportunities. Others attribute much of the difference to genetic factors. Neisser and his American Psychological Association Task Force on Intelligence (Neisser et al., 1996), however, summarized this issue as follows:

The differential between the mean intelligence scores of Blacks and Whites . . . does not result from any biases in test construction and administration, nor does it simply reflect differences in socioeconomic status. There is certainly no . . . support for a genetic interpretation. At present no one knows what causes this differential. (p. 94)

A frequently offered argument is that intelligence tests and other measures of cognitive aptitude are constructed by and for White middle-class individuals and therefore are biased against lower socioeconomic individuals and others who are not members of the majority culture. Some of this cultural bias could be found in the items on which suburban children might have more familiarity than inner-city or rural children. Children brought up using a Black dialect or nonstandard American English might be less able to comprehend the language used on such instruments. Test developers have now become extremely sensitive to this issue and have established panels of experts that include representatives from many cultural groups. Most of this content bias has therefore been eliminated from many of the current forms of these tests, although such changes have been shown to have little if any effect on the scores obtained by minority individuals (Friedenberg, 1995; Walsh & Betz, 2001).

If the validity of cognitive aptitude test results is different for majority and minority groups and if counselors encourage or discourage clients about pursuing different levels of education or types of jobs on the basis of these test results, then this type of bias could affect counseling outcomes. Numerous studies have been conducted predicting various criteria for both education and job performance for Black and White groups. In general, results have shown that ability tests are equally valid for both minority and majority groups. These studies have used IQ tests to predict school achievement, scholastic aptitude tests to predict college grades, and job-related aptitude tests to predict job success. Both correlations and regression lines tend to be similar for both groups, and in the cases in which minor differences have occurred, there has been a tendency for the test to slightly overpredict the achievement of Black students (G. L. Cohen & Sherman, 2005; Messick, 1980). As J. Fleming (2002) has stated, "Indeed, contrary to popular opinion, over-prediction (performing worse) is the most consistent occurrence in Black predictive validity studies, and few cogent explanations have been offered" (p. 283).

Latinos/Latinas

There are more than 35 million Hispanic Americans, and this number is expected to grow to 47 million (16% of the U.S. population) by the year 2020 (U.S. Census Bureau, 2006). Counselors need to recognize the diversity within this minority group both in regard to acculturation to the U.S. society and in regard to cultural background. The largest group is of Mexican origin, most of whom have settled in the southwestern states. Puerto Ricans are concentrated in the eastern states, Cubans in Miami, Florida, and Central and South Americans in Florida and Texas. Although heterogeneous in many ways, their worldview is shaped by several common influences: the Catholic religion (85%), some presence of folk beliefs, and a Hispanic group cultural identity (Dana, 1998).

Spanish-speaking individuals often share the poor economic conditions of other minorities, but their difficulties do not lie solely in their poverty. The Spanish-speaking student meets difficulties in communication and understanding from whatever social background. A Hispanic student who scores low on a standardized test in English may actually have obtained a remarkably good score if the student has been learning English for only a short period. A Latino/a client or one from another cultural background may receive a very low score on the Information subtest of the Wechsler Adult Intelligence Scale (WAIS) not because of a lack of intelligence but because the client lacks information about the total population of the United States, the number of senators, and other general knowledge expected from the average American. Similar problems would arise from the vocabulary section and scores on the Picture Completion and Picture Arrangement subtests, because they include materials that are not part of the client's culture (Paniagua, 2005). The counselor must consider individual differences and circumstances in interpreting the test results of clients for whom English is not their native language.

For Hispanic individuals, a Spanish edition of an assessment instrument may be appropriate, and Spanish language editions have been developed for most of the widely used tests, including the Strong Interest Inventory (the Strong), the Myers–Briggs Type Indicator, the Minnesota

Multiphasic Personality Inventory–2 (MMPI-2), the Wechsler intelligence scales, the Self-Directed Search, the Sixteen Personality Factor Questionnaire (16 PF), and Cattell's Culture-Fair Intelligence Test.

American Indians

In counseling Native American individuals, caution must be used in interpreting the results of various assessment procedures. There is a wide range of differences with regard to culture among various American Indian tribes, and because of such large differences few generalizations are possible. For example, Sioux children are likely to be more integrated into the U.S. society than Navajo children, who more often live on a reservation and speak primarily Navajo (Lichtenberger & Kaufman, 1998). Assessment of Native American clients should therefore begin with an attempt to understand the client's cultural identity. In norming samples of tests, very small numbers of Native Americans are likely to have been included in the sample, and even those are likely to represent only a few of the many different cultures from which Native Americans come.

As a group, American Indians have lost much of their original self-sufficient heritage and now represent major challenges for counselors and the entire mental health community because they have the highest rates of poverty, unemployment, alcohol abuse, and suicide (Dana, 1998). On the MMPI, members of several different tribes have tended to obtain higher scores on several scales including the Pd, Sc, Ma and MacAndrew Alcoholism Scale–Revised. These differences remained when matched on age, gender, and education, suggesting that they indicate real differences in behavior and symptoms—not test bias (Greene, Albaugh, Robin, & Caldwell, 2003).

In testing situations, Native Americans may underestimate the seriousness of tests, lack test-taking skills, or lack motivation to perform on tests. For some, tribal beliefs may discourage the type of competitive behavior often present in test-taking situations. They may also have learned English as a second language and learned their first language as a nonwritten language—factors that can easily affect English reading skills (Brescia & Fortune, 1989). In addition, because they often come from isolated, rural, or impoverished settings, they may lack the type of knowledge and experience expected on certain test instruments. The Native American Acculturation Scale (20 items) can be used to obtain an estimate of the extent of an individual's acculturation to U.S. society (Garrett & Pichette, 2000).

Asian Americans

Test results and the interpretations of these results vary greatly for different Asian American clients. They come from more than 20 cultural groups with widely diverse cultural backgrounds and range all the way from fourth- and fifth-generation Asian Americans to the more recent Hmong, Filipino, and Vietnamese immigrants (Teranishi, 2002).

The later generations of Japanese and Chinese Americans come from backgrounds in which the mean income level equals or surpasses that of Whites, and they hold many attitudes and values similar to the majority culture. There are aspects of their cultures, however, that influence them to place increased emphasis on the results of achievement and aptitude tests and less on other types of performance. In addition, education, especially higher education, is much valued and supported, with particular value placed on attending prestigious institutions of higher education. Thus, there is considerable pressure to attain high enough scores on academic aptitude tests to gain entrance to prominent colleges and universities.

Test results for recent Southeast Asian immigrants have much less validity because these individuals are affected by all of the language problems, vast cultural differences, and economic difficulties common to newly arrived immigrants.

Ethnicity, Social, and Educational Variables

In attempting to understand and competently interpret cognitive assessment results of clients from various backgrounds, the counselor must remember that social class is correlated with race and ethnicity and that many cultural differences disappear when socioeconomic status is controlled (Arbona, 1998). Academic aptitude and achievement test scores are far more related to school academic variables (e.g., grades achieved, types of courses taken, particular school attended) than to race or ethnicity. In a study conducted by the American College Testing Program of students in four racial/ethnic groups (African American, Hispanic/Native American, Asian American, and Caucasian), over 50% of the variance in ACT scores could be explained by high school academic variables, with an additional 15% explained by student background characteristics and noncognitive, education-related factors. Race/ethnicity or gender explained only 1% to 2% of additional variance in ACT scores over and above the other variables considered in this study (Noble, Davenport, Schiel, & Pommerich, 1999).

Culture-Fair Tests

The typical intelligence test administered in the United States assumes a relatively common cultural background found in contemporary society along with English as a native language. For tests above the lower elementary levels, literacy in reading English is also necessary to obtain valid results on most of the group-administered tests. To provide valid assessment devices useful in other cultures or for use with subcultures or minority cultures in the United States, attempts have been made to develop culture-fair tests that function independently of a specific culture, primarily by eliminating, or at least greatly reducing, language and cultural content (Samuda, 1998b).

Cattell's Culture-Fair Intelligence Test

This test is a paper-and-pencil test that has no verbal content and is designed to reduce the effects of educational background and cultural influences (R. B. Cattell, 1973). The test consists of four parts in multiple-choice formats: (a) series—a figure must be chosen to complete the series; (b) classification—the object is to choose the figure that is different from the series; (c) matrices—the pattern of change occurring in the figures must be completed; and (d) conditions—the alternative with similar conditions to the example figure must be chosen. The test is available in two parallel forms and for three different age or ability levels: (a) children ages 4 through 8 years and adults with mental retardation, (b) children ages 8 through 14 years and average adults, and (c) college students and adults with above-average intelligence. Within particular age levels, the raw scores can be converted to normalized deviation IQ scores that have a mean of 100 and a standard deviation of 16.

Raven's Progressive Matrices

Raven's Progressive Matrices is a widely used culture-fair test that requires the examinee to solve problems involving abstract figures and designs by indicating which of various multiple-choice alternatives complete a given matrix (Raven, Court, & Raven, 1993). Progressive changes occur in the vertical dimension, horizontal dimension, or both dimensions in a series of matrices. For each item, the examinee must determine the principle by which the matrices are progressively changing and select the correct alternative from six answers that are provided. It is available in two forms: a black-and-white version for Grade 8 through adulthood and the Coloured Progressive Matrices for children ages 5 to 11 years and for adults with mental retardation. Developed in England, Raven's Progressive Matrices has been used in a large number of cross-cultural studies in many countries. These studies suggest that although this test is one of the best available, it might better be described as culturally reduced rather than culture fair or culture free. Norms are based on samples of English children and adults, and one drawback for its use in the Unites States is its lack of normative U.S. data.

Naglieri Nonverbal Ability Test (NNAT)

The NNAT provides a measure of nonverbal reasoning and problem-solving ability based on the use of progressive matrices with shapes and designs that are not unique to any cultural group (Naglieri, 1996). This test can be administered at seven different levels for students in kindergarten through Grade 12. Administration time requires about 30 minutes. The test can be used with children with hearing, motor, or color vision impairments. The NNAT has been standardized for group administration. A second version of this test, the NNAT–Individual Administration form, was created for individual administration for those students who need special attention (Naglieri, 2000). Research indicates that the NNAT produces comparable results for children from different cultural backgrounds and that it can be used to provide a fair assessment of the general intelligence of both White and minority children (Naglieri & Ronning, 2000).

Wechsler Nonverbal Scale of Ability (WNV)

The WNV has been developed as a nonverbal assessment test using the types of nonverbal items found on the other Wechsler instruments. It contains six subtests similar to Wechsler measures and has a brief version using only two subtests. It is useful in schools with students from multiple language backgrounds and where traditional intellectual assessment instruments would not be appropriate due to various language-related difficulties.

Other Culture-Fair Attempts

The Beta IQ III, which was first developed as the Beta IQ test for nonreaders in the army in World War I, is language free and useful for nonreaders and those with limited English proficiency (Kellogg & Morton, 1999). The Test of Nonverbal Intelligence, which requires only pointing or gesturing responses, uses instructions and illustrative examples that can be pantomimed (L. Brown, Sherbenou, & Johnsen, 1997).

Attempts to develop culture-fair tests not only represent attempts to increase the fairness of intelligence tests but also to provide alternative ways of studying this type of ability. Most studies in the United States have found that children in lower socioeconomic groups score substantially lower than middle-class groups on these tests as well as on the more common culturally loaded intelligence tests.

A limitation of most nonverbal tests is that they tend to measure a narrow range of intellectual abilities—primarily visual processing and perhaps short-term memory and processing speed—and thus do not access the full range of intellectual functioning (Ortiz & Dynda, 2005). In addition, culture-fair tests typically do less well in predicting academic achievement or job performance than do the standard, culturally loaded tests. This is not surprising, because academic achievement and job performance often include much culturally important content. Therefore, there are serious questions regarding the use of such instruments for predicting educational or occupational criteria. According to Sternberg (2004a), intelligence cannot be meaningfully understood or assessed outside its cultural context. He argued that intelligence can be best assessed by *culture-relevant* tests instead of by culture-free or culture-fair tests, at least at the present time.

Cultural Differences

Some authorities state that test results based on norms of White middle-class students or adults cannot usually be appropriately applied to ethnic minorities and are therefore of limited usefulness for counselors with minority clients (Dana, 1993). Counselors should understand that the actual results of cognitive tests often contain less bias than that claimed by test critics. In addition, studies show that the removal of biased items does not affect overall test scores and that many cognitive tests continue to provide mostly accurate predictions for most minority clients (Groth-Marnat, 2003). For tests that emphasize the cognitive abilities used in making high-stakes employment or admissions decisions, their developers have undertaken a number of strategies to attempt to reduce racial and ethnic subgroup differences (P. R. Sackett, Schmitt, Ellingson, & Kabin, 2001). These strategies have included identifying and removing culturally biased items, experimenting with alternative modes of presenting test items, relaxing time limits, and conducting test orientation and coaching programs, but they have not resulted in substantially reducing subgroup differences.

The melting-pot philosophy of cultural assimilation of all minorities into the Anglo American culture has been generally rejected in favor of a multiethnic culture. Counselors who hold positive attitudes toward cultural differences are better able to accommodate the cultural predispositions of students from other ethnic backgrounds. The positive attitudes of counselors are more valuable than specific techniques or special materials. As students are accepted by counselors, they accept themselves and their abilities, as well as their limitations. In schools in which the counselor has considerable influence in determining guidance and testing procedures for these students, he or she can influence the adoption of appropriate programs and policies to prevent the misuse of tests and test results.

CAREER ASSESSMENT

A major question with regard to the use of vocational interest inventories is whether minority students are sufficiently familiar with the vocabulary, the examples, the occupational terms, and the situations that are used in these tests. Because many minority students differ from middle-class White students in their experiences, orientations, and values, their view of available occupations may be restricted even though the minority students' aspirations may equal or exceed those of the middle-class White student. Students from disadvantaged backgrounds are likely to be less aware of the great variety of occupations and the skills required for certain occupations. They may also view potential occupations in ways that are quite different from that which is implied in occupational literature. Minority students tend to enter narrower ranges of fields of study (Arbona, 1990; Bowman, 1995; Leong & Gim-Chung, 1995).

Within minority communities, there is often a lack of continuity of values between school and family as well as a lack of diversity in the occupations that exist as models for children from these backgrounds. Family cultures vary considerably among different ethnic groups, which influence career roles and expectations. The genogram (chapter 13) and its accompanying discussion can be a useful tool to help counselors understand the career values and motivations of minority clients (Penick, 2000). On various interest inventories, minority students may obtain relatively low scores because such students indicate liking fewer occupational titles or interests than students in the norm group.

Studies have shown that despite these differences, interest measures have similar validities among various minority groups in the United States. Interest inventories can therefore be used with minority clients with the same amount of confidence as with Whites, with the possible exception of those coming from particularly disadvantaged backgrounds. Studies have also shown that interest measures predict college majors similarly for students from various minority backgrounds. Differences have been found on interest measures among different minorities, but these differences have equal predictive value (Fouad, Harmon, & Hansen, 1994; Fouad & Mohler, 2004; Lattimore & Borgen, 1999). For example, Blacks, who tend to score higher on social interests, are more likely to enter social occupations; whereas Asian American students who obtain higher scores on biological and physical science interests and lower scores on social and sales interests, are more likely to pursue scientific occupations. Counselors should also be aware that some of the female–male differences found among Whites are similar but more extreme for Hispanic women.

There is a tendency among Asian Americans to choose vocations in business, science, mathematics, or engineering fields to the exclusion of humanities, social sciences, or law. When interpreting the results of interest inventories in educational and vocational counseling, the counselor should keep in mind this tendency by the minority client to consider a narrow range of possible career goals. Expanding the range of occupations being considered may well be one of the goals of such counseling.

For minority students, the development of appropriate attitudes and behaviors can be enhanced by using representative minority models and pointing out their accomplishments in various fields. In this way, counselors can assist minority students in understanding and appreciating the contributions that have been made and continue to be made by members of their own group.

Counselors must evaluate the testing and appraisal instruments to determine whether they meet criteria for nondiscrimination. Are data provided that assist in making sound occupational choices? What is the racial and socioeconomic makeup of the population on which the test is based?

Several interest inventories have been translated into a number of other languages. A question that needs to be asked in administering such a version of the inventory is whether the person taking the test is from a culture that has similar expectations and social customs as those for the culture in which the test was devised. Unfamiliarity with the nature and purpose of tests could be a problem, as could different ways of responding. Clients from a culture in which the emphasis is on agreeing with nearly everything (because it is considered impolite to disagree) may obtain test results that lack validity.

PERSONALITY ASSESSMENT

Although racial bias has less often been a major issue in personality measurement, there is some evidence that various minority groups obtain scores on personality inventories that differ from those typically obtained in a White majority population. For example, Asian clients are more likely to express psychological problems in terms of somatic complaints. Therefore, an elevation on the Hypochondriasis scale (Scale 1) on the MMPI-2 with Asian clients should be interpreted in light of this cultural phenomenon (Gray-Little & Kaplan, 1998; Paniagua, 2005). A Pacific Islander's deviant scores on the MMPI could easily be accounted for by cultural and language differences from the original sample on which it was normed.

Diagnoses of schizophrenia are more commonly found with Black clients than with White clients, whereas depression is reported more frequently for White clients than for Black clients (Paniagua, 2005). Differences on personality tests among minority groups and those from other cultures are to be expected, and counselors should take these into consideration in their interpretations of personality test results. Studies of various personality inventories, however, usually indicate that the scales predict the same types of behavioral and personality characteristics for both minority and majority group members, and, therefore when used with caution, these scales can be appropriately used in counseling and psychiatric situations (Duckworth & Anderson, 1995; McNulty et al., 1997; Novy, Nelson, Goodwin, & Rowzee, 1993; Timbrook & Graham, 1994).

Greene (1987), in reviewing a large number of studies examining differences between Black and White Americans on the MMPI, reported no consistent pattern to such differences on any of the standard validity and clinical scales. Although Blacks frequently score higher on the F scale and Scales 8 and 9 of the MMPI than White Americans, differences usually disappeared if the groups were matched on education and severity of psychopathology. Black Americans may also score higher on Scales 8 and 9 because of higher levels of nonconformity, alienation, or impulsivity or because of different types of values and perceptions (Gray-Little, 2002, Groth-Marnat, 2003). Timbrook and Graham (1994) also reported only small differences on MMPI-2 scales between Black and White Americans when matched by age, education, and income. Although there were some statistically significant differences—for example, Black men scoring higher on Scale 8 and Black women scoring higher on Scales 4, 5, and 9—these small differences were less than 5 T-score points and therefore of little clinical significance. They, along with Arbisi, Ben-Porath, and McNulty (2002), reported a slight underprediction of psychopathology for Black men, which is in the opposite direction of the criticisms that have been suggested in the literature.

Few consistent differences have been found in comparing Latinos/Latinas and White Americans on the MMPI scales. In most cases when bilingual Hispanics have been administered both English and Spanish versions, the resulting profiles have been similar. An exception is that those with traditional Mexican Indian spiritual beliefs tend to obtain higher scores on the Schizophrenic Scale, scores that should not be regarded as abnormal or unhealthy (Velasquez, Maness, & Anderson, 2002). A number of other variables such as socioeconomic status, education, and intelligence seem to be more important determinants of MMPI performance than ethnic status. Alcohol abuse combined with depression is more often found among Hispanic male clients compared with White male clients. Hispanic women tend to obtain scores on the Masculinity–Femininity Scale indicating greater femininity. Their expected traditional roles are often in conflict with the greater female role flexibility in U.S. society. Failure to meet these gender-specific roles as wives and mothers can lead to guilt, anger, and depression that may be revealed on personality instruments (Prieto, McNeill, Walls, & Gomez, 2001). The only nontrivial difference for Hispanic men was their scoring lower on the Masculinity–Femininity scale. This is not a pathological scale and suggests a stronger masculine identity in this group.

There is some evidence that Native Americans tend to score higher on the clinical scales on the MMPI compared with Whites, but these differences are not well understood and should be interpreted with caution (Greene, 1987). An American Indian client with particular results on a personality test might be told,

> This finding suggests that you have low self-esteem, are reserved and timid, and lack interest in activities, and that you are a shy person. My understanding, however, is that among American Indians, these behaviors are generally culturally accepted. So we probably need to talk more about these behaviors so that I can be sure that they are not part of the clinical diagnosis of the mental problems you reported to me earlier. (Paniagua, 2005, p. 150)

In a meta-analysis of 25 studies that compared the MMPI scores of African Americans, Hispanics, and European Americans, only slightly higher or lower scores were found among these groups, none of which suggested substantive statistical or clinical differences (differences of less than 5 T-score points are not felt to have much clinical significance; Nagayama Hall et al., 1999).

Asian Americans tend to underuse counseling and mental health services and share experiences and emotions less often with those outside the family (Meyers, 2006). They are more likely to express concerns in an indirect manner, such as physical symptoms. In general, however, highly acculturated Asian Americans obtain MMPI-2 scores similar to Whites. Differences are found among those less acculturated, with more elevated scores on a majority of the clinical scales. Asian Americans tend to receive lower extroversion (indicating more introversion) scores on the NEO Personality–Revised (Okazaki, Kallivayalil, & Sue, 2002). There have been few studies of the scores on personality inventories of Asian students compared with White students.

Projective techniques, personality assessment instruments that have generally not shown high validity, undoubtedly have even less value as assessment tools for minority clients. This is probably true for lower socioeconomic groups in general, because interpretations of protocols of people from different cultures or lower socioeconomic classes tend to result in diagnoses of more severe illness (Garb, 1998; Jenkins & Ramsey, 1991).

Inaccuracies in the assessment and diagnosis of mental disorders can have three consequences: overdiagnosis, underdiagnosis, and misdiagnosis. Bias in testing can be an important factor in such inaccuracies. Attempts have been made to eliminate or control bias in the assessment and diagnosis of multicultural groups by the translation of tests into the language of the group being tested or through the development of culturally appropriate norms. For example, for the 5th edition of the 16 PF, all items were reviewed for gender, racial, and cultural bias by African American and Hispanic bias consultants, with norms based on age, gender, and racial 1990 census data (Conn & Rieke, 1997). Despite these attempts, the general sense among researchers and counselors is that biases in cross-cultural testing still exist (Dana, 2000). Thus, although it is important for counselors to use tests and inventories in the assessment of multicultural groups, they need to determine how to best use these instruments with clients from different cultural backgrounds (Paniagua, 2005).

ASSESSMENT OF CLIENTS WITH DISABILITIES

According to recent estimates, nearly one fifth of the U.S. population ages 15 years and over have a physical disability (Whiston, 2000). Assessment of clients with physical disabilities in rehabilitation settings may involve three different approaches to vocational evaluation. One approach is psychological testing, a second involves the use of work activities or work samples, and the third is evaluation of actual on-the-job activities (Berven, 1980).

For some clients with disabilities, psychological testing that provides relatively objective and reliable measures of individual abilities and interests can yield sufficient data to assist in decisions regarding vocational choice, training, and job placement while avoiding the great additional amount of time and expense involved in the other types of evaluation. For others, employability can better be explored through work samples and on-the-job evaluations. Here the employer becomes directly involved with the problems of the client, client characteristics can be ascertained (particularly in relation to the ultimate objective of more independent living), and a functional appraisal of job-related characteristics can be provided. Disadvantages obviously include dependence on the goodwill of potential employers as well as insurance, wage laws, and regulations that make cooperation by employers difficult. Considerable evaluative information about clients must be obtained in advance if job tryouts are to be successful.

The Americans With Disabilities Act of 1990 includes a section that speaks directly to the testing (primarily employment testing) of individuals with disabilities. Any tests administered to a job applicant or employee who has a disability must accurately reflect the skills or aptitudes the test purports to measure rather than reflecting the individual's particular disability. In the same way that employers must make reasonable accommodations for otherwise qualified employees to perform a particular job, so must reasonable accommodations be provided in the testing process to ensure that the test accurately measures the abilities of the candidate rather than reflecting the disability (unless the disability relates directly to the skill the test measures). Reasonable accommodations can include administering tests in accessible locations or modifying the testing materials (timed vs. untimed, written vs. Braille, or oral vs. sign language; LoVerde, McMahon, & Morris, 1992).

Personality measures, interest inventories, general intelligence tests, measures of specific aptitudes, and tests of achievement or current skills have potential for use with various types of special populations. In using such instruments, however, counselors must view results with caution; for example, items related to general health and physical symptoms on a personality test may be answered in a "deviant" direction by people who are physically ill or disabled and therefore yield scores that are difficult to interpret or are easily misinterpreted. Instruments such as the Battery for Health Improvement 2 discussed in chapter 12 can assist a counselor in discovering psychological or social factors that may interfere with a rehabilitation client's recovery.

Assessment Accommodations

Section 504 of the Rehabilitation Act of 1973 requires that testing be adapted for students with disabilities so that it measures what it is designed to measure while allowing for the students' disability. For students with disabilities, academic standards should be maintained while appropriate accommodations in test administration are made. Considerable information regarding the assessment and testing of people with physical disabilities can be found in the professional literature (Frank & Elliott, 2000; Sandoval, Frisby, Geisinger, Scheuneman, & Grenier, 1998). Included in these publications are lists of assessment instruments appropriate for particular types of disabilities, with recommendations for modifications where necessary.

A cornerstone of the Education of All Handicapped Children Act of 1975 (also called P.L. 94-142) has been the requirement that an Individualized Education Program (IEP) be written for each eligible student. Renamed the Individuals With Disabilities Education Act, or IDEA, the amendments passed in 1997 (IDEA-97) placed additional emphasis on the assessment of students' needs and the evaluation of their progress toward observable goals. The team that develops the IEP now must include not only (a) the student's special education teacher, (b) the student's general education teacher, (c) the student's parents, and (d) a local education agency representative but also (e) a professional educator such as a counselor or school psychologist who has the knowledge and expertise to interpret the assessment and evaluation results (Yell, Drasgow, & Ford, 2000).

An IEP must include (a) a statement of the student's present level of performance and the student's needs, (b) the special educational services that are to be provided to meet these needs, and (c) a valid measure of annual goals and short-term objectives (Shinn & Shinn, 2000). Several test publishers (e.g., Harcourt, American Guidance Service) now provide materials to assist in the writing and assessment of IEPs that accompany their educational achievement tests.

The 1997 revision of the Individuals With Disabilities Education Act requires states and districts to devise appropriate testing procedures for students with disabilities (Azar, 1999). Recent statistics indicate that up to 15% of school children (11% because of disabilities and 4% because of limited English proficiency) will need special testing accommodations. Test experts are challenged to find ways that allow the students with disabilities to show their skills without giving them an unfair advantage. Research conducted thus far indicates that the accommodations often must be tailor-made for the student (Smith, 2002).

The IDEA-97 amendments also include requirements regarding the question of the participation of students with disabilities in statewide and districtwide assessments. Such participation becomes especially controversial when high-stakes testing programs are involved such as those required by the No Child Left Behind Act of 2002. In the past, many students with disabilities were excluded from such large-scale achievement tests, but with the emphasis on accountability for all students, their participation is now required by law.

School counselors are usually involved in and often responsible for the organization and administration of such testing and must make difficult decisions regarding which accommodations (e.g. extended time, providing a reader, using a calculator) are appropriate for particular students (Elliott, McKevitt, & Kettler, 2002). If testing, even with accommodations, is not appropriate, reasons must be given along with a statement of how the student will otherwise be assessed. In most states, the student's IEP plan must contain the appropriate accommodations in order for them to be used in the testing situation. Counselors should make it clear to the student's IEP team that this information needs to be included.

The national testing programs such as ACT and the College Board, the major achievement test publishers, and statewide testing programs provide special test forms and special testing arrangements for examinees with disabilities who are unable to take the test under standard testing conditions. These options include audiocassettes, Braille, large-type editions, magnifiers, use of a reader, use of an amanuensis to mark responses, or extended time for testing.

In general, predictions of college grades obtained from the special testing situations are less accurate, and more emphasis should be placed on other data (Laing & Farmer, 1984). When college admission tests are administered with accommodations, the resulting scores are "flagged" to indicate nonstandard conditions. This policy is consistent with standardized testing procedures (AERA, APA, & NCME, 1999) but is seen as a violation of privacy by many with disabilities and as a violation of the Americans With Disabilities Act (Mehrens & Ekstrom, 2002)

The Peabody Picture Vocabulary Test and the Raven Progressive Matrices are two intelligence tests that require only a pointing response and are useful for the assessment of individuals with cerebral palsy or other physical handicaps. Verbal scales of the Wechsler tests can also be used for severely motor-impaired clients. Some of the performance subtests are not easily adapted because they require both adequate vision and some arm and hand use.

Adaptive devices for computers can provide clients with disabilities with options other than paper-and-pencil responses or the traditional computer keyboard. As a result, individuals with disabilities can complete a test with minimal staff assistance. Examples include voice input, simplified keyboards, joysticks, pneumatic controls, head pointers, and Braille keyboards. Without the computer, individuals with disabilities have typically completed tests with the assistance of another person who read or responded to test items for the test taker. The problem with an intermediary is that that person may influence the test taker's response or the test taker may modify his or her responses because of the presence of another individual. The practice also has the potential of reinforcing dependence of people with disabilities on others (Sampson, 1990).

Visual Disabilities

People who are functionally blind must be assessed through senses other than sight, such as by auditory (readers) or tactile (Braille) means (Bradley-Johnson & Ekstrom, 1998). Fewer than 25% of those classified as legally blind (corrected visual acuity of less than 20/200, which determines eligibility for government benefits) have no usable vision. Those not functionally blind are described as low vision or partially sighted and can often use large type print or magnifiers. Extra time must be provided as these accommodations, including reading large type, are slower and reading Braille, for example, takes 2.5 times as long. A study of the SAT results of visually impaired students using different accommodations (all with extra time) yielded results comparable with those of sighted students. The only exception was that those using Braille found certain graphics or novel-content mathematics items to be more difficult (R. E. Bennett, Rock, Kaplan, & Jirele, 1988).

The verbal scales on the Wechsler Intelligence Scale for Children (WISC) and the WAIS and certain parts of the Stanford–Binet are widely used with blind and partially sighted individuals. Some of the comprehension items need rephrasing to be appropriate, and attention should be paid to the possibility that lower scores on certain subtests may result from experiential deprivation. The performance scales have less validity if visual impairment is more than minimal. Individuals born without sight who have no visual memories may have difficulty with some concepts such as color, canyon, skyscraper, or elephant. They may also find it difficult to develop competent social skills because they cannot see others' social behaviors and nonverbal communications. Interest inventories such as the Strong or the Kuder General Interest Survey are frequently used with visually impaired people by reading items aloud or by tape recording.

Hearing Disabilities

Individuals who are deaf or hard-of-hearing are also a heterogeneous population with disabilities ranging from mild, to severe, to profound. Some have been deaf since birth (congenital), others later due to disease or trauma (adventitious; Brauer, Braden, Pollard, & Hardy-Braz, 1998). Therefore, any assessment should begin with a discussion of communication preference—spoken, written, or signed. Children who are deaf are nearly always delayed in their speech and language skills, and this deficit continues into adulthood (Braden & Hannah, 1998). They develop a smaller vocabulary, which affects reading, spelling, and writing scores. Verbal IQ tests are therefore never used, but normal scores can be expected on performance tests. The performance scales on the Wechsler tests are the most commonly used. Other nonverbal IQ tests such as the Raven Progressive Matrices or the Matrix Analogies Test can be administered when appropriate.

Norms for the hearing impaired are available for the WISC and the Metropolitan and Stanford Achievement Tests. Mean ACT assessment scores of students with auditory disabilities fall below the means obtained by students with visual, motor, or learning disabilities (Laing & Farmer, 1984).

Certain tests and inventories may be administered to the population with American Sign Language (ASL), and responses can also be communicated through an ASL interpreter. The WAIS-III and the MMPI-2 are available in ASL translations.

COGNITIVE DISABILITIES

Because cognitive disabilities cause problems adjusting to the demands of the environment, the diagnosis of mental retardation is usually made not only on the basis of individual intelligence tests but also on the basis of an assessment of adaptive behavior. Intelligence and adaptive behavior are obviously closely related, but adaptive behavior is more synonymous with such terms as *social maturity, personal competence,* and *social competence,* that is, how effectively individuals cope with and adjust to the natural and social demands of their environment. Can they function and maintain themselves independently, and can they meet the culturally imposed demands of personal and social responsibility? Measures of adaptive behavior generally consist of behavioral rating scales administered in an interview or by observation (R. J. Cohen, Swerdlik, & Smith, 1992).

Vineland Adaptive Behavior Scales, Second Edition (Vineland II)

The Vineland II (Sparrow, Cicchetti, & Balla, 2006) is available in survey interview, expanded interview, and parent/caregiver and teacher rating forms. These scales were developed from the original measures designed to assess social competence by Edgar Doll of the Vineland Training School in Vineland, New Jersey. The interview, which follows a semistructured format, is conducted with the client's parents or caregivers. It is conducted without the client being present. The teacher rating form is designed to be completed by either the general schoolteacher or the special education teacher. It has a questionnaire format that deals primarily with adaptive behavior in the classroom. The parent/caregiver form uses a rating scale format that covers the same content as the interview. The Vineland-II taps four domains: daily living skills (self-care, dressing, washing), communication (receptive and expressive language), socialization (interpersonal interactions and play), and motor skills (gross and fine coordination; Sattler, 2005). The expanded form also includes the maladaptive behavior index assessing undesirable behaviors that interfere with adaptive behavior.

The standardization sample for the current version of the Vineland scales included 3,000 individuals, 100 in each of 30 age groups stratified to represent the U.S. Census population. Test–retest reliabilities are reported from .80 to over .90 and interrater reliability from .60 to .75 for the first edition of the Vineland (Sattler, 1989). As might be expected, the expanded form was the most reliable of the three forms, and the short classroom form was the least reliable. The scales are designed to assess adaptive behavior from birth to 18 years old and among low-functioning adults. The instrument is used with individuals with mental retardation and those who are emotionally disturbed or are physically, hearing, or visually impaired to develop individually educative treatment programs or vocational rehabilitation programs. Supplementary norms are available for each of these groups.

Supports Intensity Scale (SIS)

The SIS (American Association on Mental Retardation, 2006) assesses support requirements in 57 life activities and in 28 behavioral and medical areas. The SIS is useful in evaluating the practical supports that people with developmental disabilities need to lead independent lives. It consists of an eight-page interview and profile form in either print or electronic format and has become the standard evaluation instrument for many agencies, including one entire state.

ASSESSMENT OF OLDER ADULTS

The number of older people living in the world has grown dramatically. In the United States, 1 person in 7 is over 65 years old, and by the year 2025 this figure will be 1 in 5 (U.S. Census Bureau, 2006). Older adults are often divided into two cohorts—the young–old, 65 to 84 years, and the old–old, 85 years and over. The need to assess both their mental health and cognitive functioning has led to the development of instruments specifically designed for the assessment of older clients as well as guidelines for their use (American Psychological Association, 1998, 2004).

The Clinical Assessment Scales for the Elderly (CASE) provide information for diagnosing *DSM-IV-TR*, Axis I disorders (C. R. Reynolds & Bigler, 2000). There are 10 clinical scales, for example, Anxiety, Depression, Psychoticism, and Substance Abuse, along with 3 validity scales. Two forms are provided: One with 199 items (CASE-F) can be completed by the client, and a second (190 items, CASE-R) can be completed by a knowledgeable caregiver such as a spouse, son or daughter, or health care worker. Norms are based on 2,000 adults ages 55–90 matched to census data. Two brief versions, the 100-item CASE–Short Form (CASE-SF) and the 88-item CASE-SF–Form R, are also available (DePaola, 2003).

Several standardized methods that involve tasks such as drawing a clock, making change, or answering certain questions have been devised to assess cognitive functioning and cognitive deficits among older people. The most popular of these is the Mini-Mental State Examination (MMSE; Folstein, Folstein, & McHugh, 1975; Folstein, Folstein, McHugh, & Fanjiang, 2001).

The MMSE represents a brief standardized method to assess mental status and consists of 11 questions on which the maximum score for each ranges from 1 to 5 for a maximum score of 30. Following are sample questions, with the maximum score shown in parentheses after the question. "What is the [year] [season] [date] [month]?" (5). "Begin with 100 and count backward by subtracting 7. Stop at 65." (4). The individual is asked to perform the three-step command: "Take the paper in your right hand, fold it in half and put it on the floor." (3). Adults who are functioning normally usually obtain scores of 27 or higher, and 23 is the most widely accepted cutoff score, indicating some cognitive impairment (although others use cutoffs that range from 22 to 25). Scores of l0 or less indicate severe cognitive deficits. Test–retest reliabilities range from .80 to .95, and the MMSE has shown high validity (87% correct) in predicting clinically diagnosed cognitive impairment (Albanese, 2003). In use since 1975, the MMSE has been criticized for having too many easy items and too many cutoff points and no standard scores (M. N. Lopez, Charter, Mostafavi, Nibut, & Smith, 2005).

Alzheimer's disease is the most common disorder causing cognitive decline in old age and is progressive and irreversible. Therefore, if the MMSE reveals cognitive impairment, the next step is to conduct a more extensive examination of the deficit and to determine whether it is due to Alzheimer's disease or whether it is a more treatable impairment such as depression, vascular dementia, or substance abuse dementia (American Association for Geriatric Psychiatry, Alzheimer's Association, & American Geriatrics Society, 1997). The further diagnostic screening includes both medical and psychological tests often involving the administration of certain portions of the WAIS-III or the Wechsler Memory Scale (WMS-III).

The WMS-III is receiving considerable use due to the growing importance of assessing memory functions in an increasing aging population of older adults (Groth-Marnat, 2003). It is an individually administered battery designed to assess a full range of memory functions in line with current theories of memory and to distinguish normal memory loss from the early symptoms of dementia. It is composed of six primary and five optional subtests yielding eight index scores. The index scores allow a comparison between visual and auditory memory and between immediate and delayed memory. It was co-normed with the WAIS-III, which allows a direct comparison between WMS-III scores and WAIS-III IQ scores. For example, an IQ score of 20 points or more higher than the WMS-III can indicate possible brain dysfunction. The WMS-III takes 40 or more minutes to administer (although there is an abbreviated form), and norms are now available for age ranges up to 89 (Hambleton, 2005). Reliabilities of .74–.93 for the subtest scores and .82 or higher for the indexes are reported (Horton, 1999; Psychological Corporation, 1997; Wechsler, 1997b).

In assessing functional impairment, both cognitive and health status must be considered. This type of assessment usually includes an appraisal or checklist of Activities of Daily Living (ADLs; e.g., feeding, toileting) and Instrumental Activities of Daily Living (IADLs; e.g., financial management, preparing meals, shopping; Scogin & Crowther, 2003).

When assessing older clients, counselors need to be aware of possible fatigue and the influence of medications. Once tested, the resulting assessment data can serve as a baseline against which to compare future changes in cognitive functions. Reimbursement for psychological assessment is provided under Medicare and Medicaid, and to receive such compensation it is important to understand and use the Current Procedural Terminology (CTP) coding system. Additional information concerning assessment instruments that are particularly useful with geriatric patients can be obtained from the *Geropsychology Assessment Resource Guide* (U.S. Department of Veterans Affairs, 1996).

SUMMARY

1. The increasing diversity of cultural backgrounds in the U.S. population will present challenges both now and in the future; therefore, counselors who make use of psychological assessment instruments will need to become more culturally competent as the population becomes more diverse.

2. Counselors need to be aware of problems associated with the cross-cultural use of psychological tests, which include the difficulty in establishing equivalence across cultures, the difficulty of not possessing appropriate norms, differences in response sets across different cultures, the nature of the test items, and the differing attitudes toward psychological testing across cultures.

3. Cultural factors influence not only aptitude test results but also scores on interest and personality inventories.

4. When used appropriately, psychological assessment instruments such as the Wechsler Adult Intelligence Scale, the Strong Interest Inventory, and the Minnesota Multiphasic Personality Inventory have produced results that are equally valid for individuals from different racial and ethnic backgrounds.

5. With different types of accommodations, psychological test data can provide useful information in counseling individuals with disabilities, but results obtained under atypical testing conditions must be viewed with caution.

6. The need to assess the mental health and cognitive functioning of members of the increasing population of older adults has led to the development of instruments specifically designed for older adults.

17

Communication of Test Results

Counselors are constantly required to communicate assessment results both to clients and to others, including parents, agencies, and other professionals, but although the evaluation, selection, administration, and interpretation of assessment instruments receive much emphasis in texts, course curricula, and the counseling literature, one of the most important aspects of the assessment process, the communication of assessment results, typically receives scant attention. In fact, of course, it is the understanding by the client or other individual who will be making decisions on the basis of the results that will in the end determine the actual application, if any, to which the assessment results will be put.

This chapter deals with this important subject and contains four sets of guidelines for such communications. The first set lists some general guidelines regarding the communication of assessment procedures and the results. The second set pertains to the actual interpretation of tests in the interview with the client. The third discusses reporting results to children, parents, and others. In the final section, suggestions regarding the format and content of a typical written report on an assessment procedure are provided.

Most of the research studies on the interpretation of test results have been related to career counseling and have been conducted with either high school or college students as participants. These studies have usually shown that clients who receive test interpretations experience greater gains than those in control conditions who do not. Thus, counselors may have confidence that the interpretation of test results to clients generally has a positive effect. There is little research evidence that outcomes are differentially affected by one type of interpretation over another, although clients generally prefer individual integrative interpretations over self-interpretations or group interpretations (Goodyear, 1990; Swanson et al., 2006).

The counselor's theoretical orientation usually determines how the test scores are interpreted to the client. Counselors whose orientation is client-centered are likely to present clients with key scores or percentiles and encourage the clients to join in the process of interpretation. They pay particular attention to how clients feel about the test results and the interpretations. Counselors who are more directive typically review the purpose of testing, present the scores, clarify what they mean, and discuss their implications. Both types should consider assisting clients to make their own interpretations. The advantage of helping clients to interpret and react to test results is that it assists the counselor in obtaining more insight about the client. Also, clients may become accepting of the results more readily by participating in the discussion and may be more likely to use the information when making decisions. In addition, it has been found that client participation in the testing process increases the therapeutic value of the assessment itself (Finn & Tonsager, 1997). It should also assist their memory of the results, because studies of the accuracy of recall of test data have not been encouraging (Swanson et al., 2006; Zytowski, 1997). The participation of clients in the interpretations, of course, usually takes more time on the part of both the counselor and the client, and this must be weighed when determining the type of approach to be used.

It is necessary to have a thorough understanding of tests, particularly of their theoretical foundations and the attribute (such as intelligence or personality) that is being assessed if a counselor is to function as a professional interpreting the test rather than as a technician using a simple cookbook approach. Two of the most important steps in interpreting tests are, first, to understand the method used to develop the test and, second, to learn about the evidence of its reliability and validity (J. C. Hansen, 1999). Tests are used to diagnose and predict; interpretations must lead to the desired understanding and results. It must be remembered that a huge number of factors are involved in producing a particular test score. These factors include clients' inherited characteristics; their educational, cultural, family, and other experiences; their experiences with other tests, particularly psychological tests; their motivation; their test anxiety; the physical and psychological conditions under which they took the test; and the lack of consistency in the test itself.

Psychological and educational diagnoses of culturally diverse clients based on the results of testing data should be made with extreme caution. Culture has a strong influence on psychopathological expression, which can yield significant bias related to the assessment of psychopathology across cultures (Andary, Stolk, & Klimidis, 2003). Although some studies have indicated that ethnically and racially diverse individuals are more likely to receive negative psychological diagnoses, meta-analysis studies have shown no substantive differences for ethnic minorities on such instruments as the Minnesota Multiphasic Personality Inventory (Nagayama Hall et al., 1999). In any case, counselors should be knowledgeable of culture-specific behaviors that may influence the traditional diagnostic process.

In writing reports of psychological and educational assessments, counselors should be aware of the implications of test scores. All of the factors that have contributed to the scores should be considered when reporting predictions and recommendations. Counselors know very well that Miller Analogies Test or Graduate Record Examination scores account for only a small fraction of the variance in predicting which students, for example, will become skillful counselors. Therefore, test results should always include a statement about the validity of the entire testing situation. Counselors should include in their report social, ethnic, racial, and cultural variables that may affect intelligence, achievement, or personality test scores (Hinkle, 1994). Counselors should interpret cross-cultural test scores with caution and, when necessary, include a disclaimer for limitations in the report.

It is in the interpretation of the test that the various types of validity become extremely important. In every kind of test interpretation, there is the assumption of a definite relationship between the person's score or result on a test and what it is being related to in the interpretation. It is therefore important to understand the construction and development of the test as well as its validity, as determined by the relationship of the test score to that aspect or construct that the test has been designed to measure. Often this relationship is expressed in statistical terms, such as correlation coefficients, descriptive and comparative statistics, or expectancy tables. These statistics can often be presented to clients through profiles and other graphic means.

Claiborn and Hanson (1999) have argued that test interpretations offer clients alternative ways of considering their experience and constitute messages of varying discrepancy to clients about their behaviors and their relationships to the world. They give the example of a client who is interested in scientific activities and obtains a high score on the Investigative Scale of the Self-Directed Search. However, he also obtains a high score on the Realistic Scale, suggesting that design and technical aspects of science are more interesting to him than theory and research—a discrepant message for him. Such discrepancies are important variables in the counseling process to which counselors should pay particular attention.

GENERAL GUIDELINES FOR COMMUNICATING TEST RESULTS

1. Remember that an assessment procedure is generally an anxiety-producing experience for most people and usually involves a discussion of personal information; thus, clients may feel vulnerable or exposed in the process (Lewak & Hogan, 2003).
2. Professional codes of ethics and standards stipulate information that test authors and publishers should include in their manuals to facilitate test interpretation. Therefore, the first step in interpreting a test is to know and understand the test manual. In this way, the va-

lidity of a test can be related to the purpose for which the test was used. The manual is also likely to contain information regarding the limits to which the test can be used and suggestions for interpreting the results.

3. In interpreting test results, the counselor must review the purposes for which the client took the test and the strengths and limitations of the test. It is also helpful to go over with the client the questions that the client wanted answered by means of the testing process.

4. In interpreting results, the counselor must explain the procedure by which the test is scored, along with an explanation of percentile ranks or standard scores if they are to be included in the interpretation.

5. Where possible, the counselor should present results in terms of probabilities, which can be understood by clients in the same way as a weather report, rather than certainties or specific predictions. Keep in mind standard errors of measurement and the intervals they represent.

6. Unlike other testing situations, in counseling the tests are used to assist the client in his or her decision making. It is the understanding of the results by the client, not the counselor, that is ultimately important, because it is the client who will use, misuse, or ignore the results. The emphasis should be on increasing clients' understanding and, where appropriate, encouraging clients to make their own interpretations.

7. The test results should be fully integrated in relation to all other available information about the client (Lewak & Hogan, 2003).

8. The counselor should ensure that the interpretation of the test information is understood by the client and that he or she is encouraged to express reactions to the information. Remember that clients prefer an interactive interpretation over one that is simply delivered (Hanson, Claiborn, & Kerr, 1997).

9. Any relevant information or background characteristics, such as sex or disabilities, should be examined, along with any apparent discrepancies or inconsistencies that appear.

10. Both strengths and weaknesses revealed by the test results should be discussed objectively (Hanson & Claiborn, 2006).

Some of the more difficult tests to interpret are those in which a pattern or profile of scores is provided and one on which the client's pattern is a flat profile with no particularly high or low scores. In educational and vocational counseling, flat profiles on interest inventories are often encountered by the counselor because it is the client's indecision that both brings the client into counseling and yields a flat profile. In other circumstances, the individual's response set when taking the test may be a factor. The client makes little differentiation among the responses—all are high, neutral, or low. Validity indices and response patterns should therefore be examined before results are interpreted. With some inventories on which some scale scores are either slightly higher or slightly lower, there may be patterns that can be pointed out and discussed. Other relevant information such as past experiences, values, lifestyle goals, and previous work activities can be investigated.

On aptitude and achievement tests, flat profiles indicate a general level of performance in all areas that may be average, above average, or below average. Again, results from other types of tests and relevant past experiences may be taken into consideration in assisting with decision making.

GUIDELINES FOR THE TEST INTERPRETATION INTERVIEW

1. Show confidence in the client's ability to understand and make use of the test information. Emphasize the importance of adding the test data to other information that clients have about themselves. Emphasize the importance of clients, themselves, using the test information to assist them in making the decisions they are facing. Refer to the questions posed together in the test selection process (as in chapter 4). Ask about comfort, anxiety or apprehensiveness. Adjusting the interview style such as amount of eye contact, use of personal space, and rate of speech to client cultural norms can be helpful in facilitating a culturally sensitive interview.

2. Ask clients to tell how they feel about the particular tests they took before beginning the interpretation process. This may yield information about their attitudes toward the particular tests and provide information about the usefulness or validity of some of the

test results. An understanding of how clients perceive the test is often useful in the interpretation process. Stress to clients that they can ask questions and make comments; that you, as a counselor, are particularly interested in their reactions to the interpretation; and that you want to know their thoughts about the results.

3. Do not begin discussing the results of any test without reminding clients which test is being discussed. Refresh their memory about it by saying, for example, "Remember the test where you checked whether the two sets of names and numbers were exactly the same or were different? That was a test designed to measure clerical aptitude or ability. . . ." If available, it would probably help if you could show them a copy of the test itself.

4. Try to make sure that clients are involved in the interpretation process. Do not merely state the results. After refreshing the clients' memories about an instrument, ask "How do you think you did on it?" "How would you interpret this result?"

5. Be prepared with a brief, clear description of what the instrument measures, including what the results mean and what the results do not mean. For example, "These are some of the activities you indicated you liked and these are some that you said you did not like. Your interests seem to be more like those of people in social service fields and unlike those of most people in mechanical and technical occupations." Be sure to clarify the differences between interests and aptitudes or abilities and personality characteristics.

6. Emphasize the usefulness of the tests for the client's decision making rather than for information it provides to the counselor: "With this set of scores, you can see how you compare with other college-bound students regarding your ability to learn academic subject matter" rather than "These results confirm my belief that you have the ability to do well in most colleges."

7. Discuss the test results in the context of other information, particularly relating the test results to past, present, and future behavior. Past information and current test results should be related to current decisions and to future long-range plans rather than treating each of these subjects separately.

8. Present the purpose of a test in useful and understandable terms, trying to stay away from psychological jargon. Adjust the pace of the instructions and interpretations to clients' ability and understanding. Have clients summarize often to make sure the results are being understood. If necessary, additional information or alternative methods of interpretation can be used.

9. Where possible, use a graphic representation of the results in addition to a verbal explanation. Remember to turn test profiles so that clients can read them directly. If anyone is going to have to read the profile upside down, it should be counselors, who are familiar with profile sheets, rather than clients. It is probably better to position chairs so that you and your clients can go over the results together from similar angles. Complicated profile sheets should be grouped and summarized; in this way, a number of scores can be more easily assimilated by the client. It should not be assumed that most clients have the ability to do this on their own. The results should be explained simply, without the use of elaborate statistics. Verbal interpretations that can be given for particular T scores or percentile ranks, assuming they are based on appropriate norms, were presented in Table 3-1. The normal curve with 100 figures drawn on it was illustrated in Figure 3-1; when covered with plastic for continuous use, this figure is particularly helpful for interpreting scores to students and adults.

   For interpretation of test results to children (and often to parents as well), a simple line drawing of five identical children of the appropriate gender and ethnicity can be a very practical device. They can be verbally labeled from right to left (as viewed by the child) as superior, above average, average, below average, and low. The child is then asked to point to which of those children he or she is like on various characteristics. Begin with some neutral or positive characteristics to ensure the child understands—how tall, how fast a runner, how cute (most children have been told they are cute), and then move to test results. First, ask the children to point to the appropriate figure where they predict they fall in regard to reading, for example, and then you can point to what the test results indicate.

10. Avoid overidentifying with the test results. Discuss a client's rejection of low test scores. The primary concern is what the results mean to the client, not what they mean to the counselor. Low performance scores should be expressed honestly but with perspective and in

regard to the presenting question. They should not be ignored or attributed to inadequate measures or chance.

11. Listen attentively to what the client says and be alert for unexpressed or nonverbal emotional reactions, especially when the test results are not what are expected or desired. Accept the client's right not to agree with them. Consider the client's explanation for the test results. Work with clients in an empathic manner to make sense of the results. Clients may want affirmation of their self-perceptions, but they also want the opportunity to grow in terms of self-understanding and self-discovery (Finn & Tonsager, 1997).

12. Make alternative plans sound respectable without imposing the biases of the typical middle-class counselor. Encourage clients to make their own plans rather than simply agreeing with the counselor's suggestions.

13. Be certain that you and your client relate the test information to other data available on the client. For example, scholastic aptitude scores should be related to school grades. It should be remembered that the usual purpose of a scholastic aptitude test is to predict academic course grades. When such grades are available, emphasis should be placed on actual grades rather than on test results that merely predict those grades.

14. Whenever possible, use the types of norms that are most relevant to clients. When such norms are not directly appropriate, information about this should be presented to clients, and the interpretation of the results should make certain that this is clear.

15. Use only tests that you, the counselor, have personally taken, scored, and interpreted for yourself. Know the reasons a particular test was administered, what was expected from its interpretation, and the validity of the test for the purpose for which it was used.

16. Be aware that psychological tests should not be used to provide information that can be easily gathered in other ways. Only in an exceptional circumstance would a student with high academic achievement or scholastic aptitude test scores need to be administered an IQ test. Tests should not be overused.

17. Toward the end of the interview, have clients summarize the results of the entire interview rather than attempting to do this for them. Allow enough time to discuss this summarization and to discuss discrepancies or misunderstandings. Attempt to end on a positive note even though some portions of the interview have not yielded information that the client has been happy to receive. If clients have received discouraging information about educational, vocational, or other types of plans, try to broaden the scope of alternatives that might be considered. Emphasis should be placed not only on narrowing the focus of future plans but also on broadening them.

18. Remember that in counseling there is almost always an implicit future orientation. Even though the immediate goal may be to help clients to make a particular decision, clients also gain the opportunity to understand themselves better. Ultimately, the self-knowledge acquired in counseling and testing will enable individuals to pursue more effective and satisfying lives and to make wiser and more realistic plans.

GUIDELINES FOR THE CASE CONFERENCE

Counselors often meet together with other professionals and people interested in the client's welfare to discuss assessment results and their implications for treatment. Guidelines for conducting these conferences are listed below.

1. Make certain that all present are introduced. You may be familiar with everyone and their roles but others—the social worker, the parents, the school psychologist, the grandparent—may not be.

2. Structure the session by briefly outlining how you will proceed and the contributions each will be making and encourage feedback, discussion, and questions.

3. Recognize and accept the fact that, as the possessor of assessment information, you may be perceived by parents as "the enemy" or perhaps the messenger with the bad news. Point out that the main concern of all present is the welfare of the child. All are trying to help the child and thus have a common goal.

4. Begin by covering the history that leads up to the meeting and the context in which it is taking place. Summarize previous meetings or interviews. To be effective, you must be well

informed on the issue that is being assessed, such as attention-deficit disorder, not just on the test itself.

5. Draw useful nontest information from those present. The teacher sees the child in relation to many other children, and parents know much about the child's leisure-time interests and nonschool activities.

6. If the child is present, pay particular attention to him or her. It is easy for the adults present to become involved in their conversations and ignore the child.

7. In presenting information to parents, many professionals recommend the "bad news sandwich" approach: first some positive information, then any negative, and ending on a positive note. When the conference is due to a diagnosis of a child's disorder or disability, it is especially important to also focus on some of the child's abilities, not just the disabilities.

8. When finishing, summarize the assessment information and any conclusions that have been reached in the meeting. Encourage and allow time for final questions and discussion.

9. Recognize that receiving a diagnosis of a serious disorder can cause strong feelings of loss, guilt, or frustration and that additional sessions may be useful because you, as a counselor, can help those who are affected work through these issues.

GUIDELINES FOR REPORT WRITING

Counselors often need to summarize assessment results in a written report. Because such reports are often the only product of the assessment process that others see and because they are likely to have significant consequences for the examinee, they must be carefully prepared to be meaningful, readable, and well organized (Kvaal, Choca, & Groth-Marnat, 2003). The impact of the freedom of information legislation (including the Health Insurance and Portability Act [HIPAA]; American Psychological Association, 2005c) means that a written report is now more likely to eventually be read by the clients or their parents. It should be written with this in mind and include both a client's strengths and weaknesses in language that is likely to facilitate the client's growth.

In writing a report, the counselor must have some understanding of what is necessary to include and a conceptualization of the client or person about whom the report is being written. The focus of the report and the way it is to be used are the first considerations in determining its content, including the reasons for referral testing and whether the report will be primarily oriented toward an objective summary of test results or an overall description of the individual being examined. Occasionally, the report is to provide baseline information for evaluating progress after interventions have been implemented (Lichtenberger, Mather, Kaufman, & Kaufman, 2004). The purpose of the report should be clearly stated. Often there is a large amount of information available, and the report writer must decide what information should be included and what should be excluded (Drummond & Jones, 2006).

The writer should first decide the principal idea that should be communicated and what other types of information play an auxiliary role. One of the ways of emphasizing material is by the order in which it is presented, with the most important information first. Another way is through the adjectives and adverbs used in describing the person and his or her behavior. It can also be done through illustrations, by using a vivid example to point out critical information. Another mode is through repetition. Obviously, repetition needs to be handled skillfully to avoid repeating the same material more often than necessary. Repeating information in the summary or conclusion is another way of adding emphasis. The psychological test results themselves can often be used as a framework to describe the client—for example, the "Big Five" factors from the NEO Personality Inventory, the interpersonal circumplex from the Interpersonal Adjective Scales, or the Holland hexagon.

Problems that should be avoided include (a) poor organization, in which the results are not integrated as a whole; (b) use of psychological jargon that will not be understood; (c) use of terms that do not have clearly understood definitions; and (d) lack of integration between the test results and information based on other data such as observations or the client's history. Under the Administrative Simplification section of HIPAA, counselors seeking insurance reimbursement for psychological testing must learn and report the proper Current Procedural Terminology codes that are used to uniformly document why clients were seen and what was done for them. HIPAA regulations regarding the storage and especially the electronic transmission of "individually identifiable" client information is discussed in the next chapter.

What Gets Included in a Case Report

The following is an outline of a typical case report.

1. *Brief description of client.* Including some of the demographic information, a counselor might begin a report by saying, "This is a 32-year-old man of medium build, with wrinkled and soiled clothes, who was extremely verbal and articulate in the interview." This beginning gives a bit of an impression and should include some identifying information, such as age, race, occupation, or year in school.

2. *Reason for counseling or referral.* The next piece of information is the reason that the person is seeking counseling, the problem he or she presents, or the reason the person was referred for testing. A brief description of a client and a brief description of the nature of the problem and the reason for undertaking the evaluation give a general focus for the report.

3. *Relevant background information.* Next to be included might be some additional descriptive data and some of the information available from the referral source. The background information should be relevant to the purpose of the testing, should be related to the overall purpose of the report, and should be as succinct as possible. It is usually helpful to include the client's educational background, occupation, family background, health status, and current life situation. The report should also include other aspects of personal history that are related to the reason for testing and that help to place the problem or reason for testing in its proper context.

4. *Evaluation procedures.* Evaluation procedures should be briefly described, giving the rationale for testing, the names of the tests used, and why the particular tests were selected.

5. *Behavioral observations.* Specific behaviors that were observed during the interviews and during the tests can be included in this section. The way the client approached the test, any problems that arose, and any other factors that might bring into question the validity of any of the tests used should be mentioned. Only relevant observations should be included. This section is likely to be very brief if the behaviors were normal and much lengthier if behaviors were unusual.

6. *Test results and their interpretation.* Next are a report of the test results, an overall interpretation, and diagnostic impressions. The description of the test results does not necessarily need to include the actual test scores, but they should be included if the report is for other professionals who are knowledgeable about testing. The most important part of this section is the interpretation of the results. Here all of the test data are integrated, along with the behavioral observations and relevant background information. A discussion of the client's strengths and weaknesses is included. A statement regarding the client's future prospects in relation to the reason for the testing often needs to be included. This statement would include both favorable and unfavorable predictions.

7. *Recommendations.* The primary reason for testing and the subsequent case report is usually to make recommendations. Particularly if the case is a referral, recommendations can include further testing or activities that the client or others should undertake in relation to the problem. Recommendations should relate to the problem and to the general purpose of the testing and report. They should be as practical and specific as possible.

8. *Brief concluding summary.* A summary paragraph should succinctly restate the most important findings and conclusions.

Writing Style

Writing a report is often much easier if an overall case conceptualization is developed first. Reports often include the general theoretical framework that is followed by the counselor. When psychoanalytic theory was the primary theory followed by counselors, a great deal of emphasis was placed on early childhood experiences. Those who follow Rogerian theory probably pay particular attention to the person's self-concept. The Gestalt theorist looks specifically at current relationships, and the behavioral counselor will be interested in personal and environmental factors that reinforce particular behaviors. Counselors may not feel they have a particular theory of behavior, but in the case report their general theory of personality often emerges because it influences what they perceive from the interviews and test results and, therefore, what they report.

In reporting test results, it is a good idea to stay away from testing jargon. It is also important in writing a report to avoid the extremes of focusing either too much or too little on the test results themselves. It is possible to report extensive test results without relating them to the individual and the individual's situation and future plans and, thus, not offer much in the way of conclusions or practical suggestions. It is also possible to depart too much from the test results and downplay them, particularly if the test information does not come out as expected or if it is not likely to be seen in positive terms by the client.

Counselors should also remember that it is better to write a report immediately after counseling and testing rather than letting a considerable period of time go by. Counselors enjoy working with people much more than writing reports, so it is easy to put these aside. Timeliness becomes particularly important when a number of clients are seen each day. It is important to at least write down the information that will be needed to write a report, even if it is not possible to write the final report immediately. In writing a report, the counselor should say what needs to be said, making clear statements and clear recommendations. Conversely, where results must be considered inconclusive, this also needs to be reported and not ignored.

School counselors are frequently called on to discuss local or statewide testing programs, especially in regard to the No Child Left Behind Act, to Parent-Teacher Associations or other parent groups. They also interpret an individual student's test results to his or her parent or parents. Although designed for parents, the monograph titled "A Parent's Survival Guide to School Testing" (Association for Assessment in Counseling and Education, 2003a) can be a useful reference for counselors. It provides useful assessment information and includes answers to many of the questions about tests that parents are likely to ask.

SUMMARY

The influence of the counselor's theoretical orientation and the importance of case conceptualization are related both to the interpretation of the test results and to the content of a test report. Ten general guidelines for communicating test results were presented in this chapter, along with 18 counselor behaviors useful in the test interpretation interview and 9 guidelines for a case conference. A sample outline provided eight topics typically included in a written case report.

18

Ethical and Social Issues in Testing

There are a number of situations in which ethical principles are called into question when psychological tests are used in counseling and placement. In this chapter, important ethical issues related to tests are discussed, along with the accompanying ethical principles that need to be considered. The second portion of the chapter includes several social issues related to testing that have not been included in previous chapters.

PROFESSIONAL ETHICAL STANDARDS

Because of the number of cases that have arisen in the past regarding the ethical use of psychological tests, each of the professional organizations whose members make use of tests have developed, in their codes of ethics, principles that deal specifically with psychological testing. The American Counseling Association's (ACA; 2005) *ACA Code of Ethics* and the American Psychological Association's (2002) *Ethical Principles of Psychologists and Code of Conduct* each contains a section related to educational and psychological testing. ACA's relevant standards are reemphasized in the Measurement and Evaluation section of the National Board of Certified Counselors (NBCC) *Code of Conduct* (see NBCC, 2005, for the online version of the *Code of Conduct*). In addition, The Responsibilities of Users of Standardized Tests (The RUST Statement 3rd Edition; Association for Assessment in Counseling and Education, 2003b) and the Joint Committee's *Standards for Educational and Psychological Testing* (AERA, APA, & NCME, 1999), both of which were discussed in chapter 2, contain statements of test user responsibilities and ethical standards.

Counselors are obligated to use tests according to the highest professional and ethical standards (Association for Assessment in Counseling, 2002; Herlihy & Corey, 2006). The Joint Committee on Testing Practices (2004) has produced a statement on the rights and responsibilities in the testing process and outlines the responsibility of those professionals involved in the testing process and the steps they should take to ensure that test takers receive these rights (see chapter 2). ACA (2003) has also established a set of Standards for Qualifications of Test Users. Excerpts from the *ACA Code of Ethics,* the RUST Statement, and the Joint Committee Standards most relevant for test use in the counseling process are presented in Appendices A, B, and C, respectively. In their review of the codes of ethics of 13 mental health professions, Vacc, Juhnke, and Nilsen (2001) concluded that the ethical code of ACA addressed more of the assessment standards than did those of the other professional groups.

In addition to these general ethical and competency standards, several of the national specialty counseling associations have issued standards of their own in cooperation with the Association for

Assessment in Counseling and Education. The American Mental Health Counselors Association (2004) has established its own "Standards for Assessment in Mental Health Counseling." The statement of the American School Counselor Association and Association for Assessment in Counseling (1998) is titled "Competencies in Assessment and Evaluation for School Counselors." The International Association of Addictions and Offenders Counselors (2004) has its "Standards for Assessment in Substance Abuse Counseling," and the American Rehabilitation Counseling Association (2003) has titled its statement "Pre-Employment Testing and the ADA."

ETHICAL STANDARDS FOR TEST QUALITY

A portion of the *Standards for Educational and Psychological Testing* deals with the technical quality of tests and test materials and standards to be followed by test developers and test publishers before distributing the test. Test publishers and authors make money from the sales and royalties on tests that are sold, and there is an obvious temptation to exaggerate the usefulness or the validity of such tests. The committee that developed the *Standards* placed considerable emphasis on the importance of "truth in advertising" in test publishing. Test manuals should provide evidence of reliability and validity, including information regarding the methods of estimating reliability and the populations on which reliability was measured, and types of validity studies, including validity relevant to the intended use of the test.

Certain of the *Standards* are designed to prevent the premature sale of tests for general use and to specify when the test is to be released for research purposes only. The *Standards* emphasize that the test manual should not be designed to sell the test but should include adequate information about the administration, scoring, norms, and other technical data to permit the potential user to evaluate the test itself and its potential use as well as to properly interpret its results.

COUNSELOR COMPETENCE IN TESTING

An important ethical issue concerns the competence of the counselor to use the various available assessment instruments. The issue is whether those who use various tests have sufficient knowledge and understanding to select tests intelligently and to interpret their results (*ACA Code of Ethics*, E.2.). Because different tests demand different levels of competence for their use, users must recognize the limits of their competence and make use only of instruments for which they have adequate preparation and training. The administration and interpretation of individual intelligence tests such as the Stanford–Binet or the Wechsler tests, certain personality tests such as the Minnesota Multiphasic Personality Inventory (MMPI), or projective personality tests such as the Rorschach or the Thematic Apperception Test require considerable advanced training and practice to obtain the necessary background and skill for their appropriate use.

In an attempt to deal with this problem, a number of publishers will sell tests only to those who are qualified and require a statement of qualifications from purchasers of psychological tests (Association of Test Publishers, 2006). Test publishers have produced forms that must be completed by those purchasing the tests regarding their educational background and experience. Tests are graded by levels in regard to the amount of background and experience required and are sold only to those who meet the standards required for particular tests. These levels of qualifications are usually included in the test publishers' sales catalogs. In most cases, Level A tests (e.g., Iowa tests, Self-Directed Search) may be purchased by schools and other organizations with no special qualifications required. Counselors must provide relevant information regarding their qualifications before purchasing test supplies. Typically, a master's degree and a course in psychological assessment are the minimum qualifications required to purchase many of the Level B tests (e.g., Strong Interest Inventory [the Strong], Myers–Briggs Type Indicator [MBTI]) commonly used by counselors. Level C tests (e.g., Wechsler Intelligence scales, MMPI) usually require verification of a doctoral-level degree in psychology or education or licensure or certification recognized as requiring advanced training in a relevant area of assessment. Graduate students who need to purchase particular tests for training or research purposes must have the order signed by the graduate instructor, who takes on responsibility for seeing that the tests are properly used.

High standards for publishers and purchasers of tests, however, do not guarantee that tests will be properly used. The major responsibility is that of the professional who makes use of them (*ACA Code of Ethics*, E.1.–E.12.). Is the test appropriate for the person who is being tested? How are the results going to be used? Are the test scores reliable enough? Does the test possess enough validity to be used for the purpose for which it is planned? Counselors who are well trained select tests that are appropriate both for the person to whom they are administered and for the specific purpose for which the person is being tested. They are also sensitive to the many conditions that affect test performance. They are knowledgeable enough about individual differences and human behavior not to make unwarranted interpretations of test results.

CLIENT WELFARE ISSUES

Occasionally, an ethical issue arises regarding the welfare of the client in the testing process. Is the welfare of the client being taken into consideration in the choice and use of tests (*ACA Code of Ethics,* E.1.b.)? Except in such cases as court referrals, custody determinations, or institutional testing programs, this is seldom an issue in counseling because tests are usually used to help the client and not for other purposes.

Another client welfare issue deals with the questions of privacy and confidentiality (ACA *Code of Ethics,* E.3.b., E.4.; RUST). In counseling situations, clients are typically willing to reveal aspects about themselves to obtain help with their problems; thus, the invasion-of-privacy issue, often a concern in psychological testing elsewhere, is seldom a concern in counseling. Clients obviously would not wish this information to be disclosed to others. Test data, along with other records of the counseling relationship, must be considered professional information for use in counseling and must not be revealed to others without the expressed consent of the client. Certain types of test results, such as those assessing intelligence or aptitude and those that ask for or reveal emotional or attitudinal traits, often may deal with sensitive aspects of personal lives or limitations that an individual would prefer to conceal and certainly not have disclosed to others.

Problems of confidentiality often arise when the counselor is employed by an institution or organization, which can result in conflicting loyalties (to the client and to the institution or organization). In these circumstances, counselors should tell clients in advance how the test results will be used and make clear the limits of confidentiality. In general, ethical principles state that the test results are confidential unless the client gives his or her consent for the test results to be provided to someone else. The limits of confidentiality and the circumstances under which it can be broken (such as clear and present danger or court subpoena) must be communicated to and understood by the client. These issues are included in the various associations' codes of ethics (e.g., *ACA Code of Ethics,* B. E.3.b.) and in the American Psychological Association's (1996) "Statement on the Disclosure of Test Data."

In addition, the Family Education Rights and Privacy Act (1974) requires that educational institutions release test result information to parents of minor students and to students who are 18 years of age or older. In reporting results to others who have a reason and need to make use of the results, counselors must ensure that the results of assessments and their interpretations are not misused by others. Is the person receiving the information qualified to understand and interpret the results? It is incumbent on the counselor to interpret the results in a way that they can be intelligently understood by those receiving them, including teachers and parents (*ACA Code of Ethics,* E.3.b., E. 4.; RUST). In addition, the counselor has an obligation to point out the limitations of the results and any other important information about reliability or validity, as well as a description of the norms used and their appropriateness.

Clients, of course, have the right to know the results of tests, with interpretations of the results communicated to them in a language they can clearly understand. The results must be interpreted to clients in such a way that clients understand what the tests mean and also what they do not mean. It is important that clients not reach unwarranted conclusions from the interpretation that they receive (*ACA Code of Ethics,* E. 3., E. 9.; RUST).

The manner in which test results are communicated to others (when appropriate) should be carefully considered. Results should usually be presented descriptively rather than numerically. The use of labels that can be misinterpreted or damaging should be avoided. Labeling someone as *schizophrenic* or *intellectually retarded* can stigmatize a person even when such terms can be justified. They not only suggest a lack of any chance to grow or change but may also become self-fulfilling prophecies. Instead, interpretations should be presented in terms of possible ranges of achievement or formulations of interventions to assist the individual in behaving more effectively.

To help ensure confidentiality, counselors should keep test results in a place where they are accessible only to authorized individuals. They should be maintained in school or agency files only so long as they serve a useful purpose. With the advent of computerized record keeping, the difficulty of keeping test results secure and inaccessible to all but authorized users has increased. Confidentiality must be maintained across a variety of contexts, including postal, telephone, Internet, and other electronic transmissions. This includes who receives faxes and who has access to fax machines and answering machines. Effective measures for protecting the security of individual records and reports must be maintained. In those agencies falling under the Health Insurance Portability and Accountability Act (HIPAA), a number of security regulations apply and full compliance was required beginning April 2005. These regulations specify a number of administrative, physical, and technical standards that include a designated HIPAA Security Officer, locked or password protected files, and limited employee access (American Psychological Association, 2005c).

Tests must be administered in a standardized fashion if the results are to be adequately valid and interpretable (*ACA Code of Ethics,* E.7.; RUST) A potential problem dealing with test administration involves test security (*ACA Code of Ethics,* E.10.). It is obvious that test results will not be valid if people can obtain the tests in advance. For tests such as the College Board tests or the Medical College Admission Test, elaborate procedures are established to ensure that there is adequate security for these tests on which important decisions will be based. In addition, tests need to be accurately scored and accurately profiled if the results are to have valid meaning.

Another ethical issue, probably a minor one for counselors, is in regard to what might be called impersonal service in using tests. It is possible for a counselor or a psychologist to use tests in which test materials are sent to clients, returned, scored, and interpreted through the mail or over the Internet. A fee is charged, but the counselor does not meet the client face-to-face. Considerable money in fees could be generated by this service. Without knowing why the person is requesting the tests, the purposes for which test results are to be used, or the interpretation that clients could give to the results, such a practice would constitute a misuse of testing. Therefore, this practice, along with other types of impersonal psychological services, is considered unethical unless the instrument has been specifically validated for use in this manner.

The opportunity for such practices has increased with the use of computer interpretations. As noted in chapter 4, test publishers have increasingly relied on computers to prepare often elaborate narrative reports of test results. Computer interpretations of such inventories as the Strong or the MMPI can produce interpretations that run 10–20 pages in length. Such interpretations provide a distillation of the information that has been accumulated in the professional literature and of the pooled experience of a number of experts. Narrative computer printouts are obviously no better than the wisdom and clinical experience on which they are based; however, they protect the client from possible bias or inexperience of an individual counselor while expediting what can be a time-consuming and tedious chore of report writing. The client may either take the test itself on a computer or have the test scored and interpreted by a computer. These computer interpretations are, of course, based on norms, which are not necessarily appropriate for a particular individual. They should be used only in conjunction with the counselor's professional judgment. The narrative needs to be evaluated by the counselor who knows other facts about the client, the rationale for testing, and the reasons for such evaluation. The misuse of such computer-generated test interpretations has become an issue of increased concern to the counseling and psychological professions.

A final issue deals with the ethical use of psychological tests in research. When tests are given for research purposes, the first principle is that of informed consent: Having had the procedures explained to them, individuals must have the opportunity to choose whether or not to participate. Minors should also be informed, to the extent of their comprehension, and parental consent is often necessary as well. A particular problem arises in testing research when fully informed consent would provide knowledge regarding the specific objectives of a test that would have a substantial effect on the attitude of the person taking it, therefore yielding invalid research results. In research studies, there are also the ethical issues of privacy and confidentiality.

In general, counselors have had fewer ethical problems in the use of tests than have various other professionals, because counselors typically use tests in their activities on behalf of the client—to assist him or her in regard to decision making or to provide additional information for treatment and self-understanding. They do not usually use tests for "high-stakes" purposes such as selection, promotion, or placement. For school counselors, however, this role is changing because they and other educational administrators are increasingly called on to make crucial decisions regarding student retention, tracking, or graduation based on test results as a result of the No Child Left Behind Act. To make appropriate decisions, counselors must have considerable knowledge in assessment, including measurement validity, special accommodations, and unintended consequences.

CONTROVERSIAL ISSUES IN TESTING

During the past several decades, testing has been a controversial subject that has become involved with a number of social issues. Persistent controversies occur when tests are used in making high-stakes decisions. Here concerns are expressed that the tests are unfair to minorities and women, that they are too much a measure of social class or income, or that they assume special knowledge not available to many groups. Other concerns include the effect of coaching for the test, teachers teaching to the test, and tests being improperly used to judge schools and teachers (Fremer, 1992; Sternberg, 2004b). In particular, testing has been attacked for its discrimination against minority groups (see chapter 16). Tests are designed to measure differences among individuals, but when they reveal differences among ethnic or gender groups, they are often considered to be biased.

These issues have led to much disenchantment with psychological tests, particularly intelligence and academic aptitude tests. Much of the controversy has resulted when test scores have shown group differences. There is less controversy when the discussion is restricted to individual differences, and it is individual differences with which counselors are typically concerned.

Gender Bias in Aptitude Testing

There are not significant differences in men's and women's scores on intelligence tests. Mean scores for both sexes are essentially the same. On specific aptitudes, however, women tend to score higher than men on tests of verbal ability, whereas men tend to obtain higher scores on numerical and spatial aptitudes (Eagly, 1995; Halpern, 2000; Neisser et al., 1996). Women tend to achieve higher grades in elementary school, high school, and college (Han & Hoover, 1994), although the difference in college tends to diminish when controlled for types of majors and types of courses (Hood, 1968; Young, 1994).

The question regarding lower scores on mathematical ability is a controversial one; some argue that the difference is an inherent sex-related difference, whereas others argue that it is due to stereotypical attitudes on the part of parents and teachers, which result in the two sexes being differentially encouraged to learn mathematics. Recent evidence yields at least partial support for the latter explanation because the gap has decreased among adolescents over the past 40 years and has virtually disappeared in unselected populations (Eagly, 1995; Hoover & Han, 1995; Spelke, 2005). Substantial gender differences are now found only in selected populations, such as college-bound youth on the SAT or on the National Merit test. Again, this mean difference is of less consequence to counselors because they work with individual students of either sex who may obtain scores anywhere throughout the entire range.

Another controversial issue dealing with gender bias of tests is related to the awarding of scholarships to the top 1% or 2% of scorers on the basis of a scholastic aptitude test. In the case of awarding certain scholarships, this practice has resulted in a higher proportion of men receiving scholarships than do women. A major cause of this problem may be the difference in the variance on test scores between the sexes in a number of academic areas, including mathematics (Eagly, 1995; Han & Hoover, 1994). On such measures, including quantitative reasoning, men vary over a greater range than do women (Benbow, 1988; Spelke, 2005). Thus, in the same way that the top 1% contains more men than women, so does the bottom 1%. There is pressure to develop tests to qualify for scholarships that eliminate this type of bias, but if the variance hypothesis holds, this will be a difficult task. In the case of the National Merit Testing Program, different cutoff scores are already used for different states, so that the top 1% of the students in each state qualify. If this practice were extended to the sexes, then qualifying scores could be established to ensure that the top 1% of both men and women would qualify.

Gender Bias in Personality and Interest Measurement

Although most of the controversy regarding bias in tests has centered on aptitude or intelligence tests, certain tests used in counseling, such as interest and personality measures, have not been entirely free of bias. Most personality measures are scored on norms developed for each sex, and thus the bias that would result if men and women tended to score differently on a personality characteristic is eliminated. Counselors using particular tests, such as the MMPI, should be aware that behavior patterns attributed to certain profile types often differ for men and women.

During the decades of the 1960s and 1970s, charges of gender bias were leveled against vocational interest inventories and their use in the vocational and educational counseling of women. Several of the interest inventories used only male pronouns and male-oriented occupational names and listed primarily stereotypical occupations for each sex. Earlier versions of both the male and female forms of the Strong were particularly criticized for this bias. The bias that existed has been examined by several national committees, with resulting recommendations to eliminate both the sexually stereotypical language that exists among the inventories and the tendency of test results to channel students on the basis of gender into certain careers.

There are several methods by which publishers have attempted to eliminate, or at least reduce, gender bias on interest inventories. One is by using separate-sex norms. In the case of the Strong, the Occupational Scales are based on separate criterion groups for each sex. The norms for the Basic Interest Scales are based on a combined sample of men and women; however, the profile also indicates how a person's scores compare with others of the same sex as a means of taking into account gender differences. In the case of the earlier forms of the Strong, many more occupations were shown for men than for women, which had the tendency to limit the number of careers considered by women. In recent years, test authors have developed the same number and type of scales for both men and women. Virtually all inventories have eliminated sexist language, for example, replacing *policeman* with *police officer* and *mailman* with *postal worker*.

Another method by which publishers of interest inventories have attempted to make them free of gender bias has been to include only interest items that are equally attractive to both sexes. For example, on an interest inventory containing items related to the six Holland themes, many more men than women respond to a Realistic item such as "repairing an automobile" and many more women to a Social item such as "taking care of very small children." Through the elimination of items that are stereotypically masculine or feminine, such differences can be largely avoided. For example, Realistic items such as "refinishing furniture" or "operating a lawn mower" or a Social item such as "teaching in high school" tend to receive approximately equal responses from both men and women (Rayman, 1976). An interest inventory such as the unisex edition of the ACT Interest Inventory, or UNIACT (ACT, Inc., 1995), is a sex-balanced inventory that increases the probability that men will obtain higher scores on the Social scale and women on the Realistic scale and thus that each sex will be more likely to give consideration to occupations in a full range of fields.

Holland has resisted constructing sex-balanced scales on his Self-Directed Search, believing that the use of sex-balanced scales destroys much of the predictive validity of the instrument (L. S. Gottfredson, 1982; Holland & Gottfredson, 1976). An inventory that predicts that equal numbers of men and women will become automobile mechanics or become elementary school teachers is going to have reduced predictive validity given the male and female socialization and occupational patterns found in today's society. When such inventories are used primarily for vocational exploration, however, an instrument that channels individuals into stereotypical male and female fields can be criticized for containing this gender bias.

By providing the same occupational scales for both sexes, by showing norms for both sexes on interest scales, by eliminating stereotypical language, and, for some instruments, by developing sex-balanced items, gender bias in interest testing has been greatly reduced. It must be remembered, however, that gender-based restrictions in interest preferences and career choices will continue as long as societal influences limit the experiences that men and women are exposed to or are able to explore (Walsh & Betz, 2001).

TESTING AND TECHNOLOGY

The increasing automation of psychological assessment will make the administration and scoring of tests, as well as the interpretation of their results, more efficient, more extensive, and more complex. Most of the tests commonly administered by counselors are available for administration, scoring, and interpretation with a computer (e.g., California Psychological Inventory, Differential Aptitude Tests, Millon Index of Personality Styles, MMPI, MBTI, 16 Personality Factors

Questionnaire, the Strong, and the Wechsler tests). Standardized interview data can also easily be obtained through use of a computer.

The benefits of testing using the Internet are many, including speed, cost, and convenience. It can be cheaper, save time, and be more efficient. Large-scale paper-based testing programs include a number of steps that can be eliminated with Internet-based testing. When paper-and-pencil tests are administered, the test answer sheets must be scanned, then collected, checked, counted, bundled, and shipped to a scoring center prior to scoring and profiling, all of which demands considerable time and cost (Wall, 2004b). In contrast, tests administered on the Internet can be scored and interpreted for counselors and clients as fast as the last item is completed (Naglieri et al., 2004). Test publishers, stressing better and cheaper services and worldwide use, have embraced Internet testing. Revising a paper-and-pencil test requires printing and distributing new forms, answer keys, and manuals. Revisions of an Internet test can be downloaded to testing sites anywhere in moments. Internet tests can provide real-world simulations, including multimedia, three-dimensional graphics, and relevant resources, and thus assess higher order abilities and types of skills not easily measured by paper-and-pencil tests (e.g., the Test of English as a Foreign Language, which assesses listening and speaking skills over the Internet). Such processes obviously bring new challenges and problems. Various types of security must be maintained to ensure the privacy of client data and test results and to prevent the unauthorized copying of test items or the unauthorized use of testing materials. There are the other security problems of spam, viruses, hacking, cheating by examinees, and maintaining copyrights across international borders.

Because Internet-based testing does not involve the use of a test administrator, counselors cannot be sure of the circumstances under which the test was taken (Did the examinee understand the instructions? Did he or she work independently in answering the items? Was he or she distracted in any way?). Because the counselor is not present at the time of the test interpretation, the counselor is not able to discern how clients react emotionally to the results or how they will integrate the information into their lives. There are also issues in determining appropriate accommodations for examinees with disabilities.

Then there is a continuing need for the ethical and professional use of these tests supported by reliability and validity. For example, the growth of career resources on the Internet has resulted in many short career interest quizzes and brief personality measures that have no evidence of norms, reliability, or validity (Mallen, Vogel, Rochlen, & Day, 2005). The counseling profession must make it clear that these unproven instruments are no substitute for true standardized assessment instruments.

COUNSELING PROCESS ISSUES

It is probably to be expected that tests used for selection into desirable programs and occupations will be criticized, particularly by those not selected. The use of tests in counseling situations, however, has been much less controversial. Counselors and human development professionals typically use tests for problem-solving purposes to assist the client. In other settings, test results are not necessarily shared directly with clients; in counseling, test results are almost always discussed with clients because the goal of counseling is usually to assist clients in making choices and in developing self-awareness. The client is seen as the primary user of test results, with the counselor acting more as a facilitator. Although counselors use the clinical interview and behavioral observation, tests provide an opportunity to obtain standardized information concerning individual differences that can be useful both to plan counseling interventions and to promote clients' understanding of themselves. Counselors help clients explore and identify their abilities, personality characteristics, patterns of interests, and values for the purpose of making choices and changes that can improve their sense of well-being or their lifestyles.

Personality inventories reveal information that can be useful in the counseling process, and interest and aptitude test results can assist in educational and vocational planning. Diagnostic tests in academic areas such as reading or arithmetic skills can help to identify those who need special instruction in particular areas and to plan future educational programs. Because of criticisms leveled against psychological tests when used in selection procedures (and perhaps in part because of some counselors' own experiences with scholastic aptitude tests used for selection purposes), counselors occasionally develop a bias against psychological tests. They refuse to use them even in individual counseling programs, where they can often be valuable.

Some of the criticism of psychological testing and assessment and attacks on their use in educational institutions and employment situations have had constructive effects. Increased awareness of the utility and limitations of testing has resulted in the need for more carefully trained users of test results as the personal and social consequences of testing have become increasingly apparent. Consistent with these needs, the primary objective of this book has been to improve the knowledge and understanding of counselors who administer and interpret the results of these assessment procedures.

Counselors should not blame the tests themselves when they have been used inappropriately. Obviously, tests are often misused and occasionally misused by counselors and other human development professionals, but that does not mean the tests are at fault. When pliers are used on a bolt when an adjustable wrench is called for, it is not the pair of pliers or its manufacturer that is criticized.

One of the earlier criticisms of psychological tests was that they were dominating the counseling process. With the development of many new counseling theories and techniques, there are few, if any, strict practitioners of what used to be known as trait-and-factor counseling, for whom psychological tests totally dominated their counseling practices.

When using tests in counseling, the counselor must attempt to understand the client's frame of reference. If the counselor is knowledgeable about tests, the counselor can then better help the client understand the information that tests can provide. In interpreting test results, the counselor must help clients understand their implications and their limitations and help clients integrate the test information into their self-perceptions and decision-making strategies.

It has been suggested (and even mandated by legislative action) that tests should not be used because certain disadvantaged groups make poor showings on them. In these situations, the test results are often indicative of symptoms of a societal ailment, analogous to a fever thermometer that indicates an illness. When the tests reveal that the disadvantaged have not had the opportunity to learn certain concepts, there should be an attempt to provide these opportunities, not to dispose of the instruments that reveal such symptoms.

Another criticism of using tests in counseling is that validity coefficients are based on groups of individuals, and it is not possible to discern the validity of any test score for any one individual. It is in the counseling process that the counselor attempts to help clients determine the validity of that test score for that individual. To use tests properly in counseling, the counselor must know as much about the client and the client's environment as possible. Counselors must also be well informed about tests and have a basic familiarity with them. Although they may not need to have a great deal of understanding regarding the technical aspects of test development and standardization, they do need to have a clear understanding of the general purposes of the particular tests they use, the uses to which they can be put, and the role these tests can play in the counseling process.

In the information age, test results will continue to provide important data needed for many decisions. In addition to individual personal and career decisions, there will be increased reliance on tests to determine minimum skills and competencies for educational institutions, licensing and certification, and personnel selection.

FINAL STATEMENT

Psychological tests are used by personnel staff to select employees, by school psychologists to track pupils, by clinical psychologists to diagnose patients, by college admissions staff to admit students, and by forensic psychologists to determine sanity. In the counseling setting, however, psychological tests are used to help clients understand themselves. When confronted with negative attitudes toward psychological tests, counselors may be reluctant to make adequate use of them in assisting clients, but they should remember that the use of tests in counseling differs from other test use. Counselors use tests primarily to assist individuals in developing their potential to the fullest and to their own satisfaction. Test results are designed to be used by the clients themselves—and only in the ways that they decide to make use of the test results or not to make use of them. In counseling, tests are not used by others to make decisions for or against a client.

The concept of individual differences is a basic tenet of counseling. Assessment procedures enable counselors to measure and compare the different characteristics of clients and their environments. Tests and assessment data can provide important behavior samples useful in the counseling process to assist counselors to understand their clients better and clients to understand themselves.

The purpose of this volume has been to help current and future counselors, as well as others in the helping professions, become better consumers and interpreters of psychological and educational tests and assessment procedures. We have attempted to cover some of the philosophical and ethical principles related to the use of tests, basic knowledge about certain tests, when tests should be used, and how to interpret and report tests and other assessment results.

By using tests ethically, appropriately, and intelligently, counselors can assist their clients to understand their problems, make use of their potential, function more effectively, make more effective decisions, and live more satisfying lives.

SECTION

VI

APPENDIXES

A

Excerpts From the *ACA Code of Ethics* (2005)

Introduction

Counselors use assessment instruments as one component of the counseling process, taking into account the client personal and cultural context. Counselors promote the well-being of individual clients or groups of clients by developing and using appropriate educational, psychological, and career assessment instruments.

E.1. General

E.1.a. Assessment
The primary purpose of educational, psychological, and career assessment is to provide measurements that are valid and reliable in either comparative or absolute terms. These include, but are not limited to, measurements of ability, personality, interest, intelligence, achievement, and performance. Counselors recognize the need to interpret the statements in this section as applying to both quantitative and qualitative assessments.

E.1.b. Client Welfare
Counselors do not misuse assessment results and interpretations, and they take reasonable steps to prevent others from misusing the information these techniques provide. They respect the client's right to know the results, the interpretations made, and the bases for counselors' conclusions and recommendations.

E.2. Competence to Use and Interpret Assessment Instruments

E.2.a. Limits of Competence
Counselors utilize only those testing and assessment services for which they have been trained and are competent. Counselors using technology-assisted test interpretations are trained in the construct being measured and the specific instrument being used prior to using its technology-based application. Counselors take reasonable measures to ensure the proper use of psychological and career assessment techniques by persons under their supervision. *(See A.12.)*

E.2.b. Appropriate Use
Counselors are responsible for the appropriate application, scoring, interpretation, and use of assessment instruments relevant to the needs of the client, whether they score and interpret such assessments themselves or use technology or other services.

E.2.c. Decisions Based on Results
Counselors responsible for decisions involving individuals or policies that are based on assessment results have a thorough understanding of educational, psychological, and career measurement, including validation criteria, assessment

research, and guidelines for assessment development and use.

E.3. Informed Consent in Assessment

E.3.a. Explanation to Clients
Prior to assessment, counselors explain the nature and purposes of assessment and the specific use of results by potential recipients. The explanation will be given in the language of the client (or other legally authorized person on behalf of the client), unless an explicit exception has been agreed upon in advance. Counselors consider the client's personal or cultural context, the level of the client's understanding of the results, and the impact of the results on the client. *(See A.2., A.12.g., F.1.c.)*

E.3.b. Recipients of Results
Counselors consider the examinee's welfare, explicit understandings, and prior agreements in determining who receives the assessment results. Counselors include accurate and appropriate interpretations with any release of individual or group assessment results. *(See B.2.c., B.5.)*

E.4. Release of Data to Qualified Professionals

Counselors release assessment data in which the client is identified only with the consent of the client or the client's legal representative. Such data are released only to persons recognized by counselors as qualified to interpret the data. *(See B.1., B.3., B.6.b.)*

E.5. Diagnosis of Mental Disorders

E.5.a. Proper Diagnosis
Counselors take special care to provide proper diagnosis of mental disorders. Assessment techniques (including personal interview) used to determine client care (e.g., locus of treatment, type of treatment, or recommended follow-up) are carefully selected and appropriately used.

E.5.b. Cultural Sensitivity
Counselors recognize that culture affects the manner in which clients' problems are defined. Clients' socioeconomic and cultural experiences are considered when diagnosing mental disorders. *(See A.2.c.)*

E.5.c. Historical and Social Prejudices in the Diagnosis of Pathology
Counselors recognize historical and social prejudices in the misdiagnosis and pathologizing of certain individuals and groups and the role of mental health professionals in perpetuating these prejudices through diagnosis and treatment.

E.5.d. Refraining From Diagnosis
Counselors may refrain from making and/or reporting a diagnosis if they believe it would cause harm to the client or others.

E.6. Instrument Selection

E.6.a. Appropriateness of Instruments
Counselors carefully consider the validity, reliability, psychometric limitations, and appropriateness of instruments when selecting assessments.

E.6.b. Referral Information
If a client is referred to a third party for assessment, the counselor provides specific referral questions and sufficient objective data about the client to ensure that appropriate assessment instruments are utilized. *(See A.9.b., B.3.)*

E.6.c. Culturally Diverse Populations
Counselors are cautious when selecting assessments for culturally diverse populations to avoid the use of instruments that lack appropriate psychometric properties for the client population. *(See A.2.c., E.5.b.)*

E.7. Conditions of Assessment Administration
(See A.12.b., A.12.d.)

E.7.a. Administration Conditions
Counselors administer assessments under the same conditions that were established in their standardization. When assessments are not administered under standard conditions, as may be necessary to accommodate clients with disabilities, or when unusual behavior or irregularities occur during the administration, those conditions are noted in interpretation, and the results may be designated as invalid or of questionable validity.

E.7.b. Technological Administration
Counselors ensure that administration programs function properly and provide clients with accurate results when technological or other electronic methods are used for assessment administration.

E.7.c. Unsupervised Assessments
Unless the assessment instrument is designed, intended, and validated for self-administration

and/or scoring, counselors do not permit inadequately supervised use.

E.7.d. Disclosure of Favorable Conditions
Prior to administration of assessments, conditions that produce most favorable assessment results are made known to the examinee.

E.8. Multicultural Issues/ Diversity in Assessment

Counselors use with caution assessment techniques that were normed on populations other than that of the client. Counselors recognize the effects of age, color, culture, disability, ethnic group, gender, race, language preference, religion, spirituality, sexual orientation, and socioeconomic status on test administration and interpretation, and place test results in proper perspective with other relevant factors. *(See A.2.c., E.5.b.)*

E.9. Scoring and Interpretation of Assessments

E.9.a. Reporting
In reporting assessment results, counselors indicate reservations that exist regarding validity or reliability due to circumstances of the assessment or the inappropriateness of the norms for the person tested.

E.9.b. Research Instruments
Counselors exercise caution when interpreting the results of research instruments not having sufficient technical data to support respondent results. The specific purposes for the use of such instruments are stated explicitly to the examinee.

E.9.c. Assessment Services
Counselors who provide assessment scoring and interpretation services to support the assessment process confirm the validity of such interpretations. They accurately describe the purpose, norms, validity, reliability, and applications of the procedures and any special qualifications applicable to their use. The public offering of an automated test interpretations service is considered a professional-to-professional consultation. The formal responsibility of the consultant is to the consultee, but the ultimate and overriding responsibility is to the client. *(See D.2.)*

E.10. Assessment Security

Counselors maintain the integrity and security of tests and other assessment techniques consistent with legal and contractual obligations. Counselors do not appropriate, reproduce, or modify published assessments or parts thereof without acknowledgment and permission from the publisher.

E.11. Obsolete Assessments and Outdated Results

Counselors do not use data or results from assessments that are obsolete or outdated for the current purpose. Counselors make every effort to prevent the misuse of obsolete measures and assessment data by others.

E.12. Assessment Construction

Counselors use established scientific procedures, relevant standards, and current professional knowledge for assessment design in the development, publication, and utilization of educational and psychological assessment techniques.

E.13. Forensic Evaluation: Evaluation for Legal Proceedings

E.13.a. Primary Obligations
When providing forensic evaluations, the primary obligation of counselors is to produce objective findings that can be substantiated based on information and techniques appropriate to the evaluation, which may include examination of the individual and/or review of records. Counselors are entitled to form professional opinions based on their professional knowledge and expertise that can be supported by the data gathered in evaluations. Counselors will define the limits of their reports or testimony, especially when an examination of the individual has not been conducted.

E.13.b. Consent for Evaluation
Individuals being evaluated are informed in writing that the relationship is for the purposes of an evaluation and is not counseling in nature, and entities or individuals who will receive the evaluation report are identified. Written consent to be evaluated is obtained from those being evaluated unless a court orders evaluations to be conducted without the written consent of individuals being evaluated. When children or vulnerable adults are being evaluated, informed written consent is obtained from a parent or guardian.

E.13.c. Client Evaluation Prohibited

Counselors do not evaluate individuals for forensic purposes they currently counsel or individuals they have counseled in the past. Counselors do not accept as counseling clients individuals they are evaluating or individuals they have evaluated in the past for forensic purposes.

E.13.d. Avoid Potentially Harmful Relationships

Counselors who provide forensic evaluations avoid potentially harmful professional or personal relationships with family members, romantic partners, and close friends of individuals they are evaluating or have evaluated in the past.

B

Responsibilities of Users of Standardized Tests (RUST), Third Edition

Prepared by the Association for Assessment in Counseling (AAC)

Many recent events have influenced the use of tests and assessment in the counseling community. Such events include the use of tests in the educational accountability and reform movement, the publication of the *Standards for Educational and Psychological Testing* (American Educational Research Association [AERA], American Psychological Association [APA], National Council on Measurement in Education [NCME], 1999), the revision of the *Code of Fair Testing Practices in Education* (Joint Committee on Testing Practices [JCTP], 2002), the proliferation of technology-delivered assessment, and the historic passage of the *No Child Left Behind Act* (HR1, 2002) calling for expanded testing in reading/language arts, mathematics, and science that are aligned to state standards.

The purpose of this document is to promote the accurate, fair, and responsible use of standardized tests by the counseling and education communities. RUST is intended to address the needs of the members of the American Counseling Association (ACA) and its Divisions, Branches, and Regions, including counselors, teachers, administrators, and other human service workers. The general public, test developers, and policy makers will find this statement useful as they work with tests and testing issues. The principles in RUST apply to the use of testing instruments regardless of delivery methods (e.g., paper/pencil or computer administered) or setting (e.g., group or individual).

The intent of RUST is to help counselors and other educators implement responsible testing practices. The RUST does not intend to reach beyond or reinterpret the principles outlined in the *Standards for Educational and Psychological Testing* (AERA et al., 1999), nor was it developed to formulate a basis for legal action. The intent is to provide a concise statement useful in the ethical practice of testing. In addition, RUST is intended to enhance the guidelines found in ACA's *Code of Ethics and Standards of Practice* (ACA, 1997) and the *Code of Fair Testing Practices in Education* (JCTP, 2002).

Organization of Document: This document includes test user responsibilities in the following areas:

- Qualifications of Test Users
- Technical Knowledge
- Test Selection
- Test Administration
- Test Scoring
- Interpreting Test Results
- Communicating Test Results

QUALIFICATIONS OF TEST USERS

Qualified test users demonstrate appropriate education, training, and experience in using tests for the purposes under consideration. They adhere to the highest degree of ethical codes, laws, and standards governing professional practice. Lack of essential qualifications or ethical and legal compliance can lead to errors and subsequent harm to clients. Each professional is responsible for making judgments in each testing situation and cannot leave that responsibility either to clients or others in authority. The individual test user must obtain appropriate education and training, or arrange for professional supervision and assistance when engaged in testing in order to provide valuable, ethical, and effective assessment services to the public. Qualifications of test users depend on at least four factors:

- *Purposes of Testing:* A clear purpose for testing should be established. Because the purposes of testing direct how the results are used, qualifications beyond general testing competencies may be needed to interpret and apply data.
- *Characteristics of Tests:* Understanding of the strengths and limitations of each instrument used is a requirement.
- *Settings and Conditions of Test Use:* Assessment of the quality and relevance of test user knowledge and skill to the situation is needed before deciding to test or participate in a testing program.
- *Roles of Test Selectors, Administrators, Scorers, and Interpreters:* The education, training, and experience of test users determine which tests they are qualified to administer and interpret.

Each test user must evaluate his or her qualifications and competence for selecting, administering, scoring, interpreting, reporting, or communicating test results. Test users must develop the skills and knowledge for each test he or she intends to use.

TECHNICAL KNOWLEDGE

Responsible use of tests requires technical knowledge obtained through training, education, and continuing professional development. Test users should be conversant and competent in aspects of testing including:

- *Validity of Test Results:* Validity is the accumulation of evidence to support a specific interpretation of the test results. Since validity is a characteristic of test results, a test may have validities of varying degree, for different purposes. The concept of instructional validity relates to how well the test is aligned to state standards and classroom instructional objectives.
- *Reliability:* Reliability refers to the consistency of test scores. Various methods are used to calculate and estimate reliability depending on the purpose for which the test is used.
- *Errors of Measurement:* Various ways may be used to calculate the error associated with a test score. Knowing this and knowing the estimate of the size of the error allows the test user to provide a more accurate interpretation of the scores and to support better-informed decisions.
- *Scores and Norms:* Basic differences between the purposes of norm-referenced and criterion-referenced scores impact score interpretations.

TEST SELECTION

Responsible use of tests requires that the specific purpose for testing be identified. In addition, the test that is selected should align with that purpose, while considering the characteristics of the test and the test taker. Tests should not be administered without a specific purpose or need for information. Typical purposes for testing include:

- *Description:* Obtaining objective information on the status of certain characteristics such as achievement, ability, personality types, etc. is often an important use of testing.

- *Accountability:* When judging the progress of an individual or the effectiveness of an educational institution, strong alignment between what is taught and what is tested needs to be present.
- *Prediction:* Technical information should be reviewed to determine how accurately the test will predict areas such as appropriate course placement; selection for special programs, interventions, and institutions; and other outcomes of interest.
- *Program Evaluation:* The role that testing plays in program evaluation and how the test information may be used to supplement other information gathered about the program is an important consideration in test use.

Proper test use involves determining if the characteristics of the test are appropriate for the intended audience and are of sufficient technical quality for the purpose at hand. Some areas to consider include:

- *The Test Taker:* Technical information should be reviewed to determine if the test characteristics are appropriate for the test taker (e.g., age, grade level, language, cultural background).
- *Accuracy of Scoring Procedures:* Only tests that use accurate scoring procedures should be used.
- *Norming and Standardization Procedures:* Norming and standardization procedures should be reviewed to determine if the norm group is appropriate for the intended test takers. Specified test administration procedures must be followed.
- *Modifications:* For individuals with disabilities, alternative measures may need to be found and used and/or accommodations in test taking procedures may need to be employed. Interpretations need to be made in light of the modifications in the test or testing procedures.
- *Fairness:* Care should be taken to select tests that are fair to all test takers. When test results are influenced by characteristics or situations unrelated to what is being measured. (e.g., gender, age, ethnic background, existence of cheating, unequal availability of test preparation programs) the use of the resulting information is invalid and potentially harmful. In achievement testing, fairness also relates to whether or not the student has had an opportunity to learn what is tested.

TEST ADMINISTRATION

Test administration includes carefully following standard procedures so that the test is used in the manner specified by the test developers. The test administrator should ensure that test takers work within conditions that maximize opportunity for optimum performance. As appropriate, test takers, parents, and organizations should be involved in the various aspects of the testing process including:

Before administration it is important that relevant persons

- are informed about the standard testing procedures, including information about the purposes of the test, the kinds of tasks involved, the method of administration, and the scoring and reporting;
- have sufficient practice experiences prior to the test to include practice, as needed, on how to operate equipment for computer-administered tests and practice in responding to tasks;
- have been sufficiently trained in their responsibilities and the administration procedures for the test;
- have a chance to review test materials and administration sites and procedures prior to the time for testing to ensure standardized conditions and appropriate responses to any irregularities that occur;
- arrange for appropriate modifications of testing materials and procedures in order to accommodate test takers with special needs; and
- have a clear understanding of their rights and responsibilities.

During administration it is important that

- the testing environment (e.g., seating, work surfaces, lighting, room temperature, freedom from distractions) and psychological climate are conducive to the best possible performance of the examinees;
- sufficiently trained personnel establish and maintain uniform conditions and observe the conduct of test takers when large groups of individuals are tested;
- test administrators follow the instructions in the test manual; demonstrate verbal clarity; use verbatim directions; adhere to verbatim directions; follow exact sequence and timing; and use materials that are identical to those specified by the test publisher;
- a systematic and objective procedure is in place for observing and recording environmental, health, emotional factors, or other elements that may invalidate test performance and results; deviations from prescribed test administration procedures, including information on test accommodations for individuals with special needs, are recorded; and
- the security of test materials and computer-administered testing software is protected, ensuring that only individuals with a legitimate need for access to the materials/software are able to obtain such access and that steps to eliminate the possibility of breaches in test security and copyright protection are respected.

After administration it is important to

- collect and inventory all secure test materials and immediately report any breaches in test security; and
- include notes on any problems, irregularities, and accommodations in the test records.

These precepts represent the basic process for all standardized tests and assessments. Some situations may add steps or modify some of these to provide the best testing milieu possible.

TEST SCORING

Accurate measurement necessitates adequate procedures for scoring the responses of test takers. Scoring procedures should be audited as necessary to ensure consistency and accuracy of application.

- Carefully implement and/or monitor standard scoring procedures.
- When test scoring involves human judgment, use rubrics that clearly specify the criteria for scoring. Scoring consistency should be constantly monitored.
- Provide a method for checking the accuracy of scores when accuracy is challenged by test takers.

INTERPRETING TEST RESULTS

Responsible test interpretation requires knowledge about and experience with the test, the scores, and the decisions to be made. Interpretation of scores on any test should not take place without a thorough knowledge of the technical aspects of the test, the test results, and its limitations. Many factors can impact the valid and useful interpretations of test scores. These can be grouped into several categories including psychometric, test taker, and contextual, as well as others.

- *Psychometric Factors:* Factors such as the reliability, norms, standard error of measurement, and validity of the instrument are important when interpreting test results. Responsible test use considers these basic concepts and how each impacts the scores and hence the interpretation of the test results.
- *Test Taker Factors:* Factors such as the test taker's group membership and how that membership may impact the results of the test is a critical factor in the interpretation of test re-

sults. Specifically, the test user should evaluate how the test taker's gender, age, ethnicity, race, socioeconomic status, marital status, and so forth, impact on the individual's results.

- *Contextual Factors:* The relationship of the test to the instructional program, opportunity to learn, quality of the educational program, work and home environment, and other factors that would assist in understanding the test results are useful in interpreting test results. For example, if the test does not align to curriculum standards and how those standards are taught in the classroom, the test results may not provide useful information.

COMMUNICATING TEST RESULTS

Before communication of test results takes place, a solid foundation and preparation is necessary. That foundation includes knowledge of test interpretation and an understanding of the particular test being used, as provided by the test manual.

Conveying test results with language that the test taker, parents, teachers, clients, or general public can understand is one of the key elements in helping others understand the meaning of the test results. When reporting group results, the information needs to be supplemented with background information that can help explain the results with cautions about misinterpretations. The test user should indicate how the test results can be and should not be interpreted.

CLOSING

Proper test use resides with the test user—the counselor and educator. Qualified test users understand the measurement characteristics necessary to select good standardized tests, administer the tests according to specified procedures, assure accurate scoring, accurately interpret test scores for individuals and groups, and ensure productive applications of the results. This document provides guidelines for using tests responsibly with students and clients.

REFERENCES AND RESOURCE DOCUMENTS

American Counseling Association. (1997). *Code of ethics and standards of practice.* Alexandria, VA: Author.

American Counseling Association. (2003). *Standards for qualifications of test users.* Alexandria, VA: Author.

American Educational Research Association, American Psychological Association, National Council on Measurement in Education. (1999). *Standards for educational and psychological testing.* Washington, DC: American Educational Research Association.

American School Counselor Association & Association for Assessment in Counseling (1998). *Competencies in assessment and evaluation for school counselors.* Alexandria, VA: Author.

Joint Committee on Testing Practices. (2000) *Rights and responsibilities of test takers: Guidelines and expectations.* Washington, DC: Author.

Joint Committee on Testing Practices. (2002). *Code of fair testing practices in education.* Washington, DC: Author.

RUST COMMITTEE

Janet Wall, Chair
James Augustin
Charles Eberly
Brad Erford
David Lundberg
Timothy Vansickle

C

Excerpts From the *Standards for Educational and Psychological Testing*

By Committee to Develop Standards for Educational and Psychological Testing American Educational Research Association (AERA), American Psychological Association (APA), National Council on Measurement in Education (NCME) 1999

STANDARD

11.1   Prior to the adoption and use of a published test, the test user should study and evaluate the materials provided by the test developer. Of particular importance are those that summarize the test's purposes, specify the procedures for test administration, define the intended populations of test takers, and discuss the score interpretations for which validity and reliability data are available.

11.2   When a test is to be used for a purpose for which little or no documentation is available, the user is responsible for obtaining evidence of the test's validity and reliability for this purpose.

11.3   Responsibility for test use should be assumed by or delegated only to those individuals who have the training, professional credentials, and experience necessary to handle this responsibility. Any special qualifications for test administration or interpretation specified in the test manual should be met.

11.4   The test user should have a clear rationale for the intended uses of a test or evaluation procedure in terms of its validity and contribution to the assessment and decision-making process.

11.5   Those who have a legitimate interest in an assessment should be informed about the purposes of testing, how tests will be administered, the factors considered in scoring examinee responses, how the scores are typically used, how long the records will be retained, and to whom and under what conditions the records may be released.

11.6   Unless the circumstances clearly require that the test results be withheld, the test user is obligated to provide a timely report of the results that is understandable to the test taker and others entitled to receive this information.

11.7   Test users have the responsibility to protect the security of tests, to the extent that developers enjoin users to do so.

11.8   Test users have the responsibility to respect test copyrights.

11.9   Test users should remind test takers and others who have access to test materials that the legal rights of test publishers, including copyrights, and the legal obligations of other participants in the testing process may prohibit the disclosure of test items without specific authorization.

11.10   Test users should be alert to the possibility of scoring errors; they should arrange for rescoring if individual scores or aggregated data suggest the need for it.

11.11   If the integrity of a test taker's scores is challenged, local authorities, the test developer, or the test sponsor should inform the test takers of their relevant rights, including the possibility of appeal and representation by counsel.

11.12   Test users or the sponsoring agency should explain to test takers their opportunities, if any, to retake an examination; users should also indicate whether the earlier as well as later scores will be reported to those entitled to receive the score reports.

11.13   When test-taking strategies that are unrelated to the domain being measured are found to enhance or adversely affect test performance significantly, these strategies and their implications should be explained to all test takers before the test is administered. This may be done either in an information booklet or, if the explanation can be made briefly, along with the test directions.

11.14   Test users are obligated to protect the privacy of examinees and institutions that are involved in a measurement program, unless a disclosure of private information is agreed upon, or is specifically authorized by law.

11.15   Test users should be alert to potential misinterpretations of test scores and to possible unintended consequences of test use; users should take steps to minimize or avoid foreseeable misinterpretations and unintended negative consequences.

11.16   Test users should verify periodically that their interpretations of test data continue to be appropriate, given any significant changes in their population of test takers, their modes of test administration, and their purposes in testing.

11.17   In situations where the public is entitled to receive a summary of test results, test users should formulate a policy regarding timely release of the results and apply that policy consistently over time.

11.18   When test results are released to the public or to policymakers, those responsible for the release should provide and explain any supplemental information that will minimize possible misinterpretations of the data.

11.19   When a test user contemplates an approved change in test format, mode of administration, instructions, or the language used in administering the test, the user should have a sound rationale for concluding that validity, reliability, and appropriateness of norms will not be compromised.

11.20   In educational, clinical, and counseling settings, a test taker's score should not be interpreted in isolation; collateral information that may lead to alternative explanations for the examinee's test performance should be considered.

11.21   Test users should not rely on computer-generated interpretations of test results unless they have the expertise to consider the appropriateness of these interpretations in individual cases.

11.22   When circumstances require that a test be administered in the same language to all examinees in a linguistically diverse population, the test user should investigate the validity of the score interpretations for test takers believed to have limited proficiency in the language of the test.

11.23   If a test is mandated for persons of a given age or all students in a particular grade, users should identify individuals whose disabilities or linguistic background indicates the need for special accommodations in test administration and ensure that these accommodations are employed.

11.24   When a major purpose of testing is to describe the status of a local, regional, or particular examinee population, the program criteria for inclusion or exclusion of individuals should be strictly adhered to.

D

Names and Acronyms of Tests Commonly Used by Counselors and the Names and Addresses of Publishers of Those Tests

Advisor Team, Inc.
340 Brannan Street, Suite 402
San Francisco, CA. 94107
Internet: www.advisorteam.org

Keirsey Temperament Sorter-II (KTS-II)

ACT, Inc.
(formerly American College Testing Program)
P.O. Box 1008
Iowa City, IA 52243-1008
Tel: 319-337-1000 • fax: 319-337-1578
Internet: www.act.org

ACT Assessment (The "ACT" test)
ASSET
Career Planning Survey (CPS)
COMPASS
DISCOVER
English as a Second Language Placement Test (ESL)
EXPLORE
PLAN Program
Proficiency Examination Program (PEP)
WorkKeys

AGS Publishing/Pearson Assessments
(formerly American Guidance Services)
P.O. Box 1416
Minneapolis, MN 55440
Tel: 800-627-7271 • Fax: 800-632-9011
Internet: www.pearsonassessments.com

Behavior Assessment System for Children, Second Edition (BASC-2)
Harrington–O'Shea Career Decision-Making System–Revised (CDM-R)
Kaufman Adolescent and Adult Intelligence Test (KAIT)
Kaufman Assessment Battery for Children, Second Edition (KABC-II)
Kaufman Brief Intelligence Test, Second Edition (KBIT-2)
Kaufman Functional Academic Skills Test (K-FAST)
Kaufman Test of Educational Achievement, Second Edition (KTEA-II)
Peabody Individual Achievement Test-Revised-Normative Update (PIAT-R/NU)
Peabody Picture Vocabulary Test–III (PPVT-III)
Test de Vocabulario en Imágenes Peabody (TVIP)
Vineland Adaptive Behavior Scales, Second Edition (Vineland-II)
Woodcock Reading Mastery Tests-Revised-Normative Update (WRMT-R/NU)

The Ball Foundation
800 Roosevelt Road C-120, Suite E 200
Glen Ellyn, IL 60137
Tel: 800-469-TEST • fax: 6630-469-6279
Internet: www.careervision.org

Ball Aptitude Battery (BAB)

CPP, Inc.

(formerly Consulting Psychologists Press)
1055 Joaquin Road, 2nd Floor
Mountain View, CA 94043
Tel: 800-624-1765 • fax: 650-969-8608
Internet: www.cpp.com

Adjective Check List (ACL)
California Psychological Inventory (CPI)
Career Beliefs Inventory (CBI)
Career Factors Inventory (CFI)
FIRO Awareness Scales (FIRO) [Fie-Roe]
Fundamental Interpersonal Relations
    Orientation—Behavior (FIRO-B)
Guilford–Zimmerman Temperament
    Survey (GZTS)
Myers–Briggs Type Indicator (MBTI)
Problem Solving Inventory (PSI)
Rokeach Value Survey
Skills Confidence Inventory (SCI)
Strong Interest Inventory (Strong)
Thomas–Kilman Conflict Mode
    Instrument (TKI)
Values Scale (VS)

CTB/McGraw-Hill

20 Ryan Ranch Road
Monterey, CA 93940-5703
Tel: 800-538-9547• fax: 800-282-0266
Internet: www.ctb.com

Adult Language Assessment Scales
    (Adult LAS)
Primary Test of Cognitive Skills (PTCS)
TerraNova, 2nd Ed. (TerraNova CAT)
TerraNova Comprehensive Tests of Basic
    Skills (TerraNova CTBS)
Test of Cognitive Skills, 2nd Ed. (TCS/2)
Tests of Adult Basic Education 9 & 10
    (TABE 9&10)

Educational and Industrial Testing Service (EdITS)

P.O. Box 7234
San Diego, CA 92167
Tel: 800-416-1666 • fax: 619-226-1666
Internet: www.edits.net

Career Ability Placement Survey (CAPS)
Career Occupational Preference System
    Interest Inventory (COPS)
Career Orientation Placement and
    Evaluation Survey (COPES)
Comrey Personality Scales (CPS)
Dimensions of Self-Concept (DOSC)
Eysenck Personality
    Questionnaire–Revised (EPQ-R)
Junior Eysenck Personality
    Questionnaire—Revised (JEPQ-R)

Multiple Affect Adjective Check
    List–Revised (MAACL-R)
Personal Orientation Inventory (POI)
School Environment Preference Survey
    (SEPS)
Study Attitudes and Methods Survey
    (SAMS)

Educational and Psychological Consultants, Inc.

1715 W. Worley, Suite A
Columbia, MO 65203-2603
Tel: 573-446-6232 • fax: 573-446-8532
Internet: www.epc-psi.com

Personal Styles Inventory

Educational Testing Service (ETS)

Rosedale Road
Princeton, NJ 08541
Tel: 609-921-9000
Internet: www.ets.org

Academic Profile
Advanced Placement Program (AP)
College Level Examination Program
    (CLEP)
Graduate Record Examinations (GRE)
Preliminary Scholastic Aptitude Test (PSAT)
Major Field Tests (MFTs)
Measure of Academic Proficiency &
    Progress (MAPP)
National Assessment of Educational
    Progress (NAEP)
SAT Reasoning Test
SAT Subject Tests
Test of English as a Foreign Language
    (TOEFL)

H&H Publishing Co., Inc.

1231 Kapp Drive
Clearwater, FL 33765
Tel: 800-366-4079 • fax: 727-442-2195
Internet: www.hhpublishing.com

Learning and Study Strategies Inventory
    (LASSI)
Perceptions, Expectations, Emotions, and
    Knowledge about college (PEEK)
Technology and Internet Assessment (TIA)
Working

Harcourt Assessment, Inc.

(Includes The Psychological Corporation)
19500 Bulverde Road
San Antonio, TX 78259
Tel: 800-211-8378 • fax: 800-232-1223
Internet: www.harcourtassessment.com

Adaptive Behavior Assessment
    System–Second Edition (ABAS-II)

Adult Basic Learning Examination, 2nd
Ed. (ABLE-II)
Alzheimer's Quick Test
Beck Anxiety Inventory (BAI)
Beck Depression Inventory–II (BDI-II)
Beck Youth Inventories–Second Edition
(BYI-II)
Beta III
Bennett Mechanical Comprehension
Test–Second Edition
Brown Attention-Deficit Disorder Scales
(Brown ADD Scales)
Bully Victimization Scales (BVS)
Career Interest Inventory (CII)
Differential Ability Scales–Second Edition
(DAS-II)
Differential Aptitude Tests (DAT)
Dynamic Assessment of Test
Accommodations (DATA)
Gifted Rating Scales (GRS)
Metropolitan Achievement Tests, 8th Ed.
(METROPOLITAN8)
Miller Analogies Test (MAT)
Mooney Problem Checklists
Naglieri Nonverbal Ability Test (NNAT)
Otis–Lennon School Ability Test, 8th Ed.
(OLSAT8)
Pharmacy College Admission Test (PCAT)
Raven's Progressive Matrices
Resiliency Scales for Adolescents (RSA)
Rotter Incomplete Sentences Blank,
Second Edition (RISB)
Stanford Achievement Tests, 10th Ed.
(Stanford10)
Thematic Apperception Test (TAT)
Values Arrangement List (VAL)
Watson–Glaser Critical Thinking Appraisal
(WGCTA)
Wechsler Abbreviated Scale of Intelligence
(WASI)
Wechsler Individual Achievement Test-II
(WIAT-II)
Wechsler Adult Intelligence Scale–III
(WAIS-III)
Wechsler Intelligence Scale for
Children–IV (WISC-IV)
Wechsler Memory Scale–III (WMS-III)
Wechsler Nonverbal Scale of Ability
(WNV)
Wechsler Preschool and Primary Scale of
Intelligence–Third Edition (WPPSI-III)
Wide Range Interest–Opinion Test-2
(WRIOT2)

Hogan Assessment Systems

2622 East 21st Street
Tulsa, OK 74114

Tel: 800-756-0632 • fax: 918-749-0635
Internet: www.hoganassessments.com

Hogan Development Survey (HDS)
Hogan Personality Inventory (HPI)
Motives, Values, Preferences Inventory
(MVPI)

Hogrefe & Huber Publishers, Inc.

218 Main Street, Suite 485
Kirkland, WA 98033
Tel: 866-823-4726 • fax: 6173546875
Internet: www.hhpub.com

d2 Test of Attention
Family System Test (FAST)
Rorschach Inkblot Test

Inflexxion, Inc.

320 Needham St., Suite 100
Newton, MA 02464
Tel: 800-848-3895 • fax: 617-332-1820
Internet: www.inflexxion.com

Addiction Severity Index: Multimedia
Version
Health Habits Survey

Institute for Personality and Ability Testing Incorporated (IPAT)

P.O. Box 1188
Champaign, IL 61824-1188
Tel: 800-225-4728
Internet: www.ipat.com

Adult Personality Inventory
Children's Personality Questionnaire
Clinical Analysis Questionnaire (CAQ)
Culture Fair Intelligence Tests
Early School Personality Questionnaire
High School Personality Questionnaire
IPAT Work Styles Inventory
PsychEval Personality Questionnaire
(PEPQ)
16 Personality Factor Questionnaire (16 PF)

Mind Garden, Inc.

855 Oak Grove Ave., Suite 215
Menlo Park, CA 94025
Tel: 650-322-6300 • fax: 650-322-6398
Internet: www.mindgarden.com

Assessment of Personal Goals
Barron-Welsh Art Scale
Bem Sex-Role Inventory (BSRI)
Coopersmith Self Esteem Inventory
Coping Resources Inventory (CRI)
Enright Forgiveness Inventory
Family Environment Scale
Five Factor Wellness Inventory

Hoffman Vocational Values Scale
Multifactor Leadership Questionnaire
(MLQ)
Older Persons Counseling Needs Survey
Social Skills Inventory
State–Trait Anxiety Inventory (STAI)
State–Trait Anxiety Inventory for Children
(STAIC)
Test Anxiety Inventory
University Residence Environment Scale
(URES)
Ways of Coping Questionnaire
Wellness Evaluation of Life Style (WEL)

MHS (Multi-Health Systems, Inc.)

P.O. Box 950
North Tonawanda, NY 14120-0950
Tel: 800-456-3003 • fax: 800-540-4484
Internet: www.mhs.com

Anger Disorders Scale (ADS)
BarOn Emotional Quotient Inventory
(BarOn EQ-I)
Children's Depression Inventory (CDI)
Butcher Treatment Planning Inventory
(BPTI)
Conners' Adult ADHD Rating Scales
(CAARS)
Conners' Continuous Performance Test II
(CDT-II)
Conners' Rating Scales–Revised (CRS-R)
Coping Inventory for Stressful Situation
(CISS)
Coping with Health Injuries and Problems
(CHIP)
Dyadic Adjustment Scale (DAS)
Family Assessment Measure III (FAM-III)
Hare Psychopathy Checklist–Revised: 2nd
Edition (Hare PCL-R: 2nd Ed.)
Holden Psychological Screening Inventory
(HPSI)
Mayer-Salovey-Caruso Emotional
Intelligence Test (MSCEIT)
Multidimensional Anxiety Scale for
Children–Revised (MASC-R)
Profile of Mood States (POMS)
Social Problem Solving Inventory—
Revised (SPSI–R)

National Career Assessment Services, Inc.

P.O. Box 277
Adel, IA 50003
Tel: 800-314-8972 • fax: 515-993-5422
Internet: www.ncasi.com

Kuder Career Search With Person Match
(KCS)

Kuder General Interest Survey (KGIS)
Kuder Occupational Interest Survey
(KOIS)
Work Values Inventory–Revised (WVI-R)

Pearson Assessments

P.O. Box 1416
Minneapolis, MN 55440
Tel: 800-NCS-7271 • fax: 800-632-9011
Internet: www.pearsonassessments.com

Alcohol Use Inventory (AUI)
Basic Achievement Skills Inventory
(BASI)
Battery for Health Improvement 2 (BHI 2)
Brief Battery for Health Improvement 2
(BBHI 2)
Brief Symptom Inventory (BSI)
Brief Symptom Inventory 18 (BSI 18)
Campbell Interest and Skill Survey (CISS)
Career Assessment Inventory–Enhanced
Version (CAI-EV)
Career Assessment Inventory–Vocational
Version (CAI-VV)
General Ability Measures for Adults
(GAMA)
IDEAS: Interest Determination,
Exploration and Assessment System
Millon Adolescent Clinical Inventory
(MACI)
Millon Adolescent Personality Inventory
(MAPI)
Millon Clinical Multiaxial Inventory–III
(MCMI-III)
Millon Index of Personality
Styles–Revised (MIPS-R)
Millon Pre-Adolescent Clinical Inventory
(M-PACI)
Minnesota Multiphasic Personality
Inventory–2 (MMPI-2)
Minnesota Multiphasic Personality
Inventory–Adolescent (MMPI-A)
Posttraumatic Stress Diagnostic Scale (PDS)
Quality of Life Inventory (QOLI)
Quickview Social History
Symptom Checklist–90–Revised
(SCL-90-R)

PRO-ED

8700 Shoal Creek Boulevard
Austin, TX 78757-6897
Tel: 800-897-3202 • fax: 800-397-7633
Internet: www.proedinc.com

Comprehensive Test of Non-Verbal
Intelligence (CTONI)
Multidimensional Self Concept Scale
(MSCS)

Occupational Aptitude Survey and Interest Schedule-Third Edition (OASIS-3)
Self Esteem Index (SEI)
Test of Nonverbal Intelligence–3rd Ed. (TONI-3)

Psychological Assessment Resources (PAR)

16204 N. Florida Ave.
Lutz, FL 33549
Tel: 800-331-TEST • fax: 800-727-9329
Internet: www.parinc.com

ADHD Symptoms Rating Scale (ADHD-SRS)
Adolescent Drinking Index (ADI)
Career Attitudes and Strategies Inventory (CASI)
Career Decision Scale (CDS)
Career Thoughts Inventory (CTI)
Clinical Assessment of Attention Deficit-Child (CAT-C)
Clinical Assessment of Depression (CAD)
Clinical Assessment Scales for the Elderly (CASE)
College Adjustment Scales (CAS)
Coping Responses Inventory (CRI)
Dementia Rating Scale–2 (DRS-2)
Eating Disorder Inventory–3 (EDI-3)
Employee Assistance Program Inventory (EAPI)
Hamilton Depression Inventory (HDI)
Interpersonal Adjective Scales (IAS)
Life Stressors and Social Resources Inventories (LISRES)
Mental Status Checklists
Mini-Mental State Examination (MMSE)
My Vocational Situation (MVS)
NEO Five-Factor Inventory (NEO-FFI)
NEO-4
NEO Personality Inventory–Revised (NEO PI-R)
Occupational Stress Inventory–R (OSI-R)
OMNI Personality Inventory
Parenting Stress Index, 3rd Edition (PSI)
Personal History Checklists
Personality Assessment Inventory (PAI)
Personality Assessment Screener (PAS)
Position Classification Inventory (PCI)
Reynolds Intellectual Assessment Scales (RIAS)
Self-Directed Search-4th Ed. (SDS)
Social Behavior Assessment Inventory (SBAI)
State–Trait Anger Expression Inventory–2 (STAXI-2)
Suicidal Ideation Questionnaire (SIQ)

Vocational Preference Inventory (VPI)
Wide Range Achievement Test–Expanded (WRAT-Expanded)
Wide Range Achievement Test 4 (WRAT4)
Wide Range Intelligence Test (WRIT)

The Psychological Corporation (Psych Corp)

(*See* Harcourt Assessment, Inc.)

Psychological Publications, Inc.

P.O. Box 3577
Thousand Oaks, CA 91359-0577
Tel: 800-345-TEST • fax: 805-527- 9266
Internet: www.TJTA.com

Family Relationship Inventory (FRI)
Taylor–Johnson Temperament Analysis (TJTA)

Research Center for Children, Youth, & Families

One South Prospect Street
Burlington, VT 05401-3456
Fax : 802-264-6433
Internet: www.ASEBA.org

Achenbach System of Empirically Based Assessment (ASEBA)

Riverside Publishing Company

425 Spring Lake Drive
Itasca, IL 60143-2079
Tel: 800-323-9540 • fax: 630-467-7192
Internet: www. riverpub.com

Bender Visual-Motor Gestalt Test II (Bender-Gestalt II)
Cognitive Abilities Test (CogAT)
Das–Naglieri Cognitive Assessment System (CAS)
Iowa Tests of Basic Skills (ITBS)
Iowa Tests of Educational Development (ITED)
Nelson–Denny Reading Test
Scales of Independent Behavior–Revised (SIB-R)
Stanford–Binet Intelligence Scale-5 (Stanford–Binet 5)
Universal Nonverbal Intelligence Test (UNIT)
Woodcock–Johnson III Tests of Achievement
Woodcock–Johnson III Tests of Cognitive Abilities

The SASSI Institute

201 Camelot Lane
Springville, IN 47462
Tel: 800-726-0526 • fax: 800-546-7995
Internet: www.sassi.com

Adolescent SASSI (SASSI-A2)
Substance Abuse Subtle Screening
Inventory–3 (SASSI-3)

Scholastic Testing Service Incorporated

480 Meyer Road
Bensenville, IL 60106-1617
Tel: 800-642- 6787 • fax: 866-766-8054
Internet: www.ststesting.com
Educational Development Series

Hall Occupational Orientation Inventories,
4th ed. (HOOI)
Kuhlman Anderson Tests (KA)
Torrance Tests of Creative Thinking
(TTCT)

Sigma Assessment Systems Inc.

P.O. Box 610984
Port Huron, MI 48061-0984
Tel: 800-265-1285 • fax: 800-361-9411
Internet: www.sigmaassessmentsystems.com

Ashland Interest Assessment (AIA)
Basic Personality Inventory (BPI)
Career Directions Inventory (CDI)
Jackson Personality Inventory–Revised
(JPI-R)
Jackson Vocational Interest Survey (JVIS)
Multidimensional Aptitude Battery–II
(MAB-II)
Nonverbal Personality Questionnaire
(NPQ)
Personality Research Form (PRF)
Psychological Screening Inventory (PSI)
Six Factor Personality Questionnaire
(SPFQ)
Survey of Work Styles (SWS)

Slosson Educational Publications, Inc.

P.O. Box 544
East Aurora, NY 14052
Tel: 888-756-7766 • fax: 716-655-3840
Internet: www.slosson.com

Slosson Intelligence Test–Revised
(SIT-R3)
Slosson Intelligence Test–Primary
(SIT-P)

Stoelting Company

620 Wheat Lane
Wood Dale IL, 60191
Tel: 630-860-9700• fax:630-860-9775
Internet:www.stoeltingco.com

Leiter International Performance
Scale–Revised (Leiter-R)
Merrill-Palmer–Revised Scales of
Development (Merrill-Palmer-R)
Stoelting Brief Intelligence Test (S-BIT)

U.S. Department of Labor, Employment and Training Administration

200 Constitution Avenue, NW
Washington, DC 20213
Tel: 202-535-0157
Internet: www.onetcenter.org

O*NET Ability Profiler
O*NET Interest Profiler
O*NET Work Importance Profiler
O*NET Work Importance Locator

U.S. Military Entrance Processing Command (USMEPCOM)

2500 Green Bay Road
North Chicago, IL 60064-3094
Tel: 800-323-0513
Internet: www.asvabprogram.com

Armed Services Vocational Aptitude
Battery (ASVAB)

Valpar International Corporation

P.O. Box 5767
Tucson, AZ 85703
Tel: 800-528-7070 • fax: 520-292-9755
Internet: www.valparint.com

Aviator 3
Magellan
SIGI-3
Valpar Test of Essential Skills (VTES)

Vocational Research Institute

1528 Walnut St., Suite 1502
Philadelphia, PA 19102-3619
Tel: 800-874-5387
Internet: www.vri.org

CareerScope Interest Inventory
Apticom

Vocopher: The Online Career Collaboratory

Internet: www.vocopher.com

Adult Career Concerns Inventory (ACCI)
Career Development Inventory (CDI)

Career Mastery Inventory (CMAS)
(Projected 2006)
Career Maturity Inventory (CMI)
(Projected 2006)
Salience Inventory (SI) (Projected 2006)

Western Psychological Services

12031 Wilshire Boulevard
Los Angeles, CA 90025-1251
Tel: 800-648-8857 • fax: 310-478-7838
Internet: www.wpspublish.com

Aggression Questionnaire (AQ)
House–Tree–Person Projective Drawing
Technique (H-T-P)
Learning Styles Inventory (LSI)
Marital Satisfaction Inventory–Revised
(MSI-R)
Novaco Anger Scale and Provocation
Inventory (NAS-PI)
Parent–Child Relationship Inventory
(PCRI)
Personal Experience Inventory (PEI)
Personal Experience Screening
Questionnaire (PESQ)

Personality Inventory for Children, Second
Edition (PIC-2)
Personality Inventory for Youth (PIY)
Piers–Harris Children's Self-Concept
Scale, Second Edition (Piers-Harris 2)
Roberts Apperception Test for
Children–Second Edition (Roberts-2)
Shipley Institute of Living Scale
Stress Profile
Student Adaptation to College
Questionnaire (SACQ)
Suicide Probability Scale (SPS)
Tennessee Self-Concept Scale–2 (TSCS:2)

Wide Range, Inc.

(See Psychological Assessment Resources)

Wonderlic, Inc.

1795 N. Butterfield Road
Libertyville, IL 60048
Tel: 800-323-3742 • fax: 847-680-9492
Internet: www.wonderlic.com

Wonderlic Basic Skills Test (WBST)
Wonderlic Personnel Test (WPT)

Note. Tests likely to be used by counselors are listed above under their publishers. Many of the more commonly used instruments are, in addition, promoted and marketed by a number of other publishers.

Permissions

We are grateful to the following authors and publishers for permission to reproduce sample items from the assessment instruments named below:

Career Attitudes and Strategies Inventory by J. L. Holland and G. D. Gottfredson. Adapted and reproduced by special permission of the publisher, Psychological Assessment Resources, Inc., Lutz, FL 33549. Copyright © 1994 by PAR, Inc. Further reproduction is prohibited without permission from PAR, Inc.

Career Orientation Placement and Evaluation Survey (COPES) by L. Knapp, L. Knapp-Lee, and R. Knapp. Published by Educational and Industrial Testing Service (EdITS), San Diego, CA. Copyright © 1995. Reproduced with permission.

Eating Attitudes Test by David M. Garner and Paul E. Garfinkel (1979). Published by Cambridge University Press. Copyright © 1979. Reproduced with permission.

Kuder Career Search With Person Match[TM] by National Career Assessment Services, Inc[TM]. Reproduced with permission. Copyright © 1999. All rights reserved.

Minnesota Multiphasic Personality Inventory–2 (MMPI-2). Copyright © by the Regents of the University of Minnesota 1942, 1943 (renewed 1970), 1989. This booklet 1989. Reproduced with permission.

SCL-90-R by Leonard R. Derogatis. Copyright © 1975, 1983, 1990 by L. R. Derogatis, PhD, Towson, MD. Reproduced with permission. All rights reserved.

References

Abrahams, S., & Balkin, R. S. (2006). A review of the Five Factor Wellness Inventory. *Association for Assessment in Counseling and Education Newsnotes, 46,* 2–3.

Achenbach, T. M., Rescorla, L. A., McConaughey, S. H., Pecora, P. J., Wetherbee, K. M., & Ruffle, T. M. (2003). *Achenbach System of Empirically Based Assessment (ASEBA).* Burlington, VT: Research Center for Children, Youth, and Families.

ACT, Inc. (1995). *Technical manual: Revised unisex edition of the ACT Interest Inventory (UNIACT).* Iowa City, IA: Author.

ACT, Inc. (2000a). *Career Planning Survey technical manual.* Iowa City, IA: Author.

ACT, Inc. (2000b). *The World-of-Work Map* (3rd ed., Counselor version). Iowa City, IA: Author.

ACT, Inc. (2004, autumn). *National ACT scores: ACTIVITY.* Iowa City, IA: Author.

ACT, Inc. (2005a). *ACT assessment-related programs and services 2005–2006.* Iowa City, IA: Author.

ACT, Inc. (2005b). *DISCOVER: Career guidance and information system.* Retrieved August 9, 2005, from http://www.act.org/discover

ACT, Inc. (2005c). *WorkKeys occupational profiles.* Retrieved June 8, 2005, from http://www.act.org/workkeys/profiles/occuprof/wwmprof

ACT, Inc. (2005d) *WorkKeys scale score interpretation guide.* Iowa City, IA: Author.

ACT, Inc. (2005e). *The WorkKeys system.* Retrieved June 8, 2005, from http://www.act.org/workkeys

ACT, Inc. (2005f). *WorkKeys technical manuals.* Manuscripts in preparation.

ACT, Inc. (2006a). *The ASSET student success system.* Retrieved April 4, 2006, from http://www.act.org/asset

ACT, Inc. (2006b). *COMPASS with ESL and e-Write.* Retrieved April 14, 2006, from http://www.act.org/ed career/assess.html

ACT, Inc. (2006c). *It's all about productivity: Expanded WorkKeys system gives insight into job performance.* Retrieved July 11, 2006, from http://www.act.org/news/releases/2006/06-23-06.html

Adams, R. S., & Tracey, T. J. G. (2004). Three versions of the Interpersonal Adjective Scales and their fit to the circumplex model. *Assessment, 11,* 263–270.

Aegisdóttir, S., White, M. J., Spengler, P. M., Maugherman, A. S., Anderson, L. A., Cook, R. S., et al. (2006). The meta-analysis of clinical judgment project: Fifty-six years of accumulated research on clinical versus statistical prediction. *The Counseling Psychologist, 34,* 341–382.

Aiken, L. R. (1999). *Personality assessment methods and practices* (3rd ed.). Seattle, WA: Hogrefe & Huber.

Aiken, L. R. (2000). *Psychological testing and assessment.* Needham Heights, MA: Allyn & Bacon.

Albanese, M. A. (2003). Mini-Mental State Examination. In B. S. Plake, J. C. Impara, & R. A. Spies (Eds.), *The fifteenth mental measurements yearbook* (pp. 589–590). Lincoln, NE: Buros Mental Measurements Institute.

Alberti, R., & Emmons, M. (2001). *Your perfect right: Assertiveness and equality in your life and relationships* (8th ed.). Atascadero, CA: Impact.

Albion, M. J., & Fogarty, G. J. (2002). Factors influencing career decision making in adolescents and adults. *Journal of Career Assessment, 10,* 91–126.

Alexrod, B. N. (2002). Validity of the WASI and other very short forms of estimating intelligence. *Assessment, 9,* 17–23.

Alfonso, V. C., Flanagan, D. P., & Radwan, S. (2005). The impact of the Cattell-Horn-Carroll theory on test development and interpretation of cognitive and academic abilities. In D. P. Flanagan & P. L. Harrison (Eds.), *Contemporary intellectual assessment* (pp. 185–202). New York: Guilford Press.

Allen, J. P., & Wilson, V. B. (Eds.). (2003). *Assessing alcohol problems: A guide for clinicians and researchers* (2nd ed.). Rockville, MD: National Institute on Alcohol Abuse and Alcoholism.

Allport, G. W., & Vernon, P. E. (1931). A test of personal values. *Journal of Abnormal and Social Psychology, 26,* 231–248.

Allport, G. W., Vernon, P. E., & Lindzey, G. (1960). *Manual for Study of Values* (3rd ed.). Boston: Houghton Mifflin.

Alvarez-Rayón, G., Mancilla-Díaz, J. M., Vázquez-Arévalo, R., Unikel-Santoncini, C., Caballero-Romo, A., & Mercado-Corona, D. (2004). Validity of the Eating Attitudes Test: A study of Mexican eating disorders patients. *Eating and Weight Disorders, 9,* 243–248.

American Academy of Pediatrics. (2000). Diagnosis and evaluation of the child with attention-deficit/hyperactivity disorder. *Pediatrics, 105,* 1158–1170.

American Association for Geriatric Psychiatry, Alzheimer's Association, & American Geriatrics Society. (1997). Consensus statement: Diagnosis and treatment of Alzheimer disease and related disorders. *Journal of the American Medical Association, 278,* 1363–1371.

American Association of Suicidology. (2004, December). *Suicide in the U.S.A.* Retrieved March 13, 2006, from http://www.suicidology.org/associations/1045/files/Suicide2002.pdf

American Association on Mental Retardation. (2006). *Supports Intensity Scale.* Retrieved March 24, 2006, from www.siswebsite.org

American College Testing Program. (1999). *Using the ACT in advising and course placement 1999–2000.* Iowa City, IA: Author.

American Counseling Association. (2003). *Standards for qualifications of test users.* Alexandria, VA: Author.

American Counseling Association. (2005). *ACA code of ethics.* Alexandria, VA: Author.

American Educational Research Association. (2000). *AERA position statement concerning high-stakes testing in preK–12 education.* Washington, DC: Author.

American Educational Research Association, American Psychological Association, & National Council on Measurement in Education. (1999). *Standards for educational and psychological testing.* Washington, DC: American Educational Research Association.

American Guidance Service. (2005) *KABC-II sampler.* Circle Pines, MN: Author.

American Mental Health Counselors Association. (2001). Code of ethics of the American Mental Health Counselors Association: 2000 revision. *Journal of Mental Health Counseling, 23,* 2–21.

American Mental Health Counselors Association. (2004). *Standards for assessment in mental health counseling.* Alexandria, VA: Author.

American Psychiatric Association. (2000a). *Diagnostic and statistical manual of mental disorders* (4th ed., text rev.). Washington, DC: Author.

American Psychiatric Association. (2000b). *Practice guidelines for the treatment of patients with eating disorders* (2nd ed.). Retrieved April 29, 2006, from http://www.psych.org/psych_pract/treatg/pg/eating_revisebook_index.cfm

American Psychiatric Association. (2000c). *Quick reference to the diagnostic criteria from DSM-IV-TR.* Washington, DC: Author.

American Psychiatric Association. (2003). *Practice guidelines for the assessment and treatment of patients with suicidal behaviors.* Arlington, VA: Author. Retrieved March 11, 2006, from http://www.psych.org/psych_pract/treatg/pg/pg_suicidalbehaviors.pdf

American Psychological Association. (1996). Statement on the disclosure of test data. *American Psychologist, 51,* 644–648.

American Psychological Association. (1998) Guidelines for the evaluation of dementia and age-related cognitive decline. *American Psychologist, 53,* 1298–1303.

American Psychological Association. (2002). *Ethical principles of psychologists and code of conduct. American Psychologist, 57,* 1060–1073.

American Psychological Association. (2004). Guidelines for psychological practices with older adults. *American Psychologist, 59,* 236–260.

American Psychological Association. (2005a). *Appropriate use of high-stakes testing in our nation's schools.* Washington, DC: Author.

American Psychological Association. (2005b). *Guidelines for providers of psychological services to ethnic, linguistic, and culturally diverse populations.* Retrieved November 14, 2005, from www.apa.org/pi/oema/guide.html

American Psychological Association. (2005c). *HIPAA for psychologists.* Retrieved November 16, 2005, from http://www.calpsychlink.org/hipaa/files/hipaa-knapp.pdf

American Rehabilitation Counseling Association. (2003). *Pre-employment testing and the ADA.* Alexandria, VA: Author.

American Rehabilitation Counseling Association, Commission on Rehabilitation Counselor Certification, & National Rehabilitation Counseling Association. (2002). *Code of professional ethics for rehabilitation counselors.* Chicago: Author.

American School Counselor Association. (2004). *Ethical standards for school counselors.* Alexandria, VA: Author.

American School Counselor Association & Association for Assessment in Counseling. (1998). *Competencies in assessment and evaluation for school counselors.* Alexandria, VA: Author.

Americans With Disabilities Act of 1990, Pub. L. No. 101–336, § 2, 104 Stat. 328 (1991).

Anastasi, A. (1988). *Psychological testing* (6th ed.). New York: Macmillan.

Anastasi, A. (1992). What counselors should know about the use and interpretation of psychological tests. *Journal of Counseling & Development, 70,* 610–615.

Anastasi, A., & Urbina, S. (1997). *Psychological testing* (7th ed.). Upper Saddle River, NJ: Prentice Hall.

Andary, L., Stolk, Y., & Klimidis, S. (2003) *Assessing mental health across cultures.* Bowen Hills, Queensland, Australia: Australian Academic Press.

Anderson, W. (1995). Ethnic and cross-cultural differences on the MMPI-2. In J. C. Duckworth & W. P. Anderson (Eds.), *MMPI and MMPI-2 interpretation manual for counselors and clinicians* (4th ed., pp. 439–460). Bristol, PA: Accelerated Development.

Annis, H. M., Graham, J. M., & Davis, C. S. (1987). *Inventory of Drinking Situations.* Toronto, Ontario, Canada: Addiction Research Foundation.

Anton, W. D., & Reed, J. R. (1991). *College Adjustment Scales.* Odessa, FL: Psychological Assessment Resources.

Arbisi, P. A., Ben-Porath, Y. S., & McNulty, J. (2002). A comparison of MMPI-2 validity in African American and Caucasian psychiatric patients. *Psychological Assessment, 14,* 3–15.

Arbona, C. (1990). Career counseling research and Hispanics: A review of the literature. *The Counseling Psychologist, 18,* 300–323.

Arbona, C. (1998). Psychological assessment: Multicultural or universal? *The Counseling Psychologist, 26,* 911–921.

Archer, R. P. (2005). *MMPI-A: Assessing adolescent psychopathology* (3rd ed.). Mahwah, NJ: Erlbaum.

Archer, R. P., & Newsom, C. R. (2000). Psychological test usage with adolescent clients: Survey update. *Assessment, 7,* 227–235.

Association for Assessment in Counseling. (2002). *Applying the standards for educational and psychological testing—What counselors need to know* (Monograph). Alexandria, VA: Author.

Association for Assessment in Counseling. (2003). *Standards for multicultural assessments* (2nd ed.). Alexandria, VA: Author.

Association for Assessment in Counseling and Education. (2003a). *A parent's survival guide to school testing* (Monograph). Alexandria, VA: Author.

Association for Assessment in Counseling and Education. (2003b). *Responsibilities of users of standardized tests* (3rd ed.). Alexandria, VA: Author.

Association for Multicultural Counseling and Development. (1992). *Multicultural counseling competencies and standards.* Alexandria, VA: American Counseling Association.

Association of American Medical Colleges. (2000). *Medical College Admission Test.* Washington, DC: Author.

Association of Test Publishers. (2005). *Policy statement on fair access to psychological tests.* Retrieved July 13, 2006, from http://www.testpublishers.org/pubpol.htm

Attkisson, C. C., & Greenfield, T. K. (2004). The UCSF Client Satisfaction Scales: I. The Client Satisfaction Questionnaire-8. In M. E. Maruish (Ed.), *The use of psychological testing for treatment planning and outcomes assessment: Volume 3. Instruments for adults* (3rd ed., pp. 799–811). Mahwah, NJ: Erlbaum.

Azar, B. (1999, November). Fairness a challenge when developing special-needs tests. *APA Monitor, 30,* 31.

Bain, S. K., & Allin, J. D. (2005) Review of the Stanford–Binet Intelligence Scales, fifth edition. *Journal of Psychoeducational Assessment, 23,* 87–95.

Baker, H. E. (2002). Reducing adolescent career indecision: The ASVAB Career Exploration Program. *The Career Development Quarterly, 50,* 359–370.

Ball Foundation. (2002). *Ball Career System technical manual.* Glen Ellyn, IL: Author.

Bandura, A. (1986). *Social foundations of thought and action.* Englewood Cliffs, NJ: Prentice Hall.

Bandura, A. (1997). *Self-efficacy: The exercise of self-control.* New York: Freeman.

Bardos, A. N. (2004). *Information package for BASI.* Minneapolis, MN: Pearson Assessments.

Barker, R. G. (1968). *Ecological psychology: Concepts and methods for studying the environment of human behavior.* Stanford, CA: Stanford University Press.

Barkley, R. A., & Murphy, K. R. (2006). *Attention-deficit hyperactivity disorder: A clinical workbook* (3rd ed.). New York: Guilford Press.

Barrett, G. V., & Depinet, R. L. (1991). A reconsideration of testing for competence rather than for intelligence. *American Psychologist, 46,* 1012–1024.

Barrios, B. A. (1988). On the changing nature of behavioral assessment. In A. S. Bellack & M. Hersen (Eds.), *Behavioral assessment: A practical handbook* (pp. 3–41). New York: Pergamon.

Barrons Educational Series. (2004). *Profiles of American colleges 2001.* Hauppauge, NY: Author.

Barthlow, D. L., Graham, J. R., Ben-Porath, Y. S., & McNulty, J. L. (1999). Incremental validity of the MMPI-2 content scales in an outpatient mental health setting. *Psychological Assessment, 11,* 39–47.

Bartling, H. C., & Hood, A. B. (1981). An 11-year follow-up of measured interest and vocational choice. *Journal of Counseling Psychology, 28,* 27–35.

Battle, C., Imber, S., Hoen-Saric, R., Stone, A., Nash, E., & Frank, J. (1966). Target complaints as criteria of improvement. *American Journal of Psychotherapy, 20,* 184–192.

Baxter-Magolda, M. B. (1992). *Knowing and reasoning in college: Gender related patterns in students' intellectual development.* San Francisco: Jossey-Bass.

Bauman, S. (2002). Review of Substance Abuse Subtle Screening Inventory–Adolescent 2 (SASSI-2). *Association for Assessment in Counseling & Development Newsnotes,* 40(1).

Bayne, R. (2005). *Critical reflections on MBTIReg: Theory and practice.* Gainesville, FL: Center for the Application of Type.

Beck, A. T. (1996). *Beck Depression Inventory: Second edition.* San Antonio, TX: Psychological Corporation.

Beck, A. T., & Steer, R. A. (1993). *Beck Anxiety Inventory manual.* San Antonio, TX: Psychological Corporation.

Beck, A. T., Steer, R. A., & Brown, G. K. (1996). *Beck Depression Inventory–II manual.* San Antonio, TX: Psychological Corporation.

Bellah, C. G. (2005). Review of the Beta III. In R. A. Spies & B. S. Plake (Eds.), *The sixteenth mental measurements yearbook* (pp. 142–144). Lincoln, NE: Buros Institute of Mental Measurements.

Benbow, C. P. (1988). Sex differences in mathematical reasoning ability in intellectually talented preadolescents: Their nature, effects and probable causes. *Behavioral and Brain Sciences, 11,* 169–232.

Bennett, G. K., Seashore, H. G., & Wesman, A. G. (1990). *Differential Aptitude Tests* (5th ed.). San Antonio, TX: Psychological Corporation.

Bennett, R. E., Rock, D. A., Kaplan, B. A., & Jirele, T. (1988). Psychometric characteristics. In W. W. Williamham, M. Ragosta, R. Bennett, H. Braun, D. A. Rock, & D. E. Powers (Eds.), *Testing handicapped people* (pp. 83–97). Needham Heights, MA: Allyn & Bacon.

Berman, L., Berman, J., Zicak, M. C., & Marley, C. (2002). Outcome measurement in sexual disorders. In W. W. IsHak, T. Burt, & L. I. Sederer (Eds.), *Outcome measurement in psychiatry: A critical review* (pp. 273–289). Washington, DC: American Psychiatric Publishing.

Berntson, G. G., & Cacioppo, J. T. (2006). Multilevel analysis: Physiological and biochemical measures. In M. Eid & E. Diener (Eds.), *Handbook of multimethod measurement in psychology* (pp. 157–172). Washington, DC: American Psychological Association.

Berven, N. L. (1980). Psychometric assessment in rehabilitation. In B. Bolton & D. W. Cook (Eds.), *Rehabilitation client assessment* (pp. 46–64). Baltimore: University Park Press.

Betz, N. E., Borgen, F. H., & Harmon, L. W. (1996). *Skills Confidence Inventory applications and technical guide.* Palo Alto, CA: Consulting Psychologists Press.

Betz, N. E., Borgen, F. H., Rottinghaus, P., Paulsen, A., Halper, C. R., & Harmon, L. W. (2003). The Expanded Skills Confidence Inventory: Measuring basic dimensions of vocational activity. *Journal of Vocational Behavior, 62,* 76–100.

Betz, N. E., & Hackett, G. (2006). Career self-efficacy theory: Back to the future. *Journal of Career Assessment, 14,* 3–11.

Betz, N. E., Klein, K. L., & Taylor, K. M. (1996). Evaluation of a short form of the Career Decision-Making Self-Efficacy Scale. *Journal of Career Assessment, 4,* 47–57.

Betz, N. E., & Luzzo, D. A. (1996). Career assessment and the Career Decision-Making Self-Efficacy Scale. *Journal of Career Assessment, 4,* 413–428.

Betz, N. E., & Rottinghaus, P. J. (2006). Current research on parallel measures of interests and confidence for basic dimensions of vocational activity. *Journal of Career Assessment, 14,* 56–76.

Betz, N. E., & Taylor, K. M. (1994). *Manual for the Career Decision-Making Self-Efficacy Scale.* Columbus: Ohio State University, Department of Psychology.

Beutler, L. E. (2000). David and Goliath: When empirical and clinical standards of practice meet. *American Psychologist, 55,* 997–1007.

Bieling, P. J., Antony, M. M., & Swinson, R. P. (1998). The State–Trait Anxiety Inventory, trait version: Structure and content re-examined. *Behaviour Research & Therapy, 36,* 777–788.

Blacher, J. H., Murray-Ward, M., & Uellendahl, G. E. (2005). School counselors and student assessment. *Professional School Counseling, 8,* 337–343.

Bobek, B. L., & Gore, P. A. (2004). *Inventory of Work-Relevant Values: 2001 revision* (ACT Research Report Series 2004-3). Iowa City, IA: ACT.

Boggs, K. R. (2002). Review of Campbell Interest and Skill Survey (CISS). In J. T. Kapes & E. A. Whitfield (Eds.), *A counselor's guide to career assessment instruments* (4th ed., pp. 194–201). Tulsa, OK: National Career Development Association.

Bolles, R. N. (2005). *What color is your parachute? 2006.* Berkeley, CA: Ten Speed Press.

Borgen, F., & Grutter, J. (2005). *Where do I go next? Using your Strong results to manage your career* (Rev. ed.). Mountain View, CA: CPP.

Borges, N. J., Gibson, D. D., & Karnani, R. M. (2005). Job satisfaction of physicians with congruent versus incongruent specialty choice. *Evaluation & the Health Professions, 28,* 400–413.

Boughner, S. R., Hayes, S. F., Bubenzer, D. L., & West, J. D. (1994). Use of standardized assessment instruments by marital and family therapists: A survey. *Journal of Marital and Family Therapy, 20,* 69–75.

Bourque, M. L. (2005). Leave no standardized test behind. In R. P. Phelps (Ed.), *Defending standardized testing* (pp. 227–253). Mahwah, NJ: Erlbaum.

Bowman, S. L. (1995). Career strategies and assessment issues for African-Americans. In F. T. L. Leong (Ed.), *Career development and vocational behavior of racial and ethnic minorities* (pp. 137–164). Mahwah, NJ: Erlbaum.

Bozionelos, N. (2004). Socio-economic background and computer use: The role of computer anxiety and computer experience in their relationship. *International Journal of Human-Computer Studies, 61,* 725–746.

Braden, J. P., & Hannah, J. M. (1998). Assessment of hearing-impaired and deaf children with the WISC-III. In A. Prifitera & D. H. Saklofske (Eds.), *WISC-III clinical use and interpretation* (pp. 175–201). San Diego, CA: Academic Press.

Bradley, L. J., Sexton, T. L., & Smith, H. B. (2005). The American Counseling Association Practice Research Network (ACA-PRN): A new research tool. *Journal of Counseling & Development, 83,* 488–491.

Bradley-Johnson, S., & Ekstrom, R. (1998). Visual impairments. In J. Sandoval, C. L. Frisby, K. F. Geisinger, J. D. Scheuneman, & J. R. Grenier (Eds.), *Test interpretation and diversity* (pp. 271–296). Washington, DC: American Psychological Association.

Brauer, B. A., Braden, J. P., Pollard, R. Q., & Hardy-Braz, S. T. (1998). Deaf and hard of hearing people. In J. Sandoval, C. L. Frisby, K. F. Geisinger, J. D. Scheuneman, & J. R. Grenier (Eds.), *Test interpretation and diversity* (pp. 297–315). Washington, DC: American Psychological Association.

Brener, N. D., Hassan, S. S., & Barrios, L. C. (2000). Suicidal ideation among college students in the United States. *Journal of Consulting and Clinical Psychology, 67,* 1004–1008.

Brent, F. (2001). Review of the Marital Satisfaction Inventory–Revised. In B. S. Plake & J. G. Impara (Eds.), *The fourteenth mental measurements yearbook* (pp. 710–712). Lincoln, NE: Buros Institute of Mental Measurements.

Brescia, W., & Fortune, J. C. (1989). Standardized testing of American Indian students. *The College Student Journal, 23,* 98–104.

Brickman, P., Rabinowitz, V. C., Karuza, J., Coates, D., Cohn, E., & Kidder, L. (1982). Models of helping and coping. *American Psychologist, 37,* 368–384.

Brookhart, S. M. (1995). Review of the Rokeach Value Survey. In J. D. Conoley & J. D. Impara (Eds.), *The twelfth mental measurements yearbook* (pp. 878–879). Lincoln, NE: Buros Institute of Mental Measurements.

Brookhart, S. M. (1998). Review of the Iowa Tests of Basic Skills Forms K, L, & M. In J. C. Impara & B. S. Plake (Eds.), *The thirteenth mental measurements yearbook* (pp. 539–542). Lincoln, NE: Buros Institute of Mental Measurements.

Brott, P. E. (2005). A constructivist look at life roles. *The Career Development Quarterly, 54,* 138–149.

Brown, D. (1995). A values-based approach to facilitating career transitions. *The Career Development Quarterly, 44,* 4–11.

Brown, D. (2002). The role of work and cultural values in occupational choice, satisfaction, and success: A theoretical statement. *Journal of Counseling & Development, 80,* 48–56.

Brown, L., Sherbenou, R. J., & Johnsen, S. K. (1997). *Test of Nonverbal Intelligence–Third Edition.* Austin, TX: Pro-Ed.

Brown, M. B. (1998). Review of the Career Attitudes and Strategies Inventory. In J. C. Impara & B. S. Plake (Eds.), *The thirteenth mental measurements yearbook* (pp. 182–183). Lincoln, NE: Buros Institute of Mental Measurements.

Brown, M. B. (2000). Diagnosis and treatment of children and adolescents with attention-deficit/hyperactivity disorder. *Journal of Counseling & Development, 78,* 195–203.

Brown, T. E. (1996). *The Brown Attention-Deficit Disorder Scales.* San Antonio, TX: Psychological Corporation.

Brown-Chidsey, R. (Ed.). (2005). *Assessment for intervention: A problem-solving approach.* New York: Guilford.

Bruns, D., & Disorbio, P. B. (2003). *Battery for Health Improvement 2 (BHI 2) manual.* Minneapolis, MN: NCS Pearson.

Buchanan, R. D. (2002). On not "giving psychology away": The Minnesota Multiphasic Personality Inventory and public controversy over testing in the 1960s. *History of Psychology, 5,* 284–309.

Buck, J. N. (1992). *House-Tree-Person Projective Drawing Technique H-T-P: Manual and interpretive guide.* Los Angeles: Western Psychological Services.

Budman, S. H. (2000). Behavioral health care dot.com and beyond: Computer-mediated communications in mental health and substance abuse treatment. *American Psychologist, 55,* 1290–1300.

Bugbee, A. C. (2005). Review of the Iowa Tests of Educational Development Forms A and B. In R. A. Spies & B. S. Plake (Eds), *The sixteenth mental measurements yearbook* (pp. 485–488) Lincoln, NE: Buros Institute of Mental Measurements.

Bunch, M. B. (2005). Review of Occupational Aptitude Survey and Interest Schedule–Third edition. In R. A. Spies & B. S. Plake (Eds.), *The sixteenth mental measurements yearbook* (pp. 712–715). Lincoln, NE: Buros Institute of Mental Measurements.

Burns, M. (2001). Review of Personality Assessment Screener. In B. S. Plake & J. C. Impara (Eds.), *The fourteenth mental measurements yearbook* (pp. 932–934). Lincoln, NE: Buros Institute of Mental Measurements.

Buros Institute of Mental Measurements. (2005). *Test reviews online!* Retrieved June 26, 2005, from http://buros.unl.edu/buros/jsp/search.jsp

Buros Institute of Mental Measurements. (2006). *Tests in print VII.* Lincoln, NE: Author.

Busacca, L. A., & Taber, B. J. (2002). The Career Maturity Inventory–Revised: A preliminary psychometric investigation. *Journal of Career Assessment, 10,* 441–455.

Busseri, M. A., & Tyler, J. D. (2004). Client-therapist agreement on target problems, working alliance, and counseling outcome. *Psychotherapy Research, 14,* 77–88.

Butcher, J. N. (Ed.). (1997). *Personality assessment in managed health care: Using the MMPI-2 in treatment planning.* New York: Oxford University Press.

Butcher, J. N. (2005). *A beginner's guide to the MMPI-2* (2nd ed.). Washington, DC: American Psychological Association.

Butcher, J. N., Ben-Porath, Y. S., Shondrick, D. D., Stafford, K. P., McNulty, J. L., Graham, J. R., et al. (2000). Cultural and subcultural factors in MMPI-2 interpretation. In J. N. Butcher (Ed.), *Basic sources on the MMPI-2* (pp. 501–536). Minneapolis: University of Minnesota Press.

Butcher, J. N., Graham, J. R., Ben-Porath, Y. S., Tellegen, A., & Dahlstrom, W. G. (2001). *MMPI-2 manual for administration, scoring, and interpretation* (Rev. ed.). Minneapolis: University of Minnesota Press.

Butcher, J. N., Graham, J. R., Williams, C. L., & Ben-Porath, Y. (1990). *Development and use of the MMPI-2 content scales.* Minneapolis: University of Minnesota Press.

Butcher, J. N., Williams, C. L., & Fowler, R. D. (2000). *Essentials of MMPI-2 and MMPI-A interpretation* (2nd ed.). Minneapolis: University of Minnesota Press.

Butler, T., & Waldroop, J. (2004). A function-centered model of interest assessment for business careers. *Journal of Career Assessment, 12,* 270–284.

Byrum, C. N., & Tsacoumis, S. (2005, November). *O*NET analysis occupational abilities ratings: Analysis Cycle 4 results.* Raleigh, NC: National Center for O*NET Development.

Cairo, P. C., Kritis, K. J., & Myers, R. M. (1996). Career assessment and the Adult Career Concerns Inventory. *Journal of Career Assessment, 4,* 189–204.

Camera, W., Nathan, J., & Puente, A. (2000). Psychological test usage: Implications in professional psychology. *Professional Psychology: Research and Practice, 31,* 141–154.

Camp, D. C. (2000). Career decision-making difficulties in high school students: A study of reliability and validity of the Career Decision Difficulties Questionnaire. *Dissertation Abstracts International, 61*(3), 893A.

Campbell, C. A., & Ashmore, R. J. (1995). The Slossan Intelligence Test–Revised (SIT-R). *Measurement and Evaluation in Counseling and Development, 28,* 116–118.

Campbell, D. P. (1993). A new integrated battery of psychological surveys. *Journal of Counseling & Development, 71,* 575–587.

Campbell, D. P. (2002).The history and development of the Campbell Interest and Skill Survey. *Journal of Career Assessment, 10,* 150–168.

Campbell, D. P., & Borgen, F. H. (1999). Holland's theory and the development of interest inventories. *Journal of Vocational Behavior, 55,* 86–101.

Campbell, D. P., Hyne, S. A., & Nilsen, D. L. (1992). *Manual for the Campbell Interest and Skill Survey.* Minneapolis, MN: National Computer System.

Campbell, V. L., & Raiff, G. W. (2002). Review of Harrington–O'Shea Career Decision-Making System–Revised (CDM-R). In J. T. Kapes & E. A. Whitfield (Eds.), A *counselor's guide to career assessment instruments* (4th ed., pp. 228–234). Tulsa, OK: National Career Development Association.

Canals, J., Carbajo, G., & Fernández-Ballart, J. (2002). Discriminant validity of the Eating Attitudes Test according to American Psychiatric Association and World Health Organization criteria of eating disorders. *Psychological Reports, 91,* 1052–1056.

Canfield, A. A., & Canfield, J. S. (1988). *Canfield Learning Styles Inventory.* Los Angeles: Western Psychological Services.

Carney, R. N. (2005). Review of the Stanford Achievement Test, Tenth Edition. In R. A. Spies & B. S. Plake (Eds.), *The sixteenth mental measurements yearbook* (pp. 969–972). Lincoln, NE: Buros Institute of Mental Measurements.

Carroll, J. B. (1993a). *Human cognitive abilities.* New York: Cambridge University Press.

Carroll, J. B. (1993b). *Human cognitive abilities: A survey of factor-analytic studies.* Cambridge, United Kingdom: Cambridge University Press.

Cattell, R. B. (1973). *Measuring intelligence with the Culture Fair Test.* Champaign, IL: Institute for Personality and Ability Testing.

Cattell, H. E. P., & Schuerger, J. M. (2003). *Essentials of 16PF assessment.* Hoboken, NJ: Wiley.

Cesnik, B. I., & Nixon, S. K. (1977). Counseling suicidal persons. In C. Zastrow & D. H. Chang (Eds.), *Personal problem solver* (pp. 275–289). Englewood Cliffs, NJ: Prentice Hall.

Chang, E. D., D'Zurilla, T. J., & Sanna, L. J. (2004). *Social problem solving: Theory, research, and training.* Washington, DC: American Psychological Association.

Charter, R. A., & Feldt, L. S. (2002). The importance of reliability as it relates to true score confidence intervals. *Measurement and Evaluation in Counseling and Development, 35,* 104–112.

Chartrand, J. M. (1991). The evolution of trait-and-factor career counseling: A Person × Environment fit approach. *Journal of Counseling & Development, 69,* 518–524.

Chartrand, J. M., Robbins, S. B., & Morrill, W. H. (1997). *Career Factors Inventory.* Palo Alto, CA: Consulting Psychologists Press.

Cherpitel, C. J. (2000). A brief screening instrument for problem drinking in the emergency room: The RAPS4. *Journal of Studies on Alcohol, 61,* 447–449.

Cherpitel, C. J. (2002). Screening for alcohol problems in the U.S. general population: Comparison of the CAGE, RAPS4, and RAPS4-QF by gender, ethnicity, and service utilization. *Alcoholism, Clinical and Experimental Research, 26,* 1686–1691.

Chickering, A. W., & Reisser, L. (1993). *Education and identity* (2nd ed.). San Francisco: Jossey-Bass.

Chiles, J. A., & Strosahl, K. D. (2005). *Clinical manual for assessment and treatment of suicidal patients.* Washington, DC: American Psychiatric Publishing.

Chinman, M., Young, A. S., Schell, T., Hassell, J., & Mintz, J. (2004). Computer-assisted self-assessment in persons with severe mental illness. *Journal of Clinical Psychiatry, 65,* 1343–1351.

Choca, J. P. (1998). Review of the Millon Index of Personality Styles. In J. C. Impara & B. S. Plake (Eds.), *The thirteenth mental measurements yearbook* (pp. 668–670). Lincoln, NE: Buros Institute of Mental Measurements.

Choca, J. P. (2004). *Interpretive guide to the Millon Clinical Multiaxial Inventory* (3rd ed.). Washington, DC: American Psychological Association.

Cicchetti, D. V. (1994). Guidelines, criteria, and rules of thumb for evaluating normed and standardized assessment interests in psychology. *Psychological Assessment, 6,* 284–290.

Ciechalski, J. C. (2002). Review of Self-Directed Search (SDS). In J. T. Kapes & E. A. Whitfield (Eds.), *A counselor's guide to career assessment instruments* (4th ed., pp. 276–287). Tulsa, OK: National Career Development Association.

Cizek, G. J. (2005). Review of the TerraNova, Second Edition. In R. A. Spies & B. S. Plake (Eds.), *The sixteenth mental measurements yearbook* (pp. 1025–1030) Lincoln, NE: Buros Institute of Mental Measurements.

Claiborn, C. D., & Hanson, W. E. (1999). Test interpretation: A social influence perspective. In J. W. Lichtenberg & R. K. Goodyear (Eds.), *Scientist–practitioner perspectives on test interpretation* (pp. 151–166). Needham Heights, MA: Allyn & Bacon.

Clark, A. J. (2002). *Early recollections: Theory and practice in counseling and psychotherapy.* New York: Brunner-Routledge.

Cleary, T. A., Kendrick, S. A., & Wesman, A. (1975). Educational uses of tests with disadvantaged students. *American Psychologist, 30,* 15–41.

Cohen, G. L., & Sherman. D. K. (2005). Stereotype threat and the social and scientific context of the race achievement gap. *American Psychologist, 60,* 270–271.

Cohen, P. J., Glaser, B. A., & Calhoun, G. B. (2005). Examining readiness for change: A preliminary evaluation of the University of Rhode Island Change Assessment with incarcerated adolescents. *Measurement and Evaluation in Counseling and Development, 38,* 45–62.

Cohen, R. J., Swerdlik, M. E., & Smith, D. K. (1992). *Psychological testing and assessment.* Mountain View, CA: Mayfield.

College Board. (1992). *The new PSAT/NSQT.* New York: Author.

College Board. (1994). *Balancing the SAT scales.* New York: Author.

College Board. (2000). *Taking the SAT I: Reasoning Test.* New York: Author

College Board. (2002). *Facts about the Advanced Placement Program.* New York: Author.

College Board. (2004). *The CLEP advising kit.* New York: Author

College Board. (2005a). *The college handbook.* New York: Author.

College Board. (2005b). *A guide to the SAT for counselors.* Retrieved November 17, 2005, from http://www.collegeboard.com

College Board. (2005c). *Official educator guide to the PSAT.* Retrieved November 17, 2005, from http://www.collegeboard.com

College Board. (2006a). *About the SAT.* Retrieved April 12, 2006, from http://www.collegeboard.com.

College Board. (2006b). *AP update.* Retrieved April 11, 2006, from http://www.apcentral.collegeboard.com

Comas-Díaz, L., & Grenier, J. R. (1998). Migration and acculturation. In J. Sandoval, C. L. Frisby, K. F. Geisinger, J. D. Scheuneman, & J. R. Grenier (Eds.), *Test interpretation and diversity* (pp. 213–239). Washington, DC: American Psychological Association.

Conn, S. R., & Rieke, M. (1997). *16PF fifth edition technical manual.* Champaign, IL: Institute for Personality and Ability Testing.

Conners, C. K. (1997). *Conners' Rating Scales–Revised.* North Tonawanda, NY: Multi-Health Systems.

Conners, C. K., Erhardt, D., & Sparrow, E. (1998). *Conners' Adult ADHD Rating Scales.* North Tonawanda, NY: Multi-Health Systems.

Controversy follows psychological testing. (1999, December). *APA Monitor, 30,* 17.

Cooper-Patrick, L., Crum, R. M., & Ford, D. E. (1994). Identifying suicidal ideation in general medical patients. *Journal of the American Medical Association, 272,* 1757–1762.

Coopersmith, S. (1993). *Self-Esteem Inventories (SEI).* Palo Alto, CA: Consulting Psychologists Press.

Coopersmith, S., & Gilberts, R. (1982). *Professional manual: Behavioral Academic Self-Esteem (BASE), a rating scale.* Palo Alto, CA: Consulting Psychologists Press.

Corcoran, K., & Fischer, J. (2000). *Measures for clinical practice: A sourcebook—Vol. 2. Adults* (3rd ed.). New York: Free Press.

Costa, P. T., Jr., & McCrae, R. (1992). *NEO-PI-R professional manual.* Odessa, FL: Psychological Assessment Resources.

Costa, P. T., Jr., & Widiger, T. A. (Eds.). (2002). *Personality disorders and the five-factor model of personality: Second edition*. Washington, DC: American Psychological Association.

Cox, A. A. (2003). *The Wellness Evaluation of Lifestyle*. In B. S. Plake, J. C. Impara, & R. A. Spies (Eds.), *The fifteenth mental measurements yearbook* (pp. 1005–1007). Lincoln, NE: Buros Institute of Mental Measurements.

Crace, R. K., & Brown, D. (1992). *The Life Values Inventory*. Minneapolis, MN: National Computer Systems.

Craig, R. J. (1999). *Interpreting personality tests*. New York: Wiley.

Craighead, W. E., Curry, J. F., & Ilardi, S. S. (1995). Relationship of Children's Depression Inventory factors to major depression among adolescents. *Psychological Assessment, 7,* 171–176.

Crites, J. O. (1978). *Career Maturity Inventory: Theory and research handbook* (2nd ed.). Monterey, CA: CTB/McGraw-Hill.

Crites, J. O. (1993). *Career Mastery Inventory sourcebook.* Boulder, CO: Crites Career Consultants.

Crites, J. O., & Savickas, M. L. (1996). Revision of the Career Maturity Inventory. *Journal of Career Assessment, 4,* 131–138.

Crocker, L. (2005). Teaching for the test: How and why test preparation is appropriate. In R. P. Phelps (Ed.), *Defending standardized testing* (pp. 159–174). Mahwah, NJ: Erlbaum.

Cronbach, L. J. (1990). *Essentials of psychological testing* (5th ed.). New York: HarperCollins.

Cronbach, L. J., & Gleser, G. C. (1965). *Psychological tests and personnel decisions* (2nd ed.). Urbana: University of Illinois Press.

CTB/Macmillan/McGraw-Hill. (1993). *Test of Cognitive Skills test coordinator's handbook and guide to interpretation*. Monterey, CA: Author.

CTB/McGraw-Hill. (2001). *TerraNova, the second edition: Technical Bulletin 1*. Monterey, CA: Author.

CTB/McGraw-Hill. (2003). *TABE user's handbook*. Monterey, CA: Author.

Cummings, W. H. (1995). Age group differences and estimated frequencies of the Myers–Briggs Type Indicator preferences. *Measurement and Evaluation in Counseling and Development, 2,* 69–77.

D'Costa, A. (2001). Review of Career Factors Inventory. In B. S. Plake & J. C. Impara (Eds.), *The fourteenth mental measurements yearbook* (pp. 219–221). Lincoln, NE: Buros Institute of Mental Measurements.

Dagley, J. C., & Salter, S. K. (2004). Practice and research in career counseling and development—2003. *The Career Development Quarterly, 53,* 98–157.

Dana, R. H. (1993). *Multicultural assessment perspectives in professional psychology*. Boston: Allyn & Bacon.

Dana, R. H. (1998). *Understanding cultural identity in intervention and assessment*. Thousand Oaks, CA: Sage.

Dana, R. H. (2000). *Handbook of cross-cultural and multicultural personality assessment*. Mahwah, NJ: Erlbaum.

Darcy, M., & Tracey, T. J. G. (2003). Integrating abilities and interests in career choice: Maximal versus typical assessment. *Journal of Career Assessment, 11,* 219–237.

Dawis, R. V., & Lofquist, L. H. (1984). *A psychological theory of work adjustment: An individual-differences model and its applications*. Minneapolis: University of Minnesota Press.

Day, S. X., & Rounds, J. (1998). Universality of vocational interest structure among racial and ethnic minorities. *American Psychologist, 53,* 728–736.

Dean, M. A. (2004). An assessment of biodata predictive ability across multiple performance criteria. *Applied HRM Research, 9,* 1–12.

Dejong, P., & Berg, I. S. (1998). *Interviewing for solutions*. Pacific Grove, CA: Brooks/Cole.

DePaola, S. J. (2003) Clinical Assessment Scales for the Elderly. In B. S. Plake, J. C. Impara, & R. A. Spies (Eds.), *The fifteenth mental measurements yearbook* (pp. 190–193). Lincoln, NE: Buros Institute of Mental Measurements.

Derogatis, L. R. (1979). *Sexual Functioning Inventory manual.* Riderwood, MD: Clinical Psychometric Research.

Derogatis, L. R. (1993). *BSI: Administration, scoring, and procedures for the Brief Symptom Inventory* (3rd ed.). Minneapolis, MN: National Computer Systems.

Derogatis, L. R. (1994). *Administration, scoring, and procedures manual for the SCL-90-R*. Minneapolis, MN: National Computer Systems.

Derogatis, L. R. (2000). *BSI-18: Administration, scoring and procedures manual*. Minneapolis, MN: National Computer Systems.

Derogatis, L. R., & Fitzpatrick, M. (2004). The SCL-90-R, the Brief Symptom Inventory (BSI), and the BSI-18. In M. E. Maruish (Ed.), *The use of psychological testing for treatment planning and outcomes assessment: Volume 3. Instruments for adults* (3rd ed., pp. 1–41). Mahwah, NJ: Erlbaum.

Dickens, W. T., & Flynn, S. R. (2001). Heritability estimates versus large environmental effects: The IQ paradox resolved. *Psychological Review, 108,* 346–369.

Dickinson, J., & Tokar, D. M. (2004). Structural and discriminant validity of the Career Factors Inventory. *Journal of Vocational Behavior, 65,* 239–254.

DiPerna, J. C. (2005). Review of the Cognitive Abilities Test Form 6. In R. A. Spies & B. S. Plake (Eds.), *The sixteenth mental measurements yearbook* (pp. 228–231). Lincoln, NE: Buros Institute of Mental Measurements.

Division of Educational Measurements, Council on Dental Education. (1994). *Dental Admission Testing Program (DATP) overview.* Chicago: American Dental Association.

Doll, B. J. (2003). Wechsler Individual Achievement Test—Second Edition. In B. S. Plake, J. C. Impara, & R. A. Spies (Eds.), *The fifteenth mental measurements yearbook* (pp. 996–999) Lincoln, NE: Buros Institute of Mental Measurements.

Donnay, D. A. C. (1997). E. K. Strong's legacy and beyond: 70 years of the Strong Interest Inventory. *The Career Development Quarterly, 46,* 2–22.

Donnay, D. A. C., & Borgen, F. H. (1996). Validity, structure, and content of the 1994 Strong Interest Inventory. *Journal of Counseling Psychology, 43,* 275–291.

Donnay, D. A. C., & Borgen, F. H. (1999). The incremental validity of vocational self-efficacy: An examination of interest, self-efficacy, and occupation. *Journal of Counseling Psychology, 46,* 432–447.

Donnay, D. A. C., & Elliott, T. E. (2003). The California Psychological Inventory. In L. E. Beutler & G. Groth-Marnat (Eds.), *Integrative assessment of adult personality* (pp. 227–261). New York: Guilford Press.

Donnay, D. A. C., Morris, M. L., Schaubhut, N. A., & Thompson, R. C. (2005). *Strong Interest Inventory manual: Research, development, and strategies for interpretation.* Mountain View, CA: CPP.

Dorn, F. J. (1988). Utilizing social influence in career counseling: A case study. *The Career Development Quarterly, 36,* 269–280.

Drummond, P. J., & Jones, K. D. (2006). *Appraisal procedures for counselors and helping professionals* (6th ed.). Englewood Cliffs, NJ: Prentice Hall.

Duckworth, J. C., & Anderson, W. P. (1995). *MMPI and MMPI-2 interpretation manual for counselors and clinicians* (4th ed.). Bristol, PA: Accelerated Development.

Dunn, L. M., & Dunn, L. M. (1997). *The Peabody Picture Vocabulary Test—Third Edition: Examiner's manual.* Circle Pines, MN: American Guidance Service.

Dunn, R., Dunn, K., & Price, G. E. (1987). *Manual for the Learning Style Inventory (LSI).* Lawrence, KS: Price Systems.

DuPaul, G. J., Power, T. J., Anastopoulos, A. D., & Reid, R. (1998). *ADHD Rating Scale-IV: Checklists, norms, and clinical interpretation.* New York: Guilford.

D'Zurilla, T. J., & Goldfried, M. R. (1971). Problem solving and behavior modification. *Journal of Abnormal Psychology, 78,* 107–126.

D'Zurilla, T. J., & Nezu, A. M. (1999). *Problem-solving therapy: A social competence approach to clinical intervention* (2nd ed.). New York: Springer.

D'Zurilla, T. J., Nezu, A. M., & Maydeu-Olivares, A. (2002). *Social Problem-Solving Inventory–Revised (SPSI-R): Technical manual.* North Tonawanda, NY: Multi-Health Systems.

Eagly, A. H. (1995). The science and politics of comparing men and women. *American Psychologist, 50,* 145–158.

Eby, L. T., Johnson, C. D., & Russell, J. E. A. (1998). A psychometric review of career assessment tools for use with diverse individuals. *Journal of Career Assessment, 6,* 269–310.

EdITS (Educational and Industrial Testing Service). (1995). *COPSystem: A career awareness unit.* San Diego, CA: Author.

EdITS (Educational and Industrial Testing Service). (2004, Spring). New profiles with updated norms for the self-interpretation and comprehensive career guides. *Career Guidance Newsletter.* Retrieved February 24, 2006, from http://www.edits.net

Education of All Handicapped Children Act of 1975, Pub. L. No. 94-142, 20 U.S.C. 89 Stat. 773.

Educational Testing Service. (1990). *Validity of the GRE: 1988-89 summary report.* Princeton, NJ: Author.

Educational Testing Service. (2004). *Graduate Management Admission Test bulletin.* Princeton, NJ: Author.

Educational Testing Service. (2005a). *Graduate Record Examinations: Information bulletin.* Princeton, NJ: Author.

Educational Testing Service. (2005b). *TestLink: World's largest test collection database.* Retrieved June 26, 2005, from http://www.ets.org/testcoll/index.html

Educational Testing Service. (2006a). *The GRE general test*. Retrieved April 13, 2006, from http://www.ets.org

Educational Testing Service. (2006b). *TOEFL details: Learners and test takers Internet-based testing (iBT)*. Retrieved April 13, 2006, from http://www.ets.org/toefl5.html

Eggerth, D. E., Bowles, S. M., Tunick, R. H., & Andrew, M. E. (2005). Convergent validity of O*NET Holland code classifications. *Journal of Career Assessment, 13,* 150–168.

Eisen, S. V., Normand, S., Belanger, A. J., Spiro, A., & Esch, D. (2004). The Revised Behavior and Symptom Identification Scale (BASIS-R): Reliability and validity. *Medical Care, 42,* 1230–1241.

Ekstrom, R. B., Elmore, P. B., Schafer, W. D., Trotter, T. V., & Webster, B. (2004). A survey of assessment and evaluation activities of school counselors. *Professional School Counselor, 8,* 24–30.

Elliott, S. N., McKevitt, B. C., & Kettler, R. J. (2002). Testing accommodations research and decision making: The case of "good" scores being highly valued but difficult to achieve for all students. *Measurement and Evaluation in Counseling and Development, 35,* 153–166.

Elmore, P. B., Ekstrom, R. B., & Diamond, E. E. (1993). Counselors' test use practices: Indicators of the adequacy of measurement training. *Measurement and Evaluation in Counseling and Development, 26,* 116–124.

Elmore, P. B., Ekstrom, R. B., Diamond, E. E., & Whittaker, S. (1993). School counselors' test use patterns and practices. *The School Counselor, 41,* 73–80.

Emanuelson, G., Perosa, S., & Perosa, L. (2005, August). *A validation study of the SASSI-3*. Paper presented at the 113th Annual Convention of the American Psychological Association, Washington, DC.

Embertson, S. E. (1996). The new rules of measurement. *Psychological Assessment, 8,* 341–349.

Endler, N. S., & Parker, J. D. A. (1994). Assessment of multidimensional coping task, emotion, and avoidance strategies. *Psychological Assessment, 6,* 50–60.

Endler, N. S., Parker, J. D. A., & Summerfeldt, L. S. (1998). Coping with health problems: Developing a reliable and valid multidimensional measure. *Psychological Assessment, 10,* 195–205.

Erford, B. T., & Pauletta, D. (2005) Psychometric analysis of young children's responses to the Slosson Intelligence Test-Primary (SIT-P). *Measurement and Evaluation in Counseling and Development, 38,* 130–140.

Erikson, E. H. (1968). *Identity, youth and crisis*. New York: Norton.

Erwin, T. D. (1983). The Scale of Intellectual Development: Measuring Perry's scheme. *Journal of College Student Personnel, 24,* 6–12.

Evans, W. N. (1998). Assessment and diagnosis of the substance use disorders (SUDs). *Journal of Counseling & Development, 76,* 325–333.

Eveland, A. P., Conyne, R. K., & Blakney, V. L. (1998). University students and career decidedness: Effects of two computer-based career guidance interventions. *Computers in Human Behavior, 14,* 531–541.

Ewing, J. A. (1984). Detecting alcoholism: The CAGE Questionnaire. *Journal of the American Medical Association, 252,* 1905–1907.

Exner, J. E. (1993). *The Rorschach: A comprehensive system: Vol. 1. Basic foundations* (3rd ed.). New York: Wiley.

Exner, J. E. (2001). *A Rorschach workbook for the comprehensive system* (5th ed.). Odessa, FL: Psychological Assessment Resources.

Eyde, L. D., Robertson, G. J., Krug, S. E., Moreland, K. L., Robertson, A. G., Shewan, C. M., et al. (1993). *Responsible test use: Case studies for assessing human behavior*. Washington, DC: American Psychological Association.

Eysenck, H. J., & Eysenck, S. B. G. (1993). *Manual: Eysenck Personality Questionnaire (Junior & Adult)*. San Diego, CA: Educational and Industrial Testing Service.

Fals-Stewart, W., O'Farrell, T. J., Feitas, T. T., McFarlin, S. K., & Rutigliano, P. (2000). The Timeline Followback reports of psychoactive substance use by drug-abusing patients: Psychometric properties. *Journal of Consulting and Clinical Psychology, 68,* 134–144.

Family Education Rights and Privacy Act of 1974 (FERPA). Pub. L. No. 93-380 20 U.S.C. §241.

Farr, J. M., Ludden, L., & Shatkin, L. (2001). *Guide for Occupational Exploration* (3rd ed.). Indianapolis, IN: JIST Works.

Feldt, L. S. (2004). Estimating the reliability of a test battery composite or a test score based on weighted scoring. *Measurement and Evaluation in Counseling and Development, 37,* 184–190.

Feller, R., & Daly, J. (2002). Review of Career Thoughts Inventory (CTI). In J. T. Kapes & E. A. Whitfield (Eds.), *A counselor's guide to career assessment instruments* (4th ed., pp. 343–348). Tulsa, OK: National Career Development Association.

Fernandez, E. (2001). Review of the Battery for Health Improvement 2. In B. S. Plake & J. C. Impara (Eds.), *The fourteenth mental measurements yearbook* (pp. 119–121). Lincoln, NE: Buros Institute of Mental Measurements.

Fernandez, E. (2003). Review of Substance Abuse Subtle Screening Inventory–3. In B. S. Plake, J. C. Impara, & R. A. Spies (Eds.), *The fifteenth mental measurements yearbook* (pp. 914–916). Lincoln, NE: Buros Institute of Mental Measurements.

Fico, J. M., & Hogan, R. (2000). *Interpersonal Compass manual.* Tulsa, OK: Hogan Assessment Systems.

Fiedler, E. R., Oltmanns, T. F., & Turkheimer, E. (2004). *Military Medicine, 169,* 207–211.

Figler, H. E. (1993). *PATH: A career workbook for liberal arts students* (3rd ed.). New York: Sulzburger & Graham.

Finch, E. A., Linde, J. A., Jeffery, R. W., Rothman, A. J., King, C. M., & Levy, R. L. (2005). The effects of outcome expectations and satisfaction on weight loss and maintenance: Correlational and experimental analyses—a randomized trial. *Health Psychology, 24,* 608–616.

Finger, M. S., & Ones, D. S. (1999). Psychometric equivalence of the computer and booklet forms of the MMPI: A meta-analysis. *Psychological Assessment, 11,* 58–66.

Finn, S. E., & Tonsager, M. E. (1992). Therapeutic effects of providing MMPI-2 test feedback to college students awaiting therapy. *Psychological Assessment, 4,* 278–287.

Finn, S. E., & Tonsager, M. E. (1997). Information-gathering and therapeutic models of assessment: Complementary paradigms. *Psychological Assessment, 9,* 374–385.

First, M. B., & Tasman, A. (Eds.). (2004). *DSM-IV-TR mental disorders: Diagnosis, etiology and treatment.* New York: Wiley.

Fischer, J., & Corcoran, K. (2000). *Measures for clinical practice: A sourcebook: Vol. 1. Couples, families, and children* (3rd ed.). New York: Free Press.

Fitts, W. H. (1996). *Manual Tennessee Self-Concept Scale* (2nd ed.). Los Angeles: Western Psychological Services.

Fleming, J. (2002). Who will succeed in college when the SAT predicts Black students' performance. *Review of Higher Education, 25,* 281–296.

Fleming, M. F., & Barry, K. L. (1991). A three-sample test of a masked alcohol screening questionnaire. *Alcohol & Alcoholism, 26,* 81–91.

Foa, E. B., Riggs, D. S., Dancu, C. V., & Rothbaum, B. O. (1993). Reliability and validity of a brief instrument for assessing post-traumatic stress disorder. *Journal of Traumatic Stress, 6,* 459–473.

Folkman, S., & Lazarus, R. S. (1988). *Manual for the Ways of Coping Questionnaire: Research edition.* Palo Alto, CA: Consulting Psychologists Press.

Folsom, B., & Reardon, R. (2003). College career courses: Design and accountability. *Journal of Career Assessment, 11,* 421–450.

Folstein, M. F., Folstein, S. E., & McHugh, P. R. (1975). Mini-mental state: A practical method for grading the state of patients for the clinician. *Journal of Psychiatric Research, 12,* 189–198.

Folstein, M. F., Folstein, S. E., McHugh, P. R., & Fanjiang, G. (2001). *Mini-Mental State Examination user's guide.* Odessa, FL: Psychological Assessment Resources.

Fong, M. L. (1993). Teaching assessment and diagnosis within a *DSM-III-R* framework. *Counselor Education and Supervision, 32,* 276–287.

Fong, M. L. (1995). Assessment and *DSM-IV* diagnosis of personality disorders: A primer for counselors. *Journal of Counseling & Development, 73,* 635–639.

Fong, M. L., & Silien, K. A. (1999). Assessment and diagnosis of *DSM-IV* anxiety disorders. *Journal of Counseling & Development, 77,* 209–217.

Forbey, J. D., & Ben-Porath, Y. S. (2003). Incremental validity of the MMPI-A content scales in a residential treatment facility. *Assessment, 10,* 191–202.

Forgays, D. G., Forgays, D. K., & Spielberger, C. D. (1997). Factor structure of the State–Trait Anger Expression Inventory. *Journal of Personality Assessment, 69,* 497–507.

Forsyth, R. A., Ansley, T. N., Feldt, L. S., & Alnot, S. D. (2001). *Interpretive guide for teachers and counselors, Iowa Tests of Educational Development.* Chicago: Riverside.

Forsyth, R. A., Ansley, T. N., Feldt, L. S., & Alnot, S. D. (2003). *Guide to research and development, Iowa Tests of Educational Development.* Chicago: Riverside.

Fouad, N. A. (2002). Cross-cultural differences in vocational interests: Between-groups differences on the Strong Interest Inventory. *Journal of Counseling Psychology, 49,* 283–289.

Fouad, N. A., & Chan, P. M. (1999). Gender and ethnicity: Influence on test interpretation and reception. In J. W. Lichtenberg & R. K. Goodyear (Eds.), *Scientist–practitioner perspectives on test interpretation* (pp. 31–58). Needham Heights, MA: Allyn & Bacon.

Fouad, N. A., & Guillen, A. (2006). Outcome expectations: Looking to the past and potential future. *Journal of Career Assessment, 14,* 130–142.

Fouad, N. A., Harmon, L. W., & Borgen, F. H. (1997). Structure of interests in employed male and female members of U.S. racial-ethnic minority and nonminority groups. *Journal of Counseling Psychology, 44,* 339–345.

Fouad, N. A., Harmon, L. W., & Hansen, J. C. (1994). Cross-cultural use of the Strong. In L. W. Harmon, J. C. Hansen, F. H. Borgen, & A. L. Hammer (Eds.), *Strong Interest Inventory applications and technical guide* (pp. 255–280). Stanford, CA: Stanford University Press.

Fouad, N. A., & Mohler, C. J. (2004). Cultural validity of Holland's theory and the Strong Interest Inventory for five racial/ethnic groups. *Journal of Career Assessment, 12,* 423–439.

Frances, A. J., & Ross, R. (Eds.). (2002). *DSM-IV-TR case studies: A clinical guide to differential diagnosis.* Washington, DC: American Psychiatric Association.

Frank, R. G., & Elliott, T. R. (Eds.). (2000). *Handbook of rehabilitation psychology.* Washington, DC: American Psychological Association.

Frauenhoffer, D., Ross, M. J., Gfeller, J., Searight, H. R., & Piotrowski, C. (1998). Psychological test usage among licensed mental health practitioners: A multidisciplinary survey. *Journal of Psychological Practice, 4,* 28–33.

Freeman, S. J. (2003). Review of State-Trait Anger Expression Inventory–2. In B. S. Plake, J. C. Impara, & R. A. Spies (Eds.), *The fifteenth mental measurements yearbook* (pp. 875–876). Lincoln, NE: Buros Institute of Mental Measurements.

Fremer, J. (1992, August). *One hundred years of psychological testing.* Paper presented at the 100th Annual Convention of the American Psychological Association, Washington, DC.

French, J. W. (1962). Effective anxiety on verbal and mathematical examination scores. *Educational and Psychological Measurement, 22,* 553–564.

Friedenberg, L. (1995). *Psychological testing: Design, analysis, and use.* Needham Heights, MA: Allyn & Bacon.

Friedman, A. F., Lewak, R., Nichols, D. S., & Webb, J. T. (2001). *Psychological assessment with the MMPI-2.* Mahwah, NJ: Erlbaum.

Friedman, S. L., & Wachs, T. D. (1999). *Measuring environment across the life span: Emerging methods and concepts.* Washington, DC: American Psychological Association.

Frisby, C. L. (1998). Culture and cultural differences. In J. Sandoval, C. L. Frisby, K. F. Geisinger, J. D. Scheuneman, & J. R. Grenier (Eds.), *Test interpretation and diversity* (pp. 51–74). Washington, DC: American Psychological Association.

Frisch, M. B. (1994). *Manual and treatment guide for the Quality of Life Inventory.* Minneapolis, MN: National Computer Systems.

Frisch, M. B., Clark, M. P., Rouse, S. V., Rudd, M. D., Paweleck, J. K., Greenstone, A., et al. (2005). Predictive and treatment validity of life satisfaction and the Quality of Life Inventory. *Assessment, 12,* 66–78.

Galassi, J. P., & Perot, A. R. (1992). What you should know about behavioral assessment. *Journal of Counseling & Development, 70,* 624–631.

Galton, F. (1883). *Inquiries into human faculty and its development.* London: Macmillan.

Garb, H. N. (1997). Race bias, social class bias, and gender bias in clinical judgment. *Clinical Psychology: Science and Practice, 4,* 99–120.

Garb, H. N. (1998). *Studying the clinician: Judgment research and psychological assessment.* Washington, DC: American Psychological Association.

Garb, H. N., Wood, J. M., Lilienfeld, S. O., & Nezworski, M. T. (2002). Effective use of projective techniques in clinical practice: Let the data help with selection and interpretation. *Professional Psychology: Research and Practice, 33,* 454–463.

Garb, H. N., Wood, J. M., Lilienfeld, S. O., & Nezworski, M. T. (2005). Roots of the Rorschach controversy. *Clinical Psychology Review, 25,* 97–118.

Gardner, H. (1999). *Intelligence reframed: Multiple intelligences for the 21st century.* New York: Basic Books.

Garner, D. M. (2005). Eating Disorders Inventory–3. In *Catalog of selected professional testing resources* (p. 13). Lutz, FL: Psychological Assessment Resources.

Garner, D. M., & Garfinkel, P. E. (1979). The Eating Attitudes Test: An index of the symptoms of anorexia nervosa. *Psychological Medicine, 9,* 273–279.

Garrett, M. T., & Pichette, E. F. (2000). Red as an apple: Native American acculturation and counseling with or without reservation. *Journal of Counseling & Development, 78,* 3–13.

Gati, I., Kraus, M., & Osipow, S. H. (1996). A taxonomy of difficulties in career decision making. *Journal of Counseling Psychology, 43,* 510–526.

Gati, I., & Saka, N. (2001). High school students' career-related decision-making difficulties. *Journal of Counseling & Development, 79,* 331–440.

Gay, G. H. (1990). Standardized tests: Irregularities in administration of tests affect test results. *Journal of Instructional Psychology, 17,* 93–103.

Geisinger, K. F. (1998). Psychometric issues in test interpretation. In J. Sandoval, C. L. Frisby, K. F. Geisinger, J. D. Scheuneman, & J. R. Grenier (Eds.), *Test interpretation and diversity* (pp. 17–30). Washington, DC: American Psychological Association.

Gerlach, P. K. (2003). *How to make a multi-generation map ("genogram") to see who you all are.* Retrieved November 7, 2005, from http://sfhelp.org/03/geno1.htm

Geroski, A. M., Rodgers, K. A., & Breen, D. T. (1997). Using the *DSM-IV* to enhance collaboration among school counselors, clinical counselors, and primary care physicians. *Journal of Counseling & Development, 75,* 231–239.

Giannetti, R. A. (1992). *User's guide for Quickview Social History–Clinical version.* Minneapolis, MN: National Computer Systems.

Gibson, D. M. (2005). The use of genograms in career counseling with elementary, middle, and high school students. *The Career Guidance Quarterly, 53,* 353–362.

Giordano, F. G., Schwiebert, V. L., & Brotherton, W. D. (1997). School counselors' perceptions of the usefulness of standardized tests, frequency of their use, and assessment training needs. *School Counselor, 44,* 198–205.

Glavin, K. W. (2005). *Vocopher.* Retrieved June 12, 2005, http://www.vocopher.com

Goldberg, L. R. (1993). The structure of phenotypic personality traits. *American Psychologist, 48,* 26–34.

Goldenson, R. M. (Ed.). (1984). *Longman dictionary of psychology and psychiatry.* New York: Longman.

Goldfried, M. R., Stricker, G., & Weiner, I. R. (1971). *Rorschach handbook of clinical and research applications.* Englewood Cliffs, NJ: Prentice Hall.

Goldman, L. (1992). Qualitative assessment: An approach for counselors. *Journal of Counseling & Development, 70,* 616–621.

Goodwin, L. D., & Leech, N. L. (2003). The meaning of validity in the New Standards for Educational and Psychological Testing: Implications for measurement courses. *Measurement and Evaluation in Counseling and Development, 36,* 181–191.

Goodyear, R. K. (1990). Research on the effects of test interpretation: A review. *The Counseling Psychologist, 18,* 240–257.

Goonan, B. (2004). Overcoming test anxiety: Giving students at ability to show what they know. In J. E. Wall & G. R. Walz (Eds.), *Measuring up: Assessment issues for teachers, counselors, and administrators* (pp. 257–272). Greensboro, NC: CAPS Press.

Gopaul, S., & Armour-Thomas, E. (2002). *Assessment and culture: Psychological tests with minority populations.* San Diego, CA: Academic Press.

Gottfredson, G. D., & Holland, J. L. (1991). *Manual for Position Classification Inventory.* Odessa, FL: Psychological Assessment Resources.

Gottfredson, G. D., & Holland, J. L. (1996). *Dictionary of Holland occupational codes* (3rd ed.). Odessa, FL: Psychological Assessment Resources.

Gottfredson, L. S. (1982). The sex fairness of unnormed interest inventories. *Vocational Guidance Quarterly, 31,* 128–132.

Gottfredson, L. S. (2002). *g:* Highly general and highly practical. In R. S. Sternberg & E. L. Grigorenko (Eds.), *The general factor of intelligence: How general is it?* (pp. 331–380). Mahwah, NJ: Erlbaum.

Gough, H. G. (1987). *California Psychological Inventory administrator's guide.* Palo Alto, CA: Consulting Psychologists Press.

Gough, H. G. (1999). *CPI: Introduction to Form 434.* Palo Alto, CA: Consulting Psychologists Press.

Gough, H. G. (2000). The California Psychological Inventory. In C. E. Watkins & V. L. Campbell (Eds.), *Testing and assessment in counseling practice* (pp. 45–71). Mahwah, NJ: Erlbaum.

Gough, H. G., & Bradley, P. (1996). *CPI manual.* Palo Alto, CA: Consulting Psychologists Press.

Graham, J. R. (2000). *MMPI-2: Assessing personality and psychopathology* (3rd ed.). New York: Oxford University Press.

Graham, J. R. (2005). *MMPI-2: Assessing personality and psychopathology* (4th ed.). New York: Oxford University Press.

Granello, D. H., & Granello, P. F. (2001). Counseling outcome research: Making practical choices for real-world applications. In G. R. Walz & J. C. Bleuer (Eds.), *Assessment: Issues and challenges for the millennium* (pp. 163–172). Greensboro, NC: CAPS.

Grant, B. F., Stinson, F. S., Dawson, D. A., Chou, S. P., Dufour, M. C., Compton, W., et al. (2004). Prevalence and co-occurrence of substance use disorders and independent mood and anxiety disorders: Results from the national epidemiologic survey on alcohol and related conditions. *Archives of General Psychiatry, 61,* 807–816.

Gray-Little, B. (2002). The assessment of psychopathology in racial and ethnic minorities. In J. N. Butcher (Ed.), *Clinical personality assessment: Practical approaches* (pp. 171–189). New York: Oxford University Press.

Gray-Little, B., & Kaplan, D. A. (1998). Interpretation of psychological tests in clinical and forensic evaluations. In J. Sandoval, C. L. Frisby, K. F. Geisinger, J. D. Scheuneman, & J. R. Grenier (Eds.), *Test interpretation and diversity* (pp. 141–178). Washington, DC: American Psychological Association.

Green, K. E. (1998). Review of the Values Scale, Second Edition. In J. C. Impara & B. S. Plake (Eds.), *The thirteenth mental measurements yearbook* (pp. 1112–1114). Lincoln, NE: Buros Institute of Mental Measurements.

Greenberg, L. (1994). *Interpretation manual for Test of Variables of Attention.* Circle Pines, MN: American Guidance Service.

Greene, R. L. (1987). Ethnicity and MMPI performance: A review. *Journal of Consulting and Clinical Psychology, 35,* 497–512.

Greene, R. L. (1999). *The MMPI-2: An interpretive manual.* Boston: Allyn & Bacon.

Greene, R. L., Albaugh, B., Robin, R. W., & Caldwell, A. (2003). Use of the MMPI-II in American Indians: II. Empirical correlates. *Psychological Assessment 15,* 360–369.

Greenfield, T. K., & Attkisson, C. C. (2004). The UCSF Client Satisfaction Scales: II. The Service Satisfaction Scale–30. In M. E. Maruish (Ed.), *The use of psychological testing for treatment planning and outcomes assessment: Volume 3. Instruments for adults* (3rd ed., pp. 813–837). Mahwah, NJ: Erlbaum.

Gregg, N. Coleman, C., & Knight, D. (2003). Use of the Woodcock-Johnson–III in the diagnosis of learning disabilities. In F. A. Schrank & D. P. Flanagan (Eds.), *WJ-III clinical use and interpretation* (pp. 125–174). San Diego, CA: Academic Press.

Grice, J. W. (2004). Bridging the idiographic-nomothetic divide in ratings of self and others on the Big Five. *Journal of Personality, 72,* 203–241.

Gross, M. L. (1962). *The brain watchers.* New York: New American Library.

Groth-Marnat, G. (2003). *Handbook of psychological assessment* (4th ed.). New York: Wiley.

Grove, W. M., Zald, D. H., Lebow, B. S., Snitz, B. E., & Nelson, C. (2000). Clinical versus mechanical prediction: A meta-analysis. *Psychological Assessment, 12,* 19–30.

Guilford, J. P. (1959). *Personality.* New York: McGraw-Hill.

Hacker, A. (1992). *Two nations: Black and White, separate, hostile, unequal.* New York: Scribner.

Hahn, S. R., Sydney, E., Kroenke, K., Williams, J. B. W., & Spitzer, R. L. (2004). Evaluation of mental disorders with the Primary Care Evaluation of Mental Disorders and Patient Health Questionnaire. In M. Maruish (Ed.), *Use of psychological testing for treatment planning and outcomes assessment: Volume 3. Instruments for adults* (3rd ed., pp. 235–291). Mahwah, NJ: Erlbaum.

Hahn, W. K., & Marks, L. I. (1996). Client receptiveness to the routine assessment of past suicide attempts. *Professional Psychology: Research and Practice, 27,* 592–594.

Haley, M. (2004). Risk and protective factors. In D. Capuzzi (Ed.), *Suicide across the life span: Implications for counselors* (pp. 95–138). Alexandria, VA: American Counseling Association.

Hall, L. G. (2000). *Hall Occupational Orientation Inventory, fourth edition: Counselor-user's manual.* Bensenville, IL: Scholastic Testing Service.

Hall, M. E., & Rayman, J. R. (2002). Review of Career Beliefs Inventory. In J. T. Kapes & E. A. Whitfield (Eds.), *A counselor's guide to career assessment instruments* (4th ed., pp. 316–322). Alexandria, VA: National Career Development Association.

Halpern, E. (2000). *Sex differences in cognitive abilities.* Mahwah, NJ: Erlbaum.

Hambleton, R. K. (2005). Review of the WMS-3rd edition abbreviated. In R. A. Spies & B. S. Plake (Eds.), *The sixteenth mental measurements yearbook* (pp. 1097–1099). Lincoln, NE: Buros Institute of Mental Measurements.

Hammer, A. L. (Ed.). (1996). *MBTI applications: A decade of research on the Myers–Briggs Type Indicator.* Palo Alto, CA: Consulting Psychologists Press.

Hamilton, M. (1967). Development of a rating scale for primary depressive illness. *British Journal of Social and Clinical Psychology, 6,* 278–296.

Han, L., & Hoover, H. D. (1994, April). *Gender differences in achievement test scores.* Paper presented at the annual meeting of the National Council on Measurement in Education, New Orleans, LA.

Handel, R. W., Ben-Porath, Y. S., & Watt, M. (1999). Computerized adaptive assessment with the MMPI-2 in a clinical setting. *Psychological Assessment, 11,* 369–380.

Haney, W. (1981). Validity, vaudeville, and values: A short history of social concerns over standardized testing. *American Psychologist, 36,* 1021–1034.

Hansen, J. C. (1999). Test psychometrics. In J. W. Lichtenberg & R. K. Goodyear (Eds.), *Scientist–practitioner perspectives on test interpretation* (pp. 15–30). Needham Heights, MA: Allyn & Bacon.

Hansen, J. C. (2000). Interpretation of the Strong Interest Inventory. In C. E. Watkins, Jr., & V. L. Campbell (Eds.), *Testing and assessment in counseling practice* (2nd ed., pp. 227–262). Mahwah, NJ: Erlbaum.

Hansen, J. C., & Dik, B. J. (2005). Evidence of 12-year predictive and concurrent validity for SII Occupational Scale scores. *Journal of Vocational Behavior, 67,* 365–378.

Hansen, J. C., & Neuman, J. L. (1999). Evidence of concurrent prediction of the Campbell Interest and Skill Survey (CISS) for college major selection. *Journal of Career Assessment, 7,* 239–247.

Hansen, J. C., Neuman, J. L., Haverkamp, B. E., & Lubinski, B. R. (1997). Comparison of user reaction to two methods of Strong Interest Inventory administration and report feedback. *Measurement and Evaluation in Counseling and Development, 30,* 115–127.

Hansen, L. S. S. (1999). Integrative life planning: An interdisciplinary framework for aligning personal growth and organizational and social development in the 21st century. *International Medical Journal, 6,* 87–93.

Hanson, W. E., Claiborn, C. D., & Kerr, B. (1997). Differential effects of two test-interpretation styles in counseling: A field study. *Journal of Counseling Psychology, 44,* 400–405.

Hanson, W. E., & Claiborn, C. D. (2006). Effects of interpretation style and favorability in the counseling process. *Journal of Counseling & Development, 84,* 349–357.

Harcourt Assessment. (2003). *OLSAT 8 technical manual.* San Antonio, TX: Author.

Harcourt Educational Measurement. (2003). *Stanford 10 technical data report.* San Antonio, TX: Author.

Harcourt Educational Measurement. (2006). *The Miller Analogies Test.* Retrieved April 17, 2006 from http://harcourtassessment.com/HAIWEB/Cultures/en-us/dotCom/milleranalogies

Harmon, L. W., Hansen, J. C., Borgen, F. H., & Hammer, A. L. (1994). *Strong Interest Inventory applications and technical guide.* Stanford, CA: Stanford University Press.

Harrell, A. V., & Wirtz, P. W. (1989). *Adolescent Drinking Index: Professional manual.* Odessa, FL: Psychological Assessment Resources.

Harrington, T. F. (2006). A 20-year follow-up of the Harrington-O'Shea Career Decision-Making System. *Measurement and Evaluation in Counseling and Development, 38,* 198–202.

Harrington, T. F., & O'Shea, A. J. (2000). *The Harrington-O'Shea Career Decision-Making System Revised manual.* Circle Pines, MN: American Guidance Service.

Harris, E. C., & Barraclough, B. (1997). Suicide as an outcome for mental disorders: A meta-analysis. *British Journal of Psychiatry, 170,* 205–228.

Harris-Bowlsbey, J. (2005). *Take hold of your future* (5th ed.). Adel, IA: National Career Assessment Services.

Hartung, P. J., Taber, B. J., & Richard, G. V. (2005). The Physician Values in Practice Scale: Construction and initial validation. *Journal of Vocational Behavior, 67,* 309–320.

Harwell, M. R. (2005). Review of the Metropolitan Achievement Tests Eighth Edition. In R. A. Spies & B. S. Plake (Eds.), *The sixteenth mental measurements yearbook* (pp. 609–612). Lincoln, NE: Buros Mental Measurements Institute.

Hattrup, K. (2003), California Psychological Inventory–3rd Edition. In B. S. Plake, J. C.. Impara, & R. A. Spies (Eds.), *The fifteenth mental measurements yearbook* (pp. 161–163) Lincoln, NE: Buros Institute of Mental Measurements.

Hayes, J. A., Wall, T. N., & Shea, A. (1998, August). *The relationship of client–therapist attribution congruence to the working alliance and psychotherapy outcome.* Paper presented at the 106th annual convention of the American Psychological Association, San Francisco.

Heck, E. J. (1991). Developing a screening questionnaire for problem drinking in college students. *Journal of American College Health, 39,* 227–234.

Heiligenstein, E., Guenther, G., Levy, A., Savino, F., & Fulwiler, J. (1999). Psychological and academic functioning in college students with attention deficit hyperactivity disorder. *Journal of American College Health, 47,* 181–185.

Helmes, E., & Reddon, J. R. (1993). A perspective on developments in assessing psychopathology: A critical review of the MMPI and MMPI-2. *Psychological Bulletin, 113,* 453–471.

Helzer, J. E., Badger, G. J., Rose, G. L., Mongeon, J. A., & Searles, J. S. (2002). Decline in alcohol consumption during two years of daily reporting. *Journal of Studies on Alcohol, 63,* 551–557.

Hemphill, J. F. (2003). Interpreting the magnitudes of correlation coefficients. *American Psychologist, 58,* 78–79.

Heppner, M. J., Multon, K. D., & Johnston, J. A. (1994). Assessing psychological resources during career change: Development of the Career Transitions Inventory. *Journal of Vocational Behavior, 44,* 55–74.

Heppner, P. P. (1988). *The Problem-Solving Inventory: Manual.* Palo Alto, CA: Consulting Psychologists Press.

Heppner, P. P., Cook, S. W., Wright, D. M., & Johnson, W. C., Jr. (1995). Progress in resolving problems: A problem-focused style of coping. *Journal of Counseling Psychology, 42,* 279–293.

Herlihy, B., & Corey, G. (2006). *ACA ethical standards casebook* (6th ed.). Alexandria, VA: American Counseling Association.

Hess, A. K. (2001). Review of the Wechsler Adult Intelligence Scale–Third Edition. In B. S. Plake & J. C. Impara (Eds.), *The fourteenth mental measurements yearbook* (pp. 1332–1336). Lincoln, NE: Buros Institute of Mental Measurements.

Higgins, R. W. (1997). ADHD: The role of the family physician. *American Family Physician, 56,* 42–43.

Hiller, J. B., Rosenthal, R., Bornstein, R. F., Barry, D. R., & Brunell-Neuleib, T. (1999). A comparative meta-analysis of Rorschach and MMPI validity. *Psychological Assessment, 11,* 278–296.

Hinkle, J. S. (1994). Practitioners and cross-cultural assessment: A practical guide to information and training. *Measurement and Evaluation in Counseling and Development, 27,* 103–115.

Hinkle, J. S. (1999). A voice from the trenches: A reaction to Ivey and Ivey (1998). *Journal of Counseling & Development, 77,* 474–483.

Hodgson, R. J., & Rachman, S. (1977). Obsessional–compulsive complaints. *Behaviour Research and Therapy, 15,* 389–395.

Hoffman, J. A., & Weiss, B. (1986). A new system for conceptualizing college students' problems: Types of crises and the Inventory of Common Problems. *Journal of American College Health, 34,* 259–266.

Hogan, R. (1997). *Hogan Development Survey.* Tulsa, OK: Hogan Assessment Systems.

Hohenshil, T. H. (1996). Editorial: Role of assessment and diagnosis in counseling. *Journal of Counseling & Development, 75,* 64–67.

Holcomb-McCoy, C. C. (2003). Multicultural competence in school settings. In D. B. Pope-Davis, H. L. K. Coleman, W. M. Liu, & R. L. Toporek (Eds.), *Handbook of multicultural competencies in counseling and psychology* (pp. 406–419). Thousand Oaks, CA: Sage.

Holden, R. R. (1996). *Holden Psychological Screening Inventory.* Tonawanda, NY: Multi-Health Systems.

Holland, J. L. (1992). *Vocational exploration and insight kit.* Odessa, FL: Psychological Assessment Resources.

Holland, J. L. (1997). *Making vocational choices: A theory of vocational personalities and work environments* (3rd ed.). Odessa, FL: Psychological Assessment Resources.

Holland, J. L., Daiger, D. C., & Power, P. G. (1980). *My Vocational Situation.* Palo Alto, CA: Consulting Psychologists Press.

Holland, J. L., Fritzsche, B. A., & Powell, A. B. (1994). *The Self-Directed Search technical manual.* Odessa, FL: Psychological Assessment Resources.

Holland, J. L., & Gottfredson, G. D. (1976). Using a typology of persons and environments to explain careers: Some extensions and clarifications. *The Counseling Psychologist, 6,* 20–29.

Holland, J. L., & Gottfredson, G. D. (1994a, April). *Career Attitudes and Strategies Inventory: A new tool for counseling adults.* Paper presented at the annual convention of the American Counseling Association, Minneapolis, MN.

Holland, J. L., & Gottfredson, G. D. (1994b). *CASI: Career Attitudes and Strategies Inventory.* Odessa, FL: Psychological Assessment Resources.

Holland, J. L., Powell, A. B., & Fritzsche, B. A. (1994). *Self-Directed Search professional user's guide.* Odessa, FL: Psychological Assessment Resources.

Holmberg, K., Rosen, D., & Holland, J. L. (1990). *The leisure activities finder.* Odessa, FL: Psychological Assessment Resources.

Holroyd, S., & Clayton, A. H. (2000). *Measuring depression in the elderly: Which scale is best?* Retrieved April 29, 2006, from http://www.medscape.com/viewarticle/430554_4

Hood, A. B. (1968). *What type of college for what type of student?* Minneapolis: University of Minnesota Press.

Hood, A. B. (1997). *The Iowa Student Development Inventories, 2nd edition.* Iowa City, IA: Hitech Press.

Hoover, H. D., Dunbar, S. B., & Frisbie, D. A. (2003a). *Guide to research and development: Iowa Tests of Basic Skills.* Chicago: Riverside.

Hoover, H. D., Dunbar, S. B., & Frisbie, D. A. (2003b). *Interpretative guide for teachers and counselors.* Chicago: Riverside.

Hoover, H. D., & Han, L. (1995, April). *The effect of differential selection on gender differences in college admission test scores.* Paper presented at the annual meeting of the American Educational Research Association, San Francisco.

Horan, J. J. (1979). *Counseling for effective decision-making: A cognitive–behavioral perspective.* North Scituate, MA: Duxbury Press.

Horn, J. L., Wanberg, K. W., & Foster, F. M. (1986). *Alcohol Use Inventory.* Minneapolis, MN: National Computer Systems.

Horton, A. M., Jr. (1999). Test review: Wechsler Memory Scale III. *Archives of Clinical Neuropsychology, 14,* 473–477.

Horvath, A. O., & Greenberg, L. (1989). Development and validation of the Working Alliance Inventory. *Journal of Counseling Psychology*, 36, 223–232.

Howard, J. (2001). Graphic representations as tools for decision making. *Social Education, 65,* 220–223.

Hoyt, D. P. (1960). Measurement and prediction of the permanence of interests. In W. L. Layton (Ed.), *The Strong Vocational Interest Blank: Research and uses* (pp. 93–103). Minneapolis: University of Minnesota Press.

Hunsley, J., & Mash, E. J. (2005). Introduction to the special section on developing guidelines for the evidence-based assessment (EBA) of adult disorders. *Psychological Assessment, 17,* 251–255.

Hunsley, J., & Meyer, G. J. (2003). The incremental validity of psychological testing and assessment: Conceptual, methodological, and statistical issues. *Psychological Assessment, 15,* 446–455.

Ihle-Helledy, K., Zytowski, D. G., & Fouad, N. A. (2004). Kuder Career Search: Test–retest reliability and consequential validity. *Journal of Career Assessment, 12,* 285–297.

Impara, J. C., & Plake, B. S. (1995). Comparing counselors', school administrators', and teachers' knowledge in student assessment. *Measurement and Evaluation in Counseling and Development, 28,* 78–87.

Individuals With Disabilities Education Act (1997 Revision). 20 U.S.C. 1400, Pub. L. No. 105-17 111 Stat. 37 (1997).

International Association of Addictions and Offenders Counselors. (2004). *Standards for assessment in substance abuse counseling.* Alexandria, VA: Author.

Ivey, A. E., & Ivey, M. B. (1998). Reframing *DSM-IV:* Positive strategies from developmental counseling and therapy. *Journal of Counseling & Development, 68,* 334–350.

Ivey, A. E., & Ivey, M. B. (1999). Toward a developmental diagnostic and statistical manual: The vitality of a contextual framework. *Journal of Counseling & Development, 77,* 484–490.

Jackson, B., & Farrugia, D. (1997). Diagnosis and treatment of adults with attention deficit hyperactivity disorder. *Journal of Counseling & Development, 75,* 312–319.

Jackson, D. N. (1989). *Basic Personality Inventory manual.* Port Huron, MI: Sigma Assessment Systems.

Jackson, D. N. (1997a). *Jackson Personality Inventory–Revised manual.* Port Huron, MI: Sigma Assessment Systems.

Jackson, D. N. (1997b). *Personality Research Form manual.* Port Huron, MI: Research Psychologists Press.

Jackson, D. N. (1998). *Multidimensional Aptitude Battery–II manual.* Port Huron, MI: Sigma Assessment Systems.

Jackson, D. N., & Verhoeve, M. (2000). *Jackson Vocational Interest Survey manual* (2nd ed., rev.). Port Huron, MI: Sigma Assessment Systems.

Jaeger, R. M. (1985). Graduate Record Examination: General test. In J. D. Mitchell, Jr. (Ed.), *The ninth mental measurements yearbook* (pp. 624–626). Lincoln, NE: Buros Institute of Mental Measurements.

Jankowski, D. (2002). *A beginner's guide to the MCMI-III.* Washington, DC: American Psychological Association.

Jay, M., & John, O. P. (2004). A depressive symptom scale for the California Psychological Inventory: Construct validation of the CPI-D. *Psychological Assessment, 16,* 299–309.

Jenkins, J. O., & Ramsey, G. A. (1991). Minorities. In M. Herson, A. E. Kazdin, & A. S. Bellack (Eds.), *The clinical psychology handbook* (2nd ed., pp. 683–696). New York: Pergamon.

JIST Publishing. (2006). *O*NET Career Values Inventory*. Retrieved June 14, 2006, from http://www. jist.com/productDetail.asp?AID=779&ID=1198&type=sum

Johansson, C. B. (1996). *Manual for IDEAS: Interest Determination, Exploration and Assessment System*. Minneapolis, MN: National Computer Systems.

Johnson, A. K. (1997). Conflict-handling intentions and the MBTI: A construct validation study. *Journal of Psychological Types, 43,* 29–39.

Johnson, J, A., D'Amato, R. C., & Harrison, M. L. (2005) Review of the Stanford-Binet Intelligence Scales, Fifth Edition. In R. A. Spies & B. S. Plake (Eds.), *The sixteenth mental measurements yearbook* (pp. 976–979). Lincoln, NE: Buros Institute of Mental Measurements.

Johnson, R. (1989). Review of the Thomas-Kilmann Conflict Mode Instrument. In J. C. Conoley & J. L. Kramer (Eds.), *The tenth mental measurements yearbook* (pp. 868–869). Lincoln, NE: Buros Institute of Mental Measurements.

Johnson, R. W. (2001a). Review of the Career Decision-Making Self-Efficacy Scale. In B. S. Plake & J. C. Impara (Eds.), *The fourteenth mental measurements yearbook* (pp. 218–219). Lincoln, NE: Buros Institute of Mental Measurements.

Johnson, R. W. (2001b). Review of the Quality of Life Inventory. In B. S. Plake & J. C. Impara (Eds.), *The fourteenth mental measurements yearbook* (pp. 975–977). Lincoln, NE: Buros Institute of Mental Measurements.

Joiner, T. E., Jr., Walker, R. L., Rudd, M. D., & Jobes, D. A. (1999). Scientizing and routinizing the assessment of suicidality in outpatient practice. *Professional Psychology: Research and Practice, 30,* 447–453.

Joint Committee on Testing Practices. (1999). *Rights and responsibilities of test takers: Guidelines and expectations*. Retrieved April 29, 2006, from http://www.apa.org/science/jctpweb.html#publications

Joint Committee on Testing Practices. (2004). *Code of fair testing practices in education*. Washington, DC: American Psychological Association.

Joint Committee on Testing Practices. (2006). Testing and assessment. Retrieved February 14, 2006, from http://www.apa.org/science/jctpweb.html

Juhnke, G. A. (1996). The adapted–SAD PERSONS: A suicide assessment scale designed for use with children. *Elementary School Guidance and Counseling, 30,* 252–258.

Juhnke, G. A., & Hovestadt, A. J. (1995). Using the SAD PERSONS Scale to promote supervisee suicide assessment knowledge. *Clinical Supervisor, 13,* 31–40.

Juhnke, G. A., Vacc, N. A., & Curtis, R. C. (2003). Assessment instruments used by addictions counselors. *Journal of Addictions & Offender Counseling, 23,* 66–72.

Jung, C. G. (1960). *The structure and dynamics of the psyche*. New York: Bollingan Foundation.

Kagee, A. (2005). Review of Adult Manifest Anxiety Scale. In R. A. Spies & B. S. Plake (Eds.), *The sixteenth mental measurements yearbook* (pp. 29–31). Lincoln, NE: Buros Institute of Mental Measurements.

Kapes, J. T., & Vansickle, T. R. (1992). Comparing paper-and-pencil and computer-based versions of the Harrington–O'Shea Career Decision-Making System. *Measurement and Evaluation in Counseling and Development, 25,* 5–13.

Kapes, J. T., & Whitfield, E. A. (Eds.). (2002). *A counselor's guide to career assessment instruments* (4th ed.). Columbus, OH: National Career Development Association.

Karlsen, B., & Gardner, F. E. (1986). *Adult Basic Learning Examination, 2nd Edition*. San Antonio, TX: Psychological Corporation.

Karson, M., Karson, S., & O'Dell, J. (1997). *16PF interpretation in clinical practice: A guide to the fifth edition*. Champaign, IL: IPAT.

Katz, L., Joyner, J. W., & Seaman, N. (1999). Effects of joint interpretation of the Strong Interest Inventory and the Myers–Briggs Type Indicator in career choice. *Journal of Career Assessment, 7,* 281–297.

Kaufman, A. S., & Kaufman, N. L. (1993). *Manual: Kaufman Adolescent and Adult Intelligence Test*. Circle Pines, MN: American Guidance Service.

Kaufman, A. S., & Kaufman, N. L. (2002). *Kaufman Brief Intelligence Test II manual*. Circle Pines, MN: American Guidance Service.

Kaufman, A. S., & Kaufman, N. L. (2003). *K-TEA-II*. Circle Pines, MN: American Guidance Service.

Kaufman, A. S., & Lichtenberger, E. O. (1999). *Essentials of WAIS*. New York: Wiley.

Kaufman, A. S., Lichtenberger, E. O., Fletcher-Janzen, E., & Kaufman, N. L. (2005). *Essentials of KABC-II assessment*. Hoboken, NJ: Wiley.

Keirsey, D. M. (2006). *Keirsey Temperament Sorter II (KTS-II)*. Retrieved April 30, 2006, from http://www.keirsey.com

Kelley, K. N. (2005). Review of Ball Aptitude Battery Form M. In R. A. Spies & B. S. Plake (Eds.), *The sixteenth mental measurements yearbook* (pp. 77–79). Lincoln, NE: Buros Institute of Mental Measurements.

Kellogg, C. E., & Morton, N. W. (1999). *Beta III manual*. San Antonio, TX: Harcourt Educational Measurement.

Kelly, K. R. (2002a). Mapping the domain of career decision problems. *Journal of Vocational Behavior, 61,* 302–326.

Kelly, K. R. (2002b). Review of Kuder Occupational Interest Survey Form DD (KOIS-DD) and Kuder Career Search with Person Match (KCS). In J. T. Kapes & E. A. Whitfield (Eds.), *A counselor's guide to career assessment instruments* (4th ed., pp. 263–275). Tulsa, OK: National Career Development Association.

Kenrick, D. T., & Funder, D. C. (1988). Profiting from controversy: Lessons from the person–situation debate. *American Psychologist, 43,* 23–34.

Kerr, B., & Gagliardi, C. (2003). Measuring creativity in research and practice. In S. J. Lopez & C. R. Snyder (Eds.), *Positive psychological assessment* (pp. 155–169). Washington, DC: American Psychological Association.

Kessler, R. C., Berglund, P., Demler, O., Jin, R., & Walters, E. E. (2005). Lifetime prevalence and age-of-onset distributions of *DSM-IV* disorders in the national comorbidity survey replication. *Archives of General Psychiatry, 62,* 593–602.

Kessler, R. C., Chiu, W. T., Demler, O., & Walters, E. E. (2005). Prevalence, severity, and comorbidity of 12-month *DSM-IV* disorders in the national comorbidity survey replication. *Archives of General Psychiatry, 62,* 617–627.

Kessler, R. C., Demler, O., Frank, R. G., Olfson, M., Pincus, H. A., Walters, E. E., et al. (2005). Prevalence and treatment of mental disorders, 1990 to 2003. *New England Journal of Medicine, 352,* 2515–2523

Keutzer, C. S., Morrill, W. H., Holmes, R. H., Sherman, L., Davenport, E., Tistadt, G., et al. (1998). Precipitating events and presenting problems of university counseling center clients: Some demographic differences. *Journal of College Student Psychotherapy, 12,* 3–23.

Keyser, D. J. (Ed.). (2005). *Test critiques: Vol. XI.* Austin, TX: PRO-ED.

Kiesler, D. J. (1987). *Checklist of Psychotherapy Transactions–Revised (CLOPT-R) and Checklist of Interpersonal Transactions–Revised (CLOIT-R).* Richmond, VA: Virginia Commonwealth University Press.

Kiesler, D. J., Schmidt, J. A., & Wagner, C. C. (1997). A circumplex inventory of impact messages: An operational bridge between emotion and interpersonal behavior. In R. Plutchik & H. R. Conte (Eds.), *Circumplex models of personality and emotions* (pp. 221–224). Washington, DC: American Psychological Association.

King, P. M., & Kitchener, K. S. (1994). *Developing reflective judgment: Understanding and promoting intellectual growth and critical thinking in adolescents and adults.* San Francisco: Jossey-Bass.

Kinnier, R. T. (1987). Development of a values conflict resolution assessment. *Journal of Counseling Psychology, 34,* 31–37.

Kinnier, R. T. (1995). A reconceptualization of values clarification: Values conflict resolution. *Journal of Counseling & Development, 74,* 18–24.

Kinnier, R. T., & Kernes, J. L. (2002). Review of Career Values Card Sort. In J. T. Kapes & E. A. Whitfield (Eds.), *A counselor's guide to career assessment instruments* (4th ed., pp. 218–221). Tulsa, OK: National Career Development Association.

Kiresuk, T. J., Smith, A., & Cardillo, J. E. (Ed.). (1994). *Goal attainment scaling: Applications, theory, and measurement.* Hillsdale, NJ: Erlbaum.

Kitchens, J. M. (1994). Does this patient have an alcohol problem? *Journal of the American Medical Association, 272,* 1782–1787.

Kivlighan, D. M., Jr., Multon, K. D., & Patton, M. J. (2000). Insight and symptom reduction in time-limited psychoanalytic counseling. *Journal of Counseling Psychology, 47,* 50–58.

Kleiman, T., Gati, I., Peterson, G., Sampson, J., Reardon, R., & Lenz, J. (2004). Dysfunctional thinking and difficulties in career decision making. *Journal of Career Assessment, 12,* 312–331.

Klein, D. N. (2003). Patients' versus informants' reports of personality disorders in predicting 7 1/2-year outcome in outpatients with depressive disorders. *Psychological Assessment, 15,* 216–222.

Knapp, L., Knapp, R. R., & Knapp-Lee, L. (1992). *Career Ability Placement Survey technical manual.* San Diego, CA: Educational and Industrial Testing Service.

Knapp, L., Knapp-Lee, L., & Knapp, R. (1995). *Career Orientation Placement and Evaluation Survey.* San Diego, CA: Educational and Industrial Testing Service.

Knapp-Lee, L. J. (1996). Use of the COPES, a measure of work values, in career assessment. *Journal of Career Assessment, 4,* 429–443.

Knapp-Lee, L. (2000). A complete career guidance program: The COPSystem. In C. E. Watkins, Jr. & V. L. Campbell (Eds.), *Testing and assessment in counseling practice* (2nd ed., pp. 295–338). Mahwah, NJ: Erlbaum.

Knight, J. R., Wechsler, H., Kuo, M., Seibering, M., Weitzman, E. R., & Schuckit, M. A. (2002). Alcohol abuse and dependence among U.S. college students. *Journal of Studies on Alcohol, 63,* 263–270.

Knowdell, R. L. (1998). *Career Values Card Sort.* San Jose, CA: Career Research & Testing.

Kobak, K. A., Greist, J. H., Jefferson, J. W., & Katzelnick, D. J. (1996). Computer-administered clinical rating scales: A review. *Psychopharmacology, 127,* 291–301.

Kobak, K. A., & Reynolds, W. M. (2004). The Hamilton Depression Inventory. In M. E. Maruish (Ed.), *The use of psychological testing for treatment planning and outcomes assessment: Volume 3. Instruments for adults* (3rd ed., pp. 327–362). Mahwah, NJ: Erlbaum.

Kobrin, J. L., & Kimmel, E. W. (2006). *Test development and technical information on the writing section of the SAT Reasoning Test* (Research Notes RN-25). New York: College Board.

Kohlberg, L. (1969). Stage and sequence: The cognitive developmental approach to socialization. In D. Goslin (Ed.), *Handbook of socialization theory and research* (pp. 347–480). Chicago: Rand McNally.

Kohlberg, L. (1971). Stages of moral development. In C. M. Beck, V. S. Crittenden, & E. B. Sullivan (Eds.), *Moral education* (pp. 23–92). Toronto, Ontario, Canada: University of Toronto Press.

Kohn, A. (2000). *The case against standardized testing.* Plymouth, NH: Heinemann.

Kolb, D. A. (1985). *Learning Style Inventory.* Boston: McBer.

Kopelman, R. E., Prottas, D. J., & Tatum, L. G. (2004). Comparison of four measures of values: Their relative usefulness in graduate education advisement. *North American Journal of Psychology, 6,* 205–218.

Kopelman, R. E., Rovenpor, J. L., & Guan, M. (2003). The Study of Values: Construction of the fourth edition. *Journal of Vocational Behavior, 62,* 203–220.

Korotitsch, W. J., & Nelson-Gray, R. O. (1999). An overview of self-monitoring research in assessment and treatment. *Psychological Assessment, 11,* 415–425.

Kovacs, M. (1992). *Children's Depression Inventory manual.* North Tonawanda, NY: Mental Health Systems.

Kovacs, M. (2003). *CDI technical manual update.* North Tonawanda, NY: Mental Health Systems.

Kramer, J. J., & Conoley, J. C. (Eds.). (1992). *The eleventh mental measurements yearbook.* Lincoln, NE: Buros Institute of Mental Measurements.

Kraus, D. R., Seligman, D. A., & Jordan, J. R. (2005). Validation of a behavioral health treatment outcome and assessment tool designed for naturalistic settings: The Treatment Outcome Package. *Journal of Clinical Psychology, 61,* 285–314.

Kress, V. E. W., Eriksen, K. P., Rayle, A. D., & Ford, S. J. W. (2005). The *DSM-IV-TR* and culture: Considerations for counselors. *Journal of Counseling & Development, 83,* 97–104.

Krishnamurthy, R., & Archer, R. P. (2003). In L. E. Beutler & G. Groth-Marnat (Eds.), *Integrative assessment of adult personality* (pp. 262–314). New York: Guilford.

Krumboltz, J. D. (1991). *Manual for the Career Beliefs Inventory.* Palo Alto, CA: Consulting Psychologists Press.

Krumboltz, J. D., Blando, J. A., Kim, H., & Reikowski, D. J. (1994). Embedding work values in stories. *Journal of Counseling & Development, 73,* 57–62.

Krumboltz, J. D., & Worthington, R. L. (1999). The school-to-work transition from a learning theory perspective. *The Career Development Quarterly, 47,* 312–325.

Kubiszyn, T. W., Meyer, G. J., Finn, S. E., Eyde, L. D., Kay, G. G., Moreland, K. L., et al. (2000). Empirical support for psychological assessment in clinical health care settings. *Professional Psychology: Research and Practice, 31,* 119–130.

Kuder, F. (1988). *General manual for Kuder General Interest Survey, Form E.* Monterey, CA: CTB/McGraw-Hill.

Kuncel, N. R., & Hezlett, S. A. (2001). A comprehensive meta-analysis of the predictive validity of the Graduate Record Examinations: Implications for graduate student selection and performance. *Psychological Bulletin, 127,* 162–181.

Kuncel, N. R., Hezlett, S. A., & Ones, D. S. (2004). Academic performance, career potential, creativity, and job performance: Can one construct predict them all? *Journal of Personality and Social Psychology, 86,* 148–161.

Kush, J. C. (2005). Review of The Stanford–Binet Intelligence Scales, Fifth Edition. In R. A. Spies & B. S. Plake (Eds.), *The sixteenth mental measurements yearbook* (pp. 979–984). Lincoln, NE: Buros Institute of Mental Measurements.

Kvaal, S., Choca, J., & Groth-Marnat, G. (2003). The integrated psychological report. In L. E. Beutler & G. Groth-Marnat (Eds.), *Integrative assessment of adult personality* (2nd ed., pp. 398–434). New York: Guilford Press.

Kypri, K., Saunders, J. B., Williams, S. M., McGee, R. O., Langley, J. D., Cashell-Smith, M. L., et al. (2004). Web-based screening and brief intervention for hazardous drinking: A double-blind randomized controlled trial. *Addiction, 99,* 1410–1417.

LaBrie, J. W., Pedersen, E. R., Earleywine, M., & Olsen, H. (2006). Reducing heavy drinking in college males with the decisional balance: Analyzing an element of Motivational Interviewing. *Addictive Behaviors, 31,* 254–263.

Lachar, D., Espadas, A., & Bailley, S. E. (2004). The Brief Psychiatric Rating Scale: Contemporary applications. In M. E. Maruish (Ed.), *The use of psychological testing for treatment planning and outcomes assessment: Volume 3. Instruments for adults* (3rd ed., pp.153–190). Mahwah, NJ: Erlbaum.

Laing, J., & Farmer, M. (1984). *Use of the ACT assessment by examinees with disabilities* (Research Report No. 84). Iowa City, IA: American College Testing Program.

Lambert, M. J., Gregersen, A. T., & Burlingame, G. M. (2004). The Outcome Questionnaire–45. In M. E. Maruish (Ed.), *The use of psychological testing for treatment planning and outcomes assessment: Volume 3. Instruments for adults* (3rd ed., pp. 191–234). Mahwah, NJ: Erlbaum.

Lane, G. G., White, A. E., & Henson, R. K. (2002). Expanding reliability methods with KR-21 estimates: An RG study of the Coopersmith Self-Esteem Inventory. *Educational and Psychological Measurement, 62,* 685–711.

Lanier, C. W. (1994). *ACT composite scores of re-tested students.* Iowa City, IA: American College Testing Program.

Lanning, K. (2003). The Myers–Briggs Type Indicator Step II. In B. S. Plake, J. O. Impara, & R. A. Spies (Eds.), *The fifteenth mental measurements yearbook* (pp. 614–616). Lincoln, NE: Buros Institute of Mental Measurements.

Lanyon, R. I. (1978). *Manual for Psychological Screening Inventory.* Port Huron, MI: Research Psychologists Press.

Lattimore, R. R., & Borgen, F. H. (1999). Validity of the 1994 Strong Interest Inventory with racial and ethnic groups in the United States. *Journal of Counseling Psychology, 46,* 185–195.

Law, J. G., Jr. (2005). Review of Hall Occupational Orientation Inventory–4th ed. In R. A. Spies & B. S. Plake (Eds.), *The sixteenth mental measurements yearbook* (pp. 427–428). Lincoln, NE: Buros Institute of Mental Measurements.

Law School Admission Council. (2005). *LSAT/LSDAS information book.* Newton, PA: Author.

Lawyer, S. R., & Smitherman, T. A. (2004). Trends in anxiety assessment. *Journal of Psychopathology and Behavioral Assessment, 26,* 101–108.

Lazowksi, L. E., Miller, F. G., Boye, M. W., & Miller, G. A. (1998). Efficacy of the Substance Abuse Subtle Screening Inventory–3 (SASSI-3) in identifying substance dependence disorders in clinical settings. *Journal of Personality Assessment, 71,* 114–128.

Lehman, N. (1999). *The big test: The secret history of American meritocracy.* New York: Farrar, Straus, & Giroux.

Leibert, T. W. (2006). Making change visible: The possibilities in assessing mental health counseling outcomes. *Journal of Counseling & Development, 84,* 108–113.

Lent, R. W., & Brown, S. D. (2006). On conceptualizing and assessing social cognitive constructs in career research: A measurement guide. *Journal of Career Assessment, 14,* 12–35.

Lent, R. W., Brown, S. D., & Hackett, G. (1994). Toward a unifying social cognitive theory of career and academic interest, choice, and performance. *Journal of Vocational Behavior, 45,* 79–122.

Leong, F. T. L., & Gim-Chung, R. H. (1995). Career assessment and intervention with Asian Americans. In F. T. L. Leong (Ed.), *Career development and vocational behavior of racial and ethnic minorities* (pp. 193–226). Mahwah, NJ: Erlbaum.

Leonhard, C., Mulvey, K., Gastfriend, D. R., & Schwartz, M. (2000). The Addiction Severity Index: A field study of internal consistency and validity. *Journal of Substance Abuse Treatment, 18,* 129–135.

Levinson, E. M., Ohler, D. L., Caswell, S., & Kiewra, K. (1998). Six approaches to the assessment of career maturity. *Journal of Counseling & Development, 76,* 475–482.

Lewak, R. W., & Hogan, R. S. (2003). Integrating and applying assessment information. In L. E. Buetler & G. Groth-Marnat (Eds.), *Integrative assessment of adult personality* (2nd ed., pp. 356–397). New York: Guilford Press.

Lewin, K. (1935). *A dynamic theory of personality: Selected papers.* New York: McGraw-Hill.

Lewin, T. (2006, January 8). The two faces of A.P. *The New York Times Education Life,* pp. 24–28.

Lewis, P., & Rivkin, D. (2004). Improving work life decisions: O*NET career exploration tools. In J. E. Wall & G. H. Walz (Eds.), *Measuring up: Assessment issues for teachers, counselors, and administrators* (pp. 595–610). Greensboro, NC: CAPS Press.

Lichtenberger, E. O., & Kaufman, A. S. (1998). Assessment Battery for Children (K-ABC). In R. J. Samuda, R. Feuerstein, A. S. Kaufman, J. E. Lewis, R. J. Sternberg, & Associates (Eds.), *Advances in cross-cultural assessment* (pp. 56–99). Thousand Oaks, CA: Sage.

Lichtenberger, E. O., & Kaufman, A. S. (2004). *Essentials of WPPSI-III assessment.* Hoboken, NJ: Wiley.

Lichtenberger, E. O., Mather, N., Kaufman, N. L., & Kaufman, A. S. (2004). *Essentials of assessment report writing.* Hoboken, NJ: Wiley.

Lindeman, M., & Verkasalo, M. (2005). Measuring values with the short Schwartz's Value Survey. *Journal of Personality Assessment, 85,* 170–178.

Loesch, L. C., & Vacc, N. A. (1993). *A work behavior analysis of professional counselors.* Greensboro, NC: National Board for Certified Counselors.

Loew, S. A. (2003). Review of Career Planning Survey. In B. S. Plake, J. C. Impara, & R. A. Spies (Eds.), *The fifteenth mental measurements yearbook* (pp. 163–165). Lincoln, NE: Buros Institute of Mental Measurements.

Longman, R. S. (2004). Values for comparison of WAIS-III index scores with overall means. *Psychological Assessment, 16,* 323–325.

Lonner, W. J., & Ibrahim, F. A. (1996). Assessment in cross-cultural counseling. In P. Pedersen & J. G. Draguns (Eds.), *Counseling across cultures* (pp. 293–322). Thousand Oaks, CA: Sage.

Lonner, W. J., & Sundberg, N. D. (1987). Assessment in cross-cultural counseling and therapy. In P. Pedersen (Ed.), *Handbook of cross-cultural counseling and therapy* (pp. 199–205). New York: Praeger.

Lopez, M. N., Charter, R. A., Mostafavi, B., Nibut, L. P., & Smith, W. E. (2005). Psychometric properties of the Folstein Mini-Mental State Examination. *Assessment, 12,* 137–144.

Lopez, S. J., Edwards, L. M., Pedrotti, J. T., Prosser, E. C., LaRue, S., Spalitto, S. V., & Ulven, J. C. (2006). Beyond the *DSM–IV:* Assumptions, alternatives, and alterations. *Journal of Counseling & Development, 84,* 259–267.

LoVerde, M., McMahon, B. T., & Morris, G. W. (1992). Employment testing and evaluation. In N. Hablutzel & B. T. McMahon (Eds.), *The Americans With Disabilities Act: Access and accommodations* (pp. 79–88). Orlando, FL: Deutsch Press.

Lovitt, R. (1998). Teaching assessment skills in internship settings. In L. Handler & M. J. Hilsenroth (Eds.), *Teaching and learning personality assessment* (pp. 471–484). Mahwah, NJ: Erlbaum.

Lukin, L. E. (2005). Review of the Iowa Early Learning Inventory. In R. A. Spies & B. S. Plake (Eds.), *The sixteenth mental measurements yearbook* (pp. 481–483) Lincoln, NE: Buros Institute of Mental Measurements.

Lumsden, J. A., Sampson, J. P., Jr., Reardon, R. C., Lenz, J. G., & Peterson, G. W. (2004). A comparison study of the paper-and-pencil, personal computer, and Internet versions of Holland's Self-Directed Search. *Measurement and Evaluation in Counseling and Development, 37,* 85–94.

Lunneborg, P. W. (1993). *Manual for Vocational Interest Inventory–Revised.* Los Angeles: Western Psychological Services.

Luria, A. R. (1980). *Higher cortical functions in man* (2nd ed.). New York: Basic Books.

Lustman, P. J., Sowa, C. J., & O'Hara, D. J. (1984). Factors influencing college student health: Development of the Psychological Distress Inventory. *Journal of Counseling Psychology, 31,* 28–35.

Luttrell, S., Watkin, V., Livingston, G., Walker, Z., D'Ath, P., Patel, P., et al. (1997). Screening for alcohol misuse in older people. *International Journal of Geriatric Psychiatry, 12,* 1151–1154.

Luzzo, D. A. (1996). A psychometric evaluation of the Career Decision-Making Self-Efficacy Scale. *Journal of Counseling & Development, 74,* 276–279.

Luzzo, D. A. (2002). *Making career decisions that count: A practical guide* (2nd ed.). Upper Saddle River, NJ: Prentice Hall.

Maddox, T. (Ed.). (2003). *Tests: A comprehensive reference for assessments in psychology, education, and business* (5th ed.). Austin, TX: PRO-ED.

Madle, R. A. (2005). Review of the Wechsler Preschool and Primary Scale of Intelligence. In R. A. Spies & B. S. Plake (Eds.), *The sixteenth mental measurements yearbook* (pp. 1115–1118). Lincoln, NE: Buros Institute of Mental Measurements.

Mallen, M. J., Vogel, D. L., Rochlen, A. B., & Day, S. X., (2005). Online counseling: Reviewing the literature from a counseling psychology framework. *The Counseling Psychologist, 33,* 819–871.

Maller, S. J. (2005). Review of the Wechsler Intelligence Scale for Children–Fourth Edition. In R. A. Spies & B. S. Plake (Eds.), *The sixteenth mental measurements yearbook* (pp. 1092–1096). Lincoln, NE: Buros Institute of Mental Measurements.

Manages, K. J. (2001). Review of the Family Assessment Measure III. In B. S. Plake & J. G. Impara (Eds.), *The fourteenth mental measurements yearbook* (pp. 480–482). Lincoln, NE: Buros Institute of Mental Measurements.

Mancini, J. A. (2001). Review of the Family Environment Scale (third edition). In B. S. Plake & J. G. Impara (Eds.), *The fourteenth mental measurements yearbook* (pp. 482–484). Lincoln, NE: Buros Institute of Mental Measurement.

Marchetti-Mercer, M. C., & Cleaver, G. (2000). Genograms and family sculpting: An aid to cross-cultural understanding in the training of psychology students in South Africa. *The Counseling Psychologist, 28,* 61–80.

Mariani, M. (1999). Replace with a database: O*NET replaces the Dictionary of Occupational Titles. *Occupational Outlook Quarterly, 43*(1), 3–9.

Marks, I. M., & Mathews, A. M. (1978). Brief standard self-rating for phobic patients. *Behavior Research and Therapy, 17,* 263–267.

Marlatt, G. A., & Miller, W. R. (1984). *Comprehensive Drinking Profile*. Odessa, FL: Psychological Assessment Resources.

Marsh, H. W. (1985). Behavioral Academic Self-Esteem (BASE). In J. W. Mitchell (Ed.), *The ninth mental measurements yearbook* (pp. 169–170). Lincoln, NE: Buros Institute of Mental Measurement.

Marsh, H. W., & Hau, K.-T. (2003). Big-fish-little-pond effect on academic self-concept. *American Psychologist, 58,* 364–376.

Martin, D. J., Garske, J. P., & Davis, M. K. (2000). Relation of the therapeutic alliance with outcome and other variables: A meta-analytic review. *Journal of Consulting & Clinical Psychology, 68,* 438–450.

Maslow, A. H. (1987). *Motivation and personality* (3rd ed.). New York: Harper & Row.

Mau, W. (2001). Assessing career decision-making difficulties: A cross-cultural study. *Journal of Career Assessment, 9,* 353–364.

Mau, W. (2004). Cultural dimensions of career decision-making difficulties. *The Career Development Quarterly, 53,* 67–77.

McAllister, L. W. (1996). *A practical guide to CPI interpretation* (3rd ed.). Palo Alto, CA: Consulting Psychologists Press.

McCarney, S. B., & Anderson, P. D. (1996). *Adult Attention Deficit Disorders Evaluation Scale*. Columbia, MO: Hawthorne Educational Services.

McCrae, R. R., & Allik, J. (Eds.). (2002). *The five-factor model of personality across cultures*. New York: Kluwer Academic/Plenum.

McCrae, R. R., & Costa, P. T. (1986). Clinical assessment can benefit from recent advances in personality psychology. *American Psychologist, 41,* 1001–1003.

McCrae, R. R., & Costa, P. T. (1997). Personality trait structure as a human universal. *American Psychologist, 52,* 509–516.

McDivitt, P. J. (2002). Review of Career Maturity Inventory (CMI). In J. T. Kapes & E. A. Whitfield (Eds.), *A counselor's guide to career assessment instruments* (4th ed., pp. 336–342). Tulsa, OK: National Career Development Association.

McGoldrick, M., Gerson, R., & Shellenberger, S. (1999). *Genograms: Assessment and intervention* (2nd ed.). New York: Norton.

McIntosh, D. E., & Dixon, F. A. (2005). Use of intelligence tests in the identification of giftedness. In D. P. Flanagan & P. L. Harrison (Eds.), *Contemporary intellectual assessment* (pp. 545–556). New York: Guilford Press.

McLellan, A. T., Kushner, H., Metzger, D., Peters, R., Smith, I., Grissom, G., et al. (1992). The fifth edition of the Addiction Severity Index: Reliability and validity in three centers. *Journal of Nervous and Mental Disease, 173,* 412–423.

McMahon, M., Watson, M., & Patton, W. (2005). Qualitative career assessment: Developing the My System of Career Influences Reflection Activity. *Journal of Career Assessment, 13,* 476–490.

McNulty, J. L., Graham, J. R., Ben-Porath, Y. S., & Stein, L. A. R. (1997). Comparative validity of MMPI-2 scores of African American and Caucasian mental health center clients. *Psychological Assessment, 9,* 464–470.

Mehrens, W. A., & Ekstrom, R. B. (2002). Score reporting issues in the assessment of people with disabilities: Policies and practices. In R. B. Ekstrom & D. K. Smith (Eds.), *Assessing individuals with disabilities in educational, employment, and counseling settings* (pp. 87–100). Washington, DC: American Psychological Association.

Meloun, J. M. (2005). Computer anxiety: A possible threat to the predictive validity of computerized tests. *Dissertation Abstracts International, 65*(07), 3768B.

Mendelsohn, G. A., & Kirk, B. A. (1962). Personality differences not used. *Journal of Counseling Psychology, 9,* 341–346.

Messick, S. (1980). Test validity and the ethics of assessment. *American Psychologist, 35,* 1012–1027.

Messick, S. (1995). Validity of psychological assessment: Validation of inferences from person's responses and performances as scientific inquiry into score meaning. *American Psychologist, 50,* 741–749.

Meyer, G. J., Finn, S. E., Eyde, L. D., Kay, G. G., Moreland, K. L., Dies, R. R., et al. (2001). Psychological testing and psychological assessment: A review of evidence and issues. *American Psychologist, 56,* 128–165.

Meyer, P., & Davis, S. (1992). *The CPI applications guide: An essential tool for individual, group, and organizational development.* Palo Alto, CA: Consulting Psychologists Press.

Meyers, L. (2006, December). Asian-American mental health. *Monitor on Psychology, 37*(2), 44–46.

Michael, W. B. (2005). Review of O*NET Work Importance Locator. In R. A. Spies & B. S. Plake (Eds.), *The sixteenth mental measurements yearbook* (pp. 734–737). Lincoln, NE: Buros Institute of Mental Measurements.

Michael, W. B., Michael, J. J., & Zimmerman, W. S. (1988). *Study Attitudes and Methods Survey, manual of instructions and interpretations.* San Diego, CA: EdITS.

Miller, F. G., & Lazowski, L. E. (2001). *The adolescent SASSI-A2 manual: Identifying substance user disorders.* Springville, IN: SASSI Institute.

Miller, G. A. (1999). *SASSI-3 manual.* Springville, IN: SASSI Institute.

Miller, J. D., Reynolds, S. K., & Pilkonis, P. A. (2004). The validity of the five-factor prototypes for personality disorders in two clinical samples. *Psychological Assessment, 16,* 310–322.

Miller, W. R., & Muñoz, R. F. (2005). *Controlling your drinking: Tools to make moderation work for you.* New York: Guilford.

Miller, W. R., & Rollnick, S. (2002). *Motivational Interviewing: Preparing people for change* (2nd ed.). New York: Guilford.

Millon, T. (1990). *Toward a new personology: An evolutionary model.* New York: Wiley-Interscience.

Millon, T. (2003). *MIPS Revised manual.* Minneapolis, MN: Pearson Assessments.

Millon, T., & Craig, R. J. (2005). *New directions in interpreting the Millon Clinical Multiaxial Inventory–III (MCMI-III).* New York: Wiley.

Millon, T., & Davis, R. D. (1993). The Millon Adolescent Personality Inventory and the Millon Adolescent Clinical Inventory. *Journal of Counseling & Development, 71,* 570–574.

Millon, T., Davis, R. D., & Millon, C. (1997). *MCMI-III manual* (2nd ed.). Minneapolis, MN: National Computer Systems.

Millon, T., Millon, C., Davis, R., & Grossman, S. (2006). *MCMI-III: New Facet Scales help identify underlying issues.* Retrieved March 20, 2006, from http://www.pearsonassessments.com/tests/mcmi_3.htm

Miner, C. U., & Sellers, S. M. (2002). Review of Career Assessment Inventory (CAI). In J. T. Kapes & E. A. Whitfield (Eds.), *A counselor's guide to career assessment instruments* (4th ed., pp. 202–209). Tulsa, OK: National Career Development Association.

Mintz, L. B., & O'Halloran, M. S. (2000). The Eating Attitudes Test: Validation with *DSM-IV* eating disorder criteria. *Journal of Personality Assessment, 74,* 489–503.

Mintz, L. B., O'Halloran, M. S., Mulholland, A. M., & Schneider, P. A. (1997). Questionnaire for Eating Disorder Diagnoses: Reliability and validity of operationalizing *DSM-IV* criteria into a self-report format. *Journal of Counseling Psychology, 44,* 63–79.

Mitchell, L. K., & Krumboltz, J. D. (1987). The effects of cognitive restructuring and decision-making training on career indecision. *Journal of Counseling & Development, 66,* 171–174.

Moore, W. S. (1988). *The Measure of Intellectual Development: An instrument manual.* Farmville, VA: Center for the Study of Intellectual Development.

Moos, R. H. (1974). *The social climate scales: An overview.* Palo Alto, CA: Consulting Psychologists Press.

Moos, R. H., & Moos, B. S. (1994a). *Family Environment Scale manual: Development, application and research.* Palo Alto, CA: Consulting Psychologists Press.

Moos, R. H., & Moos, B. S. (1994b). *Life Stressors and Social Resources Inventory–Adult form.* Odessa, FL: Psychological Assessment Resources.

Moos, R. H., & Moos, B. S. (1994c). *Life Stressors and Social Resources Inventory–Youth form.* Odessa, FL: Psychological Assessment Resources.

Moreland, K. L., Eyde, L. D., Robertson, G. J., Primoff, E. S., & Most, R. B. (1995). Assessment of test user qualifications: A research-based measurement procedure. *American Psychologist, 50,* 14–23.

Morey, L. (1991). *Personality Assessment Inventory: Professional manual.* Odessa, FL: Psychological Assessment Resources.

Morey, L. (1998). *A user's guide: Personality Assessment Screener.* Odessa, FL: Psychological Assessment Resources.

Morey, L. C. (2003). *Essentials of PAI assessment.* Hoboken, NJ: Wiley.

Morris, M., Chartrand, J., & Donnay, D. (2002). *Instrument development: Reliability and validity of the Strong Interest Explorer.* Palo Alto, CA: Consulting Psychologists Press.

Mulholland, A. M., & Mintz, L. B. (2001). Prevalence of eating disorders among African American women. *Journal of Counseling Psychology, 48,* 111–116.

Murray, B. (1998, April). Getting smart about learning is her lesson. *APA Monitor, 29,* 36.

Murray, H. A. (1938). *Explorations in personality.* New York: Oxford University Press.

Murray, H. A. (1943). *Thematic Apperception Test manual.* Cambridge, MA: Harvard University Press.

Myers, I. B., Kirby, L. K., & Myers, K. D. (1998). *Introduction to type.* Palo Alto, CA: Consulting Psychologists Press.

Myers, I. B., McCaulley, M. H., Quenk, N. L., & Hammer, A. L. (1998). *MBTI manual: A guide to the development and use of the Myers–Briggs Type Indicator* (3rd ed.). Palo Alto, CA: Consulting Psychologists Press.

Myers, I. B., & Myers, P. B. (1995). *Gifts differing.* Palo Alto, CA: Davies-Black.

Myers, J. E., Luecht, R. M., & Sweeney, T. J. (2004). The factor structure of wellness: Reexamining theoretical and empirical models underlying the Wellness Evaluation of Lifestyle (WEL) and the five-factor model. *Measurement and Evaluation in Counseling and Development, 36,* 194–208.

Myers, J. E., & Shurts, W. M. (2002). Measuring positive emotionality: A review of instruments assessing love. *Measurement and Evaluation in Counseling and Development, 34,* 238–254.

Myers, J. E., Villalba, J., & Sweeney, T. J. (2005, April). *Determining the wellness of elementary school children and educators prior to state-standardized test administration.* Paper presented at the annual convention of the American Counseling Association, Atlanta, GA.

Nagayama Hall, G. C., Bansal, A., & Lopez, I. R. (1999). Ethnicity and psychopathology: A meta-analytic review of 31 years of comparative MMPI/MMPI-2 research. *Psychological Assessment, 11,* 186–197.

Naglieri, J. A. (1996). *Naglieri Nonverbal Ability Test–Multilevel form.* San Antonio, TX: Psychological Corporation.

Naglieri, J. A. (2000). *Naglieri Nonverbal Ability Test: Individual administration.* San Antonio, TX: Psychological Corporation.

Naglieri, J. A. (2005). *The Cognitive Assessment System.* Odessa, FL: Psychological Assessment Resources.

Naglieri J. A., & Das, J. P. (2005). Planning, attention, simultaneous, successive (PASS) theory: A revision of the concept of intelligence. In D. P. Flanagan & P. L. Harrison (Eds.), *Contemporary intellectual assessment* (pp. 120–135). New York: Guilford Press.

Naglieri, J, A., Dragow, F., Schmit, M., Handler, L., Prifitera, A., Magolis, A., et al. (2004). Psychological testing on the Internet: New problems, old issues. *American Psychologist, 39,* 150–162.

Naglieri, J. A., & Ronning, M. W. (2000). Comparison of White, African American, Hispanic, and Asian children on the Naglieri Nonverbal Ability Test. *Psychological Assessment, 12,* 328–334.

National Board of Certified Counselors. (2005). *National Board of Certified Counselors code of ethics.* Retrieved February 13, 2006, from http://www.nbcc.org/ethics2

National Career Assessment Services, Inc. (2004). *Super's Work Values Inventory–Revised.* Retrieved July 10, 2006, from http://www.kuder.com/PublicWeb/swv.aspx

National Career Assessment Services, Inc. (2006). *Kuder Online Career Portfolio.* Retrieved January 7, 2006, from https://www.kuder.com/PublicWeb/aboutus.aspx

National Career Development Association. (1997). *NCDA guidelines for the use of the Internet for provision of career information and planning services.* Retrieved November 27, 2005, from http://www.ncda.org

National Institute of Mental Health. (2004, April). *Suicide facts and statistics.* Retrieved March 11, 2006, from http://www.nimh.nih.gov/suicideprevention/suifact.cfm

National Institute on Alcohol Abuse and Alcoholism. (2005). *A pocket guide for alcohol screening and brief intervention.* Retrieved March 14, 2006, from http://pubs.niaaa.nih.gov/publications/Practitioner/Pocket Guide/pocket.pdf

Naylor, F. D., & Krumboltz, J. D. (1994). The independence of aptitudes, interests, and beliefs. *The Career Development Quarterly, 43,* 152–160.

Neimeyer, G. J. (1989). Applications of repertory grid technique to vocational assessment. *Journal of Counseling & Development, 67,* 585–589.

Neisser, V. (1998). *The rising curve: Long-term gains in IQ and related measures.* Washington, DC: American Psychological Association.

Neisser, V., Boodoo, G., Bouchardt, T. J., Boykin, A. W., Brody, N., Ceci, S. J., et al. (1996). Intelligence: Knowns and unknowns. *American Psychologist, 51,* 77–101.

Nelson, M. L. (2002). An assessment-based model for counseling strategy selection. *Journal of Counseling & Development, 80,* 416–421.

Nevill, D. D., & Calvert, P. D. (1996). Career assessment and the Salience Inventory. *Journal of Career Assessment, 4,* 312–399.

Nevill, D. D., & Kruse, S. J. (1996). Career assessment and the Values Scale. *Journal of Career Assessment, 4,* 383–397.

Nevill, D. D., & Super, D. E. (1986a). *Manual for the Salience Inventory.* Palo Alto, CA: Consulting Psychologists Press.

Nevill, D. D., & Super, D. E. (1986b). *Manual for the Values Scale.* Palo Alto, CA: Consulting Psychologists Press.

Nezu, A. M. (2004). Problem solving and behavior therapy revisited. *Behavior Therapy, 35,* 1–33.

Nezu, A. M., D'Zurilla, T. J., Zwick, M. L., & Nezu, C. M. (2004). Problem-solving therapy for adults. In E. D. Chang, T. J. D'Zurilla, & L. J. Sanna, (Eds.), *Social problem solving: Theory, research, and training* (pp. 171–191). Washington, DC: American Psychological Association.

Nezu, A. M., & Nezu, C. M. (1993). Identifying and selecting target problems for clinical interventions: A problem-solving model. *Psychological Assessment, 5,* 254–263.

Nezu, A. M., Ronan, G. F., Meadows, E. A., & McClure, K. S. (Eds.). (2000). *Practitioner's guide to empirically based measures of depression.* New York: Kluwer Academic/Plenum.

Nicholson, C. L., & Hibpshman, T. L. (1998). *Manual, Slosson Intelligence Test–Revised.* East Aurora, NY: Slosson Educational.

Niv, N., Kaplan, Z., Mitrani, E., & Shiang, J. (1998). Validity study of the EDI-2 in Israeli population. *Israel Journal of Psychiatry and Related Sciences, 35,* 287–292.

Noble, J., Davenport, M., Schiel, J., & Pommerich, M. (1999). *High school academic and noncognitive variables related to the ACT scores of racial/ethnic groups.* Iowa City, IA: American College Testing Program.

No Child Left Behind Act of 2001, 107 U.S.C. §1425 (2002).

Noel-Levitz. (2006). *College Student Inventory, Noel-Levitz Retention Management System.* Retrieved May 2, 2006, from www.noellevitz.com/Our+Services/Retention/

Novy, D. M., Nelson, D. V., Goodwin, J., & Rowzee, R. D. (1993). Psychometric comparability of the State–Trait Anxiety Inventory for different ethnic populations. *Psychological Assessment, 5,* 343–349.

Okazaki, S., Kallivayalil, D., & Sue, S. (2002). Clinical personality assessment with Asian Americans. In J. N. Butcher (Ed.), *Clinical personality assessment: Practical approaches* (pp. 135–153). New York: Oxford University Press.

Okocha, A. A. G. (1998). Using qualitative appraisal strategies in career counseling. *Journal of Employment Counseling, 35,* 151–159.

Ortiz, S. O., & Dynda, A. M. (2005). Use of intelligence tests with culturally and linguistically diverse populations. In D. P. Flanagan & P. L. Harrison (Eds.), *Contemporary intellectual assessment* (pp. 545–556). New York: Guilford Press.

Osborne, W. L., Brown, S., Niles, S., & Miner, C. U. (1997). *Career development, assessment, and counseling: Applications of the Donald E. Super C-DAC approach.* Alexandria, VA: American Counseling Association.

Osgood, C. E., & Tzeng, O. C. S. (Eds.). (1990). *Language, meaning, and culture: The selected papers of C. E. Osgood.* New York: Praeger.

Osipow, S. H. (1987). *Manual for the Career Decision Scale* (Rev. ed.). Odessa, FL: Psychological Assessment Resources.

Osipow, S. H. (1999). Assessing career indecision. *Journal of Vocational Behavior, 55,* 147–154.

Osipow, S. H., & Winer, J. L. (1996). The use of the Career Decision Scale in career assessment. *Journal of Career Assessment, 4,* 117–130.

Oswald, F. L., Schmitt, N., Kim, B. H., Ramsay, L. J., & Gillespie, M. A. (2004). Developing a biodata measure and situational judgment inventory as predictors of college student performance. *Journal of Applied Psychology, 89,* 187–207.

Othmer, E., & Othmer, S. C. (Eds.). (2001a). *The clinical interview using DSM-IV-TR: Vol. 1. Fundamentals.* Washington, DC: American Psychiatric Press.

Othmer, E., & Othmer, S. C. (Eds.). (2001b). *The clinical interview using DSM-IV-TR: Vol. 2. The difficult patient.* Washington, DC: American Psychiatric Press.

Pace, C. R. (1987). *CSEQ: Test manual and norms.* Los Angeles: University of California, Los Angeles, Center for the Study of Evaluations.

Pace, C. R., & Kuh, G. D. (1998). *College Student Experiences Questionnaire.* Bloomington: Indiana University Center for Postsecondary Research and Planning.

Paniagua, F. A. (2005). *Assessing and treating culturally diverse clients.* Thousand Oaks, CA: Sage.

Panksepp, J. (1998). Attention deficit hyperactivity disorders, psychostimulants, and intolerance of childhood playfulness: A tragedy in the making? *Current Directions in Psychological Science, 7,* 91–98.

Parker, J., & Hood, A. B. (1997). The Parker Cognitive Development Inventory. In A. B. Hood (Ed.), *The Iowa student development inventories* (2nd ed., pp. 109–133). Iowa City, IA: Hitech Press.

Parker, R. (2002). *Occupational Aptitude Survey and Interest Schedule–Third Edition (OASIS-3).* Austin, TX: PRO-ED.

Parra, G. R., Martin, C. S., & Clark, D. B. (2005). The drinking situations of adolescents treated for alcohol use disorders: A psychometric and alcohol-related outcomes investigation. *Addictive Behaviors, 30,* 1725–1736.

Parsons, F. (1909). *Choosing a vocation.* Boston: Houghton-Mifflin.

Patterson, W. M., Dohn, H. H., Bird, J., & Patterson, G. A. (1983). Evaluation of suicidal patients: The SAD PERSONS Scale. *Psychosomatics, 24,* 343–349.

Pearman, R. P., & Albritton, S. C. (1997). *I'm not crazy, I'm just not you.* Palo Alto, CA: Davies-Black.

Pearson Assessments. (2006). *MMPI-2.* Retrieved March 17, 2006, from http://www.pearsonassessments.com/tests/mmpi_2.htm

Pendergrass, L. A., Hansen, J. C., Neuman, J. L., & Nutter, K. J. (2003). Examination of the concurrent validity of scores from the CISS for student-athlete college major selection: A brief report. *Measurement and Evaluation in Counseling and Development, 35,* 212–217.

Penick, N. (2000). The genogram technique. In N. Peterson & R. C. Gonzales (Eds.), *Career counseling models for diverse populations* (pp. 137–149). Pacific Grove, CA: Brooks/Cole.

Perrone, K. M., Gordon, P. A., Fitch, J. C., & Civiletto, C. L. (2003). The Adult Career Concerns Inventory: Development of a short form. *Journal of Employment Counseling, 40,* 172–180.

Perry, W. (1970). *Forms of intellectual and ethical development in college years: A scheme.* New York: Holt, Rinehart & Winston.

Peruzzi, N., & Bongar, B. (1999). Assessing risk for completed suicide in patients with major depression: Psychologists' views of critical factors. *Professional Psychology: Research and Practice, 30,* 576–580.

Peterson, C., & Austin, J. T. (1985). Review of Coopersmith Self-Esteem Inventories. In J. V. Mitchell, Jr. (Ed.), *The ninth mental measurements yearbook* (pp. 396–397). Lincoln, NE: Buros Institute of Mental Measurements.

Peterson, C., & Seligman, M. E. P. (2004). *Character strengths and virtues: A handbook and classification.* Washington, DC: American Psychological Association.

Peterson, G. W. (1998). Using a vocational card sort as an assessment of occupational knowledge. *Journal of Career Assessment, 6,* 49–67.

Peterson, N. G., Mumford, M. D., Borman, W. C., Jeanneret, P. R., Fleishman, E. A., Levin, K. Y., et al. (2001). Understanding work using the Occupational Information Network (O*NET). *Personnel Psychology, 54,* 451–492.

Petrocelli, J. V. (2002). Processes and stages of change: Counseling with a transtheoretical model of change. *Journal of Counseling & Development, 80,* 22–30.

Phelps, R. P. (2005a). Persistently positive: Forty years of public opinion on standardized testing. In R. P. Phelps (Ed.), *Defending standardized testing* (pp. 1–22). Mahwah, NJ: Erlbaum.

Phelps, R. P. (2005b). The rich, robust research literature on testing's achievement benefits. In R. P. Phelps (Ed.), *Defending standardized testing* (pp. 55–90). Mahwah, NJ: Erlbaum.

Piaget, J. (1965). *The moral judgment of the child.* New York: Free Press.

Pickering, J. W. (1998). Test review: Career Thoughts Inventory (CTI). *AAC Newsnotes, 33*(1), 5–6.

Piers, E. B., & Harris, D. B. (1996). *Piers–Harris Children's Self-Concept Scale, Revised manual.* Los Angeles: Western Psychological Services.

Pincus, A. L., & Gurtman, M. B. (2003). Interpersonal Assessment. In J. S. Wiggins (Ed.), *Paradigms of personality assessment* (pp. 246–261). New York: Guilford Press.

Piotrowski, C. (2000). How popular is the Personality Assessment Inventory in practice and training? *Psychological Reports, 86,* 65–66.

Pittenger, D. J. (1993). The utility of the Myers–Briggs Type Indicator. *Review of Educational Research, 63,* 467–488.

Pittenger, D. J. (2003). Review of Substance Abuse Subtle Screening Inventory–3. In B. S. Plake, J. C. Impara, & R. A. Spies (Eds.), *The fifteenth mental measurements yearbook* (pp. 916–918). Lincoln, NE: Buros Institute of Mental Measurements.

Pittenger, D. J. (2005). Cautionary comments regarding the Myers–Briggs Type Indicator. *Counseling Psychology Journal: Practice and Research, 57,* 210–221.

Plake, B. S. (2002). Evaluating the technical quality of educational tests used of high-stakes decisions. *Measurement and Evaluation in Counseling and Development, 35,* 144–152.

Plake, B. S., & Parker, C. S. (1982). The development and validation of a revised version of the Mathematics Anxiety Rating Scale. *Educational and Psychological Measurement, 42,* 551–557.

Podar, I., Hannus, A., & Allik, J. (1999). Personality and affectivity characteristics associated with eating disorders: A comparison of eating disordered, weight-preoccupied, and normal samples. *Journal of Personality Assessment, 73,* 133–147.

Polanski, P. J., & Hinkle, J. S. (2000). The Mental Status Examination: Its use by professional counselors. *Journal of Counseling & Development, 78,* 357–364.

Pollak, J., Levy, S., & Breitholtz, T. (1999). Screening for medical and neurodevelopmental disorders for the professional counselor. *Journal of Counseling & Development, 77,* 350–358.

Ponterotto, J. G., Rivera, L., & Sueyoshi, L. A. (2000). The career-in-culture interview: A semi-structured protocol for the cross-cultural intake interview. *The Career Development Quarterly, 49,* 85–96.

Pope, M. (2002). Review of Kuder General Interest Survey Form E (KGIS-Form E). In J. T. Kapes & E. A. Whitfield (Eds.), *A counselor's guide to career assessment instruments* (4th ed., pp. 257–268). Tulsa, OK: National Career Development Association.

Powers, D. E., & Rock, D. A. (1998). *Effects of coaching on SAT-I: Reasoning scores* (Report No. 988-6). New York: College Board.

Prediger, D. J. (1994a). Multicultural assessment standards: A compilation for counselors. *Measurement and Evaluation in Counseling and Development, 27,* 68–73.

Prediger, D. J. (1994b). Tests and counseling: The marriage that prevailed. *Measurement and Evaluation in Counseling and Development, 26,* 227–234.

Prediger, D. J. (2002). Abilities, interests, and values: Their assessment and their integration via the World-of-Work Map. *Journal of Career Assessment, 10,* 209–232.

Prediger, D. J. (2004). Career planning validity of self-estimates and test estimates of work-relevant abilities. *The Career Development Quarterly, 52,* 202–211.

Prediger, D. J., & Swaney, K. B. (1992). *Career counseling validity of DISCOVER's job cluster scales for the revised ASVAB score report* (Report No. 92-2). Iowa City, IA: American College Testing Program.

Prieto, L. R., McNeill, B. W., Walls, R. G., & Gomez, S. P. (2001). Chicanas/os and mental health services: An overview of utilization, counselor preference, and assessment issues. *The Counseling Psychologist, 29,* 18–54.

Prince, J. P. (1998). Interpreting the Strong Interest Inventory: A case study. *The Career Development Quarterly, 46,* 339–346.

Prochaska, J. O., DiClemente, C. C., & Norcross, J. C. (1992). In search of how people change: Applications to addictive behaviors. *American Psychologist, 47,* 1102–1114.

Provost, J. A., & Anchors, S. (1987). *Applications of the Myers–Briggs Type Indicator in higher education.* Palo Alto, CA: Consulting Psychologists Press.

Pryor, R. G., & Taylor, N. B. (1986). On combining scores from interest and value measures for counseling. *Vocational Guidance Quarterly, 34,* 178–187.

Psychological Assessment Resources. (2006, January). *Catalog of selected professional testing resources.* Lutz, FL: Author.

Psychological Corporation. (1991). *Miller Analogies Test technical manual.* San Antonio, TX: Author.

Psychological Corporation. (1994). *Miller Analogies Test candidate information booklet.* San Antonio: TX: Author.

Psychological Corporation. (1997). *WAIS-III WMS-III technical manual.* San Antonio, TX: Author.

Pyle, K. R. (1984). Career counseling and computers: Where is the creativity? *Journal of Counseling & Development, 63,* 141–144.

Quenk, N. L. (2000). *Essentials of Myers–Briggs Type Indicator assessment.* New York: Wiley.

Quinn, M. T., Lewis, R. J., & Fischer, K. L. (1992). A cross-correlation of the Myers–Briggs and Keirsey instruments. *Journal of College Student Development, 33,* 279–280.

Quirk, S. W., Christiansen, N. D., Wagner, S. H., & McNulty, J. L. (2003). On the usefulness of measures of normal personality for clinical assessment: Evidence of the incremental validity of the Revised NEO Personality Inventory. *Psychological Assessment 15,* 311–325.

Randahl, G. J., Hansen, J. C., & Haverkamp, B. E. (1993). Instrumental behaviors following test administration and interpretation: Exploration validity of the Strong Interest Inventory. *Journal of Counseling & Development, 71,* 435–439.

Raths, L., Harmin, M., & Simon, S. (1978). *Values and teaching: Working with values in the classroom* (2nd ed.). Columbus, OH: Merrill.

Raven, J. C., Court, J. H., & Raven, J. (1993). *Manual for Raven's Progressive Matrices and Vocabulary Scales.* San Antonio, TX: Psychological Corporation.

Rayman, J. R. (1976). Sex and the Single Interest Inventory: The empirical validation of sex-balanced interest inventory items. *Journal of Counseling Psychology, 23,* 239–246.

Reardon, R. C., Lenz, J. G., Sampson, J. P., & Peterson, G. W. (2005). *Career development and planning: A comprehensive approach* (2nd ed.). Stamford, CT: Thomson Learning.

Rehabilitation Act of 1973, 29 U.S.C. Pub. L. No. 93-112 87 Stat 355.

Rein, J. A. (2005). Review of Ball Aptitude Battery Form M. In R. A. Spies & B. S. Plake (Eds.), *The sixteenth mental measurements yearbook* (pp. 79–81). Lincoln, NE: Buros Institute of Mental Measurements.

Renzulli, J. S., & Smith, L. H. (1978). *Learning Styles Inventory: A measure of student preference for instructional techniques.* Mansfield Center, CT: Creative Learning Press.

Rest, J. R. (1979). *Development in judging moral issues.* Minneapolis: University of Minnesota Press.

Rest, J. R., Narvaez, D., Thoma, S. J., & Bebeau, M. J. (1999). DIT2: Devising and testing a revised instrument of moral judgment. *Journal of Educational Psychology, 91,* 644–659.

Reynolds, A. L., & Pope, R. L. (2003). Multicultural competence in counseling centers. In D. B. Pope-Davis, H. L. K. Coleman, W. M. Liu, & R. L. Toporek (Eds.), *Handbook of multicultural competencies in counseling and psychology* (pp. 365–382). Thousand Oaks, CA: Sage.

Reynolds, C. R., & Bigler, E. D. (2000). *CASE/CASE–SF professional manual.* Odessa, FL: Psychological Assessment Resources.

Reynolds, C. R., & Kamphaus, R. W. (2005). *BASC-2: Behavior Assessment System for Children–Second edition.* Circle Pines, MN: American Guidance Services.

Reynolds, C. R., Richmond, B. O., & Lowe, P. A. (2003). *Adult Manifest Anxiety Scale.* Los Angeles: Western Psychological Services.

Reynolds, W. M. (1999). *Professional manual for Multidimensional Anxiety Questionnaire.* Odessa, FL: Psychological Assessment Resources.

Reynolds, W. M., & Kobak, K. A. (1995). *Professional manual for Hamilton Depression Inventory: A self-report version of the Hamilton Depression Rating Scale.* Odessa, FL: Psychological Assessment Resources.

Ridley, C. S., Li, L. C., & Hill, C. L. (1998). Multicultural assessment: Reexamination, reconceptualization, and practical application. *The Counseling Psychologist, 26,* 827–910.

Riverside Publishing Co. (2001). *Cognitive Abilities Test: Interpretive guide for teachers and counselors.* Chicago: Author.

Rochlen, A. B., Rude, S. S., & Baron, A. (2005). The relationship of client stages of change to working alliance and outcome in short-term counseling. *Journal of College Counseling, 8,* 52–64.

Rodgers, B. G. (2005). Review of the Cognitive Abilities Test Form 6. In R. A. Spies & B. S. Plake (Eds.), *The sixteenth mental measurements yearbook* (pp. 232–234). Lincoln, NE: Buros Mental Measurements Yearbook.

Rogers, J. E. (2002). Review of Armed Services Vocational Aptitude Battery Career Exploration Program (ASVAB). In J. T. Kapes & E. A. Whitfield (Eds.), *A counselor's guide to career assessment instruments* (4th ed., pp. 93–101). Tulsa, OK: National Career Development Association.

Rogers, J. R., Alexander, R. A., & Subich, L. M. (1994). Development and psychometric analysis of the Suicide Assessment Checklist. *Journal of Mental Health Counseling, 16,* 352–368.

Rogers, J. R., Lewis, M. M., & Subich, L. M. (2002). Validity of the Suicide Assessment Checklist in an emergency crisis center. *Journal of Counseling & Development, 80,* 493–502.

Roid, G. H. (2003). *Stanford–Binet Intelligence Scales, Fifth Edition, examiner's manual*. Itaska, IL: Riverside Press.

Roid, G. H., & Barram, R. A. (2004). *Essentials of Stanford–Binet Intelligence Scales (SB5) assessment*. Hoboken, NJ: Wiley.

Rokeach, M. (1973). *The nature of human values*. New York: Free Press.

Rollock, D., & Terrell, M. D. (1996). Multicultural issues in assessment: Toward an inclusive model. In J. L. DeLucia-Waack (Ed.), *Multicultural counseling competencies: Implications for training and practice* (pp. 113–153). Alexandria, VA: Association for Counselor Education and Supervision.

Rosen, D., Holmberg, K., & Holland, J. L. (1994). *The educational opportunities finder*. Odessa, FL: Psychological Assessment Resources.

Rosenthal, R. (1990). How are we doing in soft psychology? *American Psychologist, 45,* 775–776.

Rosnow, R. L., & Rosenthal, R. (1988). Focused tests of significance and effect size estimation in counseling psychology. *Journal of Counseling Psychology, 35,* 203–208.

Ross, H. E., Gavin, D. R., & Skinner, H. A. (1990). Diagnostic validity of the MAST and the Alcohol Dependence Scale in the assessment of DSM–III alcohol problems. *Journal of Studies on Alcohol, 51,* 506–513.

Rotter, J. B., Lah, M. I., & Rafferty, J. E. (1992). *Manual for the Rotter Incomplete Sentence Blank, Second Edition*. San Antonio, TX: Psychological Corporation.

Rottinghaus, P. J., Betz, N. E., & Borgen, F. H. (2003). Validity of parallel measures of vocational interests and confidence. *Journal of Career Assessment, 11,* 355–378.

Rottinghaus, P. J., Day, S. X., & Borgen, F. H. (2005). The Career Futures Inventory: A measure of career-related adaptability and optimism. *Journal of Career Assessment, 13,* 3–24.

Rottinghaus, P. J., & Zytowski, D. G. (2006). Commonalities between adolescents' work values and interests. *Measurement and Evaluation in Counseling and Development, 38,* 211–221.

Rounds, J. B. (1990). The comparative and combined utility of work value and interest data in career counseling with adults. *Journal of Vocational Behavior, 37,* 32–45.

Rubinstein, J. (2004). Test preparation: What makes it effective? In J. E. Wall & G. R. Walz (Eds.), *Measuring up: Assessment issues for teachers, counselors, and administrators* (pp. 397–415). Greensboro, NC: CAPS Press.

Ruehlman, L. S., Lanyon R. I., & Karoly, P. (1999). Development and validation of the Multidimensional Health Profile, Part I: Psychosocial functioning. *Psychological Assessment, 11,* 166–176.

Russell, M., & Karol, D. (1993). *16-PF, Fifth Edition, administrator's manual*. Champaign, IL: Institute for Personality and Ability Testing.

Sackett, S. A., & Hansen, J. C. (1995). Vocational outcomes of college freshmen with flat profiles on the Strong Interest Inventory. *Measurement and Evaluation in Counseling and Development, 28,* 9–24.

Sackett, P. R., Schmitt, N., Ellingson, J. E., & Kabin, M. B. (2001). High-stakes testing in employment, credentialing, and higher education. *American Psychologist, 56,* 302–318.

Sagiv, L. (2002). Vocational interests and basic values. *Journal of Career Assessment, 10,* 233–257.

Sagiv, L., & Schwartz, S. H. (2000). Value priorities and subjective well-being: Direct relations and congruity affects. *European Journal of Social Psychology, 30,* 177–198.

Sampson, J. P., Jr. (1990). Computer-assisted testing and the goals of counseling psychology. *The Counseling Psychologist, 18,* 227–239.

Sampson, J. P., Jr., Peterson, G. W., Lenz, J. G., Reardon, R. C., & Saunders, D. E. (1996). *Career Thoughts Inventory: Professional manual*. Odessa, FL: Psychological Assessment Resources.

Sampson, J. P., Jr., Peterson, G. W., Reardon, R. C., & Lenz, J. G. (2000). Using readiness assessment to improve career services: A cognitive information-processing approach. *The Career Development Quarterly, 49,* 146–174.

Sampson, J. P., Jr., Purgar, M. P., & Shy, J. D. (2003). Computer-based test interpretation in career assessment: Ethical and professional issues. *Journal of Career Assessment, 11,* 22–39.

Samuda, R. J. (1998a). Cross-cultural assessment: Issues and alternatives. In R. J. Samuda, R. Feuerstein, A. S. Kaufman, J. E. Lewis, R. J. Sternberg, & Associates (Eds.), *Advances in cross-cultural assessment* (pp. 1–19). Thousand Oaks, CA: Sage.

Samuda, R. J. (1998b). *Psychological testing of American minorities: Issues and consequences* (2nd ed.). Thousand Oaks, CA: Sage.

Sandene, B., Horkay, N., Bennett, R. E., Allen, N., Braswell, J., Kaplan, B., et al. (2005). *Online assessment in mathematics and writing: Reports from the NAEP Technology-Based Assessment Project, Research and Development Series* (No. NCES 2005457). Washington, DC: U.S. Department of Education.

Sandoval, J. (1998). Testing in a changing world. In J. Sandoval, C. L. Frisby, K. F. Geisinger, J. D. Scheuneman, & J. R. Grenier (Eds.), *Test interpretation and diversity* (pp. 3–16). Washington, DC: American Psychological Association.

Sandoval, J. (2003). Woodcock-Johnson III. In B. S. Plake, J. C. Impara, & R. A. Spies (Eds.), *The fifteenth mental measurements yearbook* (pp. 1024–1028) Lincoln, NE: Buros Institute of Mental Measurements.

Sandoval, J., Frisby, C. L., Geisinger, K. F., Scheuneman, J. D., & Grenier, J. R. (Eds.). (1998). *Test interpretation and diversity*. Washington, DC: American Psychological Association.

Sanford, E. E. (1995). Review of the Rokeach Value Survey. In J. C. Conoley & J. C. Impara (Eds.), *The twelfth mental measurements yearbook* (pp. 879–880). Lincoln, NE: Buros Institute of Mental Measurements.

Sanford, E. E. (2003). Review of Jackson Vocational Interest Survey. In B. S. Plake, J. C. Impara, & R. A. Spies (Eds.), *The fifteenth mental measurements yearbook* (pp. 485–487). Lincoln, NE: Buros Institute of Mental Measurements.

Sarason, I. G. (Ed.). (1980). *Test anxiety: Theory, research, and applications.* Hillsdale, NJ: Erlbaum.

Sarason, I. G., Johnson, J. H., & Siegel, J. M. (1978). Assessing the impact of life changes: Development of the Life Experiences Survey. *Journal of Consulting and Clinical Psychology, 46,* 932–946.

Satcher, D. (2000). Mental health: A report of the surgeon general—Executive summary. *Professional Psychology: Research and Practice, 31,* 5–13.

Satterthwaite, F., & D'Orsi, G. (2003). *The career portfolio workbook.* New York: McGraw-Hill.

Sattler, J. M. (1989). Vineland Adaptive Behavior Scales. In J. C. Conoley & J. J. Kramer (Eds.), T*he tenth mental measurements yearbook* (pp. 878–881). Lincoln, NE: Buros Institute of Mental Measurements.

Sattler, J. M. (2005). *Assessment of children: Behavioral and clinical applications*. La Mesa: CA: Sattler.

Saunders, J. B., Aasland, O. G., Amundsen, A., & Grant, M. (1993). Alcohol consumption and related problems among primary health care patients: WHO collaborative project on early detection of persons with harmful alcohol consumption, I. *Addiction, 88,* 349–362.

Savickas, M. L. (1993). Career counseling in the postmodern era. *Journal of Cognitive Psychotherapy, 7,* 205–215.

Savickas, M. L. (1997). Career adaptability: An integrative construct for life-span, life-space theory. *The Career Development Quarterly, 45,* 247–259.

Savickas, M. L. (2000). Assessing career decision making. In C. E. Watkins, Jr., & V. L. Campbell (Eds.), *Testing and assessment in counseling practice* (2nd ed., pp. 429–477). Mahwah, NJ: Erlbaum.

Savickas, M. L., Briddick, W. C., & Watkins, C. E. (2002). The relation of career maturity to personality type and social adjustment. *Journal of Career Assessment, 10,* 24–41.

Savickas, M. L., & Hartung, P. J. (1996). The Career Development Inventory in review: Psychometric and research findings. *Journal of Career Assessment, 4, 171–188.*

Savickas, M. L., & Taber, B. J. (2006). Individual differences in RIASEC profile similarity across five interest inventories. *Measurement and Evaluation in Counseling and Development, 38,* 203–210.

Scheuneman, J. D., & Oakland, T. (1998). High-stakes testing in education. In J. Sandoval, C. L. Frisby, K. F. Geisinger, J. D. Scheuneman, & J. R. Grenier (Eds.), *Test interpretation and diversity* (pp. 77–104). Washington, DC: American Psychological Association.

Schmidt, F. L., & Hunter, J. E. (1998). The validity and utility of selection methods in personnel psychology. *Psychological Bulletin, 124,* 262–274.

Schoemaker, C., Verbraak, M., Breteler, R., & vanderStaak, C. (1997). The discriminant validity of the Eating Disorder Inventory–2. *British Journal of Clinical Psychology, 36,* 627–629.

Schoenrade, P. (2002). Review of Values Scale (VS). In J. T. Kapes & E. A. Whitfield (Eds.), *A counselor's guide to career assessment instruments* (4th ed., pp. 298–302). Tulsa, OK: National Career Development Association.

Scholastic Testing Service. (1997). *Kuhlmann–Anderson tests manual of directions.* Bensenville, IL: Author.

Schrank, F. A. (2005). Woodcock-Johnson Tests of Cognitive Ability. In D. P. Flanagan & P. L. Harrison (Eds.), *Contemporary intellectual assessment* (pp. 371–401). New York: Guilford Press.

Schuerger, J. M. (2000). The Sixteen Personality Factor Questionnaire (16PF). In C. E. Watkins, Jr., & V. L. Campbell (Eds.), *Testing and assessment in counseling and practice* (2nd ed., pp. 73–110). Mahwah, NJ: Erlbaum.

Schultheiss, D. E. P., & Stead, G. B. (2004). Childhood career development scale: Scale construction and psychometric properties. *Journal of Career Assessment, 12,* 113–134.

Schwartz, S. H. (1994). Are there universal aspects in the structure and contents of human values? *Journal of Social Issues, 50,* 19–45.

Schwartz, S. H., & Bardi, A. (2001). Value hierarchies across cultures: Taking a similarities perspective. *Journal of Cross-Cultural Psychology, 32,* 268–290.

Schwartz, S. H., & Boehnke, K. (2004). Evaluating the structure of human values with confirmatory factor analysis. *Journal of Research in Personality, 38,* 230–255.

Schwartz, S. H., Melech, G., Lehmann, A., Burgess, S., Harris, M., & Owens, V. (2001). Extending the cross-cultural validity of the theory of basic human values with a different method of measurement. *Journal of Cross-Cultural Psychology, 32,* 519–542.

Schwartz, S. H., & Rubel, T. (2005). Sex differences in value priorities: Cross-cultural and multimethod studies. *Journal of Personality and Social Psychology, 89,* 1010–1028.

Scogin, F., & Crowther, M. R. (2003). Integrative personality assessment with older adults and ethnic minority clients. In L. E. Beutler & G. Groth-Marnat (Eds.), *Integrative assessment of adult personality* (2nd ed., pp. 338–355). New York: Guilford.

Searles, J. S., Helzer, J. E., Rose, G. L., & Badger, G. J. (2002). Concurrent and retrospective reports of alcohol consumption across 30, 90 and 366 days: Interactive voice response compared with the Timeline Follow Back. *Journal of Studies on Alcohol, 63,* 352–362.

Seligman, L. D., Ollendick, T. H., Langley, A. K., & Baldacci, H. B. (2004). The utility of measures of child and adolescent anxiety: A meta-analytic review of the Revised Children's Anxiety Scale, the State–Trait Anxiety Inventory for Children, and the Child Behavior Checklist. *Journal of Clinical Child and Adolescent Psychology, 33,* 557–565.

Selzer, M. L. (1971). The Michigan Alcoholism Screening Test: The quest for a new diagnostic instrument. *American Journal of Psychiatry, 127,* 1653–1658.

Setoodeh, R. (2006, March 20). Troubles by the score. *Newsweek, 147,* 46–48.

Sewell, T. E. (1985). Review of Coopersmith Self-Esteem Inventories. In J. V. Mitchell, Jr. (Ed.), *The ninth mental measurements yearbook* (pp. 397–398). Lincoln, NE: Buros Institute of Mental Measurements.

Shefler G., Canetti, L., & Wiseman, H. (2001). Psychometric properties of goal-attainment scaling in the assessment of Mann's time-limited psychotherapy. *Journal of Clinical Psychology, 57,* 971–979.

Shell, K. D., LeBold, W. K., & Ward, S. (1991). The Purdue Interest Questionnaire: Helping engineering and technology students make career decisions. *Proceedings of the Frontiers in Education Twenty-First Annual Conference,* 442–452.

Shinn, M. R., & Shinn, M. M. (2000). Writing and evaluating IEP goals and making appropriate revisions to ensure participation and progress in the general curriculum. In C. F. Telzrow & M. Tankersley (Eds.), *IDEA Amendments of 1997: Practice guidelines for school-based teams* (pp. 351–382). Bethesda, MD: National Association of School Psychologists.

Shrauger, J. S., & Osberg, R. M. (1981). The relative accuracy of self-predictions and judgments by others in psychological assessment. *Psychological Bulletin, 90,* 322–351.

Sigma Assessment Systems. (2005). *Jackson Vocational Interest Survey (JVIS): Extended report.* Retrieved December 6, 2005, from http://www.sigmaassessmentsystems.com/samplereports/jvisreport.pdf

Simms, L. J., Casillas, A., Clark, L. A., Watson, D., & Doebbeling, B. N. (2005). Psychometric evaluation of the Restructured Clinical Scales of the MMPI-2. *Psychological Assessment, 17,* 345–358.

Singelis, T. M. (Ed.). (1998). *Teaching about culture, ethnicity, and diversity: Exercises and planned activities.* Thousand Oaks, CA: Sage.

Sireci, S. G. (2004). Computerized adaptive testing: An introduction. In J. E. Wall & G. R. Walz (Eds.), *Measuring up: Assessment issues for teachers, counselors, and administrators* (pp. 685–6940. Greensboro, NC: CAPS Press.

Skinner, H. A., Steinhauer, P. D., & Santa-Barbara, J. (1995). *The Family Assessment Measure.* North Tonawanda, NY: Multi-Health Systems.

Slaney, R. B., & MacKinnon-Slaney, F. (2000). Using vocational card sorts in career counseling. In C. E. Watkins, Jr., & V. L. Campbell (Eds.), *Testing and assessment in counseling practice* (2nd ed., pp. 371–428). Mahwah, NJ: Erlbaum.

Smart, D. W., & Smart, J. F. (1997). *DSM-IV* and culturally sensitive diagnosis: Some observations for counselors. *Journal of Counseling & Development, 75,* 392–398.

Smart, R. M., & Peterson, C. C. (1994). Super's stages and the four-factor structure of the Adult Career Concerns Inventory in an Australian sample. *Measurement and Evaluation in Counseling and Development, 26,* 243–257.

Smith, D. K. (2002). The decision-making process for developing testing accommodations. In R. B. Ekstrom & D. K. Smith (Eds.), *Assessing individuals with disabilities in educational, employment, and counseling settings* (pp. 71–86). Washington, DC: American Psychological Association.

Snow, M., Thurber, S., & Hodgson, J. M. (2002). An adolescent version of the Michigan Alcoholism Screening Test. *Adolescence, 37,* 835–840.

Snyder, D. K. (1997). *Marriage Satisfaction Inventory manual.* Los Angeles: Western Psychological Services.

Snyder, D. K., Heyman, R. E., & Haynes, S. N. (2005). Evidence-based approaches to assessing couple distress. *Psychological Assessment, 17,* 288–307.

Sobell, L. C., Agrawal, S., Annis, H., Ayala-Velazquez, H., Echeverria, L., Leo, G. I., et al. (2001). Cross-cultural evaluation of two drinking assessment instruments: Alcohol Timeline Followback and Inventory of Drinking Situations. *Substance Use & Misuse, 36,* 313–331.

Sobell, M. B., Maisto, S. A., Sobell, L. C., Cooper, A. M., Cooper, T. C., & Sanders, B. (1980). Developing a prototype for evaluating alcohol treatment effectiveness. In L. C. Sobell, M. B. Sobell, & E. Ward (Eds.), *Evaluating alcohol and drug abuse treatment effectiveness: Recent advances* (pp. 129–150). New York: Pergamon.

Sparrow, S. S., Cicchetti, D. V., & Balla, D. A. (2006). *Vineland Adaptive Behavior Scales, Second Edition: Survey form manual.* Circle Pines, MN: American Guidance Service.

Spelke, E. S. (2005). Sex differences in intrinsic aptitude for mathematics and science? A critical review. *American Psychologist, 60,* 950–958.

Spengler, P. M., Strohmer, D. C., Dixon, D. N., & Shivy, V. A. (1995). A scientist–practitioner model of psychological assessment: Implications for training, practice, and research. *The Counseling Psychologist, 23,* 506–534.

Spielberger, C. D. (1999). *State–Trait Anger Expression Inventory–2.* Odessa, FL: Psychological Assessment Resources.

Spielberger, C. D., Gorsuch, R. L., Lushene, R., Vagg, P. R., & Jacobs, G. A. (1983). *Manual for State–Trait Anxiety Inventory.* Palo Alto, CA: Consulting Psychologists Press.

Spielberger, C. D., Reheiser, E. C., Owen, A. E., & Sydeman, S. J. (2004). In M. Maruish (Ed.), *Use of psychological testing for treatment planning and outcomes assessment: Volume 3. Instruments for adults* (3rd ed., pp. 421–447). Mahwah, NJ: Erlbaum.

Spies, R. A., & Plake, B. S. (Eds.). (2005). *The sixteenth mental measurements yearbook.* Lincoln, NE: Buros Institute of Mental Measurements.

Spitzer, R. L. (2004). *Treatment companion to the DSM-IV-TR casebook.* Washington, DC: American Psychiatric Association.

Spitzer, R. L., Kroenke, K., Williams, J. B. W., & the Patient Health Questionnaire Primary Care Study Group. (1999). Validation and utility of a self-report version of PRIME-MD. *Journal of the American Medical Association, 282,* 1737–1744.

Spitzer, R. L., Skodol, A. E., Williams, J. B. W., & First, M. B. (Eds.). (2001). *DSM-IV-TR casebook: A learning companion to the Diagnostic and Statistical Manual of Mental Disorders, Fourth Edition, Text Revision.* Washington, DC: American Psychiatric Association.

Spokane, A. R., & Catalano, M. (2000). The Self-Directed Search: A theory-driven array of self-guided career interventions. In C. E. Watkins, Jr., & V. L. Campbell (Eds.), *Testing and assessment in counseling practice* (2nd ed., pp. 339–370). Mahwah, NJ: Erlbaum.

Steenbarger, B. N., & Smith, H. B. (1996). Assessing the quality of counseling services: Developing accountable helping systems. *Journal of Counseling & Development, 75,* 145–150.

Stehouwer, R. S., & Stehouwer, J. D. (2005). Review of Beck Depression Inventory–II. In D. J. Keyser (Ed.), *Test critiques: Vol. XI* (pp. 13–20). Austin, TX: PRO-ED.

Stein, S. (2003). Review of Multidimensional Anxiety Questionnaire. In B. S. Plake, J. C. Impara, & R. A. Spies (Eds.), *The fifteenth mental measurements yearbook* (pp. 599–601). Lincoln, NE: Buros Institute of Mental Measurements.

Stelmachers, Z. T. (1995). Assessing suicidal clients. In J. N. Butcher (Ed.), *Clinical personality assessment: Practical approaches* (pp. 367–379). New York: Oxford University Press.

Sternberg, R. J. (1985). *Beyond IQ.* Cambridge, United Kingdom: Cambridge University Press.

Sternberg, R. J. (1988). *The triarchic mind.* New York: Viking Penguin.

Sternberg, R. J. (1998a). All intelligence testing is "cross-cultural": Constructing intelligence tests to meet the demands of Person ? Task ? Situation interactions. In R. J. Samuda, R. Feuerstein, A. S. Kaufman, J. E. Lewis, R. J. Sternberg, & Associates (Eds.), *Advances in cross-cultural assessment* (pp. 192–217). Thousand Oaks, CA: Sage.

Sternberg, R. J. (1998b). *Cupid's arrow: The course of love through time.* New York: Cambridge University Press.

Sternberg, R. J. (1998c). *Love is a story.* New York: Oxford University Press.

Sternberg, R. J. (2002). Beyond *g*. In R. J. Sternberg & E. L. Grigorenko (Eds.), *The general factor of intelligence: How general is it?* (pp. 447–479). Mahwah, NJ: Erlbaum.

Sternberg, R. J. (2004a). Culture and intelligence. *American Psychologist, 59,* 325–338.

Sternberg, R. J. (2004b, October 22). A dozen reasons why the No Child Left Behind Act is failing our schools. *Education Week,* 56–57.

Sternberg, R. J. (2005). The triarchic theory of successful intelligence. In D. P. Flanagan & P. L. Harrison (Eds.), *Contemporary intellectual assessment* (pp. 103–119). New York: Guilford Press.

Sternberg, R. J., Wagner, R. K., Williams, W. M., & Horvath, J. A. (1995). Testing common sense. *American Psychologist, 50,* 912–927.

Stice, E., Fisher, M., & Martinez, E. (2004). Eating Disorder Diagnostic Scale: Additional evidence of reliability and validity. *Psychological Assessment, 16,* 60–71.

Strack, S. (Ed.). (2002). *Essentials of Millon inventories assessment* (2nd ed.). New York: Wiley.

Stuart, R. B., & Jacobson, B. (1987). *Couple's Precounseling Inventory, Revised Edition.* Champaign, IL: Research Press.

Sue, D. W. (1978). Work views and counseling. *Personnel and Guidance Journal, 56,* 458–462.

Sue, D. W. (1990). Barriers to effective cross-cultural counseling. In D. W. Sue & D. Sue (Eds.), *Counseling the culturally different: Theory and practice* (pp. 27–48). New York: Wiley.

Super, D. E. (1970). *Manual for the Work Values Inventory.* Boston: Houghton-Mifflin.

Super, D. E. (1990). A life-span, life-space approach to career development. In D. Brown & L. Brooks (Eds.), *Career choice and development: Applying contemporary theories to practice* (2nd ed., pp. 197–261). San Francisco: Jossey-Bass.

Super, D. E., Osborne, W. L., Walsh, D. J., Brown, S. D., & Niles, S. J. (1992). Developmental career assessment and counseling: The C-DAC model. *Journal of Counseling & Development, 71,* 74–80.

Super, D. E., & Thompson, A. S. (1979). A six-scale, two-factor measure of adolescent career or vocational maturity. *Vocational Guidance Quarterly, 28,* 6–15.

Super, D. E., Thompson, A. S., & Lindeman, R. H. (1988). *Adult Career Concerns Inventory: Manual for research and exploratory use in counseling.* Palo Alto, CA: Consulting Psychologists Press.

Super, D. E., Thompson, R. H., Lindeman, R. H., Myers, R. A., & Jordaan, J. P. (1985). *Adult Career Concerns Inventory.* Palo Alto, CA: Consulting Psychologists Press.

Sverko, B. (1995). The structure and hierarchy of values cross-nationally. In D. E. Super & B. Sverko (Eds.), *Life roles, values, and careers: International findings of the Work Importance Study* (pp. 225–240). San Francisco: Jossey-Bass.

Swanson, J. L., & D'Achiardi, C. (2005). Beyond interests, needs/values, and abilities: Assessing other important career constructs over the life span. In S. D. Brown & R. W. Lent (Eds.), *Career development and counseling: Putting theory and research to work* (pp. 353–381). Hoboken, NJ: Wiley.

Swanson, J. L., Daniels, K. K., & Tokar, D. M. (1996). Assessing perceptions of career-related barriers: The Career Barriers Inventory. *Journal of Career Assessment, 4,* 219–244.

Swanson, J. L., Gore, P. A., Jr., Leuwerke, W., D'Achiardi, C., Edwards, J. H., & Edwards, J. (2006). Accuracy in recalling interest inventory information at three time intervals. *Measurement and Evaluation in Counseling and Development, 38,* 236–246.

Taber, B. J., & Luzzo, D. A. (1999). *A comprehensive review of research evaluating the effectiveness of DISCOVER in promoting career development* (Report No. 99-3). Iowa City, IA: ACT.

Talmon, M. (1990). *Single-session therapy.* San Francisco: Jossey-Bass.

Tareen, S. (2005, September 22). Wrong scores shake up schools. *The Oregonian,* pp. A1, A9.

Taylor, R. M., & Morrison, W. L. (1996). *Taylor–Johnson Temperament Analysis test manual.* Los Angeles: Western Psychological Services.

Teglasi, H. (2001). *Essentials of TAT and other storytelling techniques assessment.* New York: Wiley.

Teitelbaum, L., & Mullen, B. (2000). The validity of the MAST in psychiatric settings: A meta-analytic investigation. *Journal of Studies on Alcohol, 61,* 254–261.

Tellegen, A., Ben-Porath, Y. S., McNulty, J. L., Arbisi, P. A., Graham, J. R., & Kaemmer, B. (2003). *The MMPI-2 restructured clinical (RC) scales: Development, validation, and interpretation.* Minneapolis, MN: University of Minnesota Press.

Teranishi, R. (2002). The myth of the super minority. *College Board Review, 195,* 17–21.

Thomas, K. W., & Kilman, R. H. (1974). *Thomas–Kilman Conflict Mode Instrument.* Palo Alto, CA: Consulting Psychologists Press.

Thompson, A. S., Lindeman, R. H., Super, D. E., Jordaan, J. P., & Myers, R. A. (1981). *Career Development Inventory: Vol. 1. User's manual.* Palo Alto, CA: Consulting Psychologists Press.

Thorn, A. R., & Mulvenon, S. W. (2002). High-stakes testing: An examination of elementary counselors' views and their academic preparation to meet this challenge. *Measurement and Evaluation in Counseling and Development, 35,* 195–206.

Tieger, P. D., & Barron-Tieger, B. (2001). *Do what you are: Discover the perfect career through the secrets of personality type* (3rd ed.). Boston: Little-Brown.

Timbrook, R. E., & Graham, J. R. (1994). Ethnic differences on the MMPI-2? *Psychological Assessment, 6,* 212–217.

Tinsley, H. E., Tinsley, D. J., & Rushing, J. (2002). Psychological type, decision-making style, and reactions to structured career interventions. *Journal of Career Assessment, 10,* 258–280.

Toman, S. M., & Savickas, M. L. (1997). Career choice readiness moderates the effects of interest inventory interpretation. *Journal of Career Assessment, 5,* 275–291.

Toporek, R. J., & Pope-Davis, D. B. (2001). Comparison of vocational identity factor structures among African American and White American college students. *Journal of Career Assessment, 9,* 135–151.

Torrance, E. P. (1974). *Torrance Tests of Creative Thinking: Norms and technical manual.* Bensenville, IL: Scholastic Test Services.

Touliatos, J., Perlmutter, B. F., & Holdon, G. W. (Eds.). (2001). *Handbook of family measurement techniques.* Thousand Oaks, CA: Sage.

Tracey, T. J., & Rounds, J. (1999). Inference and attribution errors in test interpretation. In J. W. Lichtenberg & R. K. Goodyear (Eds.), *Scientist–practitioner perspectives on test interpretation* (pp. 113–131). Boston: Allyn & Bacon.

Tracey, T. J. G., & Schneider, P. L. (1995). An evaluation of the circular structure of the checklist of interpersonal transactions and the checklist of psychotherapy transactions. *Journal of Counseling Psychology, 42,* 496–507.

Tsai, D. C., & Pike, P. L. (2000). Effects of acculturation on the MMPI-2 scores of Asian American students. *Journal of Personality Assessment, 74,* 216–230.

Tucker, I. F., & Gillespie, B. V. (1993). Correlations among three measures of personality type. *Perceptual and Motor Skills, 77,* 650.

Turner, S. M., DeMers, S. T., Fox, H. R., & Reed, G. M. (2001). APA's guidelines for test user qualifications: An executive summary. *American Psychologist, 56,* 1099–1113.

Uffelman, R. A., Subich, L. M., Diegelman, N. M., Wagner, K. S., & Bardash, R. J. (2004). Effect of mode of interest assessment on clients' career decision-making self-efficacy. *Journal of Career Assessment, 12,* 366–380.

Ulett, G. (1994). *Rorschach introductory guide.* Los Angeles: Western Psychological Services.

Urbina, S. (1995). Review of Basic Personality Inventory. In J. C. Conoley & J. C. Impara (Eds.), *The twelfth mental measurements yearbook* (pp. 105–106). Lincoln, NE: Buros Institute of Mental Measurements.

Urbina, S. (2004). *Essentials of psychological testing.* Hoboken NJ: Wiley.

U.S. Census Bureau. (2006). *American fact-finder.* Retrieved June 1, 2006, from http://factfinder.census.gov

U.S. Department of Defense. (2005). *ASVAB counselor manual.* North Chicago, IL: U.S. Military Entrance Processing Command.

U.S. Department of Defense. (2006). *ASVAB Career Exploration Program.* Retrieved February 22, 2006, from http://www.asvabprogram.com

U.S. Department of Education, Office of Civil Rights. (2000a). *The use of tests as part of high-stakes decision-making for students: A resource guide for educators and policymakers.* Retrieved April 30, 2006, from http://www.ed.gov/legislation/FedRegister/other/2000-4/121500b.html

U.S. Department of Education, Office of Civil Rights. (2000b). *The use of tests when making high-stakes decisions for students: A resource guide for educators and policy makers.* Washington, DC: Author.

U.S. Department of Labor, Bureau of Labor Statistics. (2006). *Occupational outlook handbook: 2006-07 edition.* Retrieved January 5, 2006, from http://www.bls.gov/oco

U.S. Department of Labor, Employment and Training Administration. (2000). *Work Importance Locator user's guide* (Version 3.0). Retrieved July 9, 2006, from http://www.onetcenter.org/dl_files/WIL_zips/WIL-UG-deskp.pdf

U.S. Department of Labor, Employment and Training Administration. (2002a). *Ability Profiler user's guide.* Retrieved February 17, 2006, from http://www.onetcenter.org/AP.html

U.S. Department of Labor, Employment and Training Administration. (2002b). *Work Importance Profiler user's guide* (Version 3.0). Retrieved February 17, 2006, from http://onetcenter.org/dl_files/WIP.pdf

U.S. Department of Labor, Employment and Training Administration. (2004). *Details report for mental health counselors* (21-1014.00). Retrieved February 20, 2006, from http://online.onetcenter.org/link/details/21-1014.00

U.S. Department of Labor, Employment and Training Administration. (2005a). *O*NET career exploration tools.* Retrieved February 19, 2006, from http://www.onetcenter.org/tools.html

U.S. Department of Labor, Employment and Training Administration. (2005b). *O*NET OnLine.* Retrieved January 5, 2006, from http://online.onetcenter.org

U.S. Department of Labor, Employment and Training Administration. (2006). *O*NET OnLine: Find occupations.* Retrieved April 11, 2006, from http://online.onetcenter.org/find/

U.S. Department of Veterans Affairs. (1996). *Geropsychology assessment resource guide.* Retrieved April 30, 2006, from http://www.measurementexperts.org/instrument/book_compendium.asp?detail=11

Vacc, N. A., & Juhnke, G. A. (1997). The use of structured clinical interviews for assessment in counseling. *Journal of Counseling & Development, 75,* 470–480.

Vacc, N. A., Juhnke, G. A., & Nilsen, K. A. (2001). Community mental health service providers' codes of ethics and the standards for educational and psychological testing. *Journal of Counseling & Development, 79,* 217–224.

Velasquez, R. J., Maness, P. J., & Anderson, U. (2002). Culturally competent assessment of Latino clients: The MMPI-2. In J. N. Butcher (Ed.), *Clinical personality assessment: Practical approaches* (pp. 154–170). New York: Oxford University Press.

Valpar International Corporation. (2005). *SIGI-3: Education and career planning software for the Web.* Retrieved August 9, 2005, from http://www.valparint.com

VanDenberg, T. F., Schmidt, J. A., & Kiesler, D. J. (1992). Interpersonal assessment in counseling and psychotherapy. *Journal of Counseling & Development, 71,* 84–90.

Vansickle, T. R., & Kapes, J. T. (1993). Comparing paper-pencil and computer-based versions of the Strong–Campbell Interest Inventory. *Computers in Human Behavior, 9,* 441–449.

Vernon, A., & Clemente, R. (2005). *Assessment and intervention with children and adolescents: Developmental and multicultural approaches* (2nd ed.). Alexandria, VA: American Counseling Association.

Vernon, P. E. (1961). *The structure of human abilities* (Rev. ed.). London: Methuen.

Vilas, R. C. (1988). *Counseling outcome as related to MBTI client type, counselor type and counselor–client type similarity.* Unpublished doctoral dissertation, University of Iowa, Iowa City.

Vondracek, F. W., & Reitzle, M. (1998). The viability of career maturity theory: A developmental–contextual perspective. *The Career Development Quarterly, 47,* 6–15.

Vonk, M. E., & Thyer, B. A. (1999). Evaluating the effectiveness of short-term treatment at a university counseling center. *Journal of Clinical Psychology, 55,* 1095–1106.

Vuchinich, R. E., Tucker, J. A., & Harllee, L. N. (1988). Behavioral assessment. In D. M. Dononvan & G. A. Marlart (Eds.), *Assessment of addictive behaviors* (pp. 51–83). New York: Guilford Press.

Waldinger, R. J. (1986). *Fundamentals of psychiatry.* Washington, DC: American Psychiatric Press.

Wall, J. E. (2004a). Assessment and technology—Allies in educational reform: An overview of issues for counselors and educators. *Measurement and Evaluation in Counseling and Development, 37,* 112–127.

Wall, J. E. (2004b). Harnessing the power of technology: Testing and assessment applications. In J. E. Wall & G. R. Walz (Eds.), *Measuring up: Assessment issues for teachers, counselors, and administrators* (pp. 665–684). Greensboro, NC: CAPS Press.

Walls, R. T. (2000). Vocational cognition: Accuracy of 3rd-, 6th-, 9th-, and 12th-grade students. *Journal of Vocational Behavior, 56,* 137–144.

Walsh, W. B., & Betz, N. E. (2001). *Tests and assessment* (4th ed.). Englewood Cliffs, NJ: Prentice Hall.

Wang, L. (2002). Review of Differential Aptitude Test (DAT) and Career Interest Inventory (CII). In J. T. Kapes & E. A. Whitfield (Eds.), *A counselor's guide to career assessment instruments* (4th ed., pp. 123–131). Tulsa, OK: National Career Development Association.

Wang, S. (2004). *Online or paper: Does delivery affect results?* (Assessment Report). San Antonio, TX: Harcourt Assessment.

Watkins, C. E., Jr., Campbell, V. L., & Nieberding, R. (1994). The practice of vocational assessment by counseling psychologists. *The Counseling Psychologist, 22,* 115–128.

Wechsler, D. (1974). *Manual for the Wechsler Intelligence Scale for Children–Revised manual.* San Antonio, TX: Psychological Corporation.

Wechsler, D. (1981). *WAIS-R manual: Wechsler Adult Intelligence Scale–Revised manual.* San Antonio, TX: Psychological Corporation.

Wechsler, D. (1989). *Manual: Wechsler Preschool and Primary Scale of Intelligence.* San Antonio, TX: Psychological Corporation.

Wechsler, D. (1997a). *Wechsler Adult Intelligence Scale–Third Edition.* San Antonio, TX: Psychological Corporation.

Wechsler, D. (1997b). *WMS-III administration and scoring manual.* San Antonio, TX: Psychological Corporation.

Wechsler, D. (1999). *Wechsler Abbreviated Scale of Intelligence manual.* San Antonio, TX: Psychological Corporation.

Wechsler, D. (2001). *WIAT II examiner's manual.* San Antonio, TX: Psychological Corporation.

Wechsler, D. (2003). *WISC IV administration and scoring manual.* San Antonio, TX: Harcourt Assessment.

Weinstein, C. E. (1987). *LASSI user's manual.* Clearwater, FL: H & H.

Weinstein, C. E., Palmer, D. R., & Schulte, A. C. (1987). *Learning and Study Strategies Inventory.* Clearwater, FL: H & H.

Weinstein, C. E., Palmer, D. R., & Schulte, A. C. (1997). *The E-LASSI for Windows.* Clearwater, FL: H & H.

Weis, D. L. (1985). Review of Derogatis Sexual Functioning Inventory. In J. V. Mitchell (Ed.), *The ninth mental measurements yearbook* (pp. 455–456). Lincoln, NE: Buros Institute of Mental Measurements.

Weiss, D. J. (2004). Computerized adaptive testing for effective and efficient measurement in counseling and education. *Measurement and Evaluation in Counseling and Development, 37,* 70–84.

Weiss, L. G., Saklofske, D. H., & Prifitera, A. (2005). Interpreting the WISC-IV index scores. In A. Prifitera, D. H. Saklofske, & L. G. Weiss (Eds.), *WISC-IV clinical use and interpretation* (pp. 71–100). San Diego, CA: Academic Press.

Wells, M. G., Burlingame, G. M., Lambert, M. J., & Hoag, M. J. (1996). Conceptualization and measurement of patient change during psychotherapy: Development of the Outcome Questionnaire and Youth Outcome Questionnaire. *Psychotherapy, 33,* 275–283.

Werts, C. E., & Watley, D. J. (1969). A student's dilemma: Big fish–little pond or little fish–big pond. *Journal of Counseling Psychology, 16,* 14–19.

Westbrook, B. W. (1995). *Cognitive Vocational Maturity Test* (Rev. research ed.). Raleigh: North Carolina State University, Department of Psychology.

Westefeld, J. S., Range, L. M., Rogers, J. R., Maples, M. R., Bromley, J. L., & Alcorn, J. (2000). Suicide: An overview. *The Counseling Psychologist, 28,* 445–510.

Wettersten, K. B., Guilmino, A., Herrick, C. G., Hunter, P. J., Kim, G. Y., Jagow, D., et al. (2005). Predicting educational and vocational attitudes among rural high school students. *Journal of Counseling Psychology, 52,* 658–663.

Whiston, S. C. (2000). *Principles and applications of assessment in counseling.* Belmont, CA: Brooks/Cole.

Whiston, S. C. (2001). Selecting career outcome assessments: An organizational scheme. *Journal of Career Assessment, 9,* 215–228.

Whiston, S. C., Brecheisen, B. K., & Stephen, J. (2003). Does treatment modality affect career counseling effectiveness? *Journal of Vocational Behavior, 62,* 390–410.

Wickwire, P. N. (2002). Review of COPSystem (CAPS, COPS, and COPES). In J. T. Kapes & E. A. Whitfield (Eds.), *A counselors guide to career assessment instruments* (4th ed., pp. 210–217). Tulsa, OK: National Career Development Association.

Widaman, K. F. (2003a). Multidimensional Aptitude Battery–II. In B. S. Plake, J. C. Impara, & R. A. Spies (Eds.), *The fifteenth mental measurements yearbook* (pp. 605–607). Lincoln, NE: Buros Institute of Mental Measurements.

Widaman, K. F. (2003b). Wide Range Intelligence Test. In B. S. Plake, J. C. Impara, & R. A. Spies (Eds.), *The fifteenth mental measurements yearbook* (pp. 1015–1017). Lincoln, NE: The Buros Institute of Mental Measurements.

Widiger, T. A. (2001). Review of Millon Clinical Multiaxial Inventory-III. In B. S. Plake & J. C. Impara (Eds.), *The fourteenth mental measurements yearbook* (pp. 767–769). Lincoln, NE: Buros Institute of Mental Measurements.

Widiger, T. A. (2002). Personality disorders. In M. M. Antony & D. H. Barlow (Eds.), *Handbook of assessment and treatment planning for psychological disorders* (pp. 453–480). New York: Guilford.

Widiger, T. A., & Clark, L. A. (2000). Toward *DSM-V* and the classification of psychopathology. *Psychological Bulletin, 126,* 946–963.

Widiger, T. A., Mangine, S., Corbitt, E. M., Ellis, C. G., & Thomas, G. V. (1995). *Personality Disorder Interview–IV.* Odessa: FL: Psychological Assessment Resources.

Wiggins, J. S. (1993). *Interpersonal Adjective Scales professional manual*. Odessa, FL: Psychological Assessment Resources.

Wilkinson, G. S., & Robertson, G. J. (2005). *WRAT4 manual*. Lutz, FL: Psychological Assessment Resources.

Williamson, E. G. (1939). *How to counsel students*. New York: McGraw Hill.

Winston, R. B., Miller, T. K., & Cooper, D. L. (1999). S*tudent Developmental Task and Lifestyle Assessment*. Athens, GA: Student Development Associates.

Winters, K. C. (1991). *Personal Experience Screening Questionnaire (PESQ) manual*. Los Angeles: Western Psychological Services.

Winters, K. C. (1996). *Personal Experience Inventory for Adults manual*. Los Angeles: Western Psychological Services.

Winters, K. C. (1999). *Screening and assessing adolescents for substance use disorders: Treatment improvement protocol (TIP)* (Series No. 31). Rockville, MD: U.S. Department of Health and Human Services.

Winters, K. C., & Henley, G. A. (1989). *The Personal Experience Inventory*. Los Angeles: Western Psychological Services.

Wise, L. L. (2004). *The National Assessment of Educational Progress: What it tells educators*. In J. E. Wall & G. R. Walz (Eds.), *Measuring up: Assessment issues for teachers, counselors, and administrators* (pp. 729–741). Greensboro, NC: CAPS Press..

Wonderlic, E. F. (1999). *WPT user's manual*. Libertyville, IL: Author.

Worthington, E. L., McCullough, M. E., Shortz, J. L., Mindes, E. J., Sandage, S. J., & Chartrand, J. M. (1995). Can couples assessment and feedback improve relationships? Assessment as a brief relationship enrichment procedure. *Journal of Counseling Psychology, 42,* 466–475.

Yell, M. L., Drasgow, E., & Ford, L. (2000). The Individuals With Disabilities Education Act Amendments of 1997: Implications for school-based teams. In C. F. Telzrow & M. Tankersley (Eds.), *IDEA Amendments of 1997: Practice guidelines for school-based teams* (pp. 1–27). Bethesda, MD: National Association of School Psychologists.

Yelland, T. (1995). Review of Basic Personality Inventory. In J. C. Conoley & J. C. Impara (Eds.), *The twelfth mental measurements yearbook* (pp. 106–107). Lincoln, NE: Buros Institute of Mental Measurements.

Yesavage, J. A., Brink, T. I., Rose, T. L., Lum, O., Huang, V., Adey, M., et al. (1983). Development and validation of a geriatric depression screening scale: A preliminary report. *Journal of Psychiatric Research, 17,* 37–49.

Young, J. W. (1994). Differential prediction of college grades by gender and by ethnicity: A replication study. *Educational and Psychological Measurement, 64,* 1022–1029.

Zachar, P. (2005). Review of the Keirsey Temperament Sorter II (KTSII). In R. A. Spies & B. S. Plake (Eds), *The sixteenth mental measurements yearbook* (pp. 529–531). Lincoln, NE: Buros Institute of Mental Measurements.

Zachary, R. A. (1986). *Shipley Institute of Living Scale: Revised manual*. Los Angeles: Western Psychological Services.

Zaske, K. K., Hegstrom, K. J., & Smith, D. K. (1999, August). *Survey of test usage among clinical and school psychologists*. Paper presented at the 107th annual convention of the American Psychological Association, Boston.

Zeidner, M. (1998). *Test anxiety: The state of the art*. New York: Plenum.

Zeidner, M. (1999). The big-fish–little-pond effect for academic self-concept, test anxiety, and school grades in gifted children. *Contemporary Educational Psychology, 24,* 305–329.

Zhang, L. F., & Sternberg, R. J. (2001). Thinking styles across cultures: Their relationships with student learning. In R. J. Sternberg & L. F. Zhang (Eds.), *Perspectives on thinking, learning and cognitive styles* (pp. 197–226). Mahwah, NJ: Erlbaum.

Zierau, F., Hardt, F., Henriksen, J. H., Holm, S. S., Jorring, S., Melsen, T., et al. (2005). Validation of a self-administered modified CAGE test (CAGE-C) in a somatic hospital ward: Comparison with biochemical markers. *Scandinavian Journal of Clinical & Laboratory Investigation, 65,* 615–622.

Zimet, G. D., Dahlem, N. W., Zimet, S. G., & Farley, G. K. (1988). The Multidimensional Scale of Perceived Social Support. *Journal of Personality Assessment, 52,* 30–41.

Zimmerman, M., & Mattia, J. I. (1999). The reliability and validity of a screening questionnaire for 13 *DSM-IV* Axis I disorders (the Psychiatric Diagnostic Screening Questionnaire) in psychiatric outpatients. *Journal of Clinical Psychiatry, 60,* 677–683.

Zimny, G. H. (2002). *Updating the Medical Specialty Preference Inventory*. Retrieved December 29, 2005, from www.aamc.org/programs/cim/mspi2002.pdf

Zwi, M., Ramchandani, P., & Joughin, C. (2000). Evidence and belief in ADHD. *British Medical Journal, 321,* 975–976.

Zytowski, D. G. (1992). Three generations: The continuing evolution of Frederic Kuder's interest inventories. *Journal of Counseling & Development, 71,* 245–248.

Zytowski, D. G. (1994). A super contribution to vocational theory: Work values. *The Career Development Quarterly, 43,* 25–31.

Zytowski, D. G. (1997). *How to talk with people about their interest inventory results.* Paper presented at the conference of the Society of Vocational Psychology, Bethlehem, PA.

Zytowski, D. G. (2006). *Technical manual for Kuder® Career Search with Person Match (Version 1.1).* Retrieved January 7, 2006, from http://www.kuder.com/publicweb/kcs_manual.aspx

Zytowski, D. G., & Austin, J. T. (2001). Frederic Kuder: (1903–2000). *American Psychologist, 56,* 1170.

Zytowski, D. G., & Luzzo, D. A. (2002). Developing the Kuder Skills Assessment. *Journal of Career Assessment, 10,* 190–199.

Subject Index

Figures and tables are indicated by "f" and "t" after the page number.

Grade equivalents, 27
Graduate and professional school admissions tests, 77–79
Graduate Management Admission Test (GMAT), 78, 79
Graduate Record Examination (GRE), 28, 30, 35, 77–78
Group intelligence tests, 65–67
Guide for Occupational Exploration (GOT; Farr, Ludden, & Shatkin), 144

H

Hall Occupational Orientation Inventory (4th ed.; HOOI), 109
Hamilton Depression Inventory (HDI), 200
Hamilton Depression Rating Scale, 50, 200
Health Screening Survey–Revised, 204
Heterogeneous scales, 115
High-stakes testing, 8, 83–85
Higher education, tests for, 71–77
Hogan Development Survey (HDS), 160
Holland's My Vocational Situation, 50
Holland's theory of personality types, 119, 120*f,* 121, 166
Holland's theory of vocational choice, 129
Homogeneous scales, 115, 133
House–Tree–Person (HTP), 165

I

Idiographic assessment, 14
I'm Not Crazy, I'm Just Not You (Pearman & Albritton), 152
Impact Message Inventory, 173
Impulse-control disorder, 177
Impulsive style of problem solving, 4
Inclusion criteria for mental disorder, 180
Indecisive clients, 102
Informed self-ratings, 135, 144
Initial assessments, 39–49
Intake forms, 41–42
Intake interviews, 46–49
Intelligence, assessment of, 59–69
    advantages and disadvantages of tests, 64–65
    giftedness and creativity, 68
    group tests, 65–67
    individual tests, 60–65
    interpretation of test results, 67–68
Interest Determination, Exploration and Assessment System (IDEAS), 132
Interests, assessment of, 115–134
    counselor's interpretation of interest inventories, 131–132
    counselor's selection of interest inventories, 116–117
    popular interest inventories, 117–132
    types of interest inventories, 115–116
Interitem consistency, 31
Internal consistency, 31, 37

Interpersonal Adjective Scales (IAS), 173, 173*f*
Interpersonal relationships, 169–176
    assessment inventories, 172–174
    counselor's use of, 173–174
    genograms, 174–176, 175*f*
    marriage, couples, and family counseling, 169–172
Interviews, 177–190
    assessing problem style of individual by, 4
    client feedback interviews, 50
    guidelines, 46–48
    intake interview, 40–41, 46–49
    multicultural, 49
    specialty interview schedules, 49–50
    structured interviews, 48–49
    worksheet for, 46–47, 47*f*
Introduction to Type (I. B. Myers, Kirby, & Myers), 152
Inventories for Assessing Mental Disorders, 45
"An Inventory of Alcohol-Related Problems," 189
Inventory of Common Problems (ICP), 42–44, 43*f,* 45, 51, 196
Inventory of Work-Relevant Values (IWRV), 109
Involuntary responses, 14
Iowa Early Learning Inventory (IELI), 82
Iowa Student Development Inventories, 168
Iowa Tests of Basic Skills/Iowa Tests of Educational Development, 30, 81, 82, 84*f*
IQ (Intelligence Quotient), 28, 59

J

Jackson, Douglas, 67
Jackson Personality Inventory–Revised (JPI-R), 160
Jackson Vocational Interest Survey (JVIS), 117, 131–132
Jackson's Personality Research Form (PRF), 149
Joint Committee on Testing Practices (JCTP), 19–21
Journal of Career Assessment, 22
Journal of Counseling & Development, 22
Journal of Counseling Psychology, 22
Journal of Personality Assessment, 22
Jung's theory of personality types, 149, 151

K

Kaufman Adolescent and Adult Intelligence Test (KAIT), 63–64
Kaufman Assessment Battery for Children (KABC-II), 63–64
Kaufman batteries, 63–64
Kaufman Test of Educational Achievement–Normative Update (K-TEA-II), 87
Keirsey Temperament Sorter II (KTS-II), 153
Kohlberg's theory of ethical development, 88, 168
Koss–Butcher critical item set, 193
Kuder Career Planning System, 107, 129

Kuder Career Search with Person Match (KCS), 117, 127–129
Kuder General Interest Survey (KGIS), 127, 128
Kuder interest inventories, 9
Kuder Occupational Interest Survey (KOIS), 128
Kuder Preference Record–Vocational (KPR-V), 127
Kuder Skills Assessment (KSA), 129
Kuder–Richardson Formula 20, 31
Kuhlmann–Anderson Test, 66

L

Labeling of clients, 180
Laboratory settings, 14
Law School Admission Test (LSAT), 79
Learning and Study Strategies Inventory (LASSI), 87
Lent's social cognitive theory, 112
Life Experiences Survey, 183
Life Stressors and Social Resources Inventory–Adult or Youth Form, 183
Life Values Inventory, 114
Lifestyle Assessment Questionnaire, 167
Lorge–Thorndike Intelligence Tests, 65

M

Maintenance stage, 40
Making Career Decisions That Count: A Practical Guide (Luzzo), 136
Manual for the Campbell Interest and Skill Survey, 21
Marital Satisfaction Inventory, Revised (MSI-R), 170–171
Marriage counseling, 169–172
Mathematics Anxiety Rating Scale–Revised, 201
Maudsley Obsessional–Compulsive Inventory, 201
Maximum performance, measurement of, 16
MBTI Applications: A Decade of Research on the Myers–Briggs Type Indicator (Hammer), 152
Mean, 25
Measurement and Evaluation in Counseling and Development (journal), 22
Measures of central tendency, 24f, 25, 25f
Measures of variability, 25–26
Median, 25
Medical College Admissions Test (MCAT), 31, 35, 78, 79
Medical model, 40, 41
Medical Specialty Preference Inventory, 116
Medications taken by client, 47, 183
Mental age, 59
Mental health assessment, 9
    alcohol use, 185–189
    anger, 201–202
    anxiety and fear, 200–201
    attention deficit/hyperactivity disorder (ADHD), 206–207
    depression. *See* Depression
    eating disorders, 204–206
    general-purpose measures, 191–198

interview procedures, 177–190
    specific-purpose instruments, 198–207
    standardized inventories, 191–207
    suicide risk, 181–185
Mental Measurements Yearbook, 21
Mental self-government, 87
Mental Status Exam (MSE), 48
Meta-analyses techniques, 35
Metropolitan Achievement Tests, 81, 82–83, 87
MI theory, 67
Michigan Alcoholism Screening Test (MAST), 202, 203f
Military Entrance Score, 139
Miller Analogies Test (MAT), 78–79
Millon Adolescent Clinical Inventory (MACI), 196
Millon Clinical Multiaxial Inventory–III (MCMI-III), 9, 191, 196
Millon Index of Personality Styles–Revised (MIPS-R), 41, 160
Minnesota Importance Questionnaire (MIQ), 106
Minnesota Multiphasic Personality Inventory–2 (MMPI-2), 5, 8, 191–195
    "Big Five" factors and, 150
    clinical scales, 150
    compared to Rorschach Ink Blot Test, 164
    content scales, 149, 193
    Depression scale, 30, 36, 191, 193
    description of standard scales, 192t
    mental health counselors' use of, 9, 191
    profile for counseling client, 195f
    Restructured Clinical (RC) scales, 193
    treatment validity and, 37
    validity scales for, 192–193
Minnesota Multiphasic Personality Inventory–Adolescent (MMPI-A), 191, 195–196
Missouri Occupational Card Sort, 117
Missouri Occupational Preference Inventory, 117
Mode, 25
Models of helping and coping, 40–41
Mood disorder, 177
Moral model, 40, 41
Motivational factors, 14
Multicultural differences
    assessment standards and, 20–21
    career counseling and, 102, 113
    high-stakes testing and, 85
    interest inventories and, 121
    interviewing and, 49
    mental health assessment and, 180–181, 194
    personal values assessment and, 110
Multidimensional Anxiety Questionnaire (MAQ), 201
Multidimensional Aptitude Battery–II (MAB-II), 67
Multidimensional Scale of Perceived Social Support, 184
Multiple intelligences, theory of, 67
My Vocational Situation (MVS), 95–96, 130
Myers–Briggs Type Indicator (MBTI), 41, 133, 149, 150–153
    counselor's use of, 152–153

Specificity, 36
Split-half reliability, 31
Standard deviation, 24f, 25–26
Standard error of measurement *(SEM)*, 32–33
Standard nine, 28
Standard scores, 27–29
Standardized assessment programs, 136–144
Standardized tests, 15–16
Standards and guidelines for evaluating tests, 18–19
Standards for Educational and Psychological Testing, 6, 18–19, 21
    excerpts from, 257–258
    on reliability, 30
    on validity, 33, 34
Standards for Multicultural Assessment, 20–21
Stanford Achievement Tests, 81, 82
Stanford–Binet Intelligence Scales, 5th Ed. (SB5), 59, 60–61, 65
Stanford–Binet mean and standard deviation, 28
Stanine, 28–29
Statements of Joint Committee on Testing Practices (JCTP), 19–21
State–Trait Anger Expression Inventory–2 (STAXI-2), 201
State–Trait Anxiety Inventory (STAI), 200
State–Trait Anxiety Inventory for Children (STAIC), 201
Sternberg's thinking styles, 87
Sternberg's Triangular Love Scale (STLS), 172
Sternberg's triarchic theory of intelligence, 67
Stress
    reduction techniques, 85
    suicide and environmental stress, 183
Strong-Campbell Interest Inventory (SCII), 117
Strong Interest Inventory (SII), 8, 109, 115, 117–124, 136
    administrative indexes, 118
    Basic Interest Scales (BISs), 119–121, 149
    career counselors' use of, 9
    Expanded Skills Confidence Inventory (E-SCI), 124
    General Occupational Themes (GOTs), 119–121
    interpretation of client profile, 123–124
    Occupational Scales (OSs), 121–123
    Personal Style Scales (PSSs), 123, 133
    scores example, 119t
    Skills Confidence Inventory (SCI), 124
    Strong Interest Explorer (SIE), 124
    treatment validity and, 37
    validity of scores on, 33
Strong Interest Inventory Manual, 22
Strong Vocational Interest Blank (SVIB), 117
Structured Clinical Interview for *DSM-IV* Disorders, 48
Structured interviews, 48–49
Structured workshops, use of, 102
Stuart Couple's Precounseling Inventory, 171
Student Developmental Task and Lifestyle Assessment, 168
Study Attitudes and Methods Survey (SAMS), 87

Study habits inventories, 87–88
Study of Values (SOV), 4th Ed., 109, 111
Subjective assessment, 15
Substance abuse. *See* Alcohol abuse; Drug abuse
Substance Abuse Subtle Screening Inventory–3rd Ed. (SASSI-3), 203–204
    adolescent version (SASSI-A2), 204
Suicide Assessment Checklist (SAC), 184
Suicide risk assessment, 181–185
    aids for, 184–185
    available resources, 183–184
    environmental stress, 183
    psychological symptoms, 182–183
    self-reported risk, 181
    suicide history, 182
    suicide plan, 182
Super's model of career development, 100, 111
Symptom Check List–90–Revised (SCL-90-R), 44–45

T

T score, 27–28, 28t
Tailor-made measures, 50–51
Take Hold of Your Future (Harris-Bowlsbey), 129
Target Complaints (TC), 50–51
Taylor–Johnson Temperament Analysis (TJTA), 170
Temperamental factors, 14
Tennessee Self-Concept Scale (2nd Ed.), 161
Terman, Lewis, 59
TerraNova Tests, 81, 83
Test anxiety, 79–80, 201
Test Anxiety Scale, 201
Test-criteria relationships, 34–36
Test Critiques, 21
Test development, 38
Test of Cognitive Skills (TCS/2), 66
Test of English as a Foreign Language (TOEFL), 86
Test publishers, 21, 259–265
    requirements for, 20
Test-retest reliability, 30
Test Reviews Online, 21
Test selection, 51–52
TestLink, 21
Tests (5th Ed.), 21
Tests in Print VII, 21
Tests of Adult Basic Education 9/10 (TABE 9/10), 86
Thematic Apperception Test (TAT), 17, 164–165
Thinking Styles Inventory, 87
Thomas–Kilman Conflict Mode Instrument, 174
Torrance Tests of Creativity, 68
Treatment Companion to the DSM-IV-TR Casebook (Spitzer), 180
Treatment validity, 37–38
Triarchic theory of intelligence, 67
Types of psychological assessment methods, 15–18
Typical performance, measurement of, 16

U

Undisguised behavior, 15
UNIACT Interest Inventory, 73
Unique variables, 14
University of California, San Francisco (UCSF)
    Client Satisfaction Questionnaire–8 (CSQ-8), 49
    Service Satisfaction Scale–30 (SSS-30), 49
University of Rhode Island Change Assessment (URICA), 40
U.S. Department of Education, Office of Civil Rights, 85
U.S. Department of Labor, O*NET (Occupational Information Network), 106

V

Validity, 33–38
    evidence based on consequences of testing, 37
    evidence based on content and response processes, 34
    evidence based on internal structures, 37
    evidence based on relevant criteria and other variables, 34–37
    mental health assessment and, 192–193
    personality inventory development and, 149
    treatment validity, 37–38
Values. *See* Work and personal values
Values Conflict Resolution Assessment (VCRA), 114
Values Scale (VS), 108–109, 133
Verification, 5–6
Vocational Card Sort, 99
Vocational Interest Inventory–Revised (VII-R), 132
Voluntary responses, 14

W

Ways of Coping Questionnaire, 41
Wechsler Abbreviated Scale of Intelligence, 63
Wechsler Adult Intelligence Scale–Revised (WAIS-R), 9
Wechsler Adult Intelligence Scale–3rd Ed. (WAIS-III), 61–62, 62*f*
Wechsler Individual Achievement Test–2nd Ed. (WIAT-II), 87
Wechsler Intelligence Scale for Children–3rd Ed. (WISC-III), 9, 10
Wechsler Intelligence Scale for Children–4th Ed. (WISC-IV), 62–63
Wechsler Preschool and Primary Scale of Intelligence (WPPSI-III), 63
Wechsler scales, 61–63, 65
    mean and standard deviation for, 28
Wellness Evaluation of Lifestyle (WEL), 167
What Color Is Your Parachute? (Bolles), 136
Wide Range Achievement Test, 3rd Ed. (WRAT3), 9
Wide Range Achievement Test, 4th Ed. (WRAT4), 87
Wide Range Intelligence test (WRIT), 64
Wonderlic Personnel Test, 66–67
Woodcock–Johnson III (WJ III), 64
Work and personal values, 105–114
    values clarification exercises, 113–114
    values inventories, 105–113
        counselor's use of, 112–113
        personal values, 109–112
        work values, 105–109
Work Importance Locator (WIL-P&P), 106–107
Work Importance Profiler (WIP), 106–107, 107*t*
Work Values Inventory–Revised (WVI-R), 10, 107–108, 129
WorkKeys, 136, 140–141

Z

Z score, 27

Name Index

Association of American Medical Colleges, 79
Association of Test Publishers, 20, 236
Attkisson, C. C., 49
Austin, J. T., 127, 161
Ayala-Velazquez, H., 188
Azar, B., 221

B

Badger, G. J., 188
Bailley, S. E., 50
Bain, S. K., 61
Baker, H. E., 139, 140
Baldacci, H. B., 201
Balkin, R. S., 167
Balla, D. A., 223
Ball Foundation, 144
Bandura, A., 99
Bansal, A., 194, 219, 228
Bardash, R. J., 99
Bardi, A., 110
Bardos, A. N., 86
Barker, R. G., 166
Barkley, R. A., 206, 207
Baron, A., 39
Barraclough, B., 183
Barram, R. A., 61
Barrett, G. V., 68
Barrios, B. A., 37
Barrios, L. C., 181, 182
Barrons Educational Series, 75
Barron-Tieger, B., 152
Barry, D. R., 164
Barry, K. L., 204
Barthlow, D. L., 193
Bartling, H. C., 122
Battle, C., 51
Bauman, S., 204
Baxter-Magolda, M. B., 88
Bayne, R., 152
Bebeau, M. J., 88
Beck, A. T., 198, 199, 201
Belanger, A. J., 50
Bellah, C. G., 65
Benbow, C. P., 239
Bennett, G. K., 138
Bennett, R. E., 54, 222
Ben-Porath, Y. S., 54, 192, 193, 194, 196, 219
Berg, I. S., 46
Berglund, P., 177, 185, 198, 200
Berman, J., 171
Berman, L., 171
Berntson, G. G., 18
Berven, N. L., 220
Betz, N. E., 99, 116, 117, 124, 214, 240
Beutler, L. E., 40
Bieling, P. J., 200
Bigler, E. D., 224
Binet, A., 59
Bird, J., 184
Blacher, J. H., 10

Blakney, V. L., 136
Blando, J. A., 113
Bobek, B. L., 109
Boehnke, K., 105, 110
Boggs, K. R., 125
Bolles, R. N., 18, 113, 136
Bongar, B., 182
Boodoo, G., 211, 213, 239
Borgen, F. H., 102, 117, 119, 120, 121, 123, 124, 218
Borges, N. J., 116
Borman, W. C., 141
Bornstein, R. F., 164
Bouchardt, T. J., 211, 213, 239
Boughner, S. R., 169, 170
Bourque, M. L., 85
Bowles, S. M., 142
Bowman, S. L., 218
Boye, M. W., 204
Boykin, A. W., 211, 213, 239
Bozionelos, N., 54
Braden, J. P., 222
Bradley, L. J., 51
Bradley, P., 153, 155
Bradley-Johnson, S., 222
Braswell, J., 54
Brauer, B. A., 222
Brecheisen, B. K., 136
Breen, D. T., 180
Breitholtz, T., 47, 179
Brener, N. D., 181, 182
Brent, F., 170
Brescia, W., 215
Breteler, R., 206
Brickman, P., 40, 41, 55
Briddick, W. C., 100, 101
Briggs, K., 150
Brink, T. I., 199
Brody, N., 211, 213, 239
Bromley, J. L., 184
Brookhart, S. M., 82, 109
Brotherton, W. D., 10, 61, 143
Brott, P. E., 113
Brown, D., 113, 114
Brown, G. K., 198, 199
Brown, L., 217
Brown, M. B., 98, 206, 207
Brown, S., 133
Brown, S. D., 93, 99, 109, 112
Brown, T. E., 207
Brown-Chidsey, R., 3
Brunell-Neuleib, T., 164
Bruns, D., 167
Bubenzer, D. L., 169, 170
Buchanan, R. D., 8
Buck, J. N., 165
Budman, S. H., 187
Bugbee, A. C., 82
Bunch, M. B., 144
Burgess, S., 111
Burlingame, G. M., 5, 50
Burns, M., 197

Folsom, B., 102
Folstein, M. F., 224
Folstein, S. E., 224
Fong, M. L., 46, 47, 179
Forbey, J. D., 196
Ford, D. E., 182
Ford, L., 221
Ford, S. J. W., 180
Forgays, D. G., 201
Forgays, D. K., 201
Forsyth, R. A., 82, 83
Fortune, J. C., 215
Foster, F. M., 204
Fouad, N. A., 7, 112, 119, 121, 128, 129, 211, 218
Fowler, R. D., 193, 195
Fox, H. R., 18
Frances, A. J., 180
Frank, J., 51
Frank, R. G., 177, 221
Frauenhoffer, D., 9, 61
Freeman, S. J., 202
Fremer, J., 239
French, J. W., 79
Friedenberg, L., 214
Friedman, A. F., 193
Friedman, S. L., 14, 166
Frisbie, D. A., 82
Frisby, C. L., 85, 221
Frisch, M. B., 112
Fritzsche, B. A., 130, 131
Fulwiler, J., 206
Funder, D. C., 16, 17

G

Gagliardi, C., 68
Galassi, J. P., 7
Galton, F., 7
Garb, H. N., 7, 48, 163, 164, 220
Gardner, F. E., 86
Gardner, H., 67
Garfinkel, P. E., 205
Garner, D. M., 205, 206
Garrett, M. T., 215
Garske, J. P., 49
Gastfriend, D. R., 187
Gati, I., 95, 96, 97
Gavin, D. R., 202
Gay, G. H., 52
Geisinger, K. F., 212, 221
Gerlach, P. K., 174
Geroski, A. M., 180
Gerson, R., 174
Gfeller, J., 9, 61
Giannetti, R. A., 18, 42
Gibson, D. D., 116
Gibson, D. M., 176
Gilberts, R., 161
Gillespie, B. V., 153
Gillespie, M. A., 17
Gim-Chung, R. H., 218

Giordano, F. G., 10, 61, 143
Glaser, B. A., 40
Glavin, K. W., 97, 101, 102
Gleser, G. C., 16
Goldberg, L. R., 150
Goldenson, R. M., 200
Goldfried, M. R., 4, 164
Goldman, L., 15, 113
Gomez, S. P., 219
Goodwin, J., 219
Goodwin, L. D., 34
Goodyear, R. K., 227
Goonan, B., 80
Gopaul, S., 212
Gordon, P. A., 97
Gore, P. A., 109, 227, 228
Gorsuch, R. L., 200
Gottfredson, G. D., 97, 98, 121, 130, 133, 166, 240
Gottfredson, L. S., 60, 240
Gough, H. G., 153, 155, 156, 157
Graham, J. M., 204
Graham, J. R., 191, 192, 193, 194, 219
Granello, D. H., 49, 51
Granello, P. F., 49, 51
Grant, B. F., 188
Grant, M., 204
Gray-Little, B., 218, 219
Green, K. E., 109
Greenberg, L., 49, 54
Greene, R. L., 193, 194, 215, 219
Greenfield, T. K., 49
Gregersen, A. T., 50
Gregg, N., 64
Greist, J. H., 54
Grenier, J. R., 7, 221
Grice, J. W., 14
Grissom, G., 187
Gross, M. L., 211
Grossman, S., 196
Groth-Marnat, G., 48, 67, 154, 156, 164, 165, 217, 219, 224, 232
Grove, W. M., 7
Grutter, J., 123
Guan, M., 111
Guenther, G., 206
Guilford, J. P., 14
Guillen, A., 112
Guilmino, A., 103
Gurtman, M. B., 174

H

Hacker, A., 213
Hackett, G., 93, 99, 112
Hahn, S. R., 48, 180
Hahn, W. K., 181
Haley, M., 182
Hall, L. G., 109
Hall, M. E., 94
Halper, C. R., 124

O'Shea, A. J., 131
Osipow, S. H., 95, 96, 97
Oswald, F. L., 17
Othmer, E., 180
Othmer, S. C., 180
Owen, A. E., 198
Owens, V., 111

P

Pace, C. R., 167
Palmer, D. R., 87
Paniagua, F. A., 212, 214, 218, 219, 220
Panksepp, J., 206
Parker, C. S., 201
Parker, J., 88
Parker, J. D. A., 41, 167
Parker, R., 144
Parra, G. R., 204
Parsons, F., 115
Patel, P., 202
Patient Health Questionnaire Primary Care Study
    Group, 45, 48
Patterson, G. A., 184
Patterson, W. M., 184
Patton, M. J., 51
Patton, W., 102
Pauletta, D., 64
Paulsen, A., 124
Paweleck, J. K., 112
Pearman, R. P., 152
Pearson Assessments, 191
Pecora, P. J., 206
Pedersen, E. R., 188
Pedrotti, J. T., 180
Pendergrass, L. A., 125
Penick, N., 174, 218
Perlmutter, B. F., 171
Perosa, L., 204
Perosa, S., 204
Perot, A. R., 7
Perrone, K. M., 97
Perry, W., 88
Peruzzi, N., 182
Peters, R., 187
Peterson, C., 161, 180
Peterson, C. C., 97
Peterson, G. W., 54, 93, 94, 95, 98, 99, 103, 130,
    136
Peterson, N. G., 141
Petrocelli, J. V., 39
Phelps, R. P., 7, 8, 85
Piaget, J., 88
Pichette, E. F., 215
Pickering, J. W., 95
Piers, E. B., 161
Pike, P. L., 194
Pilkonis, P. A., 159
Pincus, A. L., 174
Pincus, H. A., 177
Piotrowski, C., 9, 61, 197

Pittenger, D. J., 151, 204
Plake, B. S., 10, 21, 83, 85, 201
Podar, I., 206
Polanski, P. J., 48
Pollak, J., 47, 179
Pollard, R. Q., 222
Pommerich, M., 216
Ponterotto, J. G., 49
Pope, M., 128, 132
Pope, R. L., 212
Pope-Davis, D. B., 95
Powell, A. B., 130, 131
Power, P. G., 95
Power, T. J., 207
Powers, D. E., 80
Prediger, D. J., 9, 135, 137, 140, 143, 212
Price, G. E., 87
Prieto, L. R., 219
Prifitera, A., 53, 54, 63, 241
Primoff, E. S., 19, 20
Prince, J. P., 133
Prochaska, J. O., 39, 40, 95
Prosser, E. C., 180
Prottas, D. J., 111
Provost, J. A., 152
Pryor, R. G., 105
Psychological Assessment Resources, 131
Psychological Corporation, 61, 78, 224
Puente, A., 9
Purgar, M. P., 55
Pyle, K. R., 136

Q

Quenk, N. L., 150, 151, 152, 169
Quinn, M. T., 153
Quirk, S. W., 159

R

Rabinowitz, V. C., 40, 41, 55
Rachman, S., 201
Radwan, S., 60
Rafferty, J. E., 165
Raiff, G. W., 131
Ramchandani, P., 206
Ramsay, L. J., 17
Ramsey, G. A., 220
Randahl, G. J., 3, 37
Range, L. M., 184
Raths, L., 113
Raven, J., 216
Raven, J. C., 216
Rayle, A. D., 180
Rayman, J. R., 94, 240
Reardon, R. C., 54, 93, 94, 95, 102, 103, 130, 136
Reddon, J. R., 194
Reed, G. M., 18
Reed, J. R., 42
Reheiser, E. C., 198
Reid, R., 207

Sexton, T. L., 51
Shatkin, L., 144
Shea, A., 40
Shefler, G., 51
Shell, K. D., 116
Shellenberger, S., 174
Sherbenou, R. J., 217
Sherman, D. K., 214
Sherman, L., 43
Shewan, C. M., 8, 19, 20
Shiang, J., 206
Shinn, M. M., 221
Shinn, M. R., 221
Shivy, V. A., 47
Shondrick, D. D., 192
Shortz, J. L., 3
Shrauger, J. S., 135
Shurts, W. M., 172
Shy, J. D., 55
Siegel, J. M., 183
Sigma Assessment Systems, 132
Silien, K. A., 47
Simms, L. J., 193
Simon, S., 113
Singelis, T. M., 113
Sireci, S. G., 78
Skinner, H. A., 172, 202
Skodol, A. E., 180
Slaney, R. B., 117
Smart, D. W., 179
Smart, J. F., 179
Smart, R. M., 97
Smith, A., 5, 51
Smith, D. K., 11, 221, 223
Smith, H. B., 5, 51
Smith, I., 187
Smith, L. H., 87
Smith, W. E., 224
Smitherman, T. A., 18
Snitz, B. E., 7
Snow, M., 202
Snyder, D. K., 169, 170, 171
Sobell, L. C., 188
Sobell, M. B., 188
Sowa, C. J., 42
Spalitto, S. V., 180
Sparrow, E., 207
Sparrow, S. S., 223
Spelke, E. S., 239
Spengler, P. M., 7, 47
Spielberger, C. D., 198, 200, 201
Spies, R. A., 21
Spiro, A., 50
Spitzer, R. L., 5, 45, 48, 180
Spokane, A. R., 129
Stafford, K. P., 192
Stead, G. B., 100
Steenbarger, B. N., 5
Steer, R. A., 198, 199, 201
Stehouwer, J. D., 199
Stehouwer, R. S., 199
Stein, L. A. R., 194, 219

Stein, S., 201
Steinhauer, P. D., 172
Stelmachers, Z. T., 181, 182
Stephen, J., 136
Sternberg, R. J., 60, 67, 85, 87, 172, 217, 239
Stice, E., 205
Stinson, F. S., 188
Stolk, Y., 228
Stone, A., 51
Strack, S., 196
Stricker, G., 164
Strohmer, D. C., 47
Strong, E. K., Jr., 117
Strosahl, K. D., 181, 182
Stuart, R. B., 171
Subich, L. M., 99, 184, 185
Sue, D. W., 212, 213
Sue, S., 220
Sueyoshi, L. A., 49
Summerfeldt, L. S., 167
Sundberg, N. D., 211, 213
Super, D. E., 93, 97, 98, 100, 105, 107, 108, 109, 111
Sverko, B., 105, 108
Swaney, K. B., 140
Swanson, J. L., 10, 103, 227, 228
Sweeney, T. J., 85, 167
Swerdlik, M. E., 223
Swinson, R. P., 200
Sydeman, S. J., 198
Sydney, E., 48, 180

T

Taber, B. J., 101, 109, 133, 136
Talmon, M., 50
Tareen, S., 55
Tasman, A., 180
Tatum, L. G., 111
Taylor, K. M., 99
Taylor, N. B., 105
Taylor, R. M., 170
Teglasi, H., 164
Teitelbaum, L., 202
Tellegen, A., 192, 193, 194
Teranishi, R., 215
Terman, L., 59
Terrell, M. D., 180
Thoma, S. J., 88
Thomas, G. V., 179
Thomas, K. W., 174
Thompson, A. S., 93, 97, 100
Thompson, R. C., 8, 22, 117, 118, 120, 121, 122, 123
Thorn, A. R., 83
Thurber, S., 202
Thyer, B. A., 44
Tieger, P. D., 152
Timbrook, R. E., 194, 219
Tinsley, D. J., 102
Tinsley, H. E., 102

Tistadt, G., 43
Tokar, D. M., 95, 96, 103
Toman, S. M., 93
Tonsager, M. E., 3, 7, 37, 51, 227, 231
Toporek, R. J., 95
Torrance, E. P., 68
Touliatos, J., 171
Tracey, T. J. G., 7, 117, 122, 172, 173
Trotter, T. V., 10, 83
Tsacoumis, S., 143
Tsai, D. C., 194
Tucker, I. F., 153
Tucker, J. A., 188
Tunick, R. H., 142
Turkheimer, E., 13
Turner, S. M., 18
Tyler, J. D., 4
Tyler, L., 117
Tzeng, O. C. S., 16

U

Uellendahl, G. E., 10
Uffelman, R. A., 99
Ulett, G., 164
Ulven, J. C., 180
Unikel-Santoncini, C., 205
Urbina, S., 5, 15, 23, 27, 35, 81, 149, 198
U.S. Census Bureau, 214
U.S. Department of Defense, 139, 140
U.S. Department of Education, Office of Civil
    Rights, 85
U.S. Department of Labor, Bureau of Labor
    Statistics, 129
U.S. Department of Labor, Employment and
    Training Administration, 106, 107, 113, 121,
    124, 130, 133, 141, 142
U.S. Department of Veterans Affairs, 224

V

Vacc, N. A., 9, 48, 49, 203, 235
Vagg, P. R., 200
Valpar International Corporation, 136
VanDenberg, T. F., 172
vanderStaak, C., 206
Vansickle, T. R., 53
Vázquez-Arévalo, R., 205
Velasquez, R. J., 219
Verbraak, M., 206
Verhoeve, M., 131
Verkasalo, M., 111
Vernon, A., 212
Vernon, P. E., 68, 111
Vilas, R. C., 152
Villalba, J., 85
Vogel, D. L., 241
Vondracek, F. W., 100
Vonk, M. E., 44
Vuchinich, R. E., 188

W

Wachs, T. D., 14, 166
Wagner, C. C., 173
Wagner, K. S., 99
Wagner, R. K., 67
Wagner, S. H., 159
Waldinger, R. J., 48
Waldroop, J., 116
Walker, R. L., 182, 184, 185
Walker, Z., 202
Wall, J. E., 54, 241
Wall, T. N., 40
Walls, R. G., 219
Walls, R. T., 98
Walsh, D. J., 109
Walsh, W. B., 214, 240
Walters, E. E., 6, 177, 180, 185, 188, 198, 200
Wanberg, K. W., 204
Wang, L., 139
Wang, S., 53, 54
Ward, S., 116
Watkin, V., 202
Watkins, C. E., 10, 100, 101
Watley, D. J., 77
Watson, D., 193
Watson, M., 102
Watt, M., 54
Webb, J. T., 193
Webster, B., 10, 83
Wechsler, D., 61, 63, 87, 224
Wechsler, H., 7, 185
Weiner, I. R., 164
Weinstein, C. E., 87
Weis, D. L., 171
Weiss, B., 42–43
Weiss, D. J., 54
Weiss, L. G., 63
Weitzman, E. R., 7, 185
Wells, M. G., 5
Werts, C. E., 77
Wesman, A. G., 74, 138
West, J. D., 169, 170
Westbrook, B. W., 98
Westefeld, J. S., 184
Wetherbee, K. M., 206
Wettersten, K. B., 103
Whiston, S. C., 49, 68, 136, 150, 220
White, A. E., 161
White, M. J., 7
Whitfield, E. A., 9, 22
Whittaker, S., 8, 10, 61
Wickwire, P. N., 143
Widaman, K. F., 64, 67
Widiger, T. A., 150, 159, 179, 196
Wiggins, J. S., 173
Wilkinson, G. S., 87
Williams, C. L., 193, 195
Williams, J. B. W., 45, 48, 180
Williams, S. M., 3
Williams, W. M., 67
Williamson, E. G., 166